THE BUILDINGS OF SCOTLAND

EDITOR: COLIN MCWILLIAM
CONSULTANT EDITOR: JOHN NEWMAN

FIFE

JOHN GIFFORD

The special costs of research and site-visiting for the whole of the *Buildings of Scotland* series are being underwritten by the National Trust for Scotland with the aid of generous grants from the Pilgrim Trust and the Scottish Arts Council, and from the Russell Trust whom it is particularly appropriate to thank in connection with the Fife volume.

Fife

BY

JOHN GIFFORD

THE BUILDINGS OF SCOTLAND

PENGUIN BOOKS

PENGUIN BOOKS
Published by the Penguin Group
27 Wrights Lane, London w8 5TZ, England

Viking Penguin Inc., 40 West 23rd Street, New York, New York 10010, USA
Penguin Books Australia Ltd, Ringwood, Victoria, Australia
Penguin Books Canada Ltd, 2801 John Street, Markham, Ontario, Canada L3R 1B4
Penguin Books (NZ) Ltd, 182–190 Wairau Road, Auckland 10, New Zealand

Penguin Books Ltd, Registered Offices: Harmondsworth, Middlesex, England

First published 1988

—

ISBN 0.14.07 10.77 9

Made and printed in Great Britain by
Butler & Tanner Ltd, Frome and London
Set in Lasercomp Plantin

DEDICATED TO
THE NATIONAL MONUMENTS RECORD
OF SCOTLAND

The numbers printed in italic type in the margin against the place names in the gazetteer of the book indicate the position of the place in question on the index map (pages 2–3), which is divided into sections by the 10-kilometre reference lines of the National Grid. The reference given here omits the two initial letters (formerly numbers) which in a full grid reference refer to the 100-kilometre squares into which the country is divided. The first two numbers indicate the *western* boundary, and the last two the *southern* boundary, of the 10-kilometre square in which the place in question is situated. For example, Auchtertool (reference 2090) will be found in the 10-kilometre square bounded by grid lines 20 and 30 on the *west* and 90 and 100 on the *south*; Falkland (reference 2000) in the square bounded by grid lines 20 and 30 on the *west* and 00 and 10 on the *south*.

The map contains all those places, whether towns, villages, or isolated buildings, which are the subject of separate entries in the text.

CONTENTS

ACCESS TO BUILDINGS 10

EDITOR'S FOREWORD
  BY COLIN MCWILLIAM 11

AUTHOR'S FOREWORD 15

ACKNOWLEDGEMENTS FOR THE PLATES 17

TOPOGRAPHY AND BUILDING MATERIALS 19

PREHISTORIC, ROMAN AND PICTISH FIFE
  BY GORDON S. MAXWELL AND J. N. GRAHAM
  RITCHIE 20

MEDIEVAL CHURCHES, MONASTERIES AND COLLEGES 29

POST-REFORMATION CHURCHES 34

CASTLES, PALACES AND TOWER HOUSES 42

COUNTRY HOUSES 44

BURGH AND VILLAGE BUILDINGS 48

RURAL BUILDINGS 55

FIFE 57

GLOSSARY 429

INDEX OF ARTISTS 453

INDEX OF PLACES 465

ACCESS TO BUILDINGS

Many of the buildings described in this book are in public places, and in some obvious cases their interiors (at least the public sections of them) can be seen without formality. But it must be emphasized that the mention of buildings or lands does not imply any right of public access to them, or the existence of any arrangements for visiting them.

Some churches are open within regular hours, and it is usually possible to see the interiors of others by arrangement with the minister or church officer. Particulars of admission to Ancient Monuments and other buildings in the care of the Secretary of State for Scotland (free to the Friends of the Scottish Monuments) are available from the Historic Buildings and Monuments Directorate, 21 Brandon Street, Edinburgh EH3 5DX. Details of access to properties of the National Trust for Scotland are available from the Trust's head office at 5 Charlotte Square, Edinburgh EH2 4DU. Admission is free to members, on whose subscriptions and donations the Trust's work depends.

Two useful current directories (1988) are *Historic Houses, Castles and Gardens Open to the Public* (British Leisure Publications), which includes many private houses, and the annual booklet listing gardens and houses open to visitors under Scotland's Gardens Scheme, available from 31 Castle Terrace, Edinburgh EH1 2EL.

EDITOR'S FOREWORD

> *Hear, Land o' Cakes, and brither Scots,*
> *Frae Maidenkirk to Johnny Groats,*
> *If there's a hole in a' your coats,*
>   *I rede you, tent it*;*
> *A chiel's amang you, taking notes,*
>   *And, faith, he'll prent it.*

Burns was writing about Captain Francis Grose, whose last work, The Antiquities of Scotland, *was printed in 1791. A* chiel *is a young lad, hence an enthusiast.*

Here are The Buildings of Fife, *and the chiel is John Gifford. Our interest is not now limited to fabrics with holes or in holes, and two men have played an important part in the change. First, in Scotland, there was Sir John Sinclair, whose Statistical Account is a late eighteenth-century planning survey, looking at buildings and everything else from the point of view of usefulness. Then, in Britain at large, came Sir Nikolaus Pevsner, who completed* The Buildings of England *and launched the equivalent* Ireland, *Scotland and* Wales. *He was no particular respecter of holes. His aim was to describe 'all buildings of architectural importance', regardless of date.*

So now we have 'the Pevsner books', as they are often called, either in preparation or already published and under revision, for the whole of the British Isles. John Newman of the Courtauld Institute of Art, himself the author of the two exemplary Kent *volumes, is the overall Consultant Editor. When the whole territory has been covered, it will at last be possible to take an equal view of the Buildings of Britain, with excellence recognized wherever it occurs, and without the mention of 'Scottish architecture' (or English, Irish or Welsh) arousing suspicions of chauvinism.*

The books are used in various ways. For reading on the spot, where one needs above all facts, and clear explanation. For advance reconnaissance, when one wants visual description (also useful for finding and identifying a building). For straight reading, even without the prospect of a visit; here too description is important, and context is specially important. And for reference. Is this building in the book? What does Pevsner (or whichever author) say about it? This is where the educational influence of the series often begins. The same questions may also be asked when a building is at risk or involved in a difficult planning application, and here they really put

---

* I warn you, see to it.

the author on the spot. He must have an eye for all sorts of architecture, and must surely be allowed a few personal quirks and pref-
erences – the more explicit the better. But his qualitative judgements
(either specific or implied) are bound to be noticed, and he must
avoid indiscriminate praise as much as careless condemnation.

What about Scotland? The McPevsner series is inevitably affected
by the Scottish background. Here we have our Royal Commission
on the Ancient and Historical Monuments of Scotland* (note the
emotive 'Ancient', distinguishing it from the equivalent English
Commission). We also have (after numerous changes in the last thirty
years) our own Historic Buildings and Monuments Directorate at
the Scottish Office, responsible for looking after Guardianship
Monuments, and for listing and grant-aiding buildings on a system
slightly different from that in England; for example, Victorian and
later architecture has been included in the Scottish lists ever since
they started forty years ago.

As to published source materials on Scottish architecture, the basic
list is very short (see the Author's Foreword). However, we have a
very great wealth of primary material, much of it housed in the
Scottish Record Office or the National Library of Scotland, and
the systematic use of it for large-scale research has been surprisingly
rare. In short, much information on Scottish buildings of all periods
has still to be discovered.

So from the start in Lothian except Edinburgh, and increasingly
in Edinburgh and the rest of the series, it has been and will be
necessary to prepare for each book not only by collecting published
information but by a great deal of research into primary sources.
The fruits of this extra effort include new and reliable attributions
of individual works to architects and craftsmen, the sorting out of
building histories (sometimes of quite well-known monuments), and
often the clothing of the bare bone of names and dates with the flesh
of context. In this role we have a particular responsibility now that
the RCAHMS, like the Royal Commission in England, has ceased the
preparation of its large blue Inventories. These, though extremely
valuable, remain incomplete in territorial as in chronological scope.

The use of a lot of new information accentuates a problem common
to the whole British series in that sources are not acknowledged
(except in a general way and sometimes in the form of thanks to
other researchers who kindly let us share their material before it is
published). This is surely reasonable; the second generation of
Pevsner books is already perilously tall, and to make them any bigger
would defeat their main purpose as handy guides for use on the spot.
The answering of the consequent queries and the corrections and
suggestions (for which we are very grateful), as well as the research
itself: all these are carried out by the Buildings of Scotland Research
Unit at the address given below. John Gifford is the Chief
Researcher, and in Fife (as in part of Edinburgh) he has also been
the author.

Such an ambitious programme cannot be contemplated without a
sympathetic sponsor. The National Trust for Scotland, which has

* Hereafter shortened to RCAHMS.

long been known for its broad view of conservation in this country, has provided the necessary security by undertaking the task of raising funds for research, and by underwriting it meantime. I am very grateful for the interested support of Lester Borley, the Trust's Director, and his staff.

Finally a short addendum to what I have already said about the inclusion and omission of buildings, but now with reference to the Scottish series. As many readers have already noticed, sometimes rather indignantly, we tend to put in certain kinds of buildings as a matter of course, e.g. practically all public buildings and churches along with others that are merely conspicuous, often with no more information than the date and the name of the architect. No claims are made for the architectural quality of a mediocre building – only for its individuality. It is probably valued by somebody, it may be the only distinctive feature of an otherwise nondescript place, and sooner or later its future may come under discussion. Perhaps this applies most of all to Victorian churches. Likewise with Victorian and later stained glass, which still awaits a comprehensive assessment, we tend to include everything for which we have the artist's name, and whatever other examples appear interesting. For the inclusion of vernacular buildings no apology is necessary, but it is worth remarking that a minor building in or near a town or village may be mentioned under that entry, while an identical example in an isolated position may not appear. More important rural buildings such as castles and country houses have individual entries in the Gazetteer. An entry in brackets shows that the building concerned has not, for whatever reason, been personally visited. These are some of our house-rules within the durable and wonderfully flexible principles and format invented by Sir Nikolaus Pevsner for the first volume in the Buildings of Britain super-series, published in 1951.

Colin McWilliam
Department of Architecture
Heriot-Watt University
The Edinburgh College of Art
Lauriston Place
Edinburgh EH3 9DF

AUTHOR'S FOREWORD

Production of this book has been a long process in which many people have taken part. Dr Gordon Maxwell and Dr Graham Ritchie of the Royal Commission on the Ancient and Historical Monuments of Scotland (RCAHMS) *wrote the introductory section and gazetteer entries for Prehistoric, Roman and Pictish Fife. Colin McWilliam, the Series Editor, not only gave welcome encouragement and advice but also, when I got stuck, undertook most of the descriptions of the 'East Neuk' burghs. John Newman, Consultant Editor to the various* Buildings of ... *series, read the typescript and made several suggestions.*

A very considerable amount of research has had to be done. The RCAHMS *Inventory of* Fife (*1933*) *and David MacGibbon and Thomas Ross's two works,* The Castellated and Domestic Architecture of Scotland (*5 vols., 1887–92*) *and* The Ecclesiastical Architecture of Scotland (*3 vols., 1896–7*), *were invaluable starting points for buildings dating from before 1707; and the Scottish Development Department's* List of Buildings of Special Architectural or Historic Interest *gives a great deal of information on Georgian and Victorian structures. Useful historical background is provided by A. H. Millar's* Fife: Pictorial and Historical (*2 vols., 1895*). *However, these works, even when added together, are far from comprehensive, and much digging had to be done. Several years ago I extracted all Scottish references from* C19 *and* C20 *architectural and building periodicals* (The Builder, The Building News, The Architect, *etc.*). *From my notes Yvonne Hillyard valiantly extracted the Fife material and arranged it by individual buildings grouped in parishes. She also greatly supplemented my notes with information collected from such sources as the various* Statistical Accounts of Scotland, C19 *gazetteers* (The Ordnance Gazetteer of Scotland, *ed. Francis H. Groome, 5 vols., 1882–5, being the fullest), and a mass of local histories and guidebooks. I in turn added to Mrs Hillyard's work my own gleanings from manuscript sources, especially ecclesiastical and estate records now housed in the Scottish Record Office, for whose staff's assistance and occasional forbearance I am very grateful. Just as long-suffering and helpful have been the staff of the National Library of Scotland, the Edinburgh Central Public Library (especially the Scottish and Fine Art Departments), the Dunfermline Public Library and the Kirkcaldy Public Library. Still greater is my gratitude to the staff of the National Monuments Record of Scotland (an integral part of the* RCAHMS), *who have cheerfully put up with my rummaging through their collection of photographs, drawings, books and pam-*

phlets. On my frequent visits Catherine Cruft and Ian Gow have often brought new information to my attention, politely questioned my more far-fetched ideas and gently suggested new interpretations of complex building histories.

Other architectural historians have been generous in sharing their own discoveries, and I must particularly thank John Frew, who, together with Ronald Cant, has done so much to document the buildings of St Andrews, Howard Colvin, Richard Fawcett, Ierne Grant, Bob Heath, Aonghus Mackechnie, Anne Riches, Joe Rock, and David Walker. The architectural staff of Fife Regional Council, Glenrothes Development Corporation, and St Andrews University have provided lists of architects' names and dates for recent buildings, as have the planning departments of Dunfermline, Kirkcaldy and North-East Fife District Councils. Above all I must thank the many ministers, priests, church officers, and the owners of country houses and other private buildings who have put themselves to considerable trouble to let me see over the buildings in their care and have often given me valuable information. I hope they will forgive me for having sometimes disagreed with their interpretation of the history of their own buildings.

The county map and town plans for this volume were specially drawn by Reg Piggott, and most of the plans of buildings by Richard Andrews, but Matthew Pease drew the plan of House of Falkland and the elevations of St Andrews Cathedral and Balcaskie. Photographs were especially taken by Douglas MacGregor and Colin McWilliam. Judith Wardman prepared the typescript for the printer, good-humouredly pointing out the inconsistencies and obvious omissions and apparently unruffled by last-minute alterations. She also compiled the Index of Buildings.

ACKNOWLEDGEMENTS FOR THE PLATES

We are grateful to the following for permission to reproduce photographs:

Edinburgh Central Library, City of Edinburgh District Council: 107
Country Life: 55, 70
Bill Hill, Pittenweem: 103
Hurd Rolland Partnership: 53
Anthony Kersting: 6, 27
Douglas MacGregor: 11, 13, 14, 15, 16, 21, 24, 29, 30, 31, 35, 37, 38, 39, 41, 43, 44, 57, 63, 65, 67, 72, 80, 81, 82, 84, 88, 91, 92, 98, 102, 110, 111, 112, 113, 114, 115, 116, 117, 120
Colin McWilliam: 1, 2, 10, 18, 20, 22, 23, 25, 26, 28, 33, 40, 42, 45, 47, 52, 54, 60, 61, 62, 66, 69, 71, 73, 76, 77, 78, 86, 87, 89, 94, 95, 97, 99, 101, 104, 105, 106, 108, 109, 118, 119, 121, 122
National Trust for Scotland: 59, 83, 90
Joe Rock: 96
Royal Commission on the Ancient and Historical Monuments of Scotland (National Monuments Record of Scotland): 3, 4, 8, 19, 34, 36, 51, 56, 64, 68, 74, 75, 79, 93
Scottish Development Department (Historic Buildings and Monuments Directorate): 5, 7, 9, 12, 17, 32, 48, 49, 50, 58
Scottish Tourist Board: 85
Wheeler & Sproson: 46, 100

The plates are indexed in the indexes of artists and buildings, and references to them are given by numbers in the margin of the text.

INTRODUCTION

TOPOGRAPHY AND BUILDING MATERIALS

FIFE is a peninsula sticking out between the Firths of Tay and
Forth into the North Sea. On the W it is almost cut off from the
rest of Scotland by the Ochil Hills, the main land routes having
to squeeze past the ends of the range. Inside this peninsula, the
ground, apart from a flat coastal strip, is broken by low hills (few
approaching 300m.) into small valleys and two large ones, the
straths of Eden and of the Leven and its tributary the Ore.

The main geological divisions run in belts from SW to NE. At
the top, the hills N of Stratheden are formed from Lower Old
Red Sandstone lavas. The broad vale of Stratheden lies on Upper
Old Red Sandstone sediments washed down by water action and
compacted to form stone. The Lomond Hills at the valley's SW   2
end are dolerite (whinstone) intrusions, the twin peaks of East
and West Lomond the eroded necks of volcanoes. Dolerites
and volcanic necks recur in S and E Fife, pushing through the
underlying carboniferous rocks to make unexpected punc-
tuations (e.g. at Kincraig Point, Elie, or The Binn behind
Burntisland) in the generally undulating landscape. This S belt
is bisected by the coal measures stretching from Culross to Largo,
whose large-scale exploitation in the late C19 and early C20
produced a string of mining villages through this predominantly
agricultural region.

Soil is generally fertile, although the heavier clay away from
the coast was hard to work before late Georgian agricultural
improvement introduced tile drains. Until then much of inland
Fife was moor, loch or bog, its contrast with the lighter, naturally
drained and arable-producing soil round the coast giving literal
meaning to James VI's description of the county as 'a beggar's
mantle fringed with gold.'

Fife's rocks and clays have produced its indigenous building
materials. Sandstone is abundant and was an C18 and C19 export
from the Cullaloe and Grange quarries to satisfy the needs of
Edinburgh's voracious building industry. The immensely hard
dolerite whinstone, too intractable for dressings, makes a dark,
almost shiny rubble. By the early C18, clay was used to make
bricks and tiles (both drainage tiles for agriculture and pantiles
for roofing buildings). The best-known brick and tile centre was
the factory at Kirkcaldy begun by William Adam, but there were
other works at Kincardine-on-Forth, Cupar and Leven. For

roofing, thatch of straw, turf or heather was common until C19, cultivation of reed beds in the Tay for a durable thatching material being started in 1776.* As well as pantiles and thatch, 'grey slates' (i.e. sandstone flags) from Angus were used as a covering in the C18, but the more prosperous Georgian and Victorian buildings were covered with 'blue' slates imported from the West Highland Easdale and Ballachulish quarries. Good-quality timber was imported from the Baltic by the C16, supplemented from the C18 by home-grown wood. But stone, tiles, slates and timber were not cheap, and until the C18 most houses were built of rough wooden crucks with walls of turf or clay, sometimes combined with boulders from the fields. The change to a general use of stone for construction in the C18 was accompanied by exploitation of Fife's plentiful limestone to produce lime for mortar and for harling (a lime-and-sand render applied to rubble walls as both a protection and an adornment). Harling or cement render, usually as a cover-up for concrete or brick, has become the C20's favourite method of suggesting that Fife's building tradition continues as a specifically local art.

PREHISTORIC, ROMAN AND PICTISH FIFE

BY GORDON S. MAXWELL AND J. N. GRAHAM RITCHIE

THE way of life of Fife's earliest settlers is unusually well documented from excavations at Morton, just above Tentsmuir at the NE tip of the Region. Here the careful recording of a series of campsites has increased our knowledge of the exploitation of natural resources about eight thousand years ago, and of the animals, including birds, fish and shellfish, on which the hunters depended for their livelihood. We also know that they tapped another resource, the flint and chert from which they worked their tiny flake tools (microliths).

During this MESOLITHIC period it is likely that Tentsmuir was covered by the sea; the little promontory at Morton on which the excavations took place would have risen slightly above the shore. Traces of about fifteen wind-breaks were found, indicated by stake-hole settings, as well as hearths and what are described as sleeping-hollows. The bones of animals recovered during excavation included red deer, otters, bears and wolves, birds (guillemot and cormorant) and fish (haddock and cod). Morton was evidently a seasonal campsite over several generations – perhaps just one site in a pattern of settlement whose different habitats were exploited at different times through the year. Evidence of further seasonal sites is provided by shell middens at various points along the shore of the inner Firth of Forth, including Torryburn.

* But 'Reed Houses' at Rossie near Auchtermuchty were thatched in 1721.

About 4000 B.C. there was an influx of new groups of people, and different skills, into E Scotland. Agriculture and stock-rearing radically changed the pattern of life, with greater emphasis on the systematic working of land rather than culling its resources. Fife, Angus and the Lothian plain have none of the chambered cairns and long mounds that are found in the N and W, but we know of the presence of contemporary NEOLITHIC activity in Fife by the discovery of distinctive tools such as stone axeheads, and from a very few chance finds of pottery, including early Neolithic ware from Barns Farm (Dalgety Bay) and Clatchard Craig (Newburgh). One of the most distinctive objects of later Neolithic date is the carved stone ball, a symbol perhaps of social or religious status. Several examples have been found in N Fife, e.g. at Grange of Lindores, Clatchard Craig and Strath-miglo, and others in the S at Dunfermline and on the Isle of Inchcolm.

Later Neolithic pottery in a style known as grooved ware was found in association with one of the most important ceremonial complexes in E Scotland, at Balfarg and Balbirnie (Glenrothes). The visible features of these twin sites are described in the Gazetteer (pp. 236–7). This area was an important focus for religious or ritual activity around the third millennium B.C. The great henge monument at Balfarg has been partly restored, and the ditch surrounding the ritual area has been dug out to give an impression of the scale of activity involved. It is very hard to estimate the amount of time and effort required for the digging of the ditch and the preparation and erection of the large timbers within it, as compared with, say, the construction of a medieval tower house. But they show a social organization in Fife at the time which is otherwise difficult to illustrate. No settlement sites are known, unless the cluster of five or six long timber structures resembling hall-houses, recorded from the air at Lathrisk, represents the remains of a contemporary village. But the presence of grooved ware at Morton indicates some activity there at the time. At Balfarg two large timber-built ritual enclosures (probably not roofed) excavated in advance of modern development, are reminders of the importance of wood in the construction of prehistoric houses (e.g. at Balbridge, Grampian).

If the henge at Balfarg and the later stone circle at Balbirnie betoken some sort of central authority, most of the sites of the second millennium B.C. seem to be of more local significance – standing stones, cupmarkings and cairns. The standing stones of Fife vary from spectacular examples, such as the setting of three at Lundin Links, to small boulders whose almost domestic significance is epitomized by the stone at Standing Stone Walk, Dunfermline, now landscaped as a feature in a housing development.

What do standing stones mean? The question is dreaded by archaeologists, for there is no single answer. It is likely that some stones were memorials to the dead, for excavation has revealed deposits of cremated human bones in the holes in which they have been set up. A cist and an 'urn' were found near the

Strathendry stone in 1760, and burials have been recorded near those at Lundin Links. Other stones may be territorial markers or meeting places, but proof is difficult. The seductive idea that some stones may have had a role in astronomical observation is equally hard to test. It has been suggested that those at Lundin Links were a lunar observatory, from which the rising moon could be seen at a particular stage, just grazing the Bass Rock. What we know of Bronze Age society suggests that while the rudimentary alignment of the site on an astronomical body was not beyond its capabilities, precise observation over many decades was improbable. The stones mentioned in the Gazetteer, while not all impressive, are a reminder of the antiquity of settlement in Fife.

Several standing stones and a number of rock outcrops are decorated with cupmarks, rings and grooves, e.g. at Pitcorthie, with about thirty-three cups, and Tulyies (Torryburn), with a profusion. Cup-and-ring markings from a cave at the former Michael Colliery at Wemyss survive only as a cast in the Royal Museum of Scotland, Edinburgh. A boulder at Lochmalony with twenty-nine cups was blown up in 1965. But a small sandstone slab from Glasslie and other slabs found on East Lomond hill in 1972 are now preserved in the Falkland Palace Museum. The boulder known as Macduff's Cross (SW of Newburgh) has cupmarks on top.

Many BRONZE AGE burials in small stone coffins (cists) have been found in the course of agricultural and industrial development. Often such burials, covered by a cairn, formed the focus of later interments, and the cairns were enlarged in the process. Frequently they have been robbed in old excavations or used for wall building, but others remain in hilltop positions such as West Lomond (now very ruinous), Green Hill (near Balmerino) and Norrie's Law. Several cairns or barrows (earthen mounds) were surrounded by ditches or set on platforms (e.g. near Collessie and Ladybank). Two on Melville Moor (N of Ladybank) were excavated c. 1870 and are now destroyed, and others are visible only as cropmarks on aerial photographs. Among the cropmark sites, special interest attaches to those of square plan which are beginning to be found in various parts of E Scotland, N of the Forth. Although it is presumed that these are of Iron Age or Early Historic origin, an earlier date cannot be entirely ruled out. Small cemeteries of round and square barrows have so far been identified with reasonable certainty at Melville House and Kinross (Tayside) to the NE and SW of Loch Leven.

But the richness of Bronze Age remains in Fife lies in the pottery and other artefacts recovered from burials in cairns and in cists found in the course of recent developments. Such objects are outside the scope of this volume, but their importance justifies their inclusion here: e.g. the beaker and dagger found at Ashgrove (Methilhill) in 1963; the dagger found at Kirkcaldy in 1931; and, in a large cist at Masterton, found in 1961 and perhaps made for a man and a woman, a dagger blade, a small bronze blade, a jet necklace and a pair of bronze armlets. A burial at Collessie included a dagger with a gold pommel mount. Food vessels were found at Pitreavie in 1885 and at Aberdour Road, Dunfermline, in 1972, and large cinerary urns at Kingskettle, Lawhead (St Andrews), Cowdenbeath and Brackmont Mill. Such cemeteries and burials give an impression of the order and stability of Bronze Age society.

The influences that began to bear on native societies in E Scotland from the C8 B.C. may not yet be clearly understood. Climatic deterioration, the appearance of new elements in the population, and the rise of iron-working technology – all could have played a part. Most of the archaeological evidence is in the upsurge of new forms of habitation. The enclosed settlements of more or less defensive character demand particular consideration, if only because of their physical size. Perhaps such strongholds were required to protect good land from annexation either by jealous neighbours or by intruders from farther afield.

Fife contains several examples of these prehistoric forts, and the best preserved are on the summits of conspicuous hills, e.g. East Lomond and Norman's Law. But many more existed on lower ground; proximity to arable terrain or richer pastures made up for their lack of natural protection, and the wasted remains of such forts may still be traced on the coastal hillss s of the Tay, on the tumbled ranges NE of Loch Leven, as well as on some of the low ridges near the SW coast and on the s side of the Eden valley. Regrettably only two examples, Craigluscar Hill and Clatchard Craig, have been excavated in recent times, and then only partially. Moreover Clatchard Craig (now demolished) appeared to have been remodelled in the Early Historic period. But in some cases the surviving remains offer clues, e.g. the weight of stony debris indicating the main line of the defences on Dunearn Hill and Norman's Law, and Black Cairn Hill above Newburgh, which suggests that these were boulder-faced, rubble-filled walls. Doubtless other examples were internally braced with timber lacing, like some forts in adjacent parts of Tayside, but, apart from Clatchard Craig, none has yet been recognized.

On sites where the geology permits, the defences may also incorporate ditches whose spoil is used to form the core of the accompanying ramparts or counterscarp banks, e.g. at Links Wood and Lady Mary's Wood (Kirkton of Cults), or in the outermost perimeter on the East Lomond. In each case it is probable that the outer face of the main defence was revetted with stone or timber, as a sheer obstacle to any assailant. And since such a barrier would have had to be manned, it must also be presumed that the superstructure included a wall-top walk with breastwork.

Other works may have consisted almost entirely of timber, and their recognition used to depend on the chances of excavation, e.g. at Craigluscar Hill. From the 1970s, however, intensive aerial survey has helped in the location of such tenuous evidence as the narrow trenches which held the upright members of a palisade, even on sites completely levelled by cultivation. Any alteration of the subsoil, by the digging of pits or post-holes or ditches, or

the laying of stony foundations, will affect the ripening process
of any crops subsequently grown above it. This can be recorded
from the air as a difference in the colour or height of the growing
plants, i.e. a cropmark. Thus it is now possible to identify a
palisaded phase in the bivallate ditched enclosure Myres Castle,
a low-lying cropmark site SW of Auchtermuchty, while smaller
palisaded works, little more than homesteads enclosing one or
two round timber houses, have been recorded at nearby Ravenshall and at Sands Farm not far from Kincardine-on-Forth.

Palisades of any date nevertheless appear at present to have
been even less popular in Fife than they were among the native
communities of the Forth, Teith or Earn, or in Lothian. There
are also fewer small earthworks of any kind than in adjacent
districts, especially those to the S and W. Two embanked homesteads, both enclosing round timber houses, have been excavated
at Green Craig and Scotstarvit. The former, roughly rectangular
in plan, may be compared with examples discovered from the air
at West Flisk and Waukmill, Crombie, while the latter is paralleled at Glenduckie Hill (though there the enclosed house is
stone-founded, which may indicate a Later Iron Age date). The
unenclosed stone-built house excavated at Drumcarrow Craig is
very like the stone houses of the Borders and SE Scotland generally, whose use extended into the Roman period and beyond; the
somewhat larger structures at Drumnod Wood near Balmerino
(also unenclosed) may be of similar date. The rash of circular
stone foundations within and overlying the fort on Norman's
Law has been cited as further evidence of the lateness of these
structures, but it must be borne in mind that hillforts in E
Scotland appear to have had a shorter occupational history than
used to be thought, passing out of use a century and more before
the first Roman invasion.

Several sites, however, display evidence of a complicated
sequence of building. Clatchard Craig was remodelled in the
Early Historic period, and a Pictish carved stone has been found
on East Lomond. The small citadel-like stone-walled enclosures
crowning the summits of Norman's Law and Dunearn Hill may
be similarly late, but it is equally possible that they represent a
phase of re-fortification which coincided roughly with the Roman
occupation. It seems most likely that it was about this time – the
late C1 or early C2 A.D. – that the broch at Drumcarrow Craig
was built. The broch had evolved in the Atlantic Province, in the
latter half of the first millennium B.C., as a type of fortified
homestead of circular plan and tower-like proportions, with an
enormously thick dry-stone wall capable of incorporating mural
passages, staircases and cells. When introduced into more
southerly parts of Scotland it was more or less fully developed,
and whether it signifies hostile penetration by northern invaders
or merely the peaceful transmission of an exotic building type
cannot yet be determined. At about the same time another cate-
gory of Atlantic Province fortification, the dun, was also introduced into the Lowlands. No authenticated examples have been
found in Fife, but it is possible that some of the small dry-stone

univallate forts may belong to a related, contemporary type, e.g. the secondary work on Dunearn Hill and the adjacent sites recently detected on the Downans, Aberdour, and Castle Hill, Fordell.

It must be admitted, however, that the archaeological evidence so far consists of unrelated fragments, without certainty of date or purpose, and the point is underlined by the doubling of the known examples of fortified and defensive enclosures in Fife by aerial survey from c.1976 to 1986.* The major impact of such survey on the archaeology of Fife is in the revelation that the defensive and enclosed sites which form the bulk of the structural evidence represent only a small part of the Region's settlements in the period 700 B.C.–A.D. 300. For every upstanding hillfort, there are about half a dozen unenclosed settlements comprising up to thirty round timber houses, mainly, it would seem, of ring-ditch type, found throughout the Region wherever drift geology and current farming practice promote the formation of crop-marks, i.e. in NE Fife and in the Kirkcaldy District away from the coal measures.

Sadly, none of these prehistoric 'deserted villages' survives as a standing monument, but the excavation of similar sites in Tayside allows us to clothe the bare bones of cropmark evidence. Individual houses ranged from c.5m. to c.18m. diameter within a low wall of earth at least 1m. thick and faced internally with panels of wattle. The main weight of the conical thatched roof was supported by a ring-beam on an internal circle of uprights, and the lower ends of the steep rafters probably overlapped the wallhead. Headroom was increased towards the periphery by excavating that part of the floor, giving the ring-ditch type its name. As such houses are sometimes found in open settlements alongside souterrains, it seems possible that their lifespan extended at least as far as the beginning of the Christian era.

Five or six souterrains have been authenticated in Fife, but only Ardross can be seen in near-original state. They are clustered between Wemyss and Elie, and seem to be closer in form to those of the Northern Isles and NE Scotland than the better-known examples in nearby Angus (Tayside). It seems only a matter of time before aerial reconnaissance locates further sites; already undoubted Angus-type souterrains have been recognized near the Regional boundary at Mugdrum, and several more resembling the smaller Grampian sites have been recorded in NE Fife, notably at Kinloch near Collessie and at Tofts Law by Newport. As to the purpose of these enigmatic structures, it can be assumed that each one is an adjunct to an unenclosed settlement of above-ground houses – hence the high probability that many more await discovery in Fife. Were they storage chambers, and if so for what commodity? Present evidence suggests that they continued in use till the early·C3 A.D., by which time the

---

* e.g. the recently discovered multivallate structures at Purin Hill and Freuchie; slighter hillforts at Lindores and Pitscottie; and coastal forts at Waukmill, Barns Mill, Randerston Castle and Guardbridge.

Roman army had thrice attempted to make s Scotland a permanent part of the province of Britannia – and failed.

The first ROMAN invasion was during the governorship of Julius Agricola (c.A.D. 77–83). There is no evidence of consequent operations in the Region, but when the army had advanced beyond the Tay it became imperative to isolate the tribesmen of Fife from contact with 'Free Caledonia' to the N, and a metalled road with watchtowers, fortlets and garrison posts was built, probably all the way from Doune to Bertha near Perth (Tayside). After Agricola's sweeping victory at Mons Graupius c.A.D. 83, the numerous garrisons of the occupying force were no doubt supplied with the help of sea transport, and the C2 map compiled by the geographer Ptolemy suggests at least a nodding acquaintance with the coastal parts of Fife. The Romans knew the Eden estuary – they called it 'the mouth of the River Tina' – and their name for the local Iron Age tribes was the Venicones, among whom lay the 'town' of Horrea Classis (Storehouses of the Fleet). It is generally assumed that Horrea was a coastal fort serving as a naval base. This may well have been the C1 forerunner of the legionary stronghold at Carpow near Newburgh (just over the Tayside boundary). But soon after A.D. 86 Agricola's northern conquests were surrendered, and by 100 most of the Roman forts N of Cheviot had been abandoned, so that the frontier of the province lay on the Tyne–Solway isthmus. Here in the reign of the emperor Hadrian (118–138) the continuous barrier known as Hadrian's Wall was gradually constructed.

Secondly, on the accession of Antoninus Pius in 138 an expansionist policy was once more adopted – at least to the extent of re-occupying Scotland as far N as the Tay. This time a running barrier, a wall of turf known as the Antonine Wall, was drawn between Forth and Clyde. To the E the coastal forts of Carriden, Cramond and Inveresk guarded the Lothian shore against possible assault from enemies in Fife. The Fife peninsula was also, as in the C1, cut off by a chain of garrisons along the military road from Camelon, near Falkirk (Central Region) to Bertha on the Tay. This occupation of central Scotland did not long outlast the reign of Antoninus (†161), but it seems clear that the area did not then cease to be influenced by Rome. Surveillance was maintained by long-range patrols, e.g. from certain outposts of Hadrian's Wall, but they did not prevent an outbreak of hostilities on the N frontier in the late C2. The unreclaimed coin hoards discovered near Rumbling Bridge (Tayside) and Pitcullo, near Leuchars, indicate unrest in and near Fife. It came from the northern tribes who had coalesced into the Maeatae (Central Region, Fife and s Tayside) and the Caledonii (probably Strathmore and beyond).

Finally, to deal with these tribes, the emperor Septimius Severus in 208 personally embarked on a series of expeditions N of Hadrian's Wall, and for the next three years fought a bitter and costly campaign whose course may be followed by recognition of the massive (25–65ha.) marching camps used by his armies. Their line of march stretches from Newstead on the Tweed, across the

Forth and Teith near Stirling, along the Antonine road to Bertha and NE to the farthest limits of Strathmore. In his first campaign, however, he diverged from this route in Strathearn to cross the Tay at Carpow (perhaps by a bridge of boats) and enter Strathmore near Brechin, via the coastal districts of Tayside.

During one of these campaigns an army group using camps 25ha. in area appears to have set out from Carpow, where soon a legionary base was to be built, and crossed the hills into the valley of the Eden in Fife. It bivouacked at Auchtermuchty and then advanced a day's march down river to Edenwood. Its objective can only be guessed, but the need for a force numbered in tens of thousands to stay close to a water source would suggest that it followed the Eden onward to its mouth (where aerial survey has revealed a concentration of native settlement, at least in earlier centuries). Possibly a part of the army penetrated into the high ground s of St Andrews, its bivouac being represented by the c.12ha. camp at Bonnytown, and eventually came to the coast of Forth, in sight of the fort of Cramond on the Lothian shore. Apart from sectors of Edenwood, none of these camps can be seen on the ground; they were detected by aerial survey. But they do amply demonstrate a Roman presence, and like the early C3 coin hoards from Craigiehill, Leuchars and Portmoak (Tayside), they suggest local hostility.

After the abandonment of the short-lived Severan bases on the Tay and Forth, and indeed long after Rome's power had waned in s Britain, the Fife peninsula continued to be debatable ground between the warring groups. Now, however, there was conflict between Pict and Briton, and a little later between Pict and Angle. The gradual evolution of Venicones into Maeatae, possibly later into Pictish Venturiones and finally into Southern Picts, is recorded by Roman and later historians – but with such tantalizing vagueness that it is impossible to see how closely it may reflect political reality.

Yet history, mythology, archaeology and place-name evidence combine to show Fife was an integral part of the PICTISH kingdom in the middle of the first millennium A.D. Traditionally the first king, Cruithni, was followed by his seven sons, and a number of their names can be identified as districts of Pictland, e.g. Caitt (Caithness) and Fib (Fife). This is mythology rather than history, but Fife does contain not only some splendid examples of Pictish carved stones but a concentration of place-names with the prefix 'Pit', which is found throughout the area of Pictish settlement.

Pictish authority in the mid-C7 was not undisputed. The Northumbrian Angles advanced into SE Scotland and Lothian, and in the later 650s their king Oswiu is said to have 'subdued and made tributary' the Picts and the Scots. It is likely that for some thirty years up to the Pictish victory at Nechtansmere near Dunnichen (Tayside) in 685, Fife at least was under Anglian sway. Thereafter, as Bede records, Angles and Picts faced each other across the Forth. Fife has plenty of the carved stones that show the Picts' artistic invention and wide cultural contacts. Two main types have been identified: slabs or boulders, often roughly dressed, with carved geometric or animal symbols (Class I), and more carefully dressed slabs which bear a cross as well as symbols (Class II). The symbols are compatible with a Christian message, and indeed it is likely that both types were artistic expressions of a Christian society. Class I stones include those from Lindores and Strathmiglo and the fragments now in the Falkland Palace Museum. Examples of Class II have been found at Scoonie and Upper Largo. They are hard to date, but Class I may be assigned broadly to the C7, Class II to the C8–early C9. One of the most assured pieces of Pictish art is the tomb-shrine of later C8 date at St Andrews, which along with a large number of cross-slabs emphasizes its early importance as an ecclesiastical centre.

The carvings in the caves at East Wemyss are an unusual and sadly neglected display of Pictish (and later) ornament. Several symbols including double discs and rectangles can clearly be seen despite Victorian scribings (including a cannon) and recent graffiti. One of the most interesting, a double disc and Z-rod from the Doo Cave, with the head of an animal almost touching it, has now been lost. But its style appears to have been very similar to that of one of the silver plaques found with the hoard from Norrie's Law 12km. to the NE. It is possible that the foreshore at Wemyss was the focus of a metal-working community in Pictish times, for quantities of slag have been found there.

The once prominent hill of Clatchard Craig SE of Newburgh has now been quarried away, and the fort on its summit destroyed; the findings of advance excavation in 1954–60 have only recently been fully published, but it is clear that an Iron Age fort with multiple defences – including two burnt timber-laced ramparts – was refurbished in the mid-first millennium A.D., with one rampart consolidated and a second built afresh. The walling, faced with stones, comprised a core of earth and stones reinforced by transverse timbers; there was no evidence of the use of nails. Several of the stone blocks had lumps of mortar adhering to them; the mortar contained a high proportion of crushed tile, and thus the stones are likely to be of Roman origin – presumably pillaged from Carpow 3.5km. to the W. There were few traces of Early Historic structures inside the fort, but a well-built rectangular stone hearth was found. A fragment of a C8 bronze-working mould was discovered beneath a paved area. It has been suggested that there was a rectangular timber hall of C8 date within the rampart. Small finds in the course of excavation imply that this was a place of high standing, comparable to Dunadd (Strathclyde) or Mote of Mark (Dumfries and Galloway); pieces of moulds for penannular brooches include a brooch-mould fragment belonging to the St Ninian's Isle group.

Fife has evidence of burial in two different traditions in the mid-first millennium. Twelve cairns at Lundin Links, found as a result of erosion of the dunes, covered burials in grave pits dating probably to the C5–7. Also at Lundin Links are some of the long cists which are the most common form of burial, as many as a hundred and forty having been excavated at the (probably contemporary) cemetery at Hallowhill near St Andrews. Here an earlier custom is represented by the inhumation of a child with a number of objects, including a Roman seal box with a *millefiori* lid. Long cist cemeteries, which have rarely been excavated with such care as at Hallowhill, have also been found in the East Neuk, e.g. at Leuchars, Kingsbarns and Crail, where the burials are laid out in two rows. Perhaps some of the cemeteries of small round and square barrows mentioned above may also belong to this general period.

The many place-names beginning with 'Pit' are today perhaps the most obvious reminder of the strong Pictish presence in Fife in the c8 and c9. 'Pit', from the Pictish *pett*, seems to mean 'share', or 'share of land', so their distribution from Easter Ross to Fife, with a concentration in the s, may indicate the heartland of the Pictish nation. Many such names have a Gaelic second element, however, and it has been suggested that they were 'coined during a bilingual period in the ninth and tenth centuries when Gaelic speakers had already settled in Pictish territory in considerable numbers.'

MEDIEVAL CHURCHES, MONASTERIES AND COLLEGES

FIFE'S earliest and most startling church is the c11 St Regulus' at St Andrews, built as a shrine for the bones of the apostle St Andrew, brought here probably in the c8. As fits its purpose, St Regulus' is a one-off, its immensely tall tower proclaiming the extraordinary importance of the relics housed in the small chancel. Beautifully constructed of ashlar, the detail is of the simplest, similar to English Anglo-Saxon work but the tower's small windows apparently designed for nook-shafts. St Regulus' is a symbol of the Scottish Church of its time, idiosyncratic almost to an extreme but on the verge of a revolution bringing it into the mainstream of west European Christianity.

The early medieval reformation of the Scottish Church, inspired by St Margaret, wife of Malcolm III, was largely carried out by her son David I (1124–53). Its three main strands were the regularization of a diocesan episcopate, the establishment of a parochial system, and the foundation of monasteries belonging to the European orders which had arisen from the work of St Benedict. New monasteries* in Fife were founded as part of this

---

* Earlier foundations of an unreformed and peculiarly Scottish type existed. The only one to continue was that of the Céli Dé at St Andrews, which had been reorganized as a college of secular canons by 1250.

process – Dunfermline (Benedictine) by St Margaret herself, c.1070; St Andrews (Augustinian), 1144, and Isle of May (Cluniac), c.1145, both by David I, who seems also to have founded Inchcolm (Augustinian); Lindores (Tironensian), New-burgh, by David, Earl of Huntingdon, c.1190; Culross (Cistercian) by Malcolm, Earl of Fife, c.1215; Balmerino (Cistercian) by Ermengarde, widow of William I, c.1225. The first Benedictines at Dunfermline were imported directly from Canterbury, the house from which Dunfermline's first abbot was brought in 1128. David I's monastery on the Isle of May was colonized by monks from Reading Abbey. Other monasteries acquired their members from houses already established in Scotland, but that did not necessarily mean that they were natives – Bishop Robert, one of the Augustinians imported to St Andrews from Scone (Tayside), had previously been a canon at Nostell Priory (Yorkshire).

The general plan of new C12 and C13 monasteries was standardized. Church and living quarters were grouped round a quadrangular cloister, the church on the N,* the chapter house and monks' dormitory on the E, their refectory on the S, and a guesthouse (e.g. Inchcolm) or lay brothers' dormitory and refectory (e.g. Culross) on the W. The church was cruciform, its S transept forming the N end of the cloister's W range, and was divided into nave and choir by a pair of solid screens (the pulpitum and rood screen) with a passage between. The nave (with its own main altar against the rood screen) was used by lay brothers, guests or parishioners; the choir was reserved for monastic offices. Size and elaboration varied. St Andrews Cathedral had a fully aisled nave and choir with an unaisled presbytery projecting a further bay E. Dunfermline's C12 plan seems to have been similar, but Culross had no aisles, Balmerino only a S nave aisle, Lindores a N nave aisle.

Acquisition of monks to form new monastic communities may not have been easy; the collection of building materials, workmen and finance to put up large buildings took time. Not surprisingly, the first manifestations of the new monasteries in Fife were additions to existing buildings. The prime requirement was a monastic choir. At Dunfermline a new choir was added, c.1070, to the small nave-tower church already there. At St Andrews, St Regulus' was enlarged by the addition of a nave, allowing the Augustinian canons to take over the chancel. The huge C12 arch made from this new nave (now vanished) into the existing tower survives. The sections of its arch mouldings and the side-by-side arrangement of the two orders so closely resemble those at the slightly earlier Wharram-le-Street (Yorkshire) that common authorship must be presumed, especially since Wharram-le-Street belonged to Nostell Priory, the house from which (via Scone) had come the Augustinian canons of St Andrews. A more thorough-going adaptation of an existing church for monastic purposes seems to have been made at Inchcolm, where, again, a

---

* At Lindores, like its mother-house of Melrose, the church is on the S and the refectory on the N.

new choir was added in the late C12. There the existing chancel became the retrochoir, its E wall remodelled as the pulpitum, its W arch filled in as the rood screen, both with acutely pointed openings; above was raised a tower, its windows crude precursors of the C13 windows in the NW tower of Holyrood Abbey, Edinburgh (another Augustinian house).

Provision of the standard monastic cloister depended on the abbey church's nave being long enough to fill its N side. That it was the requirements of living space for monks rather than more directly spiritual needs which dictated the size of monastic churches is clear at St Andrews Cathedral. Not originally planned 12 as a monastic church, its nave was extended W by four bays when it was taken over by the Augustinians, so allowing them a suitably large cloister. The first of Fife's monastic churches to allow for the building of a sizeable cloister was Dunfermline Abbey, rebuilt in the second quarter of the C12. Its surviving nave arcades are 9 very similar to those of Durham Cathedral (consecrated in 1130 and also a Benedictine house), the round piers sharing Durham's spiral and chevron ornament and carrying arcades of almost identical section. Among Dunfermline's glories are its three elaborately carved C12 doors, the S quite remarkably well preserved.

Dunfermline's external marking off of the nave bays by pilaster strips was followed later in the C12 by St Andrews Cathedral, the largest church built then or since in Scotland, but St Andrews marks the Scottish transition from purely Romanesque forms. Its nave and choir aisles were carried on octagonal piers. The presbytery's E gable had three tiers of round-arched lights, but the N wall's clearstorey windows had pointed arches, apparently a change in design and one of several made in the course of construction. The biggest changes made to the design of St Andrews before its eventual consecration in 1318 were at the W end, first lengthened c.1250, and then contracted after the collapse of the gable c.1280; the surviving SW tower gives it a uniquely war-ravaged appearance.

Of the C13 cloister buildings at St Andrews, much of the vaulted ground floor remains, the grandest apartment being the three-aisled chapter house. Another C13 chapter house survives at Inchcolm, an octagonal room, the vaulting's wall-ribs meeting at a central boss. Only a fragment of the contemporary chapter house survives at Culross, whose cloister was sited awkwardly down a steep slope.

Architectural, social and religious fashion, sometimes accompanied by political events, led to alteration of monastic churches and cloisters. At St Andrews a new chapter house was built E of the first c.1315, an example seemingly followed at Balmerino in the C15. At Dunfermline much of the cloister was destroyed by Edward I in 1304. When rebuilt in 1329 the 6 refectory was given a huge W window filled with reticulated tracery. In the C14 Inchcolm's chapter house suffered the indignity of having a warming house squashed down on top, part of a rebuilding of the cloister which unusually incorporated the cloister walk into the main buildings rather than having it as a lean-to projection into the central garth. Even more unusual was the conversion of the church's early C12 nave and retrochoir into the N range of the ambulatory, with the abbot's hall and solar above. Not surprisingly, perhaps, the surviving choir was virtually rebuilt in the next century. Almost as drastic were the alterations made to Culross Abbey, whose nave (the lay brothers' church) became redundant with the C15 restriction of membership of the monastery to choir-monks. Except for its s wall, necessary to enclose the cloister's N side, the nave was demolished and a tower built, c.1500, over the retrochoir. More significant stylistically was the C15 work at St Andrews Cathedral. There, the s transept was remodelled after the collapse of its gable in 1409. The fragment of a semi-cylindrical respond suggests that the reconstructed arcade had circular piers, an early example of their reappearance in Scottish architecture and a following of current fashion in northern Europe and particularly the Low Countries. A desire for architectural improvement without any excuse of the need to repair damage explains Prior James Haldenstone's remodelling (c.1430) of the E gable, where he punched one huge window through the two upper tiers of the C13 work.

Fife's monastic buildings could be accused of pride, and their later abbots or priors of arrogant disrespect for historic buildings. By contrast, most medieval parish churches showed excessive humility. The means to finance a regular parish system through tiends were established by David I in the early C12, and the large number of parish church consecrations by Bishop David de Bernham in the mid-C13 probably marks the end of a century of church building. Many parish livings were granted to monasteries, who enjoyed some or all of the tiend, installing a vicar or chaplain to conduct the services and minister pastorally. The churches themselves were often single-cell rectangles, the chancel marked off only by a rood beam (e.g. the C13 St Magridin, Abdie, or St Fillan, Forgan, of c.1500). Slightly grander churches had a stone chancel arch: at Aberdour (c.1140) the arch is of two orders, at the C13 St Serf, Burntisland, of only one. Grandest of all were those where the chancel was marked externally. Leuchars of c.1185, where the progressively lower, narrower and more richly decorated chancel and apse are the most sumptuous Romanesque work in Fife, is quite exceptional. The only non-monastic contemporary work and almost the only medieval work outside a burgh which can compare is the tower of Markinch built c.1200, its great height barely interrupted by stringcourses.

The late medieval popularity of votive masses and the endowment of altars and chaplains for their performance led to the extension of some parish churches by the addition of an aisle. St Serf, Burntisland, has fragments of a C15 s aisle. Much better preserved are the C15 N aisle at Kilconquhar and Aberdour's s aisle of c.1500, both with semicircular arcades carried on round piers. An alternative means of housing additional altars was by the provision of a transept, as happened at St Devenic, Creich, in the early C16.

Multiplication of altars as much as size of population explains the ambition of Fife's late medieval burgh churches. At Cupar, 20 Dysart (Kirkcaldy), Inverkeithing, Kinghorn and St Andrews, these were fully aisled. Holy Trinity, St Andrews, was the most 41 ambitious in plan, cruciform with aisled transepts. St Serf, Dysart, and Inverkeithing were simple rectangles. At Holy Trinity, St Andrews, the arcades were of standard Scottish C15 type with semicircular arches on round piers. At St Serf, Dysart, probably built in the early C16, the piers were alternately round and oblong with semicircular responds. Burgh churches' importance was emphasized by rugged late medieval towers. Inver- 15 keithing's C14 tower has buttresses at three corners and a stairtower at the fourth. At the unbuttressed tower of Holy Trinity, St Andrews, the stair is contained in a jamb with its own little spire.

An ostentatious way to provide for votive masses was to found a church for the purpose and provide the endowment for a number of chaplains who formed a 'college' or incorporation of priests. Of Fife's collegiate churches, St Monans, founded by 13 David II in 1362–70, is memorably haunting in its cliff-top churchyard. It consists of an unaisled choir and transepts; a nave was begun but quickly abandoned. Externally, the crossing tower dominates. Inside, the choir has been expensively finished with an elaborate late Gothic vault and extravagant sedilia. Crail, founded c.1517, has an aisled nave with pointed arcades but a disappointingly mean chancel.

A C15 and C16 development from the collegiate church was the college intended both for the saying of votive masses and as an incorporation of scholars. Four of these (St Salvator, St Leonard, Blackfriars and St Mary) were founded at St Andrews, already a university, between 1450 and 1538. St Salvator's was 14 built c.1450–70. There survives the chapel, consecrated in 1460, with a massive gate tower to its W. The architecture is not adventurous, the excitement provided by canopied image niches on the stepped buttresses rather than by originality of design. St Leonard's, founded in 1512, took over an existing church of c.1400, which was then remodelled and extended to provide a choir for those who belonged to the foundation. Of Blackfriars 17 there remains only the chapel's N transept of 1525. Octagonal-ended and with large loop-traceried windows, it is a tantalizing fragment. St Mary's College has kept its heavily remodelled C16 buildings but lost its chapel.

Fife's medieval churches have suffered from the attentions of devout C16 Reformers and no less high-minded C19 and C20 restorers as well as from neglect and nature. Interiors are often stripped of plaster to reveal piously pointed rubble whose intricate patterns are insufficient compensation for the lack of colour. Of painted decoration only a few fragments survive. In Dunfermline Abbey one bay of the N aisle's vault is painted with four Apostles, probably of c.1500. On the walls of Inchcolm's C14 warming house are Latin platitudes. In the ruins of that abbey's choir is the painted back of a tomb recess, probably late C13, showing a procession of (now headless) clerics.

Medieval church furnishings have with very few exceptions disappeared. In Inchcolm Abbey a late medieval altar slab found in the s transept now marks the site of the high altar. More impressive is Inverkeithing Parish Church's octagonal font of *c*.1398, decorated with angels holding coats of arms. Flying angels holding a pyx appear on the flashy sacrament house of *c*.1455 in St Salvator's College Chapel, St Andrews, its aumbry framed by a hugely crocket-finialled ogee hoodmould.

Church burials could be marked by graveslabs. Sadly few remain, but Creich Parish Church (Brunton) contains the early C15 stone to David Barclay of Luthrie and his wife, incised with portraits of a knight and his lady. Clerical figures are shown on slabs in St Salvator's College Chapel and St Leonard's Chapel, St Andrews. More expensive and more tempting to vandals were the sculptured effigies placed in tomb recesses. The best-preserved effigy but not *in situ* is the C15 figure of a knight in Ceres Parish Church. More battered but still in their recesses are the figure, also C15, of a knight in Cupar Parish Church and, in Culross Abbey, the headless effigies of John Stewart of Innermeath and his wife. Now deprived of its effigy is the grandest of these C15 tomb recesses, the monument to Bishop James Kennedy in St Salvator's College Chapel, St Andrews, richly canopied with boldly carved image niches. The inspiration must be from France, which may also have provided the craftsmen. The canopied shrine erected in 1368 over the grave at Dunfermline Abbey of Scotland's major medieval saint, St Margaret, is now represented only by two battered marble plinth stones. Of the shrine of Scotland's patron saint, St Andrew, there is nothing.

POST-REFORMATION CHURCHES

THE Scottish Reformation of 1560 was indubitably Protestant and in Fife sometimes violently iconoclastic. Monastic churches were deprived of their function as a setting for conventual worship. St Andrews Cathedral, the abbeys of Lindores, Balmerino and Inchcolm, the Franciscan houses at St Andrews and Inverkeithing, and the collegiate church of St Mary on the Rock at St Andrews were all abandoned and later used as quarries. At Dunfermline, the abbey church's nave continued in use as a parish church but the choir was abandoned; at Culross the nave was left to fall down but the choir converted to a parish church.

The post-Reformation view of a parish church's function is described by a C17 inscription in Collessie churchyard:

A.SOLEMNE.SAIT.FOR.GODS.SERVICE.PREPARD
FOR.PRAIER.PREACHING.AND.COMMVNION

The new emphasis on praying and preaching as integral parts of worship implied that the congregation had to be able to hear as well as see. The pulpit, often doubling as a reading desk, took on major importance. Despite the wishes of the leading Reformers, communion services became infrequent; for these were provided wooden tables round which the congregation could sit, stone altars having been broken up as idolatrous paraphernalia. Most medieval parish churches were aisleless rectangles and easily enough adapted to the new requirements, the pulpit frequently placed in the centre of the long s wall, with seating, sometimes supplemented by galleries, ranged round it. In places (e.g. East Wemyss or Kinglassie) the former chancel was taken over by a local landowner who set up his private gallery there, sometimes using the ground below as a family vault. Often a transeptal 'aisle' opposite the pulpit was added for the same purpose (e.g. Auchterderran, Ballingry, Culross Abbey, Forgan, and Kinglassie) making the church a T, the plan adopted for Fife's first post-Reformation parish church, Kemback, built in 1582. Often there was more than one landowner to be accommodated in a former chancel or new 'aisle', although St Bridget's Church, Dalgety Bay, is exceptional in having acquired four lairds' 'aisles' as well as a gallery in the chancel by the early C17. Exceptional too at that church is the grandeur of the Dunfermline Aisle of 33 c.1610, with its stone-panelled interior and retiring room.

A church which broke with the conventional rectangular or T plans was Burntisland of c.1592–1600, a square church built round a central tower. Inside, the tower is supported on heavy 18–19 piers linked by round arches defining the central space. For hearing and seeing the minister it works remarkably badly. Any connexion with Renaissance ideals of centrally planned churches can be tenuous at best, and as a prototype it had no successor. Probably the idea was that the central space under the tower would serve as a communion aisle (i.e. where the holy table would be placed for a communion service), the church's perimeter being used to seat the congregation during other services.

Provision of a communion aisle was much more sensibly handled at Dairsie Church, built in 1621 by Archbishop Spottiswoode, who followed contemporary Anglican practice in providing a chancel to which the communicants would move when the sacrament was celebrated. Less sensibly, perhaps, at a time when many Scots were suspicious of bishops and the Church of England, Spottiswoode raised his chancel by one step above the body of the church, from which it was divided by a 'glorious partition wall', a solid wooden screen surmounted by the royal arms; he also decorated the interior with carved croziers. The same division of nave and chancel may also have been present in the chapel built at Balcarres in 1635, where an aumbry appears in the s wall's e end. The Balcarres chapel and Dairsie Church 21 both mixed Gothic and classical detail without conscious incongruity. So too did the chapel of 1650 at Fordell Castle, whose loop tracery is as exuberantly late Gothic as the plate tracery at Dairsie.

EIGHTEENTH-CENTURY churches in Fife are few. The first
22 was the grand though not large chapel built by *Alexander McGill*
at Donibristle, Dalgety Bay, for the Earl of Moray in 1729–
32. Its punchy classicism had no successor. Since 1693 entire
responsibility for the building and upkeep of churches had been
borne by the heritors (landowners) of each parish.* Some heritors
were Episcopalians, some absentee; few cared to do more than
they were legally bound. Fife's one mid-C18 parish church,
Kilmany (of 1768), is a plain skinny rectangle whose bellcote's
obelisk-spire provides the only hint of extravagance. Rather
grander is Abbotshall, Kirkcaldy, of 1788, which has a short
tower, but at Cults, Kirkton of Cults, of 1793 the birdcage
bellcote thriftily re-used balusters taken from table stones in the
graveyard, an economy apparently repeated at Cameron in 1808.
Burgh churches were usually larger, but town councils were not
markedly more spendthrift than rural lairds. At Auchtermuchty
20 (1779), Cupar (1785) and Markinch (1786), plain boxes were
provided, civic pride satisfied by Diocletian windows (Auchtermuchty and Markinch) and urns or vases on the gables (Cupar
and Markinch).

The EARLY NINETEENTH CENTURY was a major church-
building period in Fife, perhaps a consequence of the paucity of
C18 churches. The simple rectangular or T-plan preaching box
was still the norm but often clothed in consciously ecclesiastical
dress. 'Saxon' was chosen as the style for the tower at Ceres (by
Alexander Leslie, 1805) and by *John Henderson* at Carnock in
1838. *James Gillespie Graham* used Tudor at Dalgety, 1829.
The only classical parish church was *Alexander Laing*'s Dysart,
Kirkcaldy (1801), and Abdie's Italianate bellcote (by *William
Burn*, 1826) had no imitators. The favourite style for larger
churches of the 1820s and 1830s was Perp. The prototype, of
27–8 great size and cost, was *William Burn*'s Abbey Church, Dunfermline (1818–21). Its splendour is attributable both to its being
the sole parish church of a sizeable burgh surrounded by a
prosperous rural parish and to the accepted historic importance
of its site on the foundations of the choir of the medieval abbey,
15 the burial-place of King Robert the Bruce. Inverkeithing (1826,
by *Gillespie Graham*) is the humbler product of a less important
burgh. What surprises is the ambition of such rural churches
as Kilconquhar (1819, by *R. & R. Dickson*, adapting *Richard
Crichton*'s design for Cockpen Church, Lothian), Creich Church,
Brunton (by *William Stirling I*, 1829), Kingskettle and Tulliallan, Kincardine-on-Forth (almost identical productions by
George Angus, 1831–2), and Collessie (by *R. & R. Dickson*,
1838). These buildings, all with prominent towers and costing
far more than the heritors were legally obliged to spend, testify
to the generosity and architectural interest of at least some landowners of the time.

The established Church of Scotland was not the only denomi-
nation in the C18 and early C19. Episcopalians who had rejected

---

* And remained their responsibility until 1925, when it was transferred to the
General Trustees of the Church of Scotland.

the system of Presbyterian church government imposed after the Revolution of 1688–9 were, usually rightly, seen as Jacobites and between 1746 and 1792 forbidden to hold services attended by more than five people. Of their early C19 churches, the one at St Andrews by *William Burn*, 1825 (rebuilt at Buckhaven as a Free church in 1870), was elaborately Tudor, and Trinity Chapel, Dunfermline, of 1842 is a characteristically lumpy example of *Thomas Hamilton*'s lancet style. More productive of Georgian churches in Fife than the Episcopalians were the various Secession sects which split from the Church of Scotland after 1733 over the question of patronage and with each other over less important matters. Their meeting houses are quite common in Fife but generally are small and plain. Two big ones, both classical, are worth note, the ambitious Bethelfield Church, Kirk- 24 caldy (by *George Hay*, 1830), and the temple-fronted Limekilns 23 Church of 1825.

Two events in the 1840s revolutionized the Scottish ecclesiastical scene. At the Disruption of 1843 about one-third of ministers and laity left the Church of Scotland to form the Free Church. Four years later the bulk of the Secessionists came together as the United Presbyterian Church.[*] For the rest of the C19, Presbyterianism was represented by three strong and mutually hostile denominations. The first Free churches were put up hurriedly and cheaply. Most were preaching boxes with minimal Gothic detail; the rustic Perp of Markinch Free Church (1843–4) is unusually frivolous. The United Presbyterians retained their existing meeting houses. But by the 1860s both these denominations were rebuilding their chapels on a much larger and architecturally more ambitious scale, apparently in deliberate competition with the parish churches. At Leven, the Free (now St Andrew, by *John Hay* of Liverpool, 1860–1), United Presbyterian (now St Peter (R.C.), by *Robert Baldie*, 1870–1) and Episcopal (by *Matthews & Mackenzie*, 1879) Churches all flaunt steeples in the face of the Parish Church. In Cupar, *Peddie & Kinnear*'s United Presbyterian (now Baptist) Church of 1865–6 and *Campbell Douglas & Sellars*' Free (now St John's) Church of 1875–8 sit almost next each other. Both have steeples, but the former Free Church uses its size and siting to best its rival. In Buckhaven, Church Street is a parade of denominational differences. The style is almost always Gothic, with a predilection for Dec, despite its unsuitability as a dress for broad rectangular preaching boxes. However, the front gable could be made to suggest a nave and aisles behind, either by bisecting it with a central tower (as done by *David Bryce* at Falkland in 1848–50, followed by *Campbell Douglas & Sellars* at Cupar Free Church in 1875) or by providing a stairtower (to the galleries) each side (e.g. *Peddie & Kinnear*'s Cupar United Presbyterian Church of 1865). Not much beyond the provision of buttresses could be done to disguise the bleakness of side elevations. The biggest contribution

---

[*] Most of the Secessionists who did not enter the United Presbyterian Church in 1847 joined the Free Church in 1852.

made by these Victorian Presbyterian churches has been to the townscape.

The Episcopalians built only a handful of late C19 churches, the largest *R. Rowand Anderson*'s Tractarian St Andrew's, St
40 Andrews, of 1869, the most assured the same architect's Holy Trinity, Dunfermline, of 1891. The Roman Catholics built even less, their one major building, St Margaret's, Dunfermline, again by Anderson, begun in 1889, is a sad fragment of what was intended.

The C20 has seen a drawing together of the Churches both institutionally (in 1900 the Free and United Presbyterian Churches combined to form the United Free Church, which joined the Church of Scotland in 1929*) and architecturally. The Church of Scotland was much influenced after 1886 by the neo-Anglican ideas of the Aberdeen (later Scottish) Ecclesiological Society, which advocated placing the communion table at a focal point (preferably in the chancel), flanked by the pulpit and font. At the same time, and partly as a result of the same influence, there was a new interest in specifically Scottish architectural models (although *Campbell Douglas & Sellars* had designed Dysart Free (now Parish) Church, Kirkcaldy, as a snecked rubble version of the medieval St Monans Church as early as 1872). In 1905–6 *Thoms & Wilkie* used Scottish late medieval detail at Newburgh United Free (now Parish) Church, although the pulpit, not the communion table, was given pride of place in the chancel. *P. MacGregor Chalmers* ransacked Scottish sources for
41 his virtual rebuilding in 1907–9 of Holy Trinity, St Andrews. More satisfying is his other church in the same town: St Leonard's, a completely new church, was designed in a beautifully cool early Christian or 'pre-Norman' style and arranged along the
42 best ecclesiological lines. Just as successful is his St Leonard's, Dunfermline, of 1903–4, with the design of its slim round tower taken from Brechin Cathedral.

Interwar church building in Fife was dominated by the Roman Catholics, whose favourite architect, *Reginald Fairlie*, had
43 already designed St James (R.C.), St Andrews, in 1909, small and Romanesque in crazy-paved rubble. He kept both the style and the rubble at Methil Parish Church (his one Church of Scotland commission) in 1924, but most of his designs were for cheap mission churches. Harled simplicity was the keynote, sometimes concealing surprisingly strong interiors (e.g. Our Lady and St Bride, Cowdenbeath). Fairlie's last Fife church, Our Lady Star of the Sea, Tayport, of 1938–9, presents the ideal simple Scottish country kirk of a type which never existed. Much more powerful was *J. Ninian Comper*'s vision of triumphant Episcopalianism at St Andrew and St George, Rosyth, a huge Gothic box intended to be filled with white and gold flashed with blue from stained glass in the immense windows. Never finished, it was demolished in 1986.

The post-war period has brought more redundancy and demo-

---

* Rumps of both the Free and United Free Churches refused to join the unions and have maintained their separate existence.

lition than new churches, although large housing estates have been given churches and halls, the one often undistinguishable from the other. Only *Gillespie, Kidd & Coia*'s St Paul, Glen- 47 rothes, of 1957–8 stands out, but post-Vatican II rearrangement has destroyed the impact of its toplit altar, and pink paint has given the interior a false cosiness.

FURNISHINGS are generally unexciting. Georgian grained or painted pine and Victorian pitchpine predominate, sometimes cheered up by C20 pastel shades. At Dunfermline Abbey (Parish) Church the magistrates' pew of 1610 was painted with the royal arms. Burntisland Parish Church's early C17 Artisan classical 19 gallery fronts are painted with C17 and C18 emblems of the burgh guilds. More rudimentary classicism is shown on the same church's magistrates' pew and the ignorantly pilastered back of the early C17 pulpit in St Salvator's College Chapel, St Andrews. More correct were the Corinthian pilasters of Carnock pulpit (bits surviving in the minister's chair), dated 1674. The sounding board of Kilmany Church's octagonal late C18 pulpit has a Doric frieze. Of early C19 pulpits the best are the domed canopied examples at Ceres (of 1805) and Upper Largo (formerly at 26 Newburn, of 1815), and the Gothic pulpit at Creich Church, Brunton (of 1832). Ceres has a dove finial; so too had Holy Trinity, St Andrews, where it survives above the *nouveau riche* alabaster, onyx and marble replacement of 1909. Much less flashy is the sumptuous neo-Jacobean woodwork of *Ernest George & Peto*'s pulpit introduced to Limekilns in 1883. The ensemble of pulpit and organ loved by the richer late Victorian Edinburgh and Glasgow congregations and loathed by high-minded C20 restorers is rare in Fife, but there are examples at Markinch Parish Church, Tulliallan Church (Kincardine-on-Forth) and one of the 1920s with woodwork of real quality at Methil Church (Buckhaven and Methil). Organs themselves are far from universal.

STAINED GLASS was frowned on by Presbyterians until the late C19. The earliest in Fife was apparently provided by *William Wailes* for the Episcopalians' Trinity Chapel, Dunfermline, in 1842. The first Church of Scotland stained glass is at Inverkeithing Parish Church, a brightly coloured foliage design of 1856.* Armorial glass was placed in Dunfermline Abbey's nave in 1863. Depictions of people (but not identifiable saints) appeared in 1867 with *Ward & Hughes*' window of the Acts of Charity at Kilconquhar. Dunfermline Abbey acquired Biblical scenes (by *James Ballantine & Son*) in 1871; they were joined by Scottish historical figures (again by *Ballantine*) in 1882. Much of the glass is pedestrian, but there are examples worth seeking out. *Edward Burne-Jones* designed windows at Forgan and St Brycedale, Kirkcaldy. *G. F. Bodley* produced an accomplished pair at Dunfermline Abbey in 1880–1901. Also at Dunfermline Abbey is a pre-Raphaelitish window of 1909–10 by *Henry Holiday*, whose characteristically strong colour glows in the

---

* i.e. two years after stained glass had been introduced to Glasgow Cathedral, but a year before the first Church of Scotland stained glass in Edinburgh.

chancel of St Leonard's Church and the ante-chapel of St Salvator's College Chapel, both in St Andrews. Excellent colour also characterizes *Alexander Strachan*'s windows (of *c*.1930–3) at Aberdour and Dunfermline Abbey. His brother *Douglas Strachan* provided a parade of expressionist work over a forty-year period (1910–50) at Holy Trinity, St Andrews. By comparison, *Margaret Chilton*'s precise windows at St Leonard, St Andrews, seem brittle, but at St Finnian (Episcopal), Lochgelly, she produced an unexpectedly rich light for the Lady Chapel in 1949. *William Wilson*'s brightly coloured and rather crowded windows appear frequently (e.g. at Dunfermline Abbey, Ladybank Parish Church, St Salvator's College Chapel, and Holy Trinity, St Andrews), but seem timid and provincial compared to *Gabriel Loire*'s glass for the Church of the Holy Name at Oakley.

In 1581 the reformed Church of Scotland forbade burial within churches. Although the ban was circumvented by the use of lairds' aisles as burial vaults, CHURCH MONUMENTS are fairly rare. One of the first is the wall monument of *c*.1590 to Robert Stewart, Earl of March, in St Leonard's Chapel, St Andrews, a basket-arched tomb recess with inept Corinthian pilasters. No more competently classical was the same chapel's Wilkie monument of *c*.1611. This combination of a medieval tomb recess with would-be classical detail appears at the Pitcarn monument of *c*.1585 at Dunfermline Abbey, but the same church's memorial
31 to William Schaw † 1602 is much more resolutely classical.
32 Immensely grander is Sir George Bruce of Carnock's monument in Culross Abbey Church, a huge combination of the tomb recess and aedicule, erected *c*.1630. Sculpture is prominent, with recumbent effigies of Bruce and his wife and kneeling alabaster figures of their children. *John Mercer* signed the monument, but the figures almost certainly came from England. Said to have
35 been imported from the Netherlands in 1679 is Archbishop Sharp's grandiose memorial in Holy Trinity, St Andrews, a great Corinthian aedicule framing a tomb-chest, all adorned with sculptured reliefs depicting Sharp as a martyr to Covenanting rage. After the C17 there is little of note. Mid-C18 refinement is carried almost to excess in St Salvator's College Chapel, St Andrews, where the marble tablet to John Home † 1754 is carved like an engraver's plate. More conventional is the heavy Jacobean frame for carved heraldry on Elizabeth Preston's memorial of *c*.1835 in Culross Abbey Church. In Cults Parish Church
39 (Kirkton of Cults) portrait reliefs by *Francis Chantrey* adorn the monument of 1833 to the parents of Sir David Wilkie, whose
37 adjoining relief bust of a few years later is by *Samuel Joseph*. An absurdly confident belief in Lady Augusta Stanley's acceptance into heaven is shown by *Mary Grant*'s monument of 1876 in Dunfermline Abbey. The rest is routine.

CHURCHYARDS were attached to all parish churches,* the upkeep of their walls the responsibility of the heritors. At their gates were frequently built OFFERTORY HOUSES, shelters in

---

* But sometimes when a new parish church was built on a different site the old churchyard remained in use.

which (until the Poor Law Act of 1845) church elders sat to collect money for relief of the poor. Examples survive at Kinglassie (c.1700), Abdie (1748) and Upper Largo (early C19). Usually built at the expense of the kirk session, they sometimes doubled as SESSION HOUSES where the sessions met (e.g. the Gothic session house at Torryburn of c.1800, or the Tudorish session house at Saline of 1819).

The general purpose of burial was to provide for the seemly disintegration of bodies to dust, not to give a private resting place until the General Resurrection. Monuments over tombs were the prerogative of the prosperous, and C17 town councils (e.g. Burntisland) tried to restrict memorials to the churchyard walls. The best collection of C17 WALL MONUMENTS is at St Andrews Cathedral graveyard, a display of aedicular tablets, all would-be classical, some correctly so. A grand monument of this type at Cupar commemorates William Scott † 1642 with trumpeting angels giving news of the Resurrection, but Francis Moray's monument of c.1650 at Strathmiglo shows how uncertainly the classical vocabulary could still be used in the mid-C17.

GRAVESTONES were used to proclaim the social standing of the deceased by being adorned with heraldry or trade emblems. Two from the 1630s (Agnes Lindsay at Leuchars and David Martin at Auchtertool) have life-size full-length portraits. Full-lengths of John Fortune and his wife decorate their children's headstone of c.1770 at Upper Largo. The Fortunes stand on skulls, and cheerful emblems of death abound, Auchtermuchty having the best collection of skulls, crossbones and hour-glasses on C18 stones. More sentimental is the stone at Forgan to Agnes Cunningham † 1792, its top carved with one big and three small angels to represent this mother and her three children. Much grislier is the headstone of 1792 at Cupar to three Covenanters, 38 carved with the two heads and a hand which were gathered after their execution and buried here. A few headstones are of cast-iron, like the two early C19 examples at Kinghorn with pretty Adamish decoration. Also Adamish is one of the few larger monuments of note, that to James Cheape of c.1810 in Strathmiglo, a version of the Robertson Mausoleum in Greyfriars Churchyard (Edinburgh). The Victorian repertoire of urns and crosses is amply represented, but very few have the quality of *Sydney Mitchell*'s Balfour monument in Markinch Cemetery, a free reproduction of the Kildalton Cross. Outstanding for its inventively sinuous beauty is *Charles Rennie Mackintosh*'s Johnson memorial of c.1905 in Macduff Cemetery at East 45 Wemyss.

MAUSOLEA were erected as an assertion of proprietary rights to burial plots. Most are shedlike, but at Collessie in 1609 Sir James Melville built one which attempts smartness with vestigial columns attached to the ends of its ashlar-panelled walls. The inscription relates its propaganda purpose in demonstrating that there could be an acceptable upper-class alternative to burial inside the church itself. A late C19 alternative to churchyard burial was provided by new cemeteries, the most lavish being

Vicarsford, where *T. Martin Cappon*'s French Gothic chapel of
1895–7 takes spectacular advantage of its hilltop site.

CASTLES, PALACES AND TOWER HOUSES

THE C12 transformation of Scotland begun by David I made the
Pictish earldom of Fife into a feudal holding. At the same time,
often perhaps through marriage, Norman-French knights began
to acquire land in the region. Motte-and-bailey castles (artificial
mounds topped by wooden keeps and surrounded by palisades)
were characteristic of the new social and political order. In Fife
thirteen certain or possible motte sites have been identified,*
among them Leuchars Castle, Castlehill at Cupar, Lochore
Castle, and Perdieus Mount at Dunfermline. Of the 'motte' at
Crail there is now no trace. But there is no reason to suppose
that naturally defensive sites were not used for castle building as
well as artificial mottes. Aberdour Castle, standing on a strong
rock outcrop, was the centre of a barony by 1126, when Sir
Alan de Mortimer gained possession through his marriage to the
daughter of another Norman-French knight, Sir John Vipont.
Bishop Roger built St Andrews Castle *c.* 1200 on another natural
48 stronghold. The cubed ashlar and small lancet windows of Aberdour Castle's earliest part look C12; many more C12 castles may
have been swept away by later medieval fashion.

Fife, probably because it was not a frontier region of strategic
importance, has no major C13 castle to compare with Dirleton
(Lothian), Caerlaverock (Dumfries and Galloway) or Kil-
drummy (Grampian), but the development of the curtain-walled
castle, essentially an enclosure surrounded by a stone wall against
which were built the principal buildings, affected Fife by the
C14. Ballinbreich, on the edge of a steep slope down to the Tay,
was begun probably in the early C14 for the Leslies. Its main
living quarters protrude as a tower from the curtain's SW corner,
probably protecting the original entrance. At St Andrews Castle,
rebuilt in the late C14, the entrance itself was contained in a
gatehouse tower, although one which lacked the swagger of a
gatehouse like that of Dirleton (Lothian). But at St Andrews
accommodation was dispersed among corner towers, whilst the
50 hall probably occupied the E range. At Ravenscraig Castle, Kirkcaldy, begun in 1460 for James II's queen, Mary of Gueldres,
massive drum towers (disconcertingly of different heights) guard
the ends of the curtain's front wall. Inside the W tower and the
central range, gun platforms were provided from the start. The
central range's upper floor, probably intended originally for the
hall, was made an artillery platform in the C16.

* *See* Grant G. Simpson and Bruce Webster, 'Charter Evidence and the Distribution of Mottes in Scotland', *Essays on the Nobility of Medieval Scotland*, ed.
K. J. Stringer (1985).

In the C16 defence began to take a subservient role in the
design of castles and palaces. In 1537–42 James V carried out a
massive reconstruction and enlargement of Falkland Palace, a
royal seat which had grown from the medieval castle of the Earls
of Atholl. His new gatehouse with drum towers flanking the 54
entrance looked back directly to the recently completed NW tower
at Holyroodhouse (Edinburgh) and to the earlier forework at
Stirling Castle (Central). By contrast his remodelling of the E 55
range and the new S range was in line with contemporary work in
France, the façades divided into bays by buttresses with attached
classical columns topped by upside-down consoles, whilst the
walling is studded with carved portrait roundels. Falkland's
French classicism was exceptional – in his contemporary remodelling of the Palace Block at Dunfermline Abbey, James V was 6
content to add oriels – but classicism of a sort was attempted
elsewhere. In his remodelling of the entrance front of St Andrews 56
Castle, c.1555, Archbishop John Hamilton dressed up his
entrance as a triumphal arch, a surprisingly ambitious concept
for the date. The fourth Earl of Morton's addition of c.1570 to
Aberdour Castle has windows set in aedicules with attenuated 49
Tuscan pilasters and steep pediments.

Houses such as Falkland Palace, St Andrews Castle and Aberdour Castle were the property of the Crown or political magnates,
but most Fife estates belonged to landowners of no great consequence. These could not afford, even should they so desire, to
build castles. Their dwellings until the C15 were probably largely
of wood and no more than two storeys high, perhaps given some
protection by stone dykes or palisades. A very smart example of
this tradition translated into stone is probably represented by
the C15 main block of Tulliallan Castle (Kincardine-on-Forth),
whose accommodation was pacifically arranged on two floors, the
ground floor covered with quadripartite vaulting, the first floor
probably taken up by a hall; the plan is a small-scale version of
the frater block at Culross Abbey. But Tulliallan is unusual for
its time. The standard type of laird's residence from the C15 was
the TOWER HOUSE, essentially a vertical stack of rooms, usually
on three floors, the ground floor given over to storage and frequently the kitchen, the first floor occupied by the hall, the
second floor by bedchambers. The near-universal provision of
tunnel-vaulting over the ground floor gave constructional
strength and protection against a fire in the kitchen. The wallhead
often had a corbelled and crenellated parapet, more as a symbol
of lairdly prestige than martial intent. Gunloops are common,
becoming more prolific as times grew quieter, so that a house of
c.1580 like Pittarthie Castle has pistol-holes in all the window
sills.

Tower houses varied in size and pretension with the wealth
and ambition of their owners. The simplest type is represented
by the C15 N tower of Kellie Castle, a simple rectangle with 59
the stair contained in the wall thickness. Much grander is the
austerely fastidious Scotstarvit Tower of c.1500. Beautifully built 58
of ashlar, it consists of two high tunnel-vaults, one above the

other, each divided horizontally by a wooden floor. The plan is an L, the comfortable stair filling the jamb which is given its own walltop flourish. The L-plan with the stair either contained in the jamb or placed in the inner angle became general in the c16. Placing the stair at one corner with the entrance in the inner angle (and usually commanded by a gunloop) gave some protection against unwelcome visitors and draughts. Some late c16 houses (e.g. Dairsie Castle) expanded the L into a Z by the addition of a second jamb diagonally opposite the first, containing, on the first floor, a room which opened off the hall's warmer 53 fireplace end. Rossend Castle at Burntisland, of c.1552–4, is exceptional in the grandeur of its T-plan, which provides a withdrawing room and bedchamber in the crossbar, rather awkwardly placed at the screens' end. More sophisticated was the expansion of Kellie Castle, c.1600, which placed these rooms beyond the hall dais.

Internal decoration of castles and tower houses until the mid-c17 was mostly provided by hangings. Falkland Palace chapel's compartmented oak ceiling of c.1540 is a rare covering up of floor joists. Usually these were left exposed, although by the beginning of the c17 they might be painted with heraldic decoration, as at Collairnie Castle in 1607, or with fruit and flowers, as at Rossend Castle, Burntisland, in c.1616.* The most ambitious scheme of painted decoration was provided in the Long Gallery at Earlshall in 1620. Here the boarded ceiling is painted in black, grey and white, with heraldry interspersed with animals, both arms and beasts owing much to imagination; along the walls is a painted arcade containing aphorisms. More colourful are the heraldry and texts painted on the chapel walls and ceiling at Falkland Palace in honour of Charles I's visit to Scotland in 1633. Here the decoration attempts to perfect the architecture by providing painted windows on the N wall to balance the real openings in the s. Plasterwork is rare in Scotland before the mid-c17, but the present library at Kellie Castle has a ceiling of 1617. Similar 63 but much classier is the one in the Panelled Room at Balcarres of c.1630, its strapworked compartments filled with the royal arms and roundels of four of the Nine Worthies. Probably derived from English examples, it is a surprising embellishment for what was then a modest house, perhaps indicative of burgeoning political and architectural ambition.

COUNTRY HOUSES

RESTORATION of the monarchy in 1660 restored the Scottish Parliament, Privy Council and law courts and brought to office

---

* The ceiling from Rossend is now in the Royal Museum of Scotland, Edinburgh.

nobles and gentry determined to do the best for themselves and their families after the lean years of Cromwellian military dictatorship. Consciousness of their new position was expressed by the building or reconstruction of their houses.

The largest and earliest of these RESTORATION houses in Fife was Leslie, begun by *John Mylne Jun.* in 1667 for the seventh Earl (later first Duke) of Rothes, Lord Chancellor of Scotland. Leslie was a quadrangular palace comparable in size to Holyroodhouse (Edinburgh). Externally it showed a sleepy recognition of classicism, the main front a gauche paraphrase of Clarendon House in London. The main features of its plan, however, produced a model for other late C17 houses. The ground floor, largely devoted to servants' and storage accommodation, contained in the E range (overlooking a terraced garden) the family apartment of dining room, library, drawing room, bedchambers and closets. In the first floor's S and E ranges was a state apartment, a sequence of ascending honour from the state stair through the great saloon, drawing room and ante-chamber to the state bedchamber in the centre of the E front. Also reached from the state stair was the 47.8m.-long gallery, occupying the whole of the W range and hung with full-length portraits of the Earl's ancestors. The N range and second floor were filled with bedrooms and closets. The Earl's architectural adviser was *Sir William Bruce*, who in 1668–74 enlarged an early C17 house on his own newly acquired estate of Balcaskie to produce Fife's second major Restoration house. At Balcaskie a great stair led from the entrance hall to a gallery, probably doubling as a saloon, from which was entered the state apartment of drawing room, ante-chamber, bedchamber and closet. The need for a state apartment was felt also by the second Earl of Wemyss, for whom, in 1669–72, *Robert Mylne* tacked on to Wemyss Castle an addition containing a state stair, ante-chamber (or dining room), drawing room, bedchamber and closet. Robert Mylne's son-in-law, *James Smith*, built and probably designed* Melville House for another 66 leading C17 politician, the first Earl of Melville, in 1697–1703. The house is H-plan; in the crossbar are the great stair and first-floor saloon, off which opens in each of the side-pieces a suite of drawing room, bedchamber and closet.

Externally these houses are disappointing, the exuberance of early C17 design being replaced by a stodgy symmetry, gables not pediments the dominant features.‡ The emphasis of gables may be partly conservatism. At Balcaskie it was probably largely the result of the decision to extend rather than rebuild an earlier house. In his enlargement Bruce made the existing L-plan into a U, filling the centre with a lower flat-roofed block, a development of the formula first used by John Mylne Jun. at Panmure (Tayside) in 1666. The fullest realization of this design was Bruce's enlargement of Craighall in 1697–9 (demolished 1955),

---

* *Sir William Bruce* also supplied designs for Melville House, but the executed scheme seems to be Smith's.

‡ At Melville House the side elevations are pedimented but the entrance front is not.

where he carried the centre up to the height of the flanking gables and gave it an overall segmental pediment.

It was on the interiors that most care was lavished. Balcaskie
64 has deeply modelled plaster ceilings in the state rooms, their centres (in the ante-chamber and bedchamber) filled with allegorical paintings; the plasterer of the most important ceilings here was *George Dunsterfield*, the painter probably *Jacob de Witt*, both employed by Bruce for his rebuilding of the King's palace of Holyroodhouse (Edinburgh). Plasterwork was used to similar effect in the state bedchamber and closet at Wemyss Castle and the state apartment at Kellie Castle. At Balcaskie, Wemyss Castle and Kellie Castle, the principal family rooms were also provided with enriched ceilings. Those at Balcaskie and Wemyss have a more intimate character than the state apartments' ceilings. The Vine Room's ceiling at Kellie is unusual for its studied richness, more appropriate to a state room designed for display than to a family room. At Melville House the ceilings are plain, the display of wealth concentrated on sumptuously carved woodwork.

Fife's first example of the rectangular piend-roofed house with a pedimented centre of the type introduced to England by Hugh May is Raith House, built for Lord Raith in 1693–6. *James Smith* seems to have been involved in its construction, and it is a larger and more confident version of his own house at Newhailes (Lothian) of 1686, but with the addition of flanking pavilions. Pavilions of the same sort, but placed excessively far forward, were supplied for Donibristle House, Dalgety Bay, by Smith's partner *Alexander McGill* in 1719–23. More conventionally Palladian are the mid-C18 pavilions and curving screen walls at Balcaskie. There they enclose an entrance court and probably are built on the line of earlier office buildings, such as survive at Melville House; but most C18 houses in Fife made do without pavilions. In general these C18 houses are straightforward piend-
68 roofed boxes, but Largo House, Upper Largo, of 1750 has punchy detail, and a smooth elegance appears at Dunnikier
72 House, Kirkcaldy (by *Alexander Laing*, 1791–3), and Lochore House, Ballingry (*c*.1790).

The EARLY NINETEENTH CENTURY gave Fife one neoclassical house of importance and a number of Gothic ones. In 1815–
71 19 *Richard Crichton* remodelled and enlarged Balbirnie House, Glenrothes, with projecting and recessed Ionic porticoes. More strongly Greek and much grander might have been Broomhall.
70 This was begun by *Thomas Harrison* in 1796, but between *c*.1800 and 1828 the seventh Earl of Elgin commissioned designs from no fewer than twelve architects. The failure to execute any of them was almost as big a loss to potential classicism in Fife as Elgin's sale of the Parthenon Marbles in 1816. Fife's Gothic houses had begun *c*.1785 with Torrie House, Torryburn, an agreeably light-hearted villa (demolished) whose castellated stables survive in better condition than those of the also lost Inchrye Abbey, a Batty Langleyish house of 1827. Still standing
74 is the shell of Crawford Priory, an C18 house reconstructed in 1809–13 for the strong-willed Lady Mary Lindsay Crawford,

David Hamilton adding a four-poster Gothick Hall, *James Gillespie Graham* clothing the original house in frivolous ecclesiastical dress. *William Atkinson*'s Tulliallan Castle (Kincardine-on-Forth) of 1817–20 and *R. & R. Dickson*'s Dunimarle Castle of 1839–45 are heavy-handed by comparison. 75 78

MID-NINETEENTH-CENTURY contributions are disappointing except for *William Burn*'s smooth Jacobean House of Falkland of 1839–44. Burn also added low-key additions (Baronial and Jacobean) to Kilconquhar Castle (in 1831–9) and Balcarres (in 1838–43). At both a C16 tower house was intended to provide a full stop at one end, but the tower at Kilconquhar lost all impact when reconstructed after a fire in 1978, and the tower at Balcarres was swallowed up in 1860s additions by *David Bryce*. Bryce's fiercer Baronial appears to better effect at three other houses, Inzievar (of 1855–6), Birkhill (of 1857–9) and Craigflower, Torryburn (of 1862). 81 82

The TWENTIETH CENTURY began not badly with *Paul Waterhouse*'s flat-fronted François I Craigtoun Park (formerly Mount Melville) of 1902. Three years later *Robert S. Lorimer* introduced early Georgian revival at Hill of Tarvit, whose polite exterior gives little hint of the eclecticism inside. Lorimer's friend *F. W. Deas* designed for himself Fife's best Arts and Crafts house at The Murrel, lovingly detailed in orangey rubble. More straightforward is *M. H. Baillie Scott*'s harled Sandford Hill of 1913. The Lorimer tradition was carried on by *Reginald Fairlie* with his Cape Dutch Kilmany House of 1914–27, but Fife was not favoured with interwar country houses. The post-war period has brought only one house of distinction, *Trevor Dannatt*'s austere Pitcorthie of 1967. 83

GARDENS and PARKLAND are almost invariable companions of country houses. In the unenclosed and largely treeless landscape of C16 Fife the house of pretension was given a walled garden extending from it on at least one side. The form of Aberdour Castle's late C16 terraced garden has been re-established from old plans and excavation. More formal terraces characterize the late C17 gardens at Leslie and at Balcaskie, whose symmetrical lay-out is focused on the Bass Rock. C18 enclosure created wooded parks in which the garden next the house could seem an irrelevancy; by the late C18, flower and vegetable gardens were often contained in walled enclosures sited some way from the mansion. The High Victorian love of house parties brought the formal garden (to be viewed from the drawing room) back into favour (e.g. the reconstruction of the terraces at Balcaskie and the creation of terraces and parterres at Balcarres). The late C19 reaction looked back not to the C18 park but to a C17 garden mixture of flowers, vegetables and fruit trees. This ideal, championed in Frances Hope's *Notes and Thoughts on Gardens and Woodlands* of 1881, was given practical expression in the garden at Earlshall, laid out, together with its coyly jocular buildings, by *Lorimer* in the 1890s. The same principles underlie *F. W. Deas*' garden at The Murrel of *c.*1908. Extension of the garden into the park is the keynote of *Paul Waterhouse*'s scheme at Craigtoun Park, where a cypress avenue led from the house to a temple;* beyond was an artificial lake whose island was crowned with a miniature Franco-German castle.

Gardens provided vegetables and fruit. A main source of fresh meat in winter was provided by pigeons housed in DOOCOTS, whose possession was restricted to those of lairdly position and which seem to be as concerned to proclaim status as to shelter
51 birds. The C16 beehive doocot at Aberdour Castle is prominently sited in the garden. The contemporary Bogward doocot, Doocot Road, St Andrews, is now less happily placed in a housing estate. The standard C17 and C18 doocot was of the lectern type (rectangular with a monopitch roof), its gables usually crow-stepped. One at Limekilns can be dated to 1697. The pyramid-roofed doocot built at Balcarres a century later may have been intended primarily as an architectural incident in the park. Very
65 consciously architected is the mid-C18 pair of doocots standing like tall conical-roofed lodges at the E gates to Balcaskie.

The C16 and C17 house without a parkland setting was divided from the surrounding countryside by a walled courtyard, entered through GATES designed to mark the importance of the house behind. At Earlshall the late C16 entrance in the barmkin wall has prominent gunloops. Gunloops are combined with rudimentary classical piers at the contemporary main gate to Aberdour Castle. This has been moved from its original position. So too probably
67 have the pedimented and ball-finialled gatepiers of 1671 at Leslie House's Duke's Lodge. C18 enclosure pushed gates and lodges away from the house to the edge of the park. One very elegant example of a gateway and accompanying lodge was designed by *James Playfair* in 1786 for the approach to Raith House; it is now marooned in Raith Drive, Kirkcaldy (p.287). By the early C19 the park, however small, had replaced the doocot as the symbol of gentry status, so the small villa of Whitehill, near Aberdour, has a Grecian lodge at the end of its short S drive. The opulence
80 of *Brown & Wardrop*'s coroneted gates of 1870 at the Aberdour approach to the Earl of Moray's seat at Donibristle House is an effective answer to upstart minor landowners, but *Lorimer*'s
84 North Lodge and Gates (of 1896–8) at Balcarres seem unsure whether they are to guard an earl or make a joke.

BURGH AND VILLAGE BUILDINGS

FIFE is now a region full of small towns and large villages, but in 1500 it contained only five royal burghs (one, Falkland, enjoying the title only by courtesy‡) and two burghs (Dun-

---

* The temple has been demolished. Its columns were re-used from the portico added to the former house on the site by *James Gillespie Graham* in 1821–4.
‡ Presumably because of the proximity of a royal palace.

fermline and St Andrews) technically dependent on great monastic houses but treated as royal burghs. Auchtermuchty was given the title of a royal burgh in 1517 but was never treated as one. More important was the port of Pittenweem, which became a royal burgh in 1541. Then, between c.1574 and 1594, eight more were created, all on the coast. Most flourished only briefly. Expansion of Fife's foreign trade (of which royal burghs held a monopoly until the late C17) in the late C16 was followed by late C17 decline, exacerbated by the effects of the Act of Union of 1707. Most of the new royal burghs erected in the C16 had previously been burghs of barony, dependent on a landowner or monastery but entitled to hold regular markets for the sale of domestically produced goods. New burghs of barony (e.g. Ceres, Kincardine-on-Forth, and Markinch) were created in the C17 and became local centres of trade and industry. In the C18 and C19 villages sprang up, some to house rural craftsmen and landless labourers, others for workers in a particular industry (e.g. Charlestown in the 1770s for lime workers, Ladybank in the early C19 for linen weavers, or Auchtertool in the later C19 for distillery workers). The most prominent single-industry villages (many quickly becoming towns) are the late C19 mining settlements. The promise of coal was also the reason for the foundation of Fife's C20 New Town at Glenrothes.

The characteristic symbol of burgh status is the MARKET CROSS, usually, despite the name, an octagonal shaft topped by a capital, sometimes surmounted by a finial. Of medieval crosses the best-preserved is at Inverkeithing, datable from its heraldic shields to 1398. At Kincardine-on-Forth the late C17 cross has a would-be Doric capital. Most impressive is the Culross cross, a conjectural restoration of 1902. A C20 equivalent of the market cross is the WAR MEMORIAL erected after the First World War. All towns and quite a few villages have them, although few do more than provide a bronze statue of a soldier. *H. S. Gamley* gave Cupar a huge winged Victory in 1921–2; *Taylor & Young* provided a stark cenotaph at Dunfermline in 1925.

The cross symbolized burgh status, but the TOLBOOTH gave the status practical effect. Originally, as the name suggests, the collection point for the burgh tolls or taxes, it served also as the meeting place of the burgh council (and so was often known as the Town House), and as the burgh lock-up for debtors and suspected criminals. The C16 tolbooths of Crail and Dysart (Kirkcaldy) are both square towers, Crail solid and stolid, Dysart enlivened by jumpy stringcourses. By contrast, Culross Tolbooth of 1626 is externally quite domestic, a simple crowstepped two-storey rectangle. Its ogee-roofed tower was not added until 1783, but belfry towers were common. At West Wemyss (c.1700), Auchtermuchty (1728), Strathmiglo (1734) and Newburgh (1808), they are slim protuberances rising straight from the ground. At Inverkeithing (1754) the belfry cupola sits awkwardly atop the pedimented tower; Falkland's belfry (1800) rises more comfortably above a pediment.

The Burgh Reform Acts of 1833 established a new system of

local government which stimulated rather than depressed civic pride. Two of Fife's larger burghs acquired new town houses. St Andrews' is Baronial (by *J. Anderson Hamilton*, 1858–62),
112 Dunfermline's French (by *James C. Walker*, 1875–9). These were intended not just for the transaction of council business but also to house public meetings. Homes for public meetings were provided also by other HALLS, like the steepled Cupar Corn Exchange (of 1861, by *Campbell Douglas & Stevenson*) or *R. Rowand Anderson*'s Normand Hall at Dysart (Kirkcaldy) of 1883. Villages often acquired outsize halls, e.g. Anderson's Queen's Hall at Charlestown (1887) or *James Gillespie*'s Queen Victoria Memorial Hall at Coaltown of Balgonie (1905–6). The function of these halls in providing community meeting places was shared by PUBLIC LIBRARIES, which could be financed from the rates after 1854. One of the earlier (of 1870, by *John Milne*) is the weirdly steepled Duncan Institute in Cupar. *J. C. Walker*'s Dunfermline Central Library of 1881–3, the first financed by the steel millionaire Andrew Carnegie, is sadly tame. The Carnegie Dunfermline Trust's institutes (two of them combining libraries and public baths) at Baldridgeburn (by *H. & D. Barclay*, 1908–9), Nethertown (by *James Lindsay*, 1912) and Townhill (by *Peter L. Henderson*, 1905) are more fun. Enjoyable too, though hardly
115 frivolous, is *William Williamson*'s Wrennish Burntisland Library of 1906. The Beaux Arts classicism of Kirkcaldy Public Library and Museum (by *Heiton & McKay*, 1923) is very serious but too small for the site.

The Scottish educational system from the C17 to the C19 was based on the parish and burgh schools (built by the heritors), supplemented by a few urban grammar schools. Of burgh schools, the smartest architecturally is *Thomas Hamilton*'s neo-
107 Greek Kinghorn Primary School of 1829, squashed by its top-heavy tower. More conventionally classical is the former Philp School of *c.*1830 in Kirkcaldy. Much larger is the quadrangular
110 Madras College, St Andrews, by *William Burn*, 1832–4, with relaxed Jacobean gables. The Education Act of 1872 established a national system of school boards. Of the early board schools in
111 Fife the best is *R. Rowand Anderson*'s West Primary School, Linktown, Kirkcaldy, of 1874–80, very simple Gothic with a steep *flèche*-topped roof. A little later (1883–6) and much larger is the former Dunfermline High School (now Allan Centre) by *James A. Mercer* and *F. & G. Holme*, whose great tower gives it undeniable if unwelcome presence. Friendlier are a number of early C20 schools by *William Williamson*, the best the gabled and dormered Auchterderran Junior High (1902–4) or the blocky Queen Anne Dysart Primary, Kirkcaldy (1914–15).

Fife's one UNIVERSITY, St Andrews, was restricted until the C19 to its medieval sites, and only gradually replaced its medieval
102 buildings. At St Mary's College, the W range was remodelled *c.*1620. At St Leonard's College (now School), a new s range was begun in 1617 and extended in 1655. The University Library (p. 374) was built in 1612–18 and Georgianized in 1764–7. Except for its chapel, St Salvator's College was largely rebuilt in the

mid-c18 and again, in a Jacobean manner, in 1829–46, by the
government architects *Robert Reid* and *William Nixon*. The
University's late c19 expansion brought a number of new buildings, mostly unexciting Baronial by the local firm of *James Gillespie & Scott*. Not much better was *Robert S. Lorimer's* insipid
English baroque Library addition of 1907–9, even before it was
altered in 1928–30. More recent contributions have, with one
exception, failed to add distinction. That exception is *James
Stirling's* Andrew Melville Hall (1968), a V-shaped hall of residence stepping down a hillside.

The administration of justice through Sheriff and Burgh courts
was largely localized. Purpose-built COURTHOUSES are few.
Cupar's Sheriff Court was produced by *William Burn's* adaptation in 1836 of a tenement in St Catherine Street, Dunfermline's (since replaced) by the reconstruction in 1849–50 of
Archibald Elliot's Guildhall of 1805–11. But in 1893 *James Gillespie* gave Kirkcaldy a towered Baronial court. PRISONS were
specially designed for their job, but the villa-like appearance of
James Gillespie Graham's Old Jail of 1813 at Cupar was thought 106
inappropriate, and in 1842 a less inviting block was put up in
Castlebank Road. Only the outer wall survives of the contemporary prison at Dunfermline.

Town PARKS were laid out from the mid-c19 and have preserved a number of their late Victorian BANDSTANDS (e.g. at
Cupar, Dunfermline and St Andrews). Seaside fun could be
suggested by gaily painted late Victorian cast-iron FOUNTAINS
like those at Burntisland and Newport-on-Tay, but they could
also mark the centre of a town with appropriate solemnity, as do
Alexander Roos's heraldic fountain at Falkland of 1856 and *R. W.
Edis's* Whyte-Melville Fountain of 1880 in Market Street, St
Andrews. A means to impart civic dignity and commemorate a
benefactor was to erect a STATUE. The most imposing are of
Onesiphorus Tyndall-Bruce at Falkland, a life-size bronze by
John Steell, 1864, and *Richard Goulden's* gigantic frock-coated
Andrew Carnegie (1913–14) at the entrance to Pittencrieff Park,
Dunfermline.

The architectural bulk and much of the character of towns and
villages is given by HOUSING. Until the c15, most of Fife's urban
housing was probably wood-framed, stone or clay being used as
infilling. Even the more prosperous town houses of *c.*1500 were
of only two storeys, with a hall and one or two chambers built
above ground-floor storage. Remains of c15 vaulted ground
floors survive in several St Andrews houses (e.g. No. 77 North
Street, and St John's House, South Street) which seem to have
been simple rectangular buildings, their upper floors reached by
an external wooden stair. The c16 and early c17 growth of Fife's
burghs led to existing buildings being extended towards the
street by the addition of new front blocks, and upwards by the
addition of an extra floor (often occupied as a separate flat). No.
77 North Street, St Andrews, which had a new block built across
its c15 front gable, is one example of this. Quite often a c16 tower
house's stone stairtower was given pride of place, projecting at

one corner and finished with its own crowstepped gable. This
position of the stairtower is found also in a number of con-
89 temporary town houses, but in urban examples (e.g. The Study
at Culross, Kelly Lodging at Pittenweem, Nos. 2–4 Bank Street
at Inverkeithing) the towers often rise at least one storey above
the main block, their upper floors (which contain rooms reached
by a second stair corbelled out in the inner angle) jettied out on
continuous corbelling. Jettying of upper floors could apply to
the main block as well as the stairtower (e.g. Sailors' Walk at
Kirkcaldy, Bay House at Dysart (Kirkcaldy), or St John's House,
South Street, St Andrews). But the jettying gives only a minimal
increase in floor area. Is it just a decorative device or does it
represent the translation into stone of a tradition of building in
wood? Not that timber construction was a dead tradition by the
late c16. The main structural supports of the superior house at
Nos. 339–343 High Street, Kirkcaldy, are wooden posts. That
house's c16 first-floor plan is essentially intact and remarkably
similar to that (before the 1969 reconstruction) of Bay House,
Dysart, of 1583. The first floor contained three rooms, the larger
central room seemingly a hall open to the roof, the end rooms
bedchambers with attics above.

Among the owners of town houses were landowners needing
an urban base for business or as a retreat from the rigours of
rustic life. The late c16 Kelly Lodging at Pittenweem was the
town house of the Earls of Kellie. In St Andrews, c.1575, Archbishop Adamson built himself a neat house (No. 71 North Street),
its s w tower decorated with gunloops. Humbler but just as much
a laird's house come to town is Macduff House, Auchtermuchty,
of 1597. More consciously urbane is Moncrief House, Falkland,
built for one of James VI's courtiers in 1610, symmetrically
fronted with would-be classical detail. Smarter still is the U-plan
94 Preston Lodge, Cupar, of 1623, which again attempts classicism,
its window detail remarkably close to contemporary work at
Roslin Castle (Lothian). Preston Lodge acquired a smart new N
front in the late c17 but Fordell's Lodging, Inverkeithing, of
c.1670 remained resolutely old-fashioned.

Inside these c16 and c17 town houses there could be lavish
decoration. There is a stupendous display of painted ceilings and
87 walls inside Culross Palace (c.1597–1611). Strapwork, fruit and
foliage are fairly standard motifs of c.1600, but two rooms have
88 walls painted with Scriptural and allegorical subjects, work equal
to that found in the grander tower houses. Late c17 plaster
ceilings of a quality which would not have disgraced a small
91–2 country house exist in Nos. 339–343 High Street, Kirkcaldy.
Preston Lodge, Cupar, has ambitious though provincial panelling.

Fife's burghs and villages contain plenty of c18 houses but
few which are more than humdrum. The early c19 contributed
several town houses of real distinction. In St Andrews, the Crawford Centre, North Street, was built for the Lindsays of Wormiston, c.1812, with rosette-studded friezes and a broad columnar
doorpiece. In Dunfermline the contemporary Viewfield House's

doorpiece has a Tower of the Winds order. Another Dunfermline villa (Woodhead Cottage of *c.*1830, now part of the United Free Church, Chalmers Street) is lighthearted Gothick. Rather earlier and less frivolous but unaltered is Rosemount Cottage, Rigg's Place, Cupar. Smartest of all has been the Adamish neoclassical No. 36 Crossgate, Cupar, of *c.*1815, its door and first-floor window combined as a single fanlit opening. The façade survives stuck onto a supermarket.

Fife's only Georgian attempt at unified development of the palace-fronted terrace type found in Edinburgh, Glasgow, Aberdeen or Perth was St Catherine Street, Cupar, for which *Gillespie Graham* prepared a scheme in 1810. However, financial problems forced the abandonment of strict control over elevations, and public opinion deprived it of its intended focus, Gillespie 105 Graham's jail. In St Andrews a couple of early Victorian unified schemes did appear, first *George Rae*'s Playfair Terrace, North Street (1846), its Aegypto-Greek centre squeezed by Georgian survival ends, then (from 1847) *John Chesser*'s Abbotsford Crescent development, plain terraces on a picturesque lay-out.

Any town of size acquired Victorian villas. The largest are at St Andrews, where an opulent Baronial display is strung out along The Scores. At Burntisland *F. T. Pilkington*'s double villas of 1858 in Broomhill Road are characteristically wild Ruskinian 97 Gothic. Much starker Gothic in the same town is *R. C. Carpenter*'s Old Parsonage, Leven Street, of 1854. Rather cosier has 98 been *R. Rowand Anderson*'s No. 10 East Fergus Place, Kirkcaldy, of 1881. Arts and Crafts of a sort appears with the gabled and dormered Wayside, Hepburn Gardens, St Andrews, by *Robert S. Lorimer*, 1901–4.

Workers' housing dominates many Fife towns and villages. Most is very plain, character coming from the building materials (e.g. whinstone walling at Colinsburgh) or the dominance of a detail (e.g. the parade of skewputts at Kincardine-on-Forth). Generous and imaginative lay-out on garden city lines gives Methil and Rosyth a quality independent of narrowly architectural criteria. A determinedly picturesque mining settlement is Coaltown of Wemyss, whose broad eaves and rustic porches 99 conspire to give the impression of the bucolic estate village. Dunfermline, otherwise marked by mean lay-out and uninventive design, produced a genuine attempt at originality with *Sam Bunton*'s flat-roofed housing round the huge Hoggan Crescent in 1940. By contrast, *H. J. Scrymgeour-Wedderburn*'s Memorial Square (1948) at Balmerino is *retardataire* in the Clough Williams-Ellis manner. In the 1950s *Wheeler & Sproson* undertook large-scale redevelopment of a number of burghs (e.g. Dysart and Burntisland), keeping a few old buildings as harled 100 sacred cows among the straightforward new housing. Kirkcaldy and Kincardine-on-Forth have grouped tower blocks to good effect, Glenrothes' one tower looks friendless. But tower blocks are now unfashionable, and architects or their clients have espoused a 'neo-vernacular' whose rendered brickwork and con-

crete crowsteps owe nothing to a genuine tradition and everything to the need to satisfy the planners' sensibilities.

Fife has been unlucky in its COMMERCIAL BUILDINGS. The
only bank head office is that of the former Fife Bank in Bonnygate,
Cupar, unflashy Georgian of c. 1810 with an inept doorpiece. The
Victorian branch banks are dependably worthy but without the
swaggering self-confidence of banks in the major cities. That sort
114 of show-off quality is attempted only by the Prudential Assurance
Co. in East Port, Dunfermline, a piece of premature Art Deco
classicism by *Paul Waterhouse*, 1914–16. Department stores (Co-
operative predominant) began c. 1900 but are more impressive
for size than architecture. They are now giving way to shopping
malls. *Michael Laird & Partners*' The Mercat at Kirkcaldy
(1981–3) makes some attempt to give order to shanty-town shops.
Glenrothes' Kingdom Centre begun in 1961 is shanty-town
itself. More fun have been some cinemas (e.g. Dunfermline's Art
Deco Orient Express in East Port, by *John Fraser*, 1913), but St
Andrews gentility imposed a period politeness on *Gillespie &
Scott*'s New Picture House, North Street (1930). Pubs seldom
add to Fife's visual pleasures, but Ye Olde Foresters Arms of
1911 is a jolly presence beside Inverkeithing harbour. Well worth
exploring inside for its picture-tiled walls and stained glass is the
116 Feuars Arms (c. 1890) in Bogies Wynd, Pathhead, Kirkcaldy.
More sedate are the hotels, the bigger ones built for golfers. The
Lundin Hotel, Lundin Links (by *Peter L. Henderson*, 1900),
is ridiculously tall for its cottage style, the Grand Hotel (now
Hamilton Hall) in The Scores, St Andrews (by *James M. Monro*,
1895), a huge but timid château.

Late Victorian golfers usually travelled by train, and the railways by the late C19 covered almost all the region. Of stations
the best are those designed by *Grainger & Miller* for the Edin-
108 burgh & Northern Railway in 1846–8 at Burntisland (Greek),
Markinch and Ladybank (both Italianate). Aberdour of 1890 is
cottagey, with a garden to match.

Railways (and, earlier, ships) were a main factor in the development of Fife's industry. Until well into the C19 this was concerned primarily with the manufacture of goods from agricultural
raw materials. Of INDUSTRIAL BUILDINGS one of the earliest
57 is the King's Barn at Limekilns, a massively solid early C16
warehouse. In Culross, a few miles away, Bessie Bar's Hall was
built in 1776 as a malthouse. In Pathhead, Kirkcaldy, a late
Georgian flour mill in The Path near the harbour has a classy
villa-like office block to gentrify its industrial purpose. Grain and
barley found a useful end in the making of whisky. One of the
earliest distilleries is the Grange Distillery at Burntisland, most
of its pantiled ranges dating from c. 1805. Much larger and with
its own village is the Cameron Bridge Distillery at Windygates,
founded in 1824. Maltings were sometimes separate from distilleries. Late C19 examples at Pitlessie, Ladybank and Newton
of Falkland give character to a corner of W Fife. By the late C19,
linen manufacture was one of Fife's major industries. The Eden
Valley Works at Freuchie of c. 1870 are resolutely Georgian sur-

vival. Of the Dunfermline factories the most imposing is the Italianate St Leonard's Works (now housing) of 1851. Kirkcaldy became the centre of floor-cloth and linoleum manufacture, height the main feature of the factories.

Coal mining has been undertaken in Fife since the Middle Ages, underwent a huge expansion from c.1890, but has contracted since c.1950 and is now (1988) on the brink of extinction. Its most visible relics are the string of mining communities (each with its interwar miners' institute) from Leven sw to Oakley. The Michael Colliery's simple Modern Movement pithead baths (by *J. H. Forshaw*, 1935) survive at East Wemyss. At Lochore, 120 the Mary Colliery's pithead gear of 1902 now stands in a country park. Much more emphatic are the huge concrete winding towers of the Seafield Colliery at Linktown (Kirkcaldy). 119

RURAL BUILDINGS

RURAL Fife until the C18 was essentially a medieval peasant society. Farm buildings were grouped in clusters ('ferm-touns'), each with its strips of arable, meadow and rough-grazing enclosed by a dyke to protect it from the stock (cattle more than sheep) enjoying summer grazing on the moorland outside. Replacement of this system by one which divided the land between separate and larger farms, accompanied by the drainage of waterlogged clay soil and the planting of shelter belts, was expensive for both landlord and tenant. Although the principles of 'improved' agriculture were well-known by the early C18 the necessary investment was not generally made until the last decades of the C18,* but by c.1840 almost all land was enclosed and a recognizably modern system of farms spread across the country.

Some picture of improvement in rural accommodation in the C17 and C18 can be inferred from scattered references to country manses. In 1637 Scoonie Manse had only a hall and chamber and was thatched with divots. Possibly it was built of clay, as was Logie Manse until 1736. Auchterderran Manse was rethatched with turf c.1640; Tulliallan Manse, built c.1700, was thatched with heather. However, thatch seems to have come to be regarded as unfit for a minister's residence early in the C18. Dunino and Auchtertool Manses acquired tiled roofs in 1708–9. Saline, Logie and Auchtermuchty Manses were rebuilt in 1733–6 with slated roofs. Ballingry, rethatched with reed in 1756, was probably exceptional; and in 1775 the minister of Creich complained

That it was discreditable both to the Heretors and to the Minister to make up a Cloutted Thatch [i.e. thatch mixed with clay] roof upon the

---

*An act of 1770 'to encourage the Improvement of Lands, Tenements, and Hereditaments in that Part of Great Britain called Scotland held under Settlements of strict Entail' made it much easier for many landowners to raise money for improvement.

Manse when many of the Farmers houses are now slated with Skillie [slates] ... that it is the constant Practice of the Country to cover the manse roofs with Slate scarce one manse of a 100 being thatched ...

Improvements to farmhouses probably lagged behind those to manses and the account given of their condition *c.*1780 in John Thomson's *General View of the Agriculture of the County of Fife* (1800), although perhaps deliberately bleak, is likely to be generally accurate:

> The farmer usually lived in a low smoky house, badly lighted, and without divisions or separate apartments, except such as were formed by the arrangement of the furniture. The office-houses were small, the walls low and rudely constructed, and the roofs ponderous, and with difficulty kept dry.

Thomson's description of the new farm buildings of the C18's last decades is in strong contrast:

> The dwelling-house is of two storeys, substantially built, covered with slate, neatly finished, and with every necessary convenience for the accommodation of the farmer's family. The office-houses are built in the form of a square, sometimes at the back of the dwelling-house, and including it as a part of the square; and sometimes at a little distance from it, having stables, cow-house, barn, shades for the implements of husbandry, straw-yard for feeding cattle, milk-house, log-house, &c. all built of stone and lime, covered with slate or tyle, conveniently arranged, and of sufficient dimensions for the size of the farm.

This evidence of a general rebuilding of farmhouses and steadings in the late C18 and early C19 is borne out by the parish-by-parish description produced in the 1830s for the *New Statistical Account of Scotland*. The architecture is pleasing though unremarkable, the farmhouses usually two-storey three-bay slate-roofed boxes accompanied by pantiled steadings, to which, after 1799, were almost always appended a mill, the engine power usually provided by horses walking round in an octagonal shed, although steam-driven mills became popular in the mid-C19. Many of these new farms were the work of local architect-builders like *William Lees* of Pittenweem, but some were designed by specialist farm architects from outside Fife, such as *Thomas Brown* of Uphall, responsible for new buildings on the Hopes' Rankeillour estate in 1828–33, or *Robert Bell* of Edinburgh in the 1850s. Solid worth is the keynote, but frivolity appears at two farms on the Raith estate near Kirkcaldy, Balwearie Tower, with a gable pretending to be a ruined church, and Torbain, with a crenellated tower in the steading, both built *c.*1800 for the landlord's pleasure rather than the tenant's profit.

The mechanization of late C20 farming has imposed new requirements on the design of farm steadings, most notably the need for large sheds high enough for a tractor to be driven through. The lack of planning control over most agricultural buildings has meant that some have been sited less tactfully than may be thought desirable by the urban visitor. Silage towers, the other main recent feature of the countryside, can on a misty evening give romantic punctuation to the view.

FIFE

ABDIE

Isolated ecclesiastical group of the former parish church and manse with the present parish church 0.4km. to the N.

PARISH CHURCH. 1826–7, by *William Burn*, adapting a design produced by *James Milne* in 1824. Tall sneck-harled box with mixed detail. Y-traceried round-arched windows, large Italianate E bellcote, Tudor hoodmould over the door.

Inside, an E gallery on cast-iron columns. – Oak COMMUNION TABLE, LECTERN and FONT of 1923, by *J. Jeffrey Waddell*, who also recast Burn's PULPIT in a Celtic-Romanesque manner. – Neo-Jacobean MINISTER'S CHAIR dated 1939. – STAINED GLASS. In the W gable, two windows (Christ Blessing Children; The Adoration of the Magi) by *Nathaniel Bryson*, 1899 and 1911. – War Memorial window of 1919 in the S wall.

ST MAGRIDIN'S (OLD PARISH) CHURCH. Roofless shell of a medieval country church adapted for Reformed worship. The church consecrated by Bishop David de Bernham in 1242 is an ashlar-built skinny rectangle. Several of the original stepped buttresses were replaced by massive stone shores in the C16 or C17. The C13 work survives best at the E end. In the S wall a pointed-arched priest's door, its hoodmould formed by carrying up the stringcourse which used to run round the church. Small lancets in the N and S walls. In the E gable, a group of three obtusely pointed lancets with round-headed rear arches. The gable's crude locker may have been a credence niche. Corbels in the side walls, probably to carry the rood beam. Near the W end of the S wall is a porch with stone benches along its inside walls. It may be a late medieval addition. Its rectangular door into the church is in the C13 position but looks C17, perhaps contemporary with the introduction of rectangular windows lighting the church. Beside the porch, remains of an outside stair to a W gallery, probably the loft erected by Rankeilour McGill in 1697. Also late C17 is the primitive birdcage bellcote on the W gable. The tabling and cross on the E gable came in a restoration of 1856. Crowstepped Denmylne Aisle on the N of 1661, with a large round-arched opening into the church.

MONUMENTS. Inside the Denmylne Aisle, on the N wall, an eroded late C17 tablet to Michael Balfour and his wife Katherine Napier, carved with their arms. – On the E wall, a large tablet with a Latin inscription commemorating Sir Michael and Sir James Balfour; on top, flat obelisks and a coat of arms. It is probably of 1661. – Outside, on the church's S wall, aedicular monument to Alexander Spens and Katherine Arnot of *c.*1700: very provincial, the fluted pilasters without capitals, a coat of arms on top of the cornice, the centre panel carved with a hand holding tablets and a quill. – Propped against the S and W walls, large stones (possibly the tops of table monuments) to Patrick Thomsone †1673 and Gavin Adamson †1680, carved with reminders of death. – Near the churchyard gate, an urn on a plinth erected in 1841 to commemorate the poet John Bethune. Its E face is inscribed with a verse from his *Hymns of the Church-Yard*:

> This is a place of fear: the firmest eye
> Hath quailed to see its shadowy dreariness:
> But Christian hope and heavenly prospects high,
> And earthly cares and nature's weariness,
> Have made the timid pilgrim cease to fear,
> And long to end his painful journey here.

Churchyard GATE late C17 with moulded jambs, now missing its arch. – On its N, rubble OFFERTORY HOUSE built in 1748. – To the S, an C18 GIG HOUSE. Inside, a late medieval EFFIGY of a cleric in cassock and amice. Also a GRAVESLAB, probably C14, incised with a cross whose head is formed of *fleurs de lis*.

ABDIE HOUSE (former MANSE). L-plan Tudor cottage by *Thomas Brown*, 1839–40. Stone porch a tactful addition of 1878.

KIRKSTYLE COTTAGE, beside St Magridin's Church. Broad-eaved double cottage (now a single house) with gablets over the doors. Dated 1844.

FARM

BERRYHILL, 0.8km. S. Smart piend-roofed laird's house of *c.*1820, with a Roman Doric columned doorpiece.

1080

ABERDOUR

Two roadside villages, Wester Aberdour on the edge of the Earls of Moray's Donibristle estate, and Easter Aberdour on the Earls of Morton's Aberdour Castle estate, separated by the Dour Burn. Wester Aberdour acquired an early C19 'new town' in Seaside Place and Manse Road, but Easter Aberdour was cut off from the castle by the railway in 1890. Tidal harbour to attract decorous holiday-makers, but this is no place for trippers.

CHURCHES

FORMER PARISH CHURCH, High Street. Built in 1787–90, the plan copied from Dyke Church (Grampian).* Harled rectangle

---

* The Earl of Moray was a leading heritor in both parishes.

with a domed birdcage bellcote on the W gable. The tall round-arched S openings are overpowered by the huge Lorimerian WAR MEMORIAL (by *F. W. Deas*, 1919), a static angel in its soggy pediment. Converted to church hall by *C. Scott Gullen*, 1927. – GRAVEYARD behind, with a heavy Greek GATEWAY in the N wall.

PARISH CHURCH (St Fillan), Hawkcraig Road. A friendly little church in a comfortable graveyard beside Aberdour Castle. 10

According to a charter of *c.*1180 the Church of Aberdour had belonged to the Abbey of Inchcolm in the reign of Alexander I, so it was presumably part of the abbey's endowment at its foundation *c.*1123 just before Alexander's death in 1124. The nave and chancel of the present parish church were probably built *c.*1140, perhaps by masons who had worked on the first abbey church at Inchcolm. A S aisle was added *c.*1500, a S porch soon after, and a transeptal N 'aisle' in 1608. Unroofed after the completion of a new parish church in 1790 (*see* above), St Fillan's was lovingly restored by *William Williamson* in 1925–6.

The C12 church is of cubed ashlar. Very simple, with a nave and slightly narrower and lower rectangular chancel. Narrow round-arched windows in the chancel (those in the S wall restored 1925–6) and the E bay of the N side of the nave. Internally they have deep splayed ingoes and stepped bases. Fragment of another C12 window in the W gable. Above this, a Gothic survival two-light window probably inserted in 1588, when the upper part of this gable was rebuilt with crowsteps and a pyramid-roofed birdcage bellcote. The nave's E gable was heightened and crowstepped at the same time and a new roof put on, its S pitch carried down in a single slope over the C15 aisle. This roof was restored with Angus stone slabs in 1925–6. So too were the rectangular aisle windows, whose sills alone remained. The aisle's moulded W window (blocked) is perhaps of 1588.

On the N, Phin Aisle, with a heavy stringcourse below the steeply pedimented window dated 1608.

Long early C16 S porch. Obtusely pointed arch at the entrance. Stone benches along the walls and a stoup beside the door into the church.

The interior's open timber nave and aisle roofs are really ceilings to show the roof shape before the 1588 re-roofing. Plain chancel arch of two orders, the outer with a chamfer on the E. Three-bay arcade to the S aisle, chamfered semicircular arches carried on round piers with simply moulded capitals and bases. Tunnel-vault in the Phin Aisle.

PULPIT and COMMUNION TABLE of 1926 by *Scott Morton & Co.* – CHAIRS in the nave by *Design Furniture Group*, 1973. – STAINED GLASS. All of *c.*1930. W window (St Fillan and a pilgrim) by *James Ballantine*. – NW window (a Columban missionary at Aberdour) unattributed. Very pictorial but not very good. – Chancel windows and the E windows of nave and S aisle all by *Alexander Strachan* in excellent strong colours. –

ORGAN by *J. W. Walker & Sons Ltd*, 1966. – On the w wall, brass armorial COFFIN PLATES of James, Earl of Morton (†1768), and Sholto, Earl of Morton (†1774).

CHURCHYARD MONUMENTS. On the church's s wall, strap-work-framed inscription to Robert Blair, erected in 1672. – On the e wall of the chancel two aedicules, one with Tuscan columns and a shaped pediment dated 1688, the other of 1723 with skulls on the ends of the curvy pediment. – Under the church's w window, fluted pilasters and a cornice framing the inscription:

> PANS [think].O.PILGRIM
> THAT.PASSITH.BY.THIS.WAY
> VPON.THYN.END
> AND.THOV.SAL.FEAR.TO.SIN
> AND.THINK.ALSO
> VPON.THE.LATTER.DAY
> WHEN.THOV.TO.GOD.MAN [must].COUNT
> THEN.BEST.THOV.NOW.BEGIN.

It could be mid-C16. – SW of the church, a table stone to Major Francis Cooke †1646, 'A MARTIAL MAN FOR THE SPACE OF 26 YEIRS', carved with a shield and sword. – Elegantly lettered late C18 headstone to Andrew Morison near the s wall, commemorating also his wife and 'John Morison their Son who Fell from the Hawkscraig AND was killed on the spot 20 June 1787. And others of their family who died in Infancy.' – At the churchyard entrance, a row of early C18 headstones. Rustic and vigorous carving with a cheerful collection of reminders of mortality.

ST COLUMBA (Episcopal), Inverkeithing Road. Cruciform plan, built in 1843. Tall and boxy Gothic, with lancet windows and a lumpy bellcote.

ABERDOUR CASTLE

A carefully tended Ancient Monument which rears up as a rubbly surprise above the railway cutting.

The barony of Aberdour was acquired by Sir Alan de Mortimer in 1126 on his marriage to Anicea, daughter of Sir John Vipont. In the early C14 it was granted by Robert I to Thomas Randolph, Earl of Moray, whose grandson conferred it on Sir William Douglas of Liddesdale in 1342. Nine years later Sir William made over the property to his nephew Sir James Douglas of Dalkeith but kept a life-rent of the castle. It remained in the hands of the Douglasses (Earls of Morton from 1458) until 1924, when it passed into the care of the Secretary of State. By then the castle had been abandoned for two centuries after the eighth Earl of Morton's loan of the house to three officers in Queen Anne's army, who, 'By missfortune & negligence of their servants ... brunt down my house to the ground ...'*

---

* There had been another fire not long before. In 1700 William Stewart was paid £1 for having gone to Edinburgh 'anent the Earl's replenishing after the great burning'.

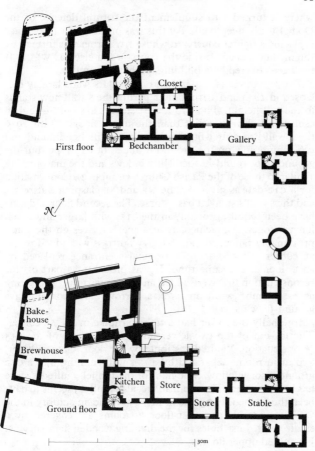

First floor
Closet
Bedchamber
Gallery

N

Bake-house
Brewhouse
Kitchen
Store
Store
Stable
Ground floor

30m

Aberdour Castle,
plans of ground and first floors

Until the railway's arrival in 1890 the main approach was from the N. It is now from the W, through a late C16 GATE originally on the N of the outer courtyard and moved here in 1890. Its heavy corniced piers (with gunloops) flanking the angular arch hint at classicism. The road* then crosses a BRIDGE built by *James Burn* of Haddington in 1798 and leads round the N side of the castle to a car park on the site of the C16 outer courtyard. W of the car park, scanty remains of the wall which divided the inner and outer courtyards. In the middle of the wall, part of the moulded jambs of a C16 GATE. At the wall's N end was a round tower. From this tower the N wall of the Inner Courtyard ran W to another round tower or bastion, now the bakehouse chimney of the kitchen offices,

* Until 1890 this was the public road between West and East Aberdour.

where it turned s to supplement the natural defence of the
Dour Burn's steep bank. All this was probably a c16 defence
replacing a tighter courtyard whose NW corner was formed by
the medieval keep. Inside the courtyard, a circular WELL. It
has been covered by a building, perhaps a laundry.

48   The NW tower is trapezoidal on plan. Its walls largely collapsed in 1844 and 1919; only a part of the s wall now stands
to the full height. The two lowest storeys are built of cubed
ashlar and clearly earlier than the upper floors. Until 1919
the s wall had a first-floor double lancet (its hoodmould and
tympanum now on the ground to the s) of c13 type, but the
ground-floor round-headed slit windows and the masonry are
similar to those of the Parish Church (*see* above). Confirmation
for a c12 date is given by the NE and SE clasping buttresses
and the s wall's splayed basecourse. The second floor and attic
have been rebuilt, probably in the c15, with larger and much
longer stones. A machicolated parapet survives on the s and
presumably ran all round. A heavy buttress was added to the
SE corner, *c.*1500, and the original s entrance replaced by
an E door at the same time. It was probably as part of this
reconstruction that were added an ashlar stairtower projecting
as a SE jamb* with, on its s, a narrow block containing a
ground-floor passage.‡

Internally the tower had a tight turnpike in the SE corner.
The lay-out of the two lower floors is the result of the c15
reconstruction. Vaulted vestibule by the door. On each floor,
two main rooms separated by a N–S wall running into a c12
ground-floor window. The floor of the tunnel-vaulted E store
has been lowered. The room above, also vaulted, seems to have
been the kitchen. Fireplace in the N wall and an aumbry in the
W. The ground- and first-floor W rooms are covered by a
single vault. Joist-holes for the dividing wooden floor survive.
Unvaulted upper floors.

The tower's size was almost doubled *c.*1570 when the fourth
Earl of Morton§ rebuilt the stairtower and s block of *c.*1500
and added a three-storey L-plan block to their s. Rubble-built
with jumping stringcourses on the s and the stairtower's E
front. The E gable, panelled by stringcourses, is a piece of
would-be classical display. First-floor window aedicule with
49   skinny pilasters, strapwork on the steep pediment. Pilastered
second-floor windows (only one jamb of the r. one surviving).¶
On the w, diagonally set gunloop at the foot of the stair.
Corbelled turret at the join of the stairtower and s block. The
SW jamb has a crowstepped lean-to gable. The lack of roofs

* The bottom of this stairtower survives as the base of the c16 stairtower of *c.*1570.
‡ Of which a door and window are visible in the N wall of the kitchen built *c.*1570.
§ Who became Chancellor in 1562, Regent in 1572, fell from power in 1578 and
was executed in 1581.
¶ These tenuously Tuscan pilasters are of the same type as those flanking the
Portcullis Gate at Edinburgh Castle, built in 1577 during Morton's regency, but
that gate's central feature is an Ionic pilastered aedicule with a Doric frieze and no
strapwork, possibly indicating a development in the Earl's architectural taste or
knowledge.

is regrettable. Originally there were a conical roof over the stairtower and pitched roofs, with a valley gutter, over the rebuilt s block of c.1500 and the new s block of c.1570. These were simplified in the c17 but even so must have added liveliness as well as a proper termination to the design.

Inside, a broad turnpike stair served all floors of both this addition and the older tower. Ground-floor passage immediately on its s. Opening off the passage is a tunnel-vaulted kitchen with a semi-elliptical arched fireplace. The round oven in its sw corner was built in 1670. Vaulted store to the e. The first floor was planned as two apartments, each consisting of a bedchamber, close garderobe and closet. The e apartment (perhaps a state apartment) was reached from the main stair by a short passage which, unlike the passage below, does not run the length of the building, since its e end is walled off to form the closet. The w apartment's closet was in the sw jamb above a stair leading from the terrace outside to the bedchamber. From this bedchamber (perhaps that of the Earl) a narrow dogleg stair in the w wall led to the bedchamber of the corresponding apartment (perhaps that of the Countess) on the second floor, where the arrangement was the same but with a further room in the nw turret.*

An L-plan range of offices was added on the w c.1600. Two ovens in the fireplace of the n bakehouse. Stone sink in the brewhouse floor.

c.1635 William, sixth Earl of Morton, built a long extension e of the c16 addition. Rectangular main block with two small n projections, the e one built against the wall of the Inner Courtyard, the w one in the centre of the courtyard's s side, its position of honour emphasized by a gable, now severely cut down so that only the bases of the top-floor window's pilasters remain. Both have been given Georgian piended roofs, probably at the same time as the main roof's pitch was lowered. Moulded second-floor windows breaking the cavetto cornice. Surely they had pedimented dormerheads? In the e gable an aediculed window, its grasp of the language of classicism still far from certain. Crowstepped se jamb with a sundial built into one corner. A lean-to stairtower on its w serves the stack of three bedrooms. On the first floor, tempera-painted wooden ceiling decorated with fruit, foliage and grotesques on the main panels; the red heart emblem of the Douglasses on the joists. The main block's ground floor is divided by a pend. Storage on the w, a stable on the e, low loft above. The whole second floor is a well-lit gallery with a large fireplace in the middle of the s wall.

c17 walled garden‡ on the e. The gate from the castle courtyard was inserted in 1740. The original entrance was from the terrace on the s through a door whose scrolly pediment is broken by the Douglas arms and strapwork. It is presumably of c.1632, the date (together with the WAM monogram for

---

* The turret was heightened to two storeys in the c17.

‡ Its n wall rebuilt to allow for the railway in 1890.

William and Anne [Earl and Countess of] Morton) above the pedimented and heavily moulded E gate to the churchyard lane. In the middle of the garden, a SUNDIAL, probably early C17, with a globe on top of a truncated pyramid. Late Victorian baluster base.

The S GARDEN was probably laid out in the 1570s. Terraces on the N and E, the retaining walls rebuilt (except the top one) in 1981, feature stone fireplaces the apparent inspiration of their hungry rubble. In the C16 they would have been harled. 51 Near the SE corner a beehive DOOCOT of four bulging stages serves both as a garden feature and a symbol of the Earl's power over his tenantry.

PERAMBULATION

Approaching from the W, a couple of landmarks on the r. First a harled C17 DOOCOT in McLAUCHLAN RISE, round but with a pitched roof of lectern type. Then the Episcopal Church (see above).

HIGH STREET takes over with the small gablets of LADY MORAY'S HOSPITAL, dated 1898 (reconstructed 1962). Beside it, the MORAY WORKSHOP with a gable to the street and the date 1713 over its first-floor door. Almost touching its S end, a crowstepped lectern DOOCOT (roofless), probably late C17. The harled and pantiled KIRK COTTAGES opposite were bought by the Kirk Session in 1735 and repaired the next year at a cost of £330 Scots. The Frenchy spire of the WOODSIDE HOTEL (by *W. L. Moffat*, 1879–80) is an inadequate balance 80 to the swagger GATES of 1870, by *Brown & Wardrop*, on the E approach to Donibristle (see p. 172), now to a housing estate. Plenty of coronets, in stone on the piers, in cast-iron on the pedestrian gates, where they form hubs for sceptred spokes. Bargeboarded EAST LODGE with stone canopies over the windows. The street now relaxes into workday vernacular. Almost opposite the former Parish Church (see above) the early C18 No. 41's door has a lugged architrave. The late Victorian bowed corner of Shore Street preludes a gable plausibly dated 1731. Low-key focal point provided by the SPENCE MEMORIAL CLOCKTOWER, built outside the former Parish Church in 1910 and moved here in 1919. Ahead are the road to Aberdour House (see below) and Castle (see above) and the entry to the RAILWAY STATION of 1890, cottage-style with a bargeboarded canopy and lovingly tended flower-beds.

(Diversion by the main road's Z-bend across the railway line to EASTER ABERDOUR. In MAIN STREET, No. 36 is mid-C18 with a Gibbsian door. Opposite, a carved piper sits on the end of the garden wall between Nos. 13 and 17. Late C19 seaside dottiness at the village's end. Nos. 69–71 are only a single storey and attic double house but adorned with shaped gablets, bracketed Gothic pediments over Roman Doric doorpieces, and capless fluted columns at the bay windows. Equally ridiculous is No. 73, with a peculiar scrolled pediment over the door, a scalloped parapet for the bay window, fluted columns, and bargeboards. More conventional seaside Art Nouveau at a double house (ARDVEICH and DALVARICH) on the corner of HOME PARK and HAWKCRAIG ROAD to the S, by *W. & C. Scott Gullen*, 1910.)

In LIVINGSTONE PLACE S of High Street, a two-storey harled and pantiled house (Nos. 6–7) of *c*.1700. Moulded ground-floor door, chamfered surround to the first-floor door reached by a forestair.

SHORE STREET goes down to the harbour. On the hill to the l., an OBELISK built by the 13th Earl of Morton in 1744; *Robert Cunningham* was the mason. In SEASIDE PLACE, the mid-C19 No. 2 has a bay window with superimposed orders (Corinthian above Doric). Earlier and more genteel is No. 1, with a skinny pilastered doorpiece and horizontal glazing. Scrolled skew-putts on Nos. 7 and 9. FORTH HOUSE opposite is of *c*.1800 but ungainly. At the end of MANSE ROAD the smart MANSE of 1802 by *Robert Burn*. At the bottom of Shore Road, ROCK-CLIFFE, mid-C19 with a tree-trunk verandah. Opposite is SEABANK HOUSE of *c*.1835. It looks like the work of *Thomas Hamilton*. Very smooth, three- by four-bay, with a Roman Doric porch on the short front. Stone canopies over the ground-floor windows. Shallow pavilion roof, the chimneys forming a central tower.

Late C18 HARBOUR with an irregularly curved rubble pier.

MANSIONS

ABERDOUR HOUSE, N end of High Street. A comfortable harled two-storey house of the C17 and C18. Crowstepped early C17 block facing E (really SE, but E for clarity). Long symmetrical front with short wings projecting at the ends. Their piended roofs are presumably C18. In 1731 the twelfth Earl of Morton consulted *James Gibbs* about remodelling the house, but only the pedimented doorpiece of the piend-roofed W block added at that time is Gibbsian. For the rest, a straightforward front of seven bays, the centre three advanced under a gable rather than the pediment one might expect.

The interior is now (1988) stripped out* and awaiting restoration. Some C17 doorways have been exposed, one in the centre ground-floor room with a roll-moulded surround, others disclosing that the C17 house had a rear jamb. Near the SW corner, small mid-C18 geometric stair with foliaged banisters.

On the lawn to the E, SUNDIAL of *c*.1640. Four balls support the square pedestal decorated with excellent carving of heraldry and, on the N face, a pair of back-to-back terms. Presumably it came from the Castle's garden.

To the S, fluted GATEPIERS with banded rustication and ball finials. They were probably among the six gatepiers for which

* Panelling was reported by the RCAHMS.

Robert Cunningham, mason, was paid in 1745. On each side, a squat obelisk, perhaps C17.

HILLSIDE, off Castle View. Early C19, the s front with a pedimented centre, the N with a Roman Doric portico and console-corniced windows. Utilitarian school additions to the N. – Broad-eaved LODGE, probably contemporary with the house.

FARMS ETC.

COCKAIRNIE, 1.9km. W. Harled mid-C18 laird's house with a rather small pedimented Doric porch *c.*1835. At the back a door lintel brought here from Otterston; it is dated 1589 and inscribed 'WELCVM.FREINDIS'.

CULLALOE, 3.2km. N. Unpretentious C18 farmhouse made into a small mansion, *c.*1830. The early C19 work, probably by *James Gillespie Graham*, was the addition of an ashlar-fronted s block; five anta-pilastered bays, the centre three slightly advanced. Set-back harled wings of 1963.

MILL FARM, 0.5km. W. Early C19, originally of three bays, later extended to four. Venetian window in the pedimented centre.

OLD WHITEHILL, 1.8km. NW. Altered mid-C19 farmhouse. To its s, a roofless lectern DOOCOT, probably late C17.

OTTERSTON, 2.2km. W. The late C16 Otterston Castle* has been demolished. One round rubble-built tower of its barmkin wall survives, perhaps of *c.*1600, but altered *c.*1800, when it was given a tall crenellated parapet. To its W, one jamb of a round-arched gateway.

WHITEHILL, 1.2km. NW. Early C19, extended W *c.*1850, when it was all given picturesque gables and bargeboards. – SOUTH LODGE of *c.*1830, with broad mutuled eaves and a pediment.

THE MURREL. *See* p. 327.

5000

AIRDRIE
4.6km. W of Crail

Harled T-plan laird's house built for the Lumsdens of Airdrie in the late C16. Plain two-storey main block, altered inside and out in the C17, C18‡ and C19. Off-centre four-storey jamb topped by a Georgian piend roof. In the l. inner angle, a big three-storey turret corbelled out above a squinch arch; more corbelling at the top to take a martial-looking square parapet. In the other inner angle, a smaller turret. The turrets' and jamb's upper floors are jettied out on continuous corbel-courses, the lower with a rope moulding. The upper jumps up above the second-floor window in the jamb's E face to frame an empty niche for a heraldic panel, its outer border carved

---

* Its door lintel (now at Cockairnie) was dated 1589. The house was enlarged in the C17 and much altered in 1851.

‡ When wings (since removed) were added, probably in *William Adam*'s alterations to the house.

with men and animals. On top of the frame, a small window flanked by triangular pedestals carved with the date 1588 and supporting human heads.

On the s approach, incongruously smart late c18 GATEPIERS showing off vermiculated rustication, a band of Greek key ornament and a swagged frieze; rather small cast-iron urns on top.

ANSTRUTHER AND CELLARDYKE *5000*

Former fishing town built in a long narrow strip along the shore. Anstruther Wester became a burgh of barony in 1541, Anstruther Easter in 1572. Both were elevated to the rank of royal burghs in the 1580s, but in 1616 neither could boast a butcher able to provide meat for a forthcoming royal visit, both protesting that they were 'mean' towns inhabited by fishermen and sailors. Their trade was badly hurt by the Act of Union in 1707, but they found some return of prosperity in the late c18 and grew further after the opening of the railway (now closed) in 1863 and the building of a harbour at Cellardyke in 1867.

CHURCHES

BAPTIST CHAPEL, East Green, Anstruther Easter. Unexciting Gothic of 1860.

CELLARDYKE PARISH CHURCH, Toll Road, Cellardyke. Craggy Gothic, 1882. A tall tower with alarmingly crow-stepped gables, and a main gable like the n front of Pittenweem Parish Church (*q.v.*), so this too could be by *James Brown.* (COMMUNION TABLE by *Robert S. Lorimer.*)

CHALMERS MEMORIAL CHURCH (originally Anstruther Free Church; now abandoned, 1988), Backdykes, Anstruther Easter. A large Gothic church by *David Henry* of St Andrews, 1889, testifying Dr Chalmers' Anstruther origin (*see also* his birthplace in Old Post Office Close, below), and acceptably dominating the town's e skyline. From closer it is ambitious but not very interesting. Nave and aisles built up from the slope, plate tracery and lancets, and a nw broach spire.

INDEPENDENT CHAPEL (now in secular use, 1988), Crail Road, Anstruther Easter. Obtuse Gothic with fancy glazing, 1833.

ST ADRIAN'S PARISH CHURCH, School Green, Anstruther Easter. Perched on its sloping churchyard above the town, it was begun in 1634, when the latter was still 'part of the parish of Kilrenny a mile distant of deep evil way in winter and rainy times'. Anstruther Easter became a separate parish in 1640 and the church and steeple were finished in 1644. Since 1970 it has served both the Anstruthers, while the Wester Parish Church has been used as a hall (*see* below).

From the s the church appears a simple rectangle, but it is in fact a stubby T-plan. Ashlar s wall, the rest harled, including the short n jamb. The w end incorporates a plain harled tower,

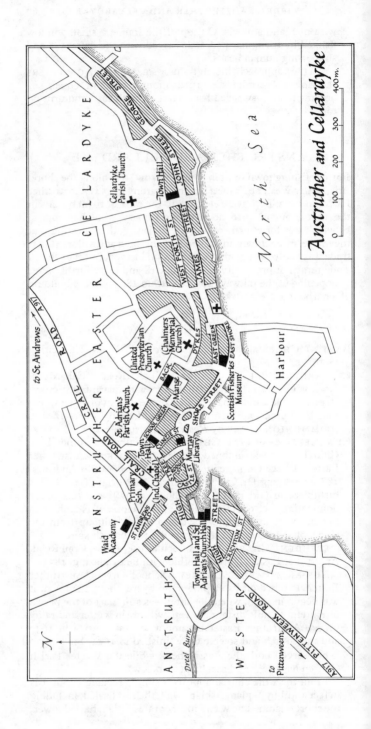

Anstruther and Cellardyke

which expands, above the main ridge, into a corbelled belfry stage and corbelled clock stage (the clock by *H. & R. Millar* of Edinburgh, 1878), and then yet more corbelling with waterspouts and a balustrade whose centre piers are carved with the anchor device of Anstruther Easter. Within them a stone spire, lucarned on the cardinal and, further up, the diagonal faces. The tower's W elevation is lopsided, for it includes a NW stair turret ending in a cap-house. In its base a large round-headed W door with roll-and-hollow moulding; the mullioned window overhead has been built up. On the S church wall, three doorways, similarly moulded, giving a number of dates. The middle one 1634, the l. one round-headed and announcing that it was blocked in 1834 (also including a resited and much weathered stone of 1675), the r. one of the same C17 type but subsequently inscribed 1934. The four windows are irregularly spaced but all of the same form, round-arched triplets with a taller light in the centre. They could be of 1834, when the interior was given its present E-facing orientation, with a gallery canted along both sides to embrace more than half the length of the church. The N jamb or Anstruther aisle was blocked up. The *New Statistical Account* (1837) said that this was 'one of the most elegant country churches anywhere to be seen'. In 1905 *McArthy & Watson* of Edinburgh carried out an elaborate scheme of redecoration and furnishing. Their PULPIT with Corinthian columns survives, but the COMMUNION TABLE is from the Chalmers Memorial Church (*see* below). – STAINED GLASS in the mullioned E window. Two lights of 1905 (SS Peter and Philip), the other four (the miraculous catch, Christ stilling the storm, SS John and Andrew) some time after 1929. – ORGAN by *Taylor of Leicester*, 1907. – MONUMENTS in the churchyard. A number of ridged tabletops, e.g. to Andrew Jameson †1646, E of the church. In the SW corner of the churchyard, a mural monument with the emblems of death on the jambs, the framed inscription starting BEATI MORTUI ... but largely defaced. Churchyard WALL by *Alexander, John & George Gilbert*, 1631.

ST ADRIAN'S CHURCH HALL (originally Parish Church), Anstruther Wester. A C16 steeple closing the view at the E end of the High Street, attached to the W end of what seems a mid-C18 church. Harled tower of four stages, the belfry stage containing pairs of little round-headed windows, of which those to the S and E have flat-topped tricuspate openings set back in the arches. Double corbels, cornice and plain balustrade in which stands a slated broach spire with fancy slating on the W side. The church is a plain harled box with smooth margins, the three S and two N windows having projecting keystones. But when was it built? There were repairs by *David Carstairs* of Largo in 1759, and the *Statistical Account* (1792) mentions re-roofing in 1761, but also describes 'a very ancient building, from the remains of a large choir and the gothic structure of the steeple'. The latter is true enough, but the first part must refer to a medieval church, and Gourlay

(*Anstruther*, 1888) says that in 1846 'the grand old relic was remodelled into the bare little church you see today'. Old-fashioned though it is, the church must surely be the result of work done in that year by *James Smith* of Edinburgh, architect, *Andrew Wilson* of Pittenweem, mason, and *Andrew Brydie* of Anstruther, wright, with *William Lees* of Pittenweem as inspector on behalf of the heritors. A resited stone on the S wall has the date 1598. Under it a tablet with the inscription ENTER IN AT YE STRAIT GET. IT IS YE VYD GET YAT LEDS TO PERDITION, and broad and narrow archways in relief. Gourlay's description was to be truer than he knew in relation to the interior, for since the adaptation of 1970 it has been quite featureless.

The churchyard is open to the sea, with just a retaining wall. The MONUMENTS include two tabletops. 'James [name defaced] mason and architect who was magistrate of this burgh † 1790 aet. 68'. 'William Taylor mason † 1807 erected by *William, James, Robert, John and Michael Taylor* all masons and surviving sons of the deceased'. The latter has crisp foli-aged squares over the balusters and fluted rosettes between. –

36   GRAVESLAB for John Fairfoul † 1626 with a primitively carved skull and Latin inscription including DISCE MORI on a little book.

UNITED PRESBYTERIAN CHURCH (now in secular use, 1988), Backdykes, Anstruther Easter. A massive stone barn by *J. Dick Peddie*, 1850. Arched door under three arched windows of the ashlar front gable.

PUBLIC BUILDINGS

FREE CHURCH SCHOOL (former), Backdykes, Anstruther Easter. 1846. One storey, with shallow-pitched overhanging gables and a little bellcote.

MURRAY LIBRARY, Shore Street, Anstruther Easter. Fussy Renaissance in red sandstone by *J. & T. W. Currie* of Elie, 1908.

PRIMARY SCHOOL, Crail Road, Anstruther Easter. 1900, by *Williamson & Inglis* of Kirkcaldy. Single-storey, nearly Art Nouveau, with symmetrical gables and a weathercocked lantern. Wilfully square two-storey addition by *Fife County Council*, 1955.

SCOTTISH FISHERIES MUSEUM, Harbourhead, Anstruther Easter. A complicated two-storey group forming a quadrangle, restored and converted to its present use by *W. Murray Jack*, 1968–70. Entrance in the S range, which is late C19 incor-porating an earlier wall. N range dated 1721 but with a pair of lancets from the medieval St Ayle's Chapel which stood on this site.* The brick E range was built as a cooperage, *c.*1850. At its end, a late C16 house with a projecting stairtower and,

---

* This chapel belonged to Balmerino Abbey. It is said to have been a long narrow rectangle with an E window of two lancet lights, a large porch, and an image niche above the W door.

inside, a large moulded fireplace. The w range, a former ship's chandler's shop and house, has a moulded doorpiece of *c.* 1700.

TOWN HALL, Cunzie Street, Anstruther Easter. 1871, by *John Harris*. Baronial in rock-faced yellow sandstone, with pompous bartizans at the corners.

TOWN HALL, High Street, Anstruther Wester. A crowstepped late C18 house attached to the N of the church tower. It was adapted for meetings in 1912 and given a steeply pedimented doorpiece.

TOWN HALL, Tolbooth Wynd and John Street, Cellardyke. 1883, by *Hall & Henry*, in place of the old Tolbooth. Feeble Gothic, with crowsteps. Attached to the w wall, the octagonal shaft of the MERCAT CROSS with egg-and-dart capital and the date 1642.

WAID ACADEMY, St Andrews Road, Anstruther Easter. 1884–6, by *David Henry*. Gabled and mullioned, with a square tower over the main door whose tympanum is carved with a ship putting to sea by *John Rhind*. Additions to the E, in polite harl and red brick by *George Sandilands*, 1930, aggressive concrete by *Fife County Council*, 1956.

DESCRIPTIONS

ANSTRUTHER WESTER

HIGH STREET is entered from the w end and leads first to the old church steeple and then, changing its name, on to the sea. The numbers are in the opposite direction. After a ragged approach, a good slate-roofed group on the N side. No. 28 with swept dormers and a moulded and lugged doorpiece dated 1702, and the smooth-rendered No. 18 and rubble-fronted DREEL TAVERN (datestone of 1734 at the back) both of three storeys. Then a continuous row of pantiled late C18 houses leading up to the late C17 BUCKIE HOUSE whose E gable, round the corner, was fantastically decorated with rows and whorls of scallop shells and buckies (whelks) by the slater *Andrew Batchelor* in the mid-C19. It was restored in 1968 by *W. Murray Jack*, and so was ELIZABETH PLACE, *c.* 1890, with its long *in situ* concrete cornice between the harling of the ground floor and the snecked stonework above. For the Town Hall attached to the church tower, *see* Public Buildings, above. The s side of High Street begins, back at the entry, with No. 43, whose mid-C18 lugged doorpiece has been altered. Nos. 25–27, FERNBANK, has three moulded doorways of the C17 or early C18, the middle one leading through to the back of No. 23, over whose door is a splendidly scrolled and vased pediment with a hammer and saw and the date 1713. Back in the street, the entry to the ESPLANADE is marked on the N side by the little early C20 splayed and piend-roofed kirk session house, followed by No. 2, with crowsteps and a formalized wheatsheaf panel, formerly an inn; and on the s side by the projecting stair-jamb of No. 15. Picturesque gentility

follows. Nos. 13 and 11, both C18, have outside stairs with
delicate cast-iron balustrades. No. 5, the OLD MANSE of 1703
with C19 extensions, narrows the view. Then No. 3, with a
lugged ogee-topped doorpiece dated 1718. Original chimney-
gable, but the wallhead each side of it has been changed. The
gable at No. 1, the WHITE HOUSE of 1760, is curvilinear. To
the SW, more whitened house fronts, which eventually merge
into sea wall, punctuated by the octagonal C19 WATCHTOWER
at the foot of the garden of No. 6 Shore Road. To the NW the
old and now practically deserted harbour, its high stone wall
interrupted by narrow sea-gates into the back gardens of the
Easter High Street. Between this wall and the slipway is the
green peninsula of the churchyard, with only a retaining wall.

ANSTRUTHER EASTER

HIGH STREET begins after the Dreel Burn which separates
Easter from Wester. The DREEL BRIDGE has an inscription
'1630, rebuilt 1795' re-sited on the present structure of 1831,
widened on the S side. To the NW the OLD CORN MILL, 1702
with a mid-C19 top floor, now a house. On the S side, the
buckie-stuck gable of No. 1 (*see* Buckie House, above) and then
the two-storey black-and-white frontage of the SMUGGLERS'
INN with two out-shots, the first a round turret carried out to
the square with triple corbelling of the late C16, the second a
pilastered and fanlit porch of the early C19, by which time it
was already a coaching inn. A wide-arched entry between
them, and plenty of hard-edged Victorian crowsteps overall.
A conventional late Georgian front, and then the plain near-
Grecian Nos. 23–25 of 1855, originally the National Bank and
probably by *J. Dick Peddie*. The N side begins in earnest with
the splendiferous house-over-shop of James Duncan, Clothier,
*c.*1880, with stone urns, elaborate mansards and cast-iron
cresting. Other notable shops of cast-iron at No. 27, mahogany
and Peterhead granite at the *c.*1900 turreted corner of Rodger
Street (Jeweller & Clockmaker) and big-scale florid ironwork
at Nos. 46–48 (Ironmonger). But older things lurk behind, all
on the S side. In WIGHTMAN'S WYND a high stone wall
ending in a crenellated tower and incorporating fragments of
DREEL CASTLE, built by *Alexander Nisbet* for Sir Philip
Anstruther in 1663. The turret and moulded doorway on the
other side belong to a snug C17 group in OLD POST OFFICE
CLOSE, where No. 3 was the birthplace in 1780 of Dr Thomas
Chalmers, leader of the Free Church. Near the E end of the
street, No. 51 has a crowstepped jamb in which a window is
crudely dated 1633. At Nos. 38–40 a re-sited semicircular
pediment with heraldry and the date 1631.

RODGER STREET steps sedately down to the harbour, the
ROYAL HOTEL looking C18 despite its smooth painted stucco
and *c.*1850 doorpiece. At No. 23 good lettering on a simple
fascia (Doig, Chemist), and at the bottom a bold baronial
TRUSTEE SAVINGS BANK dated 1870.

In St Andrews Road are the Waid Academy (*see* Public
Buildings, above) and the gabled and bargeboarded Adelaide
Lodge by *Peddie & Kinnear*, 1865. The Jacobean Clydesdale Bank of 1864 and an obliquely sited cottage mark
the junction with Crail Road, which continues E past the
Primary School and former independent Chapel (*see* Public
Buildings and Churches, above). Superior terraces sprang up
here *c*.1880, e.g. the idiosyncratic Melville Terrace with
solemn twin-arched doorways between jolly piend-roofed
bays. R. L. Stevenson spent the summer of 1868 in the late
Georgian Cunzie House.

Burial Brae runs picturesquely down past piended warehouses, the Parish Church and the Town Hall (*see* Churches
and Public Buildings, above) to the large warehouse group
(c18 and later) on the corner of Cunzie Street, a foil to the
little houses further E. Uphill again to Backdykes, notable
for its changing levels and high walls and its architectural
interludes, more or less concealed. On the N side the former
Free Church School and United Presbyterian Church (*see*
above). To the S, The Hermitage, a complicated house
originally of the early c18 and recast in 1815, when the staircase
bow was formed on the Backdykes elevation, its tall thin
window revealing cast-iron Gothick balusters; very Georgian
but also very Scottish.

93 Next is the harled and crowstepped Old Manse, built in
1590 for the minister of Kilrenny. Original L-plan of four
storeys with 'The Watch Tower' inscribed on the jamb,
and a córbelled stair turret in the angle, made into a T by the
addition of a kitchen and parlour jamb in 1753. Repairs in
1798 probably included the modification of the roof (interiors
also of this date, S.D.D.), and there was further work in 1864.
Restoration by *W. Murray Jack*, 1977–8. Crowstepped lean-
to doocot, probably early c17. Johnstone Lodge, equally
secluded, is basically a plain piend-roofed house by *George
Smith* of Edinburgh, 1829, enlivened by an artisan-Doric
porch (cf. the Lumsdaine enclosure at Kilrenny Church) which
was festooned with curvy Edwardian glazing by *Gillespie &
Scott*. Theirs also is the E wing (and elaborate interiors,
S.D.D.). Stables downhill, *c*.1800, a single block with crisp
margins, small square upper windows and spiky finials on the
gables. Finally, and far from modest, the Chalmers Memorial
Church (*see* above). In East Green, c18–19 houses, the
rubble-fronted No. 19 with a forestair, *c*.1828, was a prison
and still has two cells intact.

A walk along the harbour front from E to W. The maritime
character of East Shore is established by the two gables of
Smith & Hutton's workshop and store, one of timber in
the functional tradition, with a hoist, and its stone E neighbour
with a carved panel of a ship and the date 1737. At Harbour
Head, the Scottish Fisheries Museum (*see* Public Buildings,
above). The late c19 turret of the Ship Tavern marks the
entry to Hadfoot Wynd, whose narrow uphill view past a

corbelled C17 house is nearly blocked by the gable of No.
1, but squeezes past it towards the steeple of the Chalmers
Memorial Church. The Ship also begins the first notable
sequence of fronts in SHORE STREET. The shops are not
intrusive. No. 48 a C18 gable. Nos. 41–44 C17, with crowsteps
and dormers, a stair turret eccentrically corbelled out over the
rear archway of the central pend, and a picturesque close
enhanced by a wrought-iron lamp bracket. Plain fronts and
more pends at Nos. 36 and 34. Nos. 29–30 early C19, with
rusticated ground floor and quoins. At Nos. 21–22 a slight
kink in the building line, and another at the modest POST
OFFICE shopfront by *H.M. Office of Works*, 1934. Again an
opening is marked by a late C19 round turret, but the main
entry to Cunzie Street is a little further on, past the startling
red sandstone Murray Library (*see* Public Buildings, above,
for this and for the re-sited Mercat Cross at the harbourside).
Another kink at No. 4, the old FREEMASONS' HALL, with a
plaque inscribed 'Lodge St Ayle, 1885' in the gable. CASTLE
STREET goes on to the w, protected seaward by a massive
rubble wall. Most of the houses politely changed and whitened,
but retaining nice older features such as the basket-arched and
rusticated lintel of the doorpiece at No. 1 and the lugged and
pedimented one at No. 3. Round the corner is DREEL LODGE,
a Georgian stable block converted to a house in pre-1939
fashion. A pair of ball-topped gatepiers and a single pier of
older form.

CELLARDYKE

Two parallel streets which change their names as they run along
the contours high above the sea. In WEST FORTH STREET,
C19 fisher tenements; in EAST FORTH STREET, industrial
sheds. Downhill, JAMES STREET is mostly mid-C19. In JOHN
STREET, No. 10, a stone-fronted house and shop of *c.*1800
with a pend to the back yard. The crowstepped No. 22's lintel is
inscribed TS.MD.1709. Bullseyed chimney-gable on the brown
ashlar No. 56 of *c.*1840. On the s side, the C18 No. 17 has been
rendered and lined out to look like masonry. It has a forestair,
as do Nos. 25 and 27. For the Town Hall at the bottom of
Tolbooth Wynd, *see* Public Buildings, above. In GEORGE
STREET the houses on the s side have high garden walls to
seaward. Nos. 57–61 are of *c.*1800, built of big rust-coloured
stones, the dressings painted black. Then a whalebone arch in
the tarred wall and a surprising over-view of the C18 crowsteps
and pantiles of TOFT TERRACE, not at all the regular row one
might expect but built up every whichway from the rocky
hillside. Finally down again to SHORE STREET, whose mainly
C18 houses wind along the seafront. In HARBOUR HEAD the
two-storey C18 No. 1 has been restored by the National Trust
for Scotland. The HARBOUR, which existed by 1579, was
largely rebuilt by *Joseph Mitchell*, 1829–31, and further

improved with a new quay in 1853. In DOVE STREET, No. 1
is late C18, restored in 1967.

INNERGELLIE. *See* p. 247.

ARDROSS CASTLE
1.6km. NE of Elie

5000

Scanty remains of the castle of the Dishingtons of Ardross. There
have been two rectangular stone-built structures. Excavation
has shown that the N, perhaps C15, had a vaulted ground floor
and a stair in the thickness of the W wall.

0.6km NW, a SOUTERRAIN or earth-house, in a typical position
on the crest of a low knoll. Of a type of stone-built underground
structure more commonly found in the Northern Isles, it
consists of a twisting passage *c*. 18m. long, leading down a
flight of steps to a chamber 3.8m. by 2.2m. and 1.7m. high.
   On the S side of the road, DOOCOT of C18 lectern type.

ARNCROACH

5000

Undistinguished hamlet begun in the C18.

CARNBEE FREE CHURCH. Now a hall. Harled box of 1844–5,
with a concave-sided spired bellcote. – Contemporary SCHOOL
behind.

GIBLISTON HOUSE. *See* p. 230.
KELLIE CASTLE. *See* p. 252.

AUCHTERDERRAN, BOWHILL
AND CARDENDEN

2090

An agglomeration of mining villages developed since 1895.

AUCHTERDERRAN PARISH CHURCH, Woodend Road and Balgreggie Road. Short of charm but not of interest. The church
built in 1789 was T-plan, its main block probably a much
curtailed version of its medieval predecessor. The lower N
jamb is a transeptal aisle added to that church in the C17: large
window with Gothic survival tracery in a classical frame; ball-
finialled gable. In 1890–1 *William Constable* added the S 'nave',
replaced the C18 windows with lancets, and put red tiles on
the roof ridge. The *flèche* over the crossing must be his, and
presumably he was also responsible for the C18 birdcage
bellcote's unsuitable wooden hat.
   Interior of 1890–1, with galleries in the 'nave' and 'transepts'
and the N aisle made a chancel for the communion table. –
ORGAN by *Ingram & Co.*, 1907. – STAINED GLASS. N window
(Christ the Good Shepherd; the Risen Lord) of 1930. – In the

N aisle's E wall, three lights of stylized foliage, *c.*1890. – In the E jamb, two windows (The Good Samaritan; Sing We to the Lord) by *A. Ballantine & Son*, 1905 and 1912.

In the CHURCHYARD to the E, the piend-roofed BURIAL AISLE of the Kininmonths of that Ilk survives from the earlier church. It is probably of 1676, the date carved on the frieze of its corniced doorpiece; the pediment above containing the Kininmonth arms is not *in situ*. In the E gable, a small seg-mental-pedimented C17 monument with a prominent skull and crossbones.

BOWHILL BAPTIST CHURCH, Derran Drive. Built in 1907.

ST FOTHAD'S PARISH CHURCH, Carden Avenue. Boxy Gothic by *William Constable*, 1909–10.

ST NINIAN'S (R.C.) CHURCH, Derran Drive. By *Reginald Fairlie*, 1932. Broad synthetic stone rectangle. On the sides, straight buttresses and gabled windows. Effectively grouped with the PRESBYTERY (by *Fairlie*, 1936), pyramid-roofed, with a steep gabled porch.

AUCHTERDERRAN JUNIOR HIGH SCHOOL, Woodend Road. 1902–4, by *William Williamson*. Long single-storey block in grey ashlar. Relaxed Free style, with big gables and boat-shaped dormers. Additions, brick on the S, curtain-walled on the N, by *Fife County Council*, 1961.

BOWHILL LIBRARY, Orebank Road. Originally Miners Welfare Institute. Plain neo-Georgian in brick and harl, by *Muirhead & Rutherford*, 1932.

CARDENDEN SCHOOL, Cardenden Road. Disused. By *Lyle & Constable*, 1900–1. Jacobean of a sort. Schoolhouse in the same style next door.

CORRIE CENTRE, Carden Avenue. Originally Infant School. By *Walter Alison & Hutchison*, 1953–4. Single-storey in brick, with a shallow monopitch roof and fully glazed S wall. Curve-roofed N tower.

PRIMARY SCHOOL, Carden Avenue. Lightweight, by *Fife County Council*, 1958.

WAR MEMORIAL, head of Main Street. Classical, by *Alexander Murdoch*, 1922, the front carved with a relief of soldiers.

DESCRIPTION. In STATION ROAD, a harled *moderne* cinema (now bingo hall) of *c.*1930 and an Edwardian red sandstone pub with a domed tower on the corner of OREBANK ROAD attempt to provide a centre. For the rest, a loose-knit collection of housing, the best in BALGREGGIE ROAD and BALGREGGIE PARK, by *William Williamson & George B. Deas*, 1920, with paired centre gables.

AUCHTERMUCHTY

2010

A small town which became a royal burgh in 1517 but was never represented in Parliament or the Convention of Royal Burghs. A linen works and iron foundry were established here in the late C18 and Auchtermuchty developed as a minor industrial centre through the C19. This period of prosperity began the process of improvement or rebuilding of many houses, whose biggest consequential loss to modern eyes has been the replacement of thatch with slates or tiles.

FREE CHURCH, Croft. Now a hall. Piend-roofed whinstone box of 1843, its round-headed windows still Georgian. Harled s extension.

PARISH CHURCH, Croft. A rubble rectangle built by *Robert Wilkie*, wright in Dundee, 1779–81. In the s wall, tall round-arched windows flanking the pulpit. Diocletian windows in the gables. Tall bellcote (for two bells) with elongated Roman Doric columns; the roof is scooped up into a concave-sided spire. *Stedman Simpson* added the N aisle in 1837–8. Less happy the w porch of 1870–1.

Inside, a coved ceiling. Galleries on three sides. In the centre of the s wall, PULPIT (by *Henry W. Walker*, 1892) in front of the ORGAN (by *Ingram & Co.*, from *J. B. Lawson*'s specification, 1912–13). – PEWS of *c.*1953. – STAINED GLASS. In the windows flanking the pulpit, floral designs in deep greens and purples, of 1913. – In the s wall's outer windows, two lights ('I Ascend Unto My Father'; 'Follow Me') by *William Wilson*, *c.*1960.

CHURCHYARD with solid classical early C19 GATEPIERS. – Excellent collection of HEADSTONES (C18, except for one dated 1677) carved with jolly symbols of mortality, some having also tools of the dead man's trade. – In the SE corner, a GRAVESLAB dated 1737, again with emblems of death. – On the E wall, MONUMENT to Robert Maxwell of Broombrae, dated 1756; a big Doric aedicule. – Very similar monument to Richard Stark, dated 1759, on the church's s wall. – In the NW corner, neo-classical memorial to John Ogilvie; tall corniced plinth with a domed top.

UNITED ASSOCIATE CHAPEL, Burnside. Set high above the street behind a crenellated garden wall, it is dated 1845. T-plan with its jamb pointing forward. Tudor Gothic gable front; diamond-paned windows.

PRIMARY SCHOOL, Murray Place. Long buttressed mid-C19 front block. Rear addition of 1904–5 by *William Birrell*, who probably raised the existing windows with pedimented dormerheads at the same time. – Simple Gothic HALL (former UNITED PRESBYTERIAN CHURCH) of 1849–50 to the E.

TOWN HOUSE, High Street. Dated 1728 on the tower. The crowstepped main block has been much altered, its first-floor windows widened and given big Victorian gablets. The tower rises unbroken to a balustraded parapet; inside the parapet, a stone spire. Clockfaces dated 1897.

DESCRIPTION

CUPAR ROAD is the E approach. The rear wing of No. 26 (CAMERON HOUSE) has an early C19 anta-pilastered door-piece to the road. Its harled front block to BOW ROAD is late c18, the windows linked by lintel courses; l. skewputt carved with a head. The depth of the crowsteps shows that it used to be thatched. On the Burnside corner, VICTORIA HALL of 1865 facing the late Georgian No. 37 Cupar Road, again with lintel courses. BURNSIDE itself is a disappointment, except for the small rubble BRIDGES on its W side and the BANK OF SCOTLAND (No. 23) on the E, mid-c19 Georgian survival with consoled cornices over the windows. On Cupar Road's corner with EDEN PLACE, the mid-c19 ROYAL HOTEL, its synthetic stone E wing a recent addition. Across Eden Place, LOW ROAD begins with SOUTHPORT HOUSE of c.1800: rusticated quoins and a delicate fanlight; the window architraves have been Victorianized. THE HOLLIES is contemporary, harled with round-headed attic windows in the gable.

HIGH STREET goes uphill to the r. First, the high garden walls of a couple of late Georgian houses. On the E, the MANSE of 1793, its SE wing an addition of c.1835. On the W, No. 2 pokes a gable towards the street. Then whinstone houses and the Parish Church (see above). The harled early c19 gable of No. 9 narrows the street. Contemporary No. 11 behind a front garden; its very thin pilastered doorpiece looks an addition. The crowstepped No. 13 is mid-c18 with a lugged architrave at the door. The Tudor hoodmoulds are early c19 embellishments; so too may be the wooden pediment over the door. Narrow-fronted No. 22 opposite, late c18 with a Venetian window in its gablet.

At THE CROSS, High Street broadens to form a market place. Its W focus is the WAR MEMORIAL by *Reginald Fairlie*, 1919–20, the figure of a soldier by *Alexander Carrick*. On the S, the Town House (see above); on the N, rendered late Georgian buildings. Skewed across the NW corner, a drydashed c18 block (BRAE HOUSE), heavily restored; an inserted stone dated 1732 may belong. Then the DISTRICT COUNCIL OFFICES, late Georgian dressed up with some pompous Victorian frills. The rubble-built and crowstepped MACDUFF HOUSE opposite is dated 1597 in the curvy pediment over a blocked first-floor window. The house is L-plan with a SW jamb. Blocked segmental-arched pend under the main block's E end. Sundial in the jamb's gable. The windows have been given Georgian surrounds; c19 porch over the door in the inner angle. Inside, the main first-floor room has mid-c18 panelling. Stone stair to the first floor, its newel with vestigial bases and capitals, an early example of such detail if it is of 1597. The wooden stair to the attic's silhouette dumbbell balusters must be mid-c17. In the garden, a narrow lectern DOOCOT, probably late c17. Across the street, the late c18 ORCHARD COTTAGE and ORCHARD HOUSE. On the S side, the former CO-OPER-ATIVE SOCIETY premises, dated 1925, a half-hearted attempt at cosiness. They make one side of a little square with the unpretentious Nos. 52–56 of c.1800. Then, on the N, the late c18 crowstepped and pantiled No. 45. The c18 No. 49 still has its thatch. Much smarter is the crowstepped BRAEHEAD

HOUSE (No. 51), dated 1779 on the door lintel, set behind a small front garden whose semicircular arched gateway, perhaps C17, was rebuilt during a restoration of 1963.

In HIGH ROAD, Nos. 6–12, straightforward housing by *L. A. L. Rolland*, 1968. Fussier variant of the same formula at the MYRES VIEW development on the w. On the n, LOCHYBANK, early C19 with scrolled skewputts, but the ground-floor windows have been enlarged. In LOCKIEBANK PLACE, the late C19 No. 8; on top of one gable, half-length statue of a man. In MADRAS ROAD, the mid-Victorian MADRAS HOUSE, with plentiful Scots Jacobethan detail.

MYRES CASTLE. *See* p. 327.

ROSSIE HOUSE. *See* p. 354.

AUCHTERTOOL

2090

A straggling village along a n slope, dominated by its late C19 distillery.

PARISH CHURCH, 1.2km. to the sw. A very plain box since its thoroughgoing reconstruction in 1833. Two battlemented porches on the s side; an octagonal birdcage bellcote to the w gable. The lean-to n aisle was added in 1905–6.

In the churchyard, C17 TABLE STONES; the best (of which only the top survives) commemorates David Martin, minister of Auchtertool, † 1636, carved with a relief of Martin dressed in knee-breeches and a gown, his feet on a skull.

Very pretty Tudor MANSE of 1812 by *James Gillespie Graham* to the w. Harled back wing by *Williamson & Inglis*, 1900.

DISTILLERY. C19 group of brick and rubble buildings. Four-storey maltings range of *c.*1880, faintly Italianate in dark red and white brick. Its kilns have been demolished.

AUCHTERTOOL HOUSE. Early C19 villa, large and smart with giant anta pilasters at the corners. The Roman Doric columned doorpiece leads into a hall whose columned screen opens into the stair.

FARMS

BALMULE, 2.9km. sw. Informal farmhouse and steading of *c.*1800, partly limewashed. – C17 lectern DOOCOT, the rat-course stepping up at the gables.

EAST BALBARDIE, 2.4km. SE. Early C18 harled farmhouse with a steep roof and crowstepped gables in the centre of a U-plan rubble steading.

WEST BALBARDIE, 1.6km. SE. Laird's house dated 1638 on the r. window lintel. Originally of three bays, it was extended E by a further bay in the C18. – To the s, classy early C19 LODGE with a pediment and bowed ends.

BALMUTO. *See* p. 98.
KILRIE HOUSE. *See* p. 264.

BALBIRNIE HOUSE AND STONE CIRCLE
see GLENROTHES, p. 235

4000

BALCARRES
1 km. N of Colinsburgh

Large but surprisingly low-key mid-C19 house of the Lindsays,
built around an earlier agglomeration. The lands of Balcarres
had passed from the Earls of Fife to the Crown by the C15. In
1511 they were granted in feu ferme to Sir John Stirling of
Keir with the condition that he build and maintain a sufficient
house of stone and lime, with a hall, chamber, barn, byre,
stable, doocot, orchards, gardens, beehives, and plantations.
The house built in accordance with this charter, now swamped
by C19 additions, still shows quite clearly on the W, its sandstone masonry contrasting with the later whinstone. It is L-
plan, the jamb tenuously attached to the main block's NW
corner, the inner angle filled with a tight round stairtower.

In 1587 Balcarres was acquired by a judge, John Lindsay,
Lord Menmuir, who is said* to have built a house here in 1595,
probably an s addition to the existing house and a rectangular E
stairtower housing a much more comfortable turnpike than
the earlier one on the W.

Lord Menmuir's grandson Alexander was made first Earl
of Balcarres in 1651. After the Restoration, Colin, third Earl
of Balcarres, who inherited in 1662 at the age of ten, seems to
have begun a huge enlargement of the house by building a
four-storey L-plan block about 27m. E of the old house, which
would have been remodelled and linked to this new wing by a
great centre block. The third Earl's Jacobite sympathies and
exile in Holland from 1690 to 1700 prevented completion of
more than his E wing. Now a detached building known as the
DOWER HOUSE, it has lost its two upper floors and been
extended s. The s gable's Venetian window looks of *c.* 1800,
its crowsteps mid-C19. Inside the NW jamb the C17 scale and
platt stair survives.

Alexander, sixth Earl of Balcarres and *de jure* twenty-third
Earl of Crawford, sold the estate in 1791 to his brother, Robert
Lindsay of Leuchars, who was planning the addition of a
drawing room s of the existing house in 1804, although it was
another five years before he built it, a stolid Georgian extension
with a broad bow on the s front.

Robert Lindsay's son James inherited this ragbag in 1836.
He inherited also a scheme produced in 1834 by *William Burn*
for a massive enlargement and remodelling of the house. Burn's

---

* By Lord Lindsay, *Lives of the Lindsays*, i (1849), 376.

plans, much revised over the next two years, were executed in 1838–43. The irregular long rectangle of the existing house was made a Z by the addition of a library W of the new drawing room (itself refronted) and a family wing E of the C16 house. The C16 house's W front was altered by the insertion of a large first-floor window in the main block's gable, the addition of an oriel and pedimented dormerhead to the N jamb, and giving the W stairtower a tall conical roof. A narrow one-storey flat-roofed extension was built across the front (replacing a broader Georgian terrace or balcony). Behind the drawing room and new library, Burn placed three floors of corridor and minor rooms. A porch protruding N from the S block's W end gave a new main entrance through a curly pedimented door very similar to Burn's contemporary door at Kilconquhar Castle. All this is externally unexciting, a combination of Elizabethan bay windows with Baronial turrets. A peculiarity is Burn's failure to unify the design of the new library with the 1809 drawing-room block, which he recast by converting its bow window into a canted bay, placing strapwork pediments over the upper-floor windows, and adding crowsteps and square angle turrets.

Burn's additions were completed by building an office court E of his family wing. At its N entrance, a bellcote over the gateway. At its E, gatepiers whose swagged urns look mid-C18.

James Lindsay died in 1855, and in 1863–7 his son Sir Coutts Lindsay employed *David Bryce*, to further enlarge and remodel the house. He added a N extension (containing a dining room on the principal floor, with a studio above) to the C16 house and heightened the family wing of 1838–43. Bryce's work is more fiercely Baronial than Burn's. His N extension's crowstepped gable is gripped by fat pepperpot turrets bristling with cannon spouts. The family wing's S front became a taut group of crowstepped gables, the l. a diagonally set addition to the original house's SE corner, the centre a canted bay corbelled out to the square.

The interior's plan is essentially that created by Burn and Bryce, but the early C16 house's vaulted ground floor survives. The N jamb's room (now a wine cellar) has rectangular openings cut into the vault, possibly gunloops which have been enlarged.

The Victorian room sequence begins with the Entrance Hall, whose staircase goes up to the first-floor corridor running W into the S addition of 1595. All this is Burn Jacobean, with mean pendants on the ceilings. The library and drawing room are to the S. In both, large-scale but rather flat strapworked plaster ceilings of 1838–43. The library's marble chimney-piece, a grape-festooned goat's head under its centre pediment, has been imported from Crawford Priory; it is probably the one supplied for that house by *D. Holmes* of London in 1813. The bookcases incorporate marquetry inlay of *c.*1610 from Rubens's House in Antwerp. Very best Flemish mannerist, with attached Ionic columns and decorated with carved heads.

The drawing room still has a late Georgian feel, thanks to the internal survival of its bow window. The Frenchy chimneypiece is Burn's.

The Panelled Room N of the corridor was the C16 hall and was used as the dining room until 1863 (a use to which it has now reverted). Burn's big W window and Bryce's SE projection are incongruous but welcome for light. Splendid plaster ceiling of c. 1630,* very similar to one of c. 1610 from the 'Old Palace' at Bromley-by-Bow, now in the Victoria and Albert Museum, London. Strapworked compartments. Royal arms in the centre; portrait roundels of David, Joshua, Hector and Alexander derived from *Nicolas de Bruyn*'s engravings of the Nine Worthies‡ published at Antwerp in 1594. On the walls imported Flemish panelling carved with Biblical figures and angels holding the linenfold drapes.

The study on the N (the C16 chamber given an oriel window by Burn) serves as an ante-room to Bryce's dining room (now New Library), whose plaster frieze and enriched ceiling are based on those in the early C17 library at Winton House (Lothian). Above is Bryce's studio (now billiard room). In its E wall a tall narrow door through which paintings could be brought from outside. The stencilled strapwork frieze looks original.

The C19 family wing is entered from the Panelled Room. First comes the boudoir, its walls hung with Chinese wallpaper. Beyond were Lady Lindsay's bedroom and dressing room (now the kitchen), with Sir Coutts Lindsay's bedroom and dressing room to the N.

Second-floor bedrooms are almost entirely by Burn and Bryce, but the W room over the Panelled Room has a pretty late Georgian chimneypiece, its frieze decorated with ladies kneeling beside an urn.

The GARDEN TERRACES S of the house were begun in 1841, when the Upper Terrace with its balustraded retaining wall was made. It is divided by box hedging into two parts, fairly narrow in front of the library and drawing room block, much broader in front of the family wing, where it forms the East Court. In the late 1860s *Sir Coutts Lindsay* made the Lower Terrace. This is reached by an imperial stair on the line of a path leading from the C16 E stairtower (i.e. at the join of the reception rooms and the family wing). Parterres§ were laid out on the Lower Terrace. Lindsay seems to have been primarily responsible for the design, with *Jesse Hall* as executant architect, probably under *David Bryce*'s overlordship. In the East Court's centre, a German FOUNTAIN of c. 1550, placed here in 1873 by Sir Coutts Lindsay, who added its shell basins. –

---

* The RCAHMS reported that painted boards had been found above it.

‡ The Nine Worthies were three Jewish heroes (David, Joshua and Judas Maccabeus), three classical heroes (Hector of Troy, Alexander the Great and Julius Caesar), and three Christian heroes (Arthur, Charlemagne and Godfrey de Bouillon).

§ Three of them from designs in *Les Jardins du Roi de Pologne*.

On the Lower Terrace, a Japanese FOUNTAIN with lotus bowls. – On the Upper Terrace W of the house, an early C17 SUNDIAL with elaborately faceted shaft and head, brought from Leuchars Castle in 1873 and erected here on a new base by *Robert S. Lorimer*, 1896–7.

E of the garden, the roofless CHAPEL built for David, first Lord Lindsay of Balcarres, in 1635, an unembarrassed mixture of Gothic and classical. Three-bay rubble rectangle. Obtusely arched windows with thick Y-tracery; in the E gable, a spiral-traceried round window. At the corners, diagonal buttresses rising to window-sill level, where they change to columns topped by tall obelisk pinnacles; on the buttresses, carved emblems of death. Birdcage bellcote with Doric piers on the W gable. Attached Corinthianish columns carrying outsize balls flank the round-arched door; above are a draperied inscription, an empty frame (inserted, says the RCAHMS), and a foliated panel carved with the monogram of David, Lord Lindsay of Balcarres, and his wife Sophia, and mottoes. Inside, in the S wall's E end, an elaborately carved late Gothic aumbry; if *in situ* it is a surprising feature for a Protestant chapel of this date. Beside the chapel's door, scrolled stones carved with Tudor roses; they came from a gate on the estate.

The PARK, laid out with regular shelter belts in the early C18, owes its present well-wooded informality to Robert Lindsay's improvements of *c.* 1800. Among these was his planting around the bare outcrop of Balcarres Craig E of the chapel. On top he put a folly, the battlemented CRAIG TOWER built by *James Fisher* in 1813. Round whinstone tower with a Gothic window and huge crosslet loophole in its W face; 'ruined' screen walls go back on two sides. – The lime avenue W of the house was planted *c.* 1900. Beside it, an ivy-clad DOOCOT built by *William Wilkie*, 1797; square with a pyramid roof.

The EAST LODGE near the house was probably built by *Wilkie* in 1794; semi-octagonal ends and a rustic porch. – The WEST LODGE is a near replica of 1903. – SOUTH LODGE on the A921, red brick of 1870–1, probably by *J. Caslake* of London. Its gatepiers are by *Jesse Hall*. The delicate wrought-iron gates are Italian of *c.* 1700, imported from Cremona. – T-plan ESTATE OFFICE to the E by *Robert S. Lorimer*, 1903, with characteristic gables; big armorial carving over the W door. – NORTH GATES and LODGE on the B941 by *Lorimer*, 1896– 8. Heavy rusticated gatepiers topped by lions rampant (carved by *Stodart*). The iron gates decorated with the Crawford* arms were made by *Houston & Stewart*. Inside a screen wall, the lodge, accurately described by Lorimer as 'rather snippy in the Scots-French style à la Queen Mary's baths' (i.e. the late C16 Queen Mary's Bath at Holyrood, Edinburgh); dormer pediments carved by *William Beveridge*.

---

* James, twenty-sixth Earl of Crawford and ninth Earl of Balcarres, had bought the estate from Sir Coutts Lindsay in 1886.

5000

BALCASKIE
1.9km. N of St Monans

Large and gawky C17 house but of major importance as the first
work of *Sir William Bruce*, 'the chief introducer of architecture
in this country'.*

The starting point of the present house is a three-storey L-
plan house built for the Moncreiffs of Balcaskie shortly before
1629. Its main block is still visible on the S, where it occupies
the W third of the front. The bottom of a blocked opening
shows that its second-floor windows rose above the eaves. The
NW jamb presents its gable at the r. of the present N front. In
1665 the estate was bought by Bruce, who in 1668–74 employed
John Hamilton, mason, and *Andrew Waddell* and *Alexander
Paterson,* wrights, to enlarge the house. Bruce heightened the
NW jamb to four storeys, extended the main block E and gave
it a NE jamb. This jamb roughly balances the NW, but it is
broader and of three storeys in the height of the NW's four.
The open centre of this U-plan he filled with a two-storey
block, probably flat-roofed and balustraded. At each corner he
placed a pavilion-roofed tower. The general appearance was
very close to that of Panmure House (Tayside; demolished),
begun by John Mylne Jun. in 1666.‡

Bruce's crowstepped gables and ornamental gunloops are
courteous quotations from the early C17 house. So too may be
the moulded second-floor windows on the S front, but their
segmental pediments are similar to those provided at Leslie
House in 1667–72. More progressive (probably of French
derivation) are the N corner towers' quoins and shallowly
rusticated window margins. Characteristic of the classicism
developing in Scotland in the mid-C17 is the S doorpiece, with
panelled and banded Mannerist pilasters and a carved basket
of fruit on its segmental pediment.

In 1684 Bruce sold Balcaskie to Sir Thomas Steuart. Fourteen years later the estate was acquired by Sir Robert Anstruther. It was probably his son Sir Philip who in the mid-C18
cleared away the tight late C17 forecourt of office buildings
and replaced them with piend-roofed pavilions joined to the
main house by quadrant walls. The E (laundry) pavilion's rear
elevation has a smart pedimented centre on the axis of a new
E approach. Probably at the same time Bruce's two-storeyed
centre was largely rebuilt, raised to three storeys and with a
first-floor Venetian window its main accent.

The C18 Venetian window lost its impact when *William Burn*
punched another window each side as part of his alterations of
1830–2. At the same time he added a Jacobean porch, its
orangey stone contrasting with the C17 and C18 grey ashlar.
On the S front he lowered the sills of the first-floor windows
and introduced an iron balcony right across the main block,

---

* So said Sir John Clerk of Penicuik.
‡ Panmure's corner towers were ogee-roofed (possibly an early C18 alteration) and
overlapped the jambs.

cutting crudely across the top of Bruce's doorpiece. Less conspicuous are his twin-gabled E addition and crowstepped W
stable block. Further work was done in 1856–8 by *David Bryce*,
who gave an oriel to the SW tower and tepid Baronial additions
to the W elevation. He may also have remodelled the N quadrants, giving them niches filled with urns.★

Inside, much of Bruce's interior survives. Large entrance
hall with a chequered marble floor, the stones perhaps those
bought from James Hamilton, merchant, in 1668. At the S,
the house's spine wall is supported on mid-C18 thin Doric
columns. On the E, Jacobethan stair of 1831–2 to the first
floor, whose centre is filled by a gallery, presumably in the
position of Bruce's 'galerie', but its grained oak ceiling, decorated with lugged squares and Greek crosses, is characteristically Burn. S of the gallery the late C17 state apartment

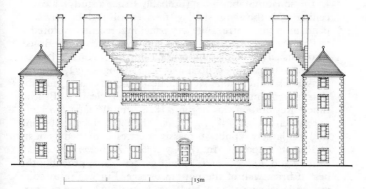

Balcaskie,
conjectural reconstruction of north front in 1674

extends the length of the house. It begins at the W with a
double-cube ante-room (made from the early C17 hall), its
ceiling enriched with rectangular panels filled with fruit and
angels' heads. In the centre, a big oval of oak leaves surrounding a pendant. More pendants in the corners. As in
almost all the rooms, the C17 chimneypiece has been replaced
by a plain marble one supplied by *David Ness* in the mid-C19.
In the drawing room (now library) next door, a much richer
ceiling, probably part of the plasterwork for which *George
Dunsterfield* was paid in 1674. In its centre, a round panel
painted with Fame seated on a cloud (probably by *Jacob de
Witt*‡), set in an octagonal frame of high-relief foliage. Octagonal border decorated with garlands and herms. All this looks
convincingly of 1674, but are the octagons in the frame and its

---

★ An engraving by Joseph Swan in John M. Leighton, *History of the County of
Fife* (1840), shows the E quadrant as a pilastered screen. It shows neither the W
quadrant nor W pavilion and may not be very accurate.

‡ There is at Balcaskie a painting, probably originally for an overmantel, signed
by de Witt. However, *T*. (? Toussaint) *Gelton* was paid 540 'rex dollars' (c. £135
sterling) 'for picters' in 1672.

guilloche enrichment late C17 or early C19 embellishment? State bedchamber (now dining room) to the E, its ceiling's octagonal centre filled with a painting of the Fall of Icarus (again probably by de Witt), set in a stucco frame decorated with rather coarse but deeply undercut foliage; four circles link the frame to the walls. This looks like *Dunsterfield*'s work of 1674, but are the rosettes inside the circles and the laurel wreaths at the corners part of his scheme or early C19 additions? In the SE tower, a closet (now serving room), its deep plaster frieze with arabesque enrichment very old-fashioned in comparison with the probable Dunsterfield work. Old-fashioned plasterwork again in two second-floor rooms. The Blue Room (probably Bruce's bedchamber) has a ceiling divided into rectangles by simply foliaged bands. In the centre, the initials of Bruce and his wife; at the sides, angels' heads. In the square Globe Room (probably Bruce's study), a coved ceiling with the same shallow foliaged ribs; globe astrolabe pendant in the centre. Late C17 panelling, recently restored.

The terraced GARDEN s of the house was laid out by Bruce, who as usual (cf. Hopetoun House, Lothian, or Kinross House, Tayside) focused its central axis on a telling object, here the Bass Rock. Alterations were made in the C18, and only the stair from the middle to the bottom terrace is clearly of Bruce's time.* Restoration was begun *c*.1826–7 by *William Burn* and the garden designer *W. S. Gilpin*. The top terrace's retaining wall was largely rebuilt, its massive buttresses topped by busts of Roman emperors. In 1836–7 *Robert Adamson*, *Alexander Watson* and *James Morris* rebuilt garden walls, probably the heated brick wall of the bottom terrace. Further restoration was undertaken *c*.1844–8 by *W. A. Nesfield*, who laid out par-terres (since partly grassed over) on the top terrace and largely rebuilt the middle terrace's retaining wall. At each end of the middle terrace he provided a great flight of stairs from above; at the top of each flight of stairs, a round-arched keyblocked gateway with ball finials on its channelled piers and rococo cast-iron gates into the park (the w into mid-air). The urns on the two upper terraces also belong to Nesfield's scheme, as may the lead statues on the top terrace. Probably also by Nesfield was the restoration of the great avenues running s of the garden and N of the house's forecourt (the court itself formalized and enlarged with a yew hedge).

To the w, the roofless ABERCROMBIE PARISH CHURCH abandoned in 1646. Probably late medieval, it is a simple rectangle built of large squared rubble blocks. It seems to have been heightened in a reconstruction of 1597–1602, when *John Wilson* made the N door from fragments of medieval tomb-stones. Probably of the same date was the w bellcote (its base surviving). The E gable's buttresses may be part of the repairs made by *Hugh Birrell* in 1843. Inside, a rectangular credence in the E gable; what may have been a stoup beside the door.

* But it is said to have been repositioned.

Placed against the W gable, heraldic TOMBSTONE of Thomas Abercrombie.

Three main drives across the park. On the W, broad-eaved WEST LODGE by *Burn & Bryce*, 1843–4. Contemporary obelisk gatepiers. – BRIDGE over the Dreel Burn with arcaded parapets and ball-finialled ends, by *Burn*, 1827–8. – NORTH LODGE of 1886, its red-tiled roof an alteration. Mid-C18 gatepiers, the wrought-iron gates by *Robert S. Lorimer*, 1912. – On the E drive, crowstep-gabled HOME FARM by *William Lees*, 1834–5. Its W wing was added by *Alexander Watson* and *Hugh Birrell* in 1842–3; the flat-roofed dormers are more recent. – Crowstepped EAST LODGE by *Burn & Bryce*, 1846. Beside it, fluted and banded gatepiers with urn finials. The S is dated 1714, perhaps the date of their erection at the house's forecourt, the S 1745, probably the date when they were moved here. They are joined by quadrants to tall round mid-C18 DOOCOTS, their conical roofs topped by square cupolas. Iron gates of 1886.

65

BALCOMIE CASTLE
2.5km. NE of Crail

6000

Bits of the S and E ranges of a large mansion built round a courtyard in the C16 and C17, mostly pulled down and rebuilt as a farmhouse and steading *c.*1800. James Learmonth of Clatto was granted the lands of Balcomie in 1526 with the condition that he erect a house, but the earliest surviving fragments look late C16. These are the remains of a U-plan S range, which seems to have had a four-storey main block with a square five-storey tower or wing projecting at each end. Only the SW tower and the main block's adjoining W bay stand to their full height, both with moulded window margins and the bases of dormer windows which presumably were topped with pediments. On the tower's S gable, a big chimney flanked by two-storey corner turrets sadly deprived of their conical roofs, but with quatrefoil gunloops still hinting at baronial class. A large gunloop at the base; more gunloops under the W front's windows. In the inner angle, a neat stair turret rising from the first to the second floor. Scanty remains of the rest of the range's vaulted ground floor and of the probably C17 thickening of the main block into a double pile infilling the area between the wings.

The E range contained the gatehouse. Its two lower floors survive. Above the elliptically arched entrance, three moulded stone panel frames under the inscription THE . LORD . BVLD . THE . HOUSE . THEY . LABOVR . IN . VAINE . THAT . BVILD . IT . The centre frame is filled by the florid heraldic achievement of the Learmonths of Balcomie, accompanied by the date 1602. In the flanking panels, the arms and initials of John Learmonth and his wife, Elizabeth Myrton. They owned Balcomie in

1602, but the carved stones are too small for the frames. Have they been re-sited here? In the gateway's r. spandrel, a sundial. Inside the transe, a gunloop each side. Vaulted porter's room on the N; garderobe in the room above.

On the courtyard's W side, an ashlar-fronted late Georgian farmhouse; on its W front, a bowed projection at the junction with the S range.

BALDRIDGEBURN see DUNFERMLINE

BALFARG see GLENROTHES, p. 237

3000

BALGONIE CASTLE
1km. W of Milton of Balgonie

52 Powerful image of baronial strength atop the steep S bank of the River Leven and poised to dominate one of Fife's main E–W routes. The lands of Balgonie were held by the Sibbald family in the early C15 when a new castle was laid out as a stone-walled enclosure with a gatehouse in the W wall, a tower house in the NW corner, and a well in the centre of the courtyard. The property passed through marriage to the Lundies in the late C15, and Sir Andrew Lundy was engaged in building work (almost certainly construction of the N range E of the tower) in 1496, when James IV ordered fourteen shillings to be given to the masons at Balgonie. In 1627 Robert Lundy sold the estate to the Boswells, from whom it was acquired eight years later by the Covenanting general Sir Alexander Leslie, who, before being created first Earl of Leven in 1641, had built or reconstructed a block in the courtyard's SE corner and remodelled the existing tower and N range.* In 1666 the seventh Earl of Rothes (guardian of the infant Margaret, Countess of Leven) repaired the house and employed *John Mylne Jun.* to design a grand stair linking the N range to the NW tower. In 1706 the third Earl of Leven completed the E range, using *Gilbert Smith* as his mason for a new building joining the N range and the early C17 SE block. During the Jacobite rising of 1715–16 Rob Roy MacGregor garrisoned the castle. The defences may have been damaged at this time, but the buildings were habitable in 1721.‡ In 1755 they were 'painted and sashed' (i.e. sash windows were introduced) in a modernization scheme by David, Lord Balgonie (later sixth Earl of Leven). The estate was sold in 1823 to James Balfour of Whittingehame, but his schemes for repair and remodelling

---

* Two ceilings in the SE block are recorded (by the RCAHMS) as having had the initials F.S.A.L. for Field Marshal Sir Alexander Leslie, so presumably dated from after Leslie's purchase of the house in 1635 and his being made an earl in 1641.

‡ An inventory of that date shows them fully furnished.

of the castle were not carried out and by 1840 it was reported★
as 'fast hastening to decay'. Restoration by *Cunningham, Jack,
Fisher & Purdom* began in 1971 with repair of the NW tower;
the re-roofing and rehabilitation of the other buildings is now
(1988) envisaged.

Rubble walls (much altered and patched) enclose the courtyard's S and W sides. Early C19 engravings show a corbelled parapet walk on the W wall; probably the S wall had
one also. In the S wall a segmental-arched pend built as part
of a gatehouse, perhaps *c.*1640, the stubs of whose projecting
walls are still visible. Above the arch, a large blocked opening,
presumably for a first-floor room. To the l., two blocked

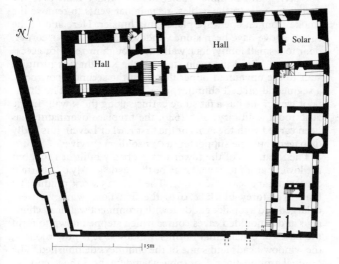

Balgonie Castle,
plan of first floor

windows of (demolished) C18 houses built against the courtyard wall.

At the W wall's S end, the C15 gatehouse. In each of the
pend's side walls a recess, the N checked for doors. On the r.,
a rectangular room. On the l., a D-plan chamber with inverted
keyhole gunloops in the bowed face; pit-prison to the N. There
has been a room above whose flat roof was reached by a
turnpike stair from the parapet walk.

The early C15 NW tower is a severe four-storey ashlar rectangle. On the N wall, two garderobe projections heavily
corbelled out, one above the other. The rather small angle
rounds, parapet studded with large ornamental spouts, and NE
cap-house are probably additions of *c.*1640 together with the
crowstepped attic. Small cusped first-floor windows. The rectangular upper-floor windows have been enlarged, perhaps in

★ By *The New Statistical Account of Scotland.*

the C17. Originally, the tower was free-standing, the doors to the ground-floor storage and first-floor hall (reached by an external wooden stair) both in the E front. These entrances were covered (the first-floor door built up) in 1666, when *John Mylne Jun.* filled the gap between the tower and N range with a stair block. The main entrance is now a lugged-architraved door at its foot.

Inside, the newel of Mylne's scale-and-platt stair (its treads replaced in wood) has carved capitals and bases of a rudimentary classical type characteristic of Mylne and his successors (cf. James Smith's service stairs at Melville House, *q.v.*). The tower's ground-floor room was a store with an obtusely pointed tunnel-vault. Round tunnel-vault over the first-floor hall. In the gables, rectangular vents to remove the smoke from an open fire placed in a brazier. Here and in the rooms above have been stone window seats. In the NE corner, door to a small lobby, its E wall cut through in 1666 for access to a room behind the main stair; on the N, tight C15 turnpike stair to the unvaulted upper floors. In the second-floor room, a segmental-arched chimneypiece; NW garderobe. The third-floor garderobe has a fat stone cornice along the N wall. In the attic room (? library) of *c.*1640, the fireplace overmantel has been carved with the arms of the first Earl of Leven; it is badly damaged, but one supporter (a C17 soldier) survives.

The N range E of the tower was probably built in 1496, but the lower part of its N wall may be the castle's early C15 curtain contemporary with the tower. The late C15 work produced a long two-storey block. *c.*1640 the first-floor windows were enlarged and a top floor added, with prominent wallhead chimneys and a moulded eaves course which stepped down to form the bases of ornamental dormer windows. It is now roofless, the window heads and some of the chimneys demolished. The original ground-floor door (now a window) near the W end has been replaced by a door one bay to the E. First-floor door in the W bay, apparently originally reached by a gallery extending from the top of the wooden stair to the tower's main entrance.

The tunnel-vaulted ground floor's W two-thirds (now two rooms) was the kitchen, perhaps serving the tower as well as this range's hall. Basket-arched fireplace in the gable; hatch in the ceiling. Round-arched doorway into the E room. In its W wall each side of the door, a large niche, round-headed on the N, pointed-arched on the S. Water inlet in the gable, drain in the N wall. Another ceiling hatch. No fireplace, so presumably this was for storage, perhaps a wine cellar.

The first floor was probably planned as a hall above the kitchen with a solar to the E. Huge N fireplace with a roll and hollow moulding, its size much reduced, probably *c.*1640, when this floor seems to have been remodelled as a grand apartment of dining room, drawing room and bedchamber. Another fireplace, its width also contracted, in the S wall. The E room's fireplace is in the partition wall.

The E range consists of two blocks. At the S, a crowstepped

two-storey building probably put up by the first Earl of Leven, *c*.1640. Chamfered window margins; tunnel-vaulted ground floor. The first floor has been reached by a forestair. The three-storey N block joining this to the N range was added by *Gilbert Smith* in 1706. It has a door to the courtyard and also a door on the E, perhaps to the garden. Turnpike stair in the SE corner with a round gunloop set high up as a reminder of the house's military character.

BALLINBREICH CASTLE   2020
4.3km. E of Newburgh

Ruined castle set off by a background of trees. The site is flat, except on the N, where it slopes to a cliff overlooking the Tay; but boggy ground, now denoted only by small burns, gave protection from attack from the E and W.

The present castle was probably begun in the C14 by the Leslies, who acquired the barony of Ballinbreich in 1312. Rubble curtain wall enclosing a roughly rectangular area; it would be about 33m. × 12m. were it not for the splayed NE corner. The enclosure's downward-sloping N quarter may have been divided off from the level S part by a wall.

The C14 living accommodation was contained in stone-built ranges against the curtain's N and W sides and in a tower projecting from its SW corner. Of the N range there survives only a stub of its S wall and one double-splayed jamb of its entrance from the W range's gable. Two blocked windows and a first-floor garderobe in the W range's N part may be C14.

Of the rectangular SW tower considerably more original work remains. It was of three storeys, rubble-built and plain externally. Inside, there was a triple-arched sedilia in the second floor's S wall; presumably this room was a chapel until the C15, when the first and second floors were thrown into one (probably as a great chamber) and covered with a pointed tunnel-vault hiding the sedilia. Presumably C15 is the large S aumbry with a flattened ogee arch. Probably also part of the C15 alterations are the flattish corbels for a parapet on the E and N faces.

Major reconstruction of the castle took place in the late C16.[*] Against the SW tower and the S curtain was built a three-storey SE block, its ashlar masonry contrasting with the C14 rubble, the join masked by a semicircular tower decorated with prominent first- and second-floor gunloops. Another gunloop in the E gable, so the lower E building, whose roof raggle is visible there, must have been added later, probably in the C17, when the C16 SE block was given an attic, its masonry not bonded

---

[*] Perhaps of *c*.1572. Charles Leslie, *Historical Records of the Family of Leslie*, ii (1869), 136, mentions the existence of an iron door-plate from the castle which bore that date and the initials A.E.R. (for Alexander (Leslie), Earl of Rothes, the then owner).

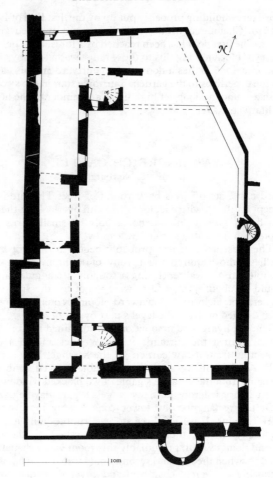

Ballinbreich Castle,
plan of ground floor

into the large C16 chimney. Inside, the SE block had a tunnel-vaulted ground floor; E fireplaces on the upper floors. First-floor door into an E range, now demolished except for the curtain, and its date unknown. Contemporary with this new SE block are the roll-moulded windows in the C14 SW tower, which was also heightened in ashlar and given a new parapet corbelled out from above the SE block's ridge.

More ambitious than the addition of the SE block was the rebuilding (except for the curtain) of the W range. On its S part was put up an L-plan block. The N wing was of only two storeys and attic, covered with a monopitch roof sloping down from corbels on the curtain wall. The four-storey S wing abuts the C14 SW tower, and its E end muscles into the courtyard. At its junction with the N wing, its upper floors' walling is carried on a segmental arch. Corbelled stair turret set diagonally across the inner angle of the S wing and SW tower. All this late C16 work is of ashlar and quite smart. Moulded stringcourses to mark off the S wing's lower floors, the second-floor stringcourse jumping up on the N front to clear the N wing's roof, the first-floor stringcourse jumping down on the surviving stub of the N wing's E front. Simple roll mouldings at the S wing's lower windows; much more elaborate the surrounds to the third-floor windows, which used to be corniced and perhaps also had pedimented dormerheads. Inside the S wing's E half has been a turnpike stair to the second floor; third-floor room above reached by the SE turret stair. In the W half has been a tunnel-vaulted ground-floor room. In the N wing was a vaulted ground-floor kitchen, its large fireplace built out behind the C14 curtain.

The late C16 reconstruction continues at the W range's N part, but its E wall was not aligned with that of the S part. Ashlar again but simpler, the only decoration at the roll-moulded or chamfered window surrounds. Gabled stairtower at the inner angle with the now demolished N range.

BALLINGRY, LOCHORE AND CROSSHILL   *1090*

Miners' housing built as three developments – Lochore and Crosshill from *c.* 1900, Ballingry from 1947 – but making a single sprawling village without a real centre.

CHURCHES

BALLINGRY PARISH CHURCH, Ballingry Road. A small T-plan kirk, the main block of 1831,* the N aisle C17, made cruciform by a large but fairly tactful S addition by *James Shearer & Annand*, 1964–6. On the W gable, a two-tier birdcage bellcote. In the N aisle's thistle-finialled gable, a window which is dated 1661 on the pilasters of the inept classical surround to the Gothic survival mullioned and transomed lights. Inside, two STAINED-GLASS windows (The Calling of St Peter; Baptism) of 1951.

In the graveyard, several C18 HEADSTONES decorated with symbols of death. – MANSE to the W by *Andrew Cumming*, 1852.

LOCHCRAIG CHURCH, Main Street. Originally United Free, opened in 1904. Plain lancet style with a gabled bellcote.

ST KENNETH'S (R.C.) CHURCH, off Main Street. Disused. Built, 1924, with an onion-domed W tower.

---

* *Ebeneezer Birrell*, of Kirkcaldy, who signed the seating plan in 1832, was possibly the architect.

PUBLIC BUILDINGS

BALLINGRY JUNIOR HIGH SCHOOL, Lochleven Road. Large
and plain, by *Andrew Scobie & Son*, 1908–11. Curtain-walled
N extension by *Fife County Council*, 1961.

CROSSHILL PRIMARY SCHOOL, Benarty Avenue. 1910, by
Andrew Scobie & Son. A long spread with some Jacobean
gables.

LOCHORE MINERS SOCIAL CLUB, Lochleven Road. By *R. H.
Motion*, 1932. Squared-up Wrenaissance in white harl and red
sandstone. Central cupola giving it a public presence.

120   MARY COLLIERY, off Mannering Street. Disused. Opened
1902. PITHEAD GEAR survives, the winding-wheel set in a
concrete frame.

LOCHORE CASTLE, off Main Street. Ruinous rubble-built tower
standing on a truncated motte surrounded by remains of a
barmkin wall. The motte was probably made in the C12 or
early C13; presumably there was a castle here by 1255, when
David de Lochore was named as one of the Scottish magnates.
The square stone tower may be C14. It has been of at least
four storeys. Second- and third-floor garderobe projection on
the E front. Unvaulted interior, with chambers in the wall
thickness. Barmkin wall probably C15.

72   LOCHORE HOUSE, off Ballingry Road. Very classy villa of
*c.*1790, with a Venetian window above the Venetian door.
Unworthy rear extension of 1969.

NAVITIE HOUSE, Navitie Drive. White-harled piend-roofed
farmhouse. In 1811 it was said to be 'newly built'.

HARE LAW, 0.8km. W. A large cairn just below the crest of
the W slope, *c.*29m. in diameter and 3m. high, but before
excavation in 1890–1 'several cartloads of stones' were
removed. Three cists were uncovered, one carefully luted with
clay and containing a metal object, the other two containing
food vessel pottery.

BENARTY HOUSE. *See* p. 99.

3020   # BALMERINO

Small agricultural village beside the Tay, a ruined abbey its most
important feature. In the C18 a harbour for corn shipments to
Dundee, in the C19 inhabited by fishermen.

BALMERINO ABBEY

Tidy but rather formless remains of the Cistercian monastery
founded by William the Lion's widow Ermengarde. She began
to acquire land for the site and endowment in 1225; the first
monks (imported from Melrose) took up residence on St
Lucy's Day, 1229; and her son Alexander II granted a foundation charter in 1231. After her death in 1233 Ermengarde
was buried in front of the high altar, so the choir and habitable

cloister buildings had presumably been completed by then,
but building work (perhaps completion of the nave and the S
aisle) seems to have been in progress in 1286, when the monks
received a grant of Nydie quarry. The abbey was burned
during the Earl of Hertford's invasion of 1547, the church
sacked by the Reformers in 1559, and John Hay was made lay
commendator two years later. In 1605 the monastic property
was made a temporal barony granted to Sir James Elphinstone,
first Lord Balmerino.

The abbey church's foundations, exposed by excavation in
1896, are now marked by humps in the lawn. The church was
cruciform, consisting of a choir, transepts, nave and S aisle.

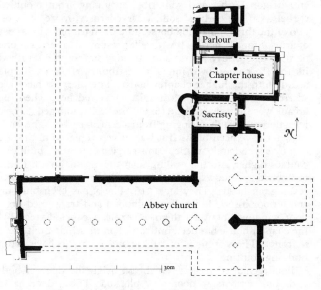

Balmerino Abbey,
plan

This aisle seems to have been an afterthought and rather
sloppily designed, since its arcade piers were not in line with
the nave's N wall-shafts. On the N side, a fair amount of the
nave wall: rubble above a slightly chamfered ashlar base. There
has been a much heavier base with a projecting upper member
round the W gable and S aisle. The gable's door had two
openings, divided by a moulded pier. In the N wall's W bay, a
triple-member wall-shaft with a waterholding base. Two more
bases further E.

Quite a lot survives of the N transept. In its W wall, one
moulded jamb of the door from the cloister. In the N wall, a
round-arched door infilled to form a segmental-arched door
under a rectangular fanlight. E of this door, an aumbry. In the
NW corner, a nook-shafted respond with a waterholding base.

As at the mother house of Melrose, the CLOISTER stood on
the church's N side. Most of the E range's ground floor survives.
Immediately N of the transept, a tunnel-vaulted room, probably the sacristy. It seems to have been converted to a kitchen
in the late C16, when this range became a house: trough in the
floor, what may have been an oven in the rebuilt W wall.
Comfortable C16 turnpike stair outside. The adjoining chapter
house contains a W vestibule, probably a C15 remodelling of
the C13 chapter house, and the chapter house itself, a C15
addition projecting E of the range's outer wall. The vestibule
is of two bays by three. Octagonal piers with moulded bases
and stiffleaf capitals. The two E bays are still covered by vaulting, quadripartite, quadripartite with ridge-ribs, transverse
and diagonal ribs, and wall ribs, springing from moulded
corbels. On the corbels' soffits, carved roses; more roses on
two of the three remaining bosses, the third carved with a coat
of arms. Stone bench on the N wall; presumably there was one
on the S also. A C16 alteration to the day stair on the N turned
its foot to come down into the vestibule's NW bay. Triple
arcade into the higher chapter house. The piers' W faces are
scarred by the marks of a fireplace inserted here when the
arcade was built up in the C16. On the walls, foliaged corbels
for a tierceron vault springing from a central corbel. The vault
may not have been built. If it was, it was replaced in the late
C16 by a wooden floor, the beams carried on corbels built two
courses higher into the walling than the original ones. Large
mullioned E windows, perhaps originally with cusping in their
rectangular heads. They look C16. The N has been built up
and a door inserted. Smaller mullioned and transomed first-
floor windows; between them, a corniced panel. Externally,
the chapter house has been buttressed on its ashlar-built E and
N fronts. The S front is of rubble and seems to have had a
building abutting.

Tunnel-vaulted parlour on the N, originally open at both
ends but with its W door now blocked. The E door has a
pointed arch; hoodmould with small foliaged label stops. Stone
benches in the N and S walls. This was probably under the
reredorter. So certainly was the N end of the range, which
projects slightly E to take in the latrine drain. W of the drain,
two cells, both with hatches from the reredorter above.
Beneath the W cell, a cellar opening off the vanished N range
of the cloister. The purpose of these cells is unclear. Possibly
they were prisons, but their lack of sanitary provision is
unusual for such a use. Perhaps they were just for storage.

NE of the cloister was the detached ABBOT'S HOUSE,
perhaps C15. Little more than a tunnel-vaulted cellar survives.

PARISH CHURCH, 1.1km. W. A sneck-harled Georgian box of
1811 recast with Gothic touches by C. & L. Ower, 1883. As
first built it was very austere*: simple rectangular windows
and doors, the only ornament a lumpy Gothic bellcote on the

---

* 'A plain building without any ornament, but considerably deficient in point of
accommodation for the parishioners', grumbled the minister in 1838.

W gable. The present pointed windows and door are all by Ower; so too must be the roof's broad eaves and the E gable's wrought-iron cross finial. The interior of 1811 had a gallery round three sides and the pulpit against the S wall. It is now all (except the acoustic tiles on the ceiling) of 1883. W gallery; large Gothic pulpit at the E. – In all the windows, STAINED GLASS of 1883: geometrical patterns in the side windows; in the E gable, a roundel of Christ in Majesty above the pulpit which is flanked by tall lights depicting Moses and St Paul. – On the N, a pretty CHURCH HALL of 1887–8, by *Ower*: Gothic, with iron cresting and a *flèche* on the broad-eaved roof.

To the W, MANSE built in 1816, its semi-octagonal porch presumably an addition.

DESCRIPTION. Coming in from the S, the DAVID SCRYM-GEOUR-WEDDERBURN MEMORIAL SQUARE stands on the r. It is by *H. J. Scrymgeour-Wedderburn*, 1948. Pantiled piend-roofed terraces on the N and E sides; in the E's centre, a Roman Doric portico of 1812–14* from Birkhill. On the S a single house and a low wall topped by lead statues. Retaining wall on the W with late Georgian cast-iron urns on the end piers. The abbey ruins (*see* above) are set back. To their N, BAL-MERINO FARM. Plain late Georgian farmhouse facing the road. Pantiled and rubble steading to its N and E. The N range includes the C15 ABBOT'S BARN. The pointed-arched S door is original. So too is the W gable's steep pitch, its inner face honeycombed with nesting boxes for pigeons, exposed by the present low-pitched roof. Against the barn's W end, a two-storey cartshed. In its gable, an inserted dormerhead, probably C16, the shield now bearing the date 1849. In the village N of the farm and down by the shore, a few C18 and early C19 vernacular houses, mostly pantiled.

DRUMNOD WOOD, 3.5km. SW. Probably an Iron Age unen-closed settlement comprising three round stone-built houses, the largest *c.* 12m. in diameter, within the ruined foundation of a dry-stone wall 1.3m. thick.

GRANGE, 2km. S. Roofless lectern DOOCOT N of the farm, prob-ably C17, its entrance placed not in the centre but at one corner.

GREEN HILL, 2.5km. SW. A cairn on the summit, 18m. in diameter and 1.9m. high. Excavation in 1899–1901 revealed several cists containing food vessels and jet beads.

NAUGHTON. *See* p. 328.

BALMULE HOUSE

1090

4km. N of Dunfermline

Large but very plain broad-eaved villa of *c.* 1890 wrapped round an earlier house whose altered S wall is still visible. This may be of *c.* 1600. Interior all of the late C19. In the inner hall, STAINED-GLASS figures emblematic of Hunting, Industry and Agriculture.

* The capitals, too badly damaged for re-use, were replaced by cast copies.

Mid-C19 STABLES to the NE. Pedimented coachhouse entrance with flight-holes for pigeons in the top. The arch's keystone is a re-used stone carved with the date 1605 and the arms and initials of Henry Wardlaw of Pitreavie and Elizabeth Wilson, his wife.

BALMUTO
2080

0.9km. S of Auchtertool

C15 and C16 house of the Boswells, freed from C18 additions and reconstructed by *The Appleton Partnership*, 1974–84. The rubble walls are now drydashed, the new work marked by concrete dressings.

The building is an irregular U-plan. On the N, a rectangular tower house of *c.*1400, its principal entrance an obtuse-arched first-floor S door, originally reached by a wooden stair. The E door on to a balcony is a Georgian insertion, made for access to the now demolished range added by *John Baxter Jun.* in 1797. Perhaps also of 1797 are the parapet's crenellations, but its widely spaced corbels are medieval. Cap-house of 1974–84: there was evidence for a medieval cap-house but not of its appearance. First- and second-floor windows enlarged in 1680, when they were given pediments with thistle, *fleur-de-lis,* rose and putti head finials. Tunnel-vaulted ground floor inside. The two upper floors had wooden ceilings, their beam ends supported on corbels. Straight stair in the thickness of the E wall.

The W range, a C16 addition, was thickened to the E in the C17 or C18. Roll-moulded window margins on the regular four-bay W front. Lower extension (of 1974–84 on earlier foundations) at the S end. Tunnel-vaulted ground-floor kitchen. In the SW first-floor room, an imported Art Nouveau chimneypiece. Two-storey S range, also a C16 addition. It has been curtailed but stubs of walling survive to the E. Tunnel-vaulted ground-floor laigh hall with a large segmental-arched fireplace at the W end. In the first-floor hall, a huge roll-moulded fireplace at the N wall's E end. The coombed wooden ceiling and W screens gallery are of 1974–84.

Built into the GARDEN WALL to the S, mid-C19 medallions carved with high-relief portraits. – Derelict STABLES to the NE, *c.*1800 with a pedimented centre. – Contemporary BRIDGE and pedimented LODGE on the E drive. – WEST LODGE on the A987, early C19 with a fluted Roman Doric portico.

BALWEARIE CASTLE
2090

2.7km. SW of Kirkcaldy

William Scott of Balwearie was granted a licence to build this plain rectangular tower in 1484. The N gable, E wall, and a stub of the s gable survive, all of good-quality ashlar masonry. The main stair seems to have risen within the wall thickness at the NW corner.

Inside, the tunnel-vaulted bottom stage has been divided horizontally by a floor: below was probably storage; at the entresol level, a room with stone benches in the window embrasures. In the N gable, a garderobe. More window seats and another garderobe in the hall above. On the second floor were probably two rooms. Large fireplace with moulded jambs in the s room; garderobe in the N room; window seats again. The top floor is now fragmentary, but it had small windows set between the corbels of the parapet walk.

To the E, a harled FARMHOUSE of the early C19, altered and enlarged in the C20. – Contemporary STEADING, partly pantiled.

BANDON TOWER   2000
3.5km. N of Glenrothes

Fragment in a field of the C16 house of the Balfours of Bandon. It has been a rectangular rubble building with a later small round tower at the NW corner. Only the N gable survives at all intact.

BENARTY HILL   1090
2.5km. NE of Kelty

A prehistoric fort of exceptional size (2.0ha.), defended by a single dry-stone wall and incorporating some massive blocks of stone, which cuts off a roughly D-shaped area of a rocky, cliff-fringed headland overlooking the s shore of Loch Leven.

BENARTY HOUSE   1090
2.1km. W of Ballingry

Country villa of c.1830–5 built for and perhaps designed by *William Briggs*, a mason turned shipowner. Two-storey *corps de logis*, the centre projecting with an Ionic portico. Short one-storey convex quadrants to taller pedimented pavilions. Rusticated quoins; urns on every pediment.

Inside, the hall's shallow coffered ceiling is intact, but almost all the other original plasterwork has been lost as a result of subsidence. Imperial stair with extravagant anthemioned balusters. Octagonal drawing room on the r.; dining room with a segmental-arched sideboard recess on the l. In the pavilions, small but well-finished front rooms; behind, a kitchen on the w, a laundry and dairy on the E.

STEADING to the N, built in several stages as a U-plan with
a detached byre on the open E side. W front of c.1840 with
three pediments, the centre containing a doocot. Octagonal NE
HORSEMILL.

Broad-eaved mid-C19 LODGE, the porch with octagonal
pillars.

2080

BENDAMEER HOUSE
1.5km. W of Burntisland

Expensive Italianate villa of c.1850. Bargeboarded LODGE.

3020

BIRKHILL
4.2km. W of Gauldry

Reconstruction of a late Georgian house as a Tudor-Baronial
manor, by *David Bryce*, 1857–9. The main block of the house
built in 1780 is still visible on the N, a plain block with a centre
bow. It was joined by quadrant colonnades to a kitchen block*
on the E and stables on the W. In 1812–14 wings were added
behind the quadrants. Bryce doubled the house's thickness to
the S, removed the colonnades, stables and old kitchen, and
shortened and remodelled the E wing, adding a new office court
on its N. His detail is routine, pedimented dormerheads the
standard feature. Hints of excitement are provided by the
balustraded SE tower over the entrance, its design based on
Castle Fraser (Grampian), and the SW pepperpot turret. On
the W front, Bryce's characteristic canted drawing room bay
window corbelled to a square crowstepped gable. In the inner
angle of the S block and the early C19 W wing, a fat conical-
roofed tower.

HOME FARM, 0.6km. S, a classical steading of 1842, the N
front with a pedimented centre and ends.

3080

BLAIR CASTLE
1.75km. W of Culross

73 Very superior early C19 three-storey house in the post-Adam
manner. Only three bays, but on a large scale. Pedimented
centrepiece with a giant Ionic order, the rusticated ground
floor breaking forward to form pedestals for the pilasters.
Between the pedestals a small portico with Adam Corinthian
columns. The same order is repeated on the pilastered three-
light window above, contained, like the flanking corniced
windows, in a segmental overarch. Under the outer windows,
panelled aprons with just a single baluster at each end. Single-
storey wings, the l. swallowed up in a drydashed addition.
Inside, an Adam Corinthian columned screen between the
vestibule and stairhall.

---

* Part of an earlier house on the site.

Contemporary STABLES to the E. Overarched ground-floor openings; pedimented centre on the S front.

BLEBOCRAIGS

4010

C19 vernacular hamlet straggling along a hillside, now hard pressed by bungaloid interlopers. At the W, THORNBANK, a Tudor house of *c.*1850, with pantiled farm offices.

BLEBO HOUSE
0.7km. S of Kemback

4010

Stolid early C19, the S front with a central bow flanked by Venetian windows. In 1903 *James Findlay* added the back wing and round NE entrance tower. Presumably the dormer windows are also his.

BOARHILLS

5010

Hamlet of vernacular rubble-built and pantiled cottages, most rather altered and with a sprinkling of recent intrusions. Winding street squashed between farm steadings.

PARISH CHURCH, 0.4km. SW. Unlovable lanceted box by *George Rae*, 1866–7. Large *fleur-de-lis* finialled W bellcote.

PRIMARY SCHOOL. Dated 1815 on a skew-end. Harled and pantiled. On the front, an ogee-topped bellcote with slim Tuscan columns. Rear addition by *George Sandilands*, 1931.

DOOCOT, N end of village. Lectern type, perhaps C17. There used to be a gableted pigeon entrance in the roof (now pantiled, formerly slated).

KENLYGREEN, 0.4km. E. Smart white-harled house of *c.*1790. Pilaster strips give the five-bay front a 2/1/2 rhythm; swagged urns on top. One-bay links (their oval windows a C20 alteration) to urn-finialled pedimented pavilions. (Inside, excellent pine and composition chimneypieces decorated with shells, urns and eagles.)

DOOCOT to W, perhaps C17, with a double-pitch roof and ball finials.

KINGASK, 2.4km. W. Small white-painted laird's house of *c.*1840. Tudor; horizontal window panes.

PEEKIE, 1.5km. SW. A tall thin slab of red sandstone, 2.7km. by 0.1m. by 0.7m., to the S of the A917 between Kingask and Kinglassie.

BOGLEYS *see* KIRKCALDY, p. 300

BOWHILL see AUCHTERDERRAN, BOWHILL AND CARDENDEN

3010   BOW OF FIFE

Small hamlet on the A91, the church a landmark.

MONIMAIL FREE CHURCH. Disused. 1897–8, by *James Gilles-pie*, using C15 Scottish Romanesque revival of the type employed by John J. Burnet at Brechin (Tayside) and Larbert (Central), but without Burnet's flair. The NE tower's red tiled roof fails to be jolly.

Behind the church, former MANSE of *c.*1845. – To its E, contemporary FREE CHURCH SCHOOL, small, with lattice glazing.

3090   BRANKSTONE GRANGE
                     4.6km. N of Culross

Unlovable Baronial in snecked grey rubble but superbly sited on a hilltop. The first part is dated 1867. Tall square tower finished with a corbelled-out crenellated parapet and SW cap-house. This is all very stark but softened by lower blocks on three sides. Crowstepped two-storey porch on the N. W range with candle-snuffered corner turrets and a fiercely detailed bay window corbelled out to the square and finished with a crowstepped gable. S front with tall pedimented dormerheads. In 1896 *R. Rowand Anderson* doubled the S range's length with a relaxed quotation from the original (smaller dormerheads but a fatter turret at the corner). Less happy is the balustraded addition of 1908 in the inner angle of the porch and tower. Interior plain and now much altered.

Outside the entrance, remarkable collection of mid–late C20 GARDEN GNOMES holding fishing rods, books, garden rakes, etc.

0080   BROOMHALL
                  0.9km. E of Charlestown

70 Coolly assured neo-classical mansion whose polished ashlar skin hides a complicated history.

In 1702 Alexander Bruce of Broomhall (later fourth Earl of Kincardine) put up a new house here. This seems to have been dignified but unambitious, with slightly projecting piend-roofed ends and a pedimented centre. *c.*1760 Charles, fifth Earl of Elgin and ninth Earl of Kincardine, built or rebuilt detached office blocks forming an open courtyard on the N. In 1766 he commissioned *John Adam* to design quadrants linking these offices to the house, which was itself to be enlarged.

Adam's scheme seems not to have been carried out, and it was only in 1794 that preparation of the ground for a s extension was begun by the seventh Earl of Elgin (Byron's 'Pictish peer' who 'basely stole what less barbarians won'). The next year Elgin commissioned designs for the enlargement and recasting of the existing house from *Thomas Harrison*, whose plans for the s addition were received in March 1796, when *James Millar* of Stirling had already been appointed the contractor. The shell of this addition was largely complete by the end of 1799, when Harrison was dismissed and Millar given sole charge of its completion. At the same time Millar recased the projecting ends of the early c18 house's N front, a preliminary to the remodelling of this façade and the construction of new wings, all to be clad in a neo-classical dress which had yet to be designed, Harrison's various proposals having been rejected by the Earl.

During the next quarter-century Lord Elgin amused himself by getting designs for the N front and wings of Broomhall. He began in 1799 with *Henry Holland*, then moved on to *Louis Damesme* (1806), *William Porden* (1807–8), *William Stark* (1808), *Robert Smirke* (1808–10), *Louis-Martin Berthault* (1815), *William Burn* (1821), *C. R. Cockerell* (1822), a 'Mr Jones', perhaps *Edward Jones* (1823), an architect in Chester, probably *Thomas Harrison* (1823–4), *William Wilkins* (1824), and *J. P. Gandy* (1826). In 1827 he asked *J. B. Papworth* for a copy of the elevations of the King of Württemberg's proposed palace at Cannstatt, explaining 'I am finishing my house in the country ...', although the only work undertaken since 1800 had been internal finishing (by *Porden*) in 1807–8 and the demolition of the mid-c18 offices in 1812. Elgin's financial embarrassment (resulting largely from the cost of acquiring and shipping the Parthenon Marbles) effectively precluded ambitious building projects, and it was only in 1865–6 that the Glasgow firm of *Thomson & Wilson* provided a new N front, the wings following in 1874.

Thomson & Wilson's N façade is flat-fronted (the projection of the c18 ends hidden by refacing), except for the three-bay centre, slightly advanced with a fussy Aegypto-Greek portico. The console-pedimented ground-floor windows are just as shown in one of Harrison's schemes, so perhaps they were re-used or copied.* Utilitarian rendered wings.

Harrison's s front is elegantly restrained, the N front's rusticated basement here becoming a full ground floor. The *piano nobile*'s windows are marked by consoled cornices, except at the segmental-bowed three-bay centre, where they are placed between attached Ionic columns and surmounted by Coade stone panels (dated 1818). On this s addition's sides, three-light windows with blind segmental fanlights, replicas of the front windows at Harrison's (demolished) Kennet House (Central) of 1793–4. The E wing's rusticated Venetian door

---

* But other designs by Harrison show only consoled cornices, as does Holland's design for completing this front.

(its design taken from William Chambers' *Treatise on Civil Architecture*) was made in the early C19 for the King's Barn at Limekilns and was moved here *c.* 1912, when *F. W. Deas* added a discreet bowed bathroom extension in the nearby inner angle.

Inside, the entrance hall was remodelled in 1890 by *R. Rowand Anderson,* who inserted the classical chimneypiece, neo-Greek niches and fragments of Greek sculpture in the walls. The trabeated ceiling looks earlier, perhaps of 1865–6. – The NW dining room's oak chimneypiece was made up, *c.* 1880, from a bed reputed to have belonged to James VI's queen, Anne of Denmark. Richly carved Jacobean Renaissance with atlantes standing on lions' heads at the sides, a relief in the centre. It contrasts oddly with the guilloche frieze of *c.* 1800. – Anthemion and palmette frieze in the drawing room to the S. White marble chimneypiece (*c.* 1800) with a relief of Pandora. The dado is a late C19 replacement. – In the S front's centre, a D-plan library, the bookcases oak-veneered in the 1890s. Another classy chimneypiece of *c.* 1800 carved with cupids, urns and gryphons. – In the room below (now Family Dining Room), a pretty pine and composition chimneypiece of *c.* 1790, imported *c.* 1912.

3020

BRUNTON

Small weaving village beside the Motray Water.

CREICH PARISH CHURCH, 1km. S. An isolated landmark by *William Stirling I,* 1829–32. Standard Georgian box but dressed up with diagonally set buttresses, Perp windows, Tudor doors, and a large Gothic parapeted tower with foliaged pinnacled buttresses.

Inside, a thinly ribbed semi-elliptical ceiling. – Triple-gableted Gothic PULPIT of 1832, its centre carried up as a very shallow sounding board. – PEWS of 1890. – STAINED GLASS. E windows (Christ's Charge to St Peter, Parable of the Sower) of 1890. – On the N side, a window ('Be Thou Faithful unto Death') signed by *A. Ballantine & Son,* 1903. – The window opposite (SS John the Baptist and Paul) is by *Nathaniel Bryson,* 1890.

In the vestibule, eroded GRAVESLAB of David Barclay of Luthrie †1400 and his wife Helen Douglas †1421: incised figures of a knight in plate armour and his lady, their heads and hands (probably of metal) now lost; tabernacle work above. – On the church's W wall, marble MONUMENT to the Baillies of Luthrie, by *James Dalziel,* 1824, with a sarcophagus in relief.

At the entrance to the small churchyard, crenellated GATE-PIERS and cast-iron Tudorish GATES of 1832.

FLISK AND CREICH FREE CHURCH, 0.3km. S. Disused. Rendered box of 1843. The round-arched windows' imposts project, but the keystones do not. On the W gable, tall birdcage bellcote with a short concave-sided spire. Elaborate shaped dormerhead on the s.

St Devenic. *See* Creich.

DESCRIPTION

Agreeable collection of early and mid-C19 whinstone cottages, their roofs slated or pantiled, arranged on an informal triangular plan. In School Row, the old Free Church School, dated 1846 on its twin-gabled e front. Creich Manse, just NW of the village, is by *Just & Carver*, 1815–16, with a Roman Doric columned doorpiece.

FARMS

Parbroath, 3.1km. s. Very smart piend-roofed farmhouse by *Thomas Brown*, 1829, the yellow freestone dressings a contrast to the cherry-cock pointed whinstone walling. Five-bay front, the centre three windows (with horizontal glazing) making a shallow bow. – In a field to the w, roofless lectern doocot, probably early C18. – To its s, part of the ground-floor vault of Parbroath Castle, built for the Setons in the C16.

Pittachope, 1.1km. NW. Whinstone group of *c.*1840. Cottage-style farmhouse with broad eaves and stone window canopies. The steading is mostly pantiled, with an octagonal horsemill on the w.

Green Craig. *See* p. 237.
Norman's Law. *See* p. 338.

BUCKHAVEN AND METHIL

3090

A former mining town which grew up from the late C19, engulfing the fishing village of Buckhaven and the small burgh of Methil. Mining is now ended; the last coal shipment from the Methil docks was in 1970. Generously laid out local authority housing of surprisingly high quality was built from 1919 (initially to a scheme by *G. C. Campbell*), but no real centre was provided.

CHURCHES

Baptist Church, College Street. By *G. C. Campbell*, 1914–15.

Buckhaven Free Church, Church Street. Being converted to secular use (1987). Originally built at St Andrews as an Episcopal chapel in 1824–5, and rebuilt at Buckhaven as a Free church, 1870, it is by *William Burn*. Crocketed pinnacled Perp front, with a rather small door under the elaborately hoodmoulded five-light window, its label stops carved with human faces. Inside, a nave and aisles; thinly detailed ribbed plaster ceiling.

BUCKHAVEN PARISH CHURCH, Church Street and Randolph Street. Big Gothic box of 1899–1902, the gable front divided by octagonal turrets into a 'nave' and 'aisles'. Octagonal bellcote corbelled out from the gable. Interior now divided by a floor at gallery level. Organ and pulpit ensemble at w end. – At the E, STAINED GLASS (Crucifixion) by *Marjorie Kemp*.

BUCKHAVEN UNITED PRESBYTERIAN CHURCH, Church Street. Now (1988) Muiredge Craft Complex. Plain Gothic of 1869, buttresses making a feeble attempt to suggest a nave and aisles behind the gable.

DENBEATH CHURCH, Barncraig Street. Scots late Gothic in red sandstone, by *Peter Sinclair*, 1931.

INNERLEVEN EAST CHURCH, Methilhaven Row. By *Esmé Gordon,* 1939–41. An awkwardly angular upturned boat with a helm-roofed tower, unappealingly rendered.

METHIL CHURCH, Wellesley Road. Large and simple Romanesque by *Reginald Fairlie*, 1924–5; flush-pointed rubble, the roofs covered with green slates. Nave and transepts, the N transept joined to the pyramid-roofed NW tower by a low 'aisle' (housing the vestry). Inside, concrete arches across the nave springing from attached stone columns, their capitals chastely carved. Segmental stone arches into the transepts, a round-headed chancel arch. The focus is the huge ORGAN (by *Rushworth & Dreaper*); its case is reminiscent of the C16 screen in the chapel of Falkland Palace, but the carved detail is Celtic. Integral elders' stalls, their arm-rests carved with beasts. – Jacobean-type PULPIT. – STAINED GLASS. In the nave's s windows, Second World War Memorial in strong blues, by *William Wilson*, 1949. – David Memorial (Christ Stilling the Sea) of *c.*1930. – The two w windows look German or Flemish, perhaps C17. – In the s transept, three lights (SS John, Andrew and Paul) of *c.*1925. – First World War memorial window in the N transept.

METHILHILL CHURCH, Chemiss Road. Cheap Gothic of 1931.

ST AGATHA (R.C.), Methil Brae. By *Reginald Fairlie*, 1923. Thrifty Romanesque in brick and concrete blockwork.

PUBLIC BUILDINGS

BUCKHAVEN COMMUNITY CENTRE, Kinnear Street and Victoria Road. Former Miners' Welfare Institute. Cottage Wrenaissance by *Peter Sinclair*, 1924–5. Cream-harled walls with red sandstone dressings, a clock-cupola on the orange pantiled roof.

BUCKHAVEN PRIMARY SCHOOL, College Street. Informal, by *G. C. Campbell*, 1907. s addition of 1928 by *George Sandilands*.

DENBEATH MINERS' WELFARE INSTITUTE, Den Walk. By *A. Stewart Tod*, 1924. An elegant pavilion, its bellcast piended roof covered with orange pantiles. On the loggiaed E front, a copper lantern.

DENBEATH PRIMARY SCHOOL, Barncraig Street. 1907–8, by *G. C. Campbell*.

KIRKLAND HIGH SCHOOL, Kirkland Road. By *Fife County Council*, 1954–7.

METHIL COMMUNITY CENTRE, Fisher Street. Former Miners' Welfare Institute. By *A. D. Haxton*, 1926–7. Tall in harl and brick, with a small cupola.

METHIL HARBOUR AND DOCKS. This is Fife's largest port. A harbour at the mouth of the Leven was begun by the second Earl of Wemyss in 1661 and linked by a wagon-way to the coalmines at Buckhaven in 1795. Development of the mines led to the harbour's rebuilding in the late C19 and early C20. First came the construction of No. 1 DOCK (by *Gibson & Hopewell*) in 1884–7, followed by the larger No. 2 DOCK to its S in 1894–1900. In 1907–13 *Blyth & Westland* added the still larger No. 3 DOCK on the N, with its own channel and sea wall parallel to the earlier docks. Concrete is the dominant material.

METHIL LIBRARY, Wellesley Road. Small-scale authoritarian in concrete block and harl, by *Edward L. Forsyth*, 1934–5.

METHIL POWER STATION. By *Stanley Ross-Smith*, 1963.

RANDOLPH WEMYSS MEMORIAL HOSPITAL, Wellesley Road. Enjoyably dotty cottage Baronial of 1909. In the centre, a Doric portico; slated steeple with gableted clock faces and a spindly vane supporting a swan (the Wemyss crest) in place of a cock. – S addition, glass-walled with fins, by *John Holt*, c.1965.

WAR MEMORIAL, Wellesley Road. By *G. C. Campbell*, c.1920. Stone statue of a kilted soldier on a big plinth.

DESCRIPTION

CHURCH STREET is the introduction to Buckhaven. Solid late Victorian housing with three churches (*see* above) to represent the Presbyterian divisions of the C19. At the end of KINNEAR STREET on the r., the Buckhaven Community Centre (*see* above). In RANDOLPH STREET, a blowsy Wrenaissance department store dated 1908. On the SE corner, ROYAL BANK OF SCOTLAND with a small tower (by *Andrew Scobie*, 1892). Church Street's line plunges down to the shore as WEST HIGH STREET, its C19 vernacular still with a fishing village flavour belied by *Wheeler & Sproson's* SHORE STREET redevelopment of c.1965–73.

COLLEGE STREET (Randolph Street's E continuation) leads to WELLESLEY ROAD slicing through Methil. Along it, a parade of late C19 and early C20 coal company and local authority housing. A small park sets off the War Memorial, the Public Library on the N and Parish Church on the E (for all these, *see* above) trying to give civic importance. Beyond the church, a long block (Nos. 193–277 Wellesley Road) on the l., of c.1910, with broad half-timbered gables at the centre and ends. Then on the r., the harled TOWER BAR of 1906, its tower cribbed from the Tolbooth at West Wemyss.

In METHILHILL on the town's NW edge, garden village miners'

housing by *A. Stewart Tod* for the Wemyss Coal Co., 1924–6; harled with tiled roofs.

BURNTISLAND

Burntisland (the derivation of the name is uncertain) was part of the Abbots of Dunfermline's estate of Wester Kinghorn. Here they had built a residence (now Rossend Castle) on the hill above the natural harbour. Extensive improvement of this harbour was begun in 1540 by James V, who founded the royal burgh of Burntisland in the next year. Despite burning of the new-built stone houses by the English in 1547 the town was sufficiently well established by 1587 to be admitted to the Convention of Royal Burghs. A new parish church in the middle of the town was begun in 1589, a tolbooth in 1605 and, in 1636, a gateway on the main landward approach, adorned with the royal and burgh arms.

After the town's surrender to the Cromwellian army in 1651 it was enclosed by a stone wall and a fort (barely visible by 1745) built on Lammerlaws Point. Like other small trading ports, Burntisland was badly affected by the Act of Union, so that in 1723 John Macky thought it 'like an old Lady in Decay ... these large Stone white Houses, which seem like Palaces afar off, prove to be Heaps of Decay when you approach them.' Late C18 attempts to provide industry with the foundation of a distillery and vitriol factory seem to have brought some return of prosperity, but it was the early C19 delight in bathing that brought about expansion outside the line of the old walls.

The building in 1842 of a pier which could be used at all states of the tide established Burntisland as the N end of the ferry route across the Forth from Granton (Edinburgh), a position consolidated with the building of the S terminus of the railway up the Fife coast here in 1847. The opening of the Forth Bridge in 1890 lessened the harbour's importance but not the town's role as a seaside playground for Edinburgh.

A large aluminium works was opened in 1914. Since 1921 a great expansion of housing to the N has more than doubled the size of the C16 burgh. Redevelopment in the 1950s of the central area has largely obliterated the old rig pattern but has been accompanied by well-meant gestures in the direction of conservation, a formula accepted at the time but now seeming needlessly brutal.

CHURCHES

ERSKINE CHURCH (United Free), Kinghorn Road. Scots Perp by *J. B. Wilson* of Glasgow, 1900–3. Gable front. On the l. a huge tower with a crocketed cap-house. Inside, a broad nave and narrow aisles. Gallery round three sides, shooting back over the vestibule at the S end. The choir gallery at the N was filled with the ORGAN (by *Hilsdon*) in 1922. – STAINED-GLASS

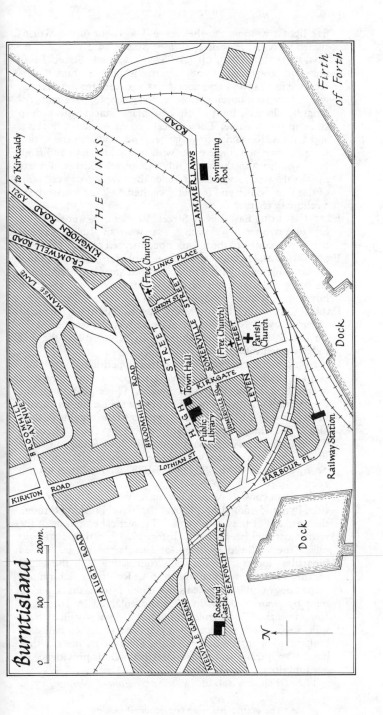

Burntisland

THE LINKS

Firth of Forth

to Kirkaldy

KINGHORN ROAD A921

CROMWELL ROAD

MANSE LANE

LAMMERLAWS ROAD

Swimming Pool

BROOMHILL ROAD

BROOMHILL AVENUE

KIRKTON ROAD

HAUGH ROAD

MELVILLE GARDENS

SEAFORTH PLACE

Rossend Castle

LOTHIAN ST.

HIGH STREET

UNION STREET

SOMERVILLE STREET

Links Place

(Free Church)

Free Church

Parish Church

Town Hall

KIRKGATE

Public Library

SOMERVILLE SQ.

LEVEN STREET

HARBOUR PL.

Railway Station

Dock

Dock

N

0   100   200 m.

five-light s window (on the theme The Light of the World) signed by *N. K. Pink* of *The Abbey Studio*, 1921.

FORMER PARISH CHURCH (ST SERF), Church Street. In an unkempt graveyard. Roofless remains of the church consecrated in 1243 and abandoned *c.*1595 except for the chancel, which became a burial enclosure. Very simple, nave and rectangular chancel, built of cubed ashlar. Lancet with a deep splay in the w gable. The chancel had no openings in the N and E walls. Remains of two lancets and a door in the s wall. Chancel arch of a single order with splayed imposts and jamb bases, built up in the C17. Only the lowest courses of a late medieval s aisle survive. This joined the nave to a C13 cell built of the same ashlar and formerly vaulted.* Could it have been a reliquary chapel?

FREE CHURCH, East Leven Street. Roofless. A warehouse of *c.*1830 converted to a church in 1843 when the Italian classical belfry was added to the s flank's pedimented centre.

FREE CHURCH, High Street. Geometric by *Patrick Wilson*, 1860. Broad gable front with a broach-spired steeple on the r. and an octagonal stairtower on the l. Converted into sheltered housing by *Wheeler & Sproson*, 1983.

18 PARISH CHURCH (ST COLUMBA), East Leven Street. An architectural as well as a navigational landmark, this was one of the earliest post-Reformation churches in Scotland and the first to have a centralized plan.

In 1589 the citizens of Burntisland petitioned the Convention of Royal Burghs 'craving support to the vpbigging of ane kirk within thair said burgh'. Three years later the Convention granted them the right to a tax on timber carried in ships using the harbour for 'supportt to the bigging of thair kirk'. The church was probably usable by 1596, when the Town Council made a final payment to *John Roche*, probably the mason, for 'ye warke wrought be him to the kirk', but *John Scott*, wright in Leith, did not finish the wooden steeple until 1600.

The plan consists of a square 'nave' with an 'aisle' on each side. Pyramid-roofed steeple over the 'nave' breaking through the pyramid of the 'aisle' roofs. The vertical emphasis of the roofs must have been stronger before 1822, when *David Virtue* raised the wallhead by 1.2m. and made the square-headed bipartite windows. Harled walls contrasting with the ashlar of the stepped diagonal buttresses. Roll-moulded round-arched door under a re-used stone dated 1592 in the w porch, built by *Andrew Alison* in 1659 and enlarged by *Alexander Hope* in 1789. Rectangular moulded s door. Against the E wall, a stone stair with panelled piers and squashed balusters built in 1679 to the Sailors' Loft. Door at its head with a lugged architrave and frieze inscribed 'Gods.providence.is. our.inheritance.June.6.1679'.

The steeple was rebuilt in stone by *Samuel Neilson*, 1748.

---

* The RCAHMS reported a pointed tunnel-vault in 1933.

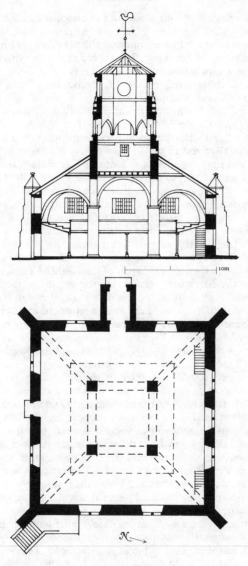

Burntisland Parish Church,
plan and section

Lower stage with heavy quoins, pointed openings and banded
pinnacles. Octagonal belfry with rusticated round openings
and a weighty cornice. Gilded weathercock of 1600.

Inside, the 'nave' is marked off by four corniced piers linked
by semicircular arches. The piers are tied to the four corners of
the church by lower elliptical arches springing from moulded
corbels.

19   Galleries on all four sides but not projecting to the front of
the 'aisles'. They were built between *c.*1602 and 1630 to a
uniform design.* Fluted columns with very Artisan Ionic capitals serving as brackets. Blind-arcaded fronts with Artisan
Composite pilasters and carved motifs (strapwork, thistles,
roses, anchors, etc.) in the spandrels. The Prime Gilt or
Sailors' Guild occupied two-thirds of the E and half of
the S gallery. In 1618 they paid *Walter Phin* for painting their
'seitt', and they paid him again in 1622 'for peantin of the
seallers Leaft'. Further payments for painting their loft were
made in 1632 and 1733. On the E gallery are painted the dates
1602 and 1733, together with four ships, a compass, and a sailor
with a cross staff, and mottoes of the Prime Gilt. On the S
gallery are shown a naval battle, a couple of sailors making a
navigation reckoning and another fathoming a rope, as well as
the inscription 'THOUGH . GODS . POUER . BE . SUF/-
THINENT . TO . GOVERNE . US . YET . FOR . MANS . INFI-
MITIE [*sic*] . / HE . APPOINTETH . HIS . ANGLS [*sic*] . / TO .
WATCHE . OVIR . US.' The ships look C17, the sailors C18. At
the W end of the S gallery, a pair of scales and a hanging balance
(?) for the Merchants' Guild. On the W gallery, the baxters'
badge of a wheatsheaf and the date 1622, although it was not
painted until 1627 and presumably repainted in 1631 after it
had been 'defacit' by some maltsters. All these panels were
restored by *Andrew Young* in 1907–10. Inscriptions on the W
gallery were painted in 1930 and 1944, and the burgh arms in
1938. Trades' insignia on the N gallery of 1967.

19   Wrapped round two sides of the NE pier is the MAGI-
STRATES' PEW, dated 1606 and with the arms and initials of
Sir Robert Melville of Burntisland and Dame Joanna Hamilton, his wife. Fluted balusters support the shallow-pitched
canopy, its frieze inlaid to suggest dentils. The frieze of the
outward sloping pew front decorated with a rudimentary guilloche pattern. Both this and the pew back are panelled with
lozenge decoration. – BOX PEWS. Most seem to be C18 (two
with painted dates, 1725 and 1742), the rest largely of 1862. A
large pew on the E has diminutive attached columns carved on
the door. Another, on the S, has urn finials. – WOODEN
PANELS. On the S wall, carved in low relief with a half-length
bearded man. Painted date, 1597, on the surround. – On the
E wall, inlaid panel of a ship at anchor, dated 1609. – PULPIT,
COMMUNION TABLE and FONT of 1926, Jacobean but
wrong. – Beautifully restrained WAR MEMORIAL PLAQUE on
NW pier, by *P. MacGregor Chalmers*, 1920. – ORGAN by
Cousans, Son & Co., 1908–9, altered 1937.

Disappointing collection of CHURCHYARD MONUMENTS.
On the E wall, Watsons of Dunnikeir, dated 1689. Aedicule
with skulls on the ends of the curvy pediment. Below the
inscription tablet, angels trying to interest a skeleton in news
of the Resurrection. – On the W wall, a simpler and more
eroded aedicule erected by George Thomson to his wife in

* The N gallery, replaced in 1822, was restored in 1967.

1722. – To the SE, table monument to David Ballantine (†1769) with stumpy baluster legs.

CHURCH HALL in West Leven Street, by *J. B. Dunn*, 1892–4, cheap Gothic.

ST SERF (Episcopal), Cromwell Road. 1903–5, by *W. R. Simpson* from a sketch design by *F. L. Pearson* of London. Awkward Gothic in hammerdressed rubble with a red-tiled roof. Double bellcote on the W gable. – STAINED GLASS. On the S, two lights (The Presentation of Christ in the Temple; The Baptism of Christ) by *J. Powell & Sons*, 1910. – One light on the N (The Light of the World), 1937.

ROSSEND CASTLE

Large white-harled mid-C16 house overlooking the harbour but 53 jostled by local authority housing behind. Its purchase in 1975 and subsequent restoration for their own use by *Robert Hurd & Partners* is the material for a conservationist's fairy story (despised frog kissed by beautiful maiden and transformed into a handsome if heavy-featured prince).

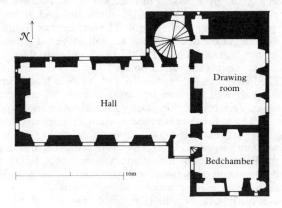

Rossend Castle,
plan of first floor

The medieval residence of the Abbots of Dunfermline was fortified by 1544, when Abbot George Durie gave its custody to Robert Durie of that Ilk. In 1552 George Durie transferred the custody to his son Peter, who seems to have built the present house, probably substantially complete by 1554. This is a T-plan with the downstroke running E–W and the crossbar at the E end. Four storeys, but the S end of the E wing has been only three, with a corbelled parapet and angle-rounds. Could this have been designed as a gun platform to cover the harbour below and deter a repetition of the English attack on Burntisland in 1547? The corner was raised to the same height as the rest of the building in the early C19 and given a second but meanly corbelled parapet. The glass-gabled cap-house is of

1976, its slated roof a sober contrast to the red pantiles put on the other roofs at the same date.

The martial character is contained by a row of ground-floor gunloops along the s side. Muddled up with them are three small lancets which could be of any date from the C13 to the C15. Their position is unrelated to the C16 store-rooms behind, so they are clearly part of an earlier house. But what did they light? If a chapel, it was very large. Perhaps, despite their size, it was a ground-floor hall.

Domestic E and N fronts with no evidence of fortification. Above the door in the N gable, a reset Gothic canopied plaque with the arms of George Durie between classicizing barley-sugar columns. Sill inscribed 'XXII MAII 1554'. Almost identical surround for the arms of St Margaret of Scotland, founder of Dunfermline Abbey, on the E wall. A pedimented dormerhead on the N wall of the main block and another, dated 1665, built into the N gable are evidence of a late C17 remodelling by General James Wemyss. Against the W gable, low tech stairtower of 1976.

All ground-floor rooms are tunnel-vaulted. Three store-rooms linked by a passage in the main block. In the E wing, kitchen and s store. Huge semi-elliptically arched kitchen fireplace. Slop sink in the E wall. The service stair from the E store-room of the main block to the hall above is built on top of an earlier stair which led to the bedchamber in the E wing. The main stair is a broad turnpike.

The hall fills the whole first floor of the main block. Simple wood and cloth partition (of 1982) to mark off the screens passage. Very broad N fireplace with masons' marks exposed above. The W fireplace is probably contemporary. Its moulding is repeated on the drawing-room fireplace in the E wing. That room's wooden ceiling, lavishly decorated c. 1616, is now in the Royal Museum of Scotland, Queen Street, Edinburgh. Bedchamber on the s, traditionally the scene of the poet Chastelard's amorous overtures to Mary, Queen of Scots, now houses early C18 panelling imported from the demolished Polton House (Lothian). It is of pine (stripped of paint) with lugged architraved doors and Corinthian pilasters flanking the basket-arched marble chimneypiece. The squidgy plaster foliage in the ceiling's corners is copied from the same room at Polton but looks a late C19 embellishment. Top-floor NE room with a C16 cavetto cornice on the W wall. Unusually it is of stone, but cf. Dunfermline Abbey Palace Block.

GARDEN WALL on the W, dated 1713. – On the s, remains of FORTIFICATIONS, perhaps those made by Sir James Melville in 1646. One triangular and two round bastions, the E one with splayed gunloops and an early C19 crenellated gazebo on top. – Self-consciously martial NE GATEWAY by *George Cousin*, 1849, with a footgate added in 1932. – OFFICES (Nos. 4–5 Melville Gardens) on the W, dated 1816. Castellated, with Tudor hoodmoulds.

HARBOUR

The 'new havin' of Burntisland was built by the Crown in 1540–
2. *Robert Orrock* was master of works and possibly the engineer
as well as paymaster. This harbour covered the area of the
present Inner Harbour and N wet dock, with a harbour wall
on the w between the shore and Familiars Rocks, and a pier
(the Iron or Heron Craig) running a short way s on the line of
the w wall of the wet dock. Frequent repairs and alterations
in the C17 and C18 replaced the largely timber quays with
stone ones.

In 1795 *William Sibbald*, Edinburgh's Superintendent of
Public Works, suggested extensive improvements, and in
1799–1800 *Thomas Hope* built a new ashlar-fronted quay SE
from the Iron Craig Pier to roughly opposite the present
railway station. A ferry pier designed by *John Henderson* was
made in 1842–3 w of the Forth Hotel. *James Leslie* added an
embankment and extension s of the E quay in 1848 and *John
Paterson* lengthened the w breakwater in 1857.

Extensive remodelling of what was still recognizable as the
1540s' harbour was carried out by *Meik & Bouch* in 1872–6,
when they divided it into the Inner Harbour, which still dried
out at low tide, and a wet dock entered from the s and with a
constant supply of deep water. A second wet dock to the s and
a new outer breakwater were made by *Thomas Meik & Sons*
in 1896–1901, with small lighthouses at the entrance. The w
side of the Inner Harbour was progressively infilled after the
foundation of the Burntisland Shipping Co. in 1918.

PUBLIC BUILDINGS

PRIMARY SCHOOL, Ferguson Place. Small-scale Tudor by
Moffat & Aitken, 1874–6. Large and plain additions by *Robert
Little*, 1899, and *W. R. Simpson*, 1911.
PUBLIC LIBRARY, High Street. By *William Williamson*, 1906. 115
Best Wrenaissance with a segmental door-hood and carved
swags at the first floor.
TOWN HALL, High Street. Tudor collegiate by *John Henderson*,
1845–6. Over-assertive and off-centre Gothic steeple.

PERAMBULATION

The best approach is by sea, landing near the RAILWAY 108
STATION. This is by *Grainger & Miller*, 1847. Friendly Greek,
the ends treated as towers with corner chimneys on the model
of Thomas Hamilton's Dean Orphanage in Edinburgh. Colonnade across the front gripped by pedimented end gateways.
The FORTH HOTEL by *William Burn*, 1823–4, was built as
the manse. Large and confident with a Doric porch. The bay
windows were probably added by *John Henderson* in 1843,
when he converted it to an hotel for the Granton ferry. The
stables behind and the harbour offices and housing on the N

are part of the same scheme. Opposite, a railway shed by *A. & A. Heiton*, 1855, with round-arched windows and ball finials. After a couple of derelict C18 cottages and a white-painted block of 1886, HARBOUR PLACE ducks under the RAILWAY VIADUCT built in 1890 to the Forth Bridge. Then an informal square with the chimney-gabled late C18 GEORGE HOTEL, followed by a pair of modern vernacular buildings (Nos. 4–13 of 1984, Nos. 1–3 of 1976).

In SEAFORTH PLACE, the ROYAL HOTEL, a classy villa with a columned doorpiece, built in 1807 for William Young, proprietor of Grange Distillery. Beside it in CASTLE STREET a slightly earlier house squashed against the railway.

HIGH STREET mixes architectural styles but has not developed a personality. The S side starts well enough with the corner turret of the GREEN TREE TAVERN, dated 1884, but the N blocks of the Somerville Square Redevelopment (by *Wheeler & Sproson*, 1957) are very weak. Mid-C19 palazzo at Nos. 90–92 with free Ionic pilastered shopfronts and a grotesque head over the common stair door. For the Public Library and Town Hall, *see* above. In SOMERVILLE SQUARE behind, 1950s redevelopment forms a morticians' slab for the embalmed and painted remains of old houses lined up on the S. The r. tenement (Nos. 25–27) belonged to Robert Clerk in 1605 and is probably late C16. Jettied upper floors and a corbelled-out stair turret. Forestair to a moulded door whose pediment is an insertion, probably an old dormerhead. The stone dated 1688 over the ground-floor door commemorates John Watson's gift of the building to the town 'for the use of Thrie widow women in the burgh of Burntisland of the Surnames of Watsone, Boswell and Orrock.' The two-storey Nos. 28–29 has been rebuilt with swept dormerheads. The MASONIC LODGE, C19 in its present form, has uncomfortably protruding skews to show its original height. On the r. of the door, eroded panel inscribed 'BLISST BE GOD/FOR AL HIS/VAGEIS'. Then MARY SOMERVILLE'S HOUSE (Nos. 30–31), a substantial late C16 tenement with a shallow projection for two staircases across three-quarters of the front. A third stair was housed in the jettied upper floors' protrusion across the E quarter. The back was regularized, *c.*1788, and a plain E extension, now harled pink to show that it is a cuckoo, built at the same time. It was probably as part of these alterations that the steep roof-pitch was lowered. Drydashed flats in SOMERVILLE STREET E of Kirkgate again by *Wheeler & Sproson*. At the bottom of UNION STREET a pantiled mid-C18 house breaks the decent but unexciting late Victorian character of this part of High Street. (For the Free Church, *see* above.)

On High Street's N side, a cement-rendered C18 block (Nos. 23–43) is followed by the sawtooth-front of Nos. 43–57, a 1960s variation of the redevelopment formula. More of the same on the corner of Lothian Street, but the crowstep-gabled STAR TAVERN allows a breathing space.

97   In BROOMHILL ROAD a polychrome pair of crowstepped Gothic

double houses dated 1858. They are by *F. T. Pilkington* and characteristically ingenious in their mixture of perversely detailed bay windows and oriels.

BANK HOUSE in High Street is a smart villa of *c.*1800 with a front garden. The curtain-walled POST OFFICE by *Stewart Sim*, 1961–3, re-establishes the street line but looks temporary. Art Deco PALACE CINEMA with a stained-glass window of frolicking deer. Then Victorian sobriety disturbed by the very reticence of the buff brick BURNTISLAND EX-SERVICE SOCIAL CLUB. ALLAN COURT, another product of the Central Area Redevelopment, is reached by a pend under a late Georgian tenement. Earlier and very vernacular L-plan tenement (Nos. 177–181) with the open part filled by a plain Victorian shop. Late C18 Artisan detail on Nos. 195–201, with rope-moulded scrolled skewputts and a baluster frieze on the r. The ROYAL BANK's palazzo of 1849 establishes a new scale, continued to the E end, where the free Flemish PORT BUILDINGS are by *Swanston & Legge*, 1899. Lively detail, with a copper-roofed corner turret squashed between gables.

At the foot of CROMWELL ROAD, a cinema by *Crawford & Fraser*, 1915. Then the Tudor MANSE by *John Henderson*, 1842–4, and a pair of 1890s double houses with half-timbered jettied upper floors.

CRAIGKENNOCHIE TERRACE is prosperous and Victorian. Trapped in it, a swishly detailed early C19 double house (Nos. 15–17). Roman Doric columns at the paired doors. Fanlight above divided by a mullion carved with a high-relief vase. Original cast-iron lamp-post in front.

At the W end of THE LINKS an enjoyable Victorian FOUNTAIN. Spired Gothic baldacchino above a cherub sitting in the middle of the basin; crocodiles inside the canopy. All gaily painted. Simple late Georgian terraces on the N side of KINGHORN ROAD as far as Erskine Church (*see* above). Then houses on both sides, Victorian on the N, single-storey villas of *c.*1830 on the S.

LOCHIES ROAD crosses The Links and goes under the railway to SEASIDE COTTAGE, early C19 with a broad-eaved verandah, overlooking a rough ashlar PIER.

In LAMMERLAWS ROAD, cheap Art Deco SWIMMING POOL by *F. A. MacDonald & Partners* of Glasgow, 1935. Then a pretty pair of cottages (ALBERT COTTAGE and VICTORIA COTTAGE), Tudor of *c.*1840, and the late Georgian NORTH VIEW HOUSE, with a terraced row (SOUTH VIEW) behind. On the point, rubbly remains of a kiln, a fragment of the VITRIOL FACTORY of *c.*1795.

LEVEN STREET's exit from the SW corner of The Links is marked by the OLD PARSONAGE. Powerful Gothic by *R. C. Carpenter*, 1854, with giant overarches in the crowstepped gables. The Ionic doorpiece of No. 24 (NELLFIELD), *c.*1800, has decidedly odd volutes. The Parish Church and Free Church (for both *see* above) confront each other at the approach to another stretch of the Central Area Redevelopment.

INDUSTRIAL BUILDINGS

ALUMINIUM WORKS, Aberdour Road. Opened 1914. At the E end, roofless lectern DOOCOT, probably C17.

GRANGE DISTILLERY, Grange Road. Founded 1786, but most of the buildings are of *c.* 1805. Solid W range incorporating the old Proprietor's House. Bonded warehouses, still with pantiled roofs, on the E.

SEA MILL, off Haugh Road. The mills existed by 1624, when the Town Council ordered their repair. Surviving rubble shed with a bullseye window in the W gable, probably late C18.

MANSIONS

COLINSWELL HOUSE, off Aberdour Road. Charmless early C19 box. Was the cresting on the roof a last-minute attempt to give it interest?

GRANGE HOUSE, off Kinmundy Drive. L-plan laird's house built for David Bonner in 1680, the date on a thistle-finialled pedimented dormerhead. Moulded door near the re-entrant angle. The top floor was added in the early C19, when the entrance was moved from the W to the S front and given a wide pilastered doorpiece (now with a glazed porch). On its l., two-storey bay window with a jolly balcony. In the billiard room added to the W in 1919, original decoration with black and gold embossed wallpaper.

Corniced GATEPIERS on the approach, dated 1740, perhaps the date of the WALLED GARDEN, whose N walls have round-arched and key-blocked niches, probably BEE-BOLLS. Attached to a cottage to the SE, a C17 lectern DOOCOT, later a laundry and now a store.

GREENMOUNT (HOTEL), Greenmount Road North. Assured Italianate with a tower. By *Thomas Gibson*, 1859.

NETHER GRANGE, Kirkbank Road. *c.* 1910. Relaxed Scots Arts and Crafts, with crowsteps and a pantiled roof.

FARM

NEWBIGGING, 1.7km. NW. Dated 1825 on the pilastered doorpiece. Two-storey main block; single-storey piend-roofed wings. To the SW, a lectern DOOCOT, probably late C17.

BENDAMEER HOUSE. *See* p. 100.
DUNEARN HILL. *See* p. 174.
EASTERHEUGHS. *See* p. 202.
STARLEY HALL. *See* p. 411.

CAIRNEYHILL

A roadside village which developed from *c.*1730. Now nothing special but with some vernacular houses, none looking earlier than the C19.

CHURCH, Main Street. Built as a Burgher chapel in 1752. Harled box with small scrolled skewputts. Ball finial on the E gable. The gable's bellcote looks mid-C19, as do the N side's hood-moulded windows. Inside, a gallery round three sides. – Two late Victorian STAINED-GLASS s lights (Acts of Charity).

CAMBO
1.2km. SE of Kingsbarns

By *Wardrop & Reid*, 1879–81. Huge-scale suburbanish villa of the faintly Italianate Georgian-survival type, built for Sir Thomas Erskine of Cambo to replace a house which had burnt down. Stugged ashlar masonry of orange-coloured Polmaise sandstone. W (entrance) front with a Roman Doric balustraded portico at the pedimented centre. Three bay windows on the s (garden) front. To the N, an extension of 1884 including a rather narrow balustraded clocktower.

The principal rooms form a U-plan first-floor suite round the stairhall. Dining room on the W, with a neo-Adamish frieze and cornice. Carved wooden neo-Jacobean chimneypiece with a canopy on baluster columns. Drawing room in the s front's centre: Frenchy plaster enrichment on the ceiling; another neo-Jacobean chimneypiece, embellished with small statues. In the billiard room on the E, soggy acanthus leaf cornice. Spindly chimneypiece with tiers of shelves at the sides, a clock in the middle; the wood is inlaid with tiles painted with mythological figures.

Late C18 Gothick DOOCOT to the NW, an octagonal tower, pinnacles on the battlemented parapet. – Contemporary STABLES to the SW, the minimally projecting ends' rusticated quoins cut into by later single-storey wings. WALLED GARDEN behind. – N of the drive, MAUSOLEUM dedicated by Bishop Low in 1821, the round-arched opening of the pedimented centre a Greek paraphrase of the Adam Mausoleum in Greyfriars Churchyard, Edinburgh. – At the entrance to the drive, corniced GATEPIERS with swagger cast-iron urns, of *c.*1800. Contemporary pedimented LODGES. – Across the A918 and half-hidden under the present road level, a GAMEKEEPER'S HOUSE of *c.*1800, happily combining a pedimented classical centre with flanking Gothick windows. – To the s, VISITORS' CENTRE (former EAST NEWHALL) converted from a late Georgian steading. Pantile-roofed L-plan, the W range dressed up with a battlemented tower and ends, the taller s range with a crenellated W gable and large octagonal horsemill (now restaurant).

4010   CAMERON

Church and manse isolated in a rural parish.

PARISH CHURCH. Georgian box of 1808 with round-headed S
    windows. The birdcage bellcote's baluster uprights seem to
    be re-used from table stones. Galleried interior altered by
    Honeyman & Keppie, 1902.
        In the churchyard, HEADSTONE to Elizabeth Guilland
    †1819, its inscription, beginning 'Meek and Gentle was her
    Spirit', copied from a stone in St Andrews Cathedral grave-
    yard.
        To the N, the manse's WALLED GARDEN of 1840 and the
    MANSE itself, built in 1798–9; the pedimented porch looks an
    addition. Late C19 W extension. – Detached U-plan steading
    of pantiled OFFICES (now a house) built in 1840.

          CARDENDEN *see* AUCHTERDERRAN,
             BOWHILL AND CARDENDEN

5000   CARNBEE

Hamlet in the centre of a rural parish.

PARISH CHURCH. Rubble box built by *Andrew Horsburgh*,
    wright in Pittenweem, who provided the design, and *David
    Ness*, mason, 1793–4. Tall bellcote with baluster sides and a
    bellcast spire; Y-tracery in the windows. The interior was
    recast in 1854 by *John Milne*, who removed end galleries, and
    in 1908 by *Robert S. Lorimer*, who designed a new PULPIT
    and re-used bits of the old as panelling. – Oak TABLET to
    Jessie Deuchar Fairweather, carved by *W. & A. Clow* from
    Lorimer's design, 1911.
CARNBEE HOUSE. Built as the manse in 1819–20 by *Thomas
    Clark* and *William Lees*. The design may be by *George Dish-
    ington*, surveyor, who inspected the work. Pleasant piend-
    roofed box with a pilastered doorpiece.
KELLIE LAW, 1.3km. W. A cairn on the summit, *c.*25m. in
    diameter and 1.4m. high.

                          CARNOCK

Little more than a hamlet, but with a prominent parish church
in the middle.

                         CHURCHES

FORMER PARISH CHURCH, off Main Street. Roofless but sub-
    stantial remains of the church built before 1250, when it was

granted by David de Bernham, Bishop of St Andrews, to the Red Friars Hospital at Scotlandwell. This simple rectangle, built of cubical ashlar, was repaired and remodelled in 1602 and 1641, the N wall and W gable apparently being rebuilt and a S porch added. It was abandoned on the opening of a new parish church in 1840.

In the E gable, a pair of obtusely pointed C13 windows with deeply splayed ingoes, the N one intact. The wall beneath them is recessed internally, presumably to take an altar; on the l. of the altar's site, a round-arched aumbry which has been altered to a cupboard. The small lancet in the N wall is also original work, probably re-used; so too is a stone carved with a small ogee-arched recess (? a stoup) built into the internal E wall of the porch. This early C17 porch is entered by a roll-moulded round-arched doorway and has another round arch into the church; the smaller door in the N wall is probably contemporary. Along the porch's E and W sides, stone benches much restored in 1921. Small segment-headed bellcote on top of the church's W gable.

The repairs of 1602 are commemorated by a stone below the SE skewputt, inscribed with the initials GB for George Bruce of Carnock and the date. Possibly referring to the work completed in 1641 are two stones* now built into the interior's N wall, one inscribed 'MR.IO.ROW./PASTOR.ANNO/DO.1638.', the other 'GEORGE./BRUCE./OF.CARNOK.' At the SW corner, a corbelled SUNDIAL, dated 1683.

Churchyard GATEPIERS very lumpy and seem to have been rebuilt, but still with ball finials. Beside them, roofless OFFERTORY HOUSE, perhaps of c.1800. – BURIAL ENCLOSURE of John Row † 1646 and his wife Grizel Ferguson † 1656, immediately E of the church. Inside, a large inscription panel under a huge steep pediment with thistle finial and scrolls on the sides, looking like an outsize dormerhead. – Just S of the church, TABLESTONE to Andrew Gibson † 1624, carved with a coat of arms and long inscription ending

> PILGRIM.IN.POL.
> FVL.20.YEARS.
> AND MOR.CAM.
> HOME.AT.LAST.
> AND.NOW.HE.R
> ESTS.IN.GLORE.

To its S, very similar stone to William Gibson † 1639. – Built against the church's W wall, a Corinthian aedicule enclosing a coat of arms, probably late C17. – A few C18 HEADSTONES with jolly emblems of mortality.

PARISH CHURCH, Main Street. By *John Henderson*, 1838–40. Cruciform, 'in the Saxon style', i.e. with innocent Romanesque detail. Entrance in the S limb, which is carried up as a tower with etiolated nook-shafts and a corbelled blocking course; small octagonal spire. Hall at the back added by *John Allan*, 1893.

* Said to have come from the church, but they were later built into the bridge.

Inside, heavy ceiling ribs over the 'crossing' meeting at a Tudor boss. S gallery under the tower. Most of the FURNISHINGS date from Allan's rearrangement. – STAINED GLASS. N window (Giving Drink to the Thirsty), Glasgow style of 1894. – Contemporary E window (Acts of Mercy). – W window (the Lamb of God) of *c.* 1960. – MINISTER'S CHAIR made up, *c.* 1840, from bits of the former pulpit dated 1674; Corinthian aediculed back with a wavy pediment.

DESCRIPTION

A small village along a winding MAIN STREET with post-war housing tucked in behind. The Parish Church (*see* above) and School (of 1865–6, with a mean harled front block dated 1907) are the chief incidents. N end closed by a straightforward late Georgian house. To the E, derelict C19 mill buildings; to the W, lane to the former Parish Church (*see* above), with, on its r., the former MANSE, plain except for large scrolled skewputts (by *John Chalmers*, 1802–4). Just outside the village to the W, the early C19 CARNOCK HOUSE.

FARMS

EASTER LUSCAR, 1.3km. NE. Harled laird's house built for the Wardlaws in 1728. One of the second-floor windows squeezed under the eaves cornice has been raised with a dormerhead. Moulded doorpiece. The drawing room mantelshelf is a marriage lintel of 1672, but with a rough block where the wife's initials should be; it came from the estate's demolished doocot. Behind, L-plan farm buildings incorporating fragments of another marriage lintel of *c.* 1700.

PITDINNIE, 2km. S. Early C19 harled farmhouse with a classical porch; piend-roofed single-storey wings of different sizes. – To the S, a lectern DOOCOT, its stringcourse carried straight across the crowstepped gables; the door lintel is dated 1799.

LUSCAR HOUSE. *See* p. 317.

CELLARDYKE *see* ANSTRUTHER AND CELLARDYKE

4010

CERES

A sizeable village which developed as a burgh of barony from 1620.

PARISH CHURCH, Main Street. By *Alexander Leslie*, 1805–6. Georgian box, the W wall's openings set in semicircular overarches. S tower with 'Saxon' windows (now all blind except at the belfry); stumpy obelisks on the machicolated and crenellated parapet. The octagonal clock stage and tower (modelled on the steeple of St Cuthbert's Church, Edinburgh) were added by *Hugh Birrell* in 1851. In 1865 *John Milne* replaced the roof's piended N end with a straight gable.

Inside, Roman Doric columns carrying a D-plan gallery, its swagged frieze a restoration by *Ian G. Lindsay*. Domed canopy with a dove finial over the PULPIT. – Original BOX PEWS; the central pews can be converted to form communion pews. – In the vestibule, remarkably well-preserved C15 EFFIGY of a recumbent knight armed with a sword and dagger, his feet resting on a lion.

E of the church, the ashlar-walled LINDSAY VAULT, now detached but added, probably in the late C16, to the previous church on the site. Roll-moulded door and window; moulded stone eaves course under the bellcast slabbed roof. Inside, large Victorian TOMB of John, twentieth Earl of Crawford, †1749. – Fragments of C16 and C17 GRAVESTONES, including one to PK and EV, dated 1579, with a well-carved coat of arms.

On the S of the churchyard, SESSION HOUSE by *William Younger*, 1868, with a small chimney gablet.

ALWYN HOUSE (former ADAMSON'S INSTITUTE), Wemysshall Road. Dated 1872. Jacobean with a lusciously corbelled chimneystack on the centre gable. Tower at the back. The recent additions are unfortunate.

PRIMARY SCHOOL, St Andrews Road and Schoolhill. Embedded in additions of 1961 by *Fife County Council* is the single-storey Tudor school by *Robert Hutchison*, 1835–6. To the N, the schoolhouse by *Hugh Birrell*, 1850, with horizontal glazing.

WAR MEMORIAL HALL, Anstruther Road. Harled box built as a Relief meeting house in 1798.

DESCRIPTION

CUPAR ROAD is the NW approach. On the l., the early C19 BRIDGEND HOUSE. Set back to its E, the contemporary CATHERINE BANK, smarter with an Ionic portico and corniced ground-floor windows. On the r., a pantiled cartshed. At the corner of New Town, classy late Georgian gatepiers with small cast-iron urns, but REDRIGGS, to which they belong, is of *c.*1900. MANSEFIELD in CURLING POND ROAD was built as the manse in 1788.

MAIN STREET mixes C18 and C19 vernacular with C20 infill, the Parish Church (*see* above) standing aloof on the N. The S view is closed by a whinstone house of *c.*1840 with a corniced doorpiece. On the l. of ST ANDREWS ROAD, GLOVERBANK, early C19 with a cast-iron columned doorpiece. A little further out, ST HELEN'S, piend-roofed with horizontal glazing, of *c.*1840, opposite the Primary School (*see* above). In ANSTRUTHER ROAD to the SE, an early–mid-C19 group on the l., ending with a store, a doocot in its gable.

HIGH STREET starts at the end of Main Street with a curiosity, the crenellated wall of a demolished house. Built into it are a pair of basket arches whose moulded columns look late medieval. They support carved female heads framing the relief of a C17 hunting scene. On top, another late medieval arch, perhaps a fireplace, in which sits an C18 Toby Jug figure labelled 'PROVOST'. The one-storey KIRPHON, dated 1744, and the C17 BRANDS INN are both much altered. Then THE WEIGH HOUSE, C17, the stone over the door carved with a balance, followed by Georgian cottages. Opposite, the mono-pitch-roofed FIFE FOLK MUSEUM, a bothy heavily reconstructed by *L. A. Rolland & Partners*, 1984, its walling very rubbly. In CASTLEGATE behind, a rubble-built and pantiled vernacular range. At the end of High Street, ST JOHN'S MASONIC LODGE of 1765 with a pedimented Ionic doorpiece. C17 BISHOP BRIDGE over the Ceres Burn, one segmental arch, the parapets triangular.

In SOUTH CROFTDYKE, a late C18 terrace of cottages, mostly pantiled. CROFT HOUSE at the end of NORTH CROFTDYKE was probably begun *c.*1785, but was extended and much altered *c.*1820, and again in 1840 and 1876. Remodelling in 1910 added shaped gablets.

0080

CHARLESTOWN

A planned village founded by Charles, fifth Earl of Elgin, in the 1770s to house labourers at his limeworks.

DESCRIPTION

77 In SALTPANS along the shore is the early C19 EASTER COT-
TAGE, a delightful *cottage orné*, the roof curving up and out as a verandah in front of the recessed centre. On EAST HARBOUR ROAD's N side, massive remains of LIMEKILNS, the first nine built in 1777–8, the other five in 1792. At the end, the HARBOUR, its inner basin begun in 1777–8, the outer basin made in the C19.

121 ROCKS ROAD leads uphill. At the top, the OLD GRANARY of 1792, its S gable carried up as a screen wall to hide the M-roof; W front with a centre gable and round-arched (now blocked) cart openings. A second granary, probably mid-C19, to the N.

The C18 village was laid out as a long rectangle (NORTH ROW and SOUTH ROW) round a green. Plain 'improved' (i.e. model) cottages, most still pantiled but some rebuilt and many altered. DOUBLE ROW exits to the E. At its end, THE QUEEN'S HALL, designed by *R. Rowand Anderson* and built in 1887 to commemorate Queen Victoria's Golden Jubilee. Colourful in harl and red Rosemary tiles; strong crowstepped gables.

BROOMHALL. See p. 102.
PITLIVER. See p. 3440.

CHARLETON
1.6km. NW of Colinsburgh

Smart mid-C18 house extended in the early C19 and remodelled at the beginning of the C20. John Thomson of Charleton bought the estate (then known as Newton) in 1740 and built a new house nine years later. In 1815–17 his grandson John Anstruther Thomson employed *Thomas Finlay* (mason) and *Alexander Leslie* (wright) to add parallel back wings of unequal length separated by a slit courtyard. Leslie was probably responsible for the design.* The house was further extended in 1832, when *William Burn*‡ added a new dining room at the E end. Major changes were made after Lieutenant-Colonel Charles Anstruther inherited the estate in 1904, *Robert S. Lorimer* being employed to form a new main entrance at the N and infill the courtyard between the early C19 wings with a gallery leading from the new front door to the main rooms in the C18 house to the S.

On the present main approach from the N, a double court. At the entrance to its first quadrangle, early C19 gatepiers re-sited and provided with restrained ironwork by *Reginald Fairlie, c.*1921. The courtyard's E and W blocks have been partly removed, so the stables' remaining centre, topped by an ogee-roofed clock turret of 1921, looks absurdly tall. Screen wall beyond with classical urns at the opening into the second court. In both courts, Egyptian statuary, placed here in the early C20.

The harled porch is off-axis and an unsatisfactory introduction. As designed by Lorimer and built in 1905–6 it was even less satisfactory, a single-storey block (the door in the recessed l. bay) too low to hide the NE wing and too short to cover the NW wing's gable. It was improved in 1907 by Mrs (*Agnes*) *Anstruther*, who added two further recessed W bays, but without achieving symmetry, and heightened it with a screen wall studded with busts of Roman emperors in oval niches; Lorimer's balustrade was reinstated on top.

The Edwardian alterations to the mid-C18 house's main (S) front have more conviction. Originally this was a straightforward six-bay elevation of polished ashlar, dignified by a broad columned and pedimented doorpiece across the two centre bays. Lorimer dressed it up by squeezing round-headed niches in between the outer ground-floor windows and in the centre of the first floor (here containing a bust). The effect of this neo-Georgian prettification is belied by the conservatory-porch slicing across the doorpiece. Burn's bay-windowed dining-room addition of 1832 (its balustrade a Lorimer addition) is tactful by comparison.

The NE wing of 1815–17 is utilitarian, but the contemporary NW wing could stand as a decent harled laird's house in its own

---

* Leslie was paid £100 'for trouble and Incidental expences' in addition to his charges for wright work.

‡ *John Lessels* was clerk of works and prepared sketches for the work.

right. Three bays with three-light windows in the advanced centre.

Inside, Lorimer's entrance hall opens into his gallery running down the middle of the house. Top-lit from cupolas, each set in a richly modelled roundel of plaster foliage. Frieze with portraits (painted by *Dorsfield Hardy*) of people connected with the house set between stumpy pilasters. On the w wall, a superb Mannerist chimneypiece made in 1907, largely of older bits. The design seems to have been chiefly the work of Mrs Anstruther. The spiralled gilded columns banded with reliefs of *putti* holding garlands could be C17 Flemish; they were imported from No. 45 Hyde Park Gate, London. Overmantel of niches framed in pilasters. Above, a pierced screen of cherubs and eagles, some of its woodwork C17, the rest of 1907. At the gallery's s end, a small C18 room (perhaps a dressing room), now windowless and with its ceiling shallowly enriched with Lorimer's characteristic vine decoration. More Lorimer ceiling enrichment (vines and birds) in a passage to its E and the adjoining Business Room (now kitchen), both in the NE wing of 1815–17.

The C18 house's main rooms are a classy mixture of original and Edwardian work. Entrance hall (now ante-room) in the centre. Its simply enriched ceiling and *trompe l'œil* mural decoration (trophies of the arts of war and peace) look mid-C18; so too does the chunky wooden chimneypiece, its centre carved with a female head. Stairhall behind, the stair with alternating turned and twisty balusters, the walls covered with *Spy* prints. Drawing room to the w, the walls hung c.1905 with Japanese painted paper whose pheasants are repeated in the centrepiece of the ceiling's restrained rococo mid-C18 enrichment. Broad Ionic columned screen at the N end, perhaps an early C19 insertion, as seems to be the simply panelled white marble chimneypiece. In the library E of the entrance hall, the frieze (boys holding garlands) and the large square ceiling rose are Lorimer embellishments. Probably contemporary but unLorimerian is the coarse chimneypiece. The Doric columned screen at the back looks early C19.

Of the original decoration of Burn's dining room only the shutters survive. Lorimer replaced the back wall with an Ionic screen to incorporate a service room behind and made the coved ceiling enriched with coats of arms and vines in his best late C17–early C18 manner. At the same time early C17 panelling was imported from Bolsover Castle (Derbyshire) and placed under a heraldic painted frieze. A much flashier importation is the gilded chimneypiece, which began its architectural career, probably in the early C18, as a doorcase. It is a huge Corinthian aedicule, the open pediment boldly bracketed. The top of the opening's round arch has been filled with an Italian *capriccio*, the bottom encloses the fireplace.

More panelling from Bolsover in the first-floor NW bedroom. In the room below, walls papered with prints; Egyptianish frieze, probably of c.1905.

The GARDEN lay-out is largely Edwardian. Terraces to the
s with pierced brick parapets on the whinstone retaining walls.
To the E, formal compartments defined by hedges. At the top
of the main path, a well, its head a carved capital; at the bottom,
iron gates decorated with Lorimerish vines.

To the E, an C18 lectern DOOCOT. – Smart late C18 GATE-
PIERS with Greek key bands across their rustication and
flaming urn finials. Formerly at Airdrie Castle, they were
placed here c.1920.

CHARLOTTETOWN   2010

Small early C19 village.

COLLESSIE FREE CHURCH. Now a hall. Built c.1845; gableted
bellcote.

COALTOWN OF BALGONIE   2090

A mining village developed from the late C18.

QUEEN VICTORIA MEMORIAL HALL, Main Street. By *James
Gillespie*, 1905–6. Bargeboarded English picturesque in glazed
red brick with a large spired *flèche*.
DESCRIPTION. Mostly late Victorian terraced cottages, some
pantiled. One early C19 double house (Nos. 88–90 MAIN
STREET) pulls out all the stops (scrolled skewputts, rusticated
quoins, and fluted friezes over doors and windows). Also late
Georgian but much plainer is BALGONIE COTTAGE at the N
end; behind, a pantiled steading of orangey rubble.

COALTOWN OF WEMYSS   3090

Picturesque estate village at the gates of Wemyss Castle, built
from the 1890s as miners' housing.

MINERS' WELFARE INSTITUTE, Main Street. By *A. Stewart
Tod*, 1924–5, with an ogee-topped lantern on the orange pan-
tiled piend roof. In the s gable, steeply pedimented WAR
MEMORIAL, also by *Tod*.
PRIMARY SCHOOL, Main Street. Tudorish, by *Alexander Tod*,
1896–7.

DESCRIPTION

The Primary School (*see* above) is the first incident on the
approach from Kirkcaldy. Then RODGER PLACE goes off to
the l., chimneyless modern vernacular, leading to LOCHEAD
CRESCENT, straight rows of cottages: on the l., pairs of semi-

detacheds linked by porches, on the r., a terrace, all harled, pantiled and crowstepped.

On MAIN STREET's s side, a row of early C19 pantiled cottages at the entry to Wemyss Castle. On the N, BARNS ROW, a broad-eaved cottage terrace of 1912 with gabled porches. Built into the end house, datestone of 1645. After the Miners'
99   Welfare Institute (*see* above), another terrace but with tree-trunk porches. Similar terrace opposite, its end gables' centres rising above the piend roof as chimney gablets with scrolled skewputts. Then, on the N, simple row of slated crowstepped cottages stepping down the slope. Round the corner, EARL DAVID HOTEL, crisp and jolly in white harl and black paint, dated 1911.

Behind Main Street's s side, PLANTATION ROW's simple Edwardian cottages, and more of the same in SOUTH ROW. In MEMORIAL SQUARE, housing of *c.*1920 with broad eaves and crowsteps, formally arranged. Rendered neo-vernacular of 1953 in CORONATION PLACE to the E.

EARLSEAT, 1.7km. N. A standing stone NE of Earlseat Farm, 1.4m. high, *c.*2.4m. maximum girth.

WEMYSS CASTLE. *See* p. 424.

WEMYSS CASTLE. *See* p. 424.

4000   COATES HOUSE
                    2.2km. NE of Upper Largo

Tall late C18 piend-roofed laird's house built of whinstone rubble. Venetian door; second-floor windows of horizontal proportion.

4000   COLINSBURGH

Roadside village founded and named after Colin, third Earl of Balcarres, in 1682 and made a burgh of barony in 1686.

PARISH CHURCH, Main Street. A broad box built as a Relief chapel, 1843–4. In the gable, depressed-arched windows; hoodmoulded door. Small birdcage bellcote.

GALLOWAY LIBRARY, Main Street. 1903, by *Charles Davidson* of Paisley. Asymmetrical front, mixing Baronial touches into a suety Wrenaissance pudding. Segmental hood over the door; first-floor balcony on corbelled rounds.

TOWN HALL, Main Street. By *A. & A. C. Dewar*, 1894–5. Timid Scots Renaissance bullied by a *porte cochère*.

DESCRIPTION

MAIN STREET begins at the E with the Town Hall. Then, terraced rows of mostly two-storey C18 and early C19 houses, built of whinstone, many with painted margins, some rendered. No. 29's widely spaced windows look mid-c18, but its anta-pilastered doorpiece is of c.1840. Beside the Parish Church, a lane to the early c19 villa housing the ROYAL BANK. In NORTH WYND opposite, mid-c19 stables (now a house) with gableted loft openings. At the wynd's end, the crow-stepped and harled FAIRFIELD of 1717, with a sundial on the r. skewputt. On its E, GRANARY, perhaps late c18, with doocot openings in the gable.

No. 30 Main Street, now covered in bullnosed render, has been a rustically smart c18 house, its door's curly lintel set in a lugged architrave. Beyond the Galloway Library (see above), No. 46 (THE COTTAGE) of c.1800, a Venetian window in its centre gablet. Rusticated doorpiece on No. 48. On the s, harled MASONIC TEMPLE of 1923. Beside it, No. 79, smart Tudorish on a small scale, c.1840. Then some pantiled cottages before the harled and crowstepped c18 No. 87.

BALCARRES. See p. 80.
PITCORTHIE HOUSE. See p. 342.

COLLAIRNIE CASTLE
7.1km. NW of Cupar

3010

Embedded in an early c19 pantiled steading, the rubble-built NE jamb and stairtower of the c16 house of the Balfours of Collairnie. Crowstepped jamb of four storeys, the roof now swept over the tops of the blocked attic windows. Pistol-holes in the NE and SE angle turrets; splayed gunloops in the (exposed) N front. Tusking on the W shows that the main block was lower. When it still existed, the effect of the stairtower rising above the jamb must have been curiously disjointed. In the jamb's s front, a moulded door, its lintel dated 1581 and with the initials DB and MW for David Balfour and his wife. Above, dogtooth ornamented frame for a heraldic panel. It is now occupied by a triangular pediment with the arms and initials of Henry Balfour and the date 1607, too large for the frame and clearly an insertion. This door gives access only to ground-floor storage. The stairtower door (probably a c19 replacement for an entrance from the main block) opens on to the anticlockwise stair to the upper floors. Early c18 basket-arched first-floor chimneypiece. In the second- and third-floor rooms, tempera-painted ceilings, the second-floor ceiling with the date 1607 and the initials HB and DB (probably for Hugh Barclay and his father, or son, David Barclay). On both ceilings the underside of the boards is decorated with coats of arms (identified by captions) on a background of leaves and fruit. The joists' sides have platitudinous inscriptions, their soffits guilloches and other patterns.

The STEADING was reconstructed in 1844 by *Archibald Mitchell*, mason, and *John Inglis*, wright, who built the thrashing barn's brick chimney. *Alexander Blyth* was probably

the architect,* as also for the 1849 reconstruction of the late
C18 farmhouse, converting its main block's s gable into the
semi-octagonal centrepiece of a smart five-bay front.

2010   COLLESSIE

Irregularly laid out village described in 1865‡ as 'a confused
collection of thatched houses, and a place of small importance.'
Most of the thatch has now gone.

PARISH CHURCH. Tall and boxy Gothic, by *R. & R. Dickson*,
1838–9. T-plan with a N aisle, fat stair turrets corbelled out
in the inner angles; shallow pulpit projection on the s. On the
E gable, a Tudor chimney. W tower decorated with blind
gunloops, the belfry openings recessed under corbelled rectangular overarches; crenellated parapet with corner pinnacles.
   Inside, a flattish ribbed plaster ceiling. Galleries on three
sides. – Furnishings largely original but the rake of the PEWS
was altered in 1911 by *James Gillespie & Scott*. – Tall PULPIT
with a double stair and sounding board. – Oil LAMPS. –
STAINED GLASS in two s windows (St Andrew, and the Good
Shepherd), colourful expressionist of 1956.
   Rubble-walled CHURCHYARD. The s GATE, a pointed arch
under a gabled parapet, is by *John Stewart*, mason, 1841. – W
of the gate, a roofless BURIAL ENCLOSURE built for Sir James
Melville in 1609. Over its roll-moulded door, a corniced panel
recording repairs in 1831. The outside wall is panelled in
ashlar, with vestigial attached columns at the ends, the cornice
jumping down in the centre to frame a (missing) heraldic
panel. An inscription commending the reformed Church of
Scotland's ban on burial inside churches begins

> DEFYLE.NOT.CHRISTS.KIRK.WITH.YOVR.CARRION
> A.SOLEMNE.SAIT.FOR.GODS.SERVICE.PREPARD
> FOR.PRAIER.PREACHING.AND.COMMVNION

– In the churchyard's NE corner, remains of a big C17 monument, with a steep pediment and scrolls. – To its s, a primitive
aedicule wall monument, probably early C17.
DESCRIPTION. Beside the church is THE GLEBE (former
MANSE) begun by *John Stewart* in 1796 and doubled in size
by *Robert Hutchison*, 1824, a three-light centre window its
main feature. To its E, a cottage (STRAD COTTAGE and
MANSE GATES), dated 1839 in its centre gablet, with stone
canopies over the windows. At the village's N end, the thatched
ROSE COTTAGE; a big sundial dated 1772 on the SW skewputt.
W of the church, a row of vernacular cottages, some pantiled.
Beyond the railway bridge over the valley below, more
cottages, one still thatched.

---

* He inspected the work in 1844 and 1849 and provided designs for two cothouses
here in 1847.
‡ By *The Imperial Gazetteer of Scotland*.

THE SCHOOLHOUSE, 0.5km. SW. Simple Gothic, by *R. & R. Dickson*, 1846. One-storey school with a schoolhouse at the back. Bellcote on the S front's central gable.

BARROW, 0.5km. N. An unusual barrow with a ditch and outer bank in the manner of a bell barrow, *c.*11m. in diameter by 0.6m. high, but now somewhat eroded.

NEWTON, 0.6km. E. A stone, very worn but incised with the figure of a man possibly bearing a shield, 2.7m. high and 2.1m. girth at the base.

MELVILLE HOUSE. *See* p.321.

COWDENBEATH   *1090*

Sizeable but not immediately attractive town which developed as a mining community from the 1870s and was made a burgh in 1890.

CHURCHES

BEATH CHURCH, Old Perth Road. Simple preaching-box of 1834–5 in a graveyard just outside the town. *James Macfarlane* was both architect and contractor. On the W gable, a fat octagonal bellcote supported by ample corbels. Tudor-arched hood-moulded windows, their mullions and transoms of wood. An incongruous conservatory-porch hides the main door. Galleried interior. The roomy PULPIT was provided as part of *John Whitelaw*'s alterations of 1884.

In the churchyard, three weathered C18 TABLE STONES to the S of the church, two of them with elegantly carved symbols of mortality. – To the church's W, C18 HEADSTONE of Isoble Hay: Ionic pilastered with a coat of arms in the curvy pediment, its top decorated with skulls.

CAIRNS CHURCH, Church Street. Originally United Presbyterian. Plain E.E. by *John Whitelaw*, 1892–3, with buttresses against the gable to suggest a nave and aisles. Tall stone-spired octagonal bellcote.

COWDENBEATH PARISH CHURCH, Broad Street. Disused. 1896–7, by *John Whitelaw*. Cheap Gothic ('partakes somewhat of the decorated style', said the *Dunfermline Journal*) enlivened by the SW tower's attempt to develop into a broached steeple, only to be squashed by a tall belfry.

MOSSGREEN CROSSGATES CHURCH, Main Street, Hill of Beath. Harled mission church dated 1901.

NORTH CHURCH, Perth Road. Built as Lumphinnans United Free Church, *c.*1900. Cement-rendered minimal Gothic.

OUR LADY AND ST BRIDE (R.C.), Stenhouse Street. By *Reginald Fairlie*, 1921–3. Shedlike exterior made unappealing by the present drydash and concrete tiles, but with a lean-to vestry to give the suggestion of a gambrel roof to the main gable. Side walls divided into panels by thin straight buttresses. Surprisingly impressive inside, with round-arched

arcades on square piers. Strong kingpost trussed roof. – ALTAR
and TABERNACLE of coloured marbles.

WEST CHURCH, Sinclair Drive. By *Wheeler & Sproson*, 1968.
Abstract in white drydash.

PUBLIC BUILDINGS

BEATH HIGH SCHOOL, Stenhouse Street. Big, blocky
Wrenaissance front in red Dumfriesshire sandstone; the harled
backside visible from a distance. By *William Birrell*, 1908–10.

BEATH HIGH SCHOOL (SENIOR BUILDING), Foulford Road
and Old Perth Road. By *Fife County Council*, 1964. Curtain-
walled, with blue coloured panels alternating with clear glass.

FOULFORD PRIMARY SCHOOL, Leuchatsbeath Drive. By *Fife
Regional Council*, 1976. Single-storey with a shallow-pitch
roof.

LUMPHINNANS PRIMARY SCHOOL, Main Street. By *John
Whitelaw*, 1892–3. Extended by *William Birrell*, 1901–3, and
by *Gilbert T. Scott*, 1909.

MINERS' WELFARE INSTITUTE, Broad Street. 1925–8, by *J. T.
Scobie*. Stripped Renaissance in stone and harl.

ST BRIDE'S SCHOOL, Barclay Street. By *G. Charles Campbell*,
1920, with a few Art Deco touches.

TOWN HOUSE, High Street. By *T. Hyslop Ure*, 1904–6. Soggy
baroque in red sandstone with a cupolaed corner tower.

FARM

CUTTLEHILL, 2.3km. S. Early C19 courtyard steading with a
pedimented S entrance.

CRAIGFLOWER *see* TORRYBURN

0090
CRAIGLUSCAR HILL
4km. NW of Dunfermline

An Iron Age hillfort partially excavated in 1944–5, *c.*53m. by
33m. within three lines of defence, the inner and outer being
dry-stone walls *c.*3.6m. thick. The middle one may have been
a twin palisade, possibly embanked. The inner E gateway
appears to have been defended by a timber tower.

4010
CRAIGTOUN PARK*
3.6km. SW of St Andrews

Huge pink sandstone Jacobean château of 1902 designed by
Paul Waterhouse for the brewer James Younger. Asymmetrical

* Formerly Mount Melville.

entrance front, the detail surprisingly small-scale and flat, perhaps to avoid the suspicion of *nouveau riche* taste. Rather stronger has been the garden front with a twin-gabled centre and conical roofed turrets at the gabled ends, but it is now overlaid with fire escapes, added since the house's conversion to a hospital in 1949.

The interior is more opulent. Entrance hall panelled in the C17 manner, its ceiling on heavy consoled beams. Arch into a stone-walled stairhall overlooked from the first-floor corridor through an arcade. The arcade's Ionic columns have marble shafts, the stair white marble treads and brown-veined alabaster balusters and handrail (the marble work all executed by *Farmer & Brindley*). At the back of the ground floor, a double drawing room, its ceiling's *pâtisserie* decoration including musical instruments in the corners; Corinthian columned screens frame the end windows.

In front of the house, a SUNDIAL, perhaps of *c.* 1700, with a polyhedron top on an octagonal shaft.

The GARDENS were laid out by Waterhouse. Beside the house, a formal flower garden with statuary, the main architectural feature a tall screen wall topped by urns and eagles, perhaps dating from *James Gillespie Graham*'s additions to the previous house in 1821–4. So too may the elegant GATEPIERS at the top of Waterhouse's cypress AVENUE. Half-way down, the fluted stone basin of a wishing well. The avenue was focused on a temple (now removed). To the w an artificial lake made by Waterhouse. On its island he provided a SUMMER-HOUSE and BOATHOUSE complex masquerading as a miniature Franco-German castle, very trim in white harl and red tiles, approached by a bridge whose heavy cutwaters give a sense of military purpose. – To the E, WALLED GARDEN, probably the one built by *Robert Hutchison* in 1826, but the domed summerhouse must be by Waterhouse. – Beside the walled garden, broad-eaved mid-C19 COTTAGES. – To their N, contemporary HOME FARM, its round horsemill dressed up by Waterhouse (converted to housing 1985). – To its E, a group of ESTATE WORKERS' COTTAGES (PROSPECT ROW), dated 1920. – Further N, STABLES by *Waterhouse*, the flat tiles of the French tower over the round-arched gateway a contrast to the flanking ranges' pantiles and heavy crowsteps.

LODGE at end of NW drive, smooth baronial, probably by *Waterhouse*. – In a field to the N, large double-chambered lectern DOOCOT, probably late C17.

CRAIL   *6000*

Picturesque small town, a royal burgh since the C12 with an adjoining royal castle to the E. Fishing, always the most important industry, gradually declined in the C19, and by the 1950s the letting of houses or rooms to holiday-makers had become 'almost

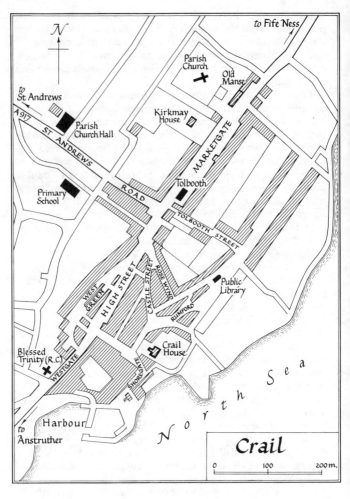

Crail

the keystone of Crail's economy'. Preservation of the town's
architectural character has been given a welcome boost by the
National Trust for Scotland's Little Houses Scheme, whose
revolving fund to finance restoration was first used here.

CHURCHES

CHURCH OF THE BLESSED TRINITY (R.C.), Westgate. Built as
   the Crail United Presbyterian Church with a firescreen Gothic
   front, 1858.
PARISH CHURCH, in a treed churchyard rising gently from the
   N side of Marketgate. A venerable church in partial Gothick
   disguise. The two-cell Norman building is represented only
   by the N wall of the chancel (now enclosed by the C20 vestry)
   and a similar stringcoursed fragment in the angle of the S

junction of chancel and nave. The tall w tower was built in the early C13. Coursed masonry divided by shallow strings into six stages, the top one with twin lancets and corbelled parapet. On the N side a staircase jamb with stone lean-to roof. This was soon followed by the new nave with N and S aisles, whose surviving w gables continue the tower's bevelled base. In the s gable a consecration cross. The church was dedicated in 1243 by the Bishop of St Andrews to the Celtic Saint Maelrubha of Applecross. But it was already known as St Mary's in 1517, when its owner, the Prioress of the Cistercian nunnery at Haddington, made a successful petition for its erection into a collegiate church.* In the early C16 the chancel was lengthened and the squat octagonal stone spire was added. On the s side the jambs of a lucarne. John Knox preached here in 1559, and in 1594 the church's assets were divided into three equal parts, for the upkeep of the minister of Crail and of students of theology at St Andrews and philosophy at Edinburgh.

Some time in the late C18 the upper part of the N aisle wall was rebuilt, the medieval lower courses being retained together with the moulded jambs of a doorway towards the w end. Was this the improvement scheme proposed by Mr *Balfour* in 1796? *Robert Balfour* (presumably the same) provided the next scheme in 1807, for two tall windows on the s side, one on each side of the pulpit. It was passed, but nothing was done till 1815, when he carried out a more radical plan with *John Bowman* as mason and *James Brown* and *David Wylie* as wrights. An accumulation of burial aisles, the loft staircase and medieval s porch were swept away, and tall pointed windows with Gothick glazing were inserted. A new roof was formed, sloping continuously from a lowered ridge to the raised wall-head of the aisles, so that from the outside there is no hint of the medieval clearstorey. In 1828 *William Lees*, wright in Pittenweem, with *James Taylor* of Anstruther, mason, short-ened the chancel and installed a gallery. A fragment of a consecration cross is built into the E gable.

Before these reordering works the interior had been lined with the lofts of the Town Council and Trades, that of the Seamen being at the E end (painted in 1765), the Tailors, Bakers and Shoemakers in the N aisle, the Magistrates, Coopers and Wrights in the s aisle, and the Weavers in the chancel. Balfour removed them and reseated the floor of the church with box pews, siting the pulpit (with ogee-topped sounding board) on the central axis, in line with the first full pier from the E. Either then or later, a w gallery was formed, two bays deep. But all these became wormy and were removed in the major restoration of 1963 by *Judith Campbell*. She unblocked the tower arch, revealing its nook-shafted piers, and repaired the rest. Six-bayed nave arcade on circular piers, triple clear-storey lancets over alternate bays (the glazing ingeniously replaced), chancel arch with leafy capitals. With white walls, a

---

* The 'ornamentis and sylver werk in the College Kirke of Caraile' were listed in the C16: Charles Rogers, *Proceedings of the Grampian Club*, 1877.

blue panelled ceiling and chestnut pews, the effect is discreetly
archaeological. – ORGAN by *Harrison & Harrison*, rebuilt by
Scovell & Co. of Edinburgh in 1936, when it was brought here
from a house in Kirkcaldy. – OAK PANEL of 1609 exhibited
in the s aisle. – STAINED GLASS in the tower by *Judith Campbell*, two lights (Creation and Redemption). In the vestry a
PAINTED PANEL from the Seamen's Loft. A man in a long
coat, with an astrolabe. In the porch, CARVED STONES, including a Celtic cross-slab with beasts, and the tomb-slab of Sir
James Ewart, chaplain of the Collegiate Church 1544–55. Also
a fragment discovered on the site of the old Grammar School
to the l. of the churchyard gate. Upper part of a tomb-slab
with incised cross, open book and chalice, a sword to one
side.

   CHURCHYARD with important collections of mural monuments. The following are described in clockwise order, starting
from the War Memorial gateway of 1921. – John Wood of
Sauchope † 1723. Grey stone, with pairs of crude Roman Doric
half-columns and a broken pediment. – Andrew Daw † 1645.
Three stages, with a Ciceronian quotation. – Patrick Hunter
† 1649. Two stages, with vestigial Ionic pilasters, the tablet
and other detail very delicately carved. – George Moncreiffe
of Sauchope † 1707. Orangey stone, with Ionic pilasters and
broken pediment. – Robert Durie † 1636. Two stages, but the
colonnettes have gone. Scrolls at the sides. – Andrew Moncreiff
† 1631. Median pilaster extending right up into the crowning
pedimental slab. – James Lumsden of Airdrie † 1598. Of engag-
ing crudity. Pairs of half-Gothic colonnettes supporting a
bulky upper stage, crowned with broached pyramids. Median
column beneath the pedimented coat of arms. – William Bruce
of Symbister † c. 1630. Figure of Bruce (now topless) as a knight
in armour, in a niche between two Corinthian pilasters which
bear trophies of war and death. All copiously inscribed, as are
the tabletop monuments. – To the N of the tower, Mrs Margaret Munro † 1792, with the inscription

34

> HERE PEACEFUL LIES CONSIGNED TO SILENT DUST
> ALL THAT WAS MORTAL OF THE GOOD & JUST.
> MODESTLY WISE BEYOND THE POMP OF ART,
> HER'S WAS THE VIRTUE THAT EXALTS THE HEART.
> THIS LED HER THROUGH THE STORMY SEANES OF LIFE
> A TENDER MOTHER A RESPECTED WIFE.
> TUTOR'D HER MIND TO KNOW THE SACRED GLOW
> OF FEELING ARDENTLY ANOTHER'S WOE,
> AND FIRM CONDUCTED O'ER THE CHEERING ROAD,
> OF PURE RELIGION TO A GRACIOUS GOD.
> GO, READER! PROVE THE LOVELY LESSON! GO,
> AND IN THY MANNERS IMITATE MUNRO.

– MORT HOUSE further to the N, against the wall, built in 1826.
PARISH CHURCH HALL, St Andrews Road. Built as the Crail
United Free Church. Late Gothic by *J. D. Cairns*, 1909, with
a big window over the entry and red-tiled spire to one side.
All the details lively and refined. Next door, the former MANSE.

PUBLIC BUILDINGS

HARBOUR. A small tidal harbour, the most picturesque in the 85
East Neuk, reached by the steep descent down Shoregate. The
hook-shaped East Pier came first. It was described in a typical
series of applications to the Convention of Royal Burghs as
'new foundit' (1610) and 'old and ruinous, a great part of it
beat down by a storme this last winter' (1707), and eventually
received a grant of £20 towards repairs in 1728. Massive
parapet on the outer side and recessed steps on the inner,
which is largely of squared stones in vertical courses. The
straight West Pier was designed by *Robert Stevenson* in 1821
and built by *John Gosman* in 1826–8 for £1,095, with a grant
of £500. Pierhead rebuilt in 1871.

PRIMARY SCHOOL, St Andrews Road. Single storey with three
gables, by *David Henry*, 1888–9.

PUBLIC LIBRARY (originally Burgh School), free-standing in
the middle of Nethergate. 1824, possibly by *Robert Balfour*.
One storey, with one end canted. Gothick glazing in the arched
windows. The gabled porch, with ball finial, dates from the
radical reconstruction by *John Gosman*, mason, and *John Balsillie*, wright, in 1852.

TOLBOOTH and TOWN HALL, Marketgate. The Tolbooth is a 103
stolid landmark in the centre of the Burgh. C16 tower of
big coursed blocks, the high-up bullseye windows inserted in
1776, when two diminishing stages were added (the upper one
with a clock) and crowned with a two-tier slated hat like a
malt-kiln. Doorway by *John Currie*, 1886. Adjacent TOWN
HALL of 1814 with big windows lighting the first-floor Council
Chamber. Re-sited datestone of 1602 with the Burgh arms,
and a lintel dated 1754. Also in Marketgate the MERCAT
CROSS, an early C17 chamfered shaft re-sited with a unicorn
finial for Queen Victoria's Golden Jubilee in 1887, and the
fountain of polychrome granite for the Diamond Jubilee in
1897.

DESCRIPTION

The E entry to Crail crosses a little burn and then climbs to
MARKETGATE, confined at first to the S by the C18 fronts of
Nos. 2–4, to the N by a retaining wall. This makes a platform
for No. 1, DENBURN HOUSE, with steep crowsteps and a
sundial of 1719 mounted on the corner, and No. 3, the OLD
MANSE by *William Lees*, 1828. *William Taylor* and *Robert
Peebles* were the masons, *John Balsillie* and *David Duncan*
the wrights. Three storeys of squared masonry with smooth
margins and an artisan classical doorpiece. The rest of the
street is a plateau, much wider than the tree-lined roadway
and defined (except for the big gap at the Parish Church, *see*
above) by an almost continuous building line. On the N side
the line is established by No. 5 and maintained by the garden
walls and gatepiers of the twin-bowed KIRKMAY HOUSE,

1817, all in smart grey ashlar except for the little cement-faced attic room, which is redeemed by its piended slate roof. E garden wall of red brick, and set in the W wall a pediment inscribed IM KP 1619. No. 9, FRIAR'S COURT, dated 1686, renovated and probably deharled in 1938. Three rubbly storeys with crowsteps and a wallhead chimney. No. 11 is politely harled before the rock-faced Victoriana of Nos. 13–15, 1896. No. 21 is dated 1811 over the door but still crowstepped to the rear. Then the polychrome pomposity of Nos. 25–29 by *John Milne*, 1886. Shallow corbelled bows and red sandstone bands, Peterhead granite colonnettes at the front doors. On the S side a forestair at No. 8, and another at the three-storeyed No. 36, which forms a centrepiece between the gabled outshots of No. 26 (straight skew) and No. 44 (crowstepped). No. 48 is a minimal vernacular parody dated 1901, and No. 52 of about the same date has a stone shopfront (Barnet, baker). Full-stop at No. 62 (1703, rebuilt 1876) behind the Tolbooth (*see* Public Buildings, above).

S by way of Tolbooth Street to NETHERGATE, which has a line of pollarded trees along the S side. The E end offers a vista of forlorn suburb, but makes a good starting point. To the S a C16 moulded doorway, walls and other fragments of the former NUNNERY, plus the beehive PRIORY DOOCOT, smothered in cement. Then THE PRIORY, a light-hearted baronial villa by *Thoms & Wilkie* for Samuel Brush of Dundee, 1915. An odd but effective composition, white-harled and red-tiled, complete with gabled tower and circular turret. DOWNIE'S TERRACE at Nos. 18–28, dated 1878, is a more serious baronial joke, each front door crowned with its own variation on the chimney-gable theme. Nos. 9–19 on the N side, all mid-C19, are a single-storey foil to these high jinks. Half-way along, the street is punctuated by the rubbly projection of No. 43, C18 but restored in 1956, answered on the S side by No. 44, which steps right forward, mid-C19 drastically updated a century later. No. 48, MILLBURN, has had a kinder facelift with a Victorian timber porch and stained glass. For the Georgian Gothick Public Library, *see* above. Its tail of houses in the middle of the street includes No. 70, recast in 1895 with a carved panel of a ship. The MARINE HOTEL is polite crowstepped classical, 1903, and No. 64, *c.*1840, has a vase on its gabled outshot. On the N side the street pushes on past the island buildings and past the Rumford gable (*see* below) into a narrow wynd, where No. 76 (the Crail Pottery) has a little square eye in its gable, half-dormers and a half-basement, the front door reached by a double forestair. RUMFORD is an important C17–18 group. Nos. 5–6 are two houses made into one by *Wheeler & Sproson*, 1961,* harled and pantiled with a corbelled SE corner.

Two streets lead back up to the Tolbooth. In the garden wall of No. 1 CASTLE STREET, a scrolled pediment carved with

---

* This was the first of the rehabilitation works carried out under the National Trust for Scotland's revolving restoration scheme.

mason's tools and the date 1643, and at No. 23 a doorpiece dated 1626, but most of the rest altered. ROSE WYND is all cottages and garden walls until the top, where No. 1, C18, has freestone margins and a forestair. Alternatively, towards the sea is CRAIL HOUSE, rock-faced and bow-windowed and something of an anticlimax after its tremendous Gothic gateway, of the same mid-Victorian period, set in an older wall which can be followed clockwise into CASTLE WALK. At the s corner a few bits of Crail Castle (originally C13) and an octagonal Victorian GAZEBO with crenellated top. Nearby is the square, piend-roofed WATCH HOUSE with pointed windows and the date 1782 carved on a re-sited C17 pediment. Both enjoy the sea view from the cliff-top.

ST ANDREWS ROAD enters Crail from the N. To the w the splayed group of houses at WINGFIELD overlooks Victoria Gardens, followed by the Primary School (for this and the Gothic Church Hall *see* Public Buildings and Churches, above). The s end widens towards the cross-roads, but unpretentiously with C19 front-gardened cottages. Straight ahead is the GOLF HOTEL, early C18 with two square eyes in its rollicking chimney-gable, two more in the gable which looks w. Its three-storey symmetry is curiously upset by the splayed NW corner, squared up by heavy corbels overhead. HIGH STREET then divides into compartments, the first brought to an end by the projection of No. 19, the second mainly a setting for No. 16, which has a lintel dated 1718 and a couple of re-sited pediments. After the picturesque view down Castle Street one is at the apex of a triangle whose N side leads into WEST GREEN, bounded by C18–19 houses and split down the middle by an island row, none very notable but all of a piece. The s side of the triangle enters the final stage of High Street, a long and gently sloping rectangle. On its N side a crowstepped outshot at Nos. 55–57, C18, and a bargeboarded outshot at No. 61 which still has part of its original C18 doorpiece. The early C19 EAST NEUK HOTEL at No. 67 defines the end of the rectangle. On the s side a succession of C18 houses with steep crowstep gables before the entry to SHOREGATE (*see* below). Then WESTGATE, which is narrower. On the N side, Nos. 7–9, with smooth margins, and Nos. 11–15, *c.* 1815 with twin gables, one of which has its original Gothick glazing. Formerly perhaps a school, now a workshop. For the R.C. Church of the Blessed Trinity *see* above. Most conspicuous on the s side is the white-harled No. 20, C18 with dormers and steep crowsteps.

From High Street the entry to SHOREGATE is well marked by the two gables of Nos. 1 and 2. Then No. 11, C17–18 with crowstepped outshot and moulded doorway, and No. 13, whose scrolled pediment dated 1632 has been re-sited in an C18 reconstruction. The crowstep gables of No. 19, originally 1613, stand up on a terrace with the late C18 No. 21. Likewise on the E side, CASTLE TERRACE, *c.* 1890, a confident pastiche of the early C18 manner with very square crowsteps over uniformly ogee-topped front doors. Shoregate steps gingerly down between the two terraces, past the forestairs of Nos. 26 and 28 and the gable of PEPPERS at No. 36 (all C18) to the harbour (*see* Public Buildings above). On the w side a sequence only a little less picturesque ends with the big full-stop of the CUSTOM HOUSE, a late C17 tenement with steep crowsteps and ground-floor and attic warehouses. Big studded doors and an oval plaque carved with a ship. Having curved round to face the water, Shoregate ends with a little raised quadrangle defined to the front by No. 37 and the crowstep gable of No. 43, both C18.

BALCOMIE CASTLE. *See* p. 87.

3010

CRAWFORD PRIORY
4.1km. SW of Cupar

74 Light late Georgian castellated-cum-Gothick with high-minded Victorian additions. The house was begun (as Crawford Lodge) by the twenty-first Earl of Crawford in 1758. An unassuming villa, it was already thought too small by the 1780s, when schemes for its enlargement or replacement were prepared for the twenty-second Earl. On his death in 1808 the title passed to a distant cousin, the estate to his sister, Lady Mary Lindsay Crawford, who the next year began to add a 'Gothick Hall' w of the existing house. Her architect was *David Hamilton*,* who designed a four-poster block with octagonal towers at the corners, slender battlemented octagonal buttresses along the S front, and round turrets flanking the main door on the W. Plain Gothic detail handled with no great sophistication, but the ogee hoodmoulds over the doors (in the centre of the W front and the r. bay of the S) hint at frivolity.

In 1810 Lady Mary changed her architect, employing *James Gillespie Graham* to complete Hamilton's work and convert the C18 house into the semblance of a 'priory'. Graham hid its S front behind a Gothick firescreen with immensely tall crocketed pinnacles on the octagonal buttresses which mark the centre and ends. Airy parapet pierced by hexagons. Three-light Perp windows rising through two storeys (the intervening floors masked by blind panels). Surprisingly powerful in this context is the Romanesque door with two orders of chevron ornament. Graham's work did not turn the corner, so the E front showed two very domestic late C18 canted bay projections.

Minor alterations were made in 1833 by Lady Mary's heir, the fourth Earl of Glasgow. In 1871 his grandson, the sixth Earl, removed the last visible signs of the C18 house, employing *William Little* to recast the E front in ecclesiastical dress, the r. bay's upper floor rebuilt as the E end of a chapel under a squat lucarned spire. At the same time Little added a large

* Assisted by *James Cleland*.

service range at the back, dominated by a tall tower with a spired angle turret. The contrast in spirit as well as detail with the work of 1809–13 is instructive, although Little's addition of a *porte cochère* to the Gothick Hall's s front was carefully detailed to be in keeping. This *porte cochère* was moved to the w front in 1920, when *Reginald Fairlie* restored the main entrance to that side. Sadly, it hides Hamilton's hoodmould.

The interior is now derelict, and a description must be more of what used to be than of what survives intact. In the Gothick Hall a plaster fan-vaulted ceiling, the fans forming a cove, central pendants hanging from the flat. This, like the other Gothick plasterwork in the house, is probably by *Andrew Bean*, who was paid for work here in 1812.* The contemporary Gothick doorpiece, blind arcading on the e wall, and s wall's canopied niches were obliterated in 1920, when *Fairlie* opened the dummy windows and introduced Lorimerian panelling. In the w window, armorial STAINED GLASS of 1812 by *W.R. Eginton.* – E of the Gothick Hall is a vestibule divided into aisles by a deep screen of clustered columns. Plaster tierceron vaults springing from corbels modelled as jolly human heads. Central door in the e wall (made in 1871 when Little formed an *enfilade* through the main rooms) to the Evening Drawing Room (former dining room). Inside, a simple ribbed ceiling and Gothic chimneypiece, both of 1871. The w wall's ogee-arched niche surrounds are of 1812, moved to their present position from the N wall in 1871. Across a lobby is the Morning Drawing Room (former Chinese Room), its chimneypiece again of 1871. Dining room (former drawing room) behind, its compartmented Gothick ceiling, doorcase and chimney-piece all of 1812. Behind the vestibule is the main stairhall, D-shaped, with the geometric stair climbing round the curve; cast-iron Gothick balustrade. Armorial STAINED GLASS of 1871; the ceiling presumably contemporary. Oak stairhall to the E, the wooden staircase an 1871 mixture of Gothic and Baroque; top-lit through abstract stained-glass panels. This was the access to the chapel of 1871. Arch-braced roof. In the semi-octagonal e end, STAINED-GLASS figures of saints. Overall STENCILLED DECORATION by *Thomas Bonnar Jun.* Two very smart bedrooms above the Gothick Hall. In the Psyche Room, wallpaper panels of Cupid and Psyche, a design first produced by *Dufour* in 1816 and perhaps placed here in 1833, a likely date for the anthemion and palmette frieze and coved ceiling. The adjoining state bedroom's opulently plastered cove is of 1871.

STABLES of c.1875 to the N, plain Gothic. – Enjoyable NORTH LODGE, a toy fort of c.1813 with a thoughtless recent addition.

MAUSOLEUM. *See* Kirkton of Cults.

* But *Alexander Arthur*, of Cupar, was also paid for plasterwork in 1813.

CREICH

Ruins of a church and tower house with only a farm for company.

CREICH PARISH CHURCH. *See* Brunton.

FLISK AND CREICH FREE CHURCH. *See* Brunton.

ST DEVENIC. Roofless. Skinny rubble-built rectangle, probably C14, with a transeptal s chapel added in the early C16. The N wall's E window is a round-headed lancet; obtusely pointed door near the s wall's W end. Both these features are probably original. The other openings are post-Reformation, some Georgian. The top of the W gable has been rebuilt incorporating a stone dated 1621.

Only the lower courses of the s chapel's ashlar walling survive. Blocked door from the church; round-arched with chamfered shafts and heavy moulded capitals. In the N wall, two round-headed tomb recesses, probably of *c.*1500. The W has two rows of rosettes on its roll and hollow mouldings; the E has lost its enrichment.

In the churchyard, well-lettered early C19 HEADSTONES. – In the SE corner, a Greek Doric aedicule to Magdalene Rachel Walker † 1874. – In the NE corner, cast-iron monument to David Wallace † 1826; undersized urn on a tall plinth.

CREICH CASTLE. Rubbly remains of a large C16 tower house sitting beside a farm steading. A 'castell' was recorded here in 1537, but the present building looks rather later. L-plan with a three-storey main block and four-storey jamb; stairtower in the inner angle. Corbelled parapet which formed rounds at the s corners. Vaulted ground floor inside. The adjoining C19 farmhouse's s gable may incorporate part of the BARMKIN wall. Also probably part of the barmkin the harled circular outbuilding to the W. – In the pantiled steading, a lectern DOOCOT dated 1723.

CROMBIE

Hamlet begun as housing for workers at the Admiralty Laboratory of 1912 to the s. Garden City whinstone-rubble housing facing the main road, by *H.M. Office of Works*, 1915.

PRIMARY SCHOOL. By *J. G. Storrar*, 1924; extended by *George Sandilands*, 1937.

CROMBIE POINT

Small C18 group beside the Forth.

Partly derelict, partly over-restored row down the hill to the shore. CROMBIE POINT HOUSE at the bottom, with scrolled skewputts. On the bank above, STRIPESIDE HOUSE pushes out a bow-ended wing. Further W, the WALLED GARDEN of

Craigflower (*see* Torryburn), with built-in heraldic stones. C18 GARDENER'S LODGE, again with scrolled skewputts.

CROSSGATES 1080

An overgrown village without much charm or any definite centre.

MOSSGREEN CROSSGATES CHURCH, Church Place. Built as a Burgher chapel, 1801–2. Minimally Gothic. Blind quatrefoil in the W gable, which supports a small birdcage bellcote.
PRIMARY SCHOOL, Dunfermline Road. By *R. H. Motion*, 1920.

CROSSHILL *see* BALLINGRY, LOCHORE AND CROSSHILL

CRUIVIE CASTLE 4020
3.8km. NW of Leuchars

Roofless remains of the L-plan tower built for the Ramsays *c.* 1500. Unusually, the first-floor entrance is not in the inner angle but near the S end of the W wall. Both in the main block and the SE jamb, the ground and first floors have been covered by a high stone vault divided horizontally by a wooden entresol. The straight stair from the first floor was contained in the thickness of the main block's E wall.

CULROSS 3080

Steeply sloping ultra-picturesque burgh beside the Forth (but separated from the water by a railway line), the showpiece of the National Trust for Scotland's early concern to preserve Scottish towns as much as the grander country houses.

The Cistercian monastery on the hilltop was founded by Malcolm, Earl of Fife, at the beginning of the C13, and the town's first formal existence was in 1490, when it was made a burgh of barony dependent on the Abbey. In 1575 the Abbey's lay commendator sold a lease of its disused colliery to George Bruce, who reopened and extended the coal workings. There followed about fifty years of prosperity, a trade in coal and salt being conducted with the Netherlands as well as other parts of Scotland. In 1592 Culross was made a royal burgh by James VI, who also granted the town a monopoly of the manufacture of iron girdles used for making scones. Decline set in after the flooding of Bruce's Moat Pit at the lowest part of the foreshore in 1625. The girdle industry, falling in importance by the late C17, lost its monopoly in 1727 and was killed by the Carron Iron Co.'s introduction of cheaper machine-made girdles. The Earl

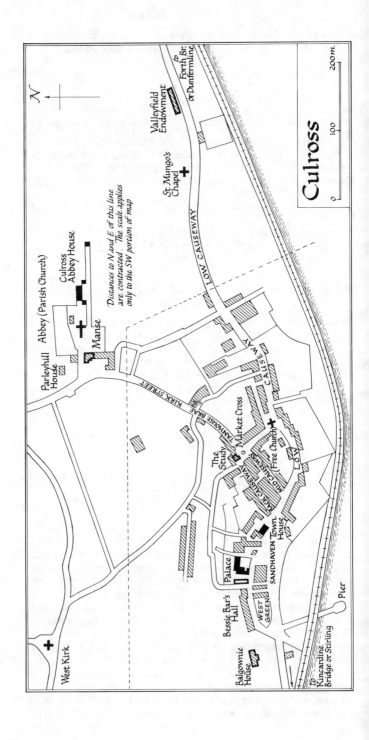

Culross

N

Distances to N and E of this line are contracted. The scale applies only to the SW portion of map

West Kirk

Parleyhill House

Culross Abbey (Parish Church)

Culross Abbey House

Manse

St Mungo's Chapel

Valleyfield Endowment

to Forth Br. or Dunfermline

LOW CAUSEWAY

KIRK STREET

TANHOUSE BRAE

The Study

Market Cross

(Free Church)

BACK CAUSEWAY

MID CAUSEWAY

LOW CAUSEWAY

Balgownie House

Bessie Bar's Hall

Palace

WEST GREEN

SANDHAVEN

Town House

to Kincardine Bridge or Stirling

Pier

0   100   200m.

View of Culross from the south, engraved by John Slezer, 1693 (RCAHMS)

of Dundonald's attempt in the late C18 to found a naphtha industry here proved unsuccessful. In 1865 *The Imperial Gazetteer of Scotland* gave a telling description of the town:

It has a picturesque and pleasing appearance as seen from the frith; but it is scattered, dingy, mean, and decayed within itself, the mere skeleton of an ancient town, almost destitute of any attraction, excepting some architectural antiquities. Most of its houses are shabby, and all its streets or lanes are in disrepair. It was once a place of great thoroughfare ... but it now sits in loneliness, encompassed in the near distance by tumultuous traffic, yet itself scarcely ever visited by either trader or tourist.

In 1909 Jessie M. King published her drawings of the burgh's buildings in romantic decay, if not actual dereliction, as *Dwellings of an Old-World Town*, but this publicity did nothing immediately to halt the decay. However, in 1932, at the urging of Dr James S. Richardson, the Inspector of Ancient Monuments for Scotland, the newly formed National Trust for Scotland acquired Culross Palace, then under threat of demolition. Next year the Trust bought another ten C16 and C17 buildings in the town's centre, and it has since restored more than thirty houses to a formula provided by *Ian G. Lindsay* which accompanied complete renewal of interiors with the lavish application of harling to the outsides. The 'little houses' thus created are instantly recognizable and internationally famous.

Culross' population is still little more than five hundred and local industry non-existent, but the working railway carrying coal along the foreshore and the dour council houses on top of the hill (the Burgh Council never showed much interest in 'conservation') preclude the town from being used as a film set.

CULROSS ABBEY (PARISH CHURCH)

Malcolm, Earl of Fife, founded the Cistercian monastery of Culross *c.*1215, the first monks being imported from Kinloss Abbey (Grampian) three years later. Originally a foundation of choir-monks and lay brothers, each group occupying its own part of the cloister and church, by the late C15 it seems to have been reorganized like other Cistercian houses as a community of choir-monks only. Consequently the nave (lay brothers' choir) became redundant and was demolished, *c.*1500, by Abbot Andrew Masoun, who finished off the choir with a tall W tower and also began the addition of a N aisle. After the Reformation the cloister buildings were abandoned and the choir taken over as the parish church, this status being legally established in 1633. The usual reconstruction of the interior to fit in galleries followed, whilst the exterior was altered to suit the new internal arrangements. In 1905–6 *R. Rowand Anderson* carried out an extensive restoration, making of the exterior a careful version of its late medieval appearance and providing a polite High Presbyterian interior.

The C13 church, unusual in that it had no aisles (but cf. Balmerino Abbey), consisted of two-bay retrochoir or vestibule and four-bay nave cut off by a rood screen and pulpitum from the four-bay monastic choir. Transepts projected from the choir, the S conventionally aligned with the E range of the cloister, whose W range abutted the retrochoir.

The S wall of the retrochoir and nave survives. At the W end, a buttress with a roll-moulded NW corner. Two doors (built up) from the retrochoir: round-arched processional door; on its E, the taller segmental-arched door from the night stair. Of the nave's chamfered wall-shafts, only the W survives as much more than a base. In the E bay, a rectangular credence

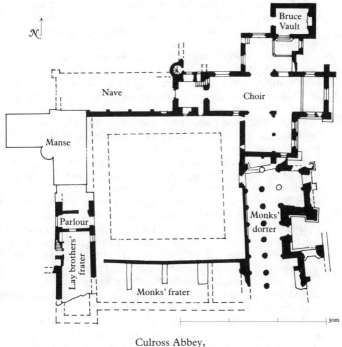

Culross Abbey,
plan

locker, originally double but converted to a single aumbry. Above, set high up so as to clear the cloister roof, part of a window jamb.

16   Abbot Masoun's tower of *c.* 1500 was built on top of existing stone walls (rood screen on the W, pulpitum on the E, and the church's side walls on N and S), which he strengthened internally. So the lower part of its W face, now the entrance front of the parish church, incorporates the late C13 rood screen. This had a door each side of the central altar, to whose S is a niche (? a piscina) heavily restored in cement. Masoun blocked the side doors and made a new opening where the altar had stood. His round-arched doorway with nook-shafts looks

C13, and he may have moved the original W door of the nave to serve as the entrance to the curtailed church. Above, he provided a semicircular niche, perhaps for a tympanum moved here from the old W front at the same time. On each side is a rectangular recess. They look like blocked doors, but if they are part of Masoun's work, what was their purpose? The blocked door beside the r. recess is clearly a post-Reformation slapping for access to a gallery. A roof raggle provided on this W front suggests that Masoun may have had some intention of rebuilding the nave. At the tower's NW corner, a round stairtower with a raggle on its E face for the roof of a N choir aisle. The aisle's W window is represented by a jamb against the stairtower. Door (now a window) into the aisle from the tower. The remainder of the aisle, perhaps never completed, has disappeared.

The tower's upper stages rise without intakes but with the belfry neatly defined by stringcourses, the upper forming a hoodmould over the round-arched openings. Above the belfry, small circular windows containing radiating and spiralling loop tracery. The corbelling of the angle rounds is of *c.*1500, but the high crenellated parapet and bartizans were added in 1823 by *William Stirling*. He placed in each bartizan a crocketed pinnacle, but these were removed in 1905.

The choir's cubical ashlar walling seems to be C13, but most of the detail is of 1905. Anderson reopened the medieval windows (themselves probably C15 insertions), which had been infilled with two tiers of openings to suit a galleried interior, and inserted new tracery. He rebuilt the S transept on the old foundations and replaced the nave's piended E end with a gable. He also rebuilt the E wall of the Bruce Aisle which had been built on the site of the medieval N transept in 1642, together with the crowstepped Bruce Vault projecting from its NE corner, these additions both having round-arched doors and Doric pilastered frames round the inscriptions recording their erection by Sir George Bruce of Carnock.

INTERIOR. Under the tower, rib-vaulted vestibule with a circular bell-hole. In the N wall, semi-elliptical headed door (now window) of three orders to the missing N aisle. Over the W wall's hoodmoulded rere-arch, Masoun's initials and coat of arms held by an angel. The panel above carved with grotesque faces gnawing a vine branch is presumably not *in situ*. The E wall is the reconstructed C13 pulpitum opening into the choir through a semicircular-arched doorway under a hood-mould whose r. corbel-stop is a battered human head.

Anderson's restoration covered the choir with a wagon roof, stripped plaster from the ashlar walls and uncovered and repaired medieval features. Two aumbries in the S wall. Arch into the S transept with keel-moulded shafts, the E capital carved with stiffleaf foliage. To its E, a broad low arch punched through the wall in the C15 to frame an effigy (now missing). To the transept's E chapel its hoodmould displays two shields, one carved with the de Quincy arms. In Anderson's reconstruction, a two-bay arcade was provided from the transept to the chapel. He did the same for the Bruce Aisle on the N. This opens into the choir by a lower arch whose shafts seem to be C14 replacements, with a filleted central roll awkwardly adjusted to the capitals. Beside it, minimally pointed arch to the E chapel, again the frame for a monument. Its ogee hoodmould and flanking pinnacled buttresses survive on the N, the buttresses half-heartedly replaced on the N. The monument is to John Stewart of Innermeath, Lord of Lorn,† 1445, and his wife. Of his armour-clad effigy the trunk survives; hers is almost complete except for the head.

The Bruce Vault of 1642 to the NE is covered with a steep-pointed tunnel-vault. Two huge and classy MONUMENTS. On the E wall, Sir George Bruce of Carnock †1625. It has the 32 inscription:

> THIS.IS.SIR.GEORGE.BRUCE.OF.CARNOCK.
> HIS.LADY.HIS.THREE.SONS.AND.FIVE.DAUG
> HTERS.THIS.TOMB.WAS.PROVIDED.BY.GEORG
> E.BRUCE.OF.CARNOCK.HIS.ELDEST.SON

On the base is recorded the name of the mason responsible: IOHN MERCER FECIT. The monument is a very grand combination of the two standard early C17 types, the tomb recess and the aedicule. Deep tomb recess framed by Doric piers containing alabaster effigies of Bruce and his wife, both looking very dead. Around the base are placed alabaster figures of his kneeling children. All these figures are highly accomplished sculpture, probably imported from England, perhaps from an artist connected with Nicholas Stone's workshop.* Above, the inscription framed by swags dangling the Bruce and Primrose arms, hourglasses, skulls and crossbones, set in a Corinthian columned aedicule, its frieze decorated with more emblems of mortality. Above the cornice, the Bruce arms in a strapwork surround flanked by obelisks. Crowning pediment broken by a finial carved with the skull and crossbones. – On the N wall, Elizabeth Preston † 1832. Crenellated octagonal buttresses gripping a Jacobean gabled frame bearing a coat of arms carved in high relief. Within, inscription panel set in a Tudor arch studded with foliaged bosses and horses' heads (the Preston crest). – On the S wall, heraldic GRAVESLAB of Edward Bruce †1565. – Next to it, an elegant brass TABLET of c.1810 commemorating the burial of Edward Lord Bruce of Kinloss's heart near this spot and depicting the 'SILVER CASE of foreign workmanship' in which it was found in 1808.

The choir FURNISHINGS completed Anderson's reconstruction and are similarly bloodless. – Oak COMMUNION TABLE, Jacobean of 1906. – Contemporary canopied Jacobean PULPIT, remodelled by *Rowand Anderson & Paul* in 1923. – ORGAN by *Norman & Beard*, 1906, in a Wrenaissance case made by *Mackay & Co.* to *P. MacGregor Chalmers'* design.

STAINED GLASS. E window (Our Lady with SS Serf and

---

* *Edward Marshall* has been suggested.

Kentigern), soppy but colourful by *A. Ballantine & Son*, 1905. – Darker and stronger the N transept window (The Presentation of Christ in the Temple; The Agony in the Garden) by *Stephen Adam*, 1906. – Gaudy window in the Bruce Aisle, *c.* 1960. – Abstract tower window (The Resurrection) by *Sadie McLennan*, 1963.

The CLOISTER lay as usual to the S of the church. The sloping ground was terraced so that the cloister garth (now the Manse's back garden) was on the same level as the church, but the surrounding buildings required very tall undercrofts to raise their upper floor to this level. The W range contained the lay brothers' frater with their dorter above. Its N part was replaced in 1637 by the parish MANSE. Originally of two storeys, the crowstepped main block was given an extra floor, probably in 1752 (the date on a dormer pediment). Crow-stepped NW wing added by *William Stirling*, 1824. The round stairtower in the inner angle is probably C17. S of the manse, C13 walling. Elaborate door to a quadripartite-vaulted manse or parlour which originally opened into a room on the N from which a stair went down to the undercroft. Rising over the doorway is the projecting line of steps of the dorter stair, climbing within the wall thickness and reached by a small door from the outer court on the W. Beside this, a larger door into the frater. Both are set in a wall recess. Of the frater's interior there remain three bays of quadripartite vaulting, the ribs springing from corbels. The room under the frater may have been the kitchen. It is tunnel-vaulted, but a corbel on the N wall suggests that applied ribs were intended. In the W wall, a slop sink beside the door into a latrine. The range has had a lean-to W wing, probably a late medieval addition.

Of the S range containing the monks' frater only the under-croft's N wall survives. The remains of corbels show that it contained two quadripartite-vaulted rooms, a seven-bay hall under the frater and a two-bay chamber, presumably under the warming room. The E range, containing the monks' dorter and chapter house, is rather more substantial. It is U-plan with two short E wings. In the undercroft, a seven-bay twin-aisled hall with the N wing making a third aisle for the end bay. Again it has been quadripartite-vaulted. Octagonal piers down the centre. Semi-octagonal wall-responds in the N wall and wing; the other responds are keel-shaped. Its N end supports a frag-ment of the chapter house's W wall containing a window and part of a door, quite elaborate, with arch mouldings of three orders and bold dogtooth ornament on the hoodmould.

GRAVEYARD to the N of the church. On the wall of the old nave, a very worn Artisan Mannerist monument, pilastered and segmental-pedimented. – Behind the N transept, tomb-stone of Martha Rich † 1820, inscribed

> A soul prepared needs no delays
> The summons comes the saint obeys
> Swift was her flight and short the road
> She closed her eyes and said my God

– Against the church's E gable, a small early C19 Gothic burial enclosure. – On the graveyard's N wall, some C18 aedicular monuments. The best, with a barley-sugar Corinthian column on the r., angels, drapery and emblems of mortality, seems to have been left unfinished. – Next to it, a big correct Corinthian aedicule to Christian Geddes † 1830.

CHURCHES

CULROSS FREE CHURCH, Low Causeway. Now flats. A big box of 1847 with sparing Jacobean detail. Chunky bellcote on the E gable. – Behind, STEPHEN MEMORIAL HALL, institutional Gothic, dated 1883.

PARISH CHURCH. *See* Culross Abbey, above.

ST MUNGO'S CHAPEL (property of the National Trust for Scotland), 0.5km. E of the town. Excavation in 1926 revealed the lower parts of the N, E and W walls of the small church built by Robert Blackadder, Archbishop of Glasgow, *c.*1500. Externally, they are ashlar-faced with a splayed basecourse. The S wall is a C20 reconstruction. Semi-octagonal E end, the chancel divided from the nave by a stone rood screen.* The high altar was raised on two steps with quirked edge rolls. The base for a stone bench survives against the nave's N wall. In the W gable, an off-centre chamfered door.

WEST KIRK, 0.8km. NW of the town. Roofless remains of the medieval parish church abandoned in the C16. It has been a skinny rectangle, but the only original detail to survive is a small rectangular window on the l. of the S door. That door and the opposite N door are insertions, perhaps early C17, their internal lintels formed by medieval graveslabs incised with swords. Other medieval fragments have been incorporated in repairs to the walls. Set into the E end, three C16 graveslabs carved with coats of arms. Crowstepped C17 burial aisle (now roofless) on the S: mullioned square-headed S and W windows; broad semi-elliptical arch into the church. In its N gable, fragments from monuments, including a Bruce coat of arms.

The surrounding GRAVEYARD contains plenty of C17 and C18 headstones decorated with skulls and crossbones. The best are on the S of the church: near its W end, pedimented stone to Robert Scott, dated 1794, carved with a ship; further E, curly topped stone dated 1722 to Robert Anderson, with a crowned hammer. Next to Anderson's stone, graveslab of John Callendar † 1664, with a coat of arms.

PUBLIC BUILDINGS

MARKET CROSS, The Cross. Octagonal four-stepped base of *c.*1600. The rest is by *J. W. Small*,‡ 1902. Chamfered shaft supporting a square pilastered top, on whose faces *Alexander Neilson* carved the arms of the burgh, of James VI (its founder),

---

* Remains of altars built against it were found in 1926.
‡ *William Gauldie* was executant architect.

of Sir James Sivewright (who financed the Cross's restoration) and of Provost Cunningham. Unicorn finial based on that of Stirling Market Cross.

86 TOWN HOUSE, Sandhaven. As built in 1626 (the date on a ground-floor lintel), this was a solidly domestic crowstepped affair of brownish stone. Symmetrical five-bay first floor with moulded window margins; attic openings squeezed under the cavetto cornice. The tall steeple added in 1783 is self-consciously smart. Polished grey ashlar with rusticated quoins; round-arched and keyblocked belfry openings; fluted frieze; steep ogee roof. Presumably the double forestair is of the same date. So too looks the bellcote on the W gable; but why the need for two bells?

Inside, first-floor vestibule, its ceiling beams painted with early C17 conventional foliage. Built into one wall, part of a C17 dormerhead carved with the burgh arms. The r. room's ceiling has more early C17 decoration, its beams and boards painted with *putti* heads and stars. Built into the E wall, a C17 stone panel vigorously carved with the arms of Sir George Bruce. Hung over the fireplace is a panel painted with the royal arms of Charles I and dated 1637. In the opposite wall, a stone panel recording Sir George Preston of Valleyfield's bequest. In the W room, panelling with a dentil cornice, perhaps of 1783.

VALLEYFIELD ENDOWMENT, Low Causeway. Almshouse founded by Sir Robert Preston of Valleyfield; now housing. Dated 1830. Long and low, with a large coat of arms in the pediment over the two-bay centre. Hoodmoulded doors and windows.

PERAMBULATION

In LOW CAUSEWAY on the approach from the E, CULROSS PRIMARY SCHOOL (by *Fife County Council*, 1961) is an unwelcoming host. NEWGATE HOUSE opposite, with scrolled skewputts and a door lintel dated 1746, introduces the thick white harl and orange pantiles which have become hallmarks of the National Trust for Scotland's restoration of Culross as a showpiece burgh. But this is still the town's outskirts, so the adjoining crowstepped house, bearing the plausible date of 1747 on an inset stone, is drydashed and slated (it must have been thatched originally). Then a very smart early C19 villa (ST KENTIGERN'S) with incised Soanean ornament on its angle pilasters. The S side begins in earnest opposite the old Free Church (*see above*) with THE HAVEN, dated 1623 on a skewputt. L-plan with the roof swept down over the projecting jamb, whose delicate moulded doorpiece looks C18. The crowstepped gable of the C18 RED LION INN makes an effective marker for the street's bend to the r. Round the corner, a couple of straightforward houses, the first dated 1788 on a lintel, the other probably contemporary but with a small inset stone carved with a monogram and the date 1676. The

crowstep-gabled house next door may date from the late
C17.

MID CAUSEWAY, uncomfortably but picturesquely cobbled,
climbs the hill to the N. On its w corner, a small C17 house
whose crowsteps appear ridiculously tall for the pantiles which
have replaced its thatched roof, was restored as an electricity
sub-station by *Ian G. Lindsay* in 1962. Another harled and
pantiled house, probably C18, on its N. Simple C18 houses on
the street's E side until BISHOP LEIGHTON'S HOUSE. This
is early C17, with its first floor partly jettied. Attached to its s
gable, a humbler contemporary; its first-floor windows squashed under the eaves may once have had dormerheads. The
house on the N is of *c*.1600, probably the remodelling of an
earlier house whose forestair has been incorporated into the
main block. Most windows with chamfered arrises, but on the
l. of the present door a moulded (blocked) door, the stones of
one of its jambs shared with a small window. The DUN-
DONALD ARMS opposite is a prosaic mid-Victorian intruder,
but C17 quaintness continues with THE ARK at the NE corner
of LITTLE CAUSEWAY, again with a roll-moulded door contrasting with the windows' chamfered arrises. Same door and
window detail on its crowstep-gable-fronted neighbour (dated
1609 on a first-floor lintel) in Little Causeway. More crowsteps
and a forestair on THE NUNNERY below.

THE CROSS forms a triangular meeting place for the streets
which have ascended from the shore. For the Market Cross
itself, *see* Public Buildings, above. On the triangle's N side, a
large-scale block of 1909 with prominent dormerheads. On the
s, a crowstepped gable-fronted house; the stone dated 1577
under its l. skewputt may be *in situ*. On the w is the harled,
crowstepped and pantiled THE STUDY. Early C17 three-   89
storey main block, with the second-floor windows rising above
the eaves as swept dormers. The fenestration was originally
arranged in a 2/1 grouping but is now disturbed by the insertion of a door and first-floor window, probably in the C18. On
the l., a projecting gabled stairtower with its jettied top floor
rising above the main block. Inside, the first-floor room's
beamed ceiling is of 1966–7, brightly painted with fruit and   90
flowers by *Alexander McNeish* under the direction of *Ian
Hodkinson*, the design supposedly a reconstruction of the original decoration, which was thought too damaged to restore.
On the tower's s front, a corbelled-out turret containing the
stair to the top.

TANHOUSE BRAE leading out of The Cross towards the Abbey
begins with a pink-harled C17 house. Projection on its r. containing a door (now a window), its lintel inscribed

Ο ΘΕΟΣ ΠΡΟΝΟΕΙ Χ. ΠΡΟΝΟΗΣΕΙ
[God provides and will provide]

After a house of *c*.1700 with a forestair, THE TANNER'S
HOUSE, with chamfered window margins and an inset stone
whose right half, inscribed I.S/I.L/1664, may give its building

date. Opposite, the single-storey and basement SHOEMAKERS COTTAGE; the lintel of its r. door is dated 1669, but the main door's keyblocked lugged architrave and the fat eaves cornice look thirty years later. Another chunky cornice on SNUFF COTTAGE, C18 in its present form, with a keyblocked segmental-arched door and another keyblock on the round-headed window squeezed under the eaves above, but a skew-putt on the S gable shows that it was originally a single-storey building, perhaps of the C17. On the corner of ERSKINE BRAE, a mid-C19 Tudor School converted into a house.

KIRK STREET makes the final ascent to the Abbey. COACH-MAN'S COTTAGE on its r., reconstructed and given a pilastered doorpiece in the early C19, has ground-floor windows of c.1600. The Abbey Church and Manse (see above) form a villagey group with the former GEDDES INSTITUTION of c.1800, a domestic-looking school (now house) whose windows have been enlarged to double lights. Further up the hill to the N, PARLEYHILL HOUSE, smart of c.1700 with flattened bullseye windows in the shaped gables and a corniced door-piece on massive brackets.

BACK CAUSEWAY leads downhill from The Cross. Set back from its W side, the harled MACDONALDS BUILDINGS by *Wheeler & Sproson*, 1970, a tall stripped version of the Culross vernacular. In the lower part of the street, more harled and pantiled C17 buildings, FERGUSON'S HOUSE at the bottom with a forestair.

86 SANDHAVEN'S E part is open to the S, with the Town House (see above) overlooking an informal square in which stands the stone base of the burgh tron. Behind the Town House and to its W, a crowstepped, harled and pantiled group leading to a late C17 house. Sundial on its crowstepped gable to the street; roll-moulded door in the close at the side. At the end of the close, a couple of stores, probably C17, their unharled rubble a welcome relief. The next house in Sandhaven is probably of c.1600 but has a second floor added in the C18.

87 CULROSS PALACE (property of the National Trust for Scotland) is a compound of buildings put up by the mine-owner George Bruce of Culross (later of Carnock) in the late C16 and early C17. Probably he acquired and developed the site piecemeal. There is no evidence of grand architectural intent, although the present harled walls and pantiled roofs give the buildings a slightly spurious unity.

To the street a screen wall with corniced ball-finialled gate-piers into a courtyard, its W and N sides filled by Bruce's buildings. The W range's S part is a roughly symmetrical U-plan whose three-storey N jamb, with smart pedimented dormerheads on its S front (the centre one carved with Bruce's initials and the date 1597), seems to contain a remodelled earlier two-storey house, apparently consisting originally of a hall and chamber above a kitchen and store. It was probably at the same time as he reconstructed this house that Bruce added to it a new two-storey L-plan block on the S, with

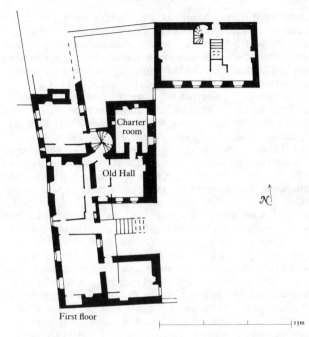

First floor

|15m

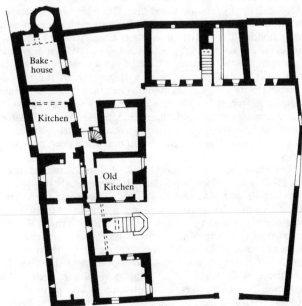

Ground floor

Culross Palace,
plans of ground and first floors

pedimented dormerheads on the S jamb's inner face and a
forestair to the centre block. Contemporary or near-con-
temporary with this work were the addition of a turnpike stair
and plain two-storey extension on the N of the original house's
hall and kitchen, and the building of a new kitchen and bakehouse range to the N of the original chamber and store.

The present principal entrance is from the forestair's
landing. A blocked door to its r. may have been the entrance
provided by Bruce. Inside, the main block's first floor was
originally a single long gallery but was divided in the early
C18. In its S room, early C18 panelling. The N room's large
moulded fireplace looks of c.1600. Off the NW corner, a garderobe. The room in the S jamb has some boards with painted
strapwork decoration of the late C16 or early C17 on its end
walls. The N jamb's room (the putative hall of the earlier
house) has more early C18 panelling but also lining and a door
with stencilled panels enclosing foliage patterns of c.1600. In
the ceiling, two short lengths of beams painted with fruit are
of the same period. Opening off this room to the N is an ashlar-
vaulted charter room with an iron door in its internal stone
porch. In the walls, a couple of aumbries which have had
doors. Tiled floor to complete the fire-proofing, but there is a
fireplace, so the room was meant for work as well as storage.
In the N room above Bruce's new kitchen, more early C18
panelling and a basket-arched fireplace in a lugged architraved
surround. On the second floor, the room added by Bruce over
the original hall has lavish painted decoration on its ceiling and
walls divided into panels filled with allegorical or Scriptural
subjects, accompanied by moralizing texts. On the ground
floor, the vaulted N room, entered from a small courtyard on
its E, was the bakehouse, with a large oven in the N wall.
Kitchen to its S with a segmental-vaulted ceiling and a huge
segmental-arched fireplace. Slop drain against the W wall.
More drains in the stone-flagged floor. Under the charter
room, another segmental-vaulted room. The self-contained
room with a fireplace in the S jamb may have been a porter's
lodge.

The main courtyard's N side is filled with a detached three-
storey four-bay block. Pedimented dormerheads dressed up
with scrolls and rose and thistle finials; one has the initials
SGB (for Sir George Bruce), another the date 1611. Lower
two-storey extension on the E. The interior is remarkable for
the surviving wealth of its painted decoration. The first-floor
W room's ceiling beams and boards are painted with fruit, very
much like the contemporary Gladstone's Land (Edinburgh).
On the E wall, traces of a painting of the Judgement of
Solomon. Central closet, its walls and ceiling painted with
strapwork. More fruit on the E room's ceiling; on its walls, a
deep frieze of foliage in strapwork panels. On the second floor,
both the main rooms have segmental-vaulted wooden ceilings
and bed-recesses in the central wall. Above the springing of
the vault, the W room's ceiling and end walls are painted with

stylized foliage in strapwork panels. Below, rectangular panels containing geometric designs. In the E room, the ceiling and upper part of the end walls painted with geometric patterns and circles of naturalistic fruit. Some arabesqued ceiling boards in the closet between.

w of Culross Palace, a sizeable malthouse (BESSIE BAR'S HALL) dated 1776, with a forestair at its gable whose top contains a pointed-arched window. To the S, a superior two-storey and attic house, its E side with two steeply pedimented dormers, the l. with a thistle finial, the r. inscribed

R

PK   MB

16   36

A first-floor door (now a window) shows that it has had a forestair. At the town's w end, octagonal pavilion (by *Robert Hurd & Partners*, 1973) containing public lavatories, followed by a large vaulted ICEHOUSE of the early C19. Opposite, BAL-GOWNIE HOUSE (now Inchkeith School), large and plain of *c*.1840 with a heavy doorpiece. On the E of its garden, remains of a rectangular house, probably C17, with a stairtower projecting from its S wall.

CULROSS ABBEY HOUSE
off Kirk Street

A recasting by *Robert Hurd & Partners*, 1954–6, of the C17 house of the Bruces of Kinloss (later Earls of Elgin). That house was L-shaped, perhaps originally intended to be a rectangular mansion round a courtyard. Its ashlar-fronted S block built by Edward, first Lord Bruce of Kinloss, was a piece of proto-classicism unparalleled in Britain. Two-storey thirteen-bay S front with a short wing projecting at each end. All absolutely regular, the ground-floor windows architraved, the first-floor windows set in aedicules whose attenuated Tuscan pilasters stand on moulded corbels; in the thistle-finialled pediments, the initials of Bruce and his wife Magdalen. First-floor stringcourse. Cannon spouts piercing the moulded eaves cornice. The N front seems to have been just as regular and has the same aedicular first-floor windows, stringcourse, and eaves cornice. *c*.1670 Robert, second Earl of Elgin, added a plain second floor and heightened the wings as four-storey ogee-roofed corner towers. Unroofed in the early C19, the main block was repaired in 1830 by Sir Robert Preston of Valleyfield, who added to the N front's pilastered doorpiece a segmental pediment carved with his coat of arms. At the same time he replaced the NW range with a piend-roofed pavilion.

In their remodelling of 1954–6 Robert Hurd & Partners removed the main block's top floor and shortened it from thirteen to nine bays, the missing ends being rebuilt as one-storey garage and kitchen links to the end towers, which were reduced to single-storey pavilions but still with ogee roofs and the lead unicorn (the Preston crest) finials of 1830 re-used. Three window aedicules from the towers were incorporated in a curvaceous attic centrepiece.

The interior is now mostly of 1954–6. C17-revival motifs applied to the coved plaster cornices of the main rooms. Wrought-iron stair balustrade decorated with roses and tulips, the design based on a stair at Caroline Park House (Edinburgh). In the drawing room, stone chimneypiece dated 1669, carved with a heavy swagged frieze and fruit on the jambs. Contemporary chimneypiece in the study, again with swags on the frieze; overmantel carved with garlands, acanthus leaves and flowers. The first-floor's s wall is stone-panelled the whole of its length. Was this side of the house (now bedrooms) a gallery in the C17? On the N wall, moulded stone window sills.

The garden on the s was terraced in the C17. At the top terrace's E end, a GARDEN HOUSE dated 1674, with fluted pilasters flanking the elliptical arch.

EAST LODGE of c. 1840, classical but with bargeboards. – Contemporary GATEPIERS surmounted by seated lions.

FARMS ETC.

BATH, 5.3km. NNW. Late C17 crowstepped and pantiled rubble-built house, its rock foundation exposed on the E. Repairs and alterations were made in 1985.

60 BLAIRHALL, 1.9km. NE. Rubble-built and harled laird's house of the late C17, characteristically narrow, with a steep-pitched roof. Moulded doorpiece on the symmetrical five-bay front. The N gable's crowsteps are missing.

EAST GRANGE, 3.4km. NE. Early C19 farmhouse with scrolled skewputts and a single-storey addition built across the front. On the w approach from the Tudor lodge of c. 1840, a large roofless lectern DOOCOT of c. 1700, with a stringcourse stepping up at the gables which contain round entry holes; a third hole above the frame for an heraldic panel over the door.

WEST GRANGE, 3.7km. N. Farmhouse of c. 1820. A smart harled villa with ashlar strip-pilasters at the corners, overarched ground-floor windows and a pilastered surround to the fanlit door. Single-storey wings.

BLAIR CASTLE. *See* p. 100.
DUNIMARLE CASTLE. *See* p. 196.

CULTS *see* KIRKTON OF CULTS

3010   CUPAR

For long the county town of Fife, Cupar was first the site of the castle of the Earls of Fife, which stood on the site of the former jail on Schoolhill. By 1213 it was the seat of a sheriff and by 1328

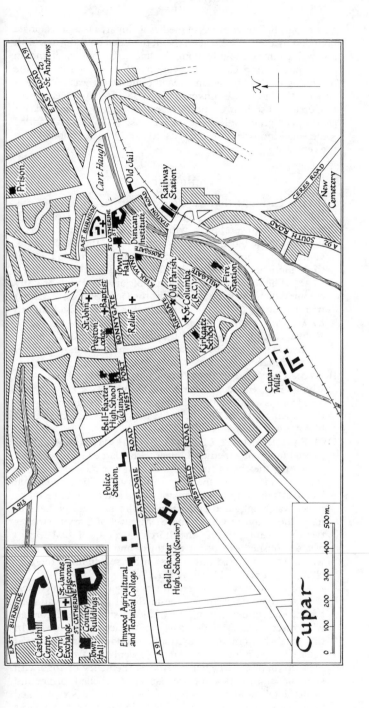

Cupar

East Burnside · A91 to St. Andrews · East Road to St. Andrews · Prison · Cart Haugh · Old Jail · Railway Station · Ceres Road · New Cemetery · South Road · A92 · East Burnside · St Catherine St. · Duncan Institute · Crossgate · Town Hall · Kirk Wynd · Fire Station · Millgate · St. John · Preston Lodge · Baptist · Bonnygate · Relief · Old Parish · St Columba (R.C.) · Kirkgate · Kirkgate School · Cupar Mills · Bell-Baxter High School (Junior) · West Port · A913 · Police Station · Carslogie Road · Westfield Road · Elmwood Agricultural and Technical College · Bell-Baxter High School (Senior) · A91

East Burnside · Castlehill Centre · Corn Exchange · St James (Episcopal) · St Catherine's · Town Hall · County Buildings

0 100 200 300 400 500 m.

N

a royal burgh. The confines of medieval Cupar, a rough rectangle bounded by the Lady Burn on the N, the Eden on the S, and with a W wall running roughly along the line of Union Street and an E wall just behind Crossgate, were hardly breached before the beginning of the C19, when St Catherine Street was laid out as an E continuation of Bonnygate. The C18 and C19 development of Cupar was solid if unspectacular as a local social and market centre, with grain milling the main industry. The C20 has added some small industries on the outskirts and plastic shopfronts in the centre.

CHURCHES

BAPTIST CHURCH (former United Presbyterian), Bonnygate. By *Peddie & Kinnear*, 1865–6. Early Gothic gable front with flanking stairtowers, the l. with a bellcast spire, the r. carried up to a gabled belfry, above which rises the slated spire. Galleried interior, the cast-iron columns going up to the roof to divide it into a wagon-roofed nave and aisles. – STAINED GLASS. The rose windows in each gable are filled with brightly coloured pictorial windows (Christ the Good Shepherd; Christ with Children) of 1875. – On the E side, King David, signed by *J. T. Stewart* of *William Meikle & Sons*, 1898. – On the W, Joshua, *c*.1950. – ORGAN by *William Hill & Son and Norman & Beard*, 1929, with a contemporary pulpit as part of the N end's arrangement.

BOSTON UNITED PRESBYTERIAN CHURCH, West Port. Now a bingo hall. Innocent Norman of 1849 by *John Dick Peddie*. The front is almost hidden by a porch added on its conversion to a cinema *c*.1920. On the gable behind, a scroll-buttressed bellcote with *fleur-de-lis* finial.

20 OLD PARISH AND ST MICHAEL OF TARVIT, Kirkgate. Disjointed union of a medieval tower with a large Georgian box.

In 1415 the site of the parish church was moved from one some distance NW of the town to Kirkgate. The new church had a 40.5 m.-long nave, flanking aisles and a NW tower. The tower was heightened and given a spire in 1620, perhaps to mark the union of Cupar and St Michael of Tarvit parishes two years before. In 1785 the church ('in a state of total decay') was demolished except for the tower and part of the N aisle, which was converted into a session house adjoining the new church designed and built by *Hay Bell*.

The unbuttressed tower built in 1415 is of rough cubical ashlar. Adjoining stump of the medieval nave's W wall containing one window jamb. This window's sill course, decorated with rosettes, is carried across the W face of the tower. In this face's bottom stage, a strange window – diamond head squashed down into a fat lancet. Deeply splayed windows high up mark the C15 belfry. Above, the belfry of 1620 with smoother stonework and paired lancets. Corbelled cornice and balustraded parapet on whose E face stands a strapworked panel dated 1620 and carved with the burgh arms. Clock faces dated 1910. Inside the parapet, a broached octagonal spire with tiers of lucarnes above and below a stone balcony.

Inside the tower, the two lower floors are vaulted. In the C15 belfry above, corbels for the bell-carriage. Bell-chamber of 1620 at the top. On the ground floor, blocked arches into the nave and aisle. On the first floor, door with a flattened ogee arch to a W nave gallery.

E of the tower is the Session House formed in 1785 from the N aisle's three W bays. The arcade to the nave survives, though built up. Octagonal W pier, the others round. Arches of two orders with chamfered edges. On the E pier, carved lion rampant supporters for a lost shield.

The church of 1785 is a broad rectangle. Perhaps it was less ungainly before the walls were raised 1.8 m. *c.* 1800. Corbelled cornice on the flanks. Urn-topped gables with small Venetian windows. Battlemented N porch added by *Morris Finlay*, 1811.

Spacious galleried interior, reseated and given a new pulpit by *James Gillespie* in 1882. – Oak FONT of 1951. – ORGAN by *Norman & Beard*, 1913; rebuilt here by *David W. Loosley*, 1983. – In the W wall, mid-C15 TOMB of a knight, covered in thick white paint. Segmental arched recess of two orders enriched with rosettes. The feet of the recumbent effigy rest on a lion eating a ram. On a shield above, arms of the Fernies of that Ilk.

STAINED GLASS. W wall. 'Love one Another' by *Stephen Adam Studios*, 1915–16. – The Good Shepherd by *A. Ballantine & Son*, 1911. – S wall. The Agony in the Garden, 1910. – The Wordie and Mackie memorials ('Render Therefore Unto Caesar'; 'Behold I Stand at the Door') are an unattributed pair of 1886–7. – Between them, the Cochrane memorials (The Maries at the Tomb; 'Suffer Little Children') by *James Ballantine & Son*, 1874–5. – Also by *James Ballantine & Son* (1882) are the Wemyss and Graham memorials at gallery level, their primary-coloured foliage a relief from the pictorial moralizing of the rest. – Moon memorial ('Blessed Are the Pure in Heart') of 1911, competent but repulsive. – E wall. Millar memorial signed by *William Meikle & Sons*, 1896.

MONUMENTS in the graveyard. Against the church's E wall, graveslab of Thomas Crichton †1619, covered with carved heraldry. – SW of the church, curly-topped stone carved in low 38 relief with two heads and a hand. The inscription explains:

Here lies Interred the Heads of LAUR.CE HAY and ANDREW PITULLOCH who Suffered martyrdom at EDIN.R July 13th 1681 for adhering to the word of GOD & Scotlands covenanted work of Reformation: and also one of the Hands of DAVID HACKSTON of Rathillot who was most cruelly murdered at EDIN.R July 30th 1680 for the same cause

On the back, another inscription:

Our persecutors fill'd with rage
Their brutish fury to aswage,
Took heads & hands of martyrs off
That they might be the peoples scoff

They Hackstons body cutt asunder
And set it up a worlds wonder
In several places to proclaim
These monsters gloryd in their shame
RE-ERECTED
July 13th 1792

– On the W, three C17 monuments. The first (to 'A.G.') is
dated 1676: aedicule with barley-sugar columns, skulls on the
ends of the curvaceous pediment. – In the enclosure behind,
ogee-pedimented Tod monument with the dates 1671 and
1685 and emblems of death in the tympanum. – To the N,
William Scott †1642, a grand aedicule with Angels of the
Resurrection trumpeting over a coat of arms.

In Kirk Wynd to the NE, SABBATH SCHOOL HALL built
in 1878 and looking like a church itself.

RELIEF CHAPEL, Provost Wynd. Secularized. Piend-roofed
two-storey rectangle of 1830. Inside, the U-plan gallery's panelled front survived conversion to an old people's centre in
1975.

ST COLUMBA (R.C.), Kirkgate. By *Peter Whiston*, 1964. Small
harled version of the Liverpool Cathedral wigwam. Prominent
slated roof and very tall central 'chimney'-spire.

ST JAMES (Episcopal), St Catherine Street. 1866, by *R. Rowand
Anderson*. Very simple; nave, W aisle and one-bay chancel. In
the S (entrance) gable, window of five lancet lights under
a small rose window. Interior lit from gables and coupled
clearstorey lights. Round-arched arcade, the piers with foliaged capitals.

PULPIT by *Anderson*, 1901, Artisan Mannerist revival. –
Brass eagle LECTERN of *c.*1890. – Richly carved ROOD SCREEN
and hanging ROOD, and a simpler wooden REREDOS, all by
Robert S. Lorimer, *c.*1920. – STAINED-GLASS N window (The
Ascension), *c.*1960, sketchily drawn and unpleasantly
coloured. – ORGAN by *J. R. Miller*, 1876.

ST JOHN, Bonnygate. Originally Cupar Free Church. Huge
snecked rubble box by *Campbell Douglas & Sellars*, 1875–8.
In the gable front's centre, a massive smooth steeple, its tall
belfry stage's octagonal shape masked by pinnacles at the
angles. Bands of quatrefoils on the spire. Transeptal stairtowers each side. Galleried interior.

ST MICHAEL, West Port. Now a school gymnasium. Built as a
chapel of ease in 1837. Buttressed box with a spired bellcote
and crenellated porch on the crowstepped gable. Inside, a S
gallery. Large Tudor Gothic ceiling rose.

PUBLIC BUILDINGS

ADAMSON HOSPITAL, Bank Street. Cottage-picturesque of
1904. W addition by *Walker & Pride*, 1935. Rather better the
brown brick HEALTH CENTRE of 1976.

BELL-BAXTER HIGH SCHOOL (JUNIOR), West Port. Begun

by *John Milne*, 1871, and much enlarged by *James Maclaren & Son*, 1889–90. W additions by *George Sandilands*, 1929.

BELL-BAXTER HIGH SCHOOL (SENIOR), off Westfield Road. 1961, by *Fife County Council*. Curtain-walled, the blue panels contrasting with harling.

CASTLEHILL CENTRE, Castlehill. Group round three sides of a courtyard. The earliest block on the E was built as Cupar Academy in 1806 by *John Davidson*, mason, and *Charles Stewart*, wright. Two-storey piend-roofed box with a pedimented centre. Over the door, the carved royal arms from the demolished Tolbooth. Large S range of 1844–6* with a three-bay pedimented centre. Roman Doric porch on the W wing's gable. E extension by *H. A. Newman*, 1908. Villagey school building on the N, dated 1867.

CASTLEHILL PRIMARY SCHOOL, Ceres Road. By *Fife Regional Council*, 1975.

CORN EXCHANGE, St Catherine Street. By *Campbell Douglas & Stevenson*, 1861–2. The steeple dominates. Unbuttressed tower with steep gableted hoodmoulds. Three-stage spire. It begins as a bellcast-eaved pyramid with tall lucarnes, but this is truncated by the wooden clock stage; on top, a repeat of the first stage but now allowed to reach a point. The hall behind was much altered inside and out by *Harvey Johnston*, 1964.

COUNTY BUILDINGS. *See* Perambulation, below.

DUNCAN INSTITUTE, Crossgate. Gothic with a Flemish accent, by *John Milne*, 1870–1. The chief feature, and the building's townscape contribution, is the tall angle-turreted tower, its eccentric angular stone spire squashed by an iron-crested stone parapet.

ELMWOOD AGRICULTURAL AND TECHNICAL COLLEGE, Carslogie Road. By *Fife County Council*, 1971–2. It stands on the site of Hope Park, a villa of *c*.1860 whose balustrade has been re-erected on the lawn, together with a STATUE of Sir Walter Scott.

FIFE REGIONAL COUNCIL OFFICES, Waterend Road. By *John Needham*, 1947. Friendly but hinting at authoritarianism. Stone-clad with a concave S front.

FIRE STATION, Millgate. By *Fife Regional Council*, 1977.

KIRKGATE SCHOOL, Lovers Lane. Begun *c*.1860. Much enlarged in 1881 by *James Maclaren & Son*; theirs is the gabled wing with a stilted Venetian window and pedimented bellcote.

NEW CEMETERY, Ceres Road. Opened 1867. Spiky Gothic gate-piers. More domestic the lodge; quatrefoils on its tower's frieze.

POLICE STATION, Carslogie Road. By *Fife County Council*, 1963.

PRISON (former), Castlebank Road. Bleak Tudor central block of 1842, given S balconies on its conversion to a militia barracks *c*.1890.

---

* By when the Academy had become a Madras Academy with a large endowment provided by Dr Bell's Trustees.

RAILWAY STATION, Station Road. Tudorish, by *Grainger &
Miller*, 1847.
ST JAMES' CHURCH SUNDAY SCHOOL, Castle Street. By
David Storrar, 1890. Economical but with presence. Built of
hammerdressed rubble with lancet windows and a copper
cupola.

PERAMBULATION

On the approach from East Road, first a detour up BOWLING
GREEN ROAD, where Nos. 23–25 are a U-plan double house.
Modern Movement of *c.*1935 in harled brick but with Art
Deco detail; semicircular canopies over the doors, covered
balconies to the garden. PITSCOTTIE ROAD crosses the Eden
by an early C19 BRIDGE, widened in the C20. At the join of
the two roads, a semi-octagonal-ended TOLLHOUSE of *c.*1825,
with a pedimented and columned doorpiece to Pitscottie Road.
A small park, the CART HAUGH, lies ahead. Octagonal BAND-
STAND of 1924 topped with a scrolled crown. To the S, the
VICTORIA BRIDGE of 1901, with lattice parapets, leads to the
106   OLD JAIL by *James Gillespie Graham*, 1813–14, a heavily
detailed villa-like building with Roman Doric columns
marking off the centre and ends: 'totally unfit for its original
purpose, having more the appearance of a gentleman's seat,
than that of a receptacle for persons who have injured society',
sniffed the *Parliamentary Gazetteer*. At Cart Haugh's W end,
WAR MEMORIAL by *John Kinross*, 1921–2; a bronze Victory
(by *H. S. Gamley*) on a fussy Greek pedestal.
EAST BURNSIDE to the NW marks the old N boundary of the
burgh. MARYBANK, *c.*1830, with a rusticated ground floor,
on the N side of the Lady Burn, is reached by a bridge whose
classy railings match those of the front garden. Crenellated
garden wall at the corner with BISHOPGATE. On the far corner,
the late Georgian hall of an Antiburgher chapel given a pend
arch on its conversion to a coach house (*c.*1870). To its W, a
single-storey building of *c.*1830 with pointed-arched windows.
Piend-roofed BISHOPGATE HOUSE to the N, *c.*1810, with a
round-arched doorpiece; stable court at the rear.
105 ST CATHERINE STREET is Cupar's formal entry. It was laid out
on the lands of Balgarvie House, which had been bought by
the banker John Ferguson in 1809 for the purpose of forming
a new street. To achieve this Ferguson also agreed to build a
new Town Hall and new County Rooms in exchange for the
site of the old, which blocked his access to Crossgate and
Bonnygate. *James Gillespie Graham* prepared designs for the
County Rooms in 1810 and also for a jail to close the street's
E end.* Probably Gillespie Graham also produced elevations
for the other buildings in the street, but control of what was
to be built broke down after Ferguson's bankruptcy in 1817,
much of the street being developed by the architect-builder
Robert Hutchison.

---

* Tenders from contractors were advertised for in January 1811, but the building
was not begun for another two years and then on a different site (*see* above).

The N side is bitty. Large ROYAL HOTEL (c. 1835) with a Greek
  Doric portico projecting across the basement area. For the
  Victorian Gothic Episcopal church (replacing a porticoed
  Georgian predecessor), see Churches, above. CLYDESDALE
  BANK (No. 16) of c. 1830 with giant angle pilasters. The plain
  Nos. 10–14 probably follow Gillespie Graham's design
  although not built until c. 1816–25 and then by Hutchison; the
  delicate Edwardian Renaissance ground floor at No. 14 was
  provided for the British Linen Bank. Set-back Corn Exchange
  (see Public Buildings, above) providing a second Victorian
  intrusion. Painted ashlar frontages at Nos. 2–8, unpretentious,
  and No. 8's smaller scale introducing a touch of humility.
The S side was originally built c. 1812–17, all or almost all by
  Hutchison, but Gillespie Graham's design seems to have been
  followed. This was a terrace of plain ashlar-fronted tenements
  but with the COUNTY ROOMS (now COUNTY BUILDINGS)
  emphasized like the central feature of a contemporary Edinburgh New Town street or square. Advanced three-bay
  centrepiece joined by two-bay links to pilastered outriggers.
  Giant pilasters on the centrepiece, whose first-floor window is
  of three lights under an overall semicircular fanlight, a detail
  perhaps consciously taken from Robert Adam's design for the
  W side of Charlotte Square, Edinburgh (then being built). It
  is a touch disconcerting that the subject of this display is not
  in the centre of the terrace.
     The rest of the terrace is not unaltered. At the E end, *Thoms
  & Wilkie* replaced the Tontine Hotel in 1924–5 with the
  COUNTY BUILDINGS EXTENSION, a pompous stripped
  classical version of the County Rooms. The next-door tenement's interior was gutted by *William Burn* on its conversion
  to a Sheriff Court in 1836; first-floor courtroom with a panelled
  segment-vaulted ceiling and anta-pilastered walls. W of the
  County Rooms, a tenement whose ground floor was built up
  with rusticated stonework when it became part of the County
  Buildings in 1960. Nos. 11–13 were given window architraves
  and a consoled cornice c. 1860 and a François I ground floor
  c. 1900, when they were premises of the Royal Bank of Scotland.
The terrace ends with the Town Hall of 1815–17 by *Robert
  Hutchison*, probably adapting a *Gillespie Graham* design. The
  lead dome topped by a tall cupola on the bowed corner wins full
  marks for townscape but was an afterthought whose provincial
  swagger is in contrast to the smooth detail of the building
  below.
At the meeting with Crossgate is the MARKET CROSS moved
  here* in 1897. Of that date are the tall pedestal and foliaged
  capital, but the shaft is dated 1683. Contemporary unicorn
  (rather battered) and relief of the burgh arms on the pedestal.
BONNYGATE continues to the W. The prevailing tone is late
  Georgian. Very heavy cornice on Nos. 3–5 on the N side.
  Discreet and undistinguished infill (Nos. 15–17) on the corner

---

* From Hill of Tarvit, where it had been taken from Cupar in 1817.

of Balmerino Place, across which the two-storey scale is broken
by Nos. 19–21 of *c*.1860. Nos. 29–31's anthemion and palmette
balconies seem to have escaped from Edinburgh's Moray
Estate. Tall No. 43 on the corner of Lady Wynd, domestic
Gothic, dated 1871.

On the S side, the corner building with Crossgate was built
c.1805, large and plain, with a small mutuled cornice and
rusticated quoins. Battlemented corner tower on the red sandstone Nos. 30–32 (dated 1912) giving an agreeable shock. The
rendered No. 38 may incorporate an earlier house, its front
wall perhaps rebuilt further out in an early C18 remodelling.
Awkward corbelling at the join with No. 40. Provincial classical
FREEMASONS' HALL, dated 1811, the upper windows of the
advanced ends framed by coupled pilasters. No. 98, on the
corner of Provost Wynd, is of *c*.1810, quite smart with a
rusticated ground floor. Ridiculously broad and stumpy-col-
umned Roman Doric doorpiece on Nos. 110–112, built as the
FIFE BANK *c*.1810. Nos. 116–120, mid-C18 with crowstepped
gables.

94 PRESTON LODGE on the N side is a C17 villa of major quality
given a deceptive blandness by Georgian remodelling. It was
begun, probably *c*.1623 (the date on a stone built into the W
wall), by James Williamson and Isobel Heggie, who built the
S half of the present house. Three-storey U-plan block, the
slightly projecting jambs probably roofed as towers, i.e. a
compact version of Culross Abbey House. Round gunloop in
the inner angle of the E jamb. The jambs' first-floor windows
are framed by skinny pilasters (their order a sort of upside-
down Tuscan) and stringcourses carried round on to the main
block, where they are stopped against another pilaster each
side. Presumably the stringcourses originally ran across the
main block but were removed during the C18 refacing. The
jambs' second-floor architraves have bead and hollow mouldings studded with rosettes, the detail very similar to contemporary work at Roslin Castle (Lothian). Ribbon-moulded
stringcourse jumping down under the window sills.

The house was bought by James Preston of Denbrae in 1690.
By 1702 he had almost doubled its size, with an extension to
the N, where he made a new entrance front. This seems to have
been of the common late C17 type, with two-bay gabled ends
gripping a one-bay flat-roofed centre. Lugged architraved
doorpiece with a heavy moulded frame for an armorial panel
above. *c*.1765 the house was remodelled for William Paston, a
London goldsmith. The S front's centre was refaced; the N
front's gables were removed, leaving stepped chimneys as
absurdly tall features; a piended roof was placed across the
whole main block, with small piend roofs over the S jambs. At
the same time a new entrance was made in the S front, although
its present Roman Doric doorpiece is early C19.

(The interior is mostly of the 1690s. On the ground floor, a
doorpiece with a Doric frieze flanked by panelled pilasters.
Staircase very grand though not very large, with pillars on

the landings and squashed balusters under a heavy moulded handrail. Consoled cornice over the door to the first-floor dining room. Adjoining doors to the drawing room and NE bedroom with bolection friezes. Above the bedroom door, an allegorical carving. The dining room itself is fully panelled, with the fireplace framed by fluted columns with ignorant Corinthian capitals.)

WEST PORT begins with two former churches and the Bell-Baxter School (*see* Churches and Public Buildings, above). Then two villas of *c*.1810. On the S, WESTON HOUSE with an open pedimented centre and Venetian windows. On the N, LADYINCH, classy, with a Roman Doric porch; Venetian windows in the set-back wings. On the corner of BALGARVIE ROAD, the wedge-shaped BLAIRNEUK of *c*.1835, with a bowed corner and prominent paired chimneys.

CARSLOGIE ROAD is the exit from town. The late Victorian DENHURST, its doorpiece carved with anthemion and rosettes, is no match for the muscular pair opposite (CASTLECRAIG and GRUINARD), *c*.1850; two-storey bay windows cantilevered to the square at first floor.

CROSSGATE, back at the beginning of Bonnygate, is the tail of Cupar's T-plan. Plain late Georgian W side jolted by the Duncan Institute (*see* Public Buildings, above) at the point where the street narrows and shifts to the W. Not so enjoyable the conscientious WOOLWORTH (1970) and the less than conscientious post-war POST OFFICE.

The E side has more variety to enliven the Georgian norm. Flat-fronted palazzo of *c*.1850 at Nos. 8–12. Contemporary Nos. 14–16 with thinly pilastered first-floor windows. ROYAL BANK of *c*.1840, its classicism rather stripped. No. 28 is punchier, domestic Gothic of *c*.1860 with steep gablets and a two-storey oriel. Then blowsy mid-C19 Renaissance at Nos. 32–34. No. 36, set well back, has been a very smart villa of *c*.1815. Pedimented centre with a quatrefoil in the tympanum; giant overarch enclosing the door and first-floor window, which are united as a triple opening under an overall fanlight. Only the façade was kept in 1984 when a crudely mansarded supermarket was built behind. Back on the street line, a stripped Jacobean TRUSTEE SAVINGS BANK (No. 46) by *William Birrell*, 1901. Roman Doric doorpiece on the early C19 No. 52. Another, with attenuated pilasters, on No. 78 (*c*.1800). The heavily restored No. 80 is late C17. Symmetrical front, the windows grouped 2/1/2; splayed window margins. The rusticated segment-headed doorpiece is mid-C18. On the South Bridge corner, mid-Victorian STATION HOTEL, boorish Baronial.

In MILLGATE, late Georgian houses. On the S side, No. 1, THE BARONY, with rusticated quoins and a lovely fanlight. At the end of the N side, BELLFIELD HOUSE of *c*.1810, with a Roman Doric porch; W addition with a bow, *c*.1830. Further out, CUPAR MILLS, large and plain of *c*.1840. In the gable, an inserted datestone of 1796.

South Bridge leads to the railway station (*see* above). At the station approach, stone STATUE of David Maitland-Makgill-Crichton of Rankeilour in a frock coat, by *John Howie*, 1862. In RIGG'S PLACE is ROSEMOUNT COTTAGE, an exceptional little whinstone villa of *c.*1810. Two-storey one-bay centre, an intricate circled fanlight in the basket-arched door. One-storey bow-fronted wings; in the front of each a big segmental-arched window. Gothick windows at the side; cast-iron Gothick gate-piers complete the ensemble.

On the corner of Ceres Road and South Road, SOUTH TOLL, a semi-octagonal-ended tollhouse of 1842. On CERES ROAD'S w side, SOUTHFIELD of *c.*1835, an almost square classical villa, its pedimented gables the main elevations. Pilastered garden front. In the back gable's tympanum, an upside-down trefoil; lions on the pediment's ends. KNOX COTTAGES in SOUTH ROAD were built as almshouses in 1836 to the designs of 'an eminent architect in London.'* Three blocks linked by porches. Picturesque with jerkin-headed gables and centre chimneys.

VILLAS

EDEN PARK, McInnes Place. Early C19. Two-storey main block and single-storey wings. Roman Doric porch; consoled cornices over the windows. Converted to flats, 1984.

PRESTON LODGE, Bonnygate. *See* Perambulation, above.

RATHCLUNAN HOUSE, Carslogie Road. (Formerly Bonvil.) Harled mid-Victorian house swamped by tepid Baronial additions of *c.*1890.

WESTFIELD HOUSE, Westfield Road. Centre block of *c.*1810; the tall parapet and bow-ended wings added *c.*1825.

FARMS ETC.

CAIRNIE LODGE, 2.5km. N. Laird's house of *c.*1770, with a pedimented centre spoilt by a C20 attic. Early C19 bow-fronted wings. – STEADING to the W. Its pantiled ranges look mid-C19, but the front and ogee-roofed tower are of *c.*1890. – Early C19 white-painted LODGE with a pedimented Doric portico.

DALGAIRN, 0.8km. N. Whinstone box of *c.*1790 and quite plain, except for a large Roman Doric columned and pedimented tripartite doorpiece.

HILTON, 2km. N. Harled house of *c.*1795 with a Roman Doric columned doorpiece. The pedimented wings are C19 additions. – Early C19 LODGE with bowed ends.

EDENWOOD. *See* p. 205.
HILL OF TARVIT. *See* p. 239.
KINLOSS HOUSE. *See* p. 277.
STRATHEDEN HOSPITAL. *See* p. 412.
TARVIT. *See* p. 415.

* So said the *New Statistical Account* (1845).

DAIRSIE   4010

Village of C18 and C19 weavers' cottages strung out along a main
street.

ST MARY'S (OLD PARISH) CHURCH, 1.3km. S. Built by John   21
Spottiswoode, Archbishop of St Andrews, in 1621 and quite
exceptionally smart for a rural church. Stylistically it mixes
Gothic survival and innocent classical without any conscious
incongruity.

The church is a buttressed ashlar-built rectangle of four
bays by two, its breadth appreciably greater than that of a
medieval kirk of the same size. Hoodmoulded three-light
windows, their huge plate-traceried heads restored by *John
Kennedy* and *John MacCulloch* in 1835–7. Sill course carried
right round, stepping up over the moulded S door. The cornice
links the windows' arched tops; small parapet. Under the
cornice, rather flat gargoyle spouts, their function lost when
the original flat lead roof was replaced by a piended slate
roof in 1794. At the SW corner, a heavily corbelled two-stage
octagonal belfry with a balustraded parapet and lucarned stone
spire. The W gable's segmental-arched door is framed by illit-
erately classical pilasters, with angels' heads for capitals.
Above, a strapworked inscription panel; on top, a heavy frame
enclosing Spottiswoode's arms and initials.

Spottiswoode's interior was remarkable for its date, the E
end raised by one or more steps and marked off as a chancel
or communion aisle by a solid wooden screen surmounted by
the royal arms. All this, regarded as superstitious, was swept
away in the 1650s.

At the CHURCHYARD entrance, corniced GATEPIERS, probably early C19. – In the NE corner, SESSION HOUSE of *c.*1830
with simple Gothic detail. – S of the church, C18 TABLE
STONES, the best that of John Finlay †1722, with a vine border
and symbols of mortality.

DAIRSIE CASTLE, 1.4km. S. Ruins of the late C16 Z-plan tower
house of the Learmonths of Dairsie. Main block of rubble,
round NE and SW towers of ashlar. Of the main block, only
the N and S walls survive. In the N wall, a tall entrance; second-
floor moulded frame for a heraldic panel. Regular two-bay S
front. Splayed oval gunloops in the corner towers, the NE
fragmentary, the SW with a second-floor stringcourse and corbelling for a rectangular cap-house.

Inside, the main block's vaulted ground floor was probably
the kitchen. There have been two first-floor rooms, the W with
a large S window (later narrowed), the E with an aumbry in the
window's l. ingo.

DAIRSIE BRIDGE, 1.3km. S. On its E side, a panel with the arms
of James Beaton, Archbishop of St Andrews 1522–38, so it is
probably of *c.*1530. Three arches, each with stout chamfered
ribs on the soffit. Heavy triangular cutwaters. The broached
ashlar parapet and W refuge are Georgian replacements.

CLAYTON HOUSE, 2 km. NE. Piend-roofed house with single-storey wings, of *c.* 1788. The Doric columned doorpiece looks an addition of *c.* 1830. Bay windows were added in 1856. To the NW, mid-C19 STEADING with a heptagonal horsemill.

MUIRHEAD, 1.8km. NE. Farmhouse dated 1860 in its central gablet. In front, a contemporary whinstone and pantiled steading.

PITCULLO. *See* p. 342.

1080   DALGETY BAY

A new town of speculative housing begun on the Donibristle estate in 1962. The first houses were completed in 1965, the year after the opening of the Forth Road Bridge. Despite some light industry on the N fringe its main function is to be a dormitory for Edinburgh.

DALGETY PARISH CHURCH, Regent's Way. Brick with a shallow monopitch roof. By *Marcus Johnston*, 1980–1.

DALGETY PARISH CHURCH, 1.5km. to the NE. Disused. Preaching box of 1829–30 by *James Gillespie Graham*. Tudor windows, battlemented porch, and a spired octagonal bellcote. Inside, a gallery round three sides, the cast-iron columns' necks decorated with individual leaves. – STAINED-GLASS window (Dorcas) of 1933.

Up the hill to the SE, the former MANSE (now ARDMHOR HOUSE), also by *Gillespie Grahame*, 1828–9, its bay windows and dormers added by *John Houston* in 1897–8.

ST BRIDGET'S CHURCH, 1.3km. to the NE. In a cliff-top graveyard overlooking the Forth, the kirk is now a roofless Ancient Monument, very kempt but still of great charm.

The rubble-built C12 or C13 church consecrated by Bishop David de Bernham in 1244 is an unpretentious single cell. Blocked rectangular doors near the N and S sides' W ends seem to be original; so too the piscina at the E end of the S wall. The S wall's arched doorway and sturdy SE buttress look considerably later, perhaps part of the post-Reformation alterations. These included the erection of an E gallery approached by a broad forestair built against the gable, probably in the late C16. Of the rather later gallery at the W end of the S wall there survive its first-floor door and the base of the forestair squeezed in beside a simple burial aisle. This gallery's N counterpart was put up in 1645 to serve the Fordell Aisle. That aisle, probably of the late C16 or early C17, is now ruinous, but the lower part of its arch into the church is visible; in the gable, a mullioned and transomed window. To its E is the slab-roofed early C17 aisle built by William Inglis of Otterston. Pointed arch into the church carried on panelled piers; pointed tunnel-vault inside. All this is Gothic survival, but on the gable's exterior a moulded stone doorpiece with a curly pediment broken by a crest.

33   The Dunfermline Aisle at the W end, built *c.* 1610 for the

first Earl of Dunfermline, is like a small but very classy tower house. Z-plan with a semi-octagonal NE stairtower and a SW jamb. Moulded window surrounds and (now empty) frames for heraldic panels. The bellcote on the main block's w gable is probably C18. Inside, ground-floor burial vaults. On the first floor of the main block, a laird's loft with a big window into the church. Stone-panelled walls and cornice; above was an elliptically vaulted plaster ceiling. Retiring room with a fireplace in the jamb.

MONUMENTS. Inside the church, graveslabs at the E end, including William Abernethy †1612. – Set in to the N wall, graveslab of William Abernethy †1540, with a vigorously carved inscription and a large coat of arms. – On the S wall, monument to Janet Inglis, dated 1681; Composite columned aedicule with a coat of arms in the curly pediment. – Outside, set into the E forestair, a small C17 aedicule with fluted pilasters

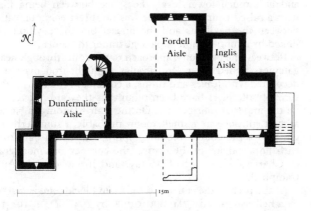

St Bridget's Church, Dalgety Bay,
plan

and a shaped pediment. – In the s wall, very rustic rectangular panel to Archibald Campbell †1714, carved with a jolly angel and skulls. – Ionic aedicule to William Henderson †1737, with an angel in the shaped broken pediment; it is badly weathered, but the pilasters' capitals must always have been soggy. – In the w wall of the Dunfermline Aisle's jamb, a large monument to Robert Meikle, dated 1685; it is suggestive of the common C17 aedicular type but lacks columns or pilasters flanking the inscription panel's frame; three angels' heads and two skulls sit on the curly broken pediment; the base is carved with bones and a skull.

A fair number of TABLE STONES, the earliest that of John Moubray of Cockairnie, dated 1665, embellished with a coat of arms. – Agreeably rustic C18 HEADSTONES, energetically carved with emblems of death.

SESSION HOUSE on the w of the churchyard. Part of its l. door jamb is an incised medieval stone.

PRIMARY SCHOOL, St Bridget's Brae. By *Fife County Council*, 1969.

DONIBRISTLE HOUSE
off Moray Way South

Forlorn reminders of the major late C17 and early C18 house created for the fifth and sixth Earls of Moray, now hemmed in by housing but the site still enjoying superb views over the Forth. The main block was burned in 1858 and later demolished. There survive the piend-roofed harled pavilions (the w roofless and with a Victorian rear extension) built in 1719–23 by *Alexander McGill*. Like the contemporary pavilions at House of Gray and Dupplin (both Tayside), the long sides are parallel to the main block's front, but here they are set exceptionally far forward (41.5m. from the main house) and at a much lower level, the space between being filled with a raised courtyard. There was no direct communication between the pavilions and the house, but the pavilions are linked by a tunnel-vaulted passage under the court.

Between the pavilions, approach to the court through heavy gatepiers joined by a semicircular wrought-iron overthrow decorated with leaves and tulips, a coronet in the centre. Presumably the piers have been rebuilt, as they are not centred on the imperial stair behind. On the stair's landing, a basket-arched entrance to a small room, probably a summerhouse. On top of the court's retaining wall, simple iron balustrade with floral finials; in the centre, the coronet and monogram of Charles, sixth Earl of Moray, and his wife Lady Anne Campbell.

At the back of the courtyard the main block's site is marked by a bellcast-roofed SUMMERHOUSE, by *F. W. Deas*, 1913; at its join with the courtyard wall, a large carved seal enjoying a fish supper.

22   In a wood to the w, the derelict but still very smart private CHAPEL built in 1729–32. *McGill* was again the architect. Tall round-arched windows with Gibbs surrounds. Channelled pilaster strips at the corners. Pedimented gables, the E simply treated with an oculus in the tympanum. The w front is much grander. Flattened oculus over the door. In the tympanum, an inscription flanked by scrolls and surmounted by a coat of arms, carved by *Robert Henderson*, mason in Stirling, from a design by *Roderick Chalmers*, herald painter. On top of the pediment, a tall octagonal belfry topped by scrolls carrying a lantern.

2010   # DENMYLNE
1.5km. SE of Newburgh

Substantial remains of a rubble-walled C16 tower house squeezed between a C19 farmhouse and its steading. The mill and lands of Denmylne were granted to John Balfour by James IV, *c.*1500, and his son Patrick's charter from James V in 1541 contained the condition that he build a hall and offices there. The present house was probably built soon after.

Irregular Latin cross on plan, with the jambs towards the main block's N end. Three storeys except for the E jamb, which contains the main stair to the second floor but has a floor above reached by a turret stair in the SE inner angle. The W jamb increases in size above the ground floor with a corbelled splay-cornered extension. At the foot of the E stairtower's N face, a moulded door guarded by splayed oval gunloops. More gun-loops in the main block's S gable and the W jamb's S front. Generous windows with rounded margins. Corbelled parapet round the S part of the main block.

Inside, each floor of the main block has contained two rooms, each with its own door (but each pair sharing a central jamb) from the stair. Tunnel-vaulted ground floor; the S room may have been a kitchen. On the second floor, remains of a fireplace in each gable, with nearby aumbries. The W jamb's projecting S part is curious. Was it for a private stair from the first-floor S room to the one above?

In a rockery in front of the farmhouse, the stone CANOPY of a late medieval piscina or credence, its front carved with tabernacle work, the soffit with spokes radiating from a central boss.

DENORK
5.9km. SW of St Andrews

4010

An Iron Age univallate stone-walled fort on a rocky knoll immediately N of the broch at Drumcarrow Craig (*q.v.*), *c.*140m. by 45m., within a heavy dry-stone wall which is built around the margin of the summit area.

DONIBRISTLE HOUSE *see* DALGETY BAY

DOWN LAW
3.5km. E of Kingskettle

3000

An Iron Age fort, roughly pear-shaped in plan, *c.*110m. by max. 60m., within defences which evidently varied in depth, being strongest on the SW, where at least two ramparts of earth and stone (with external ditches and counterscarp banks) protect the main entrance.

4010

DRUMCARROW CRAIG
4.5km. SW of St Andrews

An Iron Age broch and unenclosed round stone houses, sited on
a prominent ridge (217m. O.D.) overlooking the Eden estuary.
The broch itself has been reduced to a cairn-like round of
stony debris, in which some stones of the inner and outer wall
faces can still be seen to define an inner court 14m. in diameter
within a wall 5m. thick. A displaced lintel from the E-facing
entrance is visible in the debris.

DRUMNOD WOOD *see* BALMERINO

2010

DUNBOG

Loose-knit group of church, manse, school and one farm.

PARISH CHURCH. Disused. Plain whinstone box built by *James
Ballingal*, 1803–4, and extended E by one bay in 1851. Solid
Gothic E tower with a balustraded parapet and slated spire
added by *John Young*, 1887–8, when the W bellcote was taken
to the manse and replaced by a cross. Inside, E gallery front of
1803–4. Other FURNISHINGS, including the canopied pulpit,
of 1887. – STAINED-GLASS W windows (The Christian Soldier;
Faith, Hope and Charity) by *James Ballantine II*, 1919.

MANSE to the W. Straightforward front block built in 1776,
its harling replaced by cement render in 1884. SW addition by
Alexander Blyth, 1816.

CHURCHYARD to the N. At the gate, one gable of the WATCH
HOUSE built in 1822.

PRIMARY SCHOOL, 0.4km. N. 1839, by *John Tait* of Edinburgh
from a sketch plan by the parish schoolmaster *William Black*.
One-storey on a U-plan with the schoolhouse in the centre,
schoolrooms in the wings. The E wing's clock turret was added
in 1857, the schoolhouse's 'mansard' roof more recently.

2080

DUNEARN HILL
1.5km. NW of Burntisland

An Iron Age fort on a conspicuous craggy hill, of two periods.
First a univallate enclosure *c.*120m. by 40m., with E entrance
protected by an outer wall. Second, overlying the first, a
roughly circular enclosure *c.*36m. in diameter, in a well-built
dry-stone wall *c.*3.6m. thick. The relationship between the
secondary work and at least three round stone houses (also
post-dating the first) is indeterminate.

DUNFERMLINE   *0080*

Dunfermline Abbey	175	Pittencrieff Park	192
Churches	185	Central Area Perambulation	193
Public Buildings	187	Mansions	196

A sizeable industrial and market town which has developed around a former royal residence and Benedictine abbey. The abbey, founded by St Margaret of Scotland immediately after her marriage at Dunfermline to Malcolm III, *c.*1070, had a walled precinct enclosing the approximate area bounded by New Row, Priory Lane, Monastery Street, St Catherine's Wynd, Maygate and Canmore Street. A royal burgh mentioned *c.*1125, perhaps sited in Pittencrieff Park, seems to have been short-lived, but a 'burghal suburb' N of the abbey precinct was in existence by 1303, when Edward I ordered ditches to be made round this town (*villa*); *c.*1320 Robert I recognized it as a burgh dependent on the abbey. Later it gained gradual acceptance of the obligations and status of a royal burgh, paying a share of the *contribucio* voted by Parliament in 1424 and of stent from 1535, before admission to the Convention of Royal Burghs in 1555 and Parliament in 1594.

The medieval town extending N from the abbey precinct to Queen Anne Street was largely rebuilt after a fire in 1624. At that time it was still primarily a rural centre, but after the introduction of damask weaving in 1718 Dunfermline became the leading British town for the manufacture of table linen, the hand looms being replaced by steam looms in the mid-C19. Decline in the linen industry since 1918 has been offset by the introduction of new industries and by Dunfermline's position as a reservoir of labour for Edinburgh.

DUNFERMLINE ABBEY

Dominating the S view of Dunfermline, the abbey church and 6 monastic ruins are a monument to the revolution in Scottish Church and society traditionally associated with St Margaret, sister of Edgar Atheling and great-niece of Edward the Confessor. *c.*1070 she married Malcolm III (Canmore), King of Scots, in his palace chapel at Dunfermline. Immediately after, Margaret founded a Benedictine priory there, importing monks from Canterbury and enlarging the chapel as the community's church. In 1128 her son David I had the priory made an abbey, its first abbot Geoffrey the Prior being brought from Canterbury.* In accord with the community's new status the church was rebuilt on a much larger scale and consecrated in 1150. Within a hundred years the E end had been remodelled, the work presumably complete by 1250, when the bodies of

---

* David's charter of 1128, usually referred to as a foundation charter, is one which confirms to the monks of Dunfermline the property which they already possessed.

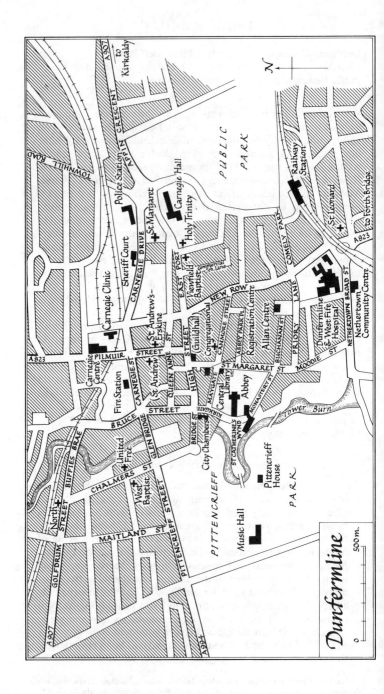

Dunfermline

500 m.

Malcolm Canmore and the newly canonized Queen Margaret were reinterred E of the high altar.

The first mention of the accompanying monastery buildings is in 1304, during the Wars of Independence, when they were partly destroyed by Edward I. The refectory was rebuilt in 1329, a probable date for the guesthouse as well. Later in the C14 a N choir aisle was added to the church, and in 1368 a new shrine was made for the body of St Margaret. Remodelling of the nave's W end, possibly begun in the C14, was certainly in progress during the abbacy of Richard de Bothwell (1446–82), who also added the N porch.

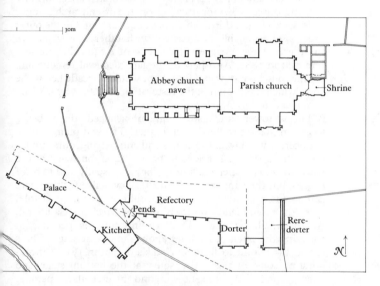

Dunfermline Abbey,
site plan

After the monastery's dissolution in 1560 the monks' quarters were left empty and soon became a quarry. The guesthouse, always a royal residence, was reconstructed in 1590–1600 as a palace for Anne of Denmark, wife of James VI. The abbey church's nave continued in use as the parish church of the burgh, but the choir was abandoned. Its E end and N aisle collapsed in 1672 and the crossing tower in 1716. In 1818–21 the ruined choir and transepts were cleared and a new parish church (designed by *William Burn*) built on the site, the old nave in turn becoming redundant except as a huge vestibule. In 1845 responsibility for the nave was taken over by the government, which has been its guardian (as also of the remains of the monastic buildings) for nearly one hundred and forty years but has yet to publish a guidebook.

The ABBEY CHURCH's combination of a medieval nave and huge Georgian Gothic parish church is impressive but dis-

concerting. Approach from St Catherine's Wynd through
GATES and up a steep flight of steps provided by *R. Rowand
Anderson*, 1891–2. The WEST FRONT's composition of the nave
gable flanked by towers at the ends of the aisles is C12, but the
gable was refronted and the towers rebuilt so as to extend
almost to the same plane, *c.* 1400. Some of this later masonry
has been peeled off the gable to reveal original stonework. Also
original is the sloping canopied PORCH containing the W door.
This is of five orders with heavily restored nook-shafts, alternately round and octagonal. Bases, where original, of two
members of elliptical section. Scalloped capitals, the middle
one on each side foliaged. Heavy star-decorated abaci forming
a stringcourse. Chevron-carving on the round arch's inner
orders, except the third, which has chip-carving. On the outer
order, grotesque heads alternate with other motifs. Above
the porch, large Y-traceried window of *c.* 1400, its transom
removed in 1882. Also part of the late medieval remodelling
are the round window and four-light window arcade below the
apex, which was rebuilt in the restoration of 1845–8 by *William
Nixon* and *Robert Matheson*.

The W towers are disturbingly unbalanced, the N being
larger on plan as well as much higher. Tall and plain, with a
Y-traceried window at the aisle's end and a stringcourse under
the belfry opening. It seems to be of *c.* 1400, but what of the
machicolated parapet and spire? They are usually said to be of
c. 1590, but the supposed documentary evidence for that date
is in fact non-existent. *c.* 1500–20 would seem more probable,
given the resemblance to the spires of St Machar's Cathedral,
Aberdeen, although the Dunfermline spire is peculiar in
changing the pitch of its sides above the lowest stage. The S
tower was rebuilt to *William Stark*'s design in 1811,[*] incorporating some of the old masonry at the bottom stage. No
attempt to challenge the N tower, and the crenellated parapet
a very weak termination.[‡]

The C12 nave was of seven bays, each marked off externally
by pilaster strips and containing an aisle window, triforium
and clearstorey. The bay rhythm was made almost absurdly
powerful by the addition of massive stepped buttresses, dated
1620 (N) and 1625 (S). On the S, frames for armorial panels on
the two centre buttresses flanking a blocked C17 door. C15 door
at the W end; beside it, arms of the first Earl of Dunfermline and
the date 1607. The E processional door into the cloister is C12.
Four orders with nook-shafts at the inner two. Elaborately
carved capitals; scroll decoration on the abaci. The arch's outer
order has rosettes, the others chevrons. Its remarkable state
of preservation is due to having been covered by a lean-to
mausoleum, the WARDLAW VAULT (dated 1617), from the
C17 until 1904–5, when the vault was reduced in size and the
door restored by *W. T. Oldrieve*.

---

[*] It had collapsed in 1807.
[‡] Perhaps not entirely the fault of Stark, who had proposed a 'minaret' which the
Heritors deleted from the scheme.

The N door is again C12. Four orders with nook-shafts. Cubical capitals. Chevron decoration on the arch. It was set in a shallow porch with blind arcading on the upper part. This is now partly hidden by a deep porch and flanking buttresses added in the C15. On the W buttress's image niche, the arms of Richard de Bothwell (Abbot of Dunfermline 1446–82). In the porch, MONUMENT to Robert Adie † 1719, Corinthianesque aedicule with a coat of arms breaking the pediment.

All the S and two of the N aisle windows are C12, set high on a sill course so as to allow room for the cloister roof on the S. Three orders with nook-shafts. Chevron and billet decoration on the round-headed arches. The N aisle's two Y-traceried W windows are C15, the deeper E window with three lancet lights perhaps C16.

The C12 triforium windows were round-arched with angle shafts. Two survive on the N side but were mutilated in the C14, when the arches were made angular and two lancet lights inserted in each opening. This treatment was copied in 1845–8 on the S side, where the triforium windows had been blocked. The narrow Romanesque revival lights in the N aisle's W bays are part of the C15 reconstruction. Round-arched C12 clearstorey windows, except in the N side's two W bays, where they have segmental arches and are presumably C15. Corbelled parapets of 1845–8, their design based on fragmentary remains on the N side.

William Burn's PARISH CHURCH of 1818–21 joins tactfully 27 enough to the medieval nave by restoring its missing E bay. But this is slightly recessed from the original building line, a difference made all too obvious by the use of yellowish droved ashlar masonry. For the rest the Perp Georgian addition is unabashedly a second church, cruciform with a three-bay nave, transepts and one-bay choir. The crossing tower is splendiferous but kitsch. Scalloped parapet with crown finials above a balustrade composed of letters spelling 'KING ROBERT THE BRUCE'. Low SESSION HOUSE at the E, perhaps intended to recall the chapel enclosing St Margaret's shrine.

The bottom courses of the S and E walls of this CHAPEL of *c.*1250 do in fact survive. Splayed base course. Round the inside, a stone seat, its moulded edge including a row of nailheads. On it sit the bases for the wall arcade's attached columns. They are of waterholding type. Three drains in the seat. The SHRINE itself is of 1368, when two stones were bought in London for the Queen's tomb. These are probably the two marble plinth blocks (the upper much damaged), which supported a stone canopy.

INTERIOR. On the floor of the medieval nave, different-coloured paving outlined with gunmetal to show the FOUNDATIONS of the first church below. The two W compartments (those of the chapel where St Margaret married Malcolm III) are C10 or C11, a square nave-tower and rectangular choir. The broader apsidal-ended E choir must have been added c.1072 to accommodate the Benedictine priory, the old choir becoming the nave.

9

The choir foundations of St Margaret's priory church were used to support some of the piers of the nave arcade of the abbey church dedicated in 1150. These are strongly reminiscent of Durham Cathedral, consecrated in 1130 and also a Benedictine house, but here the piers* are all circular, except for one composite pier (of Durham type) at the w bay of the s aisle. Chevron and spiral decoration on the e piers. Cushion capitals. Arches of almost identical section to those at Durham, three orders with a billet moulding on the outer. Stringcourses mark off the very simply treated triforium and clearstorey.

Each bay of the aisles has a wall arcade. Cushion capitals, some with fish-scale decoration. Arches with chevron carving. Between each bay, clustered shafts to carry the rib-vaults, apparently original in the e bays of the n aisle, but those of the s aisle rebuilt, probably re-using original ribs, in 1620–1 (dates on two bosses). Tauter C15 vaults in the n aisle's two w bays, whose bosses bear the arms of Richard de Bothwell and St Margaret. PAINTING of four Apostles on vault of e bay of n aisle, perhaps c.1500. Flat roof of 1845–8 over the nave, its braces springing from corbels carefully set between the holes which used to take a pitched roof's rafter ends. At e of nave, the C12 ROOD SCREEN base is effectively altar-like.

The sw tower has been vaulted, and the beginnings of the ribs survive. In its s and w walls, fragments of chevron decoration, apparently remnants of C12 doors. Stilted arch into the aisle. The arch into the nave's w bay has been built up like that of the nw tower, in whose C14 rib-vault each compartment has its own domical vault. Round hole for a bell rope in the centre.

MONUMENTS. On the s wall, South African War Memorial, very Norman in red sandstone, by *Stewart McGlashan & Son* from a design by *W. W. Robertson*, 1903. – John Gray † 1762, with a scrolled pediment. – On n wall, Durie memorial, mid-C19 ogee-arched tablet above a late C16 slab (originally in the floor) commemorating Henry Durie. – Robert Pitcarn † 1584, Gothic below, Classical above. Elliptical-arched recess. On this, pilastered inscription frame topped by scrolls holding up a steep thistle-finialled pediment containing a coat of arms. –

31

William Schaw † 1602, erected by order of Anne of Denmark, and firmly attempting classicism. Rectangular recess framed by coupled Corinthianesque pilasters. Above, heavy scrolls buttress an aediculed inscription tablet. Schaw's arms and monogram in the pediment. Urn finial.

STAINED GLASS. n aisle. Baptism of Christ, by *James Ballantine & Son*, 1873–4. – Armorial windows to Wedderburn Conway Halkett (after 1885) and Robert Durie (1933) by *Isobel Goudie*. – Narrative depictions of the Agony in the Garden (1879), Christ at the house of Martha and Mary (1873), and, at the w end, the Deposition, Entombment and Resurrection

* Three piers of the s arcade were rebuilt in 1845–8.

(1871), all by *Ballantine*. – s aisle. Carnegie memorial (Isaiah), characteristically undisciplined by *Douglas Strachan, c.*1915. – Armorial window to Queen Annabella Drummond of 1863. – Then three garish memorials, to Peter Chalmers (1870), James Douglas (1878), and Robert Douglas (1878), by *Ballantine*. – At the end, pre-Raphaelitish Christ Blessing Children, by *Henry Holiday*, 1909–10. – w window of nave (Sir William Wallace, Malcolm Canmore, St Margaret and Robert the Bruce) by *Ballantine* from a design by *Noel Paton*, 1882, mosaic character but very yellow.

The PARISH CHURCH INTERIOR is extravagantly high. The sheer walling above the nave arcades is hardly interrupted by the clearstorey. Flat stellar plaster vault. The deep gallery fronts prevent the eye from straying into the aisles and push it upward. Full-height arches into the transepts, whose end windows, like the E and W windows of the nave, take full advantage of the space. DECORATION of the plastered walls by *R. Rowand Anderson*, 1905. Lined as ashlar with a vine frieze below the clearstorey. In the choir, stencilling with a drapery-filled E arcade. – The s choir aisle was fitted up as a WAR MEMORIAL CHAPEL by *James Shearer*, 1952, wet modern-traditional.

CHOIR FURNISHINGS arranged in a Presbyterian version of the medieval E end, with Robert the Bruce's grave behind the COMMUNION TABLE a substitute for that of St Margaret. It is covered by a baldacchino doubling as a PULPIT. – FONT on the l. All these are by *Anderson*, 1890. – On the r., blocky eagle lectern of wood, carved by *Thomas Good* from a design by *Matthew M. Ochterlony* and *William Williamson*, 1931. – ROYAL PEW of 1972.

On the N transept's N wall, the elaborately panelled front of the MAGISTRATES' PEW of 1610, its centre decorated with the royal arms and initials of James VI and his queen, Anne of Denmark. On each side a shallow bow. Round-headed blind arcading on the frieze. The effect is neither Gothic nor classical.

MONUMENTS. Under the pulpit, brass incised with full-size figure of Robert the Bruce, designed by *W. S. Black* and executed by *Stewart McGlashan & Son*, 1889. It is set in a porphyry slab from an Egyptian sarcophagus. – In the N transept, Robert Stevenson, bronze plaque with a relief portrait by *George H. Paulin*, 1933. – The s transept is a shrine to the Bruce family. On the w wall, two monuments carved by *Mary Grant*, the Assumption of Lady Augusta Stanley (1876) and a more modest portrait of Lady Charlotte Locker (1882). – On the s wall, Charles Bruce, recumbent effigy backed by a flowing Angel of the Resurrection, by *Matthew Noble*, 1870. – Architectural but not literary restraint for the tablet to Charles, Earl of Elgin and Kincardine, †1771, who was 'In his Character of Husband, Father, Friend and Master, As far as human Imperfection admits, Unblemished ...'. – E wall occupied by the recumbent effigy (by *J. H. Foley*, 1863–8) of General the

Hon. Robert Bruce mourned by a veiled lady. Reliefs of incidents in his life on the tomb-chest's front.

STAINED GLASS. In the N transept, elongated figures of Scottish saints and heroes by *Gordon Webster*, 1974. – E window of nave (Last Supper and the Resurrection) of 1903 by *Ballantine & Gardiner*. – Accomplished E window of S choir aisle (Acts of Mercy) by *Alexander Strachan*, 1933. – Its S window (Poole Memorial) by *James Ballantine II*, 1914. – E and W windows of S transept (Epiphany, 1900–1; Ascension, 1880) by *G. F. Bodley*. – The narrative S window (St Margaret) of *c.*1935 by *Douglas Strachan* is crude in comparison. – S aisle. Pallid Sanders Memorial window, signed by *Ballantine*, *c.*1930, contrasting with the strong blues of the Baird Memorial by *William Wilson*, 1968.

ORGAN of 1882 by *Forster & Andrews* of Glasgow; rebuilt by *Scovell* in 1911, and again by *Walker* of Ruislip, 1967.

Of the CHURCHYARD MONUMENTS some (mostly C18, but one on the E wall of 1850) are really landmarks describing the number of 'rooms' owned by a family. – In an enclosure on the N of St Margaret's shrine, classical tomb-chest of *c.*1800 with swagged sides. – Wall monument in NE corner to Robert Gall † 1812, inscribed:

> Reader see how death all doun puls & Nought remaines
> but shanks & skulls. For the Greatest Champieon ere
> Drew Breath was all wise conquered by death.

– On the ground beside, a well-lettered inscription to Peter Williams † 1768 left plenty of room to commemorate Thomas Williams † 1784 and his wife † 1785 in a doggerel:

> of worldly cares we've had our share
> when in this world as you Now are
> But Now Our Bodys Rest in Dust
> Waiting the Rising of the Just.

– In line with the N transept, William Knox, probably late C17, would-be classical aedicule with female heads on the corners and a jolly skull and crossbones. – To its W, Joseph Neil Paton, Celtic cross in red granite, by *Noel Paton*, 1876. – Almost in a line from the centre of the nave's N side, four late C17 or early C18 stones, two with grisly reminders of mortality (one of them dated 1713), another with a scrolly pedimented aedicule, the fourth with butcher's knives. – Early C18 Corinthianesque aedicule with a coat of arms on the path to NW door. – On the path's other side, headstone of William Wellwood † 1828, inscribed:

> Tho Boreas Blasts and Neptunes Waves
> Has tost him to and fro
> Quiet by the order of Gods decree
> He harbours here below
> Where now he lies at anchor sure
> With many of the fleet
> Expecting one day to set sail
> His Admiral Christ to meet.*

* For an earlier and cruder version of this verse, *see* North Queensferry, Chapel.

The CLOISTER lay as usual S of the church, but the steeply sloping site meant that much of the building was at a far lower level. There seem to have been only a wall and presumably a covered walk on the W, the guesthouse (or Palace) being a continuation of the S range.

In 1304 Edward I destroyed 'palaces' capable of holding three kings and their retinues in the abbey precinct, probably on and near the site of the present Palace Block, leaving only 'a few houses for the monks who constituted the competent and regular staff.' These 'few houses' now survive only as the fragmentary S ends of the E range, best seen from Monastery Street. They are probably early C13. On the E the reredorter's DRAIN. Then the angle-buttressed REREDORTER, its splayed basecourse sitting on Office of Works masonry rather than the ground. Splayed lancets with stepped sills. Angular rear-arch to the door into the undercroft. This has been a two-aisle room, the vault-ribs rising directly from the chamfered wall-shafts without the interruption of capitals. Fireplace recess with a later oven in the W wall. A bridge probably gave access from the upper floor to the DORTER, whose S front's angle buttresses are supplemented by a central buttress. Hood-moulded lancets above a stringcourse. Inside, another two-aisle undercroft (its N end covered by the graveyard). Sex-partite vaulting of early C13 type. Remains of a stone bench all round.

The whole S range seems to have been rebuilt after the destruction of 1304 to provide refectory, gatehouse, kitchen and guesthouse blocks. The REFECTORY was being rebuilt in 1329. Its S front's height is emphasized by regular buttresses, across which are carried stringcourses linking the hoodmoulds of the first-floor windows and the sills of those of the hall and undercroft above and below. Stubby lancets at the lower floors. The hall is lit by tall bipartites whose mullions survive only in one of the pulpitum's paired lights. The loop tracery must be a C15 alteration. Cusped arch between two buttresses to carry the pulpitum. Much cruder are the heavy round arches carrying a passage at the two W bays. It must have looked less awkward when its E half sloped down to show the line of the stair inside.

Inside, an E lobby formed a passage from the dorter to the ground and first floors. Both had two-aisle vaulted halls. The undercroft's vault was quadripartite with ridge- and wall-ribs. In the N wall a steep stair to the cloister. In the same wall, remains of a first-floor fireplace with a drain beside it. Blocked door in the S wall into the hanging passage which gave access to the first floor of the gatehouse. SW door into the pend under the gatehouse. In its ingo, another door into a passage which has been blocked by the building of the gatehouse vault. So presumably the gatehouse is later, but the hanging passage seems to be an original part of the refectory block, and it leads to the room above this vault. Perhaps there was a change of plan while the block was being built.

The unvaulted second-floor refectory hall extended over the
E lobby with a dais lit from a huge S window. From the dais,
stair to the pulpitum, which opens into the hall through two
tall arches. The elaborate tierceron vault above looks C15. The
reticulated tracery in the seven-light W window makes a taut
contrast to the flabby loops of the S lights. Spire-roofed turnpike stair nudging into the NW corner.

The PENDS or gatehouse lacks the refectory's elegance.
Awkward butterfly plan angling the road from Monastery
Street to St Catherine's Wynd. Ribbed tunnel-vaults over the
pend's E part and the entrance to the refectory block's first
floor. Over the W part, quadripartite vault with horizontal
ridge-ribs. The pedestrian gate on the N was heightened by
R. S. Lorimer in 1909. Inside, two first-floor passage rooms.
Irregularly shaped W room with a heavy ribbed vault. The
stellar-vaulted E room links the kitchen on the S to the stair to
the refectory and to the hanging passage. In the passage,
another ribbed tunnel-vault. Quadripartite-vaulted second-
floor room. In its N wall remains of a canopied fireplace.
Grotesque human head support for a lamp bracket.

The KITCHEN block, S of the pends, served both the monastic refectory and the guesthouse. On the S front two deep
buttresses from which spring an arch to carry the wall of the
upper floors. Pointed E door into the two-aisled undercroft.
Quadripartite vaults springing from octagonal piers. Bosses
carved with human heads and roses. The original (barely traceable) stair to the first floor was in the NE corner. The tight
turnpike in the SW corner is probably C16. The first-floor
kitchen has been yet another two-aisled vaulted room. Two
fireplaces in the N wall and a huge one opposite. Only scanty
remains of the room above which has been reconstructed in
the C16.

The PALACE built in the C14 as the guesthouse (the expected
guest being the King) was reconstructed c. 1540 for James V.*
Its rise out of the glen is made even dizzier by the buttresses.
These formed a rather effete procession until the C16 reconstruction, when heavy stepped buttresses joined in to carry a
couple of oriels.

Inside, the ground floor's E part has been a vaulted twin-
aisled hall. Fireplace in the S wall with heavy corbels for a
hood. It was probably as part of the reconstruction of c. 1540
that it was divided to form four tunnel-vaulted cellars and had
a stair inserted in the NE corner. The W room is on a higher
level. Originally unvaulted, it too has been subdivided and
given tunnel-vaults. Garderobe in the SW corner; remains of
a turnpike on the N. The C16 reconstruction raised the ceiling
of the first-floor rooms and inserted tall mullioned and transomed windows pushing up through the C14 wall arcading.
The E room was the hall. Stone cornice on the S wall. Built

* In 1723 John Macky reported that the arms of James V and Mary of Guise were
'still fresh upon the Apartments', as also were those of the Earl of Arran (Regent
1542–54).

into the soffit of one window, a pediment carved with the Annunciation and the arms of George Durie (Abbot 1526–60). The w room was the Chamber, with a large rectangular oriel forming almost a separate room. The second floor seems to be almost all of *c.*1540. Mullioned and transomed windows, the large chimneypiece still very Gothic-looking.

CHURCHES

DUNFERMLINE CONGREGATIONAL CHURCH, Canmore Street. By *John Baird* of Glasgow, 1841–2. Broad box behind a Tudor-Gothic firescreen front divided into a 'nave' and 'aisles' by almost flat buttresses. On the outer buttresses, obelisk pinnacles; taller pinnacles with *fleur-de-lis* finials at the centre. Ogee hoodmould over the nave window. Galleried interior.

FREE NORTH CHURCH, Bruce Street. Secularized. By *Robert Hay*, 1849–50. Chunky Gothic, still with a Georgian accent. Pinnacled gable front whose bellcote has lost its spire.

GILLESPIE MEMORIAL CHURCH, Chapel Street. Built as a United Presbyterian chapel by *Andrew Balfour*, 1848–9. Tudor-Gothic gable front with an ogee hoodmould over the centre window, the buttresses now shorn of pinnacles. (Interior altered, 1882. – STAINED-GLASS window by *R. Douglas McLundie*, *c.*1947.)

HOLY TRINITY (Episcopal), East Port. Confidently simple late 40 Gothic, by *R. Rowand Anderson*, 1891. Nave and chancel, s transept and N porch, all of hammerdressed rubble, the roof's green slates and red-tiled ridge giving colour. The sw hall in the same manner, but placed at a lower level, was added by Anderson in 1898.

Interior with a boarded pointed tunnel roof over the nave. – Carved and gilded REREDOS designed by *Anderson* and executed by *Whytock & Reid*, 1904, its centre compartment containing two angels painted by *James Powell & Sons* of London. – Brass eagle LECTERN by *Jones & Willis*, 1891. – ORGAN by *C. & F. Hamilton*, 1894, its oak case with figures of trumpeting angels designed by *Anderson* and executed by *J. Slater*. – STAINED GLASS. Narrative E window (the Ascension) of 1904. – In the chancel, two lights (I am the Good Shepherd) by *William Wilson*, 1963. – In the nave's s wall, a four-light window* (the Transfiguration) by *James Powell & Sons (Whitefriars) Ltd*, 1950. – To its w, two lights (Simeon with the Infant Jesus; Eli with Samuel) of *c.*1950, much better than the contemporary window (S S Christopher and Michael) opposite. – Also in the N wall, a dark four-light window (the Ascension; the Supper at Emmaus) by *C. E. Kempe*, 1906.

NORTH CHURCH, Golfdrum Street. Built as a chapel of ease in 1840. Boxy with carpenter's Romanesque detail, a clock in the angular bellcote. Interior now featureless except for the semi-octagonal gallery on cast-iron columns.

---

* The window itself was opened up to receive the glass in 1950.

St Andrew, Queen Anne Street. Built as a chapel of ease in 1833 and now (1988) used as auction premises. Piend-roofed box. Unusually, the doors (to the area and galleries) are grouped together in the s gable's parapeted centre.

St Andrew's-Erskine Church, Queen Anne Street and Pilmuir Street. Built as a Burgher chapel in 1798–1800; *Alexander McFarlane* was the contractor, *David Whyte* of Edinburgh the architect. It is a large plain box ('rearing its enormous rectilinear ridge over all the other buildings in Dunfermline', complained *The New Statistical Account of Scotland*). Droved ashlar s front, the other elevations of rubble. On the gables, very small urns carved by *Robert Hutton*. In 1897–9 *John Houston* added a fussy Renaissance porch to the s vestry and an organ chamber above it. His too the cottage-Gothic ventilator on the roof.

The interior was recast in 1897–9. The semicircular gallery's cast-iron columns with Adamish capitals look re-used work of 1800; so too is probably the panelled front, but dressed up with 1890s swags. The focus is on the massive pulpit and organ (by *Ingram & Co.*, 1899). – STAINED GLASS. In the large windows flanking the pulpit, Resurrection scenes by *Heaton, Butler & Bayne*, 1903. – In the N wall, one light (Our Lord) of *c.* 1875, originally over the pulpit. – In the W porch, rustically lettered FOUNDATION STONE of the previous church on the site, dated 1747.

STATUE in front. Stone figure of Ralph Erskine by *A. Handyside Ritchie*, 1849.

42 St Leonard, Brucefield Avenue. 1903–4, by *P. MacGregor Chalmers* in his best Early Christian manner. Discreet rubbly walling, the round-arched windows quite plain. Tall N aisle with a double-pitch roof; s aisle a conventional lean-to under a clearstorey. The nave projects W for a further unaisled bay. In the angle of the s transept and E apse, a round conical-roofed tower of the Brechin Cathedral type.

The rubble walling continues inside. Round-headed cushion-capitalled arcades, tall on the N, stubby under the s clearstorey. In the N aisle, a gallery, its front decorated with the arms of great Scottish families. – On the apse ceiling, PAINTING of Our Lord and saints. – Circular stone FONT carved with interlaced arcading; spired wooden cover. – Arts and Crafts LECTERN of 1923. – ORGAN by *Henry Willis & Sons Ltd*. – STAINED GLASS. In the apse, two lights (SS Andrew and Paul), *c.* 1920. – In the N aisle, St Mungo, *c.* 1970, and Moses, by *The Abbey Studio*, 1951. – In the s aisle, David (*c.* 1930). – In that aisle's W window, an early C20 Madonna and Child, in good blues. – At the nave's W end, three windows (the Good Shepherd, the Bread of Life, and the True Vine) by *The Abbey Studio*, *c.* 1920.

St Margaret (R.C.), East Port. A huge papalist shrine of St Margaret to challenge the Presbyterians' Abbey Church (*see* Dunfermline Abbey, above) was designed by *R. Rowand Anderson* in 1889. The pinkish rubble nave and s porch (the church is orientated N–S) were completed in 1896. Very simple Transitional, based on Peterborough Cathedral but without the triforium. The porch looks bare without the pinnacled buttresses, omitted for lack of money. So too were the SE steeple, crossing tower, transepts and chancel. The chancel, built in a greyer stone with cement dressings, arrived in 1934–6, together with a sacristy and choir vestry (since remodelled) in place of the transepts.

Inside, round-arched nave arcades with the cushion capitals left in block. Semicircular tunnel-vaulted wooden ceiling intended for stencilled decoration. Extravagantly stilted central arch into the choir gallery over the porch. The chancel of 1934–6 is an anti-climax. – Wooden canopied stone REREDOS by *Reginald Fairlie*, 1939–40, with stylized statues of Scottish saints.

TOWNHILL CHURCH, Main Street. Originally Free. Mean Gothic in red sandstone, by *T. Hyslop Ure*, 1893–6.

TRINITY CHURCH (Episcopal), Pilmuir Street. Secularized. Unscholarly and not very lovable lancet style of 1842 by *Thomas Hamilton*. In the gable front a three-light window with image bases in front and a stilted hoodmould over the centre. Interior a Greek cross, with galleries on three sides inserted in 1891, when this became a Congregational chapel. – STAINED GLASS of 1842 with brightly coloured borders and roundels, by a 'Newcastle artificer', presumably *William Wailes*.

UNITED FREE CHURCH, Chalmers Street. Hall church by *David Beveridge*, 1936. It protrudes from a most enjoyable villa (Woodhead Cottage) of *c*.1830. Very Gothick, with huge crocketed finials, but the centre is pedimented and the outer windows would be Venetian did they not have ogee arches.

VIEWFIELD BAPTIST CHURCH, East Port. Lumpy Gothic, though not without ambition, by *Peter L. Henderson*, 1882–4.

WEST BAPTIST CHURCH, Chalmers Street. Plainest Gothic by *Andrew Scobie*, 1898.

PUBLIC BUILDINGS

ADMIRALTY MARINE TECHNOLOGY ESTABLISHMENT, Hospital Hill. Large and flashy late Victorian villa (St Leonard's House) engulfed in harled additions by *John Fraser & Son*, 1938.*

ALLAN CENTRE, Priory Lane. Former High School, by *James A. Mercer* and *F. & G. Holme*, all of Liverpool, 1883–6. The main block is utilitarian dressed up with crowsteps and an English baroque cupola ('Scotch Baronial adapted to modern requirements', said *The Builder*). Under the belfry opening of the tall saddlebacked E tower a huge hobgoblin carved by *Alexander Neilson* of Edinburgh gives a touch of nightmare. – The harled Primary Department on the E was added by *H. & D. Barclay* of Glasgow, 1909.

* The additions were built for the house's conversion to a teacher-training hostel.

BALDRIDGEBURN COMMUNITY CENTRE, Baldridgeburn.
Former District Library. By *H. & D. Barclay* of Glasgow,
1908–9. English picturesque in harl and red sandstone with a
tiled roof. The reading room has a skinny cupola and a parade
of gabled dormerheads down the flank.

BEANSTALK NURSERY, Fergus Place. By *Fife Regional Council*,
1975. At the w end a curved wall and a 'tower'.

BLACKLAW PRIMARY SCHOOL, Whitelaw Road. Festival of
Britain style by *Fife County Council*, 1952–3. Later glazed
additions.

BRUCE STREET HALL, Bruce Street. Built as a drill hall in 1866–
8. Institutional Gothic by *Andrew Scobie*.

BUS STATION AND CAR PARK, James Street. By *Fife Regional
Council*, 1983.

CANMORE PRIMARY SCHOOL, Evershed Drive. By *Fife
Regional Council*, 1975.

CARNEGIE CENTRE, Pilmuir Street. By *Hippolyte J. Blanc* of
Edinburgh, 1901–5. Low-key early Renaissance with a Scots
inflexion. Tall steep-gabled centre gripped by ogee-roofed
towers, long domesticated wings. Brick extension with some
high tech touches, part of the reconstruction by *James Parr
& Partners*, 1979–84. – Bronze relief PANELS flanking the
entrance ('In Infantia Pudor'; 'In Viro Virtus') by *Reginald
Goulden*, 1906.

CARNEGIE CLINIC, Pilmuir Street and Inglis Street. Stolid
Franco-Scots Renaissance by *H. & D. Barclay* of Glasgow,
1911–12.

CARNEGIE HALL, East Port. Classical-modern by *Muirhead &
Rutherford*, 1933–7, linked to a Tudor villa ('Benachie') of
c.1865.

CEMETERY, Leys Park Road. Laid out 1861–3; extended E
1899.

CENTRAL LIBRARY, Abbot Street. The first of the Carnegie
public libraries in Scotland, it is by *J. C. Walker*, 1881–3,
in subdued Gothic *hôtel-de-ville* style. Extension down St
Margaret Street in a stripped vertical variant of the same by
James Shearer, 1914–21. Inside, the Lending Library's glazed
tunnel-vault is of 1881–3. Most of the rest is of 1914–21.
Wrought-iron STAIR RAIL by *Thomas Hadden* to Shearer's
design.

112 CITY CHAMBERS, Kirkgate and Bridge Street. Formidably
French-Baronial in Polmaise sandstone, by *James C. Walker*,
1875–9. At the corner, a huge steeple. Two-stage conical-
roofed bartizans at the top of the tower. Then a spire interrupted two-thirds of the way up by a gabled clock-stage. On
the tower's face to Bridge Street, an oriel window. To Kirkgate
the tower has a cavernous entrance under a stone balcony.
The building's Kirkgate frontage continues with another stone
balcony and a corbelled stair turret, to end with an octagonal
tower; plentiful crocketed and gabled detail at the top-floor
windows. More routine elevation to Bridge Street, broken by
a crowstepped gable and ending with a turreted oriel.

COMMERCIAL and ST MARGARET'S R.C. PRIMARY SCHOOLS, off Woodmill Road. Two schools in one playground. Both are of 1970, by *Fife County Council*.

DUNFERMLINE BOWLING CLUB, Priory Lane. Picturesque pavilion by *T. Hyslop Ure*, 1895.

DUNFERMLINE HIGH SCHOOL, St Leonard's Place and Jennie Rennie's Road. By *George Sandilands*, 1934–9. Additions on NW by *Fife County Council*, 1959, and by *G. H. McConnell* of *Fife Regional Council*, 1978–83.

For the former Dunfermline High School, *see* Allan Centre above.

DUNFERMLINE AND WEST FIFE HOSPITAL, Reid Street, Nethertown Broad Street and New Row. An architectural mess. The S block of 1893–4 was designed as a cottage hospital by *Sydney Mitchell & Wilson*. Understated Queen Anne with a cupola on the pavilion-roofed centre. The same architects' additions of 1898 and 1903 stretched the design inordinately. PRIORY HOUSE on the NW, a brutalist Greek villa of c. 1835, was acquired in 1926 and given a large rear wing fronting New Row by *Muirhead & Rutherford*, 1928–31. The CASUALTY BLOCK by *John Holt*, 1955–8, stirred an indeterminate Modern Movement chunk into the mixture.

EMPLOYMENT OFFICE, Guildhall Street. 1935–6 by *H.M. Office of Works*. Weak late C17 Scots style in purplish stone.

FIRE STATION, Carnegie Drive. By *James Shearer*, 1934–6. In harl and blue brick. Quite a way after Dudok, but it reminded *The Architect* of Charles Rennie Mackintosh.

GASWORKS, Grange Road. Opened 1883, the date of the N gasholder, which has pretty latticed ironwork. The second holder and most of the other buildings were added by *Thomas Newbigging* of Manchester, 1893.

GLEN BRIDGE. Modern-traditional in concrete by *F. A. Mac-Donald & Partners*, 1930–2.

GUILDHALL, High Street. Now (1988) in commercial use. By *Archibald Elliot*, 1805–11. Solidly detailed classical block, its rock-faced basement developing to a one-storey plinth down the slope of Guildhall Street. Ground-floor windows enlarged to fill their round-headed overarches in the alterations of 1985. The front's centre bay is advanced and pedimented with pilasters and a Doric frieze. Above, a nicely complicated steeple, its stages changing from square-plan to octagonal to circular before ending with an octagonal spire.

KINGSEATHILL COMMUNITY CENTRE, Paton Street. By *Dunfermline Burgh Council*, 1975. Small, blocky and garishly painted.

LAUDER TECHNICAL SCHOOL, Priory Lane and New Row. Now (1983) Priory Lane Induction Centre. By *H. & D. Barclay* of Glasgow, 1898–9. Plain except for the ambitious turreted and pedimented centre, Jacobean with a hint of Indian. Blocky red sandstone extension to New Row by the same architects, 1907–10.

LYNBURN COMMUNITY CENTRE, Abbey View. By *Dun-*

fermline Burgh Council, 1965. Upper floor cantilevered over the entrance.

LYNBURN PRIMARY SCHOOL, Nith Street. By *Fife County Council*, 1960–1.

LYNEBANK HOSPITAL, Halbeath Road. 1965–9, by *Alison & Hutchison & Partners*. Single-storey brick wards bullied by the Administration Block's shuttered concrete. Crisply rendered staff residences.

McLEAN PRIMARY SCHOOL, Baldridgeburn. By *Andrew Scobie*, 1895–6. Relaxed with big gables, scrolly topped or pedimented with scroll supporters.

MASONIC HALL, Pilmuir Street. Two-storey villa front of 1832 with giant angle pilasters.

MASONIC LODGE (LODGE UNION 250), New Row. By *John Houston*, 1904. Small but very classical, with a Doric porch and exaggerated entasis on the dormers.

MATERNITY HOSPITAL, Izatt Avenue. Brick and harl, by *Muirhead & Rutherford*, 1934–6.

MILESMARK HOSPITAL, West Baldridge Road. Originally West of Fife Infectious Diseases Joint Hospital. By *C. S. S. Johnston* and *David B. Burnie* of Edinburgh, 1892–3. Main block of glazed red brick with a mean pediment; cottagey ward blocks. Additions to w and n by *E. Simpson* of Stirling, 1910, and *R. H. Motion*, 1915.

MILESMARK PRIMARY SCHOOL, Rumblingwell. Gothic with lots of steep gables, by *Andrew Scobie*, 1874–6.

NETHERTOWN COMMUNITY CENTRE, Nethertown Broad Street. Former Public Library and Baths. Asymmetrical English baroque by *James Lindsay* of Glasgow, 1912–18.

NORTHERN HOSPITAL, Leys Park Road. The w part was built as the poorhouse in 1843; very simple with slightly advanced ends. In 1905–7 *Muirhead & Rutherford* extended it E, disguising the join with a Wrenaissance centrepiece. Behind, the governor's house of 1843 with a block pedimented doorpiece.

PITCORTHIE PRIMARY SCHOOL, Aberdour Road. By *Fife County Council*, 1954–5.

PITREAVIE PRIMARY SCHOOL, off Pitcorthie Drive. By *Fife County Council*, 1969–70.

PITTENCRIEFF PARK. *See* p. 192.

PITTENCRIEFF PRIMARY SCHOOL, Dewar Street. Plain Wrenaissance by *H. & D. Barclay* of Glasgow, 1901–3. On the E its Gothic predecessor of 1874 by *Andrew Scobie*.

POLICE STATION, Holyrood Place and Carnegie Drive. 1972–3, by *Fife County Council*. In front, a gauche BRONZE ('Caring Philosophy') of police (one of each sex) with a small girl, by *Alistair Smart*, 1976.

POST OFFICE, Queen Anne Street and Pilmuir Street. Unadventurous Scots Renaissance of 1889–90 by *W. W. Robertson* of *H.M. Office of Works*, who extended it N in 1902 with another gabled bay and a brick garage court behind a screen wall. In this wall, two* stones, one inscribed 'SEP[E]./

* The RCAHMS reported a third, now gone.

DOCE.ET./CASTIGA.VT/VIVAT PUER.' (Be diligent to teach and beat so that the boy may live), the other carved with the burgh arms and the recut inscription 'FAVE MIHI MI DEVS 1625'. Both are from the High School which stood on the site.

POWER STATION, off Townhill Road. Opened 1905, and now derelict.

PRISON, Leys Park Road. 1842–5, presumably by *Thomas Brown Jun.* Only the outer wall with a few martial slits survives.

PUBLIC PARK, West Drive. *Joseph Paxton* was consulted on the lay-out in 1864–5 and a 'rough draft was done by himself and under his eye', the finished plan being sent to the Town Council after Paxton's death by *G. H. Stokes*, his principal assistant. This was adopted for the lay-out of the N part of the land (the S being taken by the railway) in 1866. – Ogee-roofed BANDSTAND by *Walter Macfarlane & Co.* (*Saracen Foundry*) of Glasgow, 1888. – On the N, red granite FOUNTAIN by *R. M. Cameron* of Edinburgh, 1886–7, baroque with a lion on top.

QUEEN ANNE HIGH SCHOOL, Pilmuir Street. Festival of Britain style in red brick with touches of harl, by *Harry Lind*, 1955–8. – W addition by *Fife County Council*, 1967, with a thin round-arched frame for full-height glazing.

RAILWAY VIADUCT over Woodmill Street and Bothwell Street. By *R. Young & Son*, 1874–7. A gentle curve of hammerdressed rubble; thirteen segmental arches.

REGISTRATION OFFICE, Abbot Street and Guildhall Street. Former Parish Council Offices. By *Muirhead & Rutherford*, 1912–13. Undecided between Wrenaissance and Art Nouveau.

ST COLUMBA'S R.C. HIGH SCHOOL, Woodmill Road. By *Fife County Council*, 1967–9. Sensible; glass and aggregate panels in a concrete frame. Hall with a fully glazed S wall.

ST LEONARD'S PRIMARY SCHOOL, St Leonard's Street. Small-scale but exuberant English baroque by *H. & D. Barclay* of Glasgow, 1900–2. Tall Art Nouveau wrought-iron finials on the ogee-roofed end pavilions.

ST MARGARET'S R.C. PRIMARY SCHOOL. *See* Commercial and St Margaret's R.C. Primary Schools, above.

SHERIFF COURT, Carnegie Drive. By *Property Services Agency*, 1983. Informal group of single-storey brick ranges with mon-opitch roofs, more like sheltered housing than a palace of justice.

TERRITORIAL ARMY CENTRE, 53 Elgin Street. By *Gillespie & Scott*, 1911–12. Wrenaissance drill hall (its front block with an added upper floor). Adjoining instructor's house with a segmental pedimented gablet.

TOUCH PRIMARY SCHOOL, Garvock Bank. 1970, by *Fife County Council*.

TOWNHILL COMMUNITY CENTRE, Main Street. Former Public Library and Baths. By *Peter L. Henderson* of Edinburgh, 1905–6. Cottagey, with a broad-eaved red-tile roof and small pagoda ventilators.

TOWNHILL PRIMARY SCHOOL, Chisholm Street. Chunky Gothic by *Thomas Frame & Son*, 1875.

WELLWOOD PRIMARY SCHOOL, Baldridge Place. Plain village school of 1876, with a teacher's house at one end.

WILSON'S INSTITUTION, New Row. Dated 1857. Single-storey pedimented front spoilt by over-cleaning. It was built as a replica of the School of Art on the S (by *Robert Hay*, 1854–5; made unrecognizable by *T. Waller Marwick*'s reconstruction, 1950–4).

WOMEN'S INSTITUTE, 8 Pilmuir Street. Now a pub (1988). Carefully detailed squared-up Scots Renaissance, by *Archibald Welsh*, 1911–12.

WOODMILL HIGH SCHOOL, Shields Road and Dunn Crescent. By *Fife County Council*, 1960. Straightforward three storeys with strong horizontals.

PITTENCRIEFF PARK

Pittencrieff House and its surrounding parkland were bought in 1902 by the millionaire Andrew Carnegie, who presented them to his native burgh in the next year.

N of the main path from the W, featureless fragment of MALCOLM CANMORE'S TOWER set high above the Tower Burn. The surviving rubble packing of the S and W wall shows that the structure traditionally believed to have been built by Malcolm I in the C11 was rectangular, with 3m.-thick walls. The path is carried across the burn by TOWER BRIDGE of 1788, a segmental lower arch at the level of the previous bridge of 1611, with a semicircular arch above it raising the roadway to a higher level; parapets added by *James Shearer*, 1915. Above the 1788 date stone, an inset stone from the earlier bridge inscribed 'AR [for *Anna Regina*] 1611'. On the bank to the r., an Edwardian Chinese rustic SUMMERHOUSE.

The drydashed PITTENCRIEFF HOUSE to the S was built for Sir Alexander Clerk of Pittencrieff c.1635. Clerk's house was a simple laird's house of two storeys and an attic, but an extra floor was added in 1731 (the date on the SE skewputt). Stairtower projecting from the S front's centre. In its inner angle, moulded door with the lintel inscribed PRAISED.BE. GOD.FOR.AL.HIS.GIFTES; Clerk's arms in a panel above. A segmental pedimented dormerhead should stand clear of the eaves but has been absorbed into the added top floor. Pediments of Clerk's time over second-floor windows in the gables. In 1908–11 *Robert S. Lorimer* reconstructed the interior as a club and museum, introducing new panelling and enriched plaster ceilings (by *Thomas Beattie*). Ground-floor ceiling derived from the house's former C17 dining room ceiling. In the centre first-floor room, ceiling with typically Lorimerian vine decoration around a heavy foliage circle. In the second-floor gallery, a pointed tunnel-vault with panels of lively decoration; plaster strapwork and figures of Industry, Prudence, Justice and Generosity on the end walls. At the top landing of the stair, wrought-iron balustrade with a big thistle, probably by *Thomas Hadden*. Beside the house, FOUNTAIN with Art

Nouveauish basins and a sentimental statue of a youth (Ambition), by *Richard Goulden*, 1908.

To the NW, a Cape-Baronial CAFETERIA of 1927 by *John Fraser*, extended W with a MUSIC HALL in a stronger version of the same style, by *F. A. MacDonald & Partners*, 1934. Inside the entrance hall, fountain with crouching figures by *Goulden*. To the N, DOOCOT, of *c.* 1770, like a crenellated round tower. Prominently placed huge STATUE of Andrew Carnegie in a frock coat by *Goulden*, 1913–14. At the NE corner, the LOUISE CARNEGIE MEMORIAL GATES of 1928 by *Jamieson & Arnott*, in the manner of *c.* 1700. Cushion-rusticated piers with swagged urns; wrought-iron screenwork by *Hadden*. 113

CENTRAL AREA PERAMBULATION

On the approach from the E by the A907, a roundabout to mark the central area's edge. EAST PORT ahead begins with the Carnegie Hall and a trio of churches (*see* Public Buildings and Churches, above). The N side goes on well enough with Nos. 58–62 of *c.* 1800, the ground floor built out as shops but with a pedimented doorpiece to James Street behind. The Art Deco classical ORIENT EXPRESS CINEMA by *John Fraser*, 1913, is fun. Not so the DUNFERMLINE BUILDING SOCIETY by *James Shearer & Annand*, 1979–81, whose modern-traditional front block fails to hide a huge rump.

On the S, two houses of *c.* 1830 with Doric porches, Roman at CENTURY HOUSE, attenuated Greek at Nos. 35–41. (Diversion down COMMERCIAL SCHOOL LANE, where TOWER HOUSE was built as the Commercial School Primary Department in 1892–4, a *cottage orné* with Wrenaissance detail. The old COMMERCIAL ACADEMY behind (now flatted) is of 1815–16). Staid *moderne* ELECTRICITY SERVICE CENTRE (No. 33 East Port) by *R. H. Motion*, 1938, and dour Baronial TRUSTEE SAVINGS BANK of 1873–5. (On the E side of WALMER DRIVE a classy late Georgian villa with horizontal glazing.) No. 15 114 East Port of 1914–16 was designed by *Paul Waterhouse** for the Prudential Assurance Co. Very tall and very Greek, but detail already going Art Deco; low relief of Prudentia. The BANK OF SCOTLAND by *Wheeler & Sproson*, 1977, is a blank contrast to its predecessor on the New Row corner, clumsy baroque by *James T. Scobie*, 1912.

HIGH STREET used to mix C18 vernacular with decent late Georgian and Victorian and Edwardian commercial, but developers' shanty-town has now almost taken over. On the S, a long neo-vernacular block by *Covell Matthews & Partners*, 1978, makes half-hearted concessions to planners' sensibilities but is an unworthy prelude to the old Guildhall (*see* Public Buildings, above).

The N side starts with the huge KIRKGATE SHOPPING CENTRE by *Hugh Wilson & Lewis Womersley*, 1982–5, a development stretching back to James Street, the shops served

* *James Shearer* was executant architect.

by an L-plan arcade entered through a fully glazed round arch decorated with brightly painted metalwork. Stripped Palladian former ROYAL BANK of 1906–9 by *Sydney Mitchell & Wilson*. Old COMMERCIAL BANK (No. 100), blocky Scottish by *Frank Burnet & Boston* of Glasgow, 1914. The BANK OF SCOTLAND by *David Cousin*, 1874, is Italianate. No. 66 by *Andrew Scobie*, 1901, turns the corner to Cross Wynd with a conical roofed turret and curved glass shopfront. Another turret on the CLYDESDALE BANK (built as the North of Scotland Bank, 1898, and reconstructed by *Kenneth Oliver*, 1981–2), but it is bullied by segmental pediments. The old CLYDESDALE BANK (No. 38) by *Baird & Thomson* of Glasgow, 1902, has hugely bracketed pediments over the first-floor windows. Then the DUNFERMLINE CO-OPERATIVE SOCIETY with a grim François I front block of 1901 by *Andrew Scobie* running back to modern-classical Halls on Queen Anne Street (by *John Fraser*, 1925).

For the churches and public buildings of Queen Anne Street, Pilmuir Street and Chapel Street, *see* above. Simple late Georgian houses on the N side of QUEEN ANNE STREET. The grandest (No. 40) was built as a manse in 1766–7 but given a further three storeys by *Muirhead & Rutherford*, 1915, when it became one entrance to their PALACE KINEMA, whose other entrance is a small but rich Wrenaissance block on Pilmuir Street.

BRIDGE STREET, after the huge mass of the City Chambers (*see* Public Buildings, above), is mostly small-scale Georgian with Yukon shopfronts. A couple of timidly picturesque houses (the N dated 1912) flank the grand approach to Pittencrieff Park (*see* above). More smashed Georgian in CHALMERS STREET focused on the North Church (*see* Churches, above). On the w, CANON LYNCH COURT, neo-vernacular in red brick by *Dunfermline District Council*, 1982.

Kirkgate squeezes past the City Chambers towards the Abbey (*see* above). In ST CATHERINE'S WYND, the OLD INN's late Victorian front is crisp in black and white paint. On the N side of MAYGATE, a long grey and pink block (Nos. 2–18) by *T. Hyslop Ure*, 1896; then plain late Georgian into ABBOT STREET and the Registration Office (*see* Public Buildings, above). Opposite, the ABBOT'S HOUSE, a late C16 tenement with a projecting stairtower. Above the door, recut inscription:

SEN.VORD.IS.THRALL.AND.THOCHT.IS.FRE
KEIP.VEILL.THY.TONGE.I.COINSELL.THE

On the garden side another stairtower at the E end, partly covered by a lower early C18 wing. Turrets in the inner angles. Harling was stripped and crowsteps removed in *James Shearer & Annand*'s restoration of 1963. Inside, three out of four vaulted cellars survive. Beyond the lumpy Renaissance former Commercial Bank (by *Wardrop & Reid*, 1883), the Central Library (*see* Public Buildings, above) faces across St Margaret Street to the white-painted ST MARGARET'S HOTEL of *c*. 1800.

On CANMORE STREET's N side, the ROYAL BANK, classy late Georgian with a pedimented porch and scrolled skewputts. Art Deco shop by *R. H. Motion*, 1937, beside the Congregational Church (*see* Churches, above). Beyond is the hole left by the demolition of St Paul's Church,* revealing Littlewoods' yellow backside. Opposite, a pair of houses (Nos. 27–29) of *c.*1830, with Ionic porches. At the end, ALHAMBRA THEATRE of 1922, with a mean front and vast red brick behind. On the E side of NEW ROW, COMELY PARK HOUSE, a villa of 1785 Jacobeanized in 1893. On its front lawn, a pyramid-topped SUNDIAL dated 1786.

ABBEY PARK PLACE begins badly with the nondescript TELE-PHONE EXCHANGE (by the *Ministry of Public Buildings and Works*, 1961–4). Then late Georgian prosperity. No. 12 with a Roman Doric porch and effetely consoled cornices over the ground-floor windows. No. 15 is grander; porch on the N, bowed centre to the S with cast-iron balconies. Inside, drawing room with Adamesque plasterwork. Blowsy porch on the mid-C19 No. 13. Crowsteps and a pedimented doorpiece on the late C18 No. 11. No. 5 has an attenuated Greek Doric porch, but its front has been painted. Opposite is the ABBEY CHURCH HALL, late medieval Anglo-French by *John Houston*, 1902, beside a Scots Renaissance block dated 1899.

In ST MARGARET STREET beside the churchyard's E entrance, ABBEY GARDENS COTTAGE by *Robert Bonnar*, 1841, Tudor with wavy-edged bargeboards. MONASTERY STREET has two WAR MEMORIALS. Great War cenotaph by *Taylor & Young* of Manchester, 1925; less authoritarian the Second World War memorial by *James Shearer*, 1952–3. BUCHANAN STREET has two bits of a terrace of *c.*1830 but on different building lines. At the foot of St Margaret Street, one jamb of the SOUTH PORT of the Abbey precinct, perhaps C14. In a large garden at the top of MOODIE STREET, the ABBEY MANSE by *Alexander Laing* of Edinburgh, 1814, with a pedimented S front. Opposite is the CARNEGIE BIRTHPLACE, a pantiled cottage isolated as a monument nannied by *James Shearer*'s Scots C17 style additions of 1925.

For Priory Lane's public buildings, *see* above. COMELY PARK was laid out by *Andrew Scobie* in 1875 for comfortable but unexciting villas. Off VIEWFIELD TERRACE to the N is VIEW-FIELD HOUSE of *c.*1810, tall with a pedimented centre and Tower of the Winds doorpiece.

S of the railway viaduct (*see* Public Buildings, above) the tower of St Leonard's Church is a landmark. BOTHWELL STREET is the beginning of the main road to Rosyth. On its l., THE BOTANY, a white harled and crowstepped early C18 T-plan house, now rather altered. Then the old ST LEONARDS WORKS built as a linen mill in 1851 and now housing (ERS-KINE-BEVERIDGE COURT). It is an opulent palazzo, the short front facing the street, the sides extending back for seventeen bays. Off Hospital Hill further out, ST ANDREWS STREET

* After a fire in 1976.

with pleasant interwar housing leads to the Scottish Special Housing Association's HOGGAN CRESCENT development by *Sam Bunton*, 1940. Two-storey flat-roofed blocks, the cellular concrete or brickwork walls covered with render. Flat concrete canopies over the doors. Conventionally shaped windows, some still with metal-framed horizontal glazing.

STANDING STONE, Standing Stone Walk, off Tweeddale Drive, a feature in the housing estate. A plaque 350m. to the ENE marks the discovery of a group of Bronze Age burials and cists in 1972.

MANSIONS

HILL HOUSE. *See*. p. 239.

KEAVIL HOUSE (HOTEL), 2.8km. W. Early C19 country house, but the design is so unbalanced that it looks as if something much bigger was intended. On the E (entrance) front, ignoring the S addition of 1982, the front door is on the l., then a pedimented gable with a Venetian window, then the curving service wing. A mid-C19 bay window adds to the muddle. More bay windows have been added to the harled W front.

Late Victorian bargeboarded N LODGE with half-timbering and a red-tiled roof.

PITTENCRIEFF PARK. *See* p. 192.

3080   DUNIMARLE CASTLE
                        0.8km. W of Culross

78 Spectacularly sited and picturesquely composed castle-villa of 1839–45 incorporating a small late C18 mansion house. It was designed by *R. & R. Dickson* for Mrs Magdalene Sharpe Erskine, who had recently acquired the estate.

The planned approach* is from the N along a 1.2km. avenue entered from the A985 through a martial gatehouse, its round-arched pend now infilled. The avenue ends with another gate-house, its round towers (the r. a dairy, the l. a lodge) flanking the carriage-entrance to a roughly triangular court, whose NW side is filled by the house, the others defined by steep drops towards the Forth. At the triangle's N apex, battlemented screen walls, the SE with a large turreted gateway to the garden, the NW running to the house.

At the house's NE end, a tall single-storey conservatory with slim 'Saxon' windows between crenellated buttresses. The pitched glass roof was removed *c.*1960, when the conservatory was made into a house. Then the three-storey main block of 1839. Heavy corbelled and crenellated parapet with animal gargoyles at the corners; mullioned windows. It is dominated by a projecting four-storey tower under a machicolated

* The present (1988) approach is from the B9037 to the S.

parapet. Continuous corbelled and crenellated balcony under the first-floor windows; individual stone balconies under the upper windows. In the NE face, a Romanesque door of five cushion-capitalled orders. The inner angle with the C18 house is filled by a yet taller slender stair turret. The general concept clearly derives from Nash's East Cowes Castle. The Dicksons' schemes to recase the C18 house were not carried out, and it remains a stolid two-storey three-bay box, a battlemented parapet of c.1845 its only concession to the adjoining castellated cuckoo. Service court of 1839–45 behind; most of the outbuildings were demolished c.1960.

Inside, the C18 house's ground-floor rooms are decently finished; shallow relief ceiling rose over its stair. In the tower of 1839, a D-plan entrance hall. Opposite the door, a Romanesque arched chimneypiece (containing a stove) under a huge knot-ended rope moulding. Heraldic panels on the compartmented ceiling, whose ribs are borne on corbels modelled as animal heads. The stairhall behind rises the full three storeys to a crude hammerbeam roof. Straight stair to the first floor overlooked by a second-floor balcony, both with quatrefoil-pierced oak balustrades. To the r., a ribbed tunnel-vaulted corridor to the conservatory. The identical first-floor corridor led to the conservatory's balcony. Off it, a plain ante-room opening into the boudoir. The boudoir's back part is a rectangular recess with an almost flat rib-vaulted plaster ceiling. Similar ceiling in its higher D-plan main part in the tower, the ribs springing from cherub corbels to meet at a central pendant. Sleepy cherubs carved on the white marble chimneypiece's corners. A short windowless passage hung with painted Chinese paper opens into the C18 house's first floor, whose front rooms were thrown together in the mid-C19 to form a U-plan library, re-divided by *Stewart Tod & Sons* c.1960. On each of the tower's upper floors, an octagonal room (print room and studio) with a ribbed ceiling with a central pendant.

To the W, RUINS of an earlier house built against a wall which may have been part of the medieval Dunimarle Castle. At its N end, remains of a domical-vaulted structure, probably an C18 ICEHOUSE.* – GARDEN to the E, a long terrace in front of a battlemented wall of c.1840.

ST SERF'S (EPISCOPAL) CHAPEL (disused) to the SE was built by Mrs Sharpe Erskine in 1870. Her architect was *R. Rowand Anderson*. Very simple but admirably confident Transitional buttressed box with an apsed E end. In the W gable, a wheel window beneath a blind vesica carved with an angel holding the Saltire; on top, large gabled bellcote for three bells. SW porch, the door capitals carved with friendly dragons. Red-tiled roof ridge to give a touch of colour.

The interior is a single space, the chancel and sanctuary marked off only by steps and the stiffleaf caps of the apse windows. Wooden ceiling, the pointed tunnel-vault stencilled

* But the RCAHMS thought it the ground floor of a tower.

with decorative patterns and coats of arms. More stencilling
on the walls, lined as ashlar with a delicate motif on each
'stone'; frieze of texts round the chancel and sanctuary. –
ORGAN by *D. & T. Hamilton*, now (1986) partly dismantled. –
STAINED GLASS mostly broken. Nave and chancel windows
all by *Burlison & Grylls*, the W rose window brightly coloured,
the others in *grisaille*. Apse windows by *Clayton & Bell*.

5010   # DUNINO

Isolated group of church and manse with the school on the main
road a little to the W.

PARISH CHURCH. By *James Gillespie Graham*, 1826–7. Tall
crowstepped Gothic box with hoodmoulded windows and
door. Spiky gableted bellcote on the W gable. The church was
remodelled in 1928 by *J. Jeffrey Waddell & Young*,[*] who
added the chancel and SW porch and stripped the plaster from
the interior. An agreeable touch is their decoration of window
sills with carved foliage; more foliage on lintels of the porch
and boiler room.

Furnishings all of 1928. The pine PEWS incorporate Geor-
gian woodwork. – Oak COMMUNION TABLE, PULPIT and
LECTERN by *Thomas W. Wilson*, with sparing Lorimerian
carving. – Similar PRAYER DESK by *Alexander P. Smith*. –
Pink stone FONT by *Robert S. Lorimer*, an eagle finial on its
cover. – STAINED GLASS in the chancel (the E window showing
St George and St Michael, the S Esther, the N Ruth) all by *J.
Jennings*, 1930–1.

MANSE in a large garden to the N, by *Robert Balfour*, 1819;
smart with a Roman Doric pilastered porch.

PITTARTHIE CASTLE. *See* p. 346.

DUNNIKIER HOUSE
see KIRKCALDY: NORTH, p. 294

2010   # DUNSHELT

Village of C19 whinstone cottages, several pantiled, and discreet
local authority housing (some of it by *Walker & Pride*, 1933).

EARTHWORK, probably Iron Age (but possibly much later), on
curiously low-lying ground, about 42m. by 36m. within as
many as four ramparts and ditches with an average of more
than 9m. between the two outer banks, though much of the
NE perimeter has been destroyed. SE entrance. The 13.5m.-
diameter annular bank in the middle is probably later.

---

[*] Adapting plans prepared in 1908 by *P. MacGregor Chalmers*, but omitting his
proposed transepts.

DURA HOUSE
1.1km. S of Kemback

Mid-C18 crowstep-gabled laird's house bullied by *John Milne*'s large but unexciting Baronial addition of *c.*1860.

DURIE HOUSE
1.9km. N of Leven

Smart piend-roofed box built for the Christies in 1762. Ashlar-fronted with rusticated quoins to add punch. Three-bay centre slightly advanced under an urn-finialled pediment, the tympanum carved with foliage. Pediments over the centre's first-floor windows. Venetian door dignifying the ground floor, whose square windows give it the character of a basement. Pediments, triangular and segmental, over the W gable's first-floor windows. Back wing with a crenellated parapet, probably early C19.

Small STANDING STONE 0.4km. to the E. Red sandstone, 1.3m. high, 1.7m. girth at the base.

DYSART *see* KIRKCALDY, pp. 288–91

EARLSFERRY *see* ELIE AND EARLSFERRY

EARLSHALL
1km. E of Leuchars

The C16 tower house of the Bruces of Earlshall, restored in the 1890s by *Robert S. Lorimer*, who provided it with the setting it should always have had.

According to an inscription above the Long Gallery chimneypiece, the house was begun by Sir William Bruce in 1546 and completed by his great-grandson and namesake in 1617. It is the most complete example in Fife of the late C16 grouping of house and offices round a small courtyard.

N approach through Lorimer's two-storey GATEHOUSE of 1900. Unaggressively crazy-paved whinstone rubble walls; bellcast roof. Off-centre carriage arch, a round tower projecting from the wall on its r. The drive continues past the garden wall to the house on the N side of the courtyard. C16 W BARMKIN WALL, its top corbelled for a parapet with a bartizan over the round-arched gateway. Each side of the entrance, a splayed gunloop.

The house itself is built of rubble from which Lorimer stripped the harling. Z-plan with a round NE jamb; the opposite jamb's outer wall continues the line of the W gable rather than

being projected beyond it, as was more usual. The main block
is a straightforward crowstep-gabled rectangle. On each of the
long N and S fronts, the two second-floor windows are carried
up above the eaves with dormerheads, three of them steeply
pedimented, the fourth broken by an obelisk finial. In the
pediments, the arms of Bruce and Lindsay for Sir William
Bruce II and his second wife, Agnes Lindsay, so these at least
must be part of the early C17 remodelling. So also appears to
be the top floor of the SW jamb, its W dormerhead again carved
with the Bruce and Lindsay arms. In this jamb's inner angle
with the main block, a stairtower, rectangular except for its
bowed SE corner. Above the entrance, a shield flanked by the
initials MM for Margaret Meldrum, wife of Sir William Bruce
I; higher up, another shield and the initials WB. Corbelled out
on top, a cap-house, probably early C17, with boldly projecting
rainwater spouts below its widely crenellated parapet. Stair to
the cap-house cutting across the inner angle of the stairtower
and jamb. The fat NE jamb slices into the main block's gable.
Huge NE chimney. In the SW corner, a corbelled stair turret.

The interior has tunnel-vaulted cellars under the main block
and NE jamb. Double-keyhole gunloops in the outer walls.
Under the SW jamb, a vaulted room with a fireplace in its S
gable. Sink in the W wall, so perhaps this was the C16 kitchen,
but it looks more like a porter's room.

Turnpike stair, its windows filled by Lorimer with pretty
stained glass. In the SW jamb's first-floor room, early C18
panelling. Wooden ceiling, its centre painted with a scrolled
border enclosing the impaled arms of Bruce and Lindsay and
the date 1636. Lorimer restored the main block's two W rooms
as a single hall but marked the line of the C18 partition wall
(possibly replacing a C16 screen) with a version of the chapel
screen at Falkland Palace. In the W part, red-tiled floor of the
1890s, simple early C18 panelling; the chimneypiece is by
Lorimer, of late C17 type dressed up with his favourite rosettes
and a motto. In the hall's main part to the E, a stone-flagged
floor. Large S fireplace, its lintel (renewed in cement) bearing
the arms and initials of Alexander Bruce and Euphame Leslie,
so it was introduced presumably between 1572, when they
married, and 1587, when she died. Mid-C17 plaster pendant
hanging from the ceiling. Unpainted pine panelling here and
in the adjoining drawing room. In the drawing room's SE
corner, a closet, its windows with Lorimer stained glass dated
1894. From the NE corner, access to a bedroom in the jamb
and to a private stair to the floor above.

The whole of the main block's second floor is filled with the
Long Gallery, probably the early C17 creation of Sir William
Bruce II. It is covered by a boarded elliptically vaulted ceiling.
This ceiling, the upper part of the walls and the two stone
chimneypieces are all painted in tempera, much restored in
distemper by *Nixon* of *Moxon & Carfrae* in the 1890s. Stylized
patterns on the chimneypieces. Above the larger S fireplace, a
stone shield with the initials and impaled arms of Sir William

Bruce I and his wife Margaret Meldrum; in the panel's upper part, a Latin inscription recording the house's beginning in 1546 and completion in 1617. Frieze along the side walls with a painted arcade (cf. Gladstone's Land, Edinburgh), the arches containing aphorisms (e.g. 'A . NICE . WYF . AND / A . BACK . DOORE / OFT . MAKETH . A . RICH / MAN . POORE') culled from William Baldwin's *A Treatise of Morall Philosophye ... enlarged by T. Paulfreyman* and the *Meditations* of Marcus Aurelius Antoninus. The ceiling itself is covered with painted panels arranged in rows which alternate coats of arms of the great families of Israel, Europe and Scotland with animal subjects taken from Conrad Gesner's *Historia Animalium* of 1551, interspersed with flowers. The initials of Sir William Bruce II and Agnes Lindsay appear twice, once accompanied by the date 1620. All this painted C17 decoration is in black or grey and white, the effect admirably cool. The W wall's upper part is filled with the portrait of a bloodhound* by *David Steell*, 1895, set in a border inscribed with lines from Byron's *Inscription on the Monument of a Newfoundland Dog*.

In the NE jamb's second-floor rooms, beams painted with stylized foliage. Similar painted beams in the SW jamb's room, which also has early C18 panelling with a lugged architrave round the fireplace. In the room above, another wooden ceiling painted in black and white with animal designs. At the top of the stair, a wrought-iron balustrade of the 1890s, decorated with thistles. Stairhead ceiling painted with stylized foliage.

On the courtyard's S side, an informal range. At its W end, an almost square crowstepped tower, probably C16. Next to it, a two-storey early C17 kitchen block, its pedimented dormerheads embellishments of 1891; at the same time Lorimer added a bay window on the S side. Small E block heavily reconstructed in the 1890s, with a forestair. Inside, the vaulted ground-floor kitchen has a large E fireplace. The walls and ceiling of the room above were panelled in 1891.

In the courtyard, a WELL to which Lorimer gave a decorative wrought-iron top. On the E side, which had a high wall in the C16, he placed a balustrade to contain the space but not impede views of his new topiary garden.

The large WALLED GARDEN wrapped round three sides of the C16 courtyard was intended by Lorimer to evoke the idea of an old Scottish garden integrally related to the house, quite the opposite of those parkland settings which, he complained, made Baronial houses appear as if they were engaged on a Sunday stroll. Inside the garden, the N part was laid out as a kitchen garden, the centre as a topiary garden and yew walk, the SE as a lawn and the SW an orchard.

At the NW corner, a two-storey GARDEN HOUSE. On its S front, a stone dormerhead with stone monkeys climbing up it. On the E, a forestair to a door whose pediment is carved with a basket of fruit. Inside is a first-floor room paved with black

---

* The wife of Lorimer's client R. W. R. Mackenzie was a noted breeder of these useful and affectionate creatures.

and white flags, its walls and ceiling lined in wood. – More stone monkeys on the roof of the GARDEN STORE (dated 1899) at the NE corner. – In the topiary garden's E wall, a very Lorimerian gate carved with dicky birds and inscribed

> HERE.SHALL.YE.SEE.NO.ENEMY.BVT
> WINTER.AND.ROVGH.WEATHER

– Below it, at the end of the yew alley, a semicircular SUMMERHOUSE recess with gunloops in its masonry. – In front, a SUNDIAL made up of what look like medieval fragments (a fluted column and foliaged capital). – Bellcast-roofed GARDEN PAVILION at the SE corner.

Outside the garden, immediately SW of the house, a SUNDIAL of the 1890s copied from C17 examples. – To its SW, rectangular two-storey DOOCOT. Unusually it has a double-pitch roof; also peculiar are the birds' entrances (slits into curved tunnels through the walls) each side of the ground-floor door. It is probably of c.1600, but the stone, carved with Alexander Bruce's initials and the date 1599, high in the W gable may not be *in situ*.

2080   EASTERHEUGHS
2.2km. W of Burntisland

Innocently *retardataire* curiosity of 1946–55, designed and built for himself by *William R. Thomas*.* To put up a tower house in the mid-C20 was perhaps eccentric, to begin it when government restrictions limited buildings to one storey showed either vision or pigheadedness. The construction is traditional (load-bearing stone walls pointed with lime mortar), but the floors are *in situ* concrete (the first floor served for some years as the roof), some window surrounds are re-used C16 work, others of reconstituted stone, and the pantiles (from a C19 building at Auchtertool Distillery) are hung on corrugated asbestos sheets. This mixture of old and new has a quirky integrity.

The general outline is that of the C16 laird's house, but the main block has an M-roof, and the N jamb extends back across most of its W gable, as a parapeted and flat-roofed bow-ended outshot. At the E end, a single-storey workshop, its gableted N window rebuilt here from the C16 Otterston Castle. Also from Otterston the rounded margins of the main block's N windows. The jamb mixes motifs. Round-arched door; Gibbsian window surrounds; in the inner angle, a flatly corbelled stair turret with its own cap-house. On the S front, round-arched recesses over the first-floor windows. Wallhead chimney flanked by the second-floor windows' dormerheads.

The interior is an eclectic combination of the new with late C17 oak and early C18 pine woodwork rescued from the then derelict Rossend Castle (*see* Burntisland). In the jamb, a

* *William Williamson* gave some advice and prepared the drawings for planning approval.

comfortable concrete turnpike stair, its handrail early C19. Pine-panelled first-floor bedroom. In the main block's music room, three-panelled oak doors in a lugged architraved surround. On the W wall, late C17 marble chimneypiece flanked by Corinthian pilasters, the r.'s capital a copy. Opposite, early C18 Ionic pilasters, their flat capitals endearingly provincial. Wooden shutters and cornice also from Rossend. More C18 cornicing on the bookcases in the small library to the W. The jamb's top-floor bedroom is intended to have a tunnel-vaulted ceiling with painted decoration.

EAST LOMOND   2000
1km. SW of Falkland

A multivallate Iron Age hillfort, the highest in Fife (424m. O.D.) 3 on a commanding site, measuring c.60m. by 30m., within as many as four walls or ramparts. A heavy bank and external ditch barred access from the SW, but perhaps this outermost work is later; it is tempting to associate it with the hollow glass beads, ingot mould and incised slab which give evidence of Dark Age occupation and were found within the fort in 1905–25. The slab, with the figure of a bull, was found on the S side of the fort c.1920 and is now in the Royal Museum of Scotland, Queen Street, Edinburgh. Cupmarked slabs, now in the Falkland Palace Museum, were found on the hill but are not associated with the fort.

EAST WEMYSS   3090

A small weaving centre in the C18 and C19, it became also a mining community with the opening of the Michael Colliery in 1895 (closed 1967).

WEMYSS PARISH CHURCH (former), High Street. Being converted into a recording studio (1985). Crowstep-gabled harled kirk in a small graveyard beside the harbour. The core is probably of 1528, when the church is said to have been virtually rebuilt. Typical late medieval skinny rectangle, with a small one-bay chancel at the E end. In the chancel's S wall, a late Gothic window with ogee-headed lights. The gable's round-arched door looks late C16, probably inserted after the Reformation, when the chancel was taken over as the Wemyss Aisle. On the W gable, a birdcage bellcote (its weathervane having the Wemyss crest of a swan) dated 1693, a possible date for the Gothic survival W window, although it is more likely to be of 1659, when the transeptal N and S aisles were added. Its hoodmould is probably of 1810–11, when the church was recast by *Robert Burn*, who inserted rectangular Tudor windows. Crowstepped hall infilling the NE corner, dated 1928.

WEMYSS PARISH CHURCH, High Road. Competent dead-end Gothic revival by *Peter Sinclair*, 1936–7. Red sandstone gabled front with the lower stages of a tower on the r.

MACDUFF CEMETERY, Shand Terrace. Laid out *c.*1885. In the SW corner, HEADSTONE to the Rev. Alexander Orrock Johnston † 1905. It is Fife's best early C20 monument, designed by *Charles Rennie Mackintosh* and executed by *McGilvray*. Flattened cross of Dullatur sandstone enclosing an elongated oval, its top carved with a dove floating above the inscription panel, its copper plate a replacement of *c.*1950.

PRIMARY SCHOOL, School Wynd. 1906–8, by *G. C. Campbell*. Harled, with red sandstone dressings. A few gablets to add interest.

MACDUFF'S CASTLE
off Shand Terrace

Ruin on a cliff-top site hard pressed by the cemetery to the W. The castle of East Wemyss (Macduff's Castle) was burnt by supporters of Edward I in 1306 but seems to have been rebuilt later in the C14. A large extension joining the C14 tower by a hall range to a new S tower was added, probably soon after 1530, when Sir John Colville of Ochiltree acquired the barony. Abandoned by the early C18, a large part of the ruins was demolished in 1967.

The C16 S tower still stands, though roofless and lacking most of its S wall. It is five storeys, built of now weathered ashlar. NE stairtower decorated with stringcourses and a moulded doorpiece. In the main block's N face, roof raggle of the lower-hall range, whose tunnel-vaulted S ground-floor room survives. Beside it, part of the vault (much repaired in brick) of the pend under the hall.

The late C16 BARMKIN WALL's W range is fairly intact, with wide splayed gunloops. Small conical-roofed SW tower with gunloops to N and E. Only fragments of the barmkin's other ranges. Heavy revetment on the cliff to the E.

DESCRIPTION

HIGH STREET runs from the shore. Opposite the Parish Church (*see* above), No. 11, built as the MANSE in 1791, harled, with first-floor Venetian windows and a Victorian bay window. In the rubble and pantiled outbuilding behind, a pedimented dormerhead dated 1673 from the previous manse. To its N, the WEMYSS PUBLIC HALL of 1900; jolly wooden bellcote added in 1911. In the churchyard wall, WAR MEMORIAL by *A. Stewart Tod*, *c.*1920, with a small statue of a marching soldier. BACK DYKES leads to a late Victorian textile FACTORY. In WEMYSS TERRACE beyond, the old FREE CHURCH of 1844, with a domed tower.

WEST BRAE going up the hill to the W starts with a pantiled whinstone ashlar house of *c.*1800. Secluded at the top, the former COTTAGE HOSPITAL built in 1883, harled and crow-stepped with a pantiled roof. Late C19 and early C20 miners' housing in APPROACH ROAD and RANDOLPH STREET leads s to the disused MICHAEL COLLIERY. Its two steel-girder head frames and big brick chimney are probably of 1926, when the mine was resunk. Large PITHEAD BATHS by *J. H. Forshaw*, 1935, a gentle rendered introduction to the Modern Movement.

HIGH ROAD carries the main road N. At its entry to the town, a trim little BOWLING CLUB set well back. The view to it is framed by a pair of pavilions built as housing for indigent miners. Restoration revival with overall segmental pediments towards the road, balustraded porches on the outer gables; on the inner gables, steep pediments and pious texts (NISI DOMINUS FRUSTRA, DEUS ADES LABOR ANTIBUS). All this is by *A. Stewart Tod*, *c.*1930. On the town's N edge, the cemetery and Macduff's Castle (*see* above).

On the foreshore below, CAVES with carvings in Pictish style. In COURT CAVE a figure brandishing a square, and a group of geometric markings. In the DOO CAVE, now partly collapsed, were a crescent and V-rod and an animal head. These are lost, but the pigeon nest-boxes cut out of the sandstone walls are still impressive. In JONATHAN'S CAVE is the most extensive array of carvings, including double disc symbols, a boat, and several animals and birds. In the SLOPING CAVE, difficult of access, rectangular symbols and a double disc.

EDENWOOD
2.5km. SW of Cupar

3010

A Roman marching camp discovered from the air in 1978, 630m. from NW to SE and covering 25ha. within a rampart *c.*4m. thick and a 3m. ditch. It probably housed the troops of the emperor Septimius Severus during his campaigns in E Scotland 208–211. Most of the perimeter may be seen only as a cropmark, but a section of the NE rampart and ditch appears in wooded ground near the E angle – a rare feature in Roman temporary work. At the NW end a small attached camp, a typical feature of the 25ha. series.

ELIE AND EARLSFERRY

4000

Two burghs joining hands round a natural harbour; they were formally united in 1929. Earlsferry (perhaps formerly a burgh of barony subservient to the Abbots of Culross) had been accepted as a royal burgh in 1541; Elie became a burgh of barony under the control of the lairds of Ardross in 1589. Both burghs were in decline by the C18, renewed prosperity coming with their late C19 development as seaside resorts.

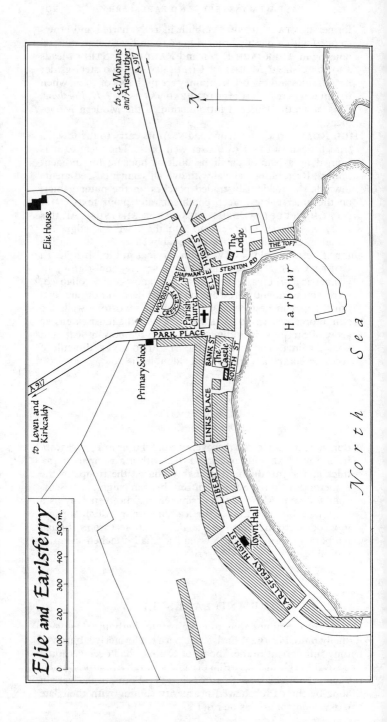

Elie and Earlsferry

to Leven and Kirkcaldy
A 917

to St Monans
and Anstruther
A 917

Elie House

Primary School

PARK PLACE

WOODSIDE CRESCENT
CHAPMAN'S
ELIE HIGH ST
Parish Church
The Lodge
STENTON RD
THE TOFT

BANK ST
The Castle
SOUTH ST

LINKS PLACE

LIBERTY

EARLSFERRY HIGH ST
Town Hall

Harbour

North Sea

0 100 200 300 400 500 m.

PARISH CHURCH, Elie High Street. The original T-plan church, paid for by William Scott of Ardross, was opened in 1639. Two years later the parish was disjoined from that of Kilconquhar. In 1726 Sir John Anstruther commissioned the tower, as recorded in a Latin inscription over the door. Grey freestone quoins, rusticated on the square base and then chamfered into an octagonal turret which is crowned with a cylindrical arcaded belfry, a stone dome and a weathercock. In 1831 the church was recast with four plain, obtusely pointed windows along the s elevation, so the effect is of a Gothic box of late Georgian type with a tall but well-fleshed early Georgian sentinel presiding in the middle. Outside stairs to the galleries were replaced by inside ones by *Currie* of Elie, wright, in 1855; traces of the old stair can be seen on the w side of the N jamb. Stripping of the harl has also revealed, in the rust-coloured walls, a C17 SW door formerly with a roll moulding and a big W window. Presumably it was done in 1905, when *Peter MacGregor Chalmers* added the E porch and NE vestry and organ chamber.

The character of the interior is that of 1831 with an obtusely pointed plaster vault, but the seating is by *John Currie*, 1885. The N jamb was cleared of a 'vault' and upstairs vestry, and the gallery moved back, by Chalmers in 1905. His are the Gothic COMMUNION TABLE and PULPIT. – STAINED GLASS. Two lights flanking the pulpit (Moses and Christ), 1891. One light (Christ the Lamb of God) in the w wall of the N jamb, by *John Blyth*, 1983. The rest was moved from the demolished Wood Memorial Church,* all of them set in blandly coloured architectural borders to fit the bigger windows here. On the N side, two lights (Michelangelesque figures with the texts 'Glory to God', 'And in Earth Peace') designed by *Edward Burne-Jones* and executed by *Morris & Co.*, 1890. – MONUMENT on the N wall to James Horsburgh, navigator, †1836, Grecian, with low relief of a ship under sail. – ORGAN by *Walker & Sons*, 1965. – MONUMENTS in the churchyard. On the E wall of the church, a large wall tablet to Thomas Turnbull of Bogmill †1650. The initials TT and IA flanking a shield over a Latin inscription, with scrolled surround and vine-border. Re-sited on the E porch wall, another, of equally assured workmanship but startling design, to his second daughter, Elizabeth Turnbull, †1658. Inscription on a convex tablet like a coffin, from which emerge the head and shoulders of a skeleton at the top, the feet at the bottom. Delicately fluted border, and an hourglass balanced on the skull. Near the gate and SESSION HOUSE (1831, now a bus shelter), a scrolled Ionic tabernacle to Alexander Gillespie †1635 and his descendants.

HARBOUR. The natural haven was developed with a grant from the Convention of Royal Burghs in 1582. Its single pier was rebuilt and lengthened *c.*1855.

---

* This church by *Sydney Mitchell & Wilson*, 1887, was in Bank Street. It has been demolished, but its octagonal Gothic font stands in the churchyard to the w of the Parish Church.

PRIMARY SCHOOL, Park Place. Jacobean of *c.*1880, its gabled
N elevation marking the entry to Elie, its two S extensions
tactful in themselves but clumsily joined.

TOWN HALL, Earlsferry. 1864–72, by *John Currie.* Single-
storey with crowsteps galore, and a little slate-spired clocktower.

DESCRIPTION

ELIE HIGH STREET begins at the E end of the town, preceded
by the long stone wall of Elie House policies (*see* below) to the
N, WADESLEA farmhouse, *c.*1830, to the S. A neat entry over
the hump of the old railway bridge, with a two-storey gable
on each side. No. 2 quite grand, *c.*1830, Nos. 1–3 originally
single-storey but built up in the late C19 to balance it. Then
older and newer things, the former a good deal altered, the
latter mostly set back behind front gardens but remembering
the building line with low walls, hedges and trees. On the N
side, No. 7, with butcher's implements and the date 1749
carved over the door, is the centrepiece of a crowstepped
trio. No. 13 grey Italianate, *c.*1880. On the S side, No. 12,
ROSEMAY, was built in 1895, though it looks earlier. Black
whin rubble relieved by bits of brown, green and orange,
the dressings and Gothic doorway grey freestone, the larger
windows divided by slim cast-iron mullions. Its near neighbour KINGSCROFT is similarly on the building line but of
plain black whin with stone mullions, dated 1862. THE LODGE
is simple Italian, *c.*1830, the ball-topped gatepiers earlier; both
belonged to Elie Lodge, built in 1807 but since demolished.
The street pulls itself together to a two-storey norm at the
junction.

To the N, CHAPMAN'S PLACE, with mid-C19 workshops and
cottages, leads to WOODSIDE PLACE and CRESCENT, whose
semi-detached houses are by *A. D. Haxton* and the Burgh
Architect *J. P. Burn,* 1930–3. Harling and large piend roofs,
mostly Welsh slate but some red tile. To the S, STENTON
ROAD, with the first-floor oriels which will become familiar
on this walk, and a gabled stone frontage complete with stone
shopfront (A. Terras, boots & shoes repaired), all *c.*1880. Then
THE TOFT. Nos. 1–5 are a fishermen's row whose mullioned
semi-dormers with pyramidal roofs seem to have been added
*c.*1860 to an earlier building. SEAFIELD BANK, a smug early
C19 cottage with a Venetian window in its central chimney-
gable, has been similarly dormered. It is flanked on one side
by its orthodox two-storey contemporary EASTFIELD, on the
other bizarrely by the tall half-timbered DALMARE, *c.*1900.
The last row starts with ADMIRALTY HOUSE, *c.*1890, but is
then basically sober under picturesque trimmings (e.g. the
little hearts cut out of the ground-floor shutters of TOFT
COTTAGE) and seaside colours. For the harbour, *see* above.

The next part of HIGH STREET is a long triangle with Stenton
Road as its base, tapering to the W. On the N side, the late

C19 QUEEN'S HOTEL, loaded with bays and dormers, whose corner turret has been a landmark all the way from the E end. Nos. 41–43 more refined Victorian, with domed bays in arched recesses. No. 49 apparently c. 1960, dry Arts-and-Crafts survival. On the S side, mostly stone wall, and none the worse for that. No. 30, the two-storey AVERNISH, built in 1824 as the manse, stands back and turns its face to the sea. In the middle is a triangle of grass with trees, a ship's mast and a cast-iron drinking-fountain-cum-lamp-post of c. 1890. The last section is bland late Georgian overseen by the Parish Church (see above) from behind its unusually eventful churchyard wall. On the opposite (S) side, a long terrace c. 1830 with skewputts discreetly emphasized. At its E end, a chemist's shop with pestle and mortar sign, at the W an odd transformation with the applied half-timbering, c. 1930, of the VICTORIA HOTEL.

RANKEILLOR STREET goes S towards the sea, past an inquisitive oriel and a near-pair of houses, c. 1840, No. 5 brown stone and partly broached dressings, No. 7 black whin and partly stugged, to the crowstepped No. 9 and the hapless WYND LODGE, covered with C20 cement 'masonry' except for the early C17 doorpiece in its projecting jamb. The street is similarly squeezed on the other side by the corner turret of WYND HOUSE. This is at the external angle of its L-plan and its corbels are C17; the upper parts and the bay-windowed S elevation are late C19. The original basement storey has been submerged by the building up of the road. (Interior Victorian. In the garden a stone dated 1568.) THE TERRACE looks S over the sea, starting with ARCHIBALD HOUSE (formerly Wade House, after the road-building General Wade*), built in 1756. Rusticated quoins and swept dormers. Then a continuous row of tall fronts stepping downhill. No. 6, c. 1760, with an outside stair to its rusticated front doorpiece. No. 7 a bit later, with architraved doorpiece and wallhead chimney-gable; the bald dormer came afterwards. No. 8, DUDDINGSTON HOUSE, late C17 with crowsteps and a heavily moulded but much eroded doorpiece. (Old dormer pediments built into back wall: S.D.D.)

SOUTH STREET continues to the W but is more level, with houses on both sides. On the N, No. 19, SOUTHGATE, has an eroded doorpiece from the Muckle Yett (see below). Console jambs, and a figure carved on the keystone of the wavy lintel. No. 25, GILLESPIE HOUSE, was rebuilt by *John Currie* (for himself) c. 1870, but retains the grand principal doorpiece of the Muckle Yett, the house of Alexander Gillespie. Roman Doric columns, the date 1682 and initials AG:CS (his wife Christian Small) between the triglyphs. Fantastically scrolled pediment containing heraldry and crowned with a hollow-faced sundial. Towards the W, plenty more oriels and a big pair at No. 29. WEST HOUSE at the far end is late C18 with later oriel bows. Between them a huge rectangular oriel, as if the whole room had pushed itself out towards the view, which is once again

* Wade recommended Elie harbour as suitable for use by the Royal Navy.

open to the s. The s side starts with a couthie C17 group, a nice foil to the dignity opposite. It consists of the harled and crowstepped EASTER GABLES and SEVEN GABLES, the former with an inviting porch of c.1900. No. 4, SEAFORT, is C17, with a big chimney on the rear projecting gable. (Original plaster and woodwork: S.D.D.) After School Wynd is the long harled front of THE CASTLE, mostly C17 but the SW stair-jamb with crowstepped garret could be earlier. (Panelling and painted ceilings: S.D.D.) Its neighbour is c.1960, brash Mediterranean villa style. Nos. 12–16 early C19, with scrolled skew-putts. The narrow SCHOOL WYND has some good C18–19 fronts on its way down to the sea, where it ends with a slipway.

PARK PLACE is the N approach to Elie. The E side all villas and cottages, with DUNCREGGAN, c.1890, authentically Baronial just after the hump crossing the railway. The W side more continuous. Nos. 7–17 late Victorian, with steep semi-dormer gables. No. 19 ingeniously quotes the chamfer of the church tower in order to widen the building line, and Nos. 33–37 are a dignified late Georgian terrace of grey stone on the upper floor, orange on the lower, which has tripartite front door-pieces. That of No. 37 has pilasters and is crowned with a big lunette on the upper level; somebody felt the need for this surprising increase in scale and prestige. For the Jacobean Primary School at the N end, see above.

BANK STREET continues the line of High Street to the W, and is built up on both sides. On the N side, two buildings with contemporary shopfronts: late Georgian rounding the corner of Park Place (Adamson, Baker) and fancy late Victorian at No. 3. Then ROSE COTTAGE, c.1820, with a central chimney-gable. Late Georgian ROYAL BANK OF SCOTLAND, with scrolled skewputts, then grey Baronial gables of 1864 just before the gap left by the demolition of the Wood Memorial Church (by *Sydney Mitchell*, 1877). The GOLF HOTEL of 1899, originally a house, is compact Baronial in pinky-grey stone. Principal tower and corbelled stair turret at the E end. On the s side, the bigger houses have their tall staircase windows to the street, their fronts to the sea. ALLANBANK, c.1820, simply presents the blank gable of its N jamb.

FOUNTAIN ROAD slips down to the sea past a late Georgian row. Then the start of LINKS PLACE is announced by the oriel of WESTERLEA, followed by the single-storey pilastered POST OFFICE of c.1920 and much grey Victorian grandeur. Two late C19 villas, THE STUDIO and OCHTERHOUSE. On the N side, the Baronial CLAREMONT by *John Currie* for himself, 1897, and a bay-windowed and gabled terrace before the sad gap where stood the Marine Hotel (by *Burnet, Son & Campbell*, 1889). The orange sandstone villa of MARION-VILLE, c.1820, with grey painted dressings, is seen through the very narrow gateway of its stone wall, crowned with a wrought-iron lamp-holder. ROCKCLIFFE COTTAGE comes nearer the street; pantiles between straight skews to the front, crowstepped to the back. The recessed bow windows are C20.

LIBERTY (more of the main street) has feudal-looking walls but nothing very distinguished behind them. To the S, the former stables, c.1900, of St Ford Cottage, harled, with red stone dressings and red roofs. FORTHSIDE to the rear was the gardener's cottage. On the N side, Liberty becomes too true to its name, but then recovers; a wobble in the road is beautifully defined by its architecture. On the S side are the former school, mid-C19 and enlarged in 1874, but now harled, and the early Victorian SALISBURY COTTAGE, mildly Tudor with big later dormers. EARLSFERRY HIGH STREET is attractively sinuous. The N side starts with a meaningless gap but order is restored by THE RIGGING and HANSEN'S HOUSE, both C18 with crowsteps. GOWANLEA, with whitewash and straight skews, is the focus of the next curve, but the senior building is the toy-Baronial Town Hall (see above). Then a picturesque constriction. On the S side THE GABLES jut out, the first one late Georgian of black whin with a Venetian window, the second a Victorian echo of it in yellow sandstone. Meanwhile on the N side a gradual narrowing towards the pantiled TWO WAYS (straight skews to front, crowstepped to rear) and the slated ASHDENE. The street widens again at STRATHNEUK, consciously picturesque early C20. A barrage of oriels at the brown stone ROSEBERIE. Then a whinstone cottage with fancy bracketed iron gutter, and the three Gothic windows of the early Victorian TURRET LODGE, smartly painted and Welsh slated. On the N side, a pretty row, all toeing the same building line while their wallheads jump up and down. Its centrepiece is a bumpily harled cottage with a forestair.

MANSION

ELIE HOUSE. A mansion with several faces. The earliest is the rubble S front of the double-pile block built by Sir William Anstruther after he bought the estate in 1697; plain with roll-moulded windows.* *William Adam* carried out work here (probably minor remodelling) c.1740 and produced a carved pediment, but his design for a new house was not executed. However, about twenty years later, a large NW wing was added, its ashlar-faced Venetian-windowed S gable uncomfortably stuck on the end of the block of c.1700. The new wing's main W front is a baldly detailed nine bays with a three-bay centre. In the pediment (is this William Adam's?), boldly carved foliage and a coat of arms. The present fussy imperial stair to the new front door is an alteration of 1854–5 replacing a straight flight of steps. At the same time Baronial dormerheads were added to the original block, and the late C18 wing's rear elevation, which now became the entrance front, was dressed up with a pompous, vaguely French porch and ogee-topped tower. Equally inappropriate but quite without pomposity the low outshots added on this side in the 1950s and the CHAPEL

* The S wall incorporates some stonework of the late C16 house on this site.

by *Peter Whiston*, 1958. (Inside, the principal floor's sw room
has rococo plasterwork.)

STEADING to the NW, built by *John Currie*, *Robert White*
and *George Forgan*, 1822–3. A castellated tower joins its w
range to a late Victorian sawmill.

To the s, a small circular DOOCOT, its ogee roof carrying a
lantern, probably late c18. – Early c19 OBELISK to the SE.

ARDROSS CASTLE. *See* p. 75.

FALKLAND

2000

A small town dominated by the linoleum factory on the s and the
Palace on the N. The Palace occupies the site of a castle which
belonged successively to the Earls of Fife and Atholl before its
acquisition by the Crown in 1437. Twenty-one years later the
adjacent village was made a royal burgh but one whose status was
largely honorific, since it was never admitted to the Convention of
Royal Burghs or Parliament. The character of dependence on a
great house was noted in 1723 by John Macky, who found it 'a
most clean little Town . . . not unlike *Woodstock* in Oxfordshire.'
Weaving became its main industry in the c18 and c19; linoleum
manufacture was introduced in the c20.

FALKLAND PALACE

c16 early Renaissance showpiece created by James IV and James
V. In 1723 John Macky* thought its courtyard 'the beau-
tifullest Piece of Architecture in *Britain*'; in 1828 C. R. Cockerell, a master of the Greek revival, confessed himself
'overwhelmed' by 'it's character it's Poetry, it's aspect & con-
venience . . .'.

For the Middle Ages Falkland's position at the meeting
point of the Howe of Fife with the w route between the Firths
of Forth and Tay was of strategic importance. There was a
castle here by 1337, when it was taken by Edward III's army
and 'levelled to the ground', but it must have been repaired or
rebuilt by 1401, when David, Duke of Rothesay, was im-
prisoned in the 'tower' of Falkland. On the execution of Walter
Stewart, Earl of Atholl, in 1437, Falkland was confiscated by
the Crown. During the next sixty years repairs and additions
were made to the castle, which developed as an irregular courtyard s of the c14 tower.

James IV began a new palace here in 1501, the same year he
started to extend Holyroodhouse (Edinburgh). At Falkland as
at Holyroodhouse the new buildings formed a quadrangle
adjoining the existing courtyard. The first part built was the
E range, for which *William Turnbull* and *John Broun* were the
masons; work must have been well advanced by January 1506,

* *A Journey through Scotland.*

when plastering was in progress, and may have been completed by July 1508, when the glazier's account was settled. In 1511–13 the N and S sides of the new courtyard were filled respectively with a hall and chapel. *William Thom* was the master mason.

For some years after James IV's death at the Battle of Flodden in 1514, Falkland suffered neglect, but in 1528 William Barclay was appointed Keeper of the Palace and the next year John Scrymgeour was acting as master of works for the completion of the E range, whose 'new galryis and crossis' (i.e. the galleries and projecting 'cross-house', on its E side)

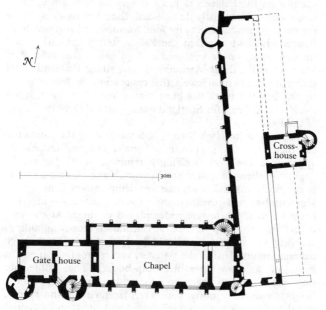

Falkland Palace,
plan of second floor (first floor of gatehouse)

were roofed in 1532, when a new stable block and aviary were also built.

James V's marriage to Madeleine de Valois* in 1537 marked the beginning of five years' remodelling of his father's work. The master masons‡ employed were *John Brounhill*, *James Black*, and two Frenchmen, *Moses Martin* and *Nicolas Roy*; *John Drummond* was master wright.§ A great SW gatehouse (probably begun a few years before) was completed, the

* She died six months later. The next year he married Mary of Guise.

‡ Other masons employed were *John Tait*, *William* and *Gilbert Masoun*, *Allister Campbell*, *Thomas Adesoun*, *Thomas French*, *Thomas Jackson*, *Nicol Black*, *John Anderson*, *Henry Bawte*, *James Staig*, *John Gady*, *John Merlioun* and *Peter Ducheman*.

§ Other wrights were *Richard Stewart*, *David Williamson*, *Alexander Ruid*, *William Meffane*, *William Morton*, *William Wright* and *Henry Lyall*.

interior of the E range was recast, and the E and S courtyard elevations were dressed in up-to-the-minute French *haute couture*. The King's death in 1542 brought work to a halt, the projected W range apparently not even begun.

Falkland's history for the next three and a half centuries was largely of decline. The Privy Council ordered repair of the Palace in 1584 and 1594, but in 1598 Fynes Morison found it 'an old building and almost ready to fall'. Repairs were finally carried out in 1625–9, and more work, including decoration of the chapel ceiling, made in 1633, when Charles I spent five nights here on his visit to Scotland. During the Cromwellian occupation the Palace's N and E ranges suffered a fire; the N range was subsequently demolished, the E left roofless. Some repairs were made in 1824 by *John Swinton* for Professor John Bruce, who had acquired the Palace four years earlier and further repairs were executed *c*.1840; but it was only after 1887, when the third Marquess of Bute added Falkland to his string of architectural jewels, that restoration (by *John Kinross*) began. Further work has been carried out since 1952, when the National Trust for Scotland was appointed Deputy Keeper of the Palace.

54   The S front (to High Street) is dominated by the gatehouse completed in 1541. Its position at one end of the front and its appearance are both strikingly reminiscent of James V's slightly earlier NW tower at Holyroodhouse (Edinburgh). It is decidedly martial, with massive drum towers flanking the segmental-arched pend. At their bases, gunloops – inverted keyholes in the l. tower, wide-splayed in the r. At the top, corbelling, the top course a continuous rope moulding, carrying the widely crenellated parapet studded with huge cannon spouts. Inside the parapet, conical-roofed turrets in front of a crowstep-gabled cap-house. The immediate impression is of symmetry, reinforced by the placing of three brightly painted armorial panels (replacements of the 1890s), but the windows are arbitrarily sized and sited, and a canted projection is corbelled out across the SE inner angle. As surprising is the realization that the gatehouse is not U- but F-plan, the tail extending E of the r. drum tower, where its termination is marked by the parapet stepping down to the wallhead of the adjoining chapel.

The chapel block of 1511–13 is late Gothic at its most stylish. Symmetrical six-bay composition, the bays marked off by stepped buttresses. In each bay, a plain ground- and first-floor window. Then a stringcourse to mark the much taller second floor containing the chapel. The chapel itself occupies the centre four bays; in each, a tall two-light window with deep splayed margins. In each of the end bays (vestry at the E, ante-chapel at the W), a smaller single window. The buttresses look very expensive. At the level of the chapel each has a tabernacle-canopied niche (the finials sadly missing), two still containing figures carved by *Peter Flemisman* in 1539; the bases are corbels decorated with angels bearing emblems of the Passion. The buttresses are finished with a second tier of canopied image niches under the crocketed pinnacles, the effect of this top stage weakened by the 1530s continuation of the gatehouse parapet across the chapel block. At the E end, a small rectangular stairtower contemporary with the chapel block, but its rubble walling an awkward contrast to the ashlar masonry of the rest. Beyond it and also of rubble is the main gable of the roofless E range built in 1501–8, large mullioned and transomed windows (probably an alteration of 1537–42) the main feature. Slightly projecting S end of the gallery addition of 1529–32. In the middle of the E range's E side, the cross-house built in 1529–32 and restored by *Kinross* in the 1890s. Crowstepped with a conical-roofed stairtower.

Entrance* to the courtyard by a vaulted passage under the gatehouse; on each side, a stone bench; there have been double doors at each end. On the gatehouse's N front, only the floor below the parapet is ashlar-faced. The rest is of rubble with corbels showing that it was meant to be the S end of a projected W range.

The courtyard's E and S ranges as remodelled in 1537–42 are the most sophisticated architectural works of that date in Britain. When first completed in 1508 the rubble-built E range was probably quite plain except perhaps for the hoodmoulds over the large first-floor windows. At the N end (filling the corner with the demolished N range), a conical-roofed tower, its top containing a doocot. James V's reconstruction applied classical detail. Between each bay, a thin buttress (inscribed I.R.S.D.G. for 'Jacobus Rex Scotorum Dei Gratia') formed of a pilaster which serves as backing for an attached column (the columns have gone) on a tall pedestal. The pilaster continues up above the column's entablature to form the back of a canopied image niche. This type of column-buttress is taken directly from contemporary French work (e.g. the Maison de François I). Was the French master mason *Moses Martin*‡ responsible for the design? Just as French are the pairs of roundels containing relief portraits (? of Roman emperors, as at Hampton Court) above each first-floor window. Also of 1537 are the elaborate second-floor windows. Only their lower parts survive to show that they were framed by pilasters standing on delicately moulded corbels, but late C17 engravings show that these carried segmental pediments rising above the wallhead.

The S range is grander still, the architectural achievement made easier because here a new though narrow tier of galleries was built in front of James IV's chapel block, whose slated roof pushes up above the shallow lead-covered slope of the lean-to addition. In the E corner, a fat conical-roofed tower. A similar tower was probably intended to be built at the W end. Between them, the five-bay ashlar façade. In each bay,

55

* Now (1988) a private entrance. The public entrance is from the E.
‡ The other French master mason, Nicolas Roy, did not arrive in Scotland until 1539.

a humble semi-basement window and four-light first-floor
window (the centre window was converted to a door, probably
in the early C19, but restored in the 1890s). Tall two-light
transomed windows lighting the chapel gallery, each flanked
by laurel wreaths enclosing more heads. Column-buttresses of
the same type as on the E range, but here they are surmounted
by inverted foliaged consoles supporting the bases (forward
projections of the moulded eaves cornice) for statues (now
lost). On the buttresses, the initials of James V, the name of
his queen, Mary of Guise, and the date 1539. Probably this is
the work of *Nicolas Roy*. On the main block behind, tall
wallhead chimneys grouped in a regular 1/2/1 arrangement
which has no relation to the galleries' front. Four segmental-
headed dormer windows; the centre two (the l. butting on to
a chimney) with carved tympana are of 1539, the unadorned
others of the 1890s.

The mid-C16 internal planning of the Palace must be partly
conjectural, but the general outline seems clear. The hall stood
on the N of the courtyard, the royal apartments were in the E
range, the chapel and courtiers' rooms in the S range, and the
gatehouse contained a sizeable lodging for the Keeper of the
Palace.

In the E range, tunnel-vaulted ground-floor stores under the
main (W) block. The N room's huge gable fireplace suggests
it was a kitchen. In the S room a garderobe and slop sink.
Unvaulted rooms under the galleries; another large fireplace
the S room, perhaps a second kitchen. The first floor probably
contained a ceremonial state suite corresponding to the one in
the W range of Holyroodhouse in the 1530s, and the second
floor an apartment for the King and a second for the Queen,
whilst on each of the cross-house's upper floors was a closet-
cum-lobby, with a stair to the garden on the E.* The gallery
extension of 1532 is 4.5m. broad, and the presence of drains
suggests that it contained an internal corridor with garderobes
against the outer wall. The cross-house's first-floor room was
fitted up as the King's bedroom‡ in 1956 by *W. Schomberg
Scott*, the walls and ceiling painted (by *David McClure*) in a
parody of early C17 work.

In the S range, a gallery or corridor on each floor, the lowest
with a C16 stone tunnel-vault, the oak ceilings and heraldic
stained glass in the upper galleries dating from the 1890s. S of
the gallery, tunnel-vaulted ground-floor cellars, the W extending under the gatehouse but clearly pre-dating it, since the
bottom of the gable cuts through its vault. Big turnpike stair
at the E decorated with a moulded necking between the first

---

* As suggested by John G. Dunbar, 'Some Aspects of the Planning of Scottish
Royal Palaces in the Sixteenth Century', *Architectural History*, xxvii (1984), 21–3.
An alternative possibility is that the whole first floor was occupied by the King's
Apartment and the whole second floor by the Queen's. If so, they were very much
larger than at any of James V's other palaces.

‡ Documentary evidence makes it clear that the King's bedchamber was not in
the cross-house in the mid-C16.

and second floors; its newel is hollow, probably to take a bell rope.

On the top landing, wrought-iron balustrade of *c.*1895, decorated with thistles. Comfortable first-floor rooms, the w probably originally a kitchen. On the second floor, the chapel. Compartmented wooden ceiling made by *Richard Stewart*, *c.*1540. Its escutcheon painted with the arms of Charles I, and the painted strapwork cartouches, royal emblems and initials (of Charles I, Henrietta Maria, and Charles, Prince of Wales) are all of 1633 but much restored in 1896. Also restored (and embellished) in 1896 were the N and S walls' friezes painted with panels containing crowned and monogrammed thistles joined by swags of fruit hanging from *trompe l'œil* consoles to cartouches inscribed with Scriptural texts. On the N wall, *trompe l'œil* windows to match the S wall's real windows. At the chapel's W end, an open screen of turned oak balusters, probably the one made by *Richard Stewart*, *c.*1540. The E wall's panelling may date from 1633. It was restored in the 1890s when the canopied Royal Pew was made, incorporating two shafts and pilasters from a C17 pew. Plain oak pulpit with a sounding board, made in the 1890s from early C17 (?) fragments.

On the chapel range's attic floor, SE library, its wooden tunnel-vaulted ceiling decorated by *Thomas Bonnar Jun.* with painted compartments filled with cherubs, peacocks, heraldry etc.; inaccurately executed *trompe l'œil* window on the N.

The gatehouse was originally the self-contained lodging of the Keeper of the Palace. On the ground floor, a vaulted room each side of the pend. Pit-prison in the SW tower. In the SE tower, a broad turnpike stair to the upper floors, their rooms' beamed ceilings mostly painted by Bonnar. On the top floor, two more ambitious ceilings, by *Andrew W. Lyon*, 1894–6: in the Priest's Room, Jacobean decoration in the manner of Pinkie House (Lothian); in David Scott's Room, panels copied from that early C19 Blakean artist's 'Monograms'.

In the garden N of the Palace, a long crowstepped stable block, perhaps the one built in 1528–31. Attached to its E side, a tennis court built in 1540–1, the internal wooden penthouses restored in the 1890s; it is of greater interest to the history of sport than of architecture.

MUSEUM in the Palace's E extension. Its archaeological exhibits include the following. Two fragments of yellow sandstone found on East Lomond Hill in 1972, the larger with at least seventeen cupmarkings (several with an encircling ring and tangential groove), the smaller with cup-and-ring motifs on both faces. A stone found at Glasslie in 1890, with cup-and-ring markings, cupmarks and gutters. Two Pictish symbol stones found on the demolition of a building at Westfield Farm, shaped to form building blocks. One with a 'mirror case' and a fragmentary double disc symbol, the other with a notched rectangle and two concentric arcs.

CHURCHES

FREE CHURCH, off New Road. Now a hall. Prominently sited simple Gothic box built in 1844–5. Small spired bellcote with gableted openings.

PARISH CHURCH, High Street. A large Early Pointed church built at the expense of Mr and Mrs Onesiphorus Tyndall-Bruce, 1848–50. *David Bryce* was the architect. Very competent, but the grey stone's texture makes it unlovable. Standard mid-C19 Presbyterian rectangle, the bulk disguised by gableted buttresses. Against the S gable, steeple with a lucarned spire, its profile a distinctive feature of the town seen from a distance.

Impressive interior. Galleries with elaborately panelled fronts round three sides. Above gallery level the supporting cast-iron columns are carried up in wood to form arches under the roof, their spandrels filled with open quatrefoils. – Mostly original FURNISHINGS, two of the PEWS adaptable as communion pews. – PULPIT cantilevered from the N gable, approached by a double stair. – STAINED GLASS. Three lights (the Nativity, Resurrection and Ascension of Our Lord) in the N gable, by *A. Ballantine & Gardiner*, 1897, the deep colours giving a welcome richness. – ORGAN in the S gallery, by *William Hill & Son and Norman & Beard*, 1930.

E of the church, STATUE of Onesiphorus Tyndall-Bruce, a life-size bronze by *John Steell*, the plinth by *David Bryce*, 1864.

PUBLIC BUILDINGS

LINOLEUM WORKS, Well Brae. Large, in red brick, by *C. H. Armour*, 1931.

TOWN HOUSE, High Street. Enjoyably unpretentious mason's classical, by *Thomas Barclay*, 1800–1. Three-bay N front with swagged urns on its centre pediment, the burgh arms carved in the tympanum. Round-arched ground-floor windows; balustered aprons at the first floor. The E front to Back Wynd is a simpler repeat but with the addition of a tower over the centre. Stone balls on its parapet; above, a spired octagonal belfry.

DESCRIPTION

On the approach from the SE, a pair of sentries on the hillside to the l. GLEBELANDS, the old Parish Manse, by *Thomas Barclay*, 1804–7. The early C19 CHAPELYARD HOUSE next door is much smarter, with a pilastered doorpiece and round-arched windows in the wings. At PLEASANCE's N end, a rubble and pantile STEADING with an octagonal horsemill. Beside it, DOVECOT of *c*.1835 with flattish gableted dormerheads of the type favoured by *Robert Hutchison*. It makes an L with the crowstepped BEECHGROVE (dated 1756), whose first-floor

windows are linked by sill and lintel courses. High above NEW
ROAD, the old Free Church (*see* above).

EAST PORT leads into the town's centre. On the r., the Palace's
garden wall interrupted by the white-harled VISITOR
CENTRE (by *W. Schomberg Scott*, 1965). HIGH STREET's first
incident on the l. is the late Victorian TORNAVEEN, Georgian
survival enlivened with lots of sculpture (by *Galloway*, an
amateur artist): almost Gothic capitals on the Composite columned doorpiece, its frieze decorated with anthemion and
palmette enrichment; skewputts carved with portraits; figures
of eagles and a sleepy lion. Of greater architectural import is
the thatched MONCRIEF HOUSE, dated 1610 on the door
lintel, built for James VI's servant Nicol Moncrief. Regular
four-bay front of roughish ashlar. Roll-moulded windows.
Above the two l. ground-floor windows, cornices supported
by small moulded capitals. In the r. bay, a blind attic window
framed by would-be classical attached columns, with corbels
for bases but now without a cornice. Below the r. first-floor
window, an inscription

AL.PRAISE TO GOD AND/THANKIS.TO THE.MOST/
EXCELLENT.MONARCHE/ [of] GREAT.BRITANE.OF WH/
OSE.PRINCELIE.LIBERA/LITIE.THIS.IS.MV.POR/
TIOVNE.DEO.LAVS./ESTO.FIDVS./ADEST.MERCES./
NICOLL.MONCREIF./1610.

In the crowstepped and pantiled FALKLAND ARMS
HOTEL's front wall, an inset heraldic stone carved with the
date 1607, likely enough for the first floor's roll-moulded
windows. Between two of them, an inserted segmental pediment, inscribed

I.R.6/GOD.SAIF.YE.KIN/G.OF.GRIT.BRITAN./
FRANCE.AND.IRLAND/.OVR SOVERAN.FOR.OF./
HIS.LIBERALITY.THIS.HO/VS.DID.I.EDIFY

The second floor is probably an early C19 addition, contemporary with the pilastered doorpieces. The BANK OF
SCOTLAND's three E bays were built as the British Linen
Bank, *c.*1845; Jacobean with gabled dormerheads. The style
was quoted, in a different stone, for the W extension of *c.*1880,
its semi-octagonal front projecting over the pavement. Large
house in BACK WYND behind, by *Harold O. Tarbolton*,
English Tudor with Arts and Crafts touches.

On High Street's N side, immediately W of the Palace, the harled
and crowstepped KEY HOUSE, set well back. Steep-pitched
roof confirming the door lintel's date of 1713. The street
line is established by ST ANDREW HOUSE, mid-C18 with a
moulded doorpiece; the first floor's swept dormerheads look a
C19 alteration. Then, the OLD POST OFFICE, a charming
early C19 toy fort, the colonetted doorpieces taken from Batty
Langley. THE SADDLERS before the churchyard is dated 1771.

High Street now becomes an informal square. In its centre, a
large FOUNTAIN by *Alexander Roos* of London, 1856. Octagonal base; on top of the buttresses red-painted lions holding

shields. Upper stage an octagon of open-cusped arches under
a crocketed spire. On the s side, squeezed by the Town House
(*see* above), the diminutive late C19 Baronial COVENANTER
BAR. COVENANTER HOTEL is dated 1771 on a gable window;
on the front, Roman Doric doorpiece with a swagged frieze.
In CROSS WYND to the s, harled C17 and C18 houses, one
with a round-headed blind window in the chimney gablet,
another dated 1686 and a third dated 1764. In High Street,
across Cross Wynd, a late Victorian front between crowstepped early C18 gables. CAMERON HOUSE'S late C19 rusticated stucco with vermiculated quoins disguises an early C17
building; formerly thatched, it is now pantiled. In the NW
corner of this 'square', the drydashed FOUNTAIN HOUSE
looks C18, but its corbelled sw corner suggests that it may be
the remodelling of an earlier house; in the w gable, an inset
stone dated 1690. Closing the E side of the 'square' is the OLD
TOWN HOUSE, tepid Baronial dated 1886. Part of a C17
doorpiece is re-used in the NW tower. On its s front, a basement
window's lintel is dated 1750. Behind it, the STAG INN,
probably late C17, its single-storey back wing to MILL WYND
dated 1680.

In the narrower w part of High Street after ROTTENROW, a
small early C18 building, externally restored in 1960 (the inside
became an electricity sub-station); forestair to the upper floor
at the E gable. Then an early C19 block, built of whinstone, on
the corner with Brunton Street. After a plain mid-C19 house
with a heavy perron, a gap. Then, a harled C18 house abutting
BRUCE'S BUILDINGS, peaceful Baronial dated 1869. Forestair
on the house opposite, whose ground-floor lintel has the date
1751. More vernacular houses, mostly C18, on both sides.

Set among them, the OLD CHURCHYARD on the s, with
plain classical gatepiers of *c.*1840. In its NW corner, headstone
of *c.*1805 to Samuel Paterson's children, inscribed

> Here innocent beauty lys who's breath
> Was snatch't by early not untimely death
> Since thy [*sic*] did go just as thy did begin
> Sorrow to know before thy knew to sin

– On the s wall, the Coll family's aedicular monument of
*c.*1690. On the base, carved drapery held by putti. The scrolly
pediment is now (1985) on the ground, its tympanum carved
with a coat of arms, the supporters angels of the Resurrection.
To the E, a similar but simpler monument dated 1696, marking
Thomas Lawson's burialplace. Several late C17 headstones
embellished with symbols of death.

High Street finishes with more vernacular, the end house (dated
1752) with big blocks of whinstone mixed into its sandstone
rubble walls. Round the corner, off LOMOND ROAD, a late
Georgian villa (MILLFIELD) with a pedimented centre; bay
windows were added to its wings in 1886.

BRUNTON STREET runs SE from High Street to form the s side
of a triangular green (Cross Wynd, *see* above, making the E

side). The harled early C18 WESTER BRUNTON HOUSE has been heavily restored. So too (by *R. Weir Schultz* in 1894–5, and again in 1970–1) has the adjoining BRUNTON HOUSE, crowstepped and with a smart armorial panel dated 1712. Humbler C18 houses follow.

In HORSEMARKET, DUNDRENNAN is dated 1694 but has acquired large Victorian oriels. Beside it, on the corner with Back Wynd, a crowstepped house of *c.*1700, with a forestair. The view E is closed by SOUTHBANK, late Georgian with a Roman Doric columned doorpiece. On SOUTH STREET's SW corner, WELLBRAE, dated 1663 but much altered and now rendered. Further E, the old BURGHER CHAPEL, a rubble box with round-arched windows, dated 1830. In WELL BRAE to the N, the large linoleum works (*see* Public Buildings, above). To its E, ROYAL TERRACE, mid-C19 pantiled cottages stepping up the hill, No. 1 with a gablet.

HOUSE OF FALKLAND
1km. W

Jacobean manor of 1839–44, designed by *William Burn* for On- 81 esiphorus Tyndall-Bruce, whose wife had inherited the Falkland estate from her uncle. In 1887 it was bought by the third Marquess of Bute, who, between 1890 and his death in 1900, employed *R. W. Schultz** to transform the interior from a display of Early Victorian opulence to one of Late Victorian idiosyncrasy.

Burn's exterior is low-key, perhaps deliberately so as not to challenge the nearby Palace. Two-storey main block; attached to its NW corner but set at a lower level, the single-storey and attic service block. N (entrance) front dominated by the projecting porch, the two towers behind insignificant accents. Symmetrical E and S elevations, each with mullioned and transomed bay windows in the gabled ends and ogee-roofed corner turrets cribbed from Audley End. The intended but unexecuted bow-fronted conservatory tying the S front's gables together would have given a much needed hint of excitement. Informally composed W front to the garden's most sheltered part. The general composition is English but there is no shortage of Scottish detail – strapworked and pierced parapets, buckle quoins, and crowstepped gables. Twisty octagonal chimneys (copied from Winton House, Lothian) appearing to best effect on the service block, where they alternate with strapwork-pedimented dormerheads.

Burn's architectural popularity in Early Victorian aristocratic circles was largely due to his ability to produce plans which systematized and integrated the main components of a country house's arrangement. House of Falkland is an exemplar of his rigorous approach to the problem of how to provide separate but linked zones for entertainment, for the family,

---

* The Marquess had employed *William Frame* in 1889 but dismissed him for drunkenness the next year.

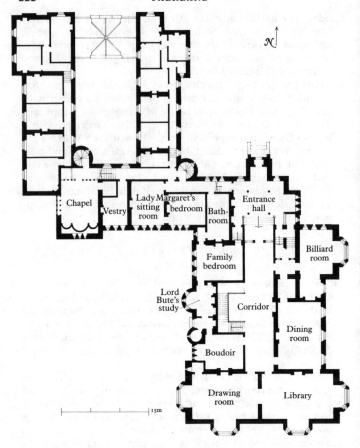

House of Falkland,
plan of ground floor in 1900

and for servants. The basement was given over to the kitchen, cellars, servants' hall, still room etc. On the main floor, the service block's E and W ranges, separated by a courtyard, contained respectively bedrooms for male and female staff. The family's private rooms made an L-plan suite of bedroom, bathroom, Mrs Tyndall-Bruce's dressing room and boudoir, and Mr Tyndall-Bruce's dressing room and sitting room, extending along most of the service block's s range and the main block's w side. A door from Mrs Tyndall-Bruce's dressing room gave access to the garden, and a door from her boudoir into the drawing room, while Mr Tyndall-Bruce's sitting or business room could be reached by a short passage from the front hall without the visitor entering any other room of the house. Along the E and s sides of the main block were the public rooms, beginning with the billiard room, separated by a dinner service room from the main suite of dining room, library and drawing room. Down the centre on the axis of the front hall extended a broad corridor with doors to the family and public rooms. On the corridor's w side a grand staircase led to the first-floor guest bedrooms.

Schultz's alterations in the 1890s made only minor amendments to Burn's plan but replaced most of the lavish 1840s decoration (by *D. R. Hay & Co.**) with equally expensive work in a more up-to-date style. The entrance hall is a mixture. Jacobean stone fireplace (now painted with a cement wash), its overmantel carved from models produced by *James Pinnan & Son* in 1843. Contemporary compartmented ceiling, but its centre was cut out in 1890 for an oval-windowed dome decorated with plaster cherubs and supported on four lumpy Corinthian columns (all this designed by *William Frame* before he was replaced by Schultz). In the dome and the main windows, heraldic glass, designed, like all the 1890s stained glass, by *H. W. Lonsdale*. Straight flight of stairs up to the Jacobean oak screen (dated 1898 but in the position of Burn's screen) into the main corridor. Here the 1840s work is intact. Jacobean ceiling of the same type as in the entrance hall; oak panelling. The huge Frenchy chimneypiece is probably one of those supplied by *Joseph Browne & Co.* of London. The Jacobean manner continues at the staircase, its great window filled in 1892 with a richly coloured arrangement of birds and animals among trees hung with the shields of successive owners of Falkland. At the top of the stair, tunnel-vaulted ceiling painted with the Eight Winds (the North Wind a portrait of Lord Bute) by *Andrew W. Lyon*, 1898.

The billiard room, off the main corridor's NE corner, was enlarged to take in part of the adjacent dinner service room in 1908, when the present panelling was installed.‡ In the dining room, *D. R. Hay & Co.*'s painted 'imitation damask' decoration of 1843. Across the house's s end, library and drawing room interconnecting through double doors. In both rooms, richly crowded Jacobean ceilings with small pendants (modelled by *James Annan & Son*). These are of the 1840s. So too are the Library's Frenchy chimneypiece and the remaining fragments of its bookcases (by *Charles Trotter*) with shell-headed niches flanking the doors. The frieze painted with *putti* holding a flower garland punctuated by coats of arms is by *Elizabeth Drake*, c.1895. Drawing room chimneypiece of two stages and two dates. The lower part, its jambs carved with winged lions, is of the 1840s. On top, *Schultz* placed Ionic columns supporting a curvy canopy above a mirrored overmantel. Also by Schultz (dated 1893) is the walls' half-height wooden lining, inlaid with mother-of-pearl flowers, fruits and insects. In the white-and-gold-painted boudoir, a rich Jacobean ceiling of the 1840s. The rest is by Schultz,§ classiest

---

* With advice from the London architect *Alexander Roos*.

‡ The big arch into the extension is now (1988) blocked.

§ Replacing or covering decoration which had been regarded as the masterpiece of *Thomas Bonnar* of *D. R. Hay & Co.*

Artisan Mannerist revival. Very broad stone chimneypiece, the deep ingoes covered with Moorish tiles. Stumpy Corinthian pilasters frame this and the overmantel's lower stage, whose round-arched mirrors are set between more pilasters. More mirrors above in square strapworked frames between terms holding musical instruments and fruit. The rest of the walling is panelled with pilastered basket-arched mirror-frames at the top. Sailing ships on the overall frieze. In Lord Bute's study (originally Mrs Tyndall-Bruce's dressing room) the frieze of cherubs holding garlands survives from *D. R. Hay & Co.*'s 1840s work. The small pieces of glass in the bow window's shutters were presumably inserted in the 1890s. More glass in the shutters of the adjoining family bedroom. Above its panelling, a deep frieze painted by *Lonsdale* in 1892 with a medieval *Corpus Christi* procession including the figure of Lord Bute. The two rooms in the w jamb of Burn's family suite (Mr Tyndall-Bruce's dressing room and sitting room) were remodelled by Schultz as a bedroom and sitting room for Lady Margaret Crichton-Stuart. Deep bed recess in the bedroom, its ceiling prettily enriched with flowers. Large stepped-top chimneypiece enclosing a very small fireplace, the mantelpiece inscribed 'Better a wee fire to warm ye / Than a big fire to burn ye.'* The sitting-room walls Schultz covered with flying seagulls realistically modelled in plaster, more a celebration of Lady Margaret's nautical interests (she was the first woman to gain a Master Mariner's certificate) than of her aristocratic good taste.

Burn had provided three bedrooms at the w end of the service block's s range. These Schultz converted to a chapel and vestry. Long tunnel-vaulted passage (chapel corridor) leading to them. On the walls and ceilings plaster vine enrichment giving way at the steps up to the chapel to inlaid wood lining (dated 1897). At the entrance, a screen made up of small openings, each with baluster mullions and fitted with shutters. At the chapel's s (liturgical e) end, an apse for the altar flanked by smaller apsidal recesses, their pierced wooden doors now removed. The ceiling's broad centre is tunnel-vaulted, the flat sides supported on elongated consoles. Walls and ceiling lined in oak inlaid with mother-of-pearl. Clearstorey lights on the w (liturgical s) side; open screen to the n (liturgical w) gallery over the entrance.

On the main block's first floor, more embellishment of the 1890s. From the stair-landing, a corridor leads s. It was decorated in 1894. Panelled walls; deep frieze and ceiling covered with a modelled plaster relief of fruit trees and birds. Top lighting from cupolas filled with abstract stained glass. At the corridor's end, the Scottish Bedroom and Dressing Room. Coved bedroom ceiling decorated with acorns and squirrels; thistles on the bay windows' soffits. Heraldic stained glass (the arms of the Bethunes of Creich, Keepers of Falkland Palace). Large wooden Jacobean chimneypiece of *c.*1845. Dressing

* Now (1988) boxed in.

room ceiling (dated 1894) with rowan-tree enrichment on the cove, thistles on the flat. The Italian Bedroom and Dressing Room on the E side were gone over in 1895. Of that date is their ceilings' vine enrichment, but the bedroom's saucer dome painted with birds and flowers looks fifty years earlier. Very smart bedroom chimneypiece carved with a relief of *putti* holding a scroll inscribed 'NOBILIS IRA'. Over the door, a round-headed niche squashing the wooden figure of a man.

CRICHTON-STUART MEMORIAL CHAPEL to the SE, a roofless shell begun by *Reginald Fairlie* in 1912 but never finished. Sturdy Scots late Gothic.

STABLES on the main approach, built by *John Swinton*, 1823, with a pediment over the pend arch. Octagonal wooden clock turret above added by *Donald A. Stewart*, c.1901. – Wavily bargeboarded mid-Victorian LODGE to their E.

TYNDALL-BRUCE MONUMENT on Black Hill, 1.4km. W, a large squat obelisk of 1855.

EAST LOMOND. *See* p. 203.
LATHRISK HOUSE. *See* p. 303.
MAIDEN CASTLE. *See*. p. 317.

FERNIE CASTLE
0.9km. E of Letham

3010

Cream-harled agglomeration of additions to a C16 tower house. This was perhaps begun by Florentin Adinulty, who was granted the lands of Fernie in feu ferme in 1510 on condition that he build a sufficient house of stone and lime; but, if so, it was probably heightened and enlarged later in the C16 by the Fernies of that Ilk.* The late C16 house was T-plan, a four-storey main block forming the tail, the crossbar made up of a taller crowstep-gabled SW stairtower and, on the NW, a round tower corbelled out to a diagonally set rectangular cap-house.

The house passed from the Fernies to the Balfours, who added a three-storey E extension, probably in the early C18. c.1815 Francis Balfour of Fernie made toy-fort additions, a porch to the stairtower, and a single-storey W extension. His son, also Francis, remodelled the C18 E extension, c.1844–9, probably employing *Alexander Blyth* as his architect.‡ In these 1840s alterations, the C18 block was given crowsteps and a new front door, a small Baronial-ecclesiastical addition was made at the back, and a conical-roofed tower placed at the NE corner. The building history has been further muddled by the recent rear addition of a round ballroom in connexion with the house's present hotel use.

---

* In whose ownership of the lands Adinulty seems to have been only a temporary intrusion.

‡ Alexander Blyth was paid for inspecting work on the new roof over the E part in 1844–5, but *Alexander Mitchell* was also paid for 'specifications & Superintendance on part of a new roof' in 1849.

Inside, a pleasant 1840s first-floor double drawing room in the E block. The adjoining room's grey marble chimneypiece seems to belong to the alterations of *c.*1815.

Early C19 STABLES to the E, with four pedimented gables facing the house.

FLISK

No village; just the church and manse of a rural parish beside the Tay.

PARISH CHURCH. Roofless shell in a small graveyard. The church was built in 1790: small rectangle, the original windows round-headed. Of the W bellcote only the base survives. The E gable's two lancets date from *T. M. Cappon*'s reconstruction of 1886, when the now fragmentary W porch was added.

Cream-harled MANSE (now WESTER FLISK) to the W, built in 1811; stone porch an addition of 1886. – Early C19 U-plan OFFICES on its NE.

BALHELVIE, 0.9km. SW. Mid-C19 farmhouse. To its N, extensive steading round a horsemill; some of the pantiled ranges were built by *Thomas Robertson*, mason, and *Alexander Kellock*, wright, 1854–5.

FLISKMILLAN, 1.8km. SW. Classy whinstone group of farmhouse and steading by *Robert Bell*, 1852–3, the house still Georgian with an anta-pilastered doorpiece and blocking course.

FORDELL CASTLE
1.8km. NE of Inverkeithing

Smart late C16 tower house built for the Hendersons, who had bought the lands of Fordell in 1511. In 1567 'Robert Peris, James Orrok and sindrye untheris masones and warkmen wer lawborand and biggand ane foundatioun of ane howse of gret quantite' at Fordell. Although in June of the next year 'James Hendersone of Fordell had hes place of Fordell brunt by ane suddaine fyre, both the old worke and the new', the house begun by *Peris* and *Orrok* in 1567 can probably be identified with the W two-thirds of the present building. It was L-plan, the square NW jamb containing a comfortable turnpike stair up to the second floor, whence a turret stair in the inner angle gave access to the corbelled-out top floor of the jamb. The jamb's present door is probably late C17; above it, a broken lintel (not *in situ*) dated 1580, and higher up an armorial stone dated 1567.

In 1580 (the date on the NE skewputt and over the door into the SE tower) the existing house was probably heightened by another floor and extended E; a second stairtower, tenuously attached to the addition's SE corner, made the L-plan into a Z.

Steep pedimented dormerheads were provided on the S front and fat turrets with pistol-holes in their corbelling at the NE and SE corners. This new work made an unpretentious house into a classy villa, the only false note the top-heaviness given the NW jamb by its extra floor, an effect accentuated by its crenellated parapet (possibly altered in the C18; the adjacent turret's conical roof was added by *Robert Hay*, *c*.1855). The SE jamb is suave, rising unbroken to eaves level, where its crowstep-gabled cap-house is minimally projected on a single corbel-course. Corbels on its N wall and tusking in the main block's E gable suggest that a larger house was contemplated. On the main block's N wall, a lead dragon gargoyle, probably mid-C19.

A peculiarity of the plan is the provision of two main stairs, each with its own door to the outside. Separate stairs, each with its own entrance, serving different floors of a tenement are common enough in contemporary urban building, but Fordell is the only example of a tower house where this occurs. Was the SE stair (originally without a door to the ground-floor rooms) designed as a private access from the upper floors to the garden? Otherwise, the interior was originally conventional. On the main block's vaulted ground floor, an E kitchen from which a passage (its brick vault probably C19) leads to the NW jamb past two stores. The W store has a tight SW stair, its top removed, built into the wall thickness, so probably this was the wine cellar with its own access to the first-floor hall. Its mid-C19 door came from the death cell in Calton Jail (Edinburgh). The hall (now drawing room) takes up the W two-thirds of the first floor. *c*.1855 *Robert Hay* removed the floor above to make it more baronial and provided a gallery on three sides. The gallery's brackets remain, but the ceiling was reinstated in 1960–7, squashing the huge chimneypiece of *c*.1855. The broad Gothic arch made by Hay in the E wall has been filled with mid-C19 doors from the demolished Fordell House, their Frenchy sophistication a touch incongruous. Dining room (the C16 chamber or withdrawing room) to the E, its ceiling by Hay again, simply compartmented, with the Henderson crest a decorative motif. The same ceiling is repeated in the second floor's W part (i.e. above the drawing room). In the library over the dining room, mid-C19 bookcases from Fordell House. In the third floor's E room, late C17 panelling with bolection-moulded friezes above the doors and chimneypiece. Simple tunnel-vaulted bedrooms on the NW jamb's two upper floors. – Iron YETT at the NW jamb's entrance door.

CHAPEL to the SW, probably built in 1650, the date on an armorial stone over the door. Simple five-bay rectangle. On the W gable, a spired bellcote with stumpy pinnacled bartizans. Three-light E window with droopy loop tracery. The two-light S windows' mullions and minimally cusped circular heads look like stone squash rackets. A classical contrast to this Gothic survival detail is given by the basket-arched door's rusticated piers and cornice. Inside, a lightweight hammerbeam roof, probably by *Robert Hay*, *c.*1855, when the vaulted crypt was made under the w end. On the walls, C19 HATCHMENTS with judges' coat of arms, brought here from the Laigh Hall of Parliament House (Edinburgh). – Lots of memorial TABLETS, the earliest C17. – German and Flemish C16 and C17 STAINED-GLASS roundels and fragments; in the e window, a Victorian scene of St Therotus' martyrdom. – ENGRAVED GLASS by *Jean Murray*.

In the garden s of the house, large URNS of *c.*1837 from the demolished New Club (Edinburgh). – SUNDIAL of *c.*1860, a copy of Pitreavie's lectern sundial of 1644. – To the N, remains of the C16 BARMKIN WALL lowered and crenellated in 1856. – Contemporary GATEPIERS to the e. – Broad-eaved NORTH LODGE of *c.*1860.

90m. w of the South Lodge, a STANDING STONE, 2m. high and 2.5m. girth at the base.

FORGAN

A rural parish, the early Victorian church 2.1km. s of Newport-on-Tay, its late medieval predecessor 1.3km. to its e.

PARISH CHURCH. Disused. By *David Bryce*, 1841. Built of coursed whinstone rubble. Tall and boxy, on a cruciform plan. Round-headed windows; conical-roofed w bellcote. Inside, gallery on three sides. At the e end, large pulpit with a sounding board. – In the windows flanking the pulpit, STAINED GLASS (Faith and Hope) designed by *Edward Burne-Jones* and made by *Morris & Co.*, 1896 and 1907.

ST FILLAN'S (OLD PARISH) CHURCH. Roofless rubble ruin. The church built *c.*1500 was an unaisled rectangle, the original openings with chamfered margins. Transeptal N 'aisle' added *c.*1600; its large semicircular arch into the church has moulded imposts and a fluted keystone.

MONUMENTS. Inside the church's w end, graveslab of Catharine Trail †1578 (?), carved with a skull and coat of arms. – Outside, w of the church, headstone of Isobel Cowan †1742, with an angel and coat of arms. – To its N, Agnes Cunningham †1792, inept classical, the fluted pilasters supporting nothing; in the curvy top, an angel with three little angels below. The inscription on the back begins

> Wep not for me my Three Children Dear
> I am not Dead but Sleeping here . . .

– To its e, stone of 1748 to the Adamson family, with a jolly angel on the top. – N of the church, a hog-backed tombstone, probably C17, with strapwork and a coat of arms.

FREUCHIE

Established as a village by the C18, it acquired late C19 prosperity when a linen factory was built, *c*. 1870.

PARISH CHURCH, High Street. By *Robert Baldie*, 1876. Three lancets in the gable front. On its l., a tower broached above the clock-stage for an octagonal spired belfry. Inside, original furnishings, the MINISTER'S CHAIR at the back of the pulpit with an ogee-arched back. – STAINED GLASS. In the s gable, two lights ('I Am the Good Shepherd'; 'Suffer the Little Children ...') of *c*. 1880, bright and bad. – In the N gable, three lights (the Transfiguration) signed by *A. Ballantine & Gardiner*, 1901. – Edwardian Adam-revival ORGAN CASE.

PRIMARY SCHOOL, Lomond Road. Mid-C19, of whinstone. One-storey, nine bays, with a chimney on the w gable. In this gable, a blocked round-arched attic window.

DESCRIPTION

Coming from the E, the ALBERT TAVERN, C18 but altered, makes a harled and pantiled landmark on the corner of High Street and Eden Valley Row. In EDEN VALLEY ROW, buildings only on the w side, austere Georgian survival houses of *c*. 1870 leading to the contemporary EDEN VALLEY LINEN WORKS, also Georgian survival but with rusticated quoins breaking the front into a ten-bay centre and three-bay ends. At the row's end, EDEN VALLEY GARDENS, 1980s bungalows around EDEN VALLEY, a large but unexciting villa dated 1887.

In HIGH STREET, the LUMSDEN MEMORIAL HALL, pompous Italian Renaissance, dated 1883. In the parallel lane behind, vernacular houses, several pantiled and with mid-C18 dates carved on their lintels. The High Street vista is closed by the LOMOND HILLS HOTEL, its centre part dated 1753, the swept dormerheads recent additions. It makes a backdrop for the war memorial, a Celtic cross of *c*. 1920. Near the village's w end, the harled and pantiled IN A NOOK is dated 1769; heavy crowsteps on its w gable. Beside it, MORISTON of *c*. 1800.

FREUCHIE MILL, 0.7km. E. Dated 1840. Four-storey cornmill with a five-storey pyramid-roofed kiln, the whinstone masonry making it a tall dark presence. Beside it, the harled C18 miller's house, now garages.

GATESIDE

Small village of vernacular C19 houses, a mill to the SE.

EDENSHEAD UNITED SECESSION CHURCH. Disused. Rubble box, dated 1823, with a diminutive birdcage bellcote. The old MANSE behind cannot be much later.

GATESIDE MILLS. The earlier part is mid-C19, built of rubble. Later s range of brick.

PRIMARY SCHOOL. Plain Board school of *c*. 1875.

3020
GAULDRY

Small village, originally a weaving settlement.

PARISH CHURCH. Built as a Free church, 1867. Very simple, with triangular tops to the windows and an E bellcote.

4000
GIBLISTON HOUSE
2km. W of Arncroach

Smart early C19 villa, its main (S) front of three broad bays. Channelled ground floor with overarches to frame the pilastered doorpiece and the three-light windows, their mullions poised on balustered aprons. Balustered bows project from the sides. Plain music room and utilitarian additions by *Robert S. Lorimer* after he bought the estate in 1915.

2010
GIFFORDTOWN

An early C19 weavers' settlement, the houses now badly altered.

HARTRIDGE, its windows enlarged, is a curiosity, built by the mason *James Scott* for himself in 1835. It is only a cottage, but the E gable sports cannon spouts and its S skewputt is topped by a bust of Scott. Carved stones built into the NE corner, one of them depicting the Annunciation.

GLASSMOUNT *see* KINGHORN

2010
GLENDUCKIE HILL
4km. NE of Newburgh

A presumed Iron Age homestead on the W spur of the hill, secondary in date to a denuded hillfort. Oval dry-stone enclosing wall *c.*2.7m. thick. Within it, a single stone-built house *c.*16m. in diameter inside a wall at least 1.8m. thick. House and enclosure are entered from the S.

2000
GLENROTHES

Town Centre	231	Pitteuchar	234
Auchmuty	232	Prestonhall	234
Cadham and Pitcoudie	233	Rimbleton	234
Collydean and Balgeddie	233	South Parks	234
Leslie Parks and Forester's		Stenton	235
Lodge	233	Tanshall and Caskieberran	235
Macedonia	233	Woodside	235
Newcastle	234	Balbirnie House	235

The second of Scotland's towns founded under the New Towns Act of 1946. The Glenrothes Development Corporation was appointed in 1948 to establish the town on a 2320ha. site. The immediate need was to house 3500 miners due to be transferred from Lanarkshire to the East Fife coalfield's new collieries at Seafield (Kirkcaldy) and Rothes, but the Corporation's Outline Plan published in 1951 tried to avoid the setting up of a single-industry community by proposing that there be eight non-miners for every miner, the town's target population being 32 000.

The 1951 Plan was the work of the New Town's first Chief Architect and Planning Officer, *Peter Tinto*.* The lay-out was based on the unit of a 'precinct' of 1150 dwellings (i.e. a population of 4000 to 5000), with a primary school, church and shop. Two or more 'precincts' made up a 'neighbourhood', with a junior secondary school and small shopping centre. The town as a whole was to be served by senior high schools, sports facilities and a commercial Town Centre.

The first houses and schools were opened in 1951, the first shops the next year and the first church in 1954, by whose end 1000 houses had been built. The Town Centre was begun in 1955. The Rothes Colliery opened two years later and the first factories were begun in 1958. In 1959 it was decided that Glenrothes should develop as a manufacturing centre to provide jobs and housing for overspill from Glasgow, the target figure for the town's eventual population being raised to 55 000.

In 1970 Tinto's successor *Merlyn C. Williams* produced a new Master Plan. The most important modifications made to the 1951 Outline Plan were for an improved road system to cater for increased car ownership, and the adoption of the 'cluster' (houses arranged along a cul-de-sac) as the basic unit, ten 'clusters' forming a 'precinct'. By the end of 1981 the population had risen to over 38 000.

The site is undramatic, though with views out to the Lomond Hills on the W and the Firth of Forth on the E; but new planting is extensive and Riverside Park (most of the parkland of Leslie House) drives a green wedge into the middle. The road system works efficiently, and the central car parks are ample. Sculptures are used with wit (*David Harding* was appointed Town Artist in 1968 and succeeded by *Malcolm Robertson* ten years later). But the architecture is at best undistinguished. In the Town Centre it is at its worst. Surely something more than a shopping mall accompanied by a few high-rise office blocks should have been thought necessary here. Just one of Edinburgh's opera house designs could have provided a sense of occasion.

TOWN CENTRE

BAPTIST CHURCH, Church Street. Formerly St Luke's (Episcopal). By *James Gillespie & Scott*, 1961–2. Hall below the

---

* *E. A. Ferriby* had been appointed Chief Architect and Planning Officer in 1950 but resigned in the same year.

oversailing church whose shallow-pitched roof rises to the E to emphasize the chancel.

46 ST COLUMBA'S PARISH CHURCH, Church Street and Rothes Road. 1960–1, by *Wheeler & Sproson*. Very boxy, with a fully glazed clearstorey. Free-standing bellcote, an open frame of steel and wood. Inside, the N wall is filled with a MURAL (The Way of the Cross) by *Alberto Morrocco*. – In front of it, a semicircular brick PULPIT. – ORGAN by *J. W. Walker & Sons Ltd.*, 1961. – HALL on the W.

RIVERSIDE PARK, Leslie Road. This was the park of Leslie
118 House. At the E end, PADDLING POOL with a group of concrete hippos, by *Stanley Bonnar*, 1972.

DESCRIPTION. The area is roughly rectangular. On the W, at the corner of CHURCH STREET and North Street, a two-storey L-plan block of flats over shops, by *Glenrothes Development Corporation*, 1955–7; The Baptist Church (*see* above) is part of this. To the N, TELEPHONE EXCHANGE by the *Ministry of Public Building and Works*, 1958–60. On NORTH STREET's N side, FIFE REGIONAL COUNCIL OFFICES (by *Glenrothes Development Corporation*, 1979–80), six storeys of precast concrete units. In front, metal SCULPTURE of a stylized flight of terns, by *Malcolm Robertson*, 1981. FIFE HOUSE is a ribbed tower by *Glenrothes Development Corporation*, 1969. On the S side, the nine-storey NEW GLENROTHES HOUSE (by *Hugh Martin & Partners*, 1975), precast concrete panels again. In FALKLAND COURT behind is the Town Artist's comment, THE HERITAGE (by *David Harding*, 1976), an assembly of concrete blocks forming columns, the detail taken from Ancient Egypt onwards. To the W, the two-storey yellow brick HANOVER COURT (by the *Multi Professional Architectural Practice of Edinburgh*, 1984), a dinky mews-style courtyard of offices and shops. L-plan ROTHESAY HOUSE (by *Glenrothes Development Corporation*, 1983), another six-storey block of precast units; flattened arches over the top-floor windows. To the S, St Columba's Church (*see* above).

The KINGDOM CENTRE fills the area's S side. Begun in 1961 by *Peter Tinto* as a pedestrian shopping mall, it is real 'Lego' architecture, a new piece being added almost every birthday. Unfortunately, no attempt seems to have been made to achieve consistency of design. The outward appearance is of big commercial backsides. Inside, it works rather better, the shopfronts giving plenty of colour. In Lyon Square, the central space, SCULPTURE by *Malcolm Robertson*, 1979, of two elderly shoppers taking the weight off their feet. Disturbingly realistic, the more so when their bronze bench is shared by live residents.

AUCHMUTY

ST LUKE'S (Episcopal) CHURCH, Ninian Quadrant. Originally Baptist. By *J. Cassells*, 1960. Monopitch-roofed drydashed shed.
47 ST PAUL'S (R.C.) CHURCH, Warout Road. By *Gillespie, Kidd*

& *Coia*, 1957–8. Trapezoidal, of white-painted brick, with a fully glazed W wall. Monopitch-roofed E tower, its W face glazed in a simple abstract pattern; off-centre wooden cross on top. The interior was designed for an altar against the E wall, flooded with light from the tower. A brick wall, some bricks set diagonally to form patterns, made a porch containing the confessionals and font. Much of the effect has been lost by liturgical rearrangement, the altar pulled out from under the tower and the font moved to the E. Repainting the white walls a salmon pink has not helped. – Above the tabernacle, elaborate spiky metal CRUCIFIX with symbols of the Passion and figures of the bystanders at Calvary, by *Benno Schotz*.

HALL on the S. – Admirably simple PRESBYTERY to the W, its 'Magnet' door not original.

AUCHMUTY HIGH SCHOOL, Auchmuty Road. 1954–7, by *Peter Tinto*.

LADYBIRD NURSERY, Stuart Road. By *Fife County Council*, 1969. The painted cement relief of sunflowers is an enjoyable touch.

WAROUT PRIMARY SCHOOL, Malcolm Road. 1956–7, by *Fife County Council*.

WAROUT STADIUM, off Warout Road. By *Glenrothes Development Corporation*, 1971–2. Metal fins on the stand's W side.

CADHAM AND PITCOUDIE

FIRE STATION, Huntsman's Road. By *Fife County Council*, 1972–3.

PITCOUDIE PRIMARY SCHOOL, off Iona Park. By *Fife County Council*, 1975–6.

COLLYDEAN AND BALGEDDIE

COLLYDEAN PRIMARY SCHOOL, Magnus Drive. 1980, by *Fife Regional Council*, 1980. Drydashed, with pavilion roofs.

PITCAIRN HOUSE, Piper Drive. Only the E gable and the bottom courses of the other three walls survive of the mid-C17 house of the Pitcairns of that Ilk. It has been a rubble-built rectangle. In the gable, a first-floor window with rounded arrises.

LESLIE PARKS AND FORESTER'S LODGE

GLENROTHES HOSPITAL, Lodge Rise. By *Scottish Health Service Common Services Agency*, 1979–80. Low, in dark brick with monopitch roofs. To the W, FORESTER'S LODGE at the old E entry to Leslie House. Early C19 with Gothic windows; the broad-eaved roof is an alteration.

MACEDONIA

GLENWOOD HIGH SCHOOL, South Parks Road. By *Fife County Council*, 1960–1.

Southwood School, Marchmont Crescent. By *Fife County Council*, 1964.

Newcastle Primary School, Muirfield Drive. By *Fife Regional Council*, 1976–7.

Church of Christ, off Blair Avenue. By *W. Stevenson*, 1975–6, with a silly version of an American Colonial spire.

Fife Institution, Viewfield. By *Fife County Council*, 1971. White-tiled swimming pool and concrete-panelled sports hall joined by a lower block. The result is lumpy.

Glamis House (Cheshire Home), off Blair Avenue. By *Wheeler & Sproson*, 1983–4. Stylish, single-storey with big pitched roofs.

Glenrothes Technical College, Stenton Road. 1966–8, by *Fife County Council*. Sensible but uninteresting.

Marigold Nursery, Glamis Avenue. By *Fife County Council*, 1970–1. Just like the Ladybird Nursery (*see* Auchmuty, above) but with a relief of marigolds.

Pitteuchar East Primary School, Glamis Avenue. By *Fife County Council*, 1969.

Pitteuchar West Primary School, Inveraray Avenue. By *Fife County Council*, 1975–6.

New Preston Centre, Alburne Park. Former Board school of 1875–6 by *W. L. Moffat & Aitken*; enlarged 1881.

In Alburne Park, Levenbank of *c*.1840, with a chimney gablet and scrolled skewputts; Tudor hoodmoulds over the ground-floor windows.

Rimbleton School, Bilsland Road. By *Fife County Council*, 1961–3.

St Paul's R.C. Primary School, Rimbleton Avenue. 1957–60, by *Fife County Council*.

Glenrothes High School, Napier Road. By *Fife County Council*, 1963–6. Curtain-walled with a glazed circular 'belvedere' on top.

Police Station, Napier Road. By *Fife County Council*, 1960.

South Parks Primary School, Napier Road. By *Fife County Council*, 1960. A pair of two-storey brick blocks joined by a lower link.

RAEBURN HEIGHTS, off ROTHES ROAD, is one of Glenrothes'
few landmarks, a sixteen-storey block of flats built in 1968
using the *Wimpey* 'no fines' method of concrete construction.

STENTON

STENTON JUBILEE CENTRE, Dunrobin Road. Mid-C19 whinstone farm steading, converted to a community centre in 1978.

TANSHALL AND CASKIEBERRAN

ST NINIAN'S PARISH CHURCH, Durris Drive. By *Rodger*,
1970. Brick hexagons containing the church and hall joined by
a one-storey link. The church roof is an eccentrically truncated
felt-covered 'tower'.
CASKIEBERRAN PRIMARY SCHOOL, Ravenswood Drive. By
Fife County Council, 1969.
GLENROTHES GOLF CLUB, Golf Course Road. 1967, by *Glenrothes Development Corporation*. Well sited and well composed,
with a boarded upper floor.
TANSHALL PRIMARY SCHOOL, off Cullen Drive. Brick and
glass; by *Fife County Council*, 1968.

WOODSIDE

ST MARGARET'S PARISH CHURCH, Woodside Road. 1953–4,
by *Peter Sinclair*. Harled, with a pyramid-roofed tower.
CARLETON PRIMARY SCHOOL, Happer Crescent. By *Fife
County Council*, 1951–2. Festival of Britain style, with a small
clocktower.
THE LOMOND CENTRE, Woodside Way. Abstract grouping of
drydashed blocks; some walls fashionably curved. By *Fife
County Council*, 1975–6.

BALBIRNIE HOUSE

Neo-classical mansion designed by *Richard Crichton* for General   71
Robert Balfour in 1815 and completed by Crichton's nephews
R. & R. Dickson four years later. A C17 house on the site had
been given a new front block in 1777–82, almost certainly by
John Baxter Jun.,* and this late C18 work was retained and
remodelled as part of the early C19 house. Baxter's addition
had a seven-bay W front with an advanced and pedimented
centre. Crichton lengthened it S by a further four bays, using
Baxter's centre as the l. bookend of a five-bay centrepiece, the
three C18 bays to its r. being given giant Ionic columns under
an attic, and the first bay of his extension being advanced as a
second bookend. Baxter's pediment was removed and each of
the advanced bays treated with coupled Ionic pilasters, three-
light windows (those of the ground floor in segmental-headed

*But *George Paterson* also submitted a scheme. *James Kay* was the mason and
David Wilkieson the wright.

overarches), and attic lunettes. The entrance was placed on the s front. Five bays, the centre three advanced with a pedimented portico, in general conception like William Chambers' Duddingston House (Edinburgh) of 1763, but the order is Ionic not Corinthian and the detail heavier, in the early C19 manner. Office court at the back, probably by *David Bryce*, *c.*1860, with a scroll-sided pedimented bellcote over the pend entry.

Inside, the entrance hall is flanked by the drawing room on the w and dining room on the e, but these are entered not from the hall but from the saloon running N of the hall behind the drawing room, library and billiard room to the stairhall. The saloon is impressive, divided by piers into four bays, each with a pendentive dome. In the e wall, lunette windows set high up; on the other walls, roundels painted in *grisaille* with cherubs. Plasterwork, as elsewhere in the house, by *Anderson & Ramage* of Edinburgh. In the stairhall, a very plain Imperial stair overlooked from the first-floor landing through a broad Ionic screen. The library has very shallow pendentives supporting a flat 'dome'. Console-corniced bookcases of 1815. The contemporary chimneypiece was supplied by *David Ness & Co.* Frenchy chimneypiece in the boudoir w of the stairhall, a replacement of 1843. The drawing room was remodelled *c.*1900. In the basement's se corner, a groin-vaulted kitchen.

A lay-out plan for the PARK was prepared by *Robert Robinson* in 1779, and the WALLED GARDEN E of the house was built in 1784–6 more or less on the site he suggested. The rest of the parkland follows *Thomas White*'s design of 1817. – Mid-C19 STABLES (now CRAFT CENTRE) with red sandstone dressings and a pedimented pend arch. – Bargeboarded SOUTH LODGE at the entry from Markinch, by *David Bryce*, dated 1861. – WEST LODGE on the A92, by *R. & R. Dickson*, 1823, in a cottage-classical manner.

0.6km. (formerly 0.72km.) NW of the house, a STONE CIRCLE, originally of ten uprights, moved to its present position in 1971, in advance of the widening of the A92. Excavation suggested a sequence of burial and ritual activity on the site in three main phases. First the erection of the stones around a rectangular stone setting. The filling of the stone-holes included cremated human bones and some fragments of grooved ware, the latter suggesting a date similar to that of the nearby henge of Balfarg (*see* below). The next stage is represented by the insertion of several cist burials within the circle, and the depositing of a Beaker pot together with a necklace of jet beads. The side slab of one of the cists is decorated with cup and cup-and-ring markings; a concrete replica of the stone may be seen on the site. Finally the interior was covered with a cairn of stones sealing the cists and masking the central setting. Several more burial deposits – perhaps as many as sixteen – were subsequently inserted into the cairn material, so the site shows continuity of burial tradition over many centuries. The finds are in the Royal Museum of Scotland, Queen Street, Edinburgh.

BALFARG, 2km. NE of Glenrothes. A ceremonial monument consisting originally of a platform *c.*16m. in diameter, surrounded by a ditch and bank, now partially restored and the ditch dug out to give an idea of the scale. On the platform was a circle of sixteen great timber posts; shorter posts are now set in the holes revealed by excavation. Subsequently two concentric rings of stones were erected, but only two survive, at the causeway entering the henge on the NW. Finally *c.*1900 B.C. a burial was inserted in the centre, accompanied by a handled Beaker and flint knife, and covered by a very large slab which still marks its position. Excavation to the E of the henge and to the N of the Balbirnie Stone Circle (*see* above), examining a cropmark in advance of housing development, revealed a roughly circular enclosure in which the post-holes of two large timber structures (*c.*19m. by 9.5m.) were found, along with some grooved ware; their function may have been both funerary and ritual.

ROTHES. A reconstructed Iron Age souterrain, or earth-house, immediately NW of Rothes House. Of elongated pear-shape plan, 12m. long. Though alleged to have been transported from near Pirnie in Wemyss parish, it is more likely to represent the fabric of a souterrain discovered closer at hand.

GRANGEMUIR HOUSE   *5000*
1.9km. N of Pittenweem

Bland late Georgian of five bays, all harled but with stone bands and cornice and a bullseyed pediment over the centrepiece, traditionally of 1807. Plasterwork of that period, but plain Grecian chimneypieces of *c.*1830. The main frontage was extended to the E at the latter time, but the bay window that interrupts it to the W must be later. Fine S outlook, but the house is now (1988) beleaguered by holiday chalets.

GRANGE OF LINDORES   *2010*

Rural hamlet developed from the early C19.

SCHOOL. Now a house. Mid-C19, Tudor, with a bellcote.

GREEN CRAIG   *3020*
0.6km. N of Brunton

A prehistoric fort on the summit, showing two phases. First, two stony ramparts enclosing an oval *c.*180m. by 100m. Second, an overlying oval *c.*30m. by 26m. within a single dry-stone wall. At the foot of the E slope is an Iron Age homestead excavated by Bersu in 1947, of rectangular plan, *c.*19m. by 16.5m., within a single stony bank. There was a single round timber house, whose lower wall was of stone bonded with the enclosing bank.

GREEN HILL *see* BALMERINO

GUARDBRIDGE

Village between the bridges which carry the W and N roads to St Andrews over the Eden and the Motray Water. A distillery built here *c.*1810 was redeveloped as a paper mill from 1872.

ST SAVIOUR'S CHURCH (Episcopal), Main Street. Now a house. Diminutive Gothic by *C. F. Anderson*, 1900–1.

GUARD BRIDGE over the Eden. Built by Bishop Henry Wardlaw in the early C15 but 'altogidder ruyneous' in 1601, when it was repaired. Further repairs are recorded in 1678–86, 1786 and 1802. Six arches (the E smaller than the others) with triangular cutwaters. The pedestrian refuges may date from one of the repairs. On both sides, frames for armorial panels, one on the N containing the arms and initials of Archbishop James Beaton (1522–39). – On the S, bridge of 1935–7 by *F. A. MacDonald & Partners*: three-span, of channel-rusticated concrete.

INNER BRIDGE over the Motray Water. Probably early C18, but the 'inner brig' was repaired in 1598. Slightly humped, of three arches with segmental cutwaters. The broached ashlar parapets presumably date from the repairs of 1804. – Now superseded by a graceless concrete bridge to the E.

INSTITUTE, Innerbridge Villas. Now housing. Light-hearted Scots Renaissance of *c.*1920.

PAPER MILL, Main Street. Very large and utilitarian complex begun in 1872–3. Mostly of brick, the earliest part of stone.

PRIMARY SCHOOL, Innerbridge Street. Dated 1889; small and stolid.

DESCRIPTION. Severe terraces of late Victorian housing for the paper mill's workers. S of the Eden, the harled GUARDBRIDGE HOTEL of *c.*1830, with a stumpy Roman Doric columned doorpiece.

SEGGIE, 0.7km. SW. Overgrown broad-eaved cottage of *c.*1860, by *Andrew Heiton Jun.*, with an Italianate tower over the entrance. – The WALLED GARDEN may be rather later: on three sides, brick walls with shaped gable features, dwarf wall (formerly with railings) on the S. – ENTRANCE LODGE contemporary with the house.

HALBEATH

Small mining village.

LAUDER TECHNICAL COLLEGE. By *Fife County Council*, 1964; extended by *Fife Regional Council*, 1976. In the grounds, FOD HOUSE of *c.*1840, with late Victorian single-storey wings.

FORMER SCHOOL, 1.1km. N. 1875–6, by *Thomas Frame & Son*.
Vaguely Ruskinian Gothic in hammerdressed rubble.

HILL HOUSE

1.4km. s of Dunfermline

0080

Laird's house built for William Monteith of Randieford in 1623,
a curious mixture of the very smart and rather gauche. On
plan it is an irregular T, the shorter but taller jamb extending
from near the crossbar's E end, the open SE angle partly filled
by a wing protruding E from the jamb, its walling shallowly
corbelled out above the ground floor. Crowsteps on the gables
of this wing and the main block, but the jamb's ashlar-fronted
S gable has straight skews. Was there a change of mind or
mason during construction?

On the approach from the SW these crudities are forgotten.
The main block's S and the jamb's W façades are ashlar-fronted.
In the inner angle, an octagonal stairtower rising a storey above
the rest and finished with a parapet of letters spelling NI DEVS
ÆDIFICET DOMVM. Inside the parapet, two tall chimneys
joined by a stone inscribed in Hebrew and Latin with a quotation from *Ecclesiasticus* ('This also is vanity and great evil').
Over the stairtower and jamb windows, finialled pediments.
The pediments above the main block's first-floor windows
have their tops sliced off by the second-floor stringcourse; in
their tympana, reliefs of a woman playing a harp and a man
holding his sides. The main block's second-floor windows
were given crowstepped gablets by *F. W. Deas* in 1912; the l.
gablet has since been altered, the r. removed. Also of 1912 is
the single-storey extension (its Baronial parapet now removed)
hiding the stairtower's entrance. Above it, a scrolled panel
with the date 1623 above a cartouche inscribed in Hebrew and
Latin with a monitory text from *Jeremiah* ('Woe unto him that
buildeth his house in unrighteousness').

HILL OF TARVIT

2.7km. s of Cupar

3010

Expensively cold-blooded Queen Anne revival villa of 1905–7 by 83
Robert S. Lorimer. When his client, the Dundee jute magnate
and collector F. B. Sharp, bought the estate (then Wemyss
Hall) in 1904, it contained an austere mansion house of 1696
to which had been added two utilitarian back wings. Lorimer
retained these additions, leaving the W wing's mid-C19
gabled dormerheads alone, adding piended bellcast-roofed
dormers to the E, and covering the court between with a glass
roof (since removed). The main block was rebuilt in a style
supposedly reminiscent of the original.*

---

* But with no resemblance of detail. The original house was of three bays with a
pedimented centre.

Lorimer's main front is to the garden on the s. Symmetrical with piend-roofed ends; in their bowed projections, three-light ground-floor windows. Set-back five-bay main range, its centre marked by a large relief of Pomona flanked by absurdly tall french windows. Entrance on the w side with a loggia across the front block, a balustraded smoking room masking the rear wing. All the new work is of harled rubble with rusticated quoins at the corners and channelled window margins.*

The entrance lobby, its Holyrood-revival ceiling the first of several, opens into the hall designed as a setting for tapestries and Jacobean furniture. Oak panelling with linenfold motifs. Ceiling also of oak, carved with Lorimer's characteristic small-scale floral decoration; this woodwork is all by *Scott Morton & Co.* Drawing room to the w, its Frenchified plasterwork (by *Thomas Beattie*) and white-painted pine panelling (by *Scott Morton*) intended to complement Sharp's collection of French furniture. E of the Hall, a groin-vaulted corridor on whose s is the library. Compartmented plaster ceiling (by *Samuel Wilson*) with vine enrichment of mid-C17 Kellie Castle type; large stone chimneypiece with onyx inlay. In the dining room to the w, a knock-out Holyrood-revival ceiling (by *Beattie*) but with some vine decoration. Late C17 style white-painted African mahogany panelling (by *Scott Morton*). On the chimneypiece, a relief of centaurs with a goat, perhaps by *Louis Deuchars*. Arches at the hall's NW corner open into the stairhall, its ceiling again Holyrood-revival (by *Wilson*). Off the half-landing, smoking room with simple rosette enrichment on the trabeated ceiling. Innocently classical stone chimneypiece dated 1627 from Scotstarvit Tower. On each jamb, a carved thistle, rose and *fleur de lis*. Thistles and shields (with the arms and initials of Sir John Scott and Dame Anne Drummond, his wife) on the frieze; scrolls flanking a steep pediment on top.

Terraced GARDENS in front and behind laid out by *Lorimer*. At the front terrace's E end, a WELL with a huge wrought-iron open cover of stylized flowers. – Sleeping stone lions on the bottom terrace's piers. – The terraces behind rise to the C18 WALLED GARDEN. Central gateway with swagged urns on the piers. Wrought-iron gates in the manner of *c.*1700 but with the addition of twee Edwardian birds. – Harled LAUNDRY to the E, again by *Lorimer*, with a bellcast roof. – To its s, mid-C19 STABLES with a tall pedimented centre and piended ends. – Adjacent late C19 crowstepped LODGE. – On the summit of the Hill of Tarvit to the N (the supposed spot of the treaty of 1559 between Mary of Guise's forces and the Lords of the Congregation), a tall stone pedestal built in 1817 as the base for the Cupar Market Cross (moved back to Cupar in 1897). – Beside it, an Iron Age HOMESTEAD, sadly wasted, originally 30m. by 24m. within a single rampart enclosing a round, stone-

---

* Most of the rubble masonry was taken from demolished buildings on the estate; some of the dressed stone came from the C17 house.

founded house, *c.*14.5m. by 12m. House entrance on the NE, in line with the main gap in the outer rampart.

INCHCOLM

1080

Island in the Firth of Forth 2.2km. S of Aberdour, now a popular resort for seals and the more discriminating tourist.

The name means Colm's island, presumably a reference to its association with a Celtic saint identified confidently, but probably wrongly, in the C12 with St Columba, to whom the Augustinian monastery here was dedicated. That abbey survived until the Reformation, after which a small part of its buildings were converted into a house and the rest left to decay until placed in government care in 1924.

Like the other islands of the Forth, Inchcolm was thought to be important in the military defence of SE Scotland. Attacked by the English in the C14, it was occupied by them during the Duke of Somerset's invasion of 1547 and by French troops the next

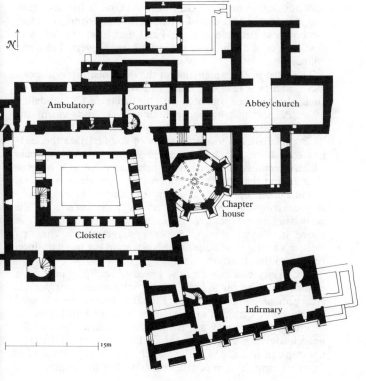

Inchcolm Abbey,
plan

year. In 1795 a gun battery was begun on the island as a defence against a Napoleonic invasion. This was dismantled in 1817, but new batteries were built during the First World War as protection against a German attack on the naval dockyard at Rosyth. These too have been abandoned, but their ruins stand as a counter-attraction to the Abbey remains.

8   INCHCOLM ABBEY. Remarkably intact remains of the Augustin-
     ian monastery founded in the C12 and abandoned after the
     Reformation of 1560.

Late medieval accounts of the convent's origin state that it was founded by Alexander I, *c.* 1123, after storms had forced him to spend three days on the island, fed and sheltered by a resident Culdee hermit. Apparent confirmation of this tra-dition is given by a charter of *c.* 1180 in which William de Mortimer admitted that the church of Aberdour had belonged to the canons of Inchcolm since the reign of Alexander I. However, a charter of *c.* 1160 records the making over to the monastery of property granted by David I to Bishop Geoffrey of Dunkeld to hold until the house of Augustinian canons had been established on the island, suggesting that the house was founded by David after 1140, when Geoffrey became bishop, and not settled on the island until *c.* 1160. It has also been suggested* that Alexander I intended to establish an Augustin-ian house at Dunkeld Cathedral and that, after the failure of that project, the funds and the canons were diverted to Inch-colm.

The most likely explanation of the documentary evidence's inconsistency is that Alexander I's foundation of a church on Inchcolm has been conflated with his or David I's foundation of an Augustinian house (including in its endowment the church of Aberdour) which finally settled on the island *c.* 1160. This explanation also makes sense of the fact that the early C12 church incorporated in the monastery is built on a plan which precludes it from having been intended as a convent church, and that the first addition to it, apparently also C12, was of a choir (the essential setting for monastic offices). Prob-ably contemporary with the choir was the conversion of the early C12 chancel into a retrochoir and the erection of a tower above it. Rather skimpy evidence suggests that the first cloister's E range was built S of this tower, in the usual position relative to the choir.

The priory was raised to the status of an abbey in 1235, a change which seems to have led to a scheme for considerable enlargement of the buildings. Probably first to be executed was the construction of a new chapter house and the beginning of a new cloister range E of the existing cloister. Work on the new cloister, however, seems to have been abandoned. Instead, a N transept was added to the church, and in 1265 Richard of Inverkeithing, Bishop of Dunkeld, doubled the length of the

* By Ian B. Cowan and D. E. Easson, *Mediaeval Religious Houses: Scotland* (2nd ed., 1976), 91.

monastic choir. Work on the cloister began again in the C14, and the new buildings were complete by its end. Included in this work was the conversion of the early C12 nave and retro-choir into the N ambulatory, with a lodging for the abbot above. This work, though it produced a comfortable cloister, entailed the contraction of the choir whose W end had to be partitioned off as a new retrochoir. Probably in consequence, the abbey church was virtually rebuilt further E from the first years of the C15. Also of the C15 was the addition of an infirmary SE of the cloister, whose interior was also improved.

The abbey had been dissolved by 1564 and the property passed to James Stewart, in favour of whose second son, Henry, Lord St Colme, the abbey and its lands were erected into a temporal lordship in 1611. The buildings were abandoned until in 1924 they were placed under the guardianship of the Secretary of State.

The early C12 CHURCH at the NW was originally very plain. Three-bay nave and narrower one-bay chancel. Ashlar-built (the masonry now much patched) with a splayed plinth and moulded stringcourse under the eaves. W door of two orders, the inner with a nook-shaft, the outer composed of plain vous-soirs. The nave had a wooden roof, the chancel may have been vaulted.

Major alterations were made in the later C12, when the monastery was established. To allow for excavation of the ground on the S to provide a level site for the cloister, this side of the nave was thickened and taken down lower. In the S wall's W bay, external traces of a round-headed door; behind it is the original S door, whose head has been lowered by the insertion of a lintel. At the same time the original chancel was reconstructed as a retrochoir (the monastic choir being added on its E), its S wall rebuilt further S, and a tower raised above it.

This TOWER is of cubical ashlar, the walling broken only by a stringcourse below the belfry. Round-arched hoodmoulds over the belfry openings, each of two lancet lights under a trefoil, a less elegant and probably earlier version of the early C13 upper windows in the NW tower of Holyrood Abbey (Edinburgh). Corbelled parapet.

In the tower's E face, a round-headed C14 arch. Above it, largely hidden by C14 or C15 masonry, the late C12 pulpitum's three acutely pointed arches, their shafts with foliaged capitals. In the W face, seen best from inside the old nave, the two arches of the rood screen's upper part. Its base (presumably with a central altar flanked by doors) was removed in the C14 when the cloister's N ambulatory was formed from the nave and retrochoir.

N of the tower, a C15 'transept' added to give extra accommodation to the abbot's lodging (by then within the upper part of the nave and tower) and, perhaps more importantly, to buttress the stone vaults inserted at the same time in the tower's upper parts. A roof raggle shows that there was an earlier transept, probably late C13, whose lean-to W aisle extended across the nave's E bay. Protruding from the tower's SE corner, a comfortable C16 stairtower.

The early C12 church's interior was transformed in the C14, when it was abandoned for worship. The nave was divided horizontally by the insertion of a stone tunnel-vault, the lower floor becoming the N ambulatory of a new cloister, the upper floor the hall or *camera* of a lodging for the abbot, with access to the guest hall in the new cloister's W range through a first-floor lobby in an addition built against the old nave's W end. The bottom part of the tower was also vaulted as part of the ambulatory, the vault cutting through the rood screen and pulpitum; its first floor became the abbot's solar.

The tower's interior was further altered in the C15, when its three upper floors were given vaults, the second floor becoming a doocot with stone nesting boxes cut in the walls, the top floor perhaps a study, its vault rising above the parapet. With the contemporary N 'transept' addition the abbot's lodging was distinctly comfortable. Hall above the C12 nave: in its W wall, scanty remains of a fireplace hood. Solar on the tower's first floor with a NE fireplace, one of its hood's corbels still surviving; stone seat in the S window. In the N 'transept', vaulted first-floor bedchamber with a fireplace, garderobe and aumbry; arched niche above the door, possibly a lampstand.

E of the tower is the late C12 MONASTIC CHOIR. Its W three-quarters, disused and probably unroofed since the C15, are now reduced to foundations, except on the S, where the choir wall formed the N end of the cloister's E range. On this side, a C12 round-arched door and a window cut across by the tower's C16 stair. Rectangular C14 door from the E ambulatory and, to its E, fragments of the contemporary stair from the monks' dormitory. On the N side, foundations of a C14 transept; its W wall, built as the E wall of the first transept extending from the tower, now serves as the E wall of the C15 'transept' added to the abbot's lodging.

The cruciform C15 ABBEY CHURCH to the E is now represented by little more than foundations, except at the S transept, the W half of whose pointed tunnel-vault still stands, with sculptural effect. The choir W of the transepts pre-dates the C15, most of it being the extension added by Bishop Richard in 1265. In its S wall, the lower part of a tomb recess, its back painted with a group of clerics: one seems to be a bishop, two others hold thuribles. This was probably the monument of John de Leycester, Bishop of Dunkeld, who was buried on the choir's S side in 1266. To its W, remains of the night stair from the monks' dormitory added in the C15, when the W end of the church was moved E, making the earlier stair unsuitable.

Doorway to the S transept with simply moulded bases and chamfered jambs. Against the transept's E wall, evidence of two altars with a plain piscina between them. In the S wall, another piscina, but more grandly sited in a trefoil-headed recess; beside it, a rectangular credence niche.

At the choir's E end, a late medieval ALTAR SLAB found in the S transept and now placed on an absurdly low plinth to mark the approximate position of the high altar.

The CLOISTER is as usual S of the church. The earliest of the existing buildings are the C13 chapter house and the short stretch of contemporary wall on the E range's side joining it to the W end of the late C12 choir. This range is not at right angles to the church but runs SE, possibly to allow an earlier chapter house to its W to remain in use during construction. The rest of the cloister buildings are C14, the E range having been completed first, followed in turn by the S and W ranges. At the same time the nave and chancel of the early C12 church were converted to form a N ambulatory with abbot's lodging above (*see* above).

The C13 CHAPTER HOUSE is octagonal, with buttresses at the corners. Pointed windows in the E, SE and S bays. The smaller NE window looks like a C14 insertion, its internal trefoil head contrasting with the simple mouldings of the others. Round SW window placed high up. Vaulted interior, the ribs springing from wall-shafts and meeting at a boss, its centre pierced so that the rope suspending a light could be hung through it. The round-arched W door's shafts have capitals but no bases; the arch mouldings continue down the jambs to stop on a broad splay. Round the walls, a stone bench, higher on the E, where it is backed by a blind arcade denoting the seats of the abbot, prior and sub-prior. A crude upper floor was dumped on the chapter house in the C14, the sailing ship weathervane of its spired roof a genteel addition by *J. Wilson Paterson*, 1931. This addition contained the WARMING HOUSE, its octagon covered internally by an awkward pointed tunnel-vault. N fireplace. The walls have been decorated with painted platitudes (e.g. STULTU(M) E(ST) TIMERE Q(UO)D VITARI NO(N) P(OTEST), 'It is foolish to fear what cannot be avoided').

The C14 cloister was unusual in that the ambulatory or monks' walk occupied the ground floor of the buildings rather than being in lean-tos built towards the central garth. A conventional lean-to walk was put up on the N side in the C15, releasing the lower part of the C12 nave and chancel for use as storage.

The cloister buildings form a severe ashlar rectangle relieved internally by the diagonal ascent of windows lighting the stair to the guest hall and refectory on the W side and by the C15 chimney of the guest hall corbelled out from the same wall. Plain first-floor windows; the dormitory's N window has been enlarged as a door. Round-arched ground-floor openings from the ambulatory, provided with stone window seats on the E and W sides. The large round-headed arches at the N ends of the E and W ranges are C15 insertions for access to the new N ambulatory. The cloister's external appearance is just as straightforward, except for the arched projection of the refectory's pulpit from the S wall, whose pointed windows are restorations of 1927. C16 stairtower with a corbelled parapet at the w end of this range.

The E range extends s of the quadrangle with a REREDORTER or latrines. The first reredorter here was joined to the dormitory in the E range by a wooden bridge for which the stone corbels survive. It seems to have been intended that the drain would be flushed by the tide, but it was built too far from the shore for the arrangement to work. Probably soon after its completion, the lower floor was converted into a cellar and the upper part, including the wooden bridge, was rebuilt as a stone extension to the dormitory, linking it to a new reredorter on the s. This dormitory extension was remodelled in the C16, presumably after the Reformation, when it was partly converted into domestic accommodation and partly unroofed and given a battlement on the E side. E of the reredorter, the C15 INFIRMARY, its exposed s wall prudently buttressed.

The interior of the cloister ambulatory is tunnel-vaulted. At its SE corner's inner side, remains of a lampstand; almost opposite in the s wall, a door which has been converted to a water trough.

On the cloister's first floor the E range contained the monks' DORMITORY (with warming house opening off it), the s their refectory, and the w the guest hall. All have pointed tunnel-vaults. In the dormitory's w wall, a round window over the door to the reredorter. The N window in its E wall was converted to a door in the C15 to give access to the new night stair made necessary by the alterations to the church.

The REFECTORY was at first a single room occupying all the s range. At the E end, dais for the high table; behind the dais, chases for panelling and lines of the high table's canopy visible in the plaster. N of the high table, a large aumbry; on the s, the pulpit. The kitchen was at the w end, originally with an open hearth under an opening in the vault. The kitchen was probably partitioned off in the C15, when a fireplace was built against the w gable, its r. jamb partly blocking a hatch to the guest hall.

GUEST HALL in the w range. Its N end is the C12 nave's s wall; in it, the top of a blocked round arch. Rather small fireplace inserted in a window embrasure in the E wall. Remains of medieval tiles on the floor.

Inside the INFIRMARY the w second-floor room opened off the dormitory; from it a turnpike stair to the room below and the cellars. The rest of the range was self-contained, with an outside stair on the N. Ground-floor cellar with an oven in a NE jamb. The first-floor E room has a pointed window in the gable and may have been a chapel.

At the NW corner of the garden w of the church, an irregularly shaped stone-roofed CELL, reputed to have been that of the Culdee hermit met here by Alexander I. The walls may be C10 or C11 work, but the pointed tunnel-vault looks C14 or C15. In the C17 it was a mortuary.

INNERGELLIE

5000

1.3km. N of Anstruther Easter

Laird's house built for the Lumisdaines in 1740, its ashlar entrance front a remarkable display of master mason's baroque. Giant Ionic pilasters frame the seven bays divided compositionally 3/1/3. In each of the outer sections, the centre is defined by a first-floor round-arched and keyblocked niche, an attic bullseye with radiating voussoirs, and a gablet suggesting an open triangular pediment. Centrepiece on the same plane. Fluted Ionic pilasters at the door; on its top, a squat Ionic aedicule containing a heraldic panel of 1650 from the previous house on the site. Figure of Mercury in the first-floor niche, whose carved head keystone breaks through the main cornice. Open segmental pediment overall, its tympanum filled with foliage. The harled W (garden) front makes no attempt to continue the display, a tall rusticated round-headed window its only concession to swagger. In the inner angle at the back, an octagonal tower given a parapeted top storey in the early C19. Inside, panelled dining room of 1740, its lugged chimneypiece framed by fluted Corinthian pilasters; more pilasters at the sideboard recess. Curiously there is only a Greek key frieze above, no proper cornice.

Lectern DOOCOT to the SW, probably rather earlier than the house.

INVERKEITHING

1080

Made a royal burgh in the late C12; its harbour on the Forth suited it well for trade. It was declining when Defoe visited in 1726, and in 1758 Sir William Burrell found it 'a mean, miserable, paultry Town'; but ironworks and a distillery were established in the late C18. Shipbuilding (followed by shipbreaking) has been another occupation. Papermaking has been the C20's main industry. The town is now also a dormitory for Edinburgh commuters.

CHURCHES

PARISH CHURCH (ST PETER), Church Street. A large Perp 15 nave and aisles box by *James Gillespie Graham*,* 1826–7, attached to a C14 tower.

The tower is beautifully strong, with a SE semi-octagonal stairtower and angle buttresses at the other three corners. Stringcourses‡ to enliven the ashlar walling, whose weathered texture seems doomed to disappear under the refacing begun by *Gordon & Dey* in 1980. Simple pointed doors and lancets at the lower stages, two-light Dec windows at the belfry. The heavy corbelled parapet is C16. Above, the squat lead-covered

* *William Stirling I* of Dunblane was executant architect.
‡ The upper one (a sill course under the belfry openings) survives only on the N face.

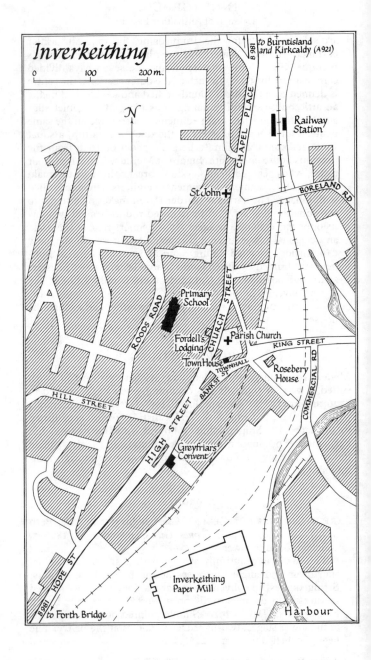

spire by *Thomas Bonnar*, 1835, replaced a similar spire of 1731. Its gabled dormers housing clock faces were added by *Andrew Scobie* in 1883. Inside the tower, angular rear-arches for the N and S doors.

The church interior was cleaned up in 1900 by *P. MacGregor Chalmers*, who imposed his standard High Presbyterian arrangement. Gillespie Graham's arcades look bald without galleries, as do the windows deprived of their tracery. – REREDOS, COMMUNION TABLE and PULPIT all of 1900. – FONT. Octagonal bowl decorated with carved angels holding armorial shields. The heraldry suggests a date of *c.*1398. The shaft of clustered columns with foliaged capitals also C14. – STAINED GLASS. E window of 1856, with bright lozenges of stylized foliage. – The N aisle's E window (The Resurrection) is signed by *A. Ballantine & Gardiner*, 1900. – Corresponding window ('Take the Helmet of Salvation ...') in S aisle, 1905. – War Memorial window of 1919. – ORGAN by *Joseph Brooke & Co.* of Glasgow.

The churchyard contains half-buried HEADSTONES, mostly worn. On the S, in line with the church's centre window, stone dated 1773 carved with a butcher's knives. – Very Artisan classical stone, probably C17, on its W; hourglass and the initials RH in the shaped pediment; skull and crossbones in the pilastered frame. – At the end of the N aisle, memorial to Mary Burns †1820, 'Who came to Inverkeithing For the recovery of her health ...'.

ST JOHN, Church Street. Built as a Burgher chapel in 1753; heightened and widened in 1798–9. Rubble box with big round-arched windows flanking the central pedimented porch.

ST PETER (Episcopal), Hope Street. By *Henry F. Kerr*, 1903, the chancel added in 1910. Rubble-built, small and villagey, with a tiled roof. Wooden bellcote corbelled out from the W gable under a stone arch. On the S side, a broad-eaved porch and semi-octagonal-ended vestry.

GREYFRIARS CONVENT (INVERKEITHING MUSEUM)
Queen Street

Only the strangely antique guesthouse fronting the street and a few cellars survive of the Franciscan house founded *c.*1350. In 1559 the buildings were sold to John Swinton, who probably reconstructed the guesthouse for his own occupation and used the rest as a quarry.

The cloister occupied the upper part of the present municipal garden. This is entered through a concretey C17 revival gateway of 1932–5. To the E, perhaps projecting beyond the original cloister, late C14 vaulted CELLARS. Pointed doorway between two of them. The range has been a double pile, but only foundations remain of the S rooms, one with a fireplace. WELL on their S.

Another well beside the GUESTHOUSE on the cloister's W side. This was altered after 1559 and later became a tenement.

An antiquarian reconstruction by *J. Wilson Paterson* in 1932–5 ruthlessly restored C14 detail for which there was any evidence, but, where evidence was lacking, C17 detail was retained or copied. The walls were stripped of harl and their rubble piously pointed, but the roof is pantiled as it has been since the C18.

The building has been cruciform, the vanished lower wings projecting from near the N end of the tall two-storey main block. Forestair (1930s copy of a C17 stair) to the pointed-arch door which opened from the first-floor hall into the W wing's attic. On its l., a rectangular window, high up so as to be above the wing's roof. On the r., a blocked window, its angular arch like the rear-arches inside the tower of the Parish Church. At the S end, a double lancet. Below, pointed-arch entrance to the pend which ran through the building and was probably the principal entrance to the cloister. Similar arrangement of openings on the E side, but there is a second ground-floor door and the pend is blocked by a C16 stairtower squashed against another two-light window. The first-floor door into the E wing looks forlorn without even a stair to it.

In the N gable, a blocked lancet set above two roof raggles. The broader is that of a C17 block demolished in 1932, the narrower that of its steep-roofed C14 predecessor, which had a first-floor door into the main block.

Twin-gabled S block of two dates. The E part is probably C15. Obtuse pointed window in the E wall, blocked shouldered-arched first-floor door in the gable. It was probably remodelled in the late C16, when the crowstepped W block filled in the open corner.

Inside, all the ground-floor rooms have tunnel-vaults, pointed over the kitchen N of the pend. Turnpike stair, whose door into the first-floor hall cuts through a lancet. The character of that room is as muddled as the elevations.

PUBLIC BUILDINGS

HIGH SCHOOL, Hillend Road. By *Fife County Council*, 1972. Large but lumpy spread of white drydash, glass, and diagonally ribbed concrete panels.

PRIMARY SCHOOL, Roods Road. Long and low, by *Brydon & Robertson* of Glasgow, 1911–14. Pagoda ventilators and a central *flèche*. On the N, plain Tudor school of 1874, by *Andrew Scobie*.

PUBLIC LIBRARY, Chapel Place. By *Frank Mears & Partners*, 1968–9. Small and shoddy. It is sunk below road level so passers-by can monitor the condition of the felt roof.

104 TOWN HOUSE, Townhall Street. The steeple was built in 1754–5 under the supervision of *John Monroe Yr.*, mason, who may have designed it. Engagingly pompous, with a pediment and ogee-roofed belfry. The three-storey block on the r. is of 1770. Plain except for a bracketed cornice over the door. *George Monroe*, mason, was paid 'for his trouble in drawing plans'.

DESCRIPTION

HOPE STREET leads in from the S, the Episcopal Church (*see* above) standing as a homely janitor. Then the old MANSE (No. 54) by *Archibald Cook*, 1796–8, squashed under the railway embankment. At the top of the hill, the piend-roofed former CORN EXCHANGE, dated 1833, with a pedimented centre and round-arched ground-floor openings, followed by the Town Hall and Greyfriars Convent (*see* above).

HIGH STREET is a pleasant informal square of little architectural distinction. Closing its short N side, a block (No. 10) of *c*.1800, with rusticated quoins, scrolled skewputts and a dentilled cornice. To its E, the exit to Bank Street is guarded by the crowstepped gable of PROVIDENCE HOUSE (Nos. 14–18), whose corniced door lintel is dated 1688 and inscribed GODS PROVIDENCE/IS MY INHERITANCE.

CHURCH STREET continues the line of High Street to the N. On the r., the Parish Church (*see* above). On the l., the gableted and oriel windowed QUEEN'S HOTEL of *c*.1870. FORDELL'S LODGING was built *c*.1670 as the town house of Sir John Henderson of Fordell; fat stairtower at its NE corner. Opposite St John's Church (*see* above), BORELAND ROAD goes downhill to the railway station. On its r., in KEITH PLACE, a late Victorian harled brick WAREHOUSE with round-arched top-floor windows.

BANK STREET slides out of High Street's NE corner. On its r., Nos. 2–4, a harled and pantiled tenement built for John Thomson in 1617 and restored in 1965. Main block of two storeys; at the S, a three-storey stairtower, its second floor (containing a room) jettied out. The tower's moulded door has a pediment enriched with scrolls and a thistle finial. Above it, a shield surmounted by a merchant's mark and flanked by the initials of Thomson and his wife. Under the shield, inscription from Psalm 137:

> EXCEPT.THE LORD.BVLD.THE.HOVS.THEY LABOVR.IN.
> VAINE.THAT.BVILD IT

Another inscription over the main block's centre window:

> CAIR.BOT.CAIR.NOT.INORDINARLIE.FOR.AL.VL.
> AS.VTHERIS.AND.VTHERIS.VIL.BE.ETC

TOWNHALL STREET is an informal triangle. On its N, the Town House (*see* above). In front of it, the MERCAT CROSS. Octagonal shaft in which have been set iron rings (? for jougs). The moulded capital bears four shields, their heraldry including the arms of Douglas and of Robert III and his queen, suggesting a date of 1398, the year when Robert's heir, David, Duke of Rothesay, married Mary Douglas. Sundial and unicorn finial added 1688.

In KING STREET, the drydashed ROSEBERY HOUSE (No. 9). It now looks plain Georgian with a pilastered doorpiece, the main block's monopitch roof its only peculiarity; at the W, a crowstepped wing running back into the garden. On this front

the main block's moulded ground-floor windows proclaim its
C16 or C17 origin. Inside, a tunnel-vaulted basement; at the
main block's W end, a transe with a simple pointed-arched
door into the adjoining chamber. On the wing's ground floor,
kitchen with a segmental-arched fireplace. In the two principal
rooms, flashy late C18 pine chimneypieces. At the SE corner,
a wall chamber at ground and first floor. Were these for a
private stair? Early C19 single-storey Gothick addition at the
NE. DRAW WELL in the garden.

COMMERCIAL ROAD goes down to the harbour. On its E, a
derelict lectern DOOCOT, perhaps late C17. At the bottom, YE
OLDE FORESTERS ARMS, jolly pub-Tudor of 1911. The huge
red brick INVERKEITHING PAPER MILL was rebuilt in 1914
after a fire. At the entrance, smart swagged GATEPIERS of
c.1800, topped by lions and vases. Originally they must have
been arranged with the two large piers in the centre forming
a carriage gate and the small piers (for foot gates) at the ends.

FORDELL CASTLE. *See* p. 226.

FORDELL CASTLE. *See* p. 226.

0080   INZIEVAR
                           1.1km. S of Oakley

82 Baronial, by *David Bryce*, 1855–6. Tall battlemented SE tower
with an ogee-roofed turret climbing in its SW corner. In the
tower's E face, a shallow two-storey porch. On the entrance
front's r., a canted bay window corbelled out to a crowstepped
gable. Another bay window and gable of the same type on the
l. of the garden (S) front. The stone balcony which joined it to
a smaller central bay window has disappeared. Stone and glass
conservatory on the W. At the back, another tower, formidably
machicolated, added in 1912. Inside, library and dining room
en suite, both with Jacobean ceilings and Frenchy chimneypieces, filling the S front and leading into the conservatory.
Simpler dining room N of the entrance hall. Converted into
flats 1985.

    Symmetrical and crowstepped STABLE COURTYARD to the
N, by *Stewart & Menzies*, 1863.

                    ISLE OF MAY *see* MAY

5000   KELLIE CASTLE
                         0.7km. E of Arncroach

59 Deceptively unified epitome of the C16 and C17 Scots mansion
house, its turreted and crowstepped silhouette rising above a
romantically formal walled garden.

    The barony of Kellie passed from the Siwards to the

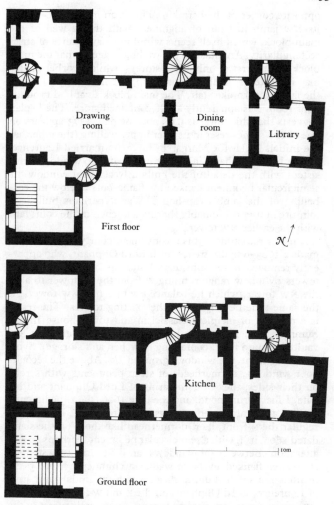

Kellie Castle,
plans of ground and first floors

Oliphants in 1361, and the present T-plan house's NW tower
may have been begun soon after, although a C15 date is likelier.
Originally it was a stolid four-storey rubble rectangle (the
parapet still traceable on the W front) standing at one corner
of a walled enclosure or barmkin which contained ancillary
buildings, including the kitchen. Inside the tower, a turnpike
stair neatly contained in the SW corner's wall thickness. The
ground and first floors each contain a vaulted room. On the
upper floors, vaulted chambers in the N wall.

The next identifiable development was the building of a
second tower some way to the SE, perhaps at the diagonally

opposite corner of the barmkin. This is an irregular L-shape, its NW jamb just out of alignment with the W wall of the main block, which itself seems wilful in its avoidance of strict rectangularity. An intake in the walling suggests that the main block was at first of only three storeys, while a corbel-course may indicate the jamb's original top, one floor higher. Inside the jamb, a turnpike stair. The main block's vaulted ground-floor room was apparently a self-contained store. The L-plan suggests that this tower is C16, and the date 1573 appears on one of two stones reset in its later upper walling (the other has the initials M.H. for Margaret Hay, who married Laurence, fourth Lord Oliphant, in that year). That date would be consistent with the detail of the bulbously classical window, its semicircular pediment flanked by 'flame-pots', below the corbelling of the jamb's cap-house. Was it perhaps built as a jointure house, presumably sharing a kitchen in the courtyard with the earlier NW tower?

A major recasting of this inconvenient courtyard house was made c. 1603–6 by Laurence, fifth Lord Oliphant, who apparently removed all the subsidiary buildings and linked the two towers by a new range running W from the SE tower to abut the NW tower, which he balanced with a new SW tower. At the same time he heightened the existing towers. The result is a mixture of incipient classicism and tower-house Indian Summer. The new range has two tall storeys above a low vaulted ground floor (containing a kitchen and storage). Symmetrical S front, the windows grouped 2/2. Above the second-floor windows, dormerheads of steep pediments with scrolls on their sides; they bear the arms of Lord Oliphant and his wife, Lilias Drummond, and the date 1606 (the r. pediment's date of 1724 presumably refers to its renewal). Rather less regular the N front, its r. dormerhead like those on the S and dated 1606, its l. with a semicircular pediment, perhaps an C18 alteration. Between the windows, an off-centre crowstepped stairtower flanked by large wallhead chimneys. More pedimented and scrolled dormerheads (with the initials and arms of Laurence, Lord Oliphant) on the E and W faces of the new SW tower; candle-snuffered S turrets, a deep stair turret in the inner angle.

In these alterations of c. 1603–6, one extra floor was added to the NW tower and two to the SE, which probably acquired at the same time a stair turret corbelled out above a squinch arch across the inner angle. The three towers (two old and one new) were now all of the same height and all finished with crowstepped gables, but symmetry is perversely avoided. The SE tower's lack of adornment makes it a quite inadequate balance to the SW tower's chunkiness, still weaker because it is slightly set back from the new main range's S front. This can be excused as an architectural failing inherent in the decision to retain both existing towers in the remodelled house, but the wilful asymmetry of the W front must stem from deliberate choice. The NW and SW towers are of the same breadth, but one presents a crowstepped gable, the other a slated roof-slope. Each has turrets at the outer corners, but the NW tower's are corbelled out further up the wall and were carried up higher. The tension between the asymmetry of detail and the basically symmetrical conception of the front is heightened by the centrepiece between the two towers, its first and second floors slightly recessed (the ground floor probably part of the earlier barmkin) but its attic jettied out so that its unnecessarily large crowstepped gable (a screen wall considerably higher than the range behind) can bully the flanking towers.

Lord Oliphant's reconstruction of Kellie probably contributed to the financial difficulties which led him in 1617 to sell the estate to Thomas Erskine, Viscount Fentoun (later first Earl of Kellie), who placed his coat of arms in the centre of the S front (the present panel a replica carved by *Hew Lorimer*). In 1661 the third Earl of Kellie and his newly acquired wife returned from Dutch exile to Kellie, the house 'being repaired by his sisters a litell before their coming.' Perhaps as part of these repairs, but more likely carried out by the Earl himself immediately after his arrival,* the main range's first-floor windows were enlarged, a prelude to a grand scheme of internal remodelling. Further alterations to the interior were made in the early C18 (probably in 1724) and *c.*1790. It was presumably in one of these C18 reconstructions that the NW tower lost the tops of its turrets and its N dormerhead, and the SE tower the roof of its stair turret. The house and earldom were inherited by the ninth Earl of Mar in 1829. For a time the castle was occupied as a farmhouse but had been abandoned by 1878, when Professor James Lorimer got a lease of it and employed *John Currie* to carry out an admirably conservative scheme of repair, his only addition the low crowstepped stables at the SE, their S opening partly screened by the DOOCOT added by *Robert S. Lorimer*, *c.*1900.

The castle's main entrance is in the SW tower's E face; above the door, a table recording Professor Lorimer's rescue of the house from rooks and owls and his dedication of it to honest ease in the midst of toils. Inside, a very broad scale-and-platt stair of 1606, with silhouette balusters, to the first floor. Here, the first 15m. of the main range are taken up by the drawing room (originally hall), the first room of the C17 state apartment.‡ Simply compartmented modelled plaster ceiling; in each main compartment, the impaled arms of the third Earl of Kellie and his second wife, Mary Dalzell, the centre dated 1676. In the E and S walls, fireplaces framed by late C17 fluted pilasters, each with an individual Doric entablature; cartouches above, carved by *W. & A. Clow* from *Robert S. Lorimer*'s design, 1897. Adamish E chimneypiece of *c.*1790; in the S fire surround, Dutch tiles introduced in 1897, when Lorimer also stripped yellow wallpaper from the C18 panelling,

---

* The windows had been enlarged by 1663, when they were specified as the model for the hall windows at Anstruther Place (now Dreel Castle).
‡ Consisting of hall (or dining room), drawing room, and bedchamber.

which he repaired and extended. The corniced doorpieces may be late C17. Small segmental-arched china cupboard in the N wall made by Lorimer from a third fireplace. In the dining room (originally drawing room) to the E, another compartmented ceiling, the centre roundel enclosing the crudely modelled arms of the third Earl of Kellie and his first wife, Mary Kirkpatrick; it must date from between 1661, when they married, and his remarriage in 1665. Doorpieces like those in the drawing room. Probably contemporary the wooden lining covering most of the walls, but its decoration of riverscapes, canal scenes, classical ruins and mountains is early C18.* The state apartment's last room is the library (originally bedchamber) in the SE tower. Modelled plaster ceiling, its strapwork enrichment forming panels in which are placed moulded human heads and lion masks; cartouches with the initials TVF (for Thomas, Viscount Fentoun) and the date 1617. Overmantel an embellishment of 1897.

The main range's two principal second-floor bedrooms have C18 panelling and late C17 straight-coved ceilings. In the Vine Room, vine branches on the coving. On the flat, a rectangular outer border of oak leaf festoons; richer inner border of fruit and foliage. More vine branches in the spandrels. In the central leafy roundel, a painting by *Jacob de Witt*, a glimpse into the sky where the inhabitants of Olympus sport on a cloud, birds perch on the opening's rim, and a pair of spaniels peers over the edge. Simpler ceiling in the Earl's Room. On each sloping side, a cherub's head set in a laurel wreath; on the flat, another laurel wreath enclosing the arms of the third Earl of Kellie and his second wife and the date 1676. In the Blue Room in the SW tower, C18 pine panelling.

WALLED GARDEN to the W and E, the lay-out of 1880 altered by *Robert S. Lorimer* when he made the long central path cutting through its compartments. Also by Lorimer the NW corner's garden house, with a carved bird on the ridge.

KELTY

A large mining village developed from the 1880s.

FREE CHURCH, Main Street. Now (1988) Kelty Community Centre. Plain Gothic by *T. Hyslop Ure*, 1895–6. Ogee-hood-moulded door in the bellcote-topped gable front; transeptal stairtowers.

PARISH CHURCH, Oakfield Street. By *John Houston*, 1894–6. Broad Gothic box dressed up with transeptal stairtowers to the W gallery. On top of the gable front, a bellcote wearing a tall slated hat.

UNITED PRESBYTERIAN CHURCH, Mossgreen Street. Disused. A small church opened in 1896. Aggressively hammerdressed

---

* In the window ingoes it covers C17 decoration.

1. Hill of Tarvit, south-eastward view from the terrace

2. The Lomond Hills from the south

3. East Lomond Hill, Iron Age hillfort

4. Lower Largo and Lundin Links, standing stones

5. St Andrews, St Regulus' Church, eleventh century

6. Dunfermline Abbey
from the south-west

7. Dunfermline
Abbey Church,
west front,
mid-twelfth century,
reconstructed *c.* 1400

8. Inchcolm Abbey,
twelfth–fifteenth centuries

9. Dunfermline
Abbey Church,
nave, mid-twelfth century

10. Aberdour Parish Church, *c.* 1140, south aisle and porch, *c.* 1500, restored by William Williamson, 1925-6

11. Leuchars Parish Church, chancel mid-twelfth century, belfry of *c.* 1700, nave by John Milne, 1857–8

12. St Andrews Cathedral, twelfth–thirteenth century

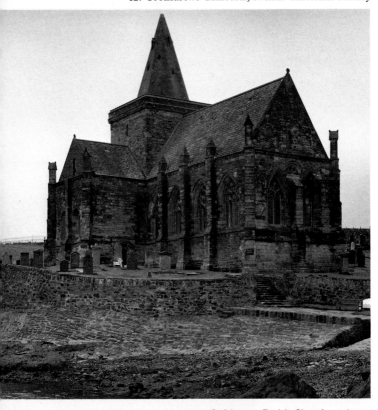

13. St Monans Parish Church, 1362–70

14. St Andrews,
St Salvator's College,
south front,
mid-fifteenth century

15. Inverkeithing
Parish Church, tower
fourteenth century,
nave by James
Gillespie Graham,
1826–7

16. Culross Abbey,
tower of *c.* 1500
incorporating
late thirteenth-
century rood screen,
parapet by
William Stirling, 1823

17. St Andrews,
Blackfriars Convent,
north transept, 1525

18. Burntisland Parish Church, 1589–1600;
steeple rebuilt by Samuel Neilson, 1748

19. Burntisland Parish Church,
magistrates' pew, 1606; galleries, c. 1602–1630,
with seventeenth- and eighteenth-century decoration

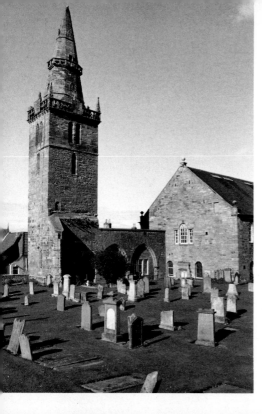

20. Cupar, Old Parish
and St Michael
of Tarvit Church,
tower, 1415,
with spire of 1620;
church by Hay Bell, 1785

21. Dairsie,
St Mary's Church, 1621

22. Dalgety Bay, Donibristle Chapel, by Alexander McGill, 1729–32

23. Limekilns Parish Church, 1825–6

24. Kirkcaldy, Bethelfield Church, by George Hay, 1830–1

25. Upper Largo,
Largo Parish Church,
by Alexander Leslie, 1816;
steeple, 1628

26. Upper Largo,
Largo Parish Church,
pulpit, 1815

27. Dunfermline
Abbey Church, choir,
by William Burn, 1818–21

28. Dunfermline
Abbey Church,
plaster vaulting, 1818–21

29. Ceres Parish Church, effigy, fifteenth century

30. St Andrews, St Salvator's College Chapel,
Bishop Kennedy's tomb and sacrament house,
mid-fifteenth century

31. Dunfermline
Abbey Church,
monument to
William Schaw † 1602

32. Culross Abbey,
monument to
Sir George Bruce,
by John Mercer,
mid-seventeenth century

33. Dalgety Bay,
St Bridget's Church,
Dunfermline Aisle,
c. 1610

34. Crail
Parish Church,
monument to
James Lumsden
of Airdrie † 1598

35. St Andrews, Holy Trinity Church, monument to Archbishop Sharp, 1679

36. Anstruther Wester
Parish Church,
headstone of
John Fairfoul † 1626

37. Kirkton of Cults,
Cults Parish Church,
monument to
Sir David Wilkie,
by Samuel Joseph, c. 1841

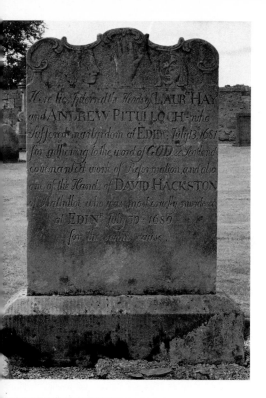

38. Cupar, Old Parish
and St Michael
of Tarvit Church,
gravestone of
Laurence Hay and
Andrew Pitulloch, 1792

39. Kirkton of Cults,
Cults Parish Church,
monument to
the Rev. David Wilkie
and Isabella Lister,
by Francis Chantrey, 1833

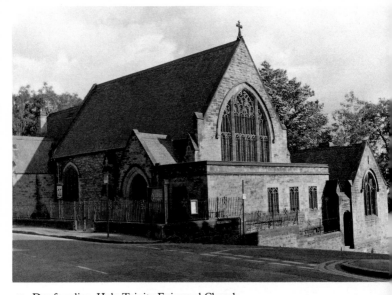

40. Dunfermline, Holy Trinity Episcopal Church,
by R. Rowand Anderson, 1891

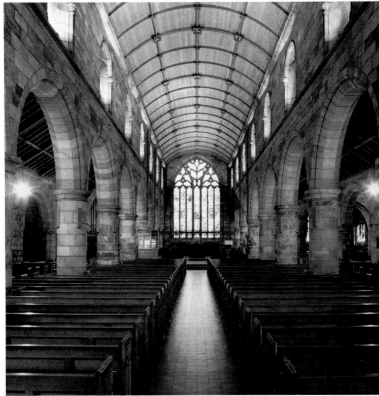

41. St Andrews, Holy Trinity Church, early fifteenth century,
reconstructed by P. MacGregor Chalmers, 1907–9

42. Dunfermline, St Leonard's Church,
by P. MacGregor Chalmers, 1903–4

43. St Andrews, St James' R.C. Church,
by Reginald Fairlie, 1909–10

44. St Andrews, All Saints' Episcopal Church,
Chapel of the Blessed Sacrament, by Paul Waterhouse, 1919–24

46. Glenrothes, St Columba's Parish Church,
by Wheeler & Sproson, 1960-1

47. Glenrothes, St Paul's R.C. Church,
by Gillespie, Kidd & Coia, 1957–8

45 (*opposite*). East Wemyss, Macduff Cemetery,
headstone to the Rev. Alexander Orrock Johnston,
by Charles Rennie Mackintosh, *c.* 1905

48. Aberdour Castle, north-west tower, twelfth century

49. Aberdour Castle, windows of *c.* 1570

50. Kirkcaldy, Pathhead, Ravenscraig Castle, 1460

51. Aberdour Castle, doocot, late sixteenth century

52. Balgonie Castle, fifteenth century

53. Burntisland, Rossend Castle, mid-sixteenth century

54. Falkland Palace, gatehouse and south front, 1537–41

55. Falkland Palace, courtyard front, 1539

56. St Andrews Castle, gatehouse, c. 1555

57. Limekilns, King's Barn, early sixteenth century

58. Scotstarvit Tower, *c.* 1500, with attic of 1627

59. Kellie Castle, fifteenth–seventeenth centuries

60. Culross, Blairhall, late seventeenth century

61. Kirkcaldy, Pathhead, Dunnikier House (now Path House),
Nether Street, 1692

62. Aberdour House, early seventeenth century
with front block added *c.* 1731

63. Balcarres, dining-room ceiling, *c.* 1630

64. Balcaskie, dining room, by Sir William Bruce, 1671–4, with plasterwork probably by George Dunsterfield

65. Balcaskie, gatepiers and doocots, early and mid-eighteenth century

66. Melville House, probably by James Smith, 1697–1703

67. Leslie House, gatepiers, 1671, with wrought-iron gates of 1906

68. Upper Largo, Largo House, 1750

69. Pitlour, by Robert Mylne, 1784

70. Broomhall, by Thomas Harrison, 1796

71. Glenrothes, Balbirnie House,
by Richard Crichton and R. & R. Dickson, 1815–19

72. Ballingry, Lochore House, *c.* 1790

73. Blair Castle, early nineteenth century

74. Crawford Priory, by David Hamilton, 1809–10,
and James Gillespie Graham, 1810–12 (photo 1869)

75. Kincardine-on-Forth, Tulliallan Castle (Scottish Police College),
by William Atkinson, 1817–20

76. Valleyfield, Woodhead, early nineteenth century

77. Charlestown, Easter Cottage, early nineteenth century

78. Dunimarle Castle, by R. & R. Dickson, 1839–45

79. Newtonhall House, by David Bryce, 1829

80. Aberdour, Donibristle East Lodge and gates,
by Brown & Wardrop, 1870

81. Falkland, House of Falkland, by William Burn, 1839–44

82. Inzievar, by David Bryce, 1855–6

83. Hill of Tarvit, by Robert S. Lorimer, 1905-7

84. Balcarres, North Lodge, by Robert S. Lorimer, 1896-8

85. Crail, harbour

86. Culross, Sandhaven, with Town House of 1626,
its steeple added 1783

87. Culross Palace, late sixteenth and early seventeenth century

88. Culross Palace, painted ceiling, *c.* 1611

89. Culross, The Study, early seventeenth century

90. Culross, The Study, painted ceiling, 1966–7, by Alexander McNeish, under the direction of Ian Hodkinson (shown in photograph)

91. Kirkcaldy, Nos. 339–343 High Street,
plaster ceiling, late seventeenth century

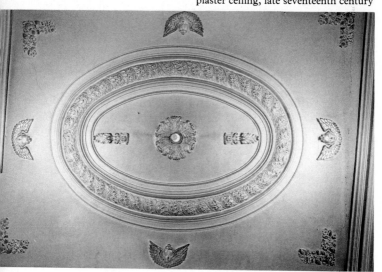

92. Kirkcaldy, Nos. 339–343 High Street,
plaster ceiling, late seventeenth century

93. Anstruther Easter, Old Manse, 1590

94. Cupar, Preston Lodge, Bonnygate,
early seventeenth century, remodelled c. 1765

95. St Andrews, South Street

96. Aberdour, Seabank House, Shore Street, *c.* 1835

97. Burntisland, Nos. 1–4 Broomhill Road, by F. T. Pilkington, 1858

98. Burntisland, Old Parsonage, by R. C. Carpenter, 1854

99. Coaltown of Wemyss, Main Street, *c.* 1900

100. Kirkcaldy, High Street, Dysart,
redevelopment by Wheeler & Sproson, 1976

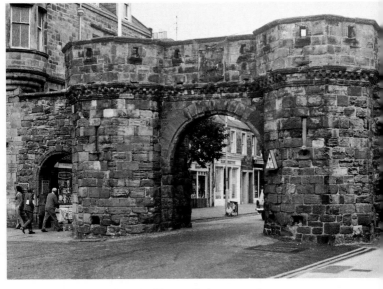

101. St Andrews, West Port, by Thomas Robertson, 1589

102. St Andrews, St Mary's College, east front, *c.* 1620

103. Crail, Tolbooth, sixteenth century

104. Inverkeithing, Town House, 1754–70

105. Cupar, St Catherine Street

106. Cupar, Old Jail, by James Gillespie Graham, 1813-14

107. Kinghorn Primary School, by Thomas Hamilton, 1829

108. Burntisland Railway Station, by Grainger & Miller, 1847

109. Upper Largo, Wood's Hospital, by James Leslie, 1830

110. St Andrews, Madras College, by William Burn, 1832–4

111. Kirkcaldy, Linktown, West Primary School, Milton Road,
by R. Rowand Anderson, 1874–80

112. Dunfermline, City Chambers, by James C. Walker, 1875–9

113. Dunfermline, Pittencrieff Park,
Louise Carnegie Memorial Gates, by Jamieson & Arnott, 1928

114. Dunfermline, No. 15 East Port, by Paul Waterhouse, 1914–16

115. Burntisland Public Library, by William Williamson, 1906

116. Kirkcaldy, Pathhead, Feuars Arms, Bogies Wynd, *c.* 1890

117. Kirkcaldy, Town House, by David Carr, 1937–56

118. Glenrothes, Riverside Park, paddling pool,
sculpture by Stanley Bonnar, 1972

119. Kirkcaldy, Linktown, Seafield Colliery, by Egon Riss, 1959

120. Ballingry, Mary Colliery, pithead gear, 1902

121. Charlestown, limekilns

122. North Queensferry, pump
by Glenfield & Kennedy, late nineteenth century

rubble walling; the Romanesque detail is belied by the bellcote's twisty wrought-iron finial.

PRIMARY SCHOOL, Main Street. Large and very boring, by *John
Houston*, 1895–7 (dated 1896), with thrifty Scots Renaissance
detail.

BUTTERCHURN, 1.1km. to the W. Early C18 crowstepped farmhouse; the steading behind looks mid-C19.

LASSODIE MILL, 1.3km. to the S. A very pretty group: the
unpretentious harled farmhouse dated 1730 on an inset stone;
rubble and pantiled steading.

BENARTY HILL. *See* p. 99.

KEMBACK   *4010*

Churches (old and new), Georgian manse, and mid-Victorian
school on the hill. A few more houses at Kemback Bridge in
the valley below, and a little milling settlement at Yoolbank
Crescent.

OLD PARISH CHURCH. Roofless remains of a T-plan church.
The date given on a door lintel is 1582, making it one of the
first post-Reformation churches in Scotland. It has been an
asymmetrical T-plan with an off-centre N 'aisle' (now demolished) which opened into the body of the church through a big
segmental arch. Rubble-built, the W gable still crowstepped.
Rectangular windows in the S wall. In each gable, a larger
transomed window, the W blocked and replaced by a Georgian
window, probably in 1760, when a second door was made in
the S side. Inside, the W gable has an aumbry checked for a
door.

PARISH CHURCH. Simple rectangle built in 1810–14, the W
wall on the main approach of ashlar, the others of rubble.
Uncomfortable acutely pointed windows. Awkward Gothic
bellcote with a stumpy spire.

The interior was refurnished *c.* 1930 (after the introduction
of a communion table in 1919). – In the E wall, a niche containing a late Georgian cast-iron swagged URN. – Large marble
wall MONUMENT to Margaret Hunter † 1843, signed by *David
Ness* of Edinburgh, early Victorian touches softening its neo-
classicism. – STAINED GLASS. In the vestibule, one light
(David) by *Ruth Walker*, 1967, messily Expressionist.

MANSE to the SW. Built by *Robert Balfour*, 1801, and quite
plain. To its N, the FORMER MANSE (now a store), probably
early C17, a small crowstepped house with a forestair. It was
thatched until 1758.

YOOLFIELD CRESCENT, 0.5km. SW. Two mid-C19 cottage terraces, the N with gabled porches; a few houses still pantiled.
At the S end, a rubble bridge to the piend-roofed MILL HOUSE
of 1839.

GROVE HOUSE, 1km. S. Mid-Victorian Baronial mill-owner's
house. L-plan with a tower in the inner angle.

KEMBACK HOUSE, 0.4km. N. Thrifty Baronial of 1907, in-

corporating an earlier house. – Half-way up the drive, late
C18 GATEPIERS with very smart fluted urn finials. – Pretty
early Victorian bargeboarded LODGE.

BLEBO HOUSE. *See* p. 101.

DURA HOUSE. *See* p. 199.

BLEBO HOUSE. *See* p. 101.

DURA HOUSE. *See* p. 199.

KENNOWAY

3000

A local malting and brewing centre on the road from Kirkcaldy
to Cupar until *c.* 1750, when the industry failed and the village
was by-passed. Prosperity returned in the late C18, when weaving
was introduced and expansion was helped by the making of a
new main road passing through the village *c.* 1800; but Kennoway
again declined in the later C19. Major new housing estates on the
E were begun in 1949 with the aim of making a new mining town
here.

ARNOT GOSPEL HALL, Cupar Road. Tall two-bay box of
orangey sandstone built as a Burgher chapel *c.* 1750. The E
gable was refaced in a greyer stone in 1870, acquiring a steep
pediment and faintly Italianate bellcote. E gallery inside. –
STAINED GLASS. Two heavily pictorial windows (Christ blessing Children; Christ the Good Shepherd) in the N wall, of
c. 1875.

FREE CHURCH, New Road. Disused. A bare box of 1848. Simple
Gothic detail; very small quatrefoil-plan bellcote.

PARISH CHURCH, Cupar Road. Thin Romanesque by *Thomas
Hamilton*, 1849–50. Nave and flat-roofed aisles. On the l. of
the nave's S gable, a skimpy tower with a small broach spire.
The result is ungainly. Datestone of 1619 in the N gable from
the church's predecessor in Causeway. Inside, tall round-
headed arcades on cast-iron columns; galleries round three
sides. – Genteel expressionist STAINED GLASS (New Testament scenes) of *c.* 1950 by *Marjorie Kemp* in the E and W aisle
windows.

PRIMARY SCHOOL, Langside Crescent. By *J. C. Cunningham*,
1959.

DESCRIPTION

The Parish Church (*see* above) commands the road junction near
the village's N end. Behind, in CUPAR ROAD, a late Georgian
house (BELVEDERE). Further out, COCKBURN HOUSE of
c. 1800, with attenuated Tuscan columns at the door and a
shallow centre pediment; each of the rusticated angle pilasters
has its own fluted frieze and a rosette. Beside the Arnot Gospel
Hall (*see* above) is the old Burgher manse (now HAWFIELD
HOUSE), early C19 with club skews. DENHEAD leads NW from
the Parish Church to LANGSIDE DRIVE, where INGOTHILL
HOUSE, hidden in its garden, was built as the parish manse in

1833: *Robert Hutchison* was the architect,[*] *James Downie* the builder. LEVEN ROAD E of the church begins with an early C19 mill, now shops. Further out, KENMOUNT of *c.*1800, drydashed and with enlarged ground-floor windows, has been quite smart. In the front's bowed centre, a Venetian window with Gothick glazing; the pedimented doorpiece looks early Victorian. Bowed stair projection at the back.

NEW ROAD leading S from the church was formed *c.*1800. On its W side, the Free Church (*see* above); on its E, an uncompleted miniature civic centre (BISHOP'S COURT) begun by the County Architect, *Maurice E. Taylor*, in 1949. The old main street was THE CAUSEWAY. At its New Road corner, the SWAN HOTEL, Jacobean of the late C19. Then some vernacular cottages, whinstone-walled and pantiled. The former MASONIC LODGE on the W is probably early C18, with a crowstepped gable to the street. On the E, the old PARISH CHURCHYARD's gatepiers and bow-fronted session house were built by *Robert Hutchison*, 1835. In SEATH HOUSE's garage front, a large heraldic stone. SETON HOUSE, late C18 with a central gablet, was extended W in 1877. Downhill, on the r., FORBES COTTAGE, mid-C19 with big scrolled skewputts. On the l., THE COTTAGE, altered, but its door lintel is dated 1766.

LANGSIDE, 1.2km. NW. Piend-roofed farmhouse of 1833, well grouped with the contemporary steading on the W.

KINGSDALE HOUSE. *See* p. 275.

NEWTONHALL HOUSE. *See* p. 338.

KETTLEBRIDGE *see* KINGSKETTLE

KILCONQUHAR 4000

Prosperous and picturesque village along a main street, with a suburb at Barnyards to the NW.

PARISH CHURCH, Main Street. High up in a graveyard. Built in 1819–21 by *R. & R. Dickson*, who used *Richard Crichton*'s design of 1818 for Cockpen Church (Lothian). Perp and cruciform, with diagonal buttresses. The tower, half engaged with the W end, where it forms a porch, starts with diagonal buttresses and continues with slim octagonal turrets – the cornerposts of the fretted parapet – terminating in flat knobs. Inside, a minimal ribbed plaster vault, springing from the four stone shafts at the corners. Galleries with Gothic fronts. – The PEWS were made less boxy when widened and lowered in 1898. – Oak PULPIT and Lorimerian LECTERN of 1921. – STAINED GLASS. Brightly coloured narrative E window (the

---

[*] Hutchison produced working drawings and specifications for a plan 'altered by the late Captain Lundin and drawn by James Fisher under his directions'.

Acts of Charity) by *Ward & Hughes*, 1867. To compensate for the loss of light caused by its introduction, N and S windows were made in the 'chancel'. The N was filled with stained glass (Pastoral Charge, Sacraments and Preaching) *c.*1918, the S (Old Testament Warriors) in 1925.

CHURCHYARD MONUMENTS. Immediately S of the church, half built into the retaining wall, a C16 slab with an incised skull and crossbones. – E of the church is the OLD PARISH CHURCH's late medieval N aisle arcade. Three bays of round piers with chamfered bases; semicircular arches. At the E end, a corbel, perhaps for the rood beam. The remains have been partly incorporated in a burial enclosure. On its floor, graveslab of James Bellenden of Kilconquhar † 1593, carved with a skull. – On its W wall, monument to John, tenth Earl of Lindsay, †1894, and his wife †1897, with bronze relief busts, his by *W. Grant Stevenson*, hers by *D. W. Stevenson*. – On top of the churchyard's S wall, a C17 steep pedimented aedicule, now with an inscription to John Fair † 1796. – Several lively but badly weathered C18 headstones.

DESCRIPTION

The Parish Church dominates the W approach. On the l., garden wall and trees hiding the former MANSE by *Alexander Leslie*, 1814–15, its front wall rebuilt and the roof pitch lowered by *George Just*, 1851–2. Vestigial pediment over the centre; weird doorpiece, its pilasters capped by consoles. Rubble-built and pantiled U-plan offices, now a house (CAMAS INAS), to the E.

MAIN STREET circles round the churchyard. On its N, the harled KINNEUCHAR INN, its E part C18, the taller and crowstepped W section a rebuild of 1962. E of the churchyard the street widens as an informal market place with a WAR MEMORIAL instead of a market cross. On the N side, the C18 ST ANNE'S of three wide bays, and the smaller COMMERCROFT, dated 1752 on the l. skew; on the S, pantiled cottages. In the prevalent vernacular mixture, THE BELL HOUSE, C18 with a moulded doorpiece renewed in cement. Further E, the C18 WOOD-LANDS, its crowstepped back skew carried down over a lean-to outshot; W addition with a jettied first floor. Beside it, THE ROUNDEL, reconstructed by *James Gillespie & Scott*, *c.*1965, as a parody of C17 burgh architecture.

BALBUTHIE ROAD exits E with a row of pantiled cottages towards the remains of LOCH FARM's early C19 steading. On the corner of ST ANDREWS ROAD, the harled and pantiled MAYVIEW, dated 1738 at the back, with a Gibbs surround to the door.

In BARNYARDS to the N, more C18 and C19 vernacular housing but also a sprinkling of recent intrusions. On the corner of KIRK WYND and GREENBRIG ROAD, the old BURGHER CHAPEL of 1795, with two big round-arched S windows. E of St Andrews Road, Kilconquhar Castle's OLD LODGE, early c19 picturesque, with semi-octagonal window heads and a rustic porch.

KILCONQUHAR CASTLE
1km. NE

Cropped remains of *William Burn*'s Baronial house built in 1831–9 for Sir Henry Bethune. The 1830s house was not entirely new. At its sw corner was a late c16 tower which had been extended E in the c18. Burn remodelled the c18 wing and added a large block N of the tower. Since a fire in 1978, most of the s part has been demolished or drastically cut down and the interior converted to flats by *Robert Fulton*.

Burn's asymmetrical entrance (N) front is intact. Two crow-stepped gables, the r. with pepperpot turrets and a two-storey rectangular bay window, the l. with a door of early c18 type, its curly segmental pediment broken by a cartouche, as at the contemporary Balcarres. To the E, single-storey crowstepped dining room addition of c.1890. The garden (w) front has suffered badly. The c16 tower, which made a five-storey stop at its s end, lost its two top floors after the fire and is now roofed as a continuation of Burn's N addition. Here the main accent is a full-height bay window corbelled out to a rec-tangular crowstepped gable. On its r., a large door pushed through the ground-floor and basement windows by Fulton. Burn's dormerheads have been renewed (without their finials), but the lack of chimneys is disconcerting. At the SE, spiky Baronial office court of 1831.

Inside, only the dining room of c.1890 survived the fire. Expensive but coarse, with a Jacobethan plaster ceiling and carved panelling.

To the NW, late c19 STABLES with a U-plan crowstepped front. – To their NE, c18 lectern DOOCOT, crowstepped, with a stringcourse jumping up at the gables; rusticated quoins an unusual embellishment. Lean-to sawmill built against the front. – On the main approach, SOUTH LODGE, domestic Baronial of c.1925. Contemporary wrought-iron gates, but their rusticated ball-finialled piers look late c18. – Some way to the N, GATEPIERS of c.1700, heavily corniced with ball finials; on the sides, pilasters with consoled tops.

MUIRCAMBUS, 1.7km. W. Cottagey house of c.1840 with crow-stepped gables and Tudor dormerheads. Small conical-roofed tower on the entrance front. Castellated addition of c.1910.

KILLERNIE CASTLE
1km. E of Saline

0090

Scant remains of an early c17 fortified house high on a steeply sloping hillside. Enough of the N and w walls' bottom courses remains to show that it has been rectangular, with a square tower projecting at the SW, and round towers at the NW and nipped-in NE corner. To the S was a large walled courtyard. Three large gunloops in the NW tower's tunnel-vaulted ground floor. Prominent gunloops again in the NE tower, which has contained a turnpike stair.

KILMANY

3020

Unselfconsciously picturesque small village.

PARISH CHURCH. Spick and span in white drydash with black-painted margins (it was formerly harled). A narrow rectangular church built in 1768, its tall birdcage bellcote topped by a stone obelisk-spire. The S wall's round-arched openings were originally for three doors and two windows, but the l. and centre doors were converted to windows in the early C19. Rectangular N windows made in 1839.

Inside, E and W galleries, the E partitioned off, the W's front with an Ionic pilastered centre. – BOX PEWS of 1860. – C18 octagonal PULPIT, a Doric frieze on its sounding board. – Marble MONUMENT to Dr David Brewster, 1899: relief bust under a consoled pediment.

In the churchyard, a good number of C18 TABLE STONES, some with deep-cut heraldry and symbols of death. – HEAD-STONE immediately NE of the church, erected by John Kinnear to his wife in 1792: agreeably old-fashioned, carved with angels carrying a crown of life.

DESCRIPTION. N of the village is Kilmany House (*see* below). On the E, EASTER KILMANY, the harled farmhouse with a tall two-storey, two-bay front dated 1802; earlier back wing. Its steading (partly built by *George Just*, mason, in 1824) introduces the whinstone walling and pantiled roofs which characterize the village buildings. Immediately W of the church, a two-storey house dated 1762. At the village's W end, the mid-C19 old SCHOOL beside the rubble BRIDGE carrying the road across the Motray Water to the former MANSE, built for Dr Thomas Chalmers in 1809–10.

KILMANY HOUSE. Agreeably rambling harled and pantiled villa of 1914–19 by *Reginald Fairlie*, who incorporated fragments of an unpretentious house 'in the Cottage style' which *Alexander Blyth* had built for John Anstruther Thomson in 1816. Fairlie's client, Colonel William Anstruther-Gray, demanded a South African look, so on the main (garden) front Fairlie provided elaborate wrought-iron wall-ties, green shutters, and a pair of Cape Dutch gables with a *stoep* to their r. At the SW corner, octagonal two-storey pavilion of 1927 (by Fairlie again), making a happy stop to this elevation. Inside, a corridor running the full length of the house designed to show off the owner's collection of armour. In the panelled dining room of 1927, a chimneypiece, probably C17, from a demolished house in Crail.

WESTER KILMANY, 0.4km. NW. Mid-C19 crowstepped and pantiled house; contemporary steading.

KILRENNY

5000

A pretty village converging downhill towards its agreeably hybrid parish church. But the approach from Anstruther is spoiled by pink-and-white houses of no distinction built in the 1980s.

PARISH CHURCH. A Georgian Gothic box whose C15 NW tower dominates the tiny village. The *New Statistical Account* (1843) says that the old church had nave arcades. Presumably it was in line with the tower, which has a pair of lancets on each side; the corbelled parapet and octagonal slated spire are of the C16, the spire repaired (and perhaps the weathercock put up) by *Robert Malcolm* in 1838. The body of the church was built in 1807–8; *Alexander Leslie* was the architect, *David Ness* and *Andrew Horsburgh* the contractors. Handsome s side of smooth ashlar with occasional vertical pinning, and four pointed windows. The rest is of fair-faced rubble, but all the corners have long-and-short rusticated quoins, and plain pinnacles crown the skews. Two windows on the N (pulpit) side, and a small thermal window at the head of each gable. The crow-stepped Romanesque porch in the s angle of tower and church is of 1932 by *Gillespie & Scott* of St Andrews, who reordered the interior with communion table and pulpit to the E and a gallery to the w. On the w wall a pointed arch, blocked. In the corners of the tower are square shafts with simple capitals; also traces of another arch in the s wall and a two-light window in the N. – MONUMENTS in the churchyard, which falls E to the Gellie burn. To the NW, the arched and domed mausoleum of Scott of Balcomie, *c*.1776. On the w face of the tower, the enclosure of Lumisdaine of Innergellie. Arched doorway and pediment to the w, but on the s side a mural monument combining C17 form with late Georgian detail, e.g. on the upper tier crude baluster-like Doric columns on each side of the quite refined Ionic order, which frames an inset armorial stone and the date 1823. To the E the rectangular Beaton enclosure, late C17 with swagged Ionic columns on each side of the moulded doorway and repeated at the angles. Against the N wall of the church a stone to Robert Ford †1672 with a ship on a wavy sea.

DESCRIPTION. The view of the church is framed by the houses of the very short main street. On the N side the former SCHOOLHOUSE of 1840, two storeys with horizontal glazing. It was designed and built by *William Lees* in 1839–40, the adjoining schoolroom by *Robert Taylor & Co.* in 1815 and extended by *Andrew Turpie*, wright in Pittenweem, in 1841. On the s side, crowstepped houses and cottages, No. 3 with straight skews to the front. KIRK WYND has single-storey cottages stepping down to the burn, and goes on over a single-arched bridge towards Innergellie (*see* above), but ROUTINE ROW climbs up again (one cottage dated 1790). Where it meets the major road, BROWNLEA COTTAGE, late C18, has cylindrical skewputts with dog-rose ornament on the sides.

RENNYHILL HOUSE, to the NW. Tall ashlar-faced mansion of *c.*1760, five bays and three storeys, with keyblocked bullseye windows in the more conspicuous W gable, a fine if austere display of mason's swank. The lugged doorway has been pushed forward by a later porch but seems always to have been in this odd position in the right-hand bay. High garden walls including an inset segmental pediment dated 1538; cylindrical GATEPIERS of the local type with half-globe tops. More of these at the FARM across the road, which has a three-bay early C19 house and steading of four parallel ranges with piended pantile roofs.

SLAB 0.5km. SW. Of whinstone, large and upright. On one face a cross formed by four pairs of 'spokes' in a double-line wheel.

WEST PITCORTHIE, 2.5km. N. Red sandstone standing stone, 2.1m. high and 2.9m. girth at the base. Cup-like markings are the result of weathering.

CORNCERES, 1km. NE. Tall steeply gabled farmhouse, Jacobean of *c.*1840, with a porch projecting diagonally from its L-plan. The jamb's bay windows have horizontal glazing.

2080

KILRIE HOUSE
2.8km. SE of Auchtertool

Large and asymmetrical Elizabethan, dated 1854. – To the W, contemporary rubble-built STEADING with an Italianate pedimented pend. – Beside the steading, ball-finialled lectern DOOCOT, the panel above the entrance dated 1684.

5010

KINALDY
3.2km. W of Dunino

Pediment-centred house of *c.*1830, extended N by *Peddie & Kinnear* in 1854–5. – C18 lectern DOOCOT.

4010

KINCAPLE HOUSE
1.6km. SE of Guardbridge

Harled laird's house built for Alexander Meldrum in 1789 (his name and the date incised on the skews), a pedimented porch the only pretension. In 1928 *J. D. Mills* made it U-plan by the addition of piend-roofed wings, the l. with a reverse-Venetian treatment (a rectangular door flanked by round-arched windows), the r. L-plan. Presumably also of 1928 the round-headed dormer windows on the main block.

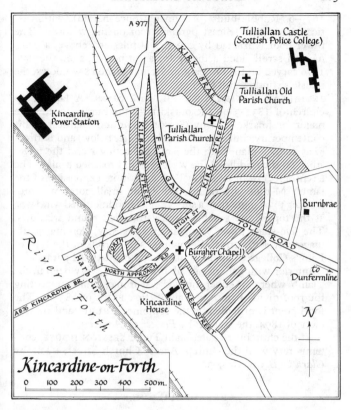

Kincardine-on-Forth

0   100   200   300   400   500m.

KINCARDINE-ON-FORTH

3080

A burgh of barony founded in 1663, the town was built largely
on marshland reclaimed from the Forth by the deposit of coal
ash from the salt pans which gave Kincardine its first industry
and earlier name of West Pans. Its position as a principal ferry
port for the shipment of goods from Fife over the Forth to sw
Scotland was strengthened by the new harbour and embankment
made in the early c19, and shipbuilding was also a main source
of employment. Opening of the Kincardine Bridge in 1936 killed
the ferry and gave the town that constant noise of traffic which
is now its dominant characteristic.

CHURCHES

BURGHER CHAPEL, Chapel Street. Disused. D-plan box of 1819.
   Slim tower built against the curved side in the mid-c19; the
   Frenchy top stage with iron cresting, giving it the look of a
   Clochemerle town hall, is of *c.*1870.
TULLIALLAN OLD PARISH CHURCH, Wood Lea. Roofless ruin
   in a graveyard. Rustic classical-Gothic survival mixture of

1675–6. Rubble-built (presumably once harled), with rusticated quoins. Bellcast pyramid roof on the w tower. The tower door is framed by channelled pilasters; above, a pedimented scroll-sided aedicule for an armorial panel, the date 1676 carved on the tympanum. Round-arched s windows, the n aisle's window still Gothic.

TULLIALLAN PARISH CHURCH, Kirk Street. A large Perp church of 1832–3 on the outskirts of the burgh, its tower a major landmark. It is by *George Angus* and identical to his contemporary churches at Kingskettle (*see* below) and Kinross (Tayside). T-plan, with the jamb projecting E and the tower stuck on the middle of the w side, all of broached ashlar. The E (entrance) front is unusually honest in its expression of the jamb's M-roof as a double gable, the small porch not pretending to be more than a shelter. Tall hoodmoulded windows; at the top of the E gables, spiral-traceried round windows. The five-stage tower (containing the vestry) dominates. Its diagonally set buttresses grow into slim turrets of the type of King's College Chapel, Cambridge. Stone latticed parapet.

Interior with galleries in all arms of the T, very deep in the E jamb, where the superimposed cast-iron columns supporting the roof divide it into two aisles. Box PEWS of 1833. – The focal point is provided by the combined PULPIT and ORGAN CASE of 1894, the ORGAN by *Forster & Andrews*.

At the churchyard gate, plain Tudor SESSION HOUSE, contemporary with the church. Across Church Street, HALL by *Clark & Blyth*, 1929–30.

PUBLIC BUILDINGS

HARBOUR. Now cut across by Kincardine Bridge. The SHIPPING PIER on the E is by *Robert Bald*, 1811–13. In 1820–2, Viscount Keith built the w EMBANKMENT from Kincardine to Kennetpans, reclaiming 61.5 ha. from the sea; the embankment was heightened in 1823 and 1836. The ramped FERRY PIER on the bridge's w replaced an earlier pier in 1826. The E EMBANKMENT to Longannet, reclaiming a further 87 ha., was built in 1829–38. PIER projecting from the w embankment added by *J. Young & Sons*, 1891.

KINCARDINE BRIDGE. By *Alexander Gibb & Partners*, 1932–6, and the earliest road crossing over the Forth built E of Stirling. Steel girders on concrete piers, the central section made to open. Quite straightforward except for the suburban Art Deco concrete decoration above bridge level.

KINCARDINE POWER STATION. By *Robert Matthew, Johnson-Marshall & Partners*, 1960.

LONGANNET POWER STATION. 1966, by *Robert Matthew, Johnson-Marshall & Partners*, a lumpier version of the same firm's Cockenzie Power Station (Lothian), but without its abstract elegance.

SCOTTISH POLICE COLLEGE (TULLIALLAN CASTLE). See p. 269.

DESCRIPTION

Kincardine's vernacular buildings had, until a few years ago, two main features – pantiles of a dark blueish colour (salt having been added to the glaze), and scrolled skewputts. The first has now (1988) been almost entirely lost, the second is still omnipresent.

Entering from Kincardine Bridge (*see* above), the former Burgher Chapel's Frenchy-topped tower provides a meeting point for several streets. To the s in SILVER STREET, a large late c18 house (later a factory) with a corniced doorpiece. In ORCHARD GROVE to its e is the crowstepped U-plan KINCARDINE HOUSE. The date of 1700 on a first-floor window lintel is plausible; the s wing's lintel date of 1664 less likely. Adding to the confusion is the door lintel of a flat-roofed outshot between the wings dated 1720.

In CHAPEL STREET just n of the church, Nos. 3–5, dated 1752, still with dark pantiles. To their w, the early c19 GARVIE'S LOUNGE BAR, closing the High Street's s end, is much more prosperous, with a Roman Doric columned doorpiece. In COOPER'S LANE to the s, No. 6, crowstepped and with a forestair, dated 1750. Of about the same date must be the pantiled cottage at the lane's w corner with EXCISE STREET, where the c18 Nos. 22–24 have forestairs and widely spaced crowsteps. In KILBAGIE STREET leading out to the NW, c18 and c19 vernacular, with lots of scrolled skewputts. On the l., the MASONIC HALL, dated 1926, stripped Scots Renaissance with a flourish at the door in Lorimer's late manner. On the r., the crowstepped No. 24 is drydashed and has late c19 dormerheads, but its r. skewputt is dated 1629. A likelier date is 1725, given on an inset stone over the door. Built into the n gable, an early c17 steep pedimented dormerhead inscribed with the Keith motto: GOD/IS MY/LYF MY/LAND/AND RENT/HIS PROMIS/IS MY EVIDENT/LAT THEM SAY.

STATION ROAD and FORTH STREET, sw of Excise Street, enclose a triangular space open to the river embankment. On the r., a long pantiled range of cottages converted to a shed and a small house, all probably late c18. At the se corner, a sizeable house of *c.*1800 with a corniced doorpiece. Forth Street continues to the e with the late Georgian SHORE HOUSE, classy despite its cement render. Enlarged ground-floor windows at the c18 No. 23; on top of a scrolled skewputt sits a sundial, its finial carved with a human face. At the e end, THE AULD HOOSE, very picturesque, with white harl and black painted margins, a lintel (? of a blocked door) dated 1734.

KEITH STREET leads n. On its w side, three late c18 houses with chimney gablets: No. 54, its three-light ground-floor windows not aligned with those above; Nos. 32–34, badly altered but with Gothick glazing in its round-arched and keyblocked attic window; No. 30, less altered except for Victorian replacement of the window margins. Then a procession of scrolled skewputts on late Georgian cottages, Nos. 19 and 17 dated 1798 and 1800.

HIGH STREET is dreary, though decent enough on the E side. The position of the MARKET CROSS of c.1670, an octagonal shaft with the suggestion of a Doric capital topped by a stone carved with the Keith arms, is challenged by the WAR MEMORIAL of c.1920. To the E, TOLL ROAD. At its exit from the town, set back on the l. is BURNBRAE, a tall villa of c.1800 with the air of wearing a city suit on a country walk. Opposite, Nos. 62–64 of 1903, Art Nouveau with a bellcast Rosemary-tiled roof and Venetian windows to the principal rooms. Some Glasgow-style stained glass in the well-finished interior.

KIRK STREET to the N of High Street has more C18 and C19 vernacular cottages, scrolled skewputts dominant. No. 24 is dated 1772; the shape of No. 26's formerly thatched roof is reproduced by shaggy pantiles. On the l., an extensive early C19 rubble-built steading with an octagonal horsemill. Then the Parish Church (*see* above). On the r., three sixteen-storey blocks of flats by *J. Fisher* of *Fife County Council*, 1969.

In KIRK BRAE, the former MANSE of 1823, with the blind centre light of a Venetian window breaking into its central S pediment.

TULLIALLAN CASTLE
off Castlepark

Ruined but substantial early C14 house concealed in a wood on the edge of the town. The position near Fife's main W ferry over the Forth has been of strategic importance, and Edward I ordered strengthening of the walls of 'Tolyalwyn' in 1304. This was probably a strengthening of the surrounding enclosure, a D-shaped ditch and outer rampart, a fairly substantial protection against attack across land which was marshy until drained in the C18. There must have been buildings within the enclosure by 1304, presumably on the rocky outcrop at the NE which provides the site of the present house.

This house may have been begun as part of Edward I's work but is probably of some years later.* As first finished it was a two-storey L-plan building of good-quality ashlar masonry. Strongly battered base all round. Main block with a corbelled parapet which has broken into a round at the SE corner, and perhaps the NE too. At the SW corner, a tower containing the main entrance, with, on its l., the main stair rising to a caphouse. The tower's W front projects as a semi-octagon almost balanced by another containing a second stair at the NW corner, beyond which extends the jamb, a few corbels of its parapet still in place. At the E front's N end, a stepped garderobe projection like a huge buttress.

The arched main entrance door is set in a rectangular overarch designed to receive a raised drawbridge; above, a single

---

* Built probably for the Douglasses, who granted a charter of the fortalice and lands of Tulliallan to Sir John Edmonstone of that Ilk in 1402.

tall slot for the bridge's chain. There has been a portcullis behind. Less obviously defensive a second entrance on the r., again with a pointed arch, defended only by double doors. Small square windows in most of the ground floor, big slits above. But the room occupying the ground floor's E two-fifths has had a large trefoil-headed window set high up to N (now hidden by the NE jamb) and S.

The interior was unusual for a fortified building in having important rooms on the ground floor. The main block's W three-fifths (entered from the principal entrance) was a twin-aisled three-bay room, the quadripartite vaults springing from octagonal piers. At the W end, a well. Grander room to the E. Only two bays, but the vaults are ribbed and the central pier has a moulded capital and base. In the N wall's W end, a fireplace whose jambs curve out to carry a stone hood. Beside it, a moulded sconce bracket. Stone seats in two of the window embrasures. The first floor may have been a single hall. In the N wall, a fireplace with evidence of an aumbry in one jamb; there has been a small window in its back. Vaulted ground-floor room in the NW jamb with a garderobe flue in the gable. The adjoining secondary stair gave access to the room above.

A narrow NE jamb was added probably in the C15, its access from the main block cut through the original E garderobes. The tunnel-vaulted ground-floor room with a hatch in the roof and a garderobe in the gable seems to have been a prison.* Major reconstruction was apparently made in the late C16. The ground floor was converted to storage, the W room being subdivided by a thick wall which supported a similar partition on the floor above. First-floor windows were enlarged. The main block's W end next the tower was heightened, while the NE jamb was thickened and had an extra floor and cap-house added, these additions utilitarian rather than decorative.

TULLIALLAN CASTLE (SCOTTISH POLICE COLLEGE)
off Kirk Brae

Castellated four-poster by *William Atkinson*, 1817–20, built for 75 Admiral Viscount Keith, who had bought the estate in 1798. Three-storey main block with a thin octagonal turret at each corner. Square tower projecting from the W (garden) front's centre. Lower set-back wings with towers at the ends. Unusually, the approach is from the back through a NE arch into a service court, where a turreted *porte cochère* pushes out from the two-storey E range.

The house was bought by the Scottish Home Department in 1950 and opened as the Scottish Police College four years later. Large harled extensions to the N have followed the new use. Dining Room, Assembly Hall and Residential Unit, 1958–60; coppery clad Recreation Block, 1966; further Residential and Teaching Accommodation on the NW, 1978, all by the

---

* In 1619 five men were tried for imprisoning another in the 'pitt of Tullieallane, quhair, throw want of intertenement, he famischet and deit of hunger'.

Ministry of Works (since 1970 the *Department of the Environment*).

The main house's interior has suffered surprisingly little from institutionalization. Entrance hall with a shallow compartmented Tudorish ceiling, perhaps of *c.*1860, when *G. P. Kennedy* did work here; the oak chimneypiece may be contemporary. Atkinson's stairhall is on the N. Almost flat rib-vaulted plaster ceiling; simple Gothick stair balustrade. Behind the principal rooms along the W front, a rib-vaulted corridor. Graham Room at the S with a late Victorian white marble chimneypiece. Kinnear Room to the N, perhaps originally two rooms. Rib-vaulted ceilings again. Black marble Tudor chimneypieces of 1820, their oak overmantels probably of *c.*1860.

Mid-C19 STABLES to the NW, converted to a driver training school, 1964. In the centre of the open court, a crowstepped C18 lectern DOOCOT. – Nearby, brick WALLED GARDEN, a late C19 greenhouse along the N wall. – At the end of the drive, huge Tudor arch, an ogee hoodmould over the opening; by *George Angus*, 1833. The Art Nouveauish iron gates and Arts and Crafts Jacobean lodge are by *Watson & Salmond*, 1903.

FARM

BORDIE, 2.5km. E. Pantiled C19 STEADING. Built into it, remains of an L-plan TOWER HOUSE, possibly the 'mansion' recorded here in 1560, but the pedimented window in the E wall looks early C17. – Lectern DOOCOT to the S, probably early C18.

2080

KINGHORN

Small coastal town beside the Forth. Kinghorn is first mentioned as a royal burgh *c.*1170 but was not granted the right to a weekly market until 1285 nor represented in Parliament until 1471. In 1723 John Macky described the town as 'well built, but decay'd', but it saw considerable rebuilding and modest prosperity in the early C19. Its main function now is as a dormitory for Kirkcaldy and Edinburgh.

CHURCHES

FREE CHURCH, Bruce Terrace. Disused. Plain lancet style by *Cousin & Gale* of Edinburgh, 1845–6, the gable front flanked by pinnacled buttresses.

PARISH CHURCH, St James Place. An economical broad box by *George Paterson* of Edinburgh, 1774, covered with orangey pebbledash in 1939. The main external interest was provided in 1894–5 by *Sydney Mitchell & Wilson*, who rebuilt the W gable with a big Venetian window and added the open-belfried ogee-roofed tower at the NW. Theirs too the rose-windowed chancel.

Plain 'aisles' (i.e. wings) of unequal size project to N and S, possibly on the site of medieval transepts. The S aisle was repaired in 1608–9 (datestone of 1609 in the gable). The N (Balmuto) aisle was rebuilt in 1774 by *James Wilkie*, mason, and *Robert Kilgour*, wright.* The event is commemorated on an elegantly lettered tablet carved by *Alexander Gowan* of Edinburgh. Also in the gable, fragments of a medieval grave-slab.

At the E end fragments of the medieval chancel, probably part of the church dedicated by Bishop David de Bernham in 1243. It has a S aisle. Shaggy E gable with an intake high up on the outside. In the N wall, a small window hard against the gable and one ingo of another further W. Piled up outside the gable are weathered bits of columns, perhaps from the nave arcades demolished in 1774.

CHURCHYARD GATEPIERS, plain classical of 1839. – The HEADSTONES include (against the S aisle) James Robertson †1702, an excruciatingly provincial stab at classicism. – At the NE, two stones with winged angel heads, one dated 1721, the other of *c.* 1731. – Two identical cast-iron monuments, early C19 by the *Kirkaldy Foundry* with fan decoration and little urns.

UNITED PRESBYTERIAN CHURCH, Rosslands Place and Burntisland Road. Now church hall. Awkward Gothic of 1865–6, with a bellcote on the gable. – In front, the burgh WAR MEMORIAL by *William Williamson* (sculptor *Alexander Carrick*), 1923. Rather small, with figures of a soldier and sailor.

PUBLIC BUILDINGS

PETTYCUR HARBOUR. Rough ashlar pier and quay built in 1810.

PRIMARY SCHOOL, Pettycur Road and Burntisland Road. The earliest (E) part is of 1829 by *Thomas Hamilton* and charac-teristically idiosyncratic. This is just a humble T-plan burgh school, but the downstroke of the T is semi-octagonal, its only opening a stone-canopied door (now a window). Incongruously massive tower over the centre. Pilastered belfry stage with a heavy Greek entablature. Then angle scrolls and round clock faces (the dials vanished) under a stepped cupola (now without its pinnacle finial). The effect is weakened by the rear addition built in 1874. – Detached INFANTS SCHOOL facing Burntisland Road, gabled, by *John Murray*, 1888. [107]

TOWN HOUSE, St Leonard's Place. Insubstantial Tudor Gothic by *Thomas Hamilton*, 1826. Three-bay main block with the centre carried up as a tower with turreted buttresses. Rich and poor detail: heavily corbelled ledge under the tower's clock, but the clock's hoodmould is as skimpy as the corbels sup-porting the stringcourses of the outer bays. Behind, roofless remains of the prison block. Crosslet loops and martial doors in its wall along North Overgate.

* Kilgour was also the wright for rebuilding the body of the church, with *Roger Black* as mason.

DESCRIPTION

At the bottom of the steeply sloping site, the Parish Church (*see* above) guards the Harbour. In NETHERGATE, an C18 vernacular group, pantiled (some of the tiles concrete) and rendered; Nos. 34–36 (dated 175–) with a broad chimney gablet, No. 38 with its gable to the street. Above, the rock-faced RAILWAY VIADUCT of 1847, four segmental arches cutting the town in two.

HIGH STREET is dull and bitty, but the former United Presbyterian Church (*see* above) holds the s entry well enough, and a jolly Edwardian block in CUINZIE NEUK enlivens the N end. For the old Town House in ST LEONARD'S PLACE, *see* above. In NORTH OVERGATE, more C18 vernacular with a couple of gable-ended houses on the w side. BRUCE TERRACE exits to the N. On the corner with East Gate, BOW BUTTS HOUSE, muddled C18 with a shallow gabled bow-fronted tower to the garden. The flanking Venetian windows look late Georgian insertions. In the garden, an octagonal DOOCOT, probably mid-C18.

GLASSMOUNT, 3km. NW. A pair of standing stones 5.8m. apart, the w one 1.8m. and the E one 1.7m. high.

MEMORIAL TO ALEXANDER III, 1.2km. w. By *Hippolyte J. Blanc*, 1886–7. A gableted Gothic shaft topped by a cross of Peterhead granite. On the pedestal, bronze low relief by *John Rhind* of the King hearing peasants' pleas during a circuit court assembly.

FARMS

BANCHORY, 1.6km. NW. Superior farmhouse with piend-roofed wings, built in 1793.

NORTH PITEADIE, 3.4km. NW. Harled and crowstepped laird's house, perhaps of 1685, the date inscribed on a Victorian stone above the door. That stone is probably of 1869, the date of the reconstruction which pushed the upper-floor windows up through the eaves course with the addition of pedimented dormerheads. Single-storey wings of *c.*1800. On the r., an early C19 outbuilding with flight-holes for pigeons in the gable; sundial finial (not *in situ*) carved with a coat of arms, perhaps C17.

PITEADIE CASTLE. *See* p. 342.
SEAFIELD TOWER. *See* p. 411.

KINGLASSIE

A roadside village laid out *c.*1800 on land belonging to the Balfours of Balbirnie. Originally it was inhabited principally by weavers. The Kinglassie Colliery opened *c.*1900, and during the C20 land behind and to the E of the Georgian settlement has been developed, mostly for good-quality local authority housing (the interwar buildings by *William Williamson*).

FREE CHURCH, Main Street. Very simple, of 1844. Y-traceried
wooden mullions in the pointed windows; a bellcote on the E
gable. The porch, dormer ventilators and red-tiled ridge must
be late C19 additions.

PARISH CHURCH, off Main Street. A plain kirk with a surprisingly complex building history. The medieval church
seems to have been a simple rectangle. After the Reformation
its chancel was taken over by the Aytouns of Inchdairnie as
their burial aisle, and a transeptal N aisle was added to the
nave. In 1773–4 *Roger Black* and *Robert Baxter*, masons, and
James Lawson, wright, put on a new roof, rebuilt the S wall,
and made new windows. The walls were heightened and
the building reroofed by *Kinnear & Peddie* in 1887–8. In
1890 *Hislop*, of Kirkcaldy, replaced the Inchdairnie Aisle
with a slightly set-back extension to the main block, the
new work repeating the existing round-arched windows (probably dating from *James Gillespie Graham*'s alterations of
1839–40). Stumpy ventilator *flèche*, presumably of 1890, in
the middle of the roof; birdcage bellcote of 1773–4 on the
W gable.

The interior is almost all of 1890–1, with a heavy pulpit at
the W end (previously the pulpit had stood in the middle of
the S wall), but the E gallery's front looks like re-used Georgian
work. – Non-figurative STAINED GLASS of 1890 in the N gable's
round window. – Marble wall MONUMENT in the N aisle to
John Aytoun of Inchdairnie † 1831, with a large coat of arms
above the inscription.

At the CHURCHYARD entry, substantial remains of a late
C17 or early C18 PORCH with a lean-to OFFERTORY HOUSE on
the N. – S of the church, GRAVESLAB of John Inglis † 1679,
with a carved angel head. – To its NW, HEADSTONE of the
Liston family, dated 1742: endearingly inept Corinthian
columns support the ogee pediment; on the front, symbols of
death under the inscription; on the back, an angel in the
pediment.

UNITED FREE CHURCH, Main Street. Secularized. Harled
brick-built Gothic box of 1911.

CLINIC, Main Street. E-plan Board school of *c.*1875. Hammerdressed rubble and spired *flèches* give it a Gothic look.

COMMUNITY CENTRE, Main Street. The single-storey W part
of exposed whinstone rubble was built by *Alexander Pierson*,
1796–7, as the PARISH SCHOOL. Porch added, 1835, by *Alexander Waterson*, wright. E extension (now harled) by *George
Anderson*, mason, and *David Wilkie & Son*, wrights, 1838. In
1856–8, *Fowler*, of Edinburgh, added the two-storey SCHOOL-
HOUSE (now harled), with a steep gabled porch.

MINERS WELFARE INSTITUTE, Main Street. Dated 1931.
Mixture of picturesque and colonial neo-Georgian, like a
superior golf club.

MITCHELL HALL, Main Street. Scots Renaissance, by *Robert
Little*, 1896–9.

PRIMARY SCHOOL, Main Street. 1912, by *G. C. Campbell*.

Squared-up Jacobean on a butterfly plan; gaily painted harled
wings and a small red sandstone centre.

DOGTON, 1.5km. S. A free-standing sandstone cross, now very
worn, but several areas of decoration can still be made out,
including a panel of key pattern, a cross with two panels in the
shaft with a horseman and beasts, and intertwined serpents.

STRATHRUDDIE, 1.3km. SW. Plain Jacobean farmhouse dated
1857. Notably intact steading of whinstone rubble, with a
pantiled octagonal horsemill.

KINGSBARNS

A weaving and agricultural village grouped round the church.

PARISH CHURCH, The Square. Harled T-plan kirk of c.1630,
much altered in 1810–11 by *Robert Balfour*, who raised the
walls by 2m., inserted round-headed windows in the front wall
and gables, and removed the stone arch which had half-blocked
the N aisle from the body of the church. The tower dominates
both church and village. Its two lowest stages are probably
C17, but advanced for the 1630s. At the bottom, a round-
headed overarch with heavy keyblock and imposts containing
the roll-moulded door. The second stage is narrower, with
scrolls at the sides and a cornice. Its round window is repeated
above, but this is probably an addition of 1789. All this lower
part is squashed by *George Rae*'s ungainly top of 1866, a tall
belfry broached to an octagon; inside its corbelled parapet, a
slated spire. Interior with E, W and N galleries.

On the CHURCHYARD's E wall, three rustically classical
MONUMENTS, dated 1638, 1652 and 1633, all rather weathered. – In the SE corner, a few C18 TOMBSTONES carved with
conventional emblems of mortality. – SESSION HOUSE at the
SW, built by *Scott & Oswald*, 1838, its broad-eaved piend roof
a C20 alteration.

PRIMARY SCHOOL, Main Street. Built by *John Cairns*, mason,
and *William Bonthron*, wright, 1822. Small and pretty, with
an ogee-roofed bellcote and intersecting tracery in the E gable's
round-arched window; open-pedimented porch.

DESCRIPTION

MAIN STREET runs through the village. Off its S end, BACK
STILE on the E leads to SOUTH QUARTER, a very plain farmhouse dated 1786, with a picturesque pantiled steading. In
a large garden E of Main Street is the MANSE by *William
Lees*, 1834–5, crowstepped with a Roman Doric columned
doorpiece. Pantiled cottages S of the Primary School. Then
THE SQUARE opens up on the r. In its middle, the village
PUMP, dated 1831, built of vertically broached ashlar, with a
stepped top. On The Square's N side, the Parish Church. On
the S, the L-plan WELLGATE, its C18 harled W block presenting

a crowstepped gable to The Square, its E jamb a bland late Georgian front. On the E side, the mid-C18 KINGSBARNS HOUSE, its dentilled main cornice almost hidden by a gutter. This was the home of the architect-builder *John Corstorphine*, who built the rear extension and, at the front, a corniced doorpiece with drawing instruments and the date 1794 carved on the frieze.

SEAGATE goes E from The Square. At its start two mid-C18 houses (MILL HOUSE and the much altered MONYPENNY HOUSE), covered with thick white harl in a reconstruction of 1976. Then a row of single-storey cottages, the first (ST ANNE'S) dated 1832.

N of The Square, STATION ROAD goes W. On its N, two plain late Georgian houses (Nos. 1–2 THE PLEASAUNCE), covered in creeper. At the W end, a SMITHY of 1834 with an obelisk finial on the gable. In Main Street, No. 4 (NORTH QUARTER), a smart early C19 farmhouse, with a pantiled steading behind. Opposite, the contemporary but plainer CAMBO ARMS HOTEL; a porch has been poked into its consoled doorpiece. In NORTH STREET, near its E end, THE OLD FORGE, dated 1792, pantiled (originally thatched), with scrolled skewputts.

FARMS

BOGHALL, 1.2km. N. House of *c.*1830; the pedimented porch looks an addition. Some of the contemporary pantiled steading survives at the rear.

SANDYHILL, 0.6km. N. Prosperous early C19 farmhouse.

CAMBO. *See* p. 119.

RANDERSTON. *See* p. 353.

KINGSDALE HOUSE
1.1km. SW of Kennoway

3000

Late C18 ashlar-fronted mansion. On the N (entrance) front, a two-bay pedimented centrepiece with a bullseye attic window. The porch is a Victorian addition. On the S front, a segmental bow flanked by pilaster strips. There was a single-storey piend-roofed pavilion each side. The E has been given a two-storey extension, the W was replaced by a bay window.

KINGSKETTLE

3000

A village clustered round the Parish Church, with two early C19 appendages, Bankton Park to the W and Kettlebridge to the S.

KETTLE PARISH CHURCH, Main Street. Perp with a prominent tower, by *George Angus*, 1831–2, and almost identical exter-nally, except for its rubble walling, to his churches at Kin-cardine-on-Forth and Kinross (Tayside). T-plan, with the jamb projecting N and the tower stuck on the middle of the S side. The N (entrance) front is unusually honest in its expression of the jamb's M-roof as a double gable, the small porch not pretending to be more than a shelter. Tall hood-moulded windows. Five-stage tower (containing the vestry), its diagonally set buttresses growing into slim turrets of the type of King's College Chapel, Cambridge. Stone latticed parapet.

Interior with galleries on three sides. These are now blocked off by a lowered ceiling over the area. – Victorian PEWS. – The PULPIT was altered by *James Gillespie & Scott*. – STAINED GLASS. On the pulpit's r., War Memorial window ('Put on the Whole Armour of God'), *c*.1920. – On its l., David, after 1928. – In the E wall, one light (The Transfiguration) of *c*.1950. – ORGAN by *Forster & Andrews*, 1902.

HALL to the SW, lumpy Gothic by *David Storrar*, 1880–2.

PARISH SCHOOL, Main Street. Now a hall. By *Robert Hutchison*, 1834. Single-storey whinstone school with a two-storey schoolhouse attached to the E. A blind quatrefoil in the school's gabled porch. Flattish gableted dormerheads on the schoolhouse.

PRIMARY SCHOOL, Rumdewan. By *G. S. Birrell*, 1876.

DESCRIPTION. The architecture of the village's main part is bitty, mostly C18 and C19 vernacular, but marred by later alterations and intrusions. In the lane between SOUTH STREET and CROWN SQUARE, a low pantiled building, now a CHAPEL, dated 1747. No. 5 SHOREHEAD (WOBURN) is of *c*.1750, with a steep pitched pantiled roof; ground-floor windows enlarged 1948–50. Single-storey former SMITHY against the E gable.

KETTLEBRIDGE to the S is a large triangular-shaped hamlet begun as a linen weavers' settlement in the early C19. Mid- and late C19 cottages along the A92. NORTH STREET runs back at the W, beginning with a substantial house (No. 78) of *c*.1800, with scrolled skewputts. Then terraced cottages, the first ones pantiled, again with scrolled skewputts. At MID STREET's N end, a small BRIDGE dated 1831. Pantiled mid-C19 cottages, No. 25 dated 1844. More of the same sort in NEEDLE STREET.

2010

KINLOCH HOUSE
3.3km. NW of Ladybank

Baronial by *Charles G. H. Kinnear* for his brother, 1859. Of the earlier house* incorporated in the Victorian work there is no sign. Kinnear's N front is dominated by the tall tower over the entrance, the height emphasized by its steep-pitched scroll-step gabled roof, the iron cresting happily intact. The effect must have been more dramatic before the recent addition of a

---

* This was very plain, of five bays by five.

discreet stone lift tower on the r., hiding the fat conical-roofed turret in the inner angle and interrupting the progression to a confident crowstep-gabled bay window and candle-snuffer angle turret. Kinnear's lower block l. of the tower was heightened in 1921–3 by *Robert S. Lorimer*, whose Baronial is much politer, with an ogee-roofed oriel giving a late C17 touch. On the oriel, a pedimented datestone inscribed 1691, presumably the putative date of the original house. The s front is an addition of 1880–1, again by *Kinnear*, with canted bay windows corbelled out to square crowstepped gables.

Routine interiors of 1881 and 1923. The best is a first-floor room by Lorimer, mixing panelling of late C17 type with a shallow-relief plaster ceiling in a rather earlier manner: on the ceiling, emblems of gardening.

FARMHOUSE to the E, early C19, with a very smart single-storey office wing. (Inside, the S.D.D. noted elaborate first-floor chimneypieces, presumably imported.)

KINLOSS HOUSE

3010

1.3km. N of Cupar

Overgrown suburban villa of *c*.1860 dumped in parkland. Symmetrical bay-windowed front. – To the E, whinstone STABLES dated 1834, with a pedimented centre.

KIRKCALDY

2090

Centre	277	Pathhead	294
Dysart	288	Sinclairtown and Gallatown	299
Linktown	291	Standing Stone	300
North	293	Farms	301

A large town incorporating three formerly separate burghs (Kirkcaldy, Dysart and Linktown) and several villages. The manufacture of floor coverings has been the principal industry since the mid-C19.

CENTRE

Kirkcaldy's nickname of 'the Lang Toun' is adequately descriptive of the town centre's shape, a skinny sausage with a winding High Street running roughly parallel to the shore. The area includes the old burgh of Kirkcaldy, which existed as a burgh of regality dependent on Dunfermline Abbey by *c*.1320. In 1451 this burgh was set in feu to its bailies and community. Kirkcaldy's formal charter as a royal burgh was not granted until 1644, but it had been admitted to the Convention of Royal Burghs seventy years before and to Parliament in 1585.

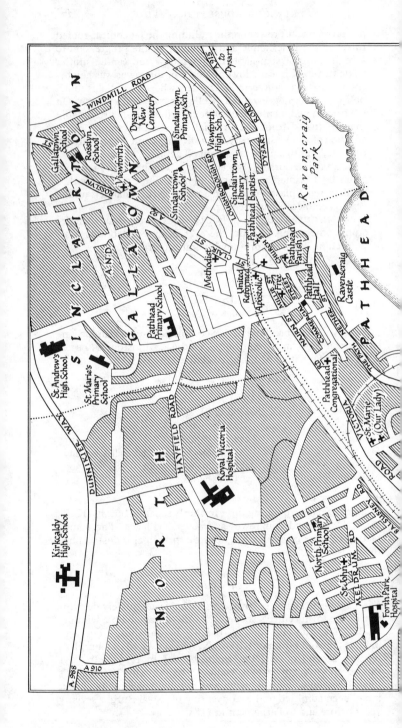

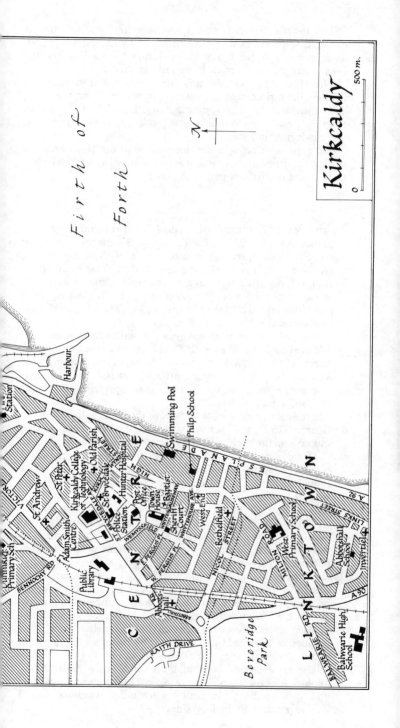

Kirkcaldy

Firth of Forth

Harbour
Station

Kinghorn Primary Sch.
St Andrew
St Peter
Kirkcaldy College of Technology
Old Parish
Adam Smith Centre
St Bryce Kirk
St Columba's
Hunter Hospital
Police Station
Post Office
Town House
Baptist
St Pet Chapel
Sheriff Court
Whytehouse Ave.
West End
Swimming Pool
Philp School

C E N T R E

Public Library
Bennochy Rd.
Wemyssfield
St Fergus Pl.
St Fergus La.
High
Nicol
Milton Road
Bethelfield
Street
Esplanade

Raith Drive
Abbots Hall
Abbotshall

Beveridge Park

L I N K T O W N

West Primary School
Abbotshall School
Invertiel
Balwearie
Links Street
A 92
A 910
Balwearie High School

N

0   500 m.

The town's first importance was as a harbour, to which a hundred ships are said to have belonged by the early C17, but its shipping suffered heavy losses during the Civil Wars, the consequent decline in trade being only gradually reversed.

The chief C18 industry was the weaving and spinning of textiles, linen becoming increasingly important from the 1730s and machinery for flax spinning being introduced *c.*1793. In 1847 the first floor-cloth factory was opened, and linoleum was first made here in 1876.

C19 expansion brought development W of the High Street, a move away from the sea institutionalized by what is effectively a civic centre in this new part of the town.

CHURCHES

ABBOTSHALL CHURCH, Abbotshall Road. Prominently sited parish kirk of 1788. Inside the W tower's machicolated and crenellated parapet, a short conical spire with oval openings; on the tower, a re-used datestone of 1674. The body of the church is a plain box, with a bowed 'aisle' (flanked by a later session room and vestry) projecting on the N. Rectangular S projection added by *John Murray* in 1898. The windows' stone mullions were inserted in 1883.

The galleried interior was recast in an up-to-date but still galleried form by *Walker & Pride*, *c.*1970. – ORGAN by *J.J. Binns*, 1898. – STAINED GLASS. Narrative windows of 1883 flanking the pulpit. They are probably by *Ballantine & Son*, who were responsible for the two lights (Spring and Autumn) of 1886 in the N gallery.

CHURCHYARD MONUMENTS. N of the church, headstone to George Nicol † 1786, carved with a hand on one side, a spade and rake on the other. – To its E, an elegant urn-topped obelisk to David Kilgour † 1812. – To the S, memorial to the child prodigy Marjory Fleming ('Pet Marjorie', 'The Youngest Immortal in the World of Letters'), a seated figure by *Pilkington Jackson*, 1930.

24 BETHELFIELD CHURCH (former Burgher), Nicol Street. By *George Hay* of Edinburgh, 1830–1. A large classical box, its two-storey gable front dressed up with a stringcourse to suggest a pediment and urns on the top. Segmental pedimented porch under an overarched Venetian window.

OLD PARISH CHURCH, Kirk Wynd. Big late Georgian ashlar box added to a medieval W tower. The rough ashlar tower may be of *c.*1500. Square and sturdy, with a single stringcourse under the original bell-chamber, which has a minimally pointed lancet in each face. Inside the uncrenellated corbelled parapet, a small mid-C18 belfry. The tower's hoodmoulded arched doorways are early C19 insertions.

The crowstepped body of the church is by *James Elliot*, 1806–8. Elegant Gothick frieze. Spired bartizans at the corners and apex of the gable. Tall hoodmoulded windows. Stolid Tudor porches on the long sides.

The interior was repaired in 1987 after a fire. (STAINED
GLASS. W windows of 1839. – E windows (Miriam, Ruth,
Moses and Elijah) by *Morris & Co.* from *Burne-Jones'* designs,
1886. – Other windows by *Alexander Gascoyne*, 1913–14.)

On the GRAVEYARD'S S and E walls, cast-iron plaques recording the ownership of lairs. – Built against the S wall, an enclosure containing classical tablets topped by heraldry to commemorate Robert Whyt † 1796 and James Townsend Oswald
of Dunnikier † 1816. – Beside it, a late C17 enclosure with
corniced dwarf walls. On its end wall, a curly pedimented
tablet to Robert Whytt † 1667 and his wife Janet Tennant
† 1670, with their arms under the inscription. – To the E, an
early C19 cast-iron 'table stone' to the Ford family. – At the N
wall's E end, large monument to Robert Philp † 1828, Gothick
but topped by a classical urn. – In this wall's centre, David
Barclay, a provincial classical tablet of *c.* 1700 embellished with
emblems of mortality. – Further W, a free-standing stone of
the Oliphant family, *c.* 1800, one side carved with masonic
emblems, the other with a grisly trophy. – Behind it, large
wall monument to Patrick Don Swan † 1889, a classical recess
containing a tomb-chest decorated with a relief bust.

OUR LADY OF PERPETUAL SUCCOUR (R.C.), Dunnikier Road.
Secularized. Lancet style of 1869. Behind, broad-eaved
SCHOOL of *c.* 1900, with a cupola.

ST ANDREW (former United Free), Victoria Road. Flabby Palladian in red sandstone by *William Dow*, 1902–3. More like a
town hall than a church.

ST BRYCEDALE (former Free Church), St Brycedale Avenue.
Geometric, by *James Matthews* of Aberdeen, 1877–81. A large
church saved from dreariness by its NE steeple (a tall angle-
buttressed tower and lucarned spire), which is excellent townscape.

Very spacious galleried interior divided into a nave and aisles
by arcades on slender cast-iron columns. Over the nave, a
wooden pointed tunnel-vault with applied ribs. A floor is being
inserted at gallery level, 1988. – ORGAN the focal point at the
S end, by *Brindley & Foster*, 1892–3. – STAINED GLASS. Rose
window at the S, a brightly coloured surround for an open
Bible, by *Adam & Small*, 1881. – N gallery window (Self-
Sacrifice), stylized social realism, by *Douglas Strachan*, 1922–
3. – Under the gallery on the E side, S window ('I am the
Resurrection and the Life') of 1887. – Beside it and much more
powerful, a window ('By the Waters of Babylon . . .') designed
by *Edward Burne-Jones* and executed by *Morris & Co.*, 1889. –
Then two routine windows (the Virtuous Mother, and the
Parable of the Talents) of *c.* 1900. – On the W side, S window
(Moses and the Burning Bush, the Burial of Moses) again by
Burne-Jones and *Morris & Co.*, 1892, with characteristic
strong colours. – Contemporary but very ordinary window
(Our Lord and Nathaniel) adjoining. – Enjoyably bad window
of *c.* 1880 commemorating the missionary Carstairs Douglas,
shown in a frock coat preaching to a bemused Chinaman.

ST MARIE (R.C., former United Free), Dunnikier Road and Victoria Road. Scots late Gothic, by *J. B. Wilson* of Glasgow, 1900–1. Nave and aisles under an overall bellcast roof. Unbuttressed NW tower with a squat octagonal spire; SW transept. Both these contain stairs to the galleries. In the W gable, empty image niche flanked by tall two-light windows; the other windows have almost flat Tudor arches. Inside, broad round-headed arcades, the gallery fronts nipped in at their piers. – STAINED GLASS. One light (Angel) in the porch.

ST PETER (Episcopal), Townsend Place. 1976, by *Wheeler & Sproson*. Self-effacing behind a car park. Harled, with a copper-covered gambrel roof.

WEST END CONGREGATIONAL CHURCH, High Street. 1874, lancet style. Tall belfry on the NW steeple.

WHYTESCAUSEWAY BAPTIST CHURCH, Whytescauseway. 1854 but still Georgian-looking, despite the Tudor detail and spired *flèche*.

PUBLIC BUILDINGS

ADAM SMITH CENTRE, Bennochy Road and St Brycedale Avenue. English baroque by *Dunn & Findlay*, 1894–9. Stodgy W front. The S elevation is much better. Pier-like ends, the l. still with its lead dome. The centre is divided into five bays by broad piers. Bullseye first-floor windows and a semicircular Ionic portico. Balustraded parapet joined to the set-back attic by heavy scrolls.

EAST SCHOOL, Glebe Park. By *John Milne*, 1876. Gothic, with a slate-roofed tower.

FIRE STATION, Dunnikier Road. 1935–8, by *George Duffus*. Art Deco touches on the hose-tower.

HARBOUR, High Street. A creation of the C19 and C20 incorporating the site of a medieval harbour at the mouth of the East Burn. A new E pier built *c*. 1600 was repaired and extended several times before 1843, when *James Leslie* again extended it and thickened its E end as a quay and railway terminus. In 1906–8 *Rendel & Robertson* lengthened the pier yet again and reconstructed the harbour as a dock and outer harbour, the dock entrance spanned by a swing bridge made by the *Brandon Bridge-building Co.* The older work is rubble-built, the newer of concrete.

HUNTER HOSPITAL, Hunter Street. The centre is St Brycedale House, a smart villa built for George Heggie in 1786; harled, with ashlar belt courses. Centre bows at front and back, the front's carried on a Roman Doric portico. Inside, oval rooms. In 1934 *W. Williamson & Hubbard* converted the house into a hospital and added the wings, parodies of the original.

KIRKCALDY COLLEGE OF TECHNOLOGY, St Brycedale Avenue. Built on the site of the High School, to which the SW block of 1926 was an addition; fag-end Beaux Arts classical. In 1966, *Fife County Council* added the nine-storey curtain-walled tower and workshops in the lightweight style of the time and now rather shabby.

PHILP SCHOOL, Thistle Street. Now a restaurant. Classical of c.1830; pedimented Roman Doric portico at the centre. The high basement makes the columns and angle pilasters appear stumpy.

POLICE STATION, St Brycedale Avenue. 1900–2, by *Williamson & Inglis*. Free English baroque; tall SE cupola an attempt to add Belcher-type panache.

POST OFFICE, Wemyssfield and Hunter Street. Plump Baronial by *H.M. Office of Works*, 1900.

PUBLIC LIBRARY AND MUSEUM, Bennochy Road. The WAR MEMORIAL of 1923 by *Heiton & McKay* of Perth was the starting point. Formal garden to the S; on its axis, a cenotaph backed by a balustraded terrace wall covered with bronze inscription tablets. On the terrace is the Museum of 1925, Beaux Arts classical, its heavy centre door continuing the axis. The Library was added in 1928, a repeat of the Museum design which ruins the effect of the War Memorial approach. The effect was further weakened by the Second World War Memorial by *Williamson & Hubbard*, 1954–8, on the E of the original.

SHERIFF COURT, Whytescauseway. By *James Gillespie*, 1893–4. The entrance is very Baronial. Balustraded tower from which grows an excessively tall steepled turret, its top stages corbelled out as an octagon. On the r., Tudorish block (the courtroom itself) with an ill-fed heraldic lion on the crow-stepped gable. Much grimmer is the E addition by the *Property Services Agency*, 1979, blank concrete walling with narrow glazed stairtowers.

SWIMMING POOL, Esplanade. White brick package by *R. Forbes Hutchison*, c.1969.

TOWN HOUSE, Wemyssfield. Designed by *David Carr* in 1937 117 but not completed until 1956. Very polite modern but carefully avoiding being Modern Movement. So the windows are traditionally proportioned and the walls are ashlar-faced. Off-centre entrance and a tall copper cupola. The result is decidedly lightweight.

VICTORIA HALLS, Victoria Road. Built as a chapel c.1881; converted to halls 1905.

DESCRIPTION

Roundabout at the S end of High Street. In NICOL STREET to the W, No. 44, late C18 with a broad chimney gablet. NEWTOWN HOUSE (No. 46) was built in 1816; large with a mutuled cornice and centre pediment. Fluted frieze over the broad door. Across the street, straightforward brick flats of the 1960s. No. 1, a less grand and more altered version of Newtown House, was built as Bethelfield Church's manse in 1804.* Beside the church (*see* above), BETHELFIELD PLACE, ashlar tenements of c.1830.

* By *Walter Beaton* and *Henry Bonthron*, masons, and *Kilgour & Nicoll*, wrights.

HIGH STREET's w side begins with a big red sandstone block of
c.1900. Pend under its French pavilion-roofed centre to the
OLYMPIA ARCADE, a covered lane with an early C19 tenement
on its s side. On High Street's s side, a warning of what is to
come: the single-storey SAFEWAY, preceded by a car park.
Shanty-town Fifth Column is well established among the solid
late Georgian and Victorian of the rest of the street. Crude
shopfront across the old ABBOTSHALL FREE CHURCH's
truncated gable of 1869. The Congregational Church (*see*
above) holds the corner of WHYTEHOUSE AVENUE, where the
early C20 No. 30 stands out from the late Victorian villas. It
is white-harled with curvilinear gablets and segment-headed
dormers.

In EAST FERGUS PLACE, superior villas. Nos. 1 and 3 mid-
Victorian, with Doric doorpieces and bay windows. Opposite,
a late Georgian couple, both harled: No. 2 with a Doric doorpiece, No. 4 with hoodmoulded tripartite windows and
anthemion decoration on its continuous cast-iron balcony.
No. 10 is by *R. Rowand Anderson*, 1881, like a Butterfield
parsonage: 'a Gothic residence, homely and unpretentious',
said *The Builder*. By contract, OSBORNE HOUSE is pompous
Renaissance of c.1850.

WHYTESCAUSEWAY passes the Sheriff Court, Town House and
Baptist Church (for all these, *see* above) on its way to High
Street. Here, WHYTEHOUSE MANSIONS by *Robert Little*,
1895–8, has a procession of crowstepped gables; thrifty bartizans on the higher corner. The large BURTON of c.1935 on
the N corner is more Deco than Art. Early C19 tenements at
Nos. 111–127, No. 125 with a columned doorpiece.

THE MERCAT opposite is an attempt by *Michael Laird & Partners*, 1981–3, to institutionalize shanty-town. One-storey
shops under a continuous arcaded concrete canopy front the
street. Behind, a mall links new shops and the back doors of
earlier stores to a multi-storey car park (its front to Esplanade
a polite shed clad in concrete bricks) and the Swimming Pool
(*see* above). The BANK OF SCOTLAND palazzo of 1887 is by
Kinnear & Peddie; carved swags and rosettes on the frieze
above the rusticated ground floor, whose windows have been
deepened to form an over-assertive arcade.

Nos. 133–135 High Street were built as the Glasgow Bank,
c.1835, suave with a balustraded cornice. The end bays are
advanced like piers gripping the centre; peculiar detail at the
first floor, where the lugs of the window architraves are supported on flat consoles. The tall three-storey scale is taken
up at the former ROYAL BANK (Nos. 151–153), Edwardian
baroque by *William Williamson*, 1905.

Nos. 148–156 on the E side form a tenement and bank development of c.1830 built by the Commercial Bank, presumably to
designs by their usual architect, *James Gillespie Graham*. Front
block with corniced first-floor windows and an overall balustrade. The shopfronts are of c.1900. So too are the granite
columns, though not their capitals, at the central pend. This

leads to the bank itself, a smart house with a Greek Doric porch. Strong Gothic block at Nos. 160–162, dated 1868, rather in the early manner of R. Rowand Anderson. Mullioned and transomed first-floor windows in pointed overarches; broad gablet flanked by battered chimneys. Late Georgian tenement on the corner of TOLBOOTH STREET, where its shopfront has a single Ionic column *in antis*. This street's s side is overawed by a flank of The Mercat. Opposite, No. 23 has been a double house, rubble-built with vertical ashlar panels linking the windows. Each house has a console-corniced doorpiece dated 1785, the r. one pedimented. The chimneys have been removed and concrete tiles added.

ROYAL BANK OF SCOTLAND (former National Bank, Nos. 191–193 High Street) of 1825; balustraded but stodgy classical, with Roman Doric porches on the advanced ends. Contemporary block at Nos. 195–199, suaver with a mutuled cornice and heavy Doric doorpiece. Nos. 211–215 of *c.*1870, enjoyably free Romanesque. No. 219 is early C18. Rendered front; lugged window architraves. Harled flank to Kirk Wynd with a rusticated doorpiece, urns on its pediment's ends. (Inside, panelled first-floor room with a bolection-moulded chimneypiece, lugged doorcases and a china cupboard. More panelling on the second floor.) On the opposite corner, the SWAN MEMORIAL HALL (now offices) of 1893–5 by *George Washington Browne*, Jacobean but spoiled by a granite shopfront of *c.*1930.

KIRK WYND focuses obliquely on the Old Parish Church's tower (*see* above). Curve-fronted TRUSTEE SAVINGS BANK, tepid baroque of *c.*1890, extended W in the same style, *c.*1905. The rather altered No. 36 is probably early C18, white-harled and crowstepped with a lean-to wing projecting into the street. Over the door, re-used heraldic stone dated 1637. Formidably Baronial CHURCH HALL, dated 1890. At the top on the corner of Townsend Place, the harled MANSE designed and built by *John Stevenson*, mason, 1808; Roman Doric doorpiece added 1839; E extension by *William Little*, 1867; neat piended dormers of 1899. In HILL STREET, large shopping development (THE POSTINGS) of 1978–84.

CLYDESDALE BANK in High Street, by *W. Dow*, 1908, with a top-heavy pediment-cum-chimney. Beside it, Nos. 218–222, smooth late Georgian with Ionic columns *in antis* at the central pend. The BANK OF SCOTLAND (Nos. 224–226) is by *William Burn*, 1833; pedimented first-floor windows and a balustraded cornice, but the ground floor remodelled. Then shanty shops halted by a massive red sandstone block of 1903–4 by *J. D. Swanston*, boring but welcome in this context.

On the N corner of Oswald Wynd, Nos. 263–265 of *c.*1800, with an absurdly deep wooden cornice. Tall pedimented gablet on the contemporary ashlar-fronted Nos. 275–277. Massive Edwardian intrusion with Nos. 287–295; three-storey bay windows in the gabled ends; Ionic centrepiece skied on the top floors. VICTORIA HOUSE (No. 295A) is blowsy Queen Anne of 1902; stained glass (a ship) in its ground-floor pub. A quieter contemporary at Nos. 299–305. Opposite, very elegant cast-iron balconies on Nos. 286–290 of *c*.1830. C18 vernacular at Nos. 305A–319; deep cornice on the late Georgian Nos. 321–323. High Street's E side marks the junction with Esplanade with a filling station.

Overlooking the Harbour (*see* above), an early pair of tenements. Nos. 333–337, late C18 with a rendered front; at the back, an earlier wing and also a cantilevered outshot, probably early C19, with Gothick windows. Cement render on the front of Nos. 339–343 masks a tenement of exceptional interest. It began as a C16 two-storey and attic block. Massive chimney corbelled out from the back wall, just like the front chimney at Bay House, Dysart (*see* Dysart: Perambulation, below). Soon after, the front wall was rebuilt 2m. further out, perhaps in wood. A jettied second floor was added either at the same time or in the late C17, when the building was refronted in ashlar. The front's central chimney gablet is a late C18 addition; so too is the broad stairtower at the rear, half-obscuring the gabled centre. Inside the first-floor flat, N room with a late C17 modelled plaster ceiling. Main compartment containing a rosette and terms set in a foliaged oval with winged *putti* heads round about; in the smaller front compartment, marked off by a guilloched beam, enrichment of different character – a square containing lions' masks and fruit, with rosettes in the guilloched lozenges each side. The S room's ceiling is again of two compartments, both coved. Panelling in the second flat's centre and S rooms. Further along, the OLDE TOUN LOUNGE, free-style Edwardian pub with an outsize egg-and-dart cornice and open pediment, all in wood; stained glass (stylized flowers) in the windows. Early C19 vernacular after Coal Wynd. HARBOUR HOUSE of *c*.1820 is set high up behind two deep pilastraded pavilions (the l. with a coach arch in the flank). The house itself is made mildly ridiculous by its centre being carried up a full extra storey as a pedimented tower. Next door, a heavy pilastered bar with a procession of window pediments, *c*.1900. No. 439, late C18, with a chimney gablet.

SAILORS' WALK (Nos. 443–447 High Street) is made up of two T-plan houses which form a rough H. They came into one ownership in 1826 and now belong to the National Trust for Scotland, for whom *Wheeler & Sproson* carried out major repairs in 1954–9. Their white harling, cement margins and red pantiles now give them a rather spurious unity. Both are probably late C16. The S house is larger. Its crossbar's crowstepped E gable has bold consoles to carry the projecting upper floors. Moulded stringcourse, perhaps early C19 over the door in the inner angle. Similar stringcourse under the second-floor windows of the N house's flat-fronted E gable. The position of a cannon spout in the inner angle shows that this wing's wallhead has been raised. On the N side, shallow projection of part of the upper floors. Small C18 addition on the NW. Inside, one room has a painted wooden ceiling, probably early C17. Arabesques with birds' and animals' heads on the boards; Biblical texts on the beams. In another room, a stone, formerly outside, carved with the arms of Charles II and the date 1662 or 1682.

Undistinguished C19 vernacular leads to ST MARY'S CANVAS WORKS. Tall main block of 1914, curving with the road to join a single-storey pilastraded block of 1864. The demolished UNION CHAPEL's crenellated screen wall of 1822, with stumpy pinnacled buttresses and hoodmoulded openings, brings High Street to a halt against the RAILWAY VIADUCT by *James Leslie*, 1843.

Back in COAL WYND, English baroque former MISSION INSTITUTE of 1909–10, by *William Williamson*. (Diversion up Dunnikier Road (for its Fire Station and churches, *see* above) to VICTORIA ROAD. To the E, ELECTRICITY STATION by *William Williamson*, 1901; shaped l. gable, the r. gable with a segmental pediment. Opposite and set well back, THE PRIORY, late Victorian by *James Gillespie*, plain Jacobean except for a vigorous coat of arms on the porch. Beside it, HALL OF RESIDENCE by *Fife Regional Council*, 1979. To the W, SOCIAL SECURITY OFFICE, U-plan in buff brick and concrete aggregate panels, by the *Property Services Agency*, 1976.)

In MITCHELL STREET, Nos. 3–5 of *c.*1820 with a centre pend. Early C19 pair of houses (Nos. 52–54) at the beginning of TOWNSEND PLACE, No. 54 with an Ionic doorpiece. Contemporary but humbler group at Nos. 32–38. The single-storey No. 30 (*c.*1840) has a centre gablet. Then comfortable Victorian villas. After the car park of St Peter's Church, Nos. 9–11, *c.*1830, with a Doric columned doorpiece. The steeple of St Brycedale Church makes a strong beginning to the parade of public buildings along ST BRYCEDALE AVENUE (for all these, *see* above, as also for the Hunter Hospital in HUNTER STREET). At the end, an early C19 double house (Nos. 6–8 St Brycedale Avenue), No. 8 still having a Doric doorpiece. Round the corner in WEMYSSFIELD, Ionic porch on No. 16 (*c.*1820). The Italianate No. 15 of *c.*1860 stands beside a large *moderne* GARAGE by *W. Williamson & Hubbard*, *c.*1938.

Large garden in front of the Public Library and Museum (*see* above). FORTH HOUSE on its W was built as the Balsusney Works in the late C19; insipid Renaissance industrial, not helped by an added top floor. ABBOTSHALL ROAD goes under the railway to Abbotshall Church (*see* above). Opposite, the BENNOCHY LINEN WORKS, dated 1865, plain classical with ball finials; brick chimney. The piend-roofed blocks behind look earlier. The former GATEWAY to Raith House on the corner of RAITH DRIVE is by *James Playfair*, 1786, and characteristically elegant. Contemporary bow-ended LODGE.

DYSART

Dysart still has something of the appearance although not the vitality of an independent small burgh, the stretch of Ravenscraig Park maintaining its physical distance from the rest of Kirkcaldy. The burgh of barony founded here by 1510 was stented as a royal burgh in 1535 and admitted to Parliament in 1594.* Salt-making was an early industry, and the town became a prosperous port for the export of coal and fish but then declined in the C18. Redevelopment since the 1950s has preserved the most important buildings as sacred cows fenced in by new housing.

CHURCHES

DYSART PARISH CHURCH (former), Townhead. Now Y.M.C.A. Hall. A smooth ashlar box of 1801–2 by *Alexander Laing*. Urns on the gables. Tall round-arched windows in the long sides; pedimented S doorpiece. The W porch and E hall are unhappy additions.

DYSART PARISH CHURCH, West Port. Originally Free. By *Campbell Douglas & Sellars*, 1872–4. A version of St Monans Parish Church (*q.v.*), but in snecked rubble. The stonework is not the only difference from the medieval prototype. The spire is slated, not stone-slabbed; the windows are all round-arched intimations of the Early Christian revival, not pointed frames for Flamboyant tracery; buttresses have been omitted but a short nave is provided. Even so, the strong squat steeple dominates to good effect.

NORMAND ROAD UNITED FREE (former United Presbyterian) CHURCH, Normand Road. 1865–7, by *James Brown* of Glasgow. Unappealing lancet style. Broach-spired steeple flush with the gable-front.

ST SERF (FORMER PARISH CHURCH), Shore Road. Gaunt landmark of a tower attached to ruins of the parish church built *c.*1500 and abandoned in 1802. The church itself has been an aisled eight-bay rectangle, the S aisle's W bay filled by the projecting tower. In the inner angle, a slab-roofed porch, perhaps an afterthought.

The aisle arcades' two W bays survive. Arches of two chamfered orders. Curiously, two out of every three of the arcades' piers are circular, but the third is oblong with bowed ends. Moulded capitals where they have not been left as bells ready for carving. Splay-margined rectangular windows in the remains of the S wall. Crowstepped W gable with a round-arched door. The E gable was apparently largely rebuilt when this end became a burial-place after the Reformation.

Above the porch entrance, an image niche. The pot of lilies on its corbel base suggests it contained a statue of Our Lady. Inside, the porch is stone vaulted. Stone benches at the E and W walls. Above the N door into the church, an ogee-headed niche, its corbel base carved with a cherub's head.

* And so treated as a royal burgh, although never officially one.

The six-storey ashlar tower is severe, very like a contemporary tower house (e.g. Scotstarvit) raised to a great
height. Stringcourses at the second and fourth floors. Tall
pointed openings mark the belfry. Individual moulded corbels
carry the uncrenellated parapet rising at the NW into a crowstepped cap-house tenuously joined to the attic. The tower's
entrance from the nave is at first-floor level, the present stone
forestair a replacement probably of a wooden stair. Inside, a
turnpike in the thickness of the NW corner's walling. Tunnel-
vaulted ground- and first-floor rooms. In the vaults, hatches
for hoisting bells.

PUBLIC BUILDINGS

DYSART PRIMARY SCHOOL, Normand Road. By *William Williamson*, 1914–15. Blocky Queen Anne with red sandstone
dressings and a central cupola.

NORMAND HALL, High Street. Early Renaissance with a French
accent, by *R. Rowand Anderson*, 1883–5. Austere High Street
front with a channelled ground floor and keyblocked first-floor
windows (bullseyes in the end bays), relieved by the red-tiled
roof and off-centre cupola. The E (entrance) gable is richer, its
pedimented Venetian window carved in low relief.

TOLBOOTH, High Street and Victoria Street. A square white-
harled tower. The lower part was built in 1576 with heavy
quoins and restless stringcourses. Round stairtower at the NE
corner. W forestair added in 1617. The upper part, wrecked
by exploding gunpowder in 1656, was rebuilt in 1707. Much
smoother, with quoin strips and segmental open pediments
over the clock faces. Above, an ogee-roofed octagonal belfry.
Council Chambers on the S, plain Renaissance of 1885 by
Campbell Douglas & Sellars.

PERAMBULATION

TOWNHEAD ROAD begins with a crowstepped lectern DOOCOT,
probably C17, beside the Parish Church. Further along, the
C18 church and United Free Church. (For all these, *see* above.)
On the E side of NORMAND ROAD, a crowstepped LODGE of
c. 1850 with stone birds on the gables. BLAIR HILL (now
Dysart Club) off HILL STREET has been a classy villa of
c. 1800, with a pedimented centre on the E front, but is spoiled
by a Victorian addition.

No. 49 EAST QUALITY STREET has a datestone of 1610, but the
house now looks late Georgian. Datestone of 1589 on the
white-harled and crowstepped No. 31. This is on the projecting jamb, which appears convincingly late C16, with a flat-
fronted projection corbelled out to contain the stair to the
attic. Lower main block, C18 in its present form. Opposite, a
Georgian group, all now part of a foundry. No. 46 with a
stairtower to the street; No. 44, large and plain of *c.* 1795, with
a corniced doorpiece; strongly detailed coachhouse on the l.;

No. 42 smaller and even plainer. Among WEST QUALITY STREET's low-rise housing by *Wheeler & Sproson*, 1964–5, the heavily restored C18 No. 11 (ORCHARD CROFT) was originally two houses; in the r. part, a corniced central door with pulvinated frieze.

RECTORY LANE curves down the hill. At its top, the late C18 OLD RECTORY with a Roman Doric doorpiece. Further down, the much restored C17 ST DAVID'S. Originally of two storeys, it was heightened *c.*1680: S front with crowstep-gabled dormers flanking a swept dormer and huge chimney. NW stairtower, its upper part corbelled out. Inside, the N room has been the kitchen, with a segmental arched fireplace. In FITZROY STREET, the L-plan Nos. 11–13 are of *c.*1700; the datestone of 1806 presumably records a reconstruction.

HIGH STREET is mostly a redevelopment by *Wheeler & Sproson*, 1976, characteristically straightforward except for one block beside the Normand Hall (*see* above) which masquerades as a pantiled tower. Heavy classical doorpiece on No. 42, *c.*1840. N of Cross Street, a harled C18 vernacular group (Nos. 43–69), much restored in 1976 and painted to resemble ice-cream. Next to the Tolbooth (*see* above) is the MECHANICS INSTITUTE with a big crowstepped and thistle-finialled gablet, by *James Aitken*, 1873–4.

McDOUALL STUART PLACE has another harled group (Nos. 1–5). No. 3's door lintel is dated 1575, but the smart curvilinear ashlar gablet at the back is of *c.*1700. THE ANCHORAGE on the S side of SHORE ROAD is dated 1582 (reconstructed 1965). L-plan with white harling and crowsteps. Much of the E front is shallowly corbelled out in an irregular manner. Further down, St Serf's Church (*see* above) on the way to the Harbour (*see* above).

PAN HA's houses were externally restored and had their guts removed by *W. Schomberg Scott*, 1968–9, as part of the National Trust for Scotland's Little Houses Scheme. BAY HOUSE at the W was built for Patrick Sinclair in 1583. Regular S front, the upper floor's two centre bays corbelled out with a large chimneystack. Human heads carved on the skewputts. Simply moulded courtyard door at the NE, its lintel inscribed MY HOIP IS IN THE LORD 1583. A round-arched door of *c.*1600 to the N served an ancillary building. The main block's rear outshot is a possibly C18 replacement for a timber gallery supported on posts. To its r., a pedimented dormerhead. The C16 lay-out of the much altered interior was established during the reconstruction of 1969. It had three ground-floor rooms, the W probably the kitchen, the others stores. First-floor hall, its ceiling coombed into the roof-space; on each side, a lower room with attic above. These flanking rooms' painted ceilings were discovered and removed in 1969. The hall's stone chimneypiece survives. Nos. 2–5 Pan Ha' are infill of 1968–9, their garage doors discreetly tucked away at the sides; harled walls, pantiled roofs, but the tiny chimneys, not even on the gables, make them irredeemably suburban. In SAUT GIRNAL

Wynd, The Salmon Fisher's House, small, of sneck-
harled orange rubble, dated 1763. Chimney gablet on No. 7
Pan Ha' (The Girnal), porch addition on No. 8; both are
mid-C18. No. 9 (The Tide-Waiter's House) is L-plan. On
the wing to Hie-Gait, a very weak Gibbsian doorpiece under
a cartouche dated 1750. Pan Ha' ends with more C18 vernacular
at Nos. 10–11.

DYSART HOUSE

Plain but complex Georgian mansion on the hill overlooking the
harbour. The earliest part is the s range's E two-thirds, built
for General James St Clair in 1755–6, the *Adam* brothers
supplying the chimneypieces and perhaps the design.* Simple
piend-roofed box with a projecting bowed centre. In 1808–14
the house was enlarged by the addition of rear wings and a w
extension: very plain except for a second bow on the w front
and three-light windows on the s, the adjacent window of the
1750s block enlarged to match. *Roger Black* was the builder,
the architect probably *Alexander Laing*.‡ Probably mid-C19
is the simple balcony under the s block's w windows.

LINKTOWN

Made a burgh of barony in 1663 but now just Kirkcaldy's s tail,
new housing along the Esplanade its chief feature. The C20's
saddest architectural loss was the early C18 Gladney House,
important not only as a major merchant's house but also as the
birthplace of Robert Adam.

CHURCHES

Invertiel Parish Church (former Free), Links Street. 1857,
by *Campbell Douglas*.
Linktown (Abbotshall) Free Church, Links Street.
Now a youth club. Incompetent Gothic of 1844. Triple-gabled
front; round pinnacles on the buttresses. The interior was
recast by *John McLachlan*, 1883. Cast-iron columns supporting the horseshoe gallery and boarded ceiling.

PUBLIC BUILDINGS

Abbotshall School, Ramsay Road. Gabled Gothic by
Robert Little, 1890–1. To the w, Infant School of 1898, blocky
English baroque with a confident cupola.
Balwearie High School, Balwearie Gardens. By *Fife
County Council*, 1964. Four- and five-storey main block, its
horizontal bands of aggregate and glass disturbed by wilful
cut-outs. N extension of 1972.

---

* But *James Campbell* seems to have been the principal contractor.
‡ Who witnessed a receipt by Black in 1808 and had been architect for the parish
church.

BEVERIDGE PARK, Abbotshall Road. Laid out by *William D. Sang*, 1891, and opened 1892. Heavy Renaissance GATEPIERS in red sandstone at the entrances. The N entrance is focused on a bargeboarded LODGE by *J. W. Hislop*, 1891, with a fat turret in the inner angle. Also by Hislop the contemporary GARDENER'S HOUSE to the w; French pavilion-roofed tower.

119 SEAFIELD COLLIERY, Kinghorn Road. Preparatory work on sinking a shaft to mine coal under the Forth began in 1954; production started in 1965 and ceased in 1988. Buildings by *Egon Riss*, the most conspicuous the winding towers of 1959, huge P shapes of precast concrete.

111 WEST PRIMARY SCHOOL, Milton Road. Long and low, by *R. Rowand Anderson*, 1874–80. Beautifully simple Gothic. Gabled ends; gable in the centre kept down in height so as not to detract from the roof, whose steep pitch is emphasized by two small dormers and a tall *flèche*. Round chimney stacks on the flanks. Also by Anderson, and just as accomplished, the schoolmaster's and janitor's houses on l. and r. Harled addition by *George Sandilands*, 1935.

PERAMBULATION

At the N end of Links Street, on the E a large supermarket (COMET) of 1986, concrete-block shed enlivened by its octagonal conservatory's red frame. On the w, MILTON ROAD begins with the green-painted ABBOTSHALL HOTEL built as Abbotshall Manse in 1772 and extended E *c.*1820. Then the West Primary School (*see* above). Picturesque group (Nos. 69–81) of *c.*1900 with red sandstone dressings and a half-timbered jettied projection to Munro Street. No. 83 by *James Gillespie*, 1895, was built as Raith Manse; squared-up Tudor with carved foliage over the door. Huge twin gables with deeply projecting bargeboarded eaves on Nos. 74–76, *c.*1890. Across the railway, at the corner of BALWEARIE ROAD and BALWEARIE CRESCENT, a double house of *c.*1900, T-plan with a half-timbered M-gable; semi-octagonal porches canted across the inner angles.

LINKS STREET starts with a late Georgian tenement (Nos. 18–24) with aproned first-floor windows. On the corner of BUTE WYND,* Nos. 78–80, a pair of late C18 houses; continuous moulded cornice, scrolled skewputts on No. 78. No. 76 is a humbler contemporary. The rest is mainly redevelopment, begun in 1930 and continued by *E. V. Collins*, 1957. Among it, a couple of Victorian churches (*see* above) and a harled cinema of 1938 by *John McKissack & Son* of Glasgow.

The huge WEST BRIDGE MILLS in BRIDGE STREET were built to spin flax in 1856; mansard-roofed with ball finials on the S gable. To the w, six-arch RAILWAY VIADUCT by *Thomas Boucher* and *Thomas Grainger*, 1845–7.

*Where Robert Adam was born in Gladney House (demolished 1927).

Except for a few villas along Bennochy Road this is almost
entirely an area of post-war housing.

CHURCHES

ST JOHN, Meldrum Road. By *Marcus Johnston*, 1976–7. Trapezoidal plan, 'Fyfestone' walls, a metal *flèche*. Inside, STAINED
GLASS by *Graham Lowe*. – Behind, the former church (now
hall) of 1908 by *William Williamson*.

TEMPLEHALL CHURCH, Beauly Place. 1955–6, by *G. B. Deas*
and *Henry Hubbard*. Unpretentious buttressed box of harled
brick. Saddleback-roofed tower to identify it as a parish kirk.

TORBAIN CHURCH, Carron Place. Abstract in white drydash;
by *Wheeler & Sproson*, 1964–8.

PUBLIC BUILDINGS

CEMETERY, Bennochy Road and Balsusney Road. Laid out
*c.*1860, and extended E *c.*1890. – MONUMENTS. In the NW
corner, John Nairn †1928; Artisan Mannerist revival, but
covered with Arts and Crafts carved foliage, peacocks and an
eagle. – W wall. John Alexander †1863; 'Greek' Thomsonesque
wall monument by *W. Galloway*, with a high-relief bronze
portrait bust signed by *C. MacCallum*, 1868. – Across the NE
corner, red sandstone Wishart Monument of *c.*1895, with a
life-size figure of Harpocrates.

FORTH PARK HOSPITAL, Bennochy Road. The starting point
was a large villa of *c.*1860, Jacobean, with shaped gables even
applied to the entrance tower. It was converted to a hospital
in 1933–5 by *W. Williamson & Hubbard*, who added a
maternity ward block. Buff brick extensions by the *South-
East Regional Hospital Board's Architect's Department* (chief
architect: *John Holt*), 1966.

ROYAL VICTORIA HOSPITAL, Dunnikier Road and Hayfield
Road. On the S, the old Infectious Diseases Hospital's brick
pavilions, by *Campbell Douglas & Morrison* of Glasgow, 1897–
9. More pavilions were added by *J. Lumsden*, 1907, and *D.
Forbes Smith*, 1912. Their small scale is no competition for the
extensions of 1955–67, all by the *South-East Regional Hospital
Board's Architect's Department* (chief architect: *John Holt*),
the dominant feature a fourteen-storey curtain-walled ward
block. On the N of Hayfield Road, low-rise block in dark brick
by *Basil Spence, Glover & Ferguson*, 1980–3.

SCHOOLS. Two Board Schools: DUNNIKIER PRIMARY by
R. M. Cameron, 1894, and NORTH PRIMARY of 1904–7, with
English baroque flourishes, by *D. Forbes Smith*. Post-war
expansion has brought several more: KIRKCALDY HIGH, on
two sites, at Templehall Avenue (1952) and Dunnikier Way
(1958); VALLEY PRIMARY, Valley Gardens (1953); TORBAIN
PRIMARY, Blairmore Road (1961); and CAPSHARD

PRIMARY, Barry Road (1970). All are by *Fife County Council* in the lightweight style of the time.

MANSION

DUNNIKIER HOUSE, off Dunnikier Way. Now a hotel. A smart house of 1791–3 built by James Townsend Oswald, whose former seat (Dunnikier House, Pathhead) 'was rendered less agreeable by its Situation in a Town'. The architect was *Alexander Laing* of Edinburgh.*

The composition is conventional: three-storey five-bay main block, its centre advanced and pedimented; one-bay links to single-storey pavilions. But the detail is sophisticated. Across the main block a deep fluted frieze, now broken by the heightening of the second-floor windows. The centre has a Venetian door. Its upper part and the pavilions are identical, except that the pavilions have no frieze. In each, a Venetian window (for which the r. pavilion has substituted a C19 bay window), and a thermal window in the pediment. Balustraded parapets on the two-storey links, but their upper floors (only a screen at the l.) may be early C19 additions, as must be their semicircular stone balconies.

The entrance was moved to the N *c.* 1885, that front acquiring pedimented gablets over the windows and a large off-centre porch. The best things inside are two large chimneypieces of continental Renaissance type, one dated 1886.

LODGE on Hayfield Road, dated 1899, a small version of old Dunnikier House.

VILLAS

BENNOCHY ROAD shows changing fashion. Nos. 24–26, absurd French châteaux of *c.* 1880. For Forth Park Hospital, *see* above. Nos. 48–50 of *c.* 1900 with large half-timbered gables. No. 52 is by *J. B. Dunn*, *c.* 1914, accomplished neo-Georgian, its purplish Hailes rubble walling a contrast to the roof's brown Caithness slates.

PATHHEAD

Once known as Dunnikier, a village whose mansion house stands isolated in builders' rubble at the top of the Path which has given the area its present name. Nail-making was a major industry in the C18, linoleum manufacture in the C19. Three tower blocks have been the late C20's contribution.

CHURCHES

APOSTOLIC CHURCH, St Clair Street. Built in 1879 for an

---

* The mason was *Roger Blane*, the wrights *Robert Kilgour* and *Peter Nicoll* of Kirkcaldy.

Original Secession congregation by *Fraser & Son* of Pathhead, who may have designed it. Small and Gothic.

FREE CHURCH, Millie Street. Squared-up late Gothic of 1910. Gable front with stairtowers masquerading as aisles. Perp window framed by the crocketed pinnacles of the flat porch. Small *flèche* on the roof.

PATHHEAD BAPTIST CHURCH, Anderson Street. 1908. Impressive surprise in a side street. Gable front with a battered N tower topped by an Art Nouveau belfry rather of the St Andrew's East (Glasgow) type.

PATHHEAD E.U. CONGREGATIONAL CHURCH, Commercial Street. Small and simple, 1869. Turret finial on the apex of the gable front; battlemented porch with hoodmoulds over the windows.

PATHHEAD PARISH CHURCH, Church Street. Built as a chapel-of-ease, 1822–3. Broad harled box with a square N tower. Crowstepped gables with small bartizans; the windows pointed with Y-tracery. The tower has a machicolated and crenellated parapet and Tudor detail.

UNITED REFORMED CHURCH, St Clair Street. Former Baptist chapel of 1870. Minimal Tudor Gothic.

PUBLIC BUILDINGS

GOSPEL UNION HALL, Commercial Street. Dated 1899. Cheap and plain, with a hoodmoulded Venetian window.

PATHHEAD HALL, Commercial Street. By *Campbell Douglas & Sellars* of Glasgow, 1882–4. Scots early C18 revival, presumably to evoke burgh tolbooths, and the tower's ogee-roofed octagonal belfry is cribbed from Dysart Tolbooth. Hall gable with channelled angle buttresses and a large tripartite window under a fanlight; it looks curiously ecclesiastical.

RAVENSCRAIG CASTLE

A romantically positioned castle, now an Ancient Monument and 50 nesting place for fulmars. It was begun as a jointure house for James II's queen, Mary of Gueldres, in 1460. The master of works, David Boys, and his chaplain, Robert Spangy, were probably administrative overseers rather than architects, and the design may have been produced by *Henry Merlioun*, who was probably the master mason,* or perhaps by *Brother Andrew* the wright. Work seems to have stopped on the Queen's death in 1463, and the first major stage may not have been completed until after the castle was granted to William Sinclair, Earl of Caithness, in 1470.

The site is a narrow triangular promontory jutting S into the Forth, vulnerable to attack only from the N, where it is overlooked by rising ground. The principal accommodation is

---

* He contracted to provide one mason or quarryman ('*latimus*' could mean either in C15 Scotland) to the work. He was probably related to the C16 masons Walter and John Merlioun, employed respectively at Edinburgh Castle and Holyrood.

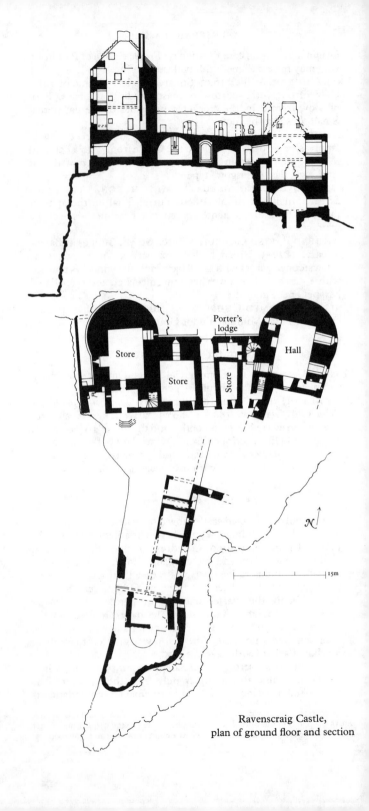

Ravenscraig Castle,
plan of ground floor and section

provided in two towers flanking a range built across this base of the triangle. Behind were ancillary buildings round two courts, ending with a third 'tower', perhaps a bastion, at the s tip of the promontory. This provision of two almost identical tower houses in one castle is peculiar. Was one, presumably the grander w tower, intended as the Queen's lodging and the other for the keeper of the castle? Architecturally even stranger is the lopsided composition produced by a sudden fall in the ground, so that the base of the E tower (a storey lower in any case) is two floors below that of the w. Design seems here to have had to defer to defence.

The approach is by a wooden bridge (now permanent, orig-inally removable) across a deep ditch cut through the rock. Ahead is the two-storey central range clasped by the bowed ends of the D-plan towers. All this is of rough ashlar, but the w tower's blackish masonry is clearly not from the same quarry as the yellowish and more weathered stone of most of the rest. It was apparently with this tower that the building work began. Intakes near the bases of the walls of the centre and towers, but they are at different levels, with no attempt to integrate them decoratively. Quite large windows, with chamfered jambs and lintels, in the sides of the towers not threatened by an enemy (E wall of the E tower, w and s walls of the w tower). In the towers and lower floor of the central range, inverted keyhole gunloops – the castle was designed from the start to be defended by artillery. Provision for artillery became still more thorough in the mid-C16, when the central block's front was heightened with a 3.5m. curtain wall containing two large gunloops of the horizontal wide-mouthed type. Its corbelled cavetto cornice was not used as an example when, probably c. 1600, the E tower was given a new parapet and the w tower's wallhead was altered to a slope covered with stone slabs (perhaps roofing over a leaking parapet walk), and both towers were given crowstepped attics.

In the front's centre a round-arched chamfered entrance into a tunnel-vaulted transe. On the l., porter's lodge with a fire-place and gunloop. It is tunnel-vaulted, as are the stores opening off the court behind. In the w store, a stepped gun platform serving the large gunloop. On the E of the centre range, a narrow transe and turnpike stair to the C16 artillery platform. Here are two deep gun embrasures in the curtain wall, each with an aumbry. Another aumbry to the w. Tusking on the w tower's E face shows that a thicker front wall (of the same thickness as the walling below) was first intended. So there is no reason to suppose that an artillery curtain here was part of the original design. A great hall may have been planned.

The w tower is self-contained. Despite the external D-plan, the main rooms are all rectangular. Tunnel-vaulted ground-floor store, its entrance from the s having had two sets of doors. Gunloops to E and w. SE forestair (originally roofed) to the first-floor hall. This has been comfortable: fireplace with one moulded jamb (a filleted edge-roll in a cavetto), stone seats in the large s and w windows, garderobe in the NE corner. The vaulted gun chamber is discreetly hidden in the N wall's thickness. Corbels for the ceiling joists survive, but all the upper floors have gone. A wall-chamber on the s of the fireplace may have been intended as a porch from the putative great hall to the E. Similarly well-appointed second- and third-floor rooms, but the fireplaces are plain (off-centre on the second floor, small on the third). No provision for a cannon – just a small wall-chamber with a gunloop for a hand-gun in the NE corner of the second floor.

The E tower's vaulted ground floor contains the well, its parapet of 1971 uncomfortably new-looking. Straight stair to the first-floor hall; large E windows with stone seats. Similar second-floor room, but with a NW wall-chamber with a gunloop. Two fireplaces in the C17 attic, so this probably contained bedrooms. On the s of this tower has been a single-storey room, apparently contemporary and with evidence of vaulting. Further s, more remains of subsidiary buildings. At a point where the site narrows sharply, a door to the beach is defended by two gunloops of the C15 inverted keyhole type set in a wall carried on three rows of corbels. At the apex of the triangle, where a 'tower' stood until the C19, rectangular room containing a stone trough. Drain in the adjoining room. Some of these buildings may have been added in the C17, when a small court was enclosed in front of the w tower.

In Ravenscraig Park to the E, a C16 beehive DOOCOT overlooking the shore. Rubble-built, with three ratcourses, but the top has been removed. – Further E, a round GAZEBO, early C19, with large keyhole 'gunloops'.

DESCRIPTION

THE PATH is the main approach. Beside the East Burn are FLOUR MILL offices of c.1800, a smart villa with Venetian windows; in the pedimented centre, elliptically arched fanlight over the door. Pavilion link with a clock to the brick and harled mill buildings which incorporate a horsemill. Across the road, late C19 MALTINGS, with two kilns with pagoda ventilators.

61 In NETHER STREET at the top of the hill is DUNNIKIER HOUSE (now PATH HOUSE), built in 1692 for John Watson and his wife, Euphan Orrock, whose initials and the date are carved on the dormerheads. L-plan main block with a conical-roofed stairtower in the internal angle. Scrolled skewputts on all gables. On the sw corner, a sundial. The s and w fronts have pedimented dormerheads with scroll enrichment. Crowstepped dormerheads at the back, the E one a replacement of 1978. Off-centre rear wing, perhaps an early C18 addition and so contemporary with the rusticated gatepiers and screen wall in front. The house stands in a wasteland. Ahead, on the N side of the street, the three fifteen-storey blocks of RAVENS CRAIG are by *Wimpey*, 1964–5. On the s overlooking Ravenscraig Castle (*see* above), a GRAVEYARD. Flashy classical tomb-

stone to James Law †1785, its inscription panel's arched top filled with carved drapery.

Not much is left of Pathhead's centre. In COMMERCIAL STREET, the CO-OPERATIVE SOCIETY premises are all by *David Forbes Smith*. Narrow three-storey building of 1905–7 at the E end, extended in 1914 with a long low block, English baroque with effectively spaced open segmental pediments. Very plain rear building to MID STREET with an absurdly small pediment. Isolated in BOGIES WYND is the red sandstone FEUARS 116 ARMS, pub-Jacobean of *c.*1890. Splendid interior with an Art Nouveau tiled bar. Tile pictures of a Shepherdess and Fool (by *Doulton & Co.*) on the walls. Stained-glass windows with coats of arms and flowers below, stylized buildings above. More stained glass in the bar gantry.

SCOTTISH LINOLEUM WORKS in VICTORIA ROAD. Main block by *Gillespie & Scott*, 1883, with round-arched windows rising through three floors. Opposite, stripped neo-Georgian office block by *James Miller* of Glasgow, 1935.

SINCLAIRTOWN AND GALLATOWN

Formerly two villages, Sinclairtown a planned village laid out *c.*1750, Gallatown older but more scattered. Little remains which is earlier than the late C19, but St Clair Street still provides a centre of sorts.

CHURCHES

LOUGHBOROUGH ROAD UNITED PRESBYTERIAN CHURCH, Loughborough Road. Disused. By *Robert Baldie* of Glasgow, 1881. A large lancet-style nave and aisles church. The 35m.-high steeple, with its tall octagonal belfry and spire, wins high marks for townscape, fewer for detail.

METHODIST CHURCH, St Clair Street. Built in 1888. Humble except for the patterned slating and red ridge tiles on the roof.

VIEWFORTH PARISH CHURCH, Viewforth Street. By *J. F. Anderson* of Dundee, 1875–8. T-plan (E transepts) and lancet windows, but still Georgian in feeling. Broad W gable. Very old-fashioned S tower with clumsy pinnacles on the crenellated parapet.

PUBLIC BUILDINGS

GALLATOWN SCHOOL, Rosslyn Street. Dated 1861. Very simple except for the polychrome slating on the E tower. W addition by *D. Forbes Smith*, 1902.

PATHHEAD PRIMARY SCHOOL, Cairns Street. 1913–15, by *William Williamson*. Stretched English baroque. Depiction of a schoolmaster and pupils on the cupola's weathervane.

ROSSLYN SCHOOL, Viewforth Terrace. By *D. Forbes Smith*, 1910. Three parallel blocks, the outer two with South African Dutch gables and cupola ventilators.

St Andrew's R.C. High School, Overton Road. By *Fife County Council*, 1959. Four boxes projecting from a long spine, all three-storey and curtain-walled. The elegance is spoiled by the authoritarian harl and red sandstone of the entrance block. Unhappy additions, both temporary and permanent.

St Marie's R.C. Primary School, Macindoe Crescent. By *Fife County Council*, 1972. Three low blocks arranged in a U. Shallow-pitched roofs and plenty of glass.

Sinclairtown Library and Clinic, Loughborough Road. By *William Williamson & Hubbard*, 1933–5.

Sinclairtown Primary School, Roomlin Gardens. By *George Sandilands*, 1930, and characteristically dreary.

Sinclairtown School (former), Viewforth Street and Rosabelle Street. *c.* 1875. Single-storey, L-plan, in hammerdressed rubble with crowstepped gables.

Viewforth High School, Loughborough Road. Blocky Wrenaissance but long and low, by *D. Forbes Smith*, 1908.

DESCRIPTION

Two main routes. St Clair Street leads N. Florid Renaissance Royal Bank of *c.* 1890. Appalling shopfront on No. 254, but above are channelled pilasters and a Second Empire dome. Next door, the old Salvation Army Citadel of 1909 by *W. Dow*, with rusticated pilasters and a steep open pediment. In Rosslyn Street, Nos. 34–42, the r. three bays dated 1895 with carved cats' heads in the pediment; four-bay extension in the same style dated 1921. Ice Rink by *Williamson & Hubbard*, 1937, a large shed with some Art Deco touches. Pantiled early C19 terrace in Doctor's Row. Interwar and post-war local authority housing to the w; more on the e, but also some late Victorian terraces stepping grimly downhill.

Solid villas on the e route along Loughborough Road. Between the Library and Viewforth High School (*see* above), Eastbank of *c.* 1870 is formidably Baronial with a top-heavy tower over the front door. Further along is Dysart New Cemetery, its crowstepped lodge dated 1881. Round the corner in Windmill Road, a double house (Nos. 56–58) of *c.* 1900; bay windows and stumpy Ionic porches in the twin-gabled centre. Off Quarry Brae, a round rubble-built Windmill tower of *c.* 1700, its early C19 brick parapet pierced by cast-iron spouts.

STANDING STONE

Bogleys, 3.9km. NW. On what is traditionally the site of a battle with the Danes. Rectangular sandstone block 1.85m. high and 2.6m. in girth at the base; one possible cupmark on the w face.

FARMS

BALWEARIE TOWER, 1.8km. SW. A plain harled farmhouse of
c.1800, except that its N gable is a folly designed as an eye-
catcher from Raith House. Beautifully detailed Gothic to
suggest that this is the surviving gable of a vanished church.
Blind ground-floor arch; above, a window with (brick) intersecting tracery; quatrefoil in the apex. Stumpy pinnacles. The
deceit even extends to the provision of tusking as if for vanished
side walls.

TORBAIN, 2.9km. W. Early C19 farmhouse and steading. Built
into the steading is a folly, a square crenellated tower with a
NE corner turret.

KIRKFORTHAR   3000
3.1km. N of Markinch

Harled mid-C19 farmhouse with a central gablet and club skewputts. – To the W, ruins of Kirkforthar House, and a C17
DOOCOT which is a cross between the beehive and lectern
types, i.e. it is round but with a pitched roof cutting across.

KIRKTON OF CULTS   3010

Just the parish church, manse and school grouped in the middle
of fields.

CULTS PARISH CHURCH. Built in 1793, small and simple. Thin
W tower topped by a birdcage bellcote whose baluster uprights
have been re-used from table stones; forestair to the belfry
door.
    Galleried interior; the end galleries of 1793, the N added in
1835. – STAINED GLASS. Window on l. of pulpit (The Good
Shepherd), c.1960. – In the tower, one light (The Burning
Bush) by *Cara McNeil*. – Two exceptional WALL MONU-
MENTS. On the r. of the pulpit, the Rev. David Wilkie and 39
Isabella Lister (Sir David Wilkie's parents) by *Francis Chantrey*, 1833, the low-relief busts carved from portraits by
Wilkie. – On the pulpit's l., Sir David Wilkie †1841, with a 37
low-relief bust by *Samuel Joseph*.
    SESSION HOUSE at the churchyard gate, probably early C19.
    To the S, former MANSE of 1795, with scrolled skewputts.
The flat-roofed dormers are an unfortunate addition. In its
garden, a lectern DOOCOT, probably early C18 despite the
inserted datestone of 1780.
    To the N, mid-C19 SCHOOL, with bracketed eaves.

LADY MARY'S WOOD, 1km. NE. An Iron Age fort c.125m. by
110m. overall, in a plantation on the crest of the W spur of
Walton Hill. The defences are severely denuded on the E side,
but on the W three lines of rampart and ditch can be discerned,

the entrance probably lying on the NW. Inside the fort stands the Crawford family's MAUSOLEUM of *c*.1760. Shedlike, but with Roman Doric columns and an open pediment stuck on the gable.

KIRKTON OF LARGO *see* UPPER LARGO

2080

KNOCKDAVIE CASTLE
3.2km. N of Burntisland

Fragmentary remains of a substantial C17 rubble-built house. It has been rectangular, with a round stairtower projecting from the N wall.

3000

LADYBANK

An early C19 planned village of linen-makers which developed from *c*.1850 as a small town whose importance came from the position at the junction of the railway lines S from Perth and Dundee. It was made a burgh in 1878.

PARISH CHURCH, Church Street. Originally a Free church. Geometric, by *Peddie & Kinnear*, 1874–6. Tower on the r. of the front gable, with a squat broach spire. Inside, a broad nave and apse-ended chancel, its arch flanked by organ pipes. – STAINED GLASS. In the porch, three lights (Scenes from the Life of Our Lord) by *William Wilson*, 1959, in his usual expressionist manner. – In the apse, five small lights (Christ the Good Shepherd, and Christian mottoes and symbols), *c*.1880. – ORGAN by *Rushworth & Dreaper*.

BONTHRONE MALTINGS, Commercial Road. Long, late C19 whinstone range; pagoda-roofed kilns placed symmetrically each side of the centre.

MASONIC HALL, Commercial Crescent. Dated 1890. Small but solid mixture of baroque and Romanesque.

RAILWAY STATION, Commercial Crescent. Designed by *Grainger & Miller* for the Edinburgh & Northern Railway, 1847–8. The main offices are on the W platform. Broad-eaved Italianate but with Tudor hoodmoulds. Acanthus leaf capitals on the canopy's columns. On the E platform, a late C19 brick waiting room, its deep valance with a fretted bottom. At the platform's E end, a Jacobean lodge of 1847–8. To the N, Engine Shed and Workshops of *c*.1850, with arched openings and diamond panes in the windows.

WATERWORKS, Beeches Road. Only the red-brick pumping tower survives. It is dated 1908. Sides panelled with giant overarches; polychrome touches.

BARROW, 1.2km. to the N, on Cairnfield Muir, *c*.16m. in diameter and 1.3 m. high, on a platform *c*.29m. overall diameter.

LADY MARY'S WOOD *see* KIRKTON OF CULTS

LAHILL
1.9km. E of Upper Largo
4000

Low-key Tudor house built in 1831 by *Hugh Birrell*, who may have designed it. Grotesque heads on the entrance porch. The garden front's bay windows look an addition.

LARGO HOUSE *see* UPPER LARGO

LARGOWARD
4000

Rather shapeless but pleasant small village on a hillside.

PARISH CHURCH. Built as a chapel-of-ease, 1835. Plain box with a small birdcage bellcote on one gable; galleried interior.
HALL. Drydashed blocky Art Nouveau, by *A. S. Macrae*, 1907.
PRIMARY SCHOOL. *c.*1840. Simple Tudor, in whinstone.

LATHRISK HOUSE
2.3km. E of Falkland
2000

Smart piend-roofed laird's house reconstructed *c.*1785. Venetian door under a three-light window in the pedimented centre. Venetian windows in the harled pavilion wings. Muddle of additions at the back. Inside, the RCAHMS reported two vaulted ground-floor rooms, probably the vaulted kitchens of the house described by the *Caledonian Mercury* in 1743 as 'lately built'.

LESLIE
2000

The village was made a burgh of barony in 1458. Major expansion to the W followed the establishment of flax mills and a bleachfield beside the Leven from *c.*1800. A police burgh from 1865 to 1975, it has just managed to elude the embrace of Glenrothes next door.

CHURCHES

BAPTIST CHURCH, North Street. 1885–6, by *John Lister*, the minister's brother. Stolid classical composition with a pedimented gable but thin Romanesque detail.
CHRIST'S KIRK ON THE GREEN, Greenside. A cheap but effective presence beside the village green. The church began as a simple T-plan built by *Thomas* or *James Barclay* in 1819–21;

Alexander Leslie was Inspector of Works and possibly the designer. In 1868–9 *J. M. Wardrop* doubled the church's size with a s extension, equally plain but for its E tower topped with a steep pyramidal roof and dressed up with gryphon gargoyles. The bargeboarded LYCHGATE abutting the w gable was added by *Rodgie* in 1875–6.

Galleried interior mostly of 1868–9, but its focal PULPIT and ORGAN (by *Scovell*) are of 1909–11. – Brightly coloured STAINED-GLASS s windows (The Feeding of the Five Thousand; Christ Blessing children) of 1889; they were memorials to Henrietta, Countess of Rothes, who is depicted in both.

In the churchyard to the N, the crowstepped Douglas and Rothes MAUSOLEA stand side by side. Both are C17 aisles added to the medieval church demolished in 1821, the probable date of their Gothic s front. – To the E of the Rothes Mausoleum, a broken monument to John Broun †1746, inscribed:

> JOHN BROUNS.DUST LAYS HERE.BELOW
> ONCE SERVED.A NOBLE.EARL.
> TO HIS.COMMANDS.HE NER.SAID NO
> HAD IT.BEEN ON.HIS PERIL
> HIS DAYS.AND YEARS.THEY WERE.SPUN OUT
> LIKE TO.A THREED.MOST FINE
> AT LAST.A PERIOD.CAME ABOUT
> SNAPT IT.AT NINTY.NINE

– E of the church itself, headstone of John Archer and his wife Agnes Walker, dated 1717 and inscribed:

> HERE LYES WITHIN THIS EARTHEN ARK
>   AN ARCHER GRAVE AND WISE
> FAITH WAS HIS ARROW CHRIST THE MARK
>   AND GLORY WAS THE PRISE
> HIS BOW IS NOW A HARP HIS SONG
>   DOTH HALLELUJAH DITE
> HIS CONSORT WALKER WENT ALONG
>   TO WALK WITH CHRIST IN WHITE

– Against the church's NE corner, an unfluted Greek Doric column put up in 1832 to commemorate Jane Watson; the overlarge obelisk finial seems not to belong. – William Clunie's headstone N of the church is dated 1817; inscription:

> Friend do not Carless [*sic*] on the road
> Oerlook this Humble Shrine
> For if thou art a Friend of God
> Here is a Friend of Thine
> His closet was a Bethel sweet
> His house a house of Prayer
> In homely strains at Jesus feet
> He wristled daily there

– Otherwise, a good but unremarkable collection of C18 headstones.

ST MARY MOTHER OF GOD (R.C.), High Street. Originally Leslie Free Church. By *R. Thornton Shiells*, 1876–9. A preaching box in spiky Gothic dress, the broad gable disguised by a transeptal stairtower on the r., a tall broach-spired steeple on the l.

TRINITY PARISH CHURCH, High Street. By the wright-architect *Henry Archibald*, 1858–9, and endearingly old-fashioned Jacobean. Spired octagonal bellcote and a loop-traceried window at the shaped gable.

DESCRIPTION

THE GREEN at the E end marks the old burgh of barony's centre with the craggy cenotaph of a WAR MEMORIAL, *c.* 1920, in place of a market cross. More unexpected is the STONE behind, said to have been used in bull-baiting and grooved by ropes used to tether the animals. The Green's N side is dominated by the Parish Church (*see* above). On its r., the broad-eaved MANSE of 1811–13, its large dormers added by *John Young*, 1868; stables behind by *Robert Hutchison*, 1836. Substantial whinstone terrace (Nos. 1–16 GREENSIDE) of *c.* 1800 across The Green. Skewputts on all the houses; skewputted gablets as well on Nos. 1–8.

HIGH STREET slips past The Green's S side. Next to Leslie House's tame Baronial lodge (*see* below), the starkly crow-stepped red sandstone gable of the CHURCH HALL by *Gillespie & Scott*, 1905, followed by piend-roofed flatted blocks (dated 1946) facing a sturdy Victorian villa (the GREENSIDE HOTEL) mocked by drydashed additions.

Ragbag vernacular ensues. On the S, Nos. 40–48, a small-scale tenement dated 1724 on a ground-floor window lintel. Contemporary Nos. 50–52, crowstepped with a moulded doorpiece on the l. Plain Gothic TOWN HALL opposite dated 1872. The harled and crowstepped Nos. 82–88, with a stairtower jutting on to the street, look late C17. Hidden behind No. 92, an early C18 rubble and pantiled house which has lost its forestair. In the gable of No. 61 (dated 1872), a stone inscribed HB 1662. A pair of late C18 pantiled cottages (Nos. 63–65) down the cobbled close give a reminder of the old rig pattern. The early C18 No. 71 presents a crowstepped gable to the street.

In closes on the S side, two former Secession chapels, both very simple rubble boxes. Behind No. 106, the painted BURGHER MEETING HOUSE, dated 1771. The ANTIBURGHER MEETING HOUSE behind No. 128, dated 1744 on the door lintel, was built by *William* and *James Gardner* and *John Jellson*, masons, and *James Robertson*, wright, in 1744–5. Inside there survive the ogee-topped sounding board of the pulpit (made by *Peter Wilkie*, 1745) and remains of the E gallery. Twin-gabled Tudor BANK OF SCOTLAND of *c.* 1840 across the road. A touch of quality at No. 222, *c.* 1800, whose doorpiece has a fluted frieze. Of No. 155's doorpiece only the anta pilasters survive, but the house makes a solid late Georgian foil to the spiky Gothic of St Mary's Church (*see* above), standing at the boundary between the old burgh and the 'New Town' which developed in the C19. Diversion down NORMAN

PLACE to FETTYKIL HOUSE, dated 1868, Baronial of the *Heiton* type, the lodge (by *R. Rowand Anderson*, 1874) relatively quiet. To its E, the immensely tall red and white brick chimney (*c*.1880) of the FETTYKIL PAPERWORKS.

High Street ends after Trinity Church (*see* above) in the PROVOSTS LAND development, sensible stripped vernacular by *L. A. Rolland & Partners*, *c*.1975. DOUGLAS ROAD on the r. leads to MANSFIELD, a row of comfortable early C19 houses overlooking the town and overlooked in turn by the contemporary MARYFIELD. To the l., GLENWOOD ROAD exits downhill past a chunky early C19 villa (No. 338 High Street) and under a curving fourteen-arch RAILWAY VIADUCT of *c*.1860. At the bottom, a picturesque gabled late Victorian terrace (Nos. 37–51 Glenwood Road) with stone canopies over the doors and windows, built as workers' housing for the adjoining PRINLAWS EAST MILL. Further out, the early C19 villa of GLENWOOD.

LESLIE HOUSE

The first impression on the approach from the W is of a benign Georgian barracks. But this long block is the much remodelled surviving range of the quadrangular palace built for the seventh Earl (later first Duke) of Rothes by *John Mylne Jun.* and his son *Robert* in 1667–72, with advice from *Sir William Bruce*. The magnificence of the interior (especially the 47.8m.-long N gallery) and of the terraced gardens was praised by contemporaries. Understandably, they were reticent about the gauchely gabled exterior, for whose remodelling *William Adam* seems to have produced an unexecuted scheme *c*.1740.

After a major fire in 1763, the eleventh Earl of Rothes demolished the N, S and E ranges, and reconstructed the W. This has a pedimented three-bay centre joined by two-bay links to advanced two-bay ends. In the C17 the centre and ends were gabled. The reconstruction of *c*.1765–7 heightened the second floor, finished the ends with piended roofs, and gave the centre a pediment. *c*.1860, a balustrade topped by dormer windows was added to the links, and it was extended across the ends in the late C19. In 1906–7 *Robert S. Lorimer* placed a coat of arms in the pediment's tympanum. The delicately moulded window surrounds must be of 1765–7 but the stringcourses above the ground and first floors are C17. So too is the centrepiece's ground-floor treatment of a tripartite frame of fluted pilasters clamped on a basket-arched arcade, an Artisan Mannerist precursor of the arcades at Holyroodhouse (Edinburgh) and Drumlanrig Castle (Dumfries and Galloway). Like those, this was a loggia front, but the C18 remodelling filled in the arches with windows and removed the scrolled pediment above the door.

On the S gable, a bay window added by Lorimer. The piend-roofed E front is very plain but not very satisfactory, the C17 rubble walling (with evidence that an earlier house is incorporated) contrasting with the C18 ashlar at the ends. C18 stair windows placed symmetrically each side of the centre, but this is marked only by a small curly pedimented doorpiece embellished with the coroneted monogram of the seventh Earl and his countess Anne Lindsay.

In the garden E of the house, remains of the C17 palace. Foundations of the W range, their W end covered by a late C19 conservatory. Vaulted basement stores of the N range, now covered by a flat roof.

The interior has been considerably altered for its present use as an eventide home. Columned screen, presumably C18, in the entrance hall. Each side, a stair of the 1760s with twisty wooden balusters, but the broad first-floor landing joining them has been filled with bathrooms.

TERRACED GARDEN on the S, still with C17 staircases connecting the different levels. – WEST LODGE at the approach from the town, pacifist Baronial, presumably by *Lorimer*, 1906–7. It incorporates a large late C17 panel bearing the arms of Rothes and Lindsay, probably from the house. – DUKE'S LODGE, hidden beneath the road from Glenrothes, dated 1906, with a crenellated parapet. – Beside it, glacial-rusticated GATEPIERS, dated 1671 and very grand with ball finials on 67 their segmental pediments. The ornate wrought-iron GATES decorated with sprays of flowers in best late C17 manner are dated 1906. The piers themselves probably stood originally at the house's E or W forecourts, which were removed in the late C18.

STRATHENDRY CASTLE. *See* p. 412.
STRATHENDRY HOUSE. *See* p. 412.

LETHAM 3010

Large hamlet, mostly of single-storey C19 cottages, several pantiled, many altered. Half-way up SCHOOL BRAE, a crowstepgabled lectern DOOCOT; another to the l. at the top. Both are probably early C18. The PRIMARY SCHOOL was built by *Robert Hutchison* in 1804 and extended by him in 1820; much altered since.

HOPETOUN MONUMENT, 3.2km. NE on the top of Mount Hill. Huge Roman Doric column containing a stair to the balcony. It was built in 1826 to commemorate John, fourth Earl of Hopetoun.

FERNIE CASTLE. *See* p. 225.

LEUCHARS 4020

Originally a medieval village round the parish church, the castle a little way to the N, it was almost entirely rebuilt from *c.*1790.

The railway got here in 1848. The Royal Air Force station opened in 1917 has become a dominant presence and been joined by housing estates to beleaguer the older core.

FREE CHURCH, Main Street. Now church hall. Broad whinstone rectangle of 1844; bellcote on N gable.

11 PARISH CHURCH (ST ATHERNASE), Schoolhill. Posed on a hill dominating the village, this church's E end is Fife's flashiest example of Romanesque architecture. The church of Leuchars was granted to the Augustinian priory of St Andrews by Nes, Lord of Lochore, with the approval of his daughter and heiress Orabilis, Countess of Mar, c. 1185.* The building was probably completed by then, and the existence on it of some of the same masons' marks as are found at Dunfermline Abbey and Dalmeny Church (Lothian) provides confirmation for a mid-C12 date.

The general massing of the C12 church was strikingly similar to that of Dalmeny and St Baldred's Church, Tyninghame (Lothian). Like them, Leuchars had a tall nave,‡ a lower, almost square chancel, and a still lower apse. Unlike those churches, Leuchars' choir and apse are richly decorated externally, each with two tiers of blind arcading separated by an ornamental stringcourse. The arches are all round-headed with cushion capitals, some with slightly voluted foliage. The apse's lower tier has coupled shafts; the upper tier's shafts are paired, but with a broad fillet between. Arches carved with billet, chevron and pearl ornament. Sawtooth ornament on the stringcourse. On the chancel's stringcourse, scroll ornament. Below, intersecting arches; the upper tier a taller version of the nave's but enriched only with cable ornament. At both chancel and apse the eaves course is projected on corbels carved with the faces of animals and grotesque humans. Chancel parapet added in 1857–8 by *John Milne*, who also restored much of the chancel's arcading and some of the apse's.

On top of the apse, an incongruous but happy belfry of c. 1700. Its lower stage is octagonal but with the NE, NW, SE and SW faces curved. Above, an octagonal stone lantern topped with a lead weathercock.

Plain nave by *John Milne*, 1857–8§; perfunctory Romanesque detail and a tall gablet over the central S door. On the N side's E end, re-used fragment of a C12 stringcourse.

The interior of Milne's nave is as unappealing as its outside. Deep W gallery continued half-way along the N side as an organ loft.

The Romanesque masonry round the chancel arch was stripped of plaster and given a wood frame by *Reginald Fairlie* in 1914. The arch itself is narrow (only 2.705m. wide), with,

---

* Nes's charter of donation can be dated 1172 × 1199; a charter of confirmation, from Bishop Hugh of St Andrews, 1178 × 1188. The church does not appear among the priory's possessions in a papal confirmation of 1183 but is in one of 1187.

‡ Early illustrations of the church showing the nave as lower than the choir post-date 1745, when the nave walls were lowered.

§ Milne's nave is 1.2m. broader than its predecessor but the same length.

on each side, a central shaft flanked by nook-shafts; the head enriched with a damier pattern, a chip-carved band, and a chevron. In the wooden-roofed chancel, a moulded sill course enriched with lozenge patterns under the nook-shafted windows.

The sanctuary arch is a smaller version of the chancel arch, decorated with a billet and chevrons. Inside the sanctuary, a short tunnel-vault halted by a transverse rib at the beginning of the apse's curve. Over the semicircular E part, vault of three webs, the stout ribs springing from wall-shafts carried on corbels carved with human and animal heads (some much restored) sitting on top of the sill course.

BAPTISTERY in the W vestibule's N half, made c.1935 when *Fairlie*'s neo-Jacobean oak screen of 1914 was moved here from the chancel arch. – Inside, alabaster and marble FONT of c.1890.

At the nave's E end, PULPIT (neo-Jacobean) and FONT (a soapy Romanesque capital but with agreeable dogs' heads on the carved oak cover) both by Fairlie, 1914. – STAINED-GLASS SE nave window ('My Peace I Give unto You') by *William Wilson*, c.1960; strongly coloured and clearly drawn.

Beside the pulpit, GRAVESLAB of Sir Robert Carnegy †1565, with a well-lettered inscription. – Two more graveslabs have been set in the S wall, each side of the central door. On the l., Sir William Bruce of Earlshall †1584, elaborately carved with a big coat of arms and inscriptions, the lowest reading:

HEIR.LYIS.OF.AL/PIETE.ANE.LA/NTERN.BRYCHT./
SCHIR.VILLZAM./BRVCE.OF.ERLISH/AL.KNY[C]HT

– On the r., Agnes Lindsay †1635, carved with a near life-size figure of the deceased. – Above the door, another stone, probably early C17, carved with would-be classical blind arcading: the outer arches contain a skull and skeleton; the centre two the inscription:

THIS./SEPITVR./THAT.ZE/HEIR.SE./
.FOR./ERLISHAL./.AND.HIS.POSTERETE.

PRIMARY SCHOOL, Pitlethie Road. By *Fife County Council*, 1965.

RAILWAY STATION, 0.9km. SW. Opened 1848, but rebuilt c.1900. Island platform reached from the E by a lattice-girder bridge. Brick station building, its asbestos-tiled roof carried out on cast-iron columns as an all-round verandah.

DESCRIPTION

The Parish Church (*see* above) stands on its hill near the village's E end. In EARLSHALL ROAD to its E, the plain whinstone MANSE built by *Robert Balfour*, 1803–5. Beside it, on the corner of Pitlethie Road, the U-plan manse OFFICES (now a house) by *Hugh Birrell*, 1844–5.

SCHOOLHILL, N of the church, is late C18 and C19 vernacular,

most of the houses single-storey and pantiled. The two-storey
No. 11 of c.1790 is grander, with a fluted frieze on its lugged
architraved doorpiece.

MAIN STREET, S of the church, vernacular again but dourer and
generally later. Touches of Edwardian frivolity on the harled
YE OLDE HOTEL. Further W, No. 78's lugged architraved
doorpiece is dated 1794. Set back on the S side, the former
Free Church (see above). Just outside the village and across
the railway, WAR MEMORIAL by *Mills & Shepherd*, c.1920:
a small tower, its top copied from the Parish Church's belfry.

MOTTE

LEUCHARS CASTLE, 0.5km. N. Large oval motte hill, probably
mid-C12, perhaps erected by Nes, Lord of Leuchars, who gave
the parish church to St Andrews priory. In the later C14 the
lands and castle of Leuchars were granted to the Ramsays of
Colluthie, from whom they passed in the C16 to the Carnegies
of Kinnaird. A late medieval tower house stood here until the
mid-C18. – To the SW, DOOCOT dated 1661. Circular, with
corbelling at the eaves for a square-plan roof. Two
stringcourses and an empty frame for a heraldic panel above
the door.

FARMS ETC.

CAST, 1.5km. N. Tudorish of c.1840, with triangular bay
windows.

COMERTON, 1.2km. E. Plain mid-C19 farmhouse with a harled
and pantiled steading to the E. The house was given a harled
upper floor and dormerheads, perhaps by *Robert S. Lorimer*,
c.1900. Of the same date the gabled farm buildings on the l.,
very picturesque, with half-timbering and bellcast roofs.

CRAIGIE, 2.9km. N. c.1840. Classy Elizabethan. In the centre, a
two-storey bay window projecting from the shaped gable.

KINSHALDY, 4km. NE. Steading dated 1878. Tudor but dressed
up with huge blind gunloops. Incongruously Italianate brick
tower on the E.

PITLETHIE, 0.7km. N. Early C19 farmhouse with a Roman Doric
columned doorpiece. In the E gable, a C17 stone with the royal
arms, from an earlier house on the site. – Largish contemporary
steading, much altered.

EARLSHALL. *See* p. 199.

EARLSHALL. *See* p. 199.

3000　　　　　　　# LEVEN

A burgh of barony since 1609; the town's expansion accompanied
the opening of a new harbour in 1880. Although the harbour
silted up and was closed in 1910, the town was established as a
mining and engineering centre. Large post-war housing estates
have been built on the W.

CHURCHES

OLD SCOONIE PARISH CHURCH, Scoonie Brae. Only a roofless ashlar-built fragment survives. It may have been the session house or vestry. Segmental-arched and keyblocked window in the s gable. In the w wall, a broad segmental-arched opening, probably an insertion of *c*.1775, when this became a burial enclosure. – To the s, GRAVESLAB of Thomas Gourlay †1641, his parents and children, carved with chunky skulls and a thin skeleton. – Nearby, rustically classical C18 HEADSTONES.

ST ANDREW, Durie Street. Originally Leven Free Church. Like an English village church. By *John Hay* of Liverpool, 1860–1, with a characteristic broach spire and Dec detail.

ST MARGARET QUEEN OF SCOTLAND (Episcopal), Victoria Road. Dec by *Matthews & Mackenzie* of Aberdeen, 1879–80. The hammerdressed rubble masonry emphasizes the disjointedness of a composition forced to include too many elements. Three-bay nave: transepts projecting from a disconcertingly low chancel; sw porch jostled by a conical-roofed steeple, seemingly placed here to group with (or challenge?) the Parish Church steeple.

The interior works much better. Wagon roofs over nave and chancel, the broad chancel arch softening the change in height. Stencilled DECORATION (*fleurs de lis* and crowns) in the chancel. – Marble ALTARPIECE of 1900 with an alabaster high relief of Christ as the Good Shepherd. – Bronze eagle LECTERN. – STAINED GLASS. E window (the Crucifixion), of 1900, effective use of very lightly decorated glass in the upper parts. – On the s of the nave, two pictorial windows (The Adoration of the Magi; Christ among the Doctors in the Temple) of *c*.1908. – More expressionist but brittler is a third (Baptism, Fasting and Temptation) by *Margaret Chilton*, 1948. – On the N side, another example (SS Brendan and Bride) of Scots expressionism, of *c*.1950. – Weak window (Christ as the Good Shepherd, and the Good Samaritan) of *c*.1930. – The w window on this side ('Let the Little Ones Come to Me') a sentimental product of the *G. Maile Studios*, *c*.1950.

ST PETER (R.C.), Durie Street. Originally United Presbyterian. Bare Gothic by *Robert Baldie* of Glasgow, 1870–1. Gable front with an octagonal-spired steeple on the r. Late Gothic detail on the HALL to the l., by *A. D. Haxton*, 1925.

SCOONIE CHURCH, Durie Street and Victoria Road. 1901–4, by *P. MacGregor Chalmers*, a disappointing example of his chaste Romanesque. The mistake may have been to keep bits of both the fabric and planning of the previous church on the site. That church had begun as a broad rectangle with a w steeple, built by *William Robertson* of Sawmill in 1775. In 1822 *Robert Balfour* made it T-plan by adding a N aisle opposite the pulpit, and in 1883–4 an organ chamber was built in the middle of the s wall behind the pulpit. Of this building Chalmers retained the steeple, the organ chamber and much of the s wall. He also provided a deep N gallery, although he put the communion table, pulpit and font at the E end.

The church now has a nave flanked by shorter independently roofed aisles. Session house clamped across the E end. N aisle with two tiers of windows. Low transeptal stairtower in the NW corner. In the SW corner is the steeple of 1775, its octagonal spire very similar to that of St Cuthbert's, Edinburgh; the clock-face pushing up into the belfry is presumably of 1901–4, when the tower was refaced with smooth stugged and squared rubble in keeping with most of the new work. The refronting of the S aisle's main wall (the S wall of the 1775 church) and organ chamber with hammerdressed rubble is an aggressive contrast. The tall round-headed windows of this aisle are presumably Georgian survivors, although the thin Romanesque tracery of the inner two is clearly by Chalmers.

The plastered interior, with tall arcades and braced roofs, is impressively simple, but the conflict of focus between the E chancel and S organ chamber is not resolved. The FUR-NISHINGS of 1904 continue the theme of simplicity. So does the chancel's oak PANELLING of 1924. – STAINED GLASS. E window (Christ in Majesty and SS Peter and Paul) by *Percy Bacon & Bros.*, 1904. – The N aisle's six E windows (the Evangelists and SS Dorcas and James) are by *Cottier & Co.*, c.1910. – To their W, The Light of the World, 1906, and 'Behold I Send You Forth', 1934. – In the N aisle, Wallace window (a knight) of 1930. – War Memorial window (Christ receiving a soldier into Paradise) by *J. Henry Dearle* of *Morris & Co.*, 1925, a slackly composed rehash of that firm's earlier work. – ORGAN by *August Gern*, c.1884.

Over-assertive HALLS of 1931, by *A. C. Dewar*, to the W.

WHITE MEMORIAL CHURCH (Baptist), off Church Road. By *A. C. Dewar*, 1914. A very red church, with its gable front of Dumfries-shire sandstone, the buttressed sides of glazed brick. Single-storey porch wrapped across the gable under a simplified Perp window.

PUBLIC BUILDINGS

GREIG INSTITUTE, Forth Street. By *Andrew Heiton* of Perth, 1872–4. A library in the garb of a large harled villa decorated with Ruskinian Gothic detail.

LEVEN PUBLIC SCHOOL (now Glenrothes and Buckhaven Technical College Annexe), Mitchell Street. Dated 1881. Unfriendly, in hammerdressed rubble. Extensive rear additions of 1892–3 (by *J. W. Hislop*) and 1910–11 (by *Haxton & Walker*).

DURIE HOUSE. *See* p.199.

LIMEKILNS

A straggling coastal village with two C18 harbours.

PARISH CHURCH, Church Street. Built as a United Associate 23
chapel in 1825–6. Temple-fronted E gable, its overall pediment
carried on giant anta pilasters; consoled pediments over the
ground-floor windows. Bellcote on the W gable added by *Hippolyte J. Blanc*, 1911. Inside, a spacious galleried interior with
a large ceiling rose. The focus is the Jacobean Renaissance
PULPIT made by *Mitchell & Kinghorn* from *Ernest George &
Peto*'s design, 1883. It is flanked by contemporary STAINED-
GLASS windows (The Three Maries at the Tomb; *Noli Me
Tangere*) by *Lavers, Barraud & Westlake*.

PRIMARY SCHOOL, Dunfermline Road. 1911–12, by *T. Hyslop
Ure & Beveridge*. Single-storey, blocky free Jacobean, with a
couple of broad gables and corner towers.

DESCRIPTION

BRUCEHAVEN HARBOUR on the E of the village was built by
Forbes of Pittencrieff, *c.*1728, probably the date of its curving
L-plan pier. Above, at the end of BRUCEHAVEN ROAD, the
harled and crowstepped FORTH CRUISING CLUB, early C18,
with a cavetto cornice.

In CHURCH STREET, the piend-roofed MANSE of 1841 and the
Parish Church (*see* above). House on the corner of SAN-
DILANDS and LOWER WELLHEADS, dated 1722 but altered;
scrolled skewputts and a Venetian window in the gable. In
THE OLD ORCHARD behind Church Lane, the harled and
crowstepped GARDEN HOUSE is perhaps late C17. On top of
the small corniced porch, a fluted frieze, its centre carved
with a human head. The gabled dormers are presumably C19
additions. In the garden behind, a lectern DOOCOT built in
1697. On the way back into Church Lane, an agreeable pantiled
house built of orangey squared rubble, *c.*1800.

MAIN STREET begins with THE BRUCE ARMS of 1899; large
stone dormerheads and a corner turret. THE TANGLES to its
W has been badly altered but looks mid-C18, with a broad
chimney gablet, lugged architraved doorpiece, and scrolled
skewputts. Behind, remains of a circular rubble tower, probably a kiln. ACADEMY SQUARE opens out informally on the
N. At its end, the KING'S BARN, an early C16 warehouse built 57
of massive rubble blocks. Forestair to the first-floor door,
whose steep pediment containing the Pitcairn arms and the
date 1581 is an insertion. (Inside, tunnel-vaults over both
floors.) Main Street ends at the C18 LIMEKILNS PIER, built of
large roughly cubed stone blocks. Only the N side of HALKETS
HALL is built on: a quite agreeable straggle of vernacular
houses, No. 13 with a marriage lintel dated 1774.

LINDORES ABBEY *see* NEWBURGH

4020

LINKS WOOD
2km. s of Newport-on-Tay

An oval fort, possibly prehistoric, in woodland on the N side of a minor road. Three well-defined earth ramparts and ditches enclosing an area *c.*90m. by 35m. Two entrances, diametrically opposed, on the NW and SE.

LINKTOWN *see* KIRKCALDY

1090

LOCHGELLY

There was a small village at Lochgelly by the late C18. Soon after 1836 a lease was granted of the mineral rights on the Lochgelly estate to a company which became the Lochgelly Iron Co. in 1851 and the Lochgelly Iron & Coal Co. in 1872, the new name denoting a change in its primary interest. Lochgelly became a burgh in 1877. Its late Victorian and Edwardian miners' dwellings have been supplemented by C20 local authority housing.

CHURCHES

MACAINSH CHURCH, Main Street. Originally Lochgelly Free Church. Innocent Tudor Gothic of 1857. The gable front's centre is slightly advanced as a porch rising into the suggestion of a tower topped by a spiky bellcote.
    Squat HALL to the W, by *William Birrell*, 1904–6.
ST ANDREW'S CHURCH, Bank Street. A plain chapel-of-ease built in 1854–5; lancets in the W gable, a bellcote on the E. It was recast and enlarged in 1915 by *P. MacGregor Chalmers*, who hid the E gable with a hall, added broad N and S aisles, and heightened the NW porch.
ST FINNIAN'S (Episcopal), Lumphinnans Road. By *Smart, Stewart & Mitchell*, 1937–8. A couthy little church, drydashed with cement dressings, but the rubbly window voussoirs are of stone. Exaggerated crowsteps; small W apse (former baptistery). Inside, a hall has been carved out of the two W bays of the nave. Its surviving half has a scissors roof. Semicircular arch into the large chancel. – STAINED GLASS. Three-light E window (Christ the High Priest) by *Margaret Chilton*, 1950; colourful but drily drawn. – In the Lady Chapel (now vestry), a single light ('*Sanctus*') of 1949, also by Chilton but much stronger.

PUBLIC BUILDINGS

LOCHGELLY HIGH SCHOOL, Station Road. By *Fife Regional Council*, 1986. Brick-built pavilions with red-tiled roofs.
MINERS' WELFARE AND WAR MEMORIAL INSTITUTE, Main Street. By *A. D. Haxton*, 1923–5. English baroque with a hint of Art Deco.

SOUTH PRIMARY SCHOOL, High Street. By *A. Scobie & Son*, 1910, with thrifty English baroque detail.

TOWN HOUSE, High Street and Hall Street. By *James T. Scobie*, 1907. Free Wrenaissance with a domed corner tower; triangular pediment on the S front, segmental pediment on the E.

WEST PRIMARY SCHOOL, School Lane off Main Street. 1901, by *William Birrell*, small and bargeboarded.

LOCHORE *see* BALLINGRY, LOCHORE AND CROSSHILL

LOGIE   4020

Settlement made up by the church, manse, school, and one farm.

PARISH CHURCH (now Elizabeth Sharp Memorial Hall). A box built in 1826. The Gothic windows in the ashlar-fronted S side are original, the others altered to match in 1893. Birdcage bellcote with a dragon weathervane on the W gable. NE vestry added in 1902.

To the E, the MANSE (now LUCKLAW HOUSE) of 1815; flat rusticated quoins and an anta-pilastered doorpiece. – L-plan OFFICES of 1828.

PARISH SCHOOL (former). Plain, of whinstone, by *John Milne*, 1858. N addition of *c.* 1930.

LOGIE HOUSE   0080
1.9km. SW of Dunfermline

Stretched-out early C19 mansion built for the Hunts. Three-storey harled centre block with stolid classical detail. Its windows' overarches are repeated on the long lower links to the end pavilions, whose ashlar fronts are prettily embellished with Adamish swags. At the back, to the garden, a full-height central bow with a smaller bow on each side. (Inside, elaborate Adamish ceiling over the stairhall.) – Contemporary STEADING to the N, the front block classical, the side ranges thinly crenellated; octagonal horsemill at the NW corner.

LORDSCAIRNIE   3010
4.3km. NW of Cupar

Ruined early C16 tower house of the Lindsays. L-plan; the rectangular NW jamb contained a turnpike stair. Rubble-built and plain except for corbelling for rounds at the S corners. The ground floor has been vaulted. In the hall above, a large S fireplace and stone window seats. More seats in the second-floor windows.

The house was joined by a barmkin wall to a NE GATEHOUSE whose ground floor survives. Bowed N front pierced by gun-loops; tunnel-vaulted interior.

To the E, two short terraces of FARM COTTAGES OF *c*. 1840, with bracketed canopies over the doors.

LOWER LARGO AND LUNDIN LINKS

4000

Lower Largo is a fishing village made a burgh of barony in 1513. It now runs into the golfers' villadom of Lundin Links.

BAPTIST CHURCH, Main Street. Small rendered box of 1868; lancet windows to show it is a church.

LARGO ST DAVID'S PARISH CHURCH, Main Street. Built for the United Presbyterians in 1871–2. Grim lancet style, with a truncated bellcote on the gable.

HARBOUR. Rubble pier of *c*. 1770, extended in the early C19. Remains of a W pier with a pantiled GRANARY (now a house) above it.

SCHOOL, Durham Wynd. Disused. Mid-C19, of whinstone. L-plan with a bellcote on the S gable.

DESCRIPTION

The CRUSOE HOTEL's mid-C19 harled lump sits beside the harbour. More agreeable are the late C18 RAILWAY INN opposite and a group of pantiled houses of *c*. 1800, one with a forestair, squashed under the four-arch RAILWAY VIADUCT of 1856–7. N of the viaduct resolutely vernacular housing of 1984; the inauthenticity of every detail is presumably delib-erate.

MAIN STREET is generally disappointing. On the r., the pantiled OLD BAPTIST MEETING HOUSE of 1789–90, small, with windows only in the S wall. After the churches (*see* above), a number of pantiled late C18 and early C19 cottages, harled or rendered. More substantial in whinstone is the late C19 block (Nos. 99–101) on the site of Alexander Selkirk's birthplace; in a first-floor niche, STATUE of Robinson Crusoe by *T. Stuart Burnett*, 1885. At the E end, CARDY HOUSE, a solid villa of 1871 with a conservatory, overlooking the CARDY WORKS of 1885, whose polychrome brick E range survives.

DRUMMOCHY ROAD W of the harbour leads to Lundin Links, a late C19 golfing settlement. Its centre is the large LUNDIN HOTEL, by *Peter L. Henderson*, 1900, on the corner of EMSDORF STREET and STATION ROAD; red brick and harl, with jerkin-headed gables. The spiritual heart of the place is the red-tiled LUNDIN GOLF CLUB off Station Road, 1896, again by *Henderson*.

On the golf course, three massive STANDING STONES; one to the

N of the site, 5.5m. high and 2.8m. girth at the base, and a close-set pair to the S, the SE stone 4.1m. high and 3.8m. girth, the SW stone (now leaning) at least 4.6m. tall. Several cists were discovered in excavation nearby.

LUNDIN TOWER. *See* below.

LUMPHINNANS *see* COWDENBEATH

LUNDIN LINKS *see* LOWER LARGO AND LUNDIN LINKS

LUNDIN TOWER   *3000*
1.2km. W of Lundin Links

Lundin House was demolished in 1876 except for this rubble-built stairtower. The lower storeys are probably C16; late C18 Gothick top with crenellated circular turrets. Attached to its S face, a Georgian Gothick single-storey outbuilding with ogee-arched openings.

To the E, late C18 crowstep-gabled DOOCOT, perhaps originally a laundry and converted to house birds in the late C19. Gothic windows, Y-traceried at the gables.

LUSCAR HOUSE   *0080*
1.1km. NE of Carnock

Long two-storey Victorian country house. The fat L-plan W part is by *David Bryce*, built in 1838 for Adam Rolland of Gask. Gabled and gableted Elizabethan in the Burn manner, with broad bay windows and diagonally set chimneys. The shouldered arched NW porch (now a room) and asymmetrical composition hint at Bryce's later Baronial style. In 1890–1 *R. Rowand Anderson* doubled the house's length to the E, repeating Bryce's polished ashlar but not his detail. Boldly projecting two-storey canted bay window in the crowstep-gabled end; scrolled foliage on the sides of the pedimented dormerheads. The house is now (1988) an old people's home, with a big fire escape across the E front and a much altered interior.

MAIDEN CASTLE   *2000*
2.5km. W of Falkland

A curious, well-preserved earthwork of unknown date on the summit of a low hillock in rough ground half-way between the E and W Lomonds. The most conspicuous defence is a single

broad ditch with external bank dug round the base of the
hillock, but faint terracing higher up the slope may show
the course of other lines since destroyed or perhaps never
completed. The summit area is *c.*140m. by 35m., and there
seem to have been entrances on the E and W.

MARKINCH

2000

A small town which was made a burgh of barony in 1673 and a
police burgh in 1892. It now struggles to preserve its independence from the spread of Glenrothes New Town.

CHURCHES

FREE CHURCH, High Street. Disused. Carpenter's Perp of 1843–
4. Gable front divided by buttresses into a 'nave' and 'aisles',
the parapet breaking into crenellation over the 'nave'. Spired
and gableted bellcote.

PARISH CHURCH, Kirk Brae. Standing on top of a hill in the
middle of the town. Large Georgian box attached to a Romanesque W tower.

The tall tower is of *c.*1200, built of cubical ashlar, the four
stages marked by stringcourses. In the top stage, two-light
belfry openings, their central and angle shafts all with cushion
capitals. The corbelled parapet and octagonal spire are by
James Barclay, 1807, replacing a 'pyramidal' spire which was
demolished as unsafe. Barclay's spire has the general appearance of that of St Cuthbert's Church, Edinburgh, but the sides
are delicately panelled with blind ovals.

The church itself was rebuilt in 1786, probably by *Thomas
Barclay*, who was working on the manse at that time. Big
rubble rectangle with a (now damaged) vase on the E gable. In
the gables, Diocletian gallery windows. In the S wall, round-
arched windows flanking the pulpit; above it a bullseye. Semi-
octagonal-fronted session house at the E, by *Robert Hutchison*,
1839. The N aisle was added by *James Barclay* in 1806; in 1884–
5 *James Gillespie* thickened it with sub-Romanesque lean-to
stairtowers.

Inside the N aisle, a stone vault, probably of 1884–5. In the
church, gallery round three sides carried on sturdy Roman
Doric columns (replacements of 1807, by *Alexander Leslie*);
simply panelled deep fronts. Ceiling enriched with little fans
at the corners. In the centre of the S wall, PULPIT, probably
part of *James Gillespie*'s alterations of 1884–5, but perhaps of
1913, when *James Gillespie & Scott* erected the ORGAN behind
it.

MONUMENTS. On the N wall, a large late C17 stone panel
carved with the arms of Alexander, second Earl of Leven, and
his wife. – On the W wall, smart neoclassical marble tablet to
the Rev. John Pinkerton † 1784, of whom the inscription relates
that:

after having spent a very chearfull evening at *Balfour House* with M^{R.}
BETHUNE and his *Family*, he was found in the morning in his bed
room sitting in a Chair by the Fire place with one stocking in his hand
Quite Dead.

STAINED GLASS. In the S wall, one light ('Suffer Little Children to Come Unto Me') of 1921. – In the N aisle's porch, a
window (The Sower) by *John Blyth*, 1985.
    CHURCHYARD. At the NW gate, crowstepped SESSION
HOUSE by *R. Rowand Anderson*, 1879. Below a window in its
W gable, a foliaged capital, probably C13; above the window,
a late medieval gableted niche canopy. – In the S of the graveyard, a couple of early C18 HEADSTONES carved with the
familiar emblems of death. In the NW corner, an old-fashioned
aedicular stone to Ann Campbell †1791, its front carved with
an anchor. – Good number of stones with elegant early C19
lettering.
UNITED PRESBYTERIAN CHURCH, Balbirnie Street. Disused.
By *Hippolyte J. Blanc*, 1896–8. A large hall, the roof swept
down over the W aisle built between a transept and porch.
Squat *flèche*. In the buttressed N front, a six-light Flamboyant
traceried window.

PUBLIC BUILDINGS

CEMETERY, Northhall Road. Opened 1853. On the hill in the
middle, MONUMENT to Lieutenant-Colonel Robert Balfour of
Balbirnie, by *Sydney Mitchell*, 1884. It is a copy of the Kildalton Cross, the missing details taken from Celtic manuscripts
and other crosses, the four central panels showing the Ascension. *Alexander Rhind* was the sculptor.
HEALTH CENTRE, Betson Street and Balgonie Place. Dated
1915. Single-storey and harled. On the corner, a grand stone
doorway, Wrenaissance thinking of going Art Deco.
MARKINCH CENTRE, Betson Street and George Street. Originally the Municipal Buildings. By *James Gillespie & Scott*,
1897–9. Chunky Scots Renaissance on a small scale.
PRIMARY SCHOOL, Betson Street. Lightweight Scandinavian
modern, by *Fife County Council*, 1949. Classrooms behind by
George Sandilands, 1929.
RAILWAY STATION, High Street. By *Thomas Grainger*, 1846–
7. Gentle Italianate broad-eaved offices on the N side. The
platforms below are joined by the contemporary road bridge
across the cutting.
TOWN HALL, Betson Street. Rendered hall built in 1857. The
stone porch and free Scots Renaissance tower were added in
1887.
WAR MEMORIAL, Balbirnie Street. By *Robert S. Lorimer*,
executed by *William Davidson*, 1920. Elongated shaft with a
small cross on top. On the shaft's front and back, figures of St
George and St Drostan.

DESCRIPTION

BETSON STREET contains most of the public buildings (*see* above) but fails to give a sense of civil importance. On the l., POST OFFICE, Scots Jacobean with an Arts and Craft flavour but no excitement, by *J. M. Scott*, 1906.

COMMERCIAL STREET continues N. On the r., RADNOR HOUSE (No. 30), very superior late Georgian. In the pedimented centre, a Roman Doric columned doorpiece; above, Venetian window with fluted Doric columns. Opposite, a plain early C19 terrace (Nos. 2–10 CROFT ROAD), its ground floor rusticated. A few more early C19 buildings. Nos. 27–29 Commercial Street with scrolled skewputts; No. 43, single-storey and pantiled. The GALLOWAY HOTEL in KIRK STREET closes the view; scrolled skewputts and a pilastered doorpiece.

SCHOOL STREET is plain late Georgian. Set back on its N side, the long single-storey Nos. 11–11A were begun as the PARISH SCHOOL by *Niel Ballingal*, 1800–1, and extended in 1825 and 1835 by *Robert Hutchison*. (Diversion along NORTHALL ROAD to the NE. No. 19, a mid-C19 ashlar-fronted cottage with a Greek key frieze under the eaves.) In MANSE ROAD to the S, the rendered MANSEFIELD, built as the PARISH MANSE in 1655, was reconstructed by *Thomas Barclay*, 1785–6. Its successor is in KIRK WYND, Scots Jacobean by *James Gillespie & Scott*, 1901–2.

MIDDLE MILL, 1.6km. S. Early C19 group. Long range of pantiled cottages and barns. To their S, the three-storey mill, now gutted and without its wheel.

RAILWAY VIADUCT, 1.6km. S. By *Thomas Grainger*, 1847. Masonry viaduct of ten segmental arches.

6090   MAY, ISLE OF

Bare island in the Firth of Forth, the home of monks in the Middle Ages, of lighthouse-keepers since the C17.

ST ADRIAN'S CHAPEL. Rubbly ruin of a building of the Cluniac priory founded by David I *c.*1145. Simple rectangle, with a couple of lancet windows near the W wall's N end and a third in the N gable. A C13 date seems likely, that it was a chapel less so. The island was granted to Patrick Learmonth of Dairsie in 1550, and it was probably he who added a round tower at the SW corner and a two-storey vaulted addition at the N.

LIGHTHOUSES. Building of a BEACON lighthouse on the Isle of May was entrusted to James Maxwell of Innerwick, Alexander Cunningham of Barnes and his son John, the feuar of the island, in 1636. This was a square, rubble-built tower supporting a brazier. Now lopped to half its original 12m. height, it was given a crenellated parapet in 1886. Moulded panel space over the door now framing part of a pediment carved with the sun in glory and the date 1636, and two bits of a heraldic water spout; these may have come from the tower's demolished upper part. Inside, a vaulted ground-floor room, its corniced chimneypiece's frieze carved with a cartouche bearing the Cunningham arms and flanked by the initials A C. – To the W, LIGHTHOUSE of 1815–16, by *Robert Stevenson*. Toy fort with Gothic windows in the tower, the domed lantern rising inside the corbelled battlement. – To the S, plain block of KEEPERS' HOUSE AND MACHINERY BUILDINGS built in 1885. – To the NE, the LOW LIGHT of 1844, a round tower with a corbelled parapet and domed lantern; keepers' cottages beside it.

MELVILLE HOUSE
2010

1.4km. E of Collessie

A showhouse built for George, first Earl of Melville and President 66 of the Privy Council, in 1697–1703. *James Smith* was the mason and seems to have been responsible for the design*; *Kenneth McKenzie* was the wright, *John Carnaby* the plumber, *James Hutchison* and *James Innes* the slaters, *Robert Bannatyne* the glazier, and *Thomas Alborn*, *John Melville* and *John Christie* the plasterers.

The original drive ran along a beech avenue on the main axis from the S, and the best approach is still from this direction. At the entrance to a large forecourt, square-plan ogee-roofed pavilions, their weathervanes dated 1697. Between them, gatepiers of diamond-faced ashlar, with C19 vase finials. Sadly, the courtyard's sense of enclosure has been lowered along with its screen walls. At the end of each side, a piend-roofed harled office block (the E for the brewhouse, coachhouse and stable, the W for the dairy and laundry) linked by niched screen walls topped by stone balls and swagged urns to the tall H-plan main block. Its S front is austere, the present cement render an unappealing substitute for the earlier harling. Three-storey and basement; recessed five-bay centre between two-bay piended ends. Ogee-roofed cupola in the centre of the piended pavilion roof. Stringcourses at each floor; rusticated quoins at the corners. All except the basement windows have lugged architraves. So does the door (now a window), Smith's intended segmental pediment apparently not executed‡; its wrought-iron balustraded perron looks a mid-C18 replacement.

The main block's N (present entrance) front is a repeat of

---

* *James Smith* and *Sir William Bruce* produced rival designs (Bruce's actually drawn by *Alexander Edward*) in 1697. The contract elevations are in Smith's hand, and Colen Campbell in *Vitruvius Britannicus* (1717) ascribed the design to Smith. The earliest attribution of the executed design to Bruce is by Thomas Pennant in 1772.

‡ It is shown in the contract elevation and (rather differently) in *Vitruvius Britannicus*, but does not seem to be mentioned in the building accounts for the house.

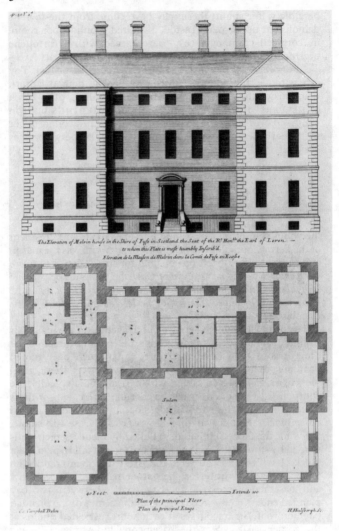

Melville House,
elevation and plan of first floor illustrated in
Colen Campbell, *Vitruvius Britannicus*, ii (1717)

the s but with plain margins at the second-floor windows.
Heavy early C19 pedimented porch put up when the entrance
was moved to this side. On the side elevations, projecting two-
bay centres; bullseyes in the tympana of their pediments which
have Smith's characteristic detail of the corona running
beyond the sloping cymatium. Ground- and first-floor
windows again with lugged architraves. Some small bathroom
windows have been inserted to fit the house for its present
function as a school.

The INTERIOR's first and second floors were planned with the public rooms grouped in the double-pile centre. On each side was an apartment of drawing room, bedchamber, dressing room and closet, the rooms overlooking one of the gardens which were laid out each side. The entrance hall of 1697–1703 was enlarged in the C19 to take in the adjoining parlour, this new room becoming a library. It has been again divided, but the C19 bookcases and routine Jacobean ceiling survive. The ground-floor W drawing room was recast in the mid-C19 in plain Georgian survival fashion. In the E drawing room, original panelling, the fireplace framed by swagged Ionic pilasters, perhaps made by *Thomas Kyle**; lugged and corniced doorpiece. The E wall's sideboard recess was presumably formed in the C19 when this became the dining room. Stairhall behind the entrance hall, with a black and white marble floor. The oak stair itself, with an awkwardly lozenged balustrade, is a C19 replacement. It leads to the first-floor ante-room: partly oak-panelled, the empty spaces formerly filled with stamped leather panels. More Ionic pilasters at the off-centre chimneypiece. Immense oak-panelled saloon occupying the whole centre of the S front. Simple lugged architraves at the doors; rosettes on the bracketed cornice's soffit. White and grey veined marble chimneypiece, its overmantel set between swags carved by *William Morgan*, the whole framed by Corinthian pilasters (again perhaps by *Kyle*). The mantelshelf with Jacobean-type carving and the date 1702 is a C19 insertion. The state apartment on the W begins with the drawing room, its walls part oak-panelled, part intended for tapestries. Corinthian pilasters at the fireplace. Marble chimneypiece under a foliaged bolection mantelshelf; overmantel surrounded by carved swags and jolly cherubs supporting the Earl's coroneted monogram (the carving all by *Morgan*). The state bedroom beyond is not quite as rich and misses its intended focus, the state bed covered in crimson velvet. Swagged Ionic pilasters at the black and yellow marble chimneypiece. E of the saloon is the other first-floor apartment, its drawing room (Wainscot Room) a plainer pine-panelled version of the state drawing room. The bedroom has been subdivided. More original panelling on the second floor, the SW room having Corinthian pilasters at the fireplace and pedimented doorpieces. Service stairs from top to bottom of the house at the NE and NW, their stone newels with moulded caps and bases. Tunnel-vaulted basement kitchen (sub-divided) at the NE.

Immediately E of the house, plain late Georgian STABLES (now converted to classrooms and a games hall). – NORTH LODGE at the top of the drive, early C19 Tudor with hood-moulds and lattice glazing.

METHIL *see* BUCKHAVEN AND METHIL

---

* Kyle was paid in 1701 for providing Ionic and Corinthian capitals to the Earl of Melville.

METHILHILL see BUCKHAVEN AND METHIL

MILTON OF BALGONIE

The village grew up round the flax-spinning mill founded in 1807 and enlarged thirty years later. It closed in 1886.

PARISH CHURCH, Main Street. Built as a T-plan chapel-of-ease, 1835–6. Tall, with Tudor-arched windows; rather small crowsteps on the gables. Spired bellcote.

PRIMARY SCHOOL, Main Street. Harled front block of 1902; the back part was begun as a subscription school in 1823 and reconstructed in 1876.

DESCRIPTION. Predominantly C19 vernacular cottages, many pantiled, some with club skews. Group at the w end of MAIN STREET with bows to front and back. The late Georgian MILTON HOUSE (Main Street) is grander: two storeys with a pedimented centre.

BALGONIE CASTLE. See p. 88.

MONIMAIL

Just a handful of buildings at the main entrance to Melville House.

PARISH CHURCH. Straightforward T-plan kirk built of whinstone by the mason-architect *Thomas Falconer*,* 1794–7. A few touches of sophistication, e.g. the long s wall's Venetian window (its centre light blind, because of the pulpit inside), ogee Gothick glazing, and belted ball finials on the gables. The E tower was finished in 1811 by *Robert Hutchison*, with advice from *James Gillespie Graham*. Apparently it was a reconstruction of Falconer's tower; perhaps that is why it seems too slim for its pinnacled angle buttresses and corbelled parapet. 'Saxon' openings in the s face.

Inside, semi-octagonal gallery on pot-bellied Tuscan columns. – PULPIT, probably by *John Bell*, with a pilastered back; it has lost its sounding board. – STAINED GLASS. Two lights (The Sower; St Andrew) of 1950, by *William Wilson*, drily expressionist.

CHURCHYARD, 0.3km. w of the Parish Church. In the centre, remains of the OLD PARISH CHURCH. The chancel is reduced to low rubble walls. In the N wall, a round-arched tomb recess; beside it, a sacrament house with an ogee-arched aumbry under two shields, the r. carved with the royal arms and surmounted by a crown. These look C15. The early C17 N (Melville) aisle is intact, its harled s gable presumably built up when the church was abandoned in 1797. Built into it, the coroneted monogram of George, Earl of Melville, of c.1700.

---

* *John Bell* was the wright.

The other walls are of ashlar. Moulded eaves courses on W and
E. In the W wall, broad door flanked by two (blocked) windows,
all moulded. In the E wall, a blocked double window (moulded
again), the r. light containing a fragmentary panel (not *in
situ*) carved with the arms of Bethune of Balfour. (Inside, the
RCAHMS reported a graveslab of David Melville, dated 1594.) –
Near the churchyard's E wall, curly pedimented headstone to
Margaret Lees, dated 1743, with cherub heads on the ends.

MONIMAIL TOWER, 0.4km. W of the Parish Church. A classy
fragment of the palace of the Archbishops of St Andrews which
was acquired by Sir James Balfour of Pittendreich in 1564.
The palace was probably quadrangular, its W and N ranges
apparently of three storeys. The surviving NW corner tower is
a storey higher, rubble-built, with stringcourses across the N
and W fronts, breaking up over the second-floor window on
the W and forming a sill to the N front's empty armorial
panel-frame. Uncrenellated parapet on continuous corbelling,
swelling into corner rounds and a large octagonal NE cap-
house, its lucarned stone spire now truncated. On two faces of
the cap-house, roundels carved with heads in relief. In a
roundel on the parapet's E front, Sir James Balfour's initials
and the date 1578 (probably the date of this tower); on the W
front, a coat of arms. Cannon spouts at the rounds; small
inverted keyhole gunloops in the straight sides.

Inside, the semi-basement was converted to an icehouse,
probably in the C18, with a hatch in the kitchen fireplace flue.
On the top floor, early C18 panelling.

MOONZIE   3010

Just the church, manse, school and a stolid Victorian farm in the
centre of a small upland parish.

PARISH CHURCH. Low crowstepped rectangle in a windy hilltop
graveyard. Birdcage bellcote on the W gable, ball finial on the
E. An intake on the E gable suggests that there may be medieval
masonry under the harling, but the rest is probably of *c.*1625,
when the parish was disjoined from Cupar. Moulded frame for
an armorial panel in the S wall, probably C17; the rectangular
windows are Georgian, perhaps dating from the repairs of
1821. SW porch of 1906. (Interior given an open timber roof by
William Little & Son, 1881. – STAINED GLASS. One window of
1889.)

MANSE (now MOONZIE HOUSE). T-plan, the crossbar built in
1804, the downstroke protruding from the front added by
William Ramsay and *John Brunton** in 1848. Horizontal
glazing in the extension. – L-plan office court of 1806 on the
E.

FORMER SCHOOL. Schoolhouse of 1804, its upper floor added

---

* They were paid 'for the plans and specifications'; *Robert* and *George Just* were
the contractors.

by *John Inglis* in 1853–4. Single-storey schoolroom on the w designed by the schoolmaster *Robert Morrison*, 1856.

COLLUTHIE, 1.6km. N. Agreeable hotch-potch. The house's plain Georgian s front is of 1823, with an anta-pilastered doorpiece. w addition of *c.*1850; on its l., a single-storey outbuilding with a carved head skewputt. Pantiled E wing. The house was turned round in 1883, when *James Maclaren & Son* added a new block on the N: angular Baronial with a French spired tower slicing across the r. gable. On the s, steading of *c.*1800, mostly pantiled; horsemill in the centre.

MOSSMORRAN

1090

3.1km. SE of Cowdenbeath

PETROCHEMICAL WORKS. Built in 1981–4. Large and functional but not without elegance. *Morris & Steedman* were the architects.

MOUNTQUHANIE

3020

4.1km. W of Kilmany

Long spread of a house built for David Gillespie of Mountquhanie *c.*1820. Two-storey and basement main block with a fluted parapet and Roman Doric portico. Monogrammed stone recording a charter of the lands granted in 1353. Single-storey and basement wings with pedimented centres. The side and rear elevations were utilitarian even before recent alterations. Bow-ended projection at the r. of the main block's backside.

Grand entrance hall with a screen of scagliola Ionic columns to the imperial stair. On the l., library with a black marble console-corniced chimneypiece and contemporary bookcases. The chimneypiece in the bow-ended dining room behind is an Edwardian replacement. The drawing room in the W wing has been subdivided as a flat. The main floor's E side contained the principal bed and dressing rooms, with a schoolroom (perhaps originally billiard room) in the wing.

STABLES to the N. Front block dated 1811; the pediments over its centre and ends were removed in 1947. Back range dated 1774. Lower crowstepped DOOCOT at its E end. This range incorporates a gateway dated 1683, the entrance to the barmkin enclosure of MOUNTQUHANIE CASTLE to the S. The roofless C16 tower survives. Simple three-storey rectangle; it had corner turrets and a corbelled parapet. Vaulted ground floor inside. No sign of a stair, so presumably it was on the fragmentary N side. An L-plan W extension was added in the C17. Its two-storey jamb still stands as a separate house. Conical-roofed SW tower incorporating a doocot.

WALLED GARDEN to the E, probably early C19.

MUGDRUM

2010

0.8km. w of Newburgh

Informal harled house of early C18 origin, much reconstructed
*c.*1790 and again *c.*1840.

CROSS 350m. to the SW, worn, but with panels of ornament still
visible on the front, including a horseman, another with a
spear, and two horsemen with hounds chasing stags. Two
panels of key pattern and scrollwork on one side. At its foot,
another cross fragment, formerly the lintel of a well at Carpow
and carved with animals including a stag, intertwined beasts
and interlaced ornament.

THE MURREL

1080

1.4km. N of Aberdour

Arts and Crafts villa designed in 1908 by *F. W. Deas* for himself.
He was a bachelor, and the house was intended to be staffed
only by a married couple. Main block at the SW. Attached to
the kitchen at its NE corner, a broad V of outbuildings ending
with a squash court and garage at the SE. The V's open mouth
to the S is closed by a screen wall, allowing the servants to use
the courtyard without disturbing their master's enjoyment of
the open views from his terraced main garden. All this is built
of orangey rubble, the curvaceously swept roofs covered with
red pantiles. The appearance is cottagey, the restlessness of the
main house's V-plan entrance front calmed by the projecting
sweep of the service range. On the garden fronts to W and S,
big bay windows for the original sitting room and dining room.
The open loggia beside the dining room (designed as a place
to breakfast in summer) has been built up. Inside, beautifully
executed but simple oak panelling. A small-scale Lorimerian
flourish at the plasterwork of the staircase ceiling.

MYRES CASTLE

2010

0.8km. s of Auchtermuchty

Unpretentious harled house which developed from a C16 laird's
house into a small C19 mansion. The earliest part is at the SE,
a tower house probably built *c.*1540 for John Scrymgeour, the
King's macer and James V's Master of Works at Holyroodhouse and Falkland Palace. This house was of two storeys,
probably with an attic; Z-plan, the jamb lying NW of the main
block. Round tower with two tiers of gunloops (rectangles
above ovals) at the SE corner; another at the jamb's NW corner;
stairtower (the door at its base) in the NE inner angle. Garderobe turret projecting from above the ground floor at the
NE. There were towers at the other corners.

The estate was bought by Stephen Paterson, notary public
and sheriff clerk of Fife, in 1611. Five years later he heightened

the main block to three storeys and corbelled out a rectangular two-storey addition, its top floor slightly jettied, on top of the SE tower. This new top to the tower is distinctly smart, its grey ashlar contrasting with the ochre harling of the rest. Deep corbelled parapet decorated with garlands containing shields, the initials and monogram of John Paterson and his wife Elizabeth Mure, and the date 1616. Conical-roofed cap-house in the SW corner.

In 1634 Myres was sold to the Covenanting general John Leslie, whose descendant Colonel George Moncrieff added a plain N wing in the mid-C18 and perhaps made the present front door in the C16 jamb's S face. Professor John Bruce bought the estate (together with Falkland Palace) in 1820 and in 1825 employed the architect-contractor *John Swinton* to build a straightforward W extension. Probably at the same time a bay window was added to the dining room in the C18 N wing, and a coachhouse and stable were built to its E. In 1873 *James C. Walker* made extensive repairs, added a pepperpot turret to the 1825 addition's SW corner, heightened the dining-room bay window by a further storey under a spired roof, and made a short extension to the N wing. Of the same date is the carved coat of arms of the then owner, Colonel Walter Hamilton Bruce, on the S front. James Fairlie, a Roman Catholic convert and papal Chamberlain, bought the house and parkland in 1887 and in 1888–90 employed *Henry W. Walker* to convert the coachhouse into a chapel, with a sharply angled external stair, and to extend the SW turret of 1873 downwards as a small tower, on which he placed panels carved by *John McFarlane* with a mace* and the Fairlie arms.

The interior is mostly plain work of 1825, with touches of 1873, but two tunnel-vaulted ground-floor rooms survive in the C16 house's main block. Drawing room in the W addition, its simple Jacobean ceiling probably of 1873; the patterned parquet floor was imported from a demolished house in Madeira, *c.*1970. The chapel of 1890 was provided with top lighting in case the house should be sold or let to a Protestant requiring a billiard room. It is now a store. The N sanctuary was blocked off *c.*1965, when the adjacent stable block was converted to a flat, but its gilded *putti*-studded frieze has been repositioned on the new wall. W family gallery with a panelled front. Much of the original wallpaper by *Morris & Co.* survives.

WALLED GARDEN immediately W of the house, its layout of *c.*1890 based on a part of the Vatican Gardens.

NAUGHTON
1.6km. E of Balmerino

A crisply harled piend-roofed house built for James Morison in 1793. In the S front's centre, a balustraded bow containing the pilastered front door, reached by an imperial stair. Rear wings

---

* In the mistaken belief that he had acquired the macership with the house.

were added *c.*1890, the w heightened *c.*1900, when an ogee-roofed tower was placed between them and a small Baronial turret built on the E.

Entrance hall ceiling with shallow-relief husk enrichment (a hollow-sided rectangle containing a circle and rose). In the round stairhall beyond, another enriched ceiling (a circle of swagged husks round a polygon). SE dining room with a cornice of erect acanthus leaves. The late C18 pine and composition chimneypiece decorated with billing doves was imported from a bedroom of the demolished Tarvit House, *c.*1963. In the sw drawing room, the same cornice, but the Jacobean compartmented ceiling and white marble chimneypiece are of *c.*1845, when the w window was enlarged. In the first-floor bedrooms, some late C18 pine and composition chimneypieces.

The back drive behind the house passes under a cast-iron FOOTBRIDGE (by the *Durie Foundry*, 1818) to a Gothick LAUNDRY of *c.*1830 and conical-roofed GAME LARDER of *c.*1870. – The footbridge carries a path up to a garden made in the remains of NAUGHTON CASTLE, whose big SE tower, probably built by the Crichtons of Naughton in the C16, was demolished *c.*1790. On the N, remains of the walls of a roughly rectangular house, perhaps added by Peter Hay of Durie after his purchase of the estate in 1621. Now built into the E gable is a tablet describing his work:

PETRVS.HAY.FILIVS.GEO/RGI.HAY/.HOC.ÆDIFICIVM.EXSTRV/
XIT.1625/DOMINE.FILII.SERVORVM/TVORVM./INHABITEBVNT

At the NW corner, remains of a round tower. – Outside the buildings on the S, a DRAW WELL. – At the W, an early C19 GARDEN HOUSE, its gablets made up of late medieval traceried window heads, possibly from Balmerino Abbey. – Some way further w, a rectangular crowstep-gabled double DOOCOT, presumably built for James Morison in 1750. His initials and that date are carved on the r. door's lintel; on the l. door lintel, worn remains of initials and the date 1636.

WALLED GARDEN E of the house, dated 1900. Coats of arms on the iron gates. – Beside the tennis court, a pretty mid-C19 GARDEN HOUSE, harled and thatched, with a treetrunk verandah.

At the main drive's S end, quatrefoil-plan GATEPIERS of *c.*1830. – Contemporary LODGE with a semi-octagonal Roman Doric porch, rebuilt on the opposite side of the road *c.*1900.

NETHERTOWN *see* DUNFERMLINE

NEWARK CASTLE
0.8km. sw of St Monans

5000

Battered fragments on a promontory jutting into the Forth. The castle's earliest part, perhaps C15, was at the S: remains of three vaulted cellars and part of the E wall. Probably in the late C16, the house was extended N, the addition ending with a large round NE tower with wide splayed gunloops. At the same time, walls were built or rebuilt to enclose a courtyard on the W. In 1649 the castle was bought by General Sir David Leslie, who was made Lord Newark in 1661, a plausible date for the remodelling of the C16 addition's main block as a smart house with shaped chimney gables (the N partly standing). To the NW and below the promontory have been outbuildings reached by a stair built against the cliff face. C16 beehive DOOCOT to the E.

2010

NEWBURGH

There was a settlement here by 1266, when Alexander III gave the monks of Lindores Abbey (founded seventy-five years earlier) leave to make their town (*villam*) into a burgh with a weekly market. Newburgh became a royal burgh in 1631 but was never admitted to the Convention of Royal Burghs or represented in Parliament. In the early C19 the inhabitants were salmon fishers in summer and weavers in winter. Linoleum manufacture was established in 1891, when the Tayside Floorcloth Company's works were begun.

LINDORES ABBEY

Fragmentary remains of the Tironensian monastery founded by David, Earl of Huntingdon, *c.*1190. The first abbot, Guido, brought here from Kelso, is said by the *Scotichronicon* to have 'built the place from the foundations' before his death in 1219, and the surviving buildings appear to be of *c.*1200, all built of local red sandstone ashlar.

Large trees grow out of the Abbey Church CHOIR's E gable. This is heavily buttressed, probably to support a vault. At the W, bases of the crossing responds. In the ground, two tiny COFFINS, perhaps for Earl David's children.

The TRANSEPTS, each of two bays by three, made the usual provision for chapels. Enough remains to show that these were covered by quadripartite vaults springing from wall-shafts. In the N transept's S wall, a double piscina and an aumbry checked for a door. Against its N wall, another stone coffin. In the S transept's S wall, another aumbry, again checked for a door.

The NAVE has a N aisle, perhaps an afterthought during construction. An even stronger appearance of a change of plan is given by the NW TOWER. Of all this, just bits of masonry; but the nave's S wall seems to have had blind arcading inside and out and a stone bench on its cloister side.

The CLOISTER was on the church's S. Quite a lot of the E range survives. Abutting the S transept is a two-bay passage. Pointed-arched E door. Both bays had quadripartite vaulting,

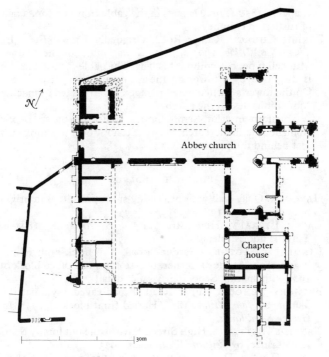

Lindores Abbey,
plan

the heavy ribs springing from moulded corbels. Part of the W compartment's ribs remains; the E compartment's vault is intact. Outside, one moulded corbel for the cloister roof. Chapter house to the S, now featureless except for the NW respond's base. Immediately to its S, clear evidence of the day stair which filled the NW corner of a room under the reredorter. E of this room has been another, probably an addition. Of the cloister's S and W ranges, only fragments. At the S range's E end, the waterholding base of a door jamb.

The abbey was enclosed by an OUTER WALL, whose round-arched hoodmoulded SW gateway survives. Across the road, to the S, more fragments of monastic buildings. In the garden of a cottage, a vaulted rubble structure. In the field to its S, one wall of what may have been a C13 BARN.

CHURCHES

BAPTIST CHURCH, High Street. Lanceted box, dated 1881.

BURGHER CHAPEL, Clinton Street. Secularized. Built in 1786 and reconstructed in 1836. Two-storey, with round-arched windows. Inside, a floor has been inserted at gallery level.

CONGREGATIONAL CHURCH, Clinton Street. Built as a Relief

chapel in 1850. Three lancets in the gable front; on top, a pair of rusticated chimneys.

PARISH CHURCH, Cupar Road. Originally United Free. By *Thoms & Wilkie*, 1905–6. Late Scots Gothic of the Sydney Mitchell type, but without his flair. The gable front's breadth is disguised by a tower on the r. and the parapet on the l. On the tower's battlemented parapet, fat crocketed pinnacles. More pinnacles on the porch.

Cruciform interior. Semi-elliptical arches into the transepts; Romanesque chancel arch. Perp oak canopy over the minister's seat behind the pulpit.

PUBLIC BUILDINGS

HARBOUR. Quay wall with projecting stone piers; C18 in origin but now mostly C19.

LAING LIBRARY, High Street. By *T. S. Anderson*, 1894–6. Timid Tudorish detail.

LINOLEUM FACTORY, Gardens Road. Tall brick-built ranges begun 1891. At the SE corner, one-storey stone office block of 1906 with sparing Scots Renaissance detail.

PRIMARY SCHOOL, Cupar Road. Broad-eaved asymmetrical Tudor, by *John Milne*, 1863. Harled front block of 1938, by *George Sandilands*.

TAYSIDE INSTITUTE, High Street. Small-scale but lumpy Scots Renaissance, by *William Williamson*, 1923.

TOWN HOUSE, High Street. By *John Speed*, mason, 1808. Simple piend-roofed block built of poor-quality ashlar. Central tower with an overarched ground-floor door and first-floor Venetian window. Ungainly broaching to carry the octagonal belfry, a stone spire rising within its crenellated parapet.

DESCRIPTION

In ABBEY ROAD, on the approach from the NE, Lindores Abbey (*see* above). Beside it, ABBEY HOUSE, C18 dressed up with a medievalizing Victorian wing. Opposite, LINDORES ABBEY FARM's mid-C19 U-plan steading. At the junction with CUPAR ROAD, the wooden ST KATHARINE's (Episcopal) CHURCH of 1897. For the Parish Church and Primary School, *see* above. Then substantial houses set back from the road. One on the r., early C19, of whinstone. On the l., TAYBANK and GUTHRIE LODGE, both of *c.* 1840 with broad-eaved roofs; between them, DUNVEGAN, built as the manse in 1786 and later extended. At the end of Cupar Road, C18 rubble-built pub (THE ABBEY), its top floor a C19 addition. Opposite, a lumpy Gothic DRINKING FOUNTAIN of 1887.

HIGH STREET's N side begins with the GEORGE HOTEL of 1811, with a Doric pilastered doorpiece. On the s, Nos. 1–3, C18 with crowstepped gables. The street's general character is Georgian vernacular, but punctuated by agreeable incidents. Early C19 No. 32 (N), with a Venetian window and late Vic-

torian Scots Renaissance door. No. 27 (s), C18, with a forestair
to the centre door. Much grander is IVYBANK at No. 42 (N),
of c.1830, with a rusticated ground floor and fluted Doric
columns at the recessed door. Open pedimented centre on the
late C18 No. 50 (N). Over No. 60's door, large stone panel
carved with a sailing ship, nautical instruments, the names of
Thomas Sanderson and Janet Williamson, and the date 1752.
No. 64 (N), late Georgian, with quatrefoils on the friezes of its
angle pilasters. Gibbsian doorpiece on the C18 No. 49 (s). For
the Town House, *see* above.

The neo-vernacular TOLBOOTH CLOSE development by
L. A. Rolland & Partners, 1981, pushes a gable towards the
street. Suave late Georgian No. 81 (s); Ionic columns at the
door and a mutuled cornice. Nos. 89–91 were built in 1840
with a channelled ground floor; aprons below the architraved
first-floor windows, horizontal glazing in the bowed dormers.
ST KATHARINE'S COURT (N), by *L. A. Rolland & Partners*,
1971, L-plan with a gable to the street and a segmental arcade,
adjoins the Laing Library (*see* above). On the corner of MASON
STREET, LODGE LINDORES, very best artisan classical of
1815. The ground floor is an arcaded base for the excitement
above. On the first floor, thin attached columns at the ends,
fluted pilasters and frieze at the centre. Tudor hoodmoulds
over the outer windows. Blind fanlight over the three-light
centre window; beneath it, a panel carved with a handshake.
Carved heads below the pilasters.

Beside the Baptist Church (*see* above), No. 150 (N), small-
scale Edwardian pomposity, dated 1907. Thatched roof on the
C18 Nos. 165–171 (s). Mid-C18 block at Nos. 190–192 (N) with
a Gibbsian doorpiece and first- and second-floor lintel courses.
No. 194 is contemporary; Venetian door under a Venetian
window. At the end of the street, two opposing early C19 inns,
the TAYVIEW HOTEL (N), with rusticated quoins and door,
and the TAYBRIDGE TAVERN, with a pilastered ground floor.
Blocking the view w is *James B. Dunn*'s WAR MEMORIAL of
1922, the statue of a soldier in the Black Watch sculpted by
Alexander Carrick. Beside it, screen-walled VICTORY FOUN-
TAIN by *William Williamson*, 1923.

FARM

PARKHILL, 0.7km. E. Picturesque whinstone and pantiled steading of C18 origin, extended in 1858–9, perhaps the date of the
three-storey MILL on the w, its waterwheel still in place. –
Villa FARMHOUSE across the road, by *Robert Bell*, 1858.

BLACK CAIRN HILL, 1km. S. A univallate Iron Age fort, with
denuded defences but of considerable size (1.2ha.), commanding wide views in all directions. Ruined dry-stone wall
originally c.3m. thick.

MACDUFF'S CROSS, 1.7km. SW. Large sandstone boulder with
eight cupmarks on top. The suggestion that it once served as
a cross-base has been discounted.

DENMYLNE. *See* p. 172.
MUGDRUM. *See* p. 327.

DENMYLNE. *See* p. 172.
MUGDRUM. *See* p. 327.

4000   NEWBURN

Rural parish without a village. The two former churches and
manse (now Newburn House) are strung along a back road
behind the A921 between Upper Largo and Colinsburgh.

OLD PARISH CHURCH. Roofless ruin in a graveyard. Rubble-
built, on an irregular T-plan. The body's narrower E part is
probably late medieval. In its S wall, remains of a pointed-
arched piscina. On the N wall, a pointed-arched aumbry (possibly a sacrament house) above a rectangular locker. The
church's W part is probably a post-Reformation reconstruction, but the S door is in the standard pre-Reformation
position and its chamfered arch looks medieval. On the W
gable, two-tiered balustered bellcote with an urn on top, probably mid-C18. The N aisle is presumably a post-Reformation
addition, early C18, to judge from the keyblocked round-
headed door. Rather later the NE burial enclosure, with rusticated piers at the entrance.
    MONUMENTS. In the church's E gable, a weathered curly
pedimented aedicule of *c.*1700, the fluted columns' capitals
perhaps meant to be Corinthian. – S of the church, a few
rustic classical headstones of the 1730s and 1740s. – In the
churchyard's SW corner, Arts and Crafts Jacobean memorial
to Professor James Lorimer by his son *Robert S. Lorimer*,
1890, carved with coats of arms and rosettes on the frieze.
PARISH CHURCH (now KIRK HOUSE). Smart piend-roofed
whinstone box, by *Alexander Leslie*, 1813–15. E steeple, the
octagonal spire rising within the tower's battlemented parapet.
On the S side, big Gothick windows flanking the single-storey
vestry. Converted to a house by *L. A. Rolland & Partners*,
1970.
NEWBURN HOUSE (former MANSE). Piend-roofed and whin-
stone-fronted, with a pilastered doorpiece. Built 1818–19.

4020   NEWPORT-ON-TAY

A town which began as the S end of the ferry to Dundee. A pier
and inn were built here by the Guildry of Dundee in 1713–15
and the place was grandly christened New Dundee. Houses were
being built in the 1790s, but development as a bathing resort for
the citizens of Dundee followed the construction of Telford's
steamboat pier in 1823. Further growth as an appendage of
Dundee followed the opening of the ill-fated Tay Bridge in 1878
and its successor nine years later.

CHURCHES

CONGREGATIONAL CHURCH, Kilnburn. Disused. By *David Mackenzie II*, 1868. Buttressed and lanceted rubble box. The gable front's width is disguised by the end bay on the l. being roofed as an aisle; on the r., a steeple with octagonal gableted belfry and fishscale slated spire.

PARISH CHURCH, Blyth Street. Bare Gothic, by *Alexander Johnston*, 1869–70. Martial-looking NE tower with angle buttresses and an aggressively corbelled parapet. The church was extended S by *Johnston & Baxter*, 1901.

Internally, a huge nave, two-bay transepts, and chancel. – STAINED GLASS. S window (the Evangelists), garishly coloured and lumpily drawn, *c.*1880. – In the round window over the chancel arch, a dove, *c.*1905. – A window by *G. W. Mottashaw* is to be erected on the l. of the chancel arch (1985). – In the nave's W wall, a two-light window (Acts of Charity), after 1907, probably by *William S. Black*.* – To its N, War Memorial window, *c.*1920. – In the N gable, three-light window (The Transfiguration) by *Black*, 1914, flanked by St Nathaniel (by *A. Ballantine & Son*, 1907) and St Thomas (by *Black*, 1914). – In the nave's E wall, one pictorial window ('What Doth the Lord Require of Thee?'), *c.*1925. – ORGAN by *Henry Willis & Sons*.

MANSE on the W, by *Johnston & Baxter*, 1901.

ST MARY (Episcopal), High Street. Simple but picturesque, by *T. M. Cappon*, 1886–7. Bellcote on the N gable; sturdy NE porch with a jerkin-headed roof. Inside, a five-bay nave and apse-ended chancel. – Wooden ROOD SCREEN, its figures carved by *William Lamb*, 1940. – STAINED GLASS. In the chancel, five lights (Scenes from the Life of Christ), *c.*1890. – Two windows (The Apostles at the Gate Beautiful; St Peter's Liberation by an Angel) in the chancel's W wall, of *c.*1930; they may be *Walter E. Tower*. – In the nave's W wall, three windows (Christ at the House at Bethany; Prophets (?); The Calling of St Peter) of *c.*1890, the middle one signed by *A. Vincent Hart*. – War Memorial window of *c.*1920. – In the nave's E wall, one light ('Touch Me Not'), *c.*1890. – Two-light window, its l. half (The Good Shepherd) by *Tower*, c.1930, the r. (St Peter) by *Alexander L. Russell*, c.1950. – Awkwardly pictorial N window (The Nativity) by *Russell*, *c.*1950. – Bronze eagle LECTERN, 1904. – ORGAN by *J. R. Miller*, 1904.

TRINITY CHURCH (United Free), W end of High Street. Spiky Gothic and effective townscape, by *C. & L. Ower*, 1881–2. Cruciform, with semi-octagonal ends to the transepts. A second pair of transepts, but not projecting, at the E. On the front's r., an octagonal slate-roofed steeple.

WORMIT PARISH CHURCH, Riverside Road. Originally Free. Late Gothic, by *James Maclaren & Sons*, 1898–1901. Battlemented tower with a small needle spire; big flight of steps to the porch.

---

* Black's designs were executed by *A. Ballantine & Son*.

PUBLIC BUILDINGS

BLYTH HALL, Blyth Street. Tepid Baronial of 1877. The front, a crowstepped gable between thin drum towers, is not improved by the recent drydash and blockwork porch. s extension by *J. Weekes Jun.*, 1913.

NEWPORT HARBOUR, Boat Road. Designed by *Thomas Telford* for the steamboat ferry to Dundee, 1823. Carriage ramps each side of a central pier. At the landward end, a late Victorian gabled office with a semicircular canopy each side (the r. opening bricked up). To the w, single-storey offices by *C. & L. Ower*, c. 1880, with Ruskinian Gothic detail. To the E, an elegantly lettered cast-iron MILESTONE, dated 1824 and signed ALEX[R]. RUSSELL/KIRKALDY FOUNDRY.

PRIMARY SCHOOL, Cupar Road. By *Fife Regional Council*, 1977. Classrooms projecting from a circular centre.

DESCRIPTION

TAY STREET leads in from the E with villas enjoying the view over the Tay. Nos. 60–64 of c. 1840 form a broad-eaved Italianate triple house, the asymmetrical two-storey end blocks joined by a single-storey centre. Contemporary No. 58, Georgian survival, but with a finial on its gablet. No. 56 (CANISBAY LODGE), bargeboarded and bay-windowed of c. 1860, with a Tudorish porch. The next incident comes on the N, a domed cast-iron DRINKING FOUNTAIN of 1882, adorned with dragons and shields. Then more bay-windowed houses of c. 1840: No. 12 with a pilastered doorpiece, Nos. 8–10 with V-plan windows and consoled keystones on the porch. (Diversion up WILLIAM STREET to the RIO COMMUNITY CENTRE, 1930s jazz-modern cinema front with awkward fins. In CUPAR ROAD to the SE, No. 63 on the Victoria Street corner, late C19 with a squashed ogee-roofed tower against a Jacobean gablet, and a pretty wooden porch.)

BLYTH STREET's collection of churches and public buildings (*see* above) fails to add up to a town centre. The Episcopal Church pokes through to HIGH STREET, small-scale commercial, focused on Trinity U.F. Church (*see* above). Beside the late Victorian Rectory, a diminutive early C19 temple (Nos. 4–6) built as the Tayfield estate office. On the corner of BOAT ROAD, the NEWPORT HOTEL, its render painted black and white, is dated 1806.

No. 2 WEST ROAD was built as the Tayfield dower house in 1840. Very pretty, with the roof carried out over Roman Doric columns to make a semicircular central porch; stone canopies over the horizontally glazed windows. In the new housing of KINBRAE PARK on the hill above, two large Italianate villas: ST SERF'S, by *Andrew Heiton Jun.*, 1865–6, asymmetrical with a tower, and the contemporary but more opulent BALMORE. Nos. 9–11 West Road are a villa of c. 1840, gableted, with vestigially pedimented ground-floor windows and a console-capitalled pilastered doorpiece of a type which recurs at

Nos. 15–17. On the N side, two pairs of semi-detached houses (Nos. 28–36), pretty Jacobean, dated 1854, followed by the set-back Nos. 44–46 of 1828, with an Italianate tower. More console-capitals on Nos. 48–50's doorpieces. On the S, a plain early C19 whinstone row (Nos. 21–27) followed by a WELL dated 1832. Opposite, HONEYSTONE HOUSE (Nos. 54–58), an early C19 double house. Then No. 70 on the corner of Riverside Lane, a smart early Victorian villa, channelled ashlar with an Ionic portico. Yet another console-capitalled doorpiece on No. 74. On the corner of Castle Brae, THE CASTLE, an early C19 harled toy fort; pedimented porch at the back.

RIVERSIDE ROAD begins with No. 92 (WOODHAVEN), an early C19 farmhouse and steading. On the path down to Woodhaven Harbour, the harled late Georgian No. 97 (MARS COTTAGE). Built into the bank, a large WORKSHOP of 1799, with an oculus in the gable. Further along Riverside Road, Wormit Parish Church (see above). In BAY ROAD, almost under the Tay Bridge, the former PARISH CHURCH by T. M. Cappon, 1894–5, with ogee-headed windows and a domed ventilator. In NAUGHTON ROAD, No. 15, on the corner of Mount Stewart Road, dated 1895, a bit of seaside fun with a cupolaed lantern.

TAYFIELD

off Cupar Road and High Road

Late C18 laird's house enlarged and recast in 1829–30. John Berry bought the estate in 1787. The next year he built a new house, for which *Robert Anderson* seems to have been the architect.* This was a harled two-storey and basement three-bay block, with twin bows on the rear (N) elevation. In 1829–30 Berry's son William employed *George Smith* to extend the building S and clothe the existing house in Elizabethan dress. The asymmetrical entrance front is all by Smith. Narrow gabled projecting bay containing the Tudor-arched front door under an oriel. On the l., a corbelled chimney stack; on the r., a corbelled gablet. Horizontal glazing in the windows, the ground-floor ones with hoodmoulds. On the W front, Smith provided gables and bay windows both for his addition and the C18 house. The addition's E front has another bay window, but the earlier house was adorned only with a corbelled gablet. Gablet of the same type but with a chimney (removed) in the centre of the N front, whose bows were given smaller gablets. Probably at the same time‡ the r. bow's Venetian window lost its arched top and gained a balcony under its lowered sill.

The interior is almost entirely Smith's. Straight flight of stairs from the front door to the *piano nobile*'s hall, in whose walls are placed early C19 plaster casts of the C16 oak bosses carved with portraits in the King's Presence Chamber at Stirling Castle (Central). More 'Stirling Heads' in the oak-grained

---

* Drawings and specifications for the house are accompanied by a note entitled 'Explanation of the Plan by Robᵗ Anderson'.

‡ But Smith's elevations do not show this alteration.

library on the r. In the billiard room (the C18 drawing room
and now a bedroom) behind, large white marble chimneypiece
of 1830. Smith's dining room is at the sw, austere, with a black
marble chimneypiece. The C18 dining room at the NW became
the drawing room in 1830, when its w bay window was added.
Contemporary plasterwork with a deep *rinceau* frieze and
simple ceiling rose. Heavy entasis on the white marble chimneypiece, which contains a neo-Egyptian cast-iron fire surround.

SOUTH LODGE at the Cupar Road entrance, probably by
Smith, *c*.1830, with stone canopies over the windows. –
NORTH LODGE to High Road, of 1821 by *James Gillespie
Graham*: broad-eaved with a semi-octagonal end and lattice
glazing.

LINKS WOOD. *See* p. 314.
SANDFORD HILL. *See* p. 409.
VICARSFORD CEMETERY. *See* p. 423.

LINKS WOOD. *See* p. 314.
SANDFORD HILL. *See* p. 409.
VICARSFORD CEMETERY. *See* p. 423.

NEWTONHALL HOUSE
1.7km. w of Kennoway

3000

79 A small country house of 1829 by *David Bryce*, in the smooth
Jacobean manner of his master William Burn. On the E, a
gabled porch and diagonally set chimneys corbelled out from
the wall. Asymmetrical s front with a large mullioned and
transomed window in the gabled r. bay and a low office wing
on the l. Dormerheads with decorative carved finials. Inside,
thin ribbed ceilings in the main rooms.

NEWTON OF FALKLAND

2000

Small C18 and C19 weaving and malting village, described, rather
unfairly, by *The Imperial Gazetteer* of 1865 as 'an irregularly
built, disagreeable place'.

BONTHRONE MALTINGS, Main Street. Late C19, rubble-built,
with a pagoda-roofed kiln.

NORMAN'S LAW
1.9km. w of Brunton

3020

A spectacular Iron Age fort crowning a conspicuous summit
(285m. O.D.) overlooking the Firth of Tay and Howe of Fife.
Three distinct structural elements. First, a heavy dry-stone
wall enclosing the whole upper summit area of *c*.220m. by
75m. Second, another stout wall taking in the two lower shelves
to s and w of the summit. Third, a kidney-shaped univallate

fort roughly 50m. by 30m. within a solid dry-stone wall $c.$3m. to 5m. thick. This overlies the first enclosure and is therefore later, as are the numerous unenclosed round stone houses, which are clearly built over the ruins of the earlier fort wall.

NORRIE'S LAW
4km. NNW of Upper Largo

4000

A cairn apparently of both earth and stone, and although dug into in the past still measuring $c.$18m. in diameter and 3.5m. high. A hoard of silver found in a sandpit at the base of the Law in 1819–22 included silver brooches or neck ornaments, leaf-shaped plaques, pins and rings, ranging in date from a late Roman spoon to pins of $c.$700 (now in the Royal Museum of Antiquities of Scotland, Queen Street, Edinburgh).

NORTH QUEENSFERRY

1080

For long the N landing-point of the ferry across the Forth, taking traffic from Edinburgh to Dunfermline and Perth, North Queensferry lost this function with the opening of the Forth Road Bridge in 1964. In the C19 it was also a fishing village and bathing resort. Now it is principally a dormitory of Edinburgh.

CHAPEL (St James), Chapel Place. Only a fragment at the NW corner of a small graveyard.

The chapel of North Queensferry was granted by Robert I to Dunfermline Abbey $c.$1320–3. The chaplainry was founded anew by Abbot Henry Creichton in 1479 and the chapel apparently rebuilt then or soon after. All that remains are the rubble-built W gable and some of the N wall. Two-light rectangular window in the gable. Round-arched door (blocked) near W end of the wall.

The GRAVEYARD walls can probably be dated from a stone beside the S gate, inscribed: THIS . IS . DONE . BY / THE . SAILERS . IN / NORTH . FERRIE / 1752. Second stone dated 1752 on inside of the chapel's gable. – TOMBSTONES. Very crudely lettered slab with the initials WB, MS, and date 1735, inscribed:

heier ue lay at anker with the manie in ouer fleet in hopes to uay at the last day ouer admirel Christ to meet.

Below is scratched an anchored ship with its sails set. – To its NE, curly-topped stone dated 1727, carved with a skull biting a swag of drapery.

PRIMARY SCHOOL, Whinneyknowe and Brock Street. Blocky red sandstone Art Nouveau on a butterfly plan. By *Andrew Scobie & Son*, 1912–14.

RAILWAY STATION, off Ferryhill Road. Opened 1890. Wooden

bridge joining the platforms. The E one still has its canopied waiting room and ticket office.

DESCRIPTION. The village cowers under the Forth Railway Bridge. The Road Bridge on the W is a relatively benign boundary. At the PIERHEAD, two harbour buildings of c. 1810. TOWER HOUSE was the ferry office, a castellated octagon with a small tower on the w. Dreary N addition of c. 1875. Hexagonal SIGNAL HOUSE with a glass-sided copper-domed lantern with a flue poking out of the top.

In and around the s stretch of MAIN STREET, an irregular collection of houses, their date and style ranging from late C17 vernacular to 1970s Civic Trust approved neo-vernacular. The late Georgian ALBERT HOTEL has acquired Edwardian recessed bow windows. No. 26 Main Street, harled and crow-stepped, is of 1693, with a triangular pediment over one window. Good group in POST OFFICE LANE, with one house dated 1776. At Main Street's N end, the curvy WATERLOO WELL, dated 1816, rusticated stone front, its inset triangular plaque carved with a ship at anchor. Behind, Victorian iron PUMP, cast by *Glenfield & Kennedy* of Kilmarnock, the spout sticking out as a tongue from a lion's mask. On the wall above, cast-iron door with reliefs of a quarrelling sailor and fishwife and of Europa and the Bull. In THE BRAE, pantiled cottages with forestairs leading towards the OLD SCHOOLHOUSE built by public subscription in 1827. On Main Street's W progress along the harbour, a pair of houses (BRAE HOUSE and WHITE HOUSE) dated 1771 and 1778 with a first-floor sundial.

ST MARGARET'S HOPE. *See* p. 403.

122

0080

OAKLEY

Begun as a village for the Forth Ironworks, which opened in 1846 (but closed in 1869), and redeveloped as C20 miners' housing.

CHURCH OF THE HOLY NAME (R.C.), Station Road. By *Charles W. Gray*, 1958. White-harled Early Christian with a very Scottish saddleback tower over the W entrance. Very simple interior an admirable container for the superb STAINED GLASS. This is all by *Gabriel Loire* of Chartres. In the E clearstorey, stylized and brightly coloured Scenes from the Life of Our Lord. – In the W windows, symbols of the Euchar-ist in blues and golds. – Our Lady in the W transept window. – Two armorial windows in its N chapel. – The choir's high-set windows are filled with yellow and gold abstract designs. – Pale colouring in the apse windows. – Contemporary STATIONS OF THE CROSS, also by Loire.

INZIEVAR SCHOOL, Station Road. By *Fife County Council*, 1954.

BLAIR HOUSE, 0.7km. N. Modestly pretentious of c. 1815, with a cornice and blocking course. Off-centre portico. – To the E, a battlemented early C19 round TOWER.

INZIEVAR. *See* p. 252.

OTTERSTON *see* ABERDOUR

OVER RANKEILLOUR
4.6km. W of Cupar

Chaste classical spread of 1796–1800 by *Alexander Laing* executing and perhaps adapting a slightly earlier design by *James McLeran*. Nine-bay S front with giant Ionic pilasters marking the pedimented centrepiece; balustraded parapet. The entrance was moved to the E gable later in the C19.

PATHHEAD *see* KIRKCALDY

PITCAIRLIE HOUSE
3.2km. N of Auchtermuchty

Harled laird's house whose successive owners seem never to have been able to realize their quite modest ambitions for its reconstruction. It began as a late C16 L- or Z-plan building, the SW jamb's upper floors jettied out under a deep ashlar parapet, its shallow projecting angle-rounds enlivened by prominent spouts. In the jamb's S face, C18 bee-bolls. *c.*1730 the main block was extended W and thickened to the N to make a double-pile. Clearly this was intended to have a seven-bay N front, but the two E bays were not built. In the three-bay 'centre', a Venetian door whose ashlar surround sweeps up to the pedimented first-floor window. In 1740 a large piend-roofed pavilion was added at the SW. It looks rather isolated, but presumably was meant to be balanced by another at the SE. The pavilion was tied more securely to the main block in 1815, when *Just & Carver*, 'Architects & Builders at Woodhaven', added a corridor on its N, screened from the approach by a wall pierced with semi-elliptical arches. At the same time they added a full-height bow to the early C18 extension's E gable. The bow was given a two-storey bay-window pimple in 1833; its balustrade may be a still later embellishment.

Inside the C16 S part, two vaulted ground-floor rooms. In its jamb's second-floor room, a moulded late C17 chimneypiece and mid-C18 pine panelling. In the extension of *c.*1730, a twisty balustered staircase. The first-floor drawing room at the NE was probably panelled in the mid-C18. Of that date survives the chimneypiece, its frieze decorated with rococo tendrils which reappear on the overmantel's scrolled frame topped by a deeply modelled flower basket. This now forms the setting for a pastoral scene in the Watteau-revival manner of *D. R. Hay*. More neo-Watteau pastoral panels on the rest of the walls, all probably of 1833. Panelled room of *c.*1730 on the floor above.

4000

PITCORTHIE HOUSE
1.3km. E of Colinsburgh

Very accomplished single-storey house set in mature parkland*;
by *Trevor Dannatt*, 1967. Stone walls, shallow metal roofs.
Austere entrance court on the N; on the S, a fully glazed
projecting gallery linking the main rooms. A tall off-centre
chimneystack counterbalances the horizontals.

STANDING STONE 0.9km. E. An impressive stone, *c*.2.4m. high
and 3.1m. maximum girth, with at least thirty-three cupmarkings and two dumbbell-shaped motifs on its S face. In the
mid-C19, the farmer found it was set into a hole about 0.6m.
deep, with a filling of cremated bones.

4010

PITCULLO
2km. N of Dairsie

Harled and crowstepped late C16 laird's house dramatically sited
on a hillside. L-plan with a turret stair corbelled out in the
inner angle of the main block and SW jamb. Less conventional
is the bowed stairtower projecting on the N side, its top jettied
out as a rectangular cap-house. The lower part of the jamb's
SE corner is chamfered, the main block's N corners rounded.
On the jamb's SW corner, a conical-roofed bartizan, perhaps
an early C17 embellishment. Wide-splayed gunloop beside the
door. All this was roofless until *R. C. Spence*'s conservative
restoration of 1971. More conjectural has been *Ian Begg*'s
subsequent addition of missing upper parts.

  Inside, the main stair to the first floor is in the jamb; service
stair in the N tower. Behind the main stair, a small segmental-
vaulted porter's room. In the main block, two tunnel-vaulted
ground-floor rooms. The W was the kitchen; large fireplace
with an oven in the l. ingo, a slit window in the r. From the E
room, straight stair down to the unvaulted undercroft. Ceilings
have been painted by *Michael Pinfold* with decorative designs
in imitation of late C16 or early C17 work since *c*.1985.

2080

PITEADIE CASTLE
2.6km. NW of Kinghorn

Ruined late C15 L-plan tower standing in a large walled garden.
The house is built of good-quality rubble, with ashlar work at
the corners. The rectangular SE jamb contains the stair; its top
is corbelled out to support a crowstepped cap-house. At the
NE and SW corners of the main block, corbelled rounds; the
deeper SW round seems to have contained the stair to an attic.
The original entrance was at first-floor level on the S side. Two
corbels, presumably for a fixed wooden stair, survive below

---

* The early C19 mansion house formerly on the site was demolished after a fire.

the blocked round-arched doorway into which a window was inserted, perhaps in the late C17, but its plain margins, like those of the S wall's other windows, suggest an C18 date. Probably contemporary is the lean-to filling the jamb's inner angle and serving as a porch to the ground-floor door, which has been made to the stair.

Inside, the ground floor was a store covered by a shallow tunnel-vault. The upper floors show evidence of a late C17 reconstruction.

In the garden wall immediately to the E, round-arched GATEWAY under a pediment carved with a coat of arms and, much more faintly, the date 1686 and the initials W.C. for the house's then owner William Calderwood, apothecary and burgess of Edinburgh.

To the N, the harled PITEADIE HOUSE, probably late C18, but its front altered c.1840. – Mid-C19 pantiled range of FARM OFFICES to its NW.

PITFIRRANE
3.2km W of Dunfermline

0080

The tall and bleak tower house of the Halket family, now a golf club which has wrapped a single-storey extension across the S front. Very plain rectangular tower of c.1500, harled except for the ashlar S side. Ashlar third floor with W corner turrets added in 1583. Also of 1583 is the SE jamb, containing a turnpike stair to the second floor and a turret stair corbelled out in the inner angle to the floors above. On the jamb's W face, above its door, boldly carved panels containing the Halket arms and the royal arms. SE corner scarred by the marks of a demolished E wing of c.1680. Round NE tower and low servants' wing added in 1854 by *David Bryce*, who was probably responsible also for the conical roofs on the turrets of 1583. On the wall beside the early C19 hoodmoulded W door, a C16 iron yett which used to protect the entrance to a self-contained ground-floor room.

Inside, the windows of the jamb's broad turnpike contain some pieces of Flemish stained glass of c.1600 set in late C19 borders. First-floor dining room (originally the hall) a spectacular muddle of C18 and C19 work. Mid-C18 bracketed cornice with egg-and-dart enrichment. Contemporary female heads in swags on the soffits of the window embrasures. The ceiling's plaster roundels and small pendants are probably part of the plasterwork for which *Alexander Henderson* was paid in 1840. The heraldic decoration presumably dates from the same time. Panelling in a smart C16 Renaissance manner was introduced in the 1880s – some panels could be genuine C16. Also of the 1880s is the wooden surround to the sideboard recess, vigorously carved with foliage, rams' heads and eagles. Contemporary chimneypiece with human heads and dolphins on the jambs.

On the N approach, late Georgian rusticated GATEPIERS with swagged urn finials.

PITLESSIE

Small village built on an irregular plan.

BONTHRONE MALTINGS, Cupar Road. By *Robert Hamilton-Paterson*, 1890. Straightforward, of whinstone, with a pyra-mid-roofed kiln to the S.
PRIMARY SCHOOL, Ladybank Road. Plain lump, dated 1911.
SIR DAVID WILKIE MEMORIAL HALL, Ladybank Road. Built in 1897 to look like a piend-roofed Georgian chapel.

PITLIVER
1.6km. N of Charlestown

C17 laird's house, enlarged in the C18 and half-heartedly Bar-onialized in the C19. It was probably begun soon after 1623, when James Leslie acquired the property, and, as first built, seems to have been a straightforward rubble box with a taller stairtower projecting from the centre of the N side. In the C18, an L-plan extension was wrapped round the building, its W jamb projecting N of the original house as a gabled wing. The windows of the addition's harled S front (some enlarged in 1935–6) are arranged in a symmetrical 1/2/1 grouping. Mid-C19 Baronialism arrived on the N with a large tower, a gabled cap-house on top of its heavy corbelled parapet, filling the inner angle of the C17 stairtower and C18 wing. At the base of the tower, a curly pedimented front door. At the same time the wing's N gable was embellished with an outsize tablet commemorating the Wellwoods, who had bought the estate in 1733. Interior mostly neo-Georgian of 1935–6 by *James Shearer*.

PITLOUR
0.8km. N of Strathmiglo

69 Stolid but smart villa perched on a hill-slope. It was built in 1784 for Colonel Philip Skene, whose brother, General Robert Skene, had commissioned designs for the house from *Robert Mylne* in 1775–6. Mylne laid out the approach in 1783, and the front (E) elevation is almost identical to one of the drawings he produced almost ten years before. Five bays with a bullseyed pediment over the broad three-bay centre. Front door in a round-headed overarch. Aprons under the ground-floor win-dows.

Expensively finished interior. Entrance hall with a round-headed niche (the r. very shallow) in the centre of each long wall. Marbled pilasters (the screen between a recent addition) to the inner hall in the house's centre, its plaster groin vault dressed up with husks and a centre rose. Deep stairhall to the N; niches in its bow end decorated with husk festoons. Ceiling above with a swagged circle of husks round the rose and fans at the corners. In the ground-floor drawing room's long S wall, a niche each side of the centre window. White marble chimneypiece opposite, the central panel carved with a hound. Dining room at the SW. More niches in its bowed N wall. Their painted decoration of fruit-filled shells is presumably contemporary with the ceiling's early C19 painted centre rose and arabesque panels adorned with swans, eagles and nosegays.

To the NW, a two-chamber ICEHOUSE, the outer compartment tunnel-vaulted, the inner conical. – To the NE, a courtyard of STABLES and offices with Venetian doors and windows in the centre range. Cartshed at the E end. Over the E front's pend, an ogee-roofed doocot tower. Some of this at least was built by *William Simson* in 1827. – By the walled garden to the SW, an early C19 Gothick-windowed COTTAGE. – EAST LODGE, picturesque-classical of *c.*1840.

PITREAVIE
1.5km. N of Rosyth

Austere but classy, almost classical, ashlar-fronted house built for Sir Henry Wardlaw, Chamberlain to Anne of Denmark, *c.*1630, and reconstructed and extended in Baronial fashion by *C. G. H. Kinnear*, 1885. Wardlaw's house was of four storeys, U-plan, with the wings projecting N. In the inner angles, small round towers serve as stems for fat candle-snuffered stair turrets corbelled out from a stringcourse. In the towers, slit windows, their sills decorated with shotholes. Second-floor garderobes slicing across the inner angles of the turrets and wings. In the courtyard front of each wing was a moulded door (the E now a window), its pediment carved with Wardlaw's initials. Horizontal ground-floor windows, the windows above of generous size. The alterations of 1885 converted the main block from a U- to an H-plan, added a dining-room xtension on the E, and gave the E wing a balustraded porch and mullioned stair window above. On the new S front, two-storey canted bay windows at the projecting ends and a second-floor balcony across the centre.

(Interior now almost all of 1885. On the first floor, E 'Chapel', oak-panelled with moralistic texts on the frieze. Library in the centre. L-plan partly panelled drawing room at the SW.)

Harled lectern DOOCOT to the NE, probably C18.

PITTARTHIE CASTLE
2.5km. SW of Dunino

Substantial remains of the hilltop house built for James Monypenny of Pitmilly *c.*1580. L-plan with the SW jamb (its NW
corner bowed) tenuously attached to the main block, and a
stairtower in the inner angle. The stonework is good-quality
rubble with ashlar dressings but much coarser masonry
appears at the bottom of the S wall, possibly evidence of an
earlier building. Wonderful display of fairly useless defences –
gunloop beside the roll-moulded door, pistol-holes in all the
window sills.

The estate was bought by the Bruces *c.*1636, and the house
was remodelled by William Bruce of Pittarthie in 1682, the
date carved, together with his arms and initials, on a segmental
pediment over the first-floor hall's S window. This window,
like most of the others, has typically late C17 rounded arrises.
Perhaps also late C17 was the addition of a N stair turret.

Derelict interior. In the tunnel-vaulted jamb, kitchen with
a huge N fireplace; water inlet in the W wall.

PITTENCRIEFF HOUSE *see* DUNFERMLINE,
p. 192

PITTENWEEM

Fishing town which became a burgh of barony of its Augustinian
priory and a royal burgh in 1541. Two centres, the High Street
with a market town character, the Harbour almost self-consciously picturesque.

PITTENWEEM PRIORY

The Augustinian Priory was moved from the Isle of May to
Pittenweem in the C13, and some of its church is incorporated
in the present Parish Church (*see* below). The conventual
accommodation was rebuilt on a grand scale in the C15 and can
be seen, or discovered, on three sides of the large quadrangle to
the S of the churchyard. To the E the C15 GATEHOUSE of
large masonry with a round-arched entry, the square holes
suggesting some sort of timber gallery, although the big double
corbels, rounded at the corners, imply a parapet walk not
far overhead. The W range was probably the dormitory and
refectory but was recast *c.*1588 as the Manse, now the GREAT
HOUSE. On the E elevation, the middle part has a big C16 oriel,
and a pantiled roof with slate skirt going half-way up. To the
l. a smaller oriel, to the r. a swelling in the wall, carefully
detailed to mask a stair. Central pend, emerging through a
(C16?) arch to Cove Wynd, where the middle part of the W
elevation has a C17–18 aspect, with swept dormers which may

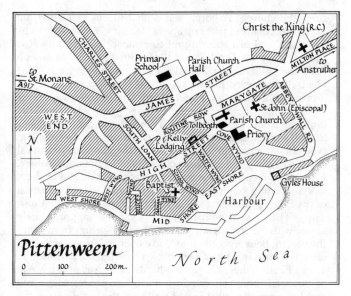

Pittenweem

0   100   200 m.

be part of the restoration by *Robert S. Lorimer*, 1921. To the
r. the ashlar façade of the former TOWN HALL (now a house),
built on the site of the refectory in 1821. Big round-arched
windows over small ones, all with Gothick glazing. Monumental entrance with diamond rustication added in the late
C19. The s range is the former PRIOR'S LODGING, largely
C16–17. s elevation with pedimented dormers and an oriel of
*c.*1840, when the building was converted into a rectory.
Vaulted C15 ground floor, but the upper rooms mainly C19
superseding C18 work. On the main floor within the N wall,
one jamb of a large fireplace of C15 type. Two orders of slim
shafts, moulded at the base and over the trumpet capitals. The
N elevation is covered by a lean-to range of the first half of the
C19.

In the garden to the s of the Prior's Lodging, a stair down
to a vaulted subterranean chamber, and thence a steep stair
down to ST FILLAN'S CAVE, traditionally the chapel and
dwelling of the C7 missionary saint. The direct entry from
Cove Wynd leads first to an outer cave, then to two forked
chambers in the l. of which are signs of a well.

CHURCHES

BAPTIST CHURCH, School Wynd. Flat Gothic of 1906.
CHRIST THE KING (R.C.), Milton Place. A solid piend-roofed
villa of *c.*1830 with an advanced and pedimented centre, the
outer margins emphasized by big plain pilasters whose slightly
Soanean finials above the cornice are in fact chimneys. Some
of the original horizontal glazing survives. In 1935 the ground
floor's two front rooms were combined with the vestibule to

form the church. A porch was added in 1954, but the old porch's entablature sticks up above, and on it is a stone SCULPTURE of Our Lord standing robed against the Cross, by *Hew Lorimer*, 1952. – Inside, a smaller stone figure of St Joseph with the child Christ holding a saw, again by Lorimer. – Central-chimneyed LODGE just inside the drive entrance.

PARISH CHURCH, at the E end of the High Street, where the Tolbooth (*see* below) merges into its gable and gives the impression of being its w tower. Tolbooth and church are both harled, and the latter has tall pointed lancets of late Georgian type. Investigation in 1981 (aided by the temporary removal of the harling) provided three clues about its previous history. First, a fragment of a doorway of *c.*1200 at the E end of the N side, indicating a church of earlier date than the C13 foundation of the Priory, extending much further to the E than what now exists. Then a large pointed arch in the S wall, approximately in line with the second lancet from the l. It springs from about the present floor level and must have opened into a s jamb (this jamb is shown in a block plan drawn by Alexander Morton in 1813). Finally, there is a square-headed doorway at the w end of this wall (now concealed by the boiler-house) whose roll moulding matches what is still visible in the lower part of the second lancet. A window was found in the w gable, on the same level as the second-floor Tolbooth window, and these are both of the same roll-moulded design. It is hard to decide whether they are of late C16 (post-Reformation) date or, as has been suggested, *c.*1532, which is the date on a stone in the centre of the S wall, one year before Pittenweem became a separate parish.

Entry on the N side in the middle of an elaborate Gothic gable designed by the church's own Session Clerk *James Brown*, 1882. Gallery-stairs on each side. The interior is long and narrow, with a coomb ceiling from end to end. Carpenter's Gothic pulpit of that date against the S wall, the other three sides lined with galleries on slim cast-iron columns. Two-storey offices to the NE by *F. Boyter*, 1939. – STAINED GLASS. In the S wall, one light (Hope) by *James Ballantine & Son*, 1882. – In the N wall, three lights by *William Wilson* (four Evangelists, 1959; The Miraculous Draft of Fishes, 1963; The Sermon from the Boat, after 1958), and one by *W. Blair & J. Blyth* (Christ walking on the Water, 1974). – MONUMENTS in the churchyard. On the S wall of the church, George Hamilton of Cairns †1677. Mural monument with the motto LEGO CREDO and an open Bible above his coat of arms. – Tabletop to 'Wm Watson sometime Bailie of this Burgh' †1657, with his recumbent figure. – James Richardsone, 'huiusci burgi olim bailius', †1652. – 'A famous man David Binning Skipper and late Bailie of this Burgh' †1675.

PARISH CHURCH HALL, James Street. 1846, designed by *George Forgan* as a Relief church. Plain but not simple Gothic gable set back from the street, where the two clustered piers were once connected by iron railings and gates.

St John the Evangelist (Episcopal), Marygate. The original building of 1805 is a simple harled oblong with a stone N gable to Marygate, innocent Gothic with round corner-shafts and conical pinnacles. These are repeated on the tiny s sanctuary, whose gable has a mitre at the apex. But in 1869–70 the N porch was added and the oblong became a T, with a new E sanctuary. Inside, the N gallery was removed and the roof transformed with fancy hammerbeam trusses. STAINED GLASS. The two lights in the old sanctuary and three in the new are of 1870. Lancets on each side of the porch (SS Hubert and John the Baptist) by *Herbert Hendrie*, 1925. On the w wall a two-light window (SS Adrian and Margaret) of similar character. They go with *Robert Lorimer*'s enlargement of the vestry and refurnishing of the sanctuary with oak dado, altar and pulpit in 1924, all carved by *W. & A. Clow*. – STONE TABLETS. One on the E inside wall to Bishop Forman; another on the w outside wall to James Kennedy, Bishop of St Andrews, †1465.

PUBLIC BUILDINGS

Harbour. Well used, with often as many as fifty trawlers berthed, mostly registered KY for Kirkcaldy. A port was mentioned in a charter of 1228, and the Exchequer Rolls show fishing customs returns from the 1470s, rising sharply by 1541, when Pittenweem's royal charter granted permission to build a harbour; the confirmation charter of 1633 refers to 'ane good and safe harbour' built at the Burgh's expense. The Convention of Royal Burghs commended many of its applications to James VI for leave to impose levies for repair, and made grants for this purpose in 1697 and 1701. It was probably the EAST PIER that was extended by *George Cowie* and *Alexander Gilbert* in 1641, repaired by *Thomas Coventry* in 1688, when 36.5m. were taken down and rebuilt, and again repaired after the storm of 1702. The masonry is squared but only roughly coursed, its E parapet swelling into a rounded platform, gained by steps, for a light. Paving of whinstone strips from end to end, in crosswise courses. The E basin, in front of the Gyles, has a narrow slipway and a wall of short soldier-courses. The WEST PIER, or rather the central one, was being built in 1724 by *William Aitken* following consultation with *William Adam*; but it was rebuilt in 1822 and is now faced with concrete, though still paved with whin setts. Almost all the central basin is similarly faced. On its w side, the FISH MARKET of *c*.1800, three storeys and five bays with roofs of slightly shallower pitch than its skews, which have the stumps of what were probably ball finials. The C20 buildings around it are messy but useful, including a public lavatory and an ice plant. The w basin is contained by the SOUTH PIER with formidable Victorian masonry and rusticated parapet. Paving of whin strips. Further to the w, and beginning with an interesting bulge of random masonry, a retaining wall wanders along between town and sea. The former BOAT HARBOUR consists of a low, half-natural pier. On its W side a gap in the rocks, and a slipway. The rocks resume and make bookends for the crowstepped S gable (and the N gable too) of the windswept ROCKVILLE in front of Mid Shore.

TOLBOOTH, at the E end of the High Street. A square tower integrated with the W gable of the Parish Church (see above), of 1588 or possibly earlier. Vaulted ground floor, Council Chamber above. Two more storeys below the unharled clock-stage, corbelled out. This and the further corbelled balustrade and lucarned octagonal spire are all in early C17 style. One bell by '*Joran Puttensen's widow* and successor' is dated 1663, the other was recast in 1742. CLOCK by *John Smith* of Pittenweem, 1773. WEATHERCOCK, 1739.

DESCRIPTION

Pittenweem's excellent town centre is bypassed by the main road, which skirts it on the N side as JAMES STREET. At the W end the semi-detached housing scheme of UNIVERSITY PARK by *J. C. Cunningham* of St Andrews, 1935. Harl and slate, and sometimes double dormers with hoists for fishing-gear to the rear, intended to tempt fishermen from the obsolete houses along the shore. Then a nicely curved house-over-shop at the entry to South Loan, and in James Street itself a single-storey bowed shop and row of cottages, dated 1832. For the Parish Church Hall on the N side, *see* above. The early C19 PARK HOUSE and ABBEY LODGE (the latter much altered) mark the junction, with the late C18 ST MARGARET'S and its former farm buildings beyond. In MARYGATE some good C20 housing. Semi-detached with twin gables by *William Walker* of St Andrews, 1920, one and two storeys by *L. A. L. Rolland*, 1971, good neighbours to St John's Episcopal Church (*see* above). On the N side, the early C19 CORNER BAR and then an up-and-down mixture of one and two storeys, mostly early C19 too. At No. 18 a wallhead chimney-gable. ROUTINE ROW is just what it says – a narrow service-street with one or two C19 industrial buildings. No. 7 with clapboard first floor, and at the end a rambling warehouse (David Taylor, Fresh Fish). To the N the former School, with two gables and a steep entrance-gable, *c.*1880, subsequently the Picture House and now the Scout Hall. SOUTH LOAN then runs S to High Street, past the 'Elie oriel' of No. 28, the forestair of No. 2, and finally a little shop with a pediment and ball finial.

The N entry to the town is down CHARLES STREET, beginning with the ANCHOR INN of *c.*1810, with a pediment and fancy fanlit doorpiece. The rest consists of C19 single-storey rows of various dates, all ponderously and uniformly dormered, with the exception of No. 28, with its scrolled skewputts, and No. 22, whose builder *c.*1840 decided on three storeys and a much larger scale.

The W end of HIGH STREET is not so much an entry as a

sneak-in from the shore, by way of West Wynd. First a little triangular space overlooked by the gable of No. 58 and on the s side by that of No. 52, with scrolled skewputts. Then No. 40, C18 with smooth margins and a bold corbelled corner to the rear; No. 42 and its chimney-gabled neighbour were built in the early C19 as its farm.* MARKET PLACE, set back behind a row of trees, is an interlude. An absurdly crenellated shopfront conceals its proper building line (and the gable of No. 7 School Wynd), but the other buildings are worthy of the site. Nos. 4 and 5 mid-C19 grey ashlar, with a scrolled chimney stalk at the wallhead, Nos. 2 and 3 painted, and No. 1 bringing Market Place back to the line of High Street, which now aims straight for the Tolbooth steeple (*see* above). On the N side, Nos. 31–39 are C17 with crowstep gables, but cement-faced in the late C19, Nos. 25–27 dated 1635 but similarly refaced. KELLY LODGING at No. 23 was the Pittenweem residence of the Earls of Kellie, built mainly in the late C16. Near-ashlar front of three storeys with projecting stair-jamb and cap-house, whose corbels run into the circular corbelled base of its own little stair turret. A late C19 shop straightened the ground-floor building line and was removed in the restoration of 1969, but the new work does not match the old in quality, let alone in detail (for which cf. Kellie Castle near Pittenweem; *see* p. 252). Finally both sides of the street have a two-storey sequence and three-storey termination before the steeple.

COVE WYND leads down past the Great House, the former Town Hall and St Fillan's Cave (*see* The Priory, above), with the C17 BINNY COTTAGE to the r. and 7m. retaining wall to the l., to the Harbour (*see* above). The buildings of the waterfront are described from E to W, interrupted by the numerous wynds that climb back to Marygate and High Street.

THE GYLES project seaward, but GYLES HOUSE looks back towards the harbour, a three-storey sea-captain's house of 1626, white-harled and pantiled. Slated eaves course running down on to a stair-jamb whose doorway and window are roll-moulded. To the r., a wallhead chimney-stalk over a blank wall with storehouse door at the bottom. The other houses are at right angles to it. No. 7 set back, so that its rear wall springs from the rock. Nos. 3–6 of three storeys with a big chimney-gable at the wallhead and a forestair to the l. *Wheeler & Sproson* in their restoration in 1962 (for the National Trust for Scotland) could not preserve the function of the projecting stair turret but marked the points where timber stumps were found in the wall to the r. These, like the corbels on the end gable, seem to have supported wooden galleries.

ABBEY WALL ROAD climbs to the N. Forestair of No. 34 jammed against the cliff which continues upwards as a wall. On the

---

* This is now (1988) the workshop of H. Lawson, joiner and picture framer, whose founder patented a frame-making device still widely used (e.g. seen recently in Florence). The large sign, framed like a picture, was painted by the Pittenweem signwriter *Mr Paterson*.

other side, No. 75 is the former RELIEF CHURCH of 1777, a plain harled box half-turned to meet worshippers from downhill. Nos. 55–57 are a terrace of *c.*1890 with dormer hoists. But the entry at the bottom is effectively marked by the late C19 No. 4 EAST SHORE and its sharply corbelled corner. No. 5 is a double house of *c.*1820 with rusticated quoins and twin front doors, No. 10 of ashlar *c.*1840. After Cove Wynd (*see* above) the curve of East Shore continues with worthy Victorian stone fronts, No. 16 with a hoist sticking out of the top of a dormer. Then No. 18, traditionally C17 but more likely early C18. Rebuilding of 1972 retained the beautiful shape of its curvilinear chimney-gable but lost its authenticity; only the skewputts and the little platform over the crowning window are original. No. 20 returns to reality with a late C19 stone oriel and bargeboards over a shop (Fishermen's Mutual, selling marine hardware).

WATER WYND climbs up past two brightly painted fronts, No. 7 and the chimney-gabled No. 8. A very steep section with split whin pavement against a high wall reaches a derelict house with forestair near the top. Then MID SHORE starts with the generously curved corner of the FO'C'SLE CAFÉ, *c.*1840. At No. 4 the best of the harbour fronts, three ashlar storeys including a shop (David Gerard, wholesale fish merchant), crowned by a Venetian window and chimney-gable complete with hoist, all late C18.

SCHOOL WYND. Another steep ascent between high walls to the Baptist Church (*see* above). Then past a winding row of house-fronts to High Street. Back in Mid Shore, No. 9 has a datestone of 1888, paired with a re-sited lintel of 1624, the figures carved on false voussoirs with a monogrammed keystone surprisingly refined for that date. Nos. 11–12, C18 with a chimney-gable, set back behind a forecourt. No. 28, past the bulge of the building-line, has a 'masonry' cement front and a dormer with a hoist. Pillared forestair and surviving skewputts at No. 36.

CARMAN'S WYND gives access to a parallel row behind Mid Shore, which goes on with No. 38, early C19 with a pend arch. Butchered ashlar front, the cement render having been removed *c.*1975. After BRUCE'S WYND and WEST WYND, the C18 No. 40 allows the road to squeeze past its corbelled corner into WEST SHORE, the gaily painted tail of the waterfront. Forestairs at Nos. 6, 7 and 16, and a chimney-gable at No. 10 which is dated 1858 but looks earlier. No. 12 leans drunkenly seawards. Another forestair at No. 18, ending the row, which is protected by a continuous sea wall.

RAITH HOUSE

1.9km. W of Kirkcaldy

Large but neat villa built for Alexander Melville, Lord Raith, Treasurer-Depute of Scotland, in 1693–6 by *Alexander Gavin-*

lock, mason,* and *Thomas Kyle*, wright. *William Rowan* is named as 'Overserer' but the design is probably by *James Smith*.‡ Reticent harled and piend-roofed box, the main (N) front's three-bay centrepiece slightly advanced under a pediment. Rusticated quoins. In the pediment, a coat of arms flanked by scrolled cartouches by *James Thomson* and *Alexander Baxter*.

In 1785 *James Playfair* remodelled the interior and added five-bay pavilions joined to the main block by quadrant links. These are very restrained, much in Smith's own manner of seventy years before (e.g. Dupplin, Tayside), but the late C18 date is proclaimed by the overarches in the W pavilion's end bays. An Ionic portico added *c*. 1800 has been replaced by a Victorian porch. Presumably also Victorian is the balcony stretched across the plain S front. More unwelcome the haphazard additions at each gable of the main block and the removal of glazing bars.

The interior is mostly Playfair's (very smart marble chimneypieces in the principal rooms), but the C17 stair survives, its light wrought-iron balustrade worked with foliage and the coronetted initials of Alexander Melville and his wife Barbara Dundas; *James Horne* may have been the smith.§

Immediately to the W, a solid castle-style early C19 ICE-HOUSE, its upper floor a game larder. – Beside it, STABLE COURT of *c*. 1800, the whinstone E front with pedimented ends and ground-floor niches. – On Cormie Hill, an early C19 brick-built and harled Gothicky TOWER.

RANDERSTON
1.9km. SE of Kingsbarns

5010

Crowstep-gabled C16 laird's house on the edge of a C19 farm steading. The Myretons or Mortons acquired the lands of Randerston in 1429 and a fortalice is mentioned here in 1567, although the present house looks a little later. Three storeys; L-plan with the SE jamb tenuously joined to the main block. In the inner angle, a rounded stairtower corbelled out to a rectangular cap-house. NW and SE corner turrets, their tops removed and the roof swept over them. Vaulted ground floor. Very plain single-storey extension to the jamb, probably C19.

RAVENSCRAIG CASTLE *see* KIRKCALDY: PATHHEAD, p. 295

ROSSEND CASTLE *see* BURNTISLAND

---

* Another mason employed (on fairly minor work) was *John Adam*, probably William Adam's father and Robert Adam's grandfather.

‡ Smith measured some of the work and was contractor for the 'yeat'.

§ He was paid for making 'ye ryvell of ye open stair' in 1695.

ROSSIE HOUSE
2.6km. E of Auchtermuchty

Harled laird's house built for the Cheapes of Rossie, who bought
the estate in 1669. The present three-bay main block was
put up c.1700 by Bailie Ballingall, mason (probably *James
Ballingall*, bailie of Strathmiglo), as the W extension of an
earlier house.* Quite plain except for a pediment over the
door. The window architraves seem to date from the alterations
made by *David Wishart*, mason, in 1752; flat-roofed dormer
of 1938 an unwelcome intrusion. The piending of the W gable
is an early C19 modification. The original house was removed
in or before 1767, when the shallowly projecting E addition
was built. Was a balancing W extension intended?‡ Late C19
conservatory on the W. On the E, farm offices (much altered),
hidden by a crenellated link and arch to a curving whinstone
screen wall which is shown as existing on an estate plan of
1830.

Inside the house, the SW ground-floor room was thrown in
with the entrance hall, c.1920, this new sitting-hall being given
thinly Jacobean panelling. Fireplace surround made up of bits
of C17 woodwork. In the overmantel, carved relief of the
Annunciation, perhaps C17 Spanish. Broad stone turnpike
stair, its newel's moulded caps and bases of the same late
C17–early C18 type as at Balgonie Castle and Melville House.
Unusually, it is placed in the middle of the double-pile. On
the first-floor sitting room's W wall, simple pine panelling of
c.1700. In the drawing room of 1767, a Leith-type pine and
gesso chimneypiece decorated with thistles, sheaves and shells.
Are this and the upright acanthus-leaf cornice of 1767, or do
they belong to a slightly later refitting? In the SW room, another
pine and gesso chimneypiece, imported in 1938. Late C18
coombed ceilings in the main second-floor rooms. Attic bathroom of 1938, its best-quality fitments and linoleum all intact.

Roofless MAUSOLEUM in Tomb Wood to the SE, probably
mid-C17. Rubble-built, with a small window in the E gable; W
door with chamfered jambs.

ROSYTH

Two settlements, divided by Admiralty Road and Castlandhill
Road. On the S is Rosyth Dockyard, its associated housing built
mostly since 1950. On the N, a garden city begun by the Scottish
National Housing Co. c.1915, but whose intended development
was thwarted by the dockyard's closure between 1925 and 1938.
A. H. Mottram was architect for almost all the well-mannered
interwar development, generously laid out and well provided
with trees and churches, but lacking a clear centre.

* The building accounts among the Cheape of Rossie papers in St Andrews
University Library are unfortunately undated.

‡ *George Paterson* had prepared a scheme for the addition of two-storey pavilions
joined to the main block by colonnaded quadrants in 1753. It was not executed.

CHURCHES

ROSYTH BAPTIST CHURCH, Queensferry Road. Opened 1923.

ROSYTH METHODIST CHURCH, Queensferry Road. By *Alan Mercer*, 1970. Tent-shaped, with a concrete-tiled roof.

ROSYTH PARISH CHURCH, Queensferry Road. By *A. H. Mottram*, 1929–31. Buttressed rectangle with neo-Georgian detail. Venetian window in the piended entrance gable. SE tower with curvaceous belfry.

ST COLUMBA, Torridon Place. By the *Ministry of Public Buildings and Works*, 1969. Drydashed box with an M-roofed clear-storey stuck on top.

ST JOHN AND ST COLUMBA (R.C.), Crossroads Place and Admiralty Road. 1926, by *A. H. Mottram*, a humbler version of his Parish Church and with no tower.

ST MARGARET (Anglican), Hilton Road. By the *Ministry of Public Buildings and Works*, Edinburgh (senior architect: *J. R. Johnston*), 1968–9, with a fashionably swept-up roof.

ROSYTH CASTLE
0.6km. S

C15 tower marooned inside the dockyard. Sir James Stewart's lands of Rosyth were created a barony in 1428, and the present house was begun probably about half a century later. Its site was a small island approachable by a causeway from the N. On this island were erected buildings round a courtyard whose NE corner was filled by the tower house.

The ashlar-built tower house is L-plan, the minimally protruding SE jamb containing the stair. Externally it is austere, the walling broken only by narrow windows with chamfered jambs and lintels; much larger mullioned and transomed first-floor gable windows were inserted in 1635 (the date inscribed, together with the initials I.S.M.N. for James Stewart and his wife Margaret Napier, on a transom of the W window). Barely projecting parapet with none of the elaborate corbelling characteristic of later tower houses. In the inner angle, a seg-mental-arched door opening into a small lobby from which is reached the turnpike stair in the jamb to the r. Ahead, the main block's ground floor was occupied by a tunnel-vaulted store, originally divided horizontally by an entresol of which the wooden floor's stone corbels survive. From the entresol's SE corner, a service stair to the first-floor hall. Like the ground-floor storage, the hall is tunnel-vaulted and was originally divided by an entresol, presumably removed in 1635, when the tall gable windows were inserted. Small C15 N window, originally with stone window seats. To its r., an aumbry. In the S wall, segment-arched buffet recess. The moulded fireplace beside it looks a C17 remodelling; locker in its W jamb. Next to the E window, a wall-chamber, probably originally a garderobe. Just above the entresol level, a garderobe in the E wall entered from the stair (now non-existent above first floor). At the second floor the stair gave access to a chamber in the s wall as well as to the solar. The solar is unvaulted; stone cornice on its long walls. NE garderobe. Beside the w fireplace, a vaulted lobby to the barmkin's C15 parapet walk. Roofless attic.

Tusking on the tower's w and s faces shows that the C15 barmkin was of exceptional height (12–15m.). It was replaced by lower ranges, probably in 1561 (the date carved, together with the garlanded royal arms and initials MR for *Maria Regina*, on a semi-classically framed panel over the entrance). Much of the N range, which perhaps contained a C16 first-floor hall, survives. Entrance in a porch whose hood looks old-fashioned for 1561. Is this C15 work re-used? In the porch's sides, diagonally set gunloops. More loops in the main wall. At the corners of the range, remains of corbelled turrets. The l., in the inner angle with the tower, contained a stair from first to second floor (there was presumably an external stair from the courtyard to the first floor); the r. terminated the second-floor parapet walk.

To the N and outwith the dockyard, a square C16 DOOCOT; double-pitch roof with gableted crowsteps and skewputts carved with human heads.

DOCKYARD

The decision to build a naval dockyard on the E coast of Scotland was taken in 1903 and the necessary land at Rosyth bought by the government. The TIDAL BASIN and two GRAVING DOCKS were built by *Easton, Gibb & Son Ltd* 1909–14. – OIL FUEL DEPOT, with a concrete tank for 250 000 tons and thirty-seven steel tanks, each for 5000 tons, 1914. – Dockyard WORKSHOPS begun 1915. – Short-time working at the yard was introduced in 1921, and the yard closed in 1925. Reopening of the yard in 1938 was accompanied by further workshop development which continued after the Second World War.

PUBLIC BUILDINGS

CAMDEAN PRIMARY SCHOOL, King's Road. By *Fife County Council*, 1946–67.

KING'S ROAD PRIMARY SCHOOL, King's Crescent. Harled and red-tiled, by *R. H. Motion*, 1920–1.

MASONIC HALL, Parkgate. By *Robert F. Shearer*, 1917. Blocky, with squat crowstepped gables.

ROSYTH HEALTH CENTRE, Park Road. By *Scottish Health Service Common Services Agency*, 1982–3. Single-storey in white blockwork, the lead roof rising to a clearstorey over the entrance.

ROSYTH INSTITUTE, Parkgate. 1925–6. Would-be picturesque but joyless, in red brick.

PITREAVIE. *See* p. 345.

ROTHES *see* GLENROTHES

ST ANDREWS 5010

St Regulus' Church,
   Cathedral and Priory   259
St Andrews Castle   369
University Buildings   372

Churches   378
Public Buildings   384
Streets   389

A former cathedral city and Scotland's main medieval pilgrimage place, St Andrews is now more famed for its university and golf courses.

A monastery in the Celtic tradition of St Columba was founded at St Andrews* by Oengus I, King of Picts,‡ in the mid-c8. This foundation has traditionally been associated with St Regulus' bringing several bones of the apostle St Andrew to Scotland and the erection of a shrine to house them. The monastery was well established by *c.*940, when Constantine III abdicated and became its abbot. By that time St Andrews had become the seat of a bishop, apparently accorded primacy over the other Scottish bishops. By 1124 the monastery seems to have divided into two sections, neither of them rigorously monastic. One group consisted of married clergy who provided hospitality for pilgrims and strangers. The other group (Céli Dé) held prebends in the cathedral church (now St Regulus') by hereditary right but failed to provide a regular service at its high altar. After David I's foundation of an Augustinian priory here in 1144, a bull of Pope Eugenius III and a royal mandate provided for the Augustinians to take over the revenues and possessions of the Céli Dé on the death of the existing prebends. However, the Céli Dé continued and had been reorganized as a college of secular canons possessing the Church of Blessed Mary on the Rock by 1250, about the same time as the Augustinians prepared to move into the cloister attached to the new cathedral begun by Bishop Arnold in 1162.

There was a settlement of sorts attached to the Celtic monastery, probably on the site of the present Cathedral precinct, but *c.*1130 David I gave Bishop Robert leave to found a new burgh. It appears from a charter of *c.*1170 that the nucleus of this burgh lay w of the Cathedral precinct, along Castle Street and perhaps North Street, possibly with an unrecorded predecessor of the present Castle (begun by Bishop Roger in 1200) as its original focal point. If that were so, the burgh's lay-out must have been altered after the new cathedral's foundation to provide two main streets (North Street and South Street) forming two sides of a triangle with the cathedral at its apex. The town developed to

---

*Then known as Cenn-rigmonaid (Head of the King's Mount) and later as Cill-rigmonaid (Church of the King's Mount).

‡Or possibly by Oengus II, *c.*830; but a mention of the death of the Abbot Tuathalan in 747 is some confirmation of an c8 date.

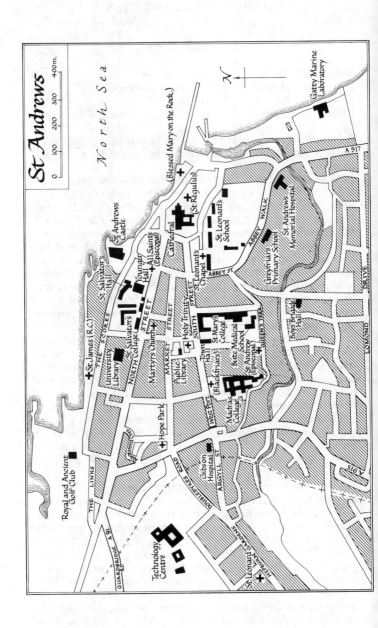

St Andrews

North Sea

0 100 200 300 400m.

N

Royal and Ancient
Golf Club

The Links

GUARDBRIDGE A 91

DOUBLEDYKES ROAD

Technology
Centre

ARGYLE ST.

Gibson
Hospital

St Leonard's

HEPBURN GARDENS

A 915

St James (R.C.)
THE SCORES
University
Library
North College
St Salvator's
St Salvator's Hall
Younger Hall
All Saints
(Episcopal)
St Andrews Castle
Cathedral
(St Regulus)
(Blessed Mary on the Rock.)
St Leonard's
Chapel
St Leonard's
School
ABBEY ST.
ABBEY WALK
Greyfriars
Primary School
St Andrews
Memorial Hospital

Martyrs Church
MARKET STREET
SOUTH STREET
Holy Trinity
Hope Park
West Port
Public Library
Town Hall
Blackfriars
St Mary's College
Bute Medical School
St Andrew (Episcopal)
Madras College
QUEEN'S TERR.
Boys Brigade Hall

LOMOND DRIVE
A 917

Gatty Marine
Laboratory

the W, a market place W of Union Street having been formed by
the C14; by the C16, the N boundary ran along the S side of The
Scores, the S along the Kinness Burn, and the West Port marked
the burgh's W end. The burgh of St Andrews was represented
in the General Council held at Scone in 1357, contributed substantially to royal customs *c.* 1362, was admitted to Parliament in
1456, and paid taxation from 1483. However, it was not formally
made a royal burgh until 1620, when its commercial importance,
at its height in the C15 and C16, was already declining. Since
then it has never been more than a local centre.

The University, now dominating the town's life, began as a
society of scholars granted a charter of incorporation by Bishop
Wardlaw in 1412. Foundation of colleges followed from the mid-
C15, and St Andrews had become a centre of Protestant theology
a century later when the Reformation brought about the abandonment and subsequent destruction of the Cathedral. Since
then the University has been the town's chief source of employment.

Golf was played at St Andrews by the late C15. The Society
of St Andrews Golfers was founded in 1754; in 1834 it changed
its name to the The Royal and Ancient Golf Club and opened
its first clubhouse. A new clubhouse was begun in 1853, the year
after the opening of the railway to Leuchars Junction had made St
Andrews an easily accessible resort from Dundee and Edinburgh.
Mid-C19 development on the lines of Edinburgh's later New
Town areas was followed from the 1890s by the building of
large villas along The Scores and Hepburn Gardens and hotels
overlooking the Links. Many of these have now been taken over
as accommodation for the University, the town's recent expansion being contained in a cluster of housing estates to the S.

ST REGULUS' CHURCH, CATHEDRAL AND PRIORY

ST REGULUS' (ST RULE'S) CHURCH

One of Fife's strangest sights, the C11 shrine-church built to
house St Andrew's relics and as a landmark for pilgrims. The
shrine is just a small chancel (7.9m. × 6m.), the landmark an
immensely tall W tower, both built of beautifully dressed local
grey ashlar. Only the original church survives, but after the
foundation of the Augustinian priory it was extended W and E
in the early C12 by the addition of a nave and new chancel.

The tower rises sheer for 33m., barely interrupted by the
stringcourses defining its three stages. The buttresses protruding N and S from the lowest stage are probably part of the
demolished nave's E wall. Very tall second stage, with small
round-headed windows. Short belfry, its two-light openings
sitting on the stringcourse. These windows' jambs are recessed
as though for nook-shafts, a divergence from contemporary
Anglo-Saxon work. Another difference from Anglo-Saxon
towers is that the central shafts are placed not in the middle

of the wall thickness but near the outer face. Above, in each face a round-headed window, like those of the second stage. Corbelled eaves course marking the original wallhead. Above it, a C17 corbelled parapet.

In the tower's W face, huge arch from the nave, its head slightly horseshoe-shaped. The arch cuts into the corbelling of the lowest stringcourse. Clearly it is an insertion of the early C12. Shafted jambs supporting capitals which develop from a rounded section at the base to a square shape under the abacus. The arch itself is of two orders, the outer plain, the inner with roll-and-hollow mouldings. The mouldings' section and the unusual arrangement of the two orders side by side instead of one above the other are paralleled at Wharram-le-Street Church (Yorkshire). That church was built in the early C12 after it had been granted to Nostell Priory, the convent from which, by way of Scone, Alexander I brought monks to St Andrews. One of these monks, Robert, who became Bishop of St Andrews shortly before 1124, is recorded in the C13 *Legend of St Andrew* as having undertaken 'the enlargement of his church and its dedication to divine worship.' The inference seems clear that it was Bishop Robert who enlarged the church, employing masons from Nostell who had previously worked on Wharram-le-Street. The arch was narrowed in the C13, the lower courses of this work still visible, and was then built up in the C16, probably at the same time as a round-headed door (itself now blocked) was slapped in the S face.

In the tower's E face, a tall round-headed arch (now blocked) into the chancel. In contrast to the elaborately moulded orders of the E arch, its two orders are of plain square section. The outer order and its jambs seem to be contemporary with the main C11 fabric, the jambs' coursing following that of the walling. The differently coursed jambs of the inner order appear to be an insertion, perhaps of the C13.

The tower's lower stringcourse continues as an eaves course round the roofless chancel. This is almost square, of two bays with round-headed windows. Three raggles on the tower's E face show successive roof pitches, the middle one apparently representing the original, the upper a C12 or C13 heightening, and the lower, which was set for a parapet gutter, may show the roof constructed by Prior William de Lothian in the mid-C14. Covered by the roof has been a small door, presumably into a loft. In the chancel's E wall, the great arch inserted in the early C12, when a new chancel was added. The similarity to Wharram-le-Street is again marked. A nook-shaft on each side of the jambs; attached shaft between them. Boldly moulded arch head, its upper part and the stonework above probably part of the repairs of 1789 recorded on an inscription on the outside wall.

MONUMENTS. On the chancel's N wall, William Preston †1657. Tomb-recess type, the base carved with a skeleton reclining in a drapery hammock; strapworked inscription panel in the pilastered recess; strapworked armorial cartouche on top. – Anna Halyburton † 1653 and John Comrie. Tall aedicule, the attached columns developing into caryatids of Justice; coats of arms in the obelisk-finialled steep pediment. – On the outside of the chancel's s wall, an eroded moulded frame, probably for an heraldic panel. – On the tower's s face, panel to the wife of G. Puas, probably late C16, with an almost illegible inscription round a coat of arms.

CATHEDRAL CHURCH AND PRIORY

Arnold, Bishop of St Andrews, founded the cathedral church 12 probably in 1162. This foundation seems to have marked the beginning of construction, after materials had been collected, so the design had presumably been decided upon a few years earlier. Bishop Arnold's church was conceived on a scale unequalled in Scotland and closely comparable to Durham Cathedral in its Romanesque form. The architectural detail is advanced. By contrast, the plan was conservative – a thin ten-bay aisled nave, transepts, and an aisled choir with the presbytery projecting beyond. No provision was made for a cloister, so the original intention seems to have been that the church would be served by secular canons (cf. Glasgow

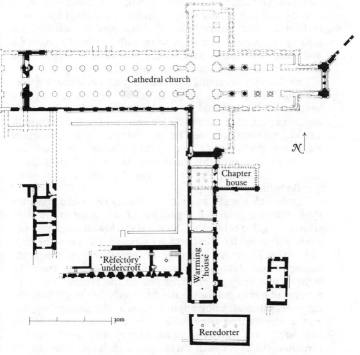

St Andrews Cathedral Church and Priory,
plan

Cathedral). The building must have been partly completed and in use by 1238, when Bishop Malvoisin was buried there (his predecessor Roger Beaumont † 1202 having been buried in St Regulus' Church). c.1250 the Augustinian priory at St Regulus' was transferred to the new cathedral church, whose presumably uncompleted nave was then extended W by a further four bays to allow sufficient length for the cloister. The W front was blown down by a gale c.1280, and then rebuilt two bays to the E, the abandoned W bays being filled with a narthex. In 1318 the church was consecrated.

After a major fire in 1378, repair and partial reconstruction continued until c.1400. Further repairs were made to the S transept after its gable was destroyed by a gale in 1409. The final major medieval work was Prior James Haldenstone's reconstruction of the great E gable c.1430.

Abandoned after the Reformation of 1560, the cathedral seems to have been used as a quarry by 1577, when the Crown ordered 'the priour of Sanctandrois [Lord James Stewart] and all uthiris demolesaris of the cathederall kirk thairof to desist and ceis from all forder douncasting thairof.' However, in 1649 Parliament gave the burgh leave to take stones from the church for fortification of the town against the Cromwellian army. Thirty years later, no more than the present fragments survived. Government consolidation of what remained began in 1805, but it was only after 1893, when the third Marquess of Bute bought Priory House, whose garden included the cloister and whose hothouses were built against the nave's S wall, that full repair could be carried out. The church and cloister are now unmistakably an Ancient Monument.

The church's surviving parts (the E gable, half the W gable, and most of the nave's S wall) have the ugly fascination of a bombed city. Of the single-storey NARTHEX made in the nave's two W bays during the post-1280 contraction of the church, much of the S wall survives. Its responds show that the narthex was of two vaulted bays. In the E bay, a blocked pointed arch into the cloister, probably made after the narthex's demolition c.1380, and replacing a taller doorway of which one nook-shaft is still visible.

The church's WEST FRONT was heavily reconstructed after 1378, but the general composition of octagonal stairtowers gripping a gable is late C13. So too is the lowest stage's stonework, with two-tier blind arcades across the faces of the aisle and tower. Door into the nave of several orders, the shafts having waterholding bases and bell capitals with traces of stiffleaf foliage; dogtooth ornament on the arches. To its r., remains of a respond for the narthex vault. In the gable above the door, blind arcading applied when a wall passage's openings to the narthex were built up in the late C14; it relates awkwardly to the earlier arcading. Above, two tiers of traceried windows, the lower each three-light, the upper two-light. A wall passage joining the towers at clearstorey level has crossed the upper windows. Presumably there was a rose window or

St Andrews Cathedral,
conjectural reconstruction of the east front of *c.*1200

St Andrews Cathedral,
conjectural reconstruction of the late thirteenth-century west front
as altered in the late fourteenth century

vesica in the gable's apex. The surviving s tower is topped by a belfry with gabled openings and a small stone spire.

Of the NAVE ARCADES, only the bases of four octagonal piers on the N survive. Their eke towards the nave suggests that they may have been intended to have shafts to carry a nave vault, although such a vault was never erected. The foundations show that the E arch on each side has been infilled, probably to strengthen the central tower after the fire of 1378. The s arcade's late C13 W respond has a semicircular major order and keel-shaped minor orders; dogtooth ornament on the hollow outer order; bell-shaped capitals.

The nave's SOUTH WALL is of pier-and-panel construction, i.e. with broad piers carrying the main load, and thinner masonry panels between. Internally, all the piers appear as pilaster strips to which the responds for the aisle vaulting are attached. In the two w bays added in the mid-C13 the responds have bases of waterholding type. Responds of the next bay w survive inside the present W front's walling. Like the earlier E part of the aisle, these bays have had quadripartite vaults but at a lower level. No windows in these bays (the N end of the cloister's W range abutted), but the walling's weight is relieved in each bay by an off-centre blind arch, the E acutely pointed.

The ten bays to the E are of *c.*1170. Deep respond bases having two demi-rolls separated by a quirk and with a quite steeply curving lower torus. In the six w of these bays, respond shafts with wall-ribs but no capitals; probably they are late C14 replacements. The wall-panels of these w bays seem to have been rebuilt, probably *c.*1250 but possibly in the late C14, with windows (now Y-traceried) set high up to clear the cloister roof. In their w bay, the cloister's off-centre W processional door, originally elliptically arched, but it has been filled in with a smaller round-arched opening of *c.*1400.

In the nave's four E bays, the responds have the same bases as those to the w, but also have capitals carved with tightly curled crocketed foliage. These probably represent the design built *c.*1170, as do the tall round-arched windows, whose lower part was blocked when the cloister was added outside. The same base design again at the respond of the arch into the crossing. That arch's stonework courses through with the adjacent window in the SOUTH TRANSEPT, so they must be contemporary. This and the transept's other round-arched W windows (their lower part blocked for the cloister) have nook-shafts and mouldings identical to those of the original windows in the presbytery's E gable. But this window detail seems to belong to a first phase of the cathedral's design, while the respond base belongs to a second phase (cf. the bases of the responds and arcades of the choir). The conclusion must be that the second phase (probably of *c.*1170) introduced only partial modification of the original concept. Above and below the windows, Romanesque blind arcading. The transept has had an arcade into three E chapels. Only the s respond, part of the gable's rebuilding after 1409, survives.

In the SW corner, fragmentary remains of the door to the night stair.

In the CHOIR, the bases of the arcades' pillars are of the same design as the bases of the responds of the nave's S wall, but the choir's triple-shafted responds have much shallower bases. Assuming that the building sequence consisted of construction of the choir walls first, followed by the nave walls, followed by the choir arcades, the bases' different detail suggests a modification of the design immediately after completion of the choir walls.

The PRESBYTERY has begun in the choir's E bay where the arcade was replaced by solid walls, marking off the E bays of the aisles as chapels, and then thrust E for a further unaisled bay.* Its E gable is almost intact, framed by square corner towers which are finished with dumpy octagonal spires above the belfry stage. Corbelling below the belfry carries across the gable's wallhead. The stringcourses which divided the front into four tiers were also carried across the towers and gable. Above the windowless lowest storey each tier contained three round-arched windows. The bottom windows survive, their jambs set in slightly recessed orders with nook-shafts; the upper windows were almost identical but with angle-rolls. In the reconstruction carried out by Prior James Haldenstone, c. 1430, the two upper tiers of windows were replaced by one great E window set just above the triforium passage and cutting through the clearstorey passage. Probably also part of this reconstruction were the addition of the large angle buttress on the N and the removal of arcading from the lowest stage of the gable's W face.

The stumps of the presbytery's N and S walls contain the jambs of their triforium and clearstorey windows. Round-arched triforium windows. The clearstorey windows' pointed arches must be a modification of the original design (presumably they were at first intended to have round-arched heads like the windows in the top tier of the gable); but this change of design must have been agreed before the E gable had been completed, since the shafts in the turrets' inner angles slope back to allow for the clearstorey's new triple-arcaded design.

The CLOISTER BUILDINGS S of the church were begun in the mid-C13. Most of their ground floor survives. On the nave's S side, corbels for the CLOISTER WALK's roof. In the E bay, round-arched E processional door. The paired round-arched recesses in the transept's W wall were probably BOOK-PRESSES. S of the transept, a round-headed door with shafted jambs into a passage (formerly vaulted). Traces of a stone bench along one wall and interlaced arcading on the N side.

Richly treated door from the cloister walk into the C13 CHAPTER HOUSE. This has been a three-aisled vaulted room. On the N wall, remains of seats and the bases of a wall arcade.

---

* It is possible but unlikely that the original, quickly discarded, intention was to continue the presbytery one bay further W into the choir.

This chapter house became a vestibule when a new chapter house was built to its E *c.*1315. The new chapter house was unaisled, vaulted in two bays. Arcaded seat recesses in the S wall. S of the chapter house, a formerly vaulted room, its door from the cloister walk with a flattened trefoil head. Beyond the day-stair passage to the now vanished dormitory above is the WARMING HOUSE, its exterior refaced, *c.*1900, in horribly red sandstone. Quadripartite-vaulted double-aisled interior, with a large fireplace near the E wall's S end. The warming house projects beyond the cloister's S range. Even further S, the REREDORTER (or latrines), again with much red sandstone refacing. Double-aisle plan, with an ample drain on the S. To the E, two vaulted basement rooms of a detached, formerly L-plan building. It is perhaps C15.

The cloister's S range contained the REFECTORY. The only surviving feature of the hall itself is the bowed S projection for the *pulpitum*, but the undercroft survives, again clad in Edwardian red sandstone. Inside, two rooms. In the E, four compartments of quadripartite vaulting springing from corbels and a central shafted column. Wheel stair in the SW corner. The six-bay W room is three-aisled, with quadripartite vaults. In the SW corner, a passage leading up to a room at cloister level. In the WEST RANGE, tunnel-vaulted rooms, their present appearance with doors to E and W unlikely to be earlier than the C16.

PRECINCT WALL

The Priory property was surrounded by a wall by the C14. In the early C16 the wall was reconstructed by Priors John and Patrick Hepburn, and most of their work survives enclosing a large area bounded by the Cathedral on the N, The Shore on the E, and Abbey Walk on the SW. It is a serious fortification, with a corbelled parapet breaking forward into bracketed rounds between the towers which punctuate its length. Martine recorded sixteen towers in 1683; there are now thirteen, and the position of a fourteenth (in Abbey Walk) can be traced. Two of the towers are rectangular, the rest round. All have tabernacled image niches and keyhole gunloops.

Of the gates, the simplest is in the short stretch of wall which runs E from the cathedral's NE buttress (the cathedral itself seems to have been the N defence). Round-arched door under an image niche containing the lower part of a seated figure; to the l., a double keyhole gunloop and the Hepburn arms. In The Shore, at the SE end of Pends Road, which runs through the precinct, is the MILL PORT or SEA YETT, its segmental-arched opening flanked by gunloops. The TIENDS GATE in Abbey Walk served the tiends barn which stood behind. Above its entrance, remains of a gatehouse. Very much grander than these C16 entrances is the C14 NW gateway, THE PENDS. Gabled buttresses flank its front to the town; blind cusped arcading above the broad arch. Inside, four vaulted bays, the ribs springing from corbels. The N bay is taller and separately vaulted. Does this mean that it was built in two stages?

GRAVEYARD MONUMENTS

Huge collection of tombstones and monuments, mostly of the C18 and C19, fairly few worth individual mention.

Excellent series of memorials on the N wall, E of the Cathedral. Under a tablet to John Small of Foodie †1862, an eroded early C17 monument, a classicizing version of the medieval tomb recess, with coupled Corinthianish pilasters and a scrolled pediment broken by an oblong panel containing two coats of arms. – In the face of the precinct wall's tower to the E, Katharine Clephane, a segmental pedimented Corinthian aedicule dated 1609. – Katharine Duddingston † 1614, very badly worn bracketed aedicule with scrolls on the steep pediment. – James Sword, dated 1657 and very old-fashioned. Tomb-recess type, the coupled pilasters far from being correctly classical, the inscription tablet set in strapwork. On top, a would-be Ionic aedicule containing a coat of arms. – Eroded early C17 Composite aedicule, now with an inscription to Andrew Hay †1832. – Helen Myrton, a small Corinthian pilastered aedicule dated 1609, the shaped pediment skied above three coats of arms. – Next door, a worn segmental pedimented aedicule, again early C17. – Adam Ferguson † 1816, large Aegypto-Greek monument with a carved relief portrait. – Clement Cor †1608, aedicular with a steep pediment. – Tall Doric aedicule to Norman Macleod of Macleod † 1772. – A little to the E, Sir Hugh Lyon Playfair †1861, a large Gothic recess enclosing a trophy-topped sarcophagus, with a relief of Playfair framed in a laurel wreath. – Across the NE corner, Gothic shrine to John Whyte Melville †1883.

On the S wall, large Composite aedicule for John Lepar, dated 1646, the steep pediment broken by a coat of arms. Relief showing the Last Trump being blown at a recumbent skeleton. On the base, Time and (?) Justice. – Kitsch memorial to Tommy Morris †1875, with a golfer in high relief. – On the graveyard wall W of St Regulus' Church, Mary Lyon Campbell †1809, elegant with an urn. The monument was erected by her husband, who wrote the inscription:

> Meek and Gentle was her Spirit
> Prudence did her life adorn
> Modest she disclaimed all Merit
> Tell me am not I forlorn
> Yet I must and will resign her
> She's in better hands than mine
> But I hope again to join her
> In the realms of love divine.

TOMBSTONES. N of the Cathedral, early C19 headstone to John, Jean and Catherine McDonald, incorporating a C17 strapworked coat of arms of the Elphinstone family. – To its SE, stone to — Youll †1748, with an angel's head in the curly top and symbols of death at the bottom. – In line with the N transept, stone for James and Laurence Porterfield † 1774 and 1776, with a crowned rounding-knife.

Beside the N wall of St Regulus' Church, coped table stone of Andrew Mason † 1691, carved with trade emblems; it was restored in 1880. – E of St Regulus', Agness Cairncross † 1830, a tall pedestal with a crisply carved urn. – To its E, headstone of Elizabeth Hamilton † 1841, erected by her husband Thomas Key, wright, the inscription framed by carved curtains. – S of St Regulus', table stone to Laurence Horsburgh, dated 1816 and characteristic of St Andrews gentility in that it has a carved tablecloth. – SW of St Regulus', headstone of Samuel Rutherfoord † 1661, but probably erected c.1712, inscribed:

> what tongu what Pen or Skill of Men
> Can Famous Rutherfoord Commend
> His Learning justly rasid his Fame
> True Godliness Adornd His Name
> He did Converse with things Above
> Acquainted with Emmanuels Love
> Most orthodox He was And sound
> And Many Errours Did confound
> For Zions King and Zions cause
> And Scotlands covenanted LAWS
> Most constantly he Did contend
> Until His Time was At An End
> Than He Wan to the Full Fruition
> Of That Which He Had Seen in vision

– NW of St Regulus', table stone to Andrew Walker, dated 1816 and very like that of Laurence Horsburgh. – Beside it, slab to Thomas Duncan † 1668, raised on legs when it was renewed by John Duncan in 1729. Coats of arms at one end, symbols of death at the other. – Coped table stone to John Duncan † 1711; recut inscription:

> HERE LIES BENEATH THIS STONE CONFIN'D
> JOHN DUNCAN LAIRD OF STONY WYND
> HE WAS A MAN OF GREAT RENOWN
> GUILD BROTHER OF ST ANDREWS TOWN
> HE HAD EVERY VIRTUE THAT CAN
> DENOMINATE AN HONEST MAN

ST ANDREWS CASTLE

Tidy remains of the castle of the bishops (from 1471, arch-bishops) of St Andrews. The site's natural strength (a headland with sheer drops to the sea on the N and E) was supplemented by ditches probably from c.1200, when Bishop Roger de Beaumont built the first castle here. Bishop Roger's castle, damaged during the Wars of Independence, was rebuilt by the English Lords de Beaumont and de Ferrers in 1336, but their work was demolished by Sir Andrew Moray the next year. According to the *Scotichronicon* it was rebuilt 'from the foundations' during the episcopate of Bishop Walter Traill (1385–1401). Cardinal

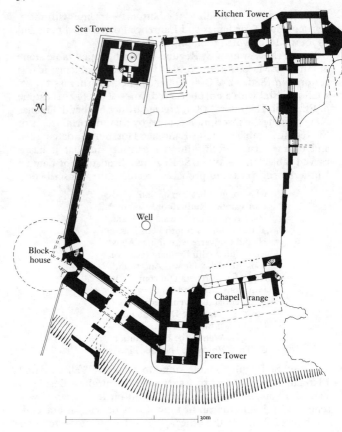

St Andrews Castle,
plan of ground floor

David Beaton was engaged in strengthening the castle's foundations in 1546 when he was murdered there and the castle was taken over by anti-government forces. In the ensuing siege the defences were, according to John Knox, 'razed to the ground'. The castle was again rebuilt by Archbishop John Hamilton, *c.*1555, but the abolition of episcopacy in 1560 brought its function as an episcopal palace to an end. Transferred to the Crown by the Act of Annexation of 1587, it was granted to the Earl of Dunbar in 1606 but restored to the revived archbishopric six years later. However, in 1654 part of its materials was used for repair of the harbour and it was clearly ruinous by the late C17. In 1911 it became an Ancient Monument.

The approach across a fixed bridge leads to Archbishop Hamilton's ENTRANCE FRONT of *c.*1555. This is a major piece of prototype Scottish classicism, its architectural effect now weakened as much by the pious pointing of its rubble walls (originally harled) as by the fragmentary state of its l. part. It has been symmetrical, the flanking ranges' corbelled parapet breaking out on each side into two projections for aediculed dormers whose column bases survive. The centrepiece is an attempt at a triumphal arch, with superimposed columns in the corners. Above the round-arched gateway, the date 1555 under a corbelled-out panel for a coat of arms. Frieze decorated with Archbishop Hamilton's device of a cinquefoil. Rectangular panels on the parapet. Immediately E of the centrepiece, a postern gate.

SE of Hamilton's entrance front is the FORE TOWER. Its battered base is of c.1390. So too, peeping through mid-c16 recasing, are the jambs of an entrance and a second-floor drawbridge slot. The rest dates from Hamilton's reconstruction. Parapet carried on chequer corbels; rounds at the corners and a crowstep-gabled attic. Large armorial panel joining the first- and second-floor windows.

The c16 entrance pend is tunnel-vaulted, with stone seats built into the walls. On each side, a tunnel-vaulted room. In the l. room's w wall, a gunloop; another gunloop covering the approach is set in the back of the fireplace. Both rooms contain shafts sunk by the castle's defenders during the siege of 1546–7 in an attempt to discover the position of their enemies' mine under the castle. The range's upper floors were reached by a turnpike stair in the courtyard's SW corner. The stair is built into a bowed projection. This is the surviving fragment of a great round tower or 'blokhous', probably of c.1500, which was destroyed together with a SE tower in 1547. The first floor probably contained the archbishop's lodging, probably a hall (the floor rising over the pend may have been a dais) with withdrawing room to the E. In the W wall, a door jamb, perhaps the entrance to a garderobe. In the E wall, a low door into the Fore Tower.

Inside the Fore Tower, clear evidence of the blocked late c14 drawbridge opening in the s wall. The ground-floor crosswall seems to have been the outside wall of 1336 and contained the original entrance. The N room's fragmentary tunnel-vault is an insertion, presumably of c.1555, when Archbishop Hamilton altered the tower's floor levels to correspond more closely with those of his entrance range.

E of the Fore Tower was the CHAPEL range, now very fragmentary. There have been two vaulted ground-floor rooms. Surviving column bases show that there was a cloister walk or loggia on the N side. Slezer's engraving of 1718 depicts the first-floor chapel windows as having tracery similar to that in the windows of St Leonard's Chapel, so perhaps this range was of the early c16 rather than part of Hamilton's work.

In the middle of the courtyard, a WELL. No evidence of buildings on the W side, whose wall is probably late c14, with a projecting salient in the centre. At the NW corner, the roughly rectangular SEA TOWER, late c14 but heavily reconstructed after the siege of 1546–7. Fat roll-and-hollow moulding on the surviving bit of its W door jamb. Inside, two tunnel-vaulted ground-floor rooms. The E room was a prison in the C14, when it was windowless, air being provided by a ventilation flue in the E wall which was blocked, probably in the C15, when the vault was inserted and a window made in the N wall. In the floor, opening to a bottle dungeon excavated in the rock below. There have been two first-floor rooms. In the W room's NW corner, a garderobe. In the E room, niche in the N wall; stair to the second floor corbelled out at the NE corner.

The courtyard's N range now consists of no more than the lower part of the N wall, perhaps of *c.* 1500. At the NE corner is the late C14 KITCHEN TOWER. Two vaulted ground-floor rooms. The first-floor room was probably the kitchen. Not much more than its E wall, with a big late C16 revetment against it, survives. The courtyard's E range seems to have contained the castle's great hall, but almost all of the buildings on this side collapsed into the sea in 1801. C19 revetment to prevent further collapse.

Outside the ditch, SE of the Fore Tower, entrance to a mine begun by the castle's besiegers in 1546. It runs for about 19m. towards the Tower. Immediately E of the Tower is the countermine made by the defenders.

UNIVERSITY BUILDINGS

The first of the Scottish universities, St Andrews had its beginning in 1410, when a group of masters, mainly graduates of Paris, founded a school of higher studies in the city. By February 1412, Bishop Henry Wardlaw had granted them a charter of incorporation as a society, and this charter was confirmed and amplified by a series of papal bulls in the next year. The first college to be founded was St Salvator's (1450), followed by St Leonard's (1512), Blackfriars (1516) and St Mary's (1538), all intended for education of the clergy.

The University suffered the loss of the Blackfriars convent at the hands of a Protestant mob in 1559. Twenty years later a commission appointed by the Crown and Privy Council made a belated post-Reformation reorganization. All responsibility for teaching was given to the individual colleges, St Salvator's and St Leonard's becoming colleges of philosophy or arts, St Mary's a college of theology. The foundation of the University Library in 1611 was an isolated admission that the University was more than a loose confederation of colleges, but the early C18 decline in the standard and number of students brought about the union of St Leonard's College with St Salvator's in 1747.

The C19 saw the establishment of the authority of the University over the colleges. Recommendations made in 1830 by the Royal Commission on the Scottish Universities were finally given effect in modified form by the Universities (Scotland) Act of 1858, which gave St Andrews a University Court as its governing body. The Court's powers were increased further by a second act in 1889, since when St Mary's College has been little more than a synonym for the Faculty of Divinity, all other members of the University being gathered under the nominal protection of the United College of St Salvator and St Leonard.

Since the C17 the colleges have had no important residential function, unlike the colleges at Oxford and Cambridge. Instead, lodgings in the town have been supplemented by halls of residence, the earliest, St Leonard's Hall, being opened in 1861, the most interesting architecturally, Andrew Melville Hall, in 1968.

ANDREW MELVILLE HALL, off Guardbridge Road. By *James Stirling*, 1964–8. Huge V-shape confidently stepping down the slope in blocks of ribbed concrete articulated by continuous glazing and canted bays.

BOTANIC GARDENS. *See* Streets: Queen's Terrace, below.

BUCHANAN BUILDING. *See* Streets: Market Street, below.

BUTE MEDICAL SCHOOL, AND BELL-PETTIGREW MUSEUM (DEPARTMENT OF ZOOLOGY), Greenside Place. The Medical School is of 1897–9, by *James Gillespie & Scott*. Tall Elizabethan of only three bays, each with a shaped gable, the centre flanked by seated gryphons. A tower was intended but not built. In 1907–9, Gillespie & Scott tacked on the Bell-Pettigrew Museum (now Department of Zoology) behind; stripped Jacobean in yellowish stone. Plain interwar addition (Anatomy and Experimental Pathology) to the N.

COLLEGE GATE. *See* Streets: North Street, below.

CRAWFORD CENTRE. *See* Streets: North Street, below.

DAVID RUSSELL HALL, Buchanan Gardens. By *Cunningham, Jack, Fisher & Purdom*, 1971. Three-storey harled blocks on a Y-plan linked by open-sided covered ways. At the SE, central facilities in a two-storey block, a spire on its roof.

GATTY MARINE LABORATORY, off Woodburn Place. By *James Gillespie & Scott*, 1895–6. Very plain single-storey Jacobean, like a Board school.

HAMILTON HALL. *See* Streets: The Scores, below.

HEPBURN HALL. *See* Streets: Hepburn Gardens, below.

KENNEDY HALL. *See* Streets: The Scores, below.

OBSERVATORY, Buchanan Gardens. By *Gillespie & Scott*, 1964.

THE PRINCIPAL'S HOUSE. *See* Streets: The Scores, below.

ST LEONARD'S CHAPEL. *See* Public Buildings: St Leonard's School and Chapel, below.

ST MARY'S COLLEGE, SOUTH STREET LIBRARY, AND DEPARTMENT OF PSYCHOLOGY, South Street. A hybrid of dates and functions, but in common ownership and making a single quasi-collegiate group.

The College of the Assumption of the Blessed Virgin Mary was founded as a hall for secular clergy by Archbishop James Beaton in 1538, and buildings were put up over the next five years. *Thomas French* was the master mason, but advice was also sought from 'the French masons coming from Falkland' (i.e. presumably *Nicolas Roy* among others). Further construction began in 1552, but the chapel had not been completed by the Reformation in 1560.

The college's w range survives. Its South Street front has been rendered and Georgianized, but the tall moulded shafts with torch-like finials framing three of the first-floor windows must be part of the C16 work. The panel under the centre window carved with the royal arms and the date 1612 (altered to 1613) was probably originally on the South Street Library and moved here when that building was reconstructed in 1764–7. On the l., gateway by *Robert Reid*, 1829–30. Stumpy obelisk finials on the steep pediment, its base dressed up with a C16 foliaged corbel, its front carved with the royal arms. On the gateway's s front to the court, more obelisk finials on the very steep open pediment, which contains a C16 corbelled and canopied image niche.

The college's courtyard frontages were remodelled by Principal Robert Howie *c.*1620. Large ogee-roofed stairtower in the inner angle; strapworked cartouche over the basket-arched door; *fleurs de lis* in the window pediment above. The main block's E front is divided by a crowstep-gabled tower topped by an ogee-roofed birdcage bellcote. The N part is symmetrical; alternating heraldic stones and pediments over the ground-floor windows; reversed alternation of pediments and skimpy cornices above the first-floor windows; three pedimented dormerheads cutting through the cavetto eaves cornice at the top. The range's s continuation is plain, with a couple of Georgian piend-roofed dormers.

102

South Street Library E of the gateway was built as the University Library in 1612–18. In 1764–7 it was reconstructed by the wright-architect *John Gairdner*, who refronted the South Street elevation, giving it a pedimented centre and ends with first-floor keyblocked niches in the links. In 1829–30 *Robert Reid* added two further w bays, carefully copying Gairdner's work, but the fourth pediment stretches the design beyond its strength. By Reid also the first-floor frieze carved with coats of arms of the University's Chancellors. The C17 ashlar masonry is visible on the s (courtyard) side. So too is one original mullioned window. The round-arched first-floor windows with projecting keyblocks and imposts were made by Gairdner (and copied by Reid on the w). Between the windows, corbels from late medieval image niches (the two w corbels copies of 1829–30). Inside, on the ground floor, the Parliament Hall, simply panelled in 1929. The first-floor Upper Hall (or Old Library) was fitted out by Gairdner in 1767, its gallery carried on tall fluted Doric columns.

Detached s addition of the library (now Department of Psychology) added by *W.W. Robertson*,* 1889–90. Large-scale Jacobean Renaissance with end towers, ogee-roofed on the l., crowstepped on the r. In the w front, a couple of medieval corbels, one carved with the *Arma Christi*. *Robert S. Lorimer* doubled the size of Robertson's extension in 1907–9

---

* *Jesse Hall* was the executant architect.

by adding a tame baroque block to the S, the centrepiece's main accent a very tall window whose steep pediment pushes into the balustrade. Coats of arms with angel supporters on the coupled end pilasters; grotesque gargoyles in the inner angles. The symmetry of Lorimer's design was ruined in 1928–30 by *J. Donald Mills*, who brought the two l. bays forward to the centrepiece's building line. *Walker & Pride*'s addition of a mansard roof made things worse; *Reginald Fairlie & Partners*' full-height S extension of 1958 in a different coloured stone was the death-blow.

On the lawn beside the College's W range, a large corniced SUNDIAL dated 1664. The supporting fat column's top suggests a Doric capital. The lawn continues S as a garden. At its top end, a C16 doorway with a roll-and-hollow moulding. Further down, a chamfered doorway under a panel carved with Robert Howie's arms and initials; it originally stood further N but was moved here in 1889. The line of the College's S boundary is marked by an isolated ivy-clad C16 gateway rebuilt here in 1907–9. It is semi-octagonal-headed (cf. St Leonard's Chapel). Above the N side have been placed a panel bearing the arms and initials of Bishop Henry Wardlaw, possibly from his Pedagogy Building of *c.*1430 which stood on the South Street Library's site, and a C17 panel carved with Robert Howie's initials. On the N side, a dormerhead with the cinquefoil of Archbishop Hamilton, who completed the College's foundation in the 1550s.

Further S, a small lectern DOOCOT, perhaps of *c.*1702, when the College's NW corner was fitted up as the Principal's House. Large crowsteps; obelisk pinnacles on the parapet.

ST REGULUS HALL, Queen's Gardens and Queen's Terrace. 1864–5, probably by *George Rae*. Stark Baronial, the verticality emphasized by very steep crowstepped gables and slim pepperpot turrets. Feeble E addition by *Gillespie & Scott*, 1951.

ST SALVATOR'S COLLEGE, North Street. The College was [14] founded in 1450 by James Kennedy, Bishop of St Andrews, as an establishment containing a Provost who was to be a Doctor of Theology, one Licentiate and one Bachelor of Theology, four Masters of Arts who were to study for theology degrees, and six choristers who were to study for arts degrees. As early as 1452 Sir David Dunbar of Ochtermoonzie expanded the college by founding a chaplainry, and Bishop Kennedy's revised foundation charter of 1458 gave explicit sanction to the addition of chaplainries whose holders could study at St Andrews. By 1475 thirty chaplainries had been endowed, and there were more than a hundred at the Reformation of 1560. After the Reformation, St Salvator's continued as an arts college, although its chapel was taken over by the burgh as a Commissary Court in 1563. In 1761 the chapel was restored to ecclesiastical use as the church of St Leonard's parish, and in 1904 it became the 'University Chapel'.

The GATE TOWER, probably built in the 1460s, rises sheer to a sill course under the tall belfry windows, each of two lights

with trefoil heads and a traceried transom. Above the belfry,
a corbelled parapet (restored by *Robert Matheson*, 1851) within
which stands a stunted octagonal spire with two tiers of
lucarnes built by Archbishop John Hamilton *c.*1550. It
replaced a spire (perhaps of timber) erected *c.*1530 and burnt
in 1547, but probably a spire was intended from the first.
Above the off-centre pend arch, Bishop Kennedy's coat of
arms with angel supporters, flanked by tall pinnacled image
niches. Tunnel-vaulted pend with stone benches; on its w side,
an aumbry checked for doors.

Rubble-built HEBDOMADAR'S BUILDING on the l. of the
Gate Tower. Its two lower storeys may also be of the 1460s;
the top floor was added and the building altered, probably as
part of the reconstruction of the College buildings by Provost
Skene (with advice from *James Smith*) in 1683–90. Attached
to the lean-to back wing, a late Georgian PORTER'S LODGE,
crowstepped, with a birdcage bellcote on the N gable.

In front of the Chapel is a small CEMETERY laid out *c.*1459,
when it extended further s. It was narrowed in 1906, the date
of the axe-head railings. Its late C15 entrance gateway opposite
the Chapel's s door was rebuilt at the same time. This seems
originally to have formed part of the cloister court and been
moved to the cemetery in 1761. Bishop Kennedy's arms are
set in the hugely pinnacled ogee hoodmould above the gate's
basket arch.

The CHAPEL itself was built in 1450–60. Seven bays with
an apsed E end. On the street side, stepped buttresses, their
tall gabled finials provided by *Robert Matheson*, 1861–3.
On the buttresses, canopied image niches, their corbel bases
carved with foliage, except at the buttresses gripping the
quadripartite vaulted porch, where the corbels are larger and
carved with human heads. The late Gothic window tracery is
all by Matheson. The Chapel's N side is covered by the Tudorish cloister added (on the site of the medieval cloister) by
William Nixon in 1845–9. Obelisk pinnacles with *fleur-de-
lis* finials on the buttresses and ogee hoodmoulds with small
pinnacles over the round-arched openings. The chapel buttresses' bristly crocketed pinnacles are of 1861–3.

N and s doors to the Chapel have semi-octagon heads (cf. St
Leonard's Chapel); so does the sacristy door further E. The
interior was stone-vaulted until 1773, when *James Craig*
produced the present wooden roof, its braces springing from
the vault-ribs' tall corbels. The two-bay ante-chapel is divided
from the Chapel by a stone SCREEN of 1928–31, by *Reginald
Fairlie*, apparently in the position of the C15 screen. Above
the ante-chapel is the organ loft (ORGAN by *Hradetzky*, 1974),
with carved and painted coats of arms on its panelled front. –
The apse's round-arched blind arcading and the stone COM-
MUNION TABLE are by *P. MacGregor Chalmers*, 1921, their
mosaic panels by *Douglas Strachan*.

Oak STALLS by *Fairlie*, 1928–31, with some routine carving
of sub-Lorimer type.– Early C17 PULPIT, the would-be Com-

posite pilasters on the back apparently intended to support a sounding board.

STAINED GLASS. In the ante-chapel, an armorial window, after 1930. – In the chapel's s wall, Shairp Memorial (Virtue; Faith; Knowledge), designed by *Henry Holiday* and made by *Powell & Sons*, 1886. – Bright narrative windows (The Sermon on the Mount; Joseph Sold into Captivity) by *Hardman*, 1863. – Christ Preaching from a Boat, by *William Wilson*, 1967. – War Memorial window of *c.*1950, by *Gordon Webster*. – Colourful E window (Crucifixion) by Webster, 1957, with small-scale drawing.

In the corner of the N wall and the apse, a SACRAMENT HOUSE of the 1450s. The recess is framed by an ogee hood-mould springing from moulded shafts and rising through blind Perp arcading to an outsize crocketed finial. On the corbel-course under the sill, (headless) angels holding a pyx. On the concave canopy, shields with the royal arms and those of Bishop Kennedy.

MONUMENTS. In the Chapel's N wall, Bishop Kennedy's tomb. It fits awkwardly into the chapel and may have first been intended to go in the Cathedral choir. If so, it was erected here probably between the Chapel's consecration in 1460 and Kennedy's death five years later. The design is of French inspiration, and the craftsmen may also have been French, although the stone seems to have come from Angus. The scale is huge, the detail elaborate. Rectangular frame of clustered shafts, the hollows between carved with diminutive image niches, supporting a richly decorated canopy of image niches with boldly undercut carving. Within the frame, a tomb-chest, its top of black marble, its bronze front a conjectural restoration by *Fairlie* with small statues of saints. The tomb-chest's recess is apsidal and has been vaulted. In its walls, niches like radiating side-chapels. – In the ante-chapel's w wall, an elliptically arched tomb recess of *c.*1500. – Against the w wall, framed graveslab of Hugh Spens †1534, incised with the figure of a priest. – Very classy marble wall monument on the s to John Home †1754, the inscription set in a drapery surround with a coat of arms above; the exceptionally shallow carving makes it look like an engraving. – On the N, wall monument to Andrew Lang by *William B. Richmond*, 1913, with a bronze portrait relief.

The N part of the College's E range is by *Robert Reid*, 1829–31, Jacobean with a shaped centre gable and buckle quoins. The parapet jumps up to form small shaped gablets containing coats of arms; cornice beneath studded with pedimented gargoyle heads. s extension in the same style but with a narrower projecting gable, by *Gillespie & Scott*, 1904–6, its canted s end derived from Adam Bothwell's House (Edinburgh).

The N range of 1845–6 by *William Nixon* is again Jacobean but much more confident. Grand doorpiece with lion and unicorn supporters standing on the Roman Doric columns. Nixon completed the court's enclosure with a screen wall to the w, pierced by a simple Tudor arcade, and along the boundary with Butt's Wynd.

SOUTH STREET LIBRARY. *See* St Mary's College, above.

TECHNOLOGY CENTRE, off Guardbridge Road. Group in a parkland setting. PHYSICS (1965), MATHEMATICS (1967) and CHEMISTRY (1968) blocks all by *William Holford & Associates*. – COMPUTING, elegant in dark brick with a glazed clearstorey under a deep fascia, is by *Williamson, Faulkner-Brown & Partners*, 1971.

UNIVERSITY HALL, St Leonard's Road. By *James Gillespie & Scott*, 1895–6; built as a hall of residence for women students. Pacific Baronial with lots of crowsteps. *Mills & Shepherd* more than doubled its size in 1910–11. Lightweight block to the w by *Gauldie, Hardie Wright & Needham*, 1962.

UNIVERSITY LIBRARY, off North Street. By *Faulkner-Brown, Hendy, Watkinson, Stonor*, 1972–6. Three tiers of ribbed concrete shelves boldly projected on heavy beam ends from the curtain glazing behind. Almost but not quite elegant.

For the old University Library (now South Street Library), *see* St Mary's College, above.

WARDLAW HALL. *See* Streets: Kennedy Gardens, below.

YOUNGER HALL, North Street. By *Paul Waterhouse*,* 1923–9. Art Deco classical, building up from projecting two-storey wings, the inner angles filled by convex 'quadrants', to the four-storey temple centrepiece, whose Portland-stone detail contrasts with the walling's Cullalo stone. Giant order of thin piers supporting the pediment; upstanding acroterion on the apex and ends. The channelled ashlar porch topped by flattened swagged urns (carved by *Alexander Carrick*) serves as a base. Inside, the main block is filled by the galleried Graduation Hall; dry classical detail.

CHURCHES

ALL SAINTS (Episcopal), North Castle Street. Complex of church, hall, rectory and club, with orange pantiled roofs and lots of crowsteps. The idiom is Scottish vernacular, the flavour gay Italian.

Main approach through a twee courtyard. On the N, CASTLE WYND HOUSE, rubbly C17 with a crowstepped E tower added by *Paul Waterhouse* on its conversion to a club in 1921. Straight ahead, the low HALL (again of 1921, by Waterhouse), with very large crowstepped dormers and a Doric porch serving also as entrance to the church. This fills the s side. Slated chancel and bell tower by *John Douglas* of Chester,‡ 1906–9. The rest is by Waterhouse, 1919–24. Aisled nave with broad battered buttresses; large crowsteps on the N transept.

Inside, two-bay chancel, the sanctuary marked off by a tall round-headed arch. There are two chancel arches, one of 1906–9 and conventionally moulded, the other of 1919–24 and

---

* Completed after his death in 1924 by *Michael Waterhouse*.

‡ *Charles F. Anderson* was executant architect.

unmoulded. Waterhouse placed the nave a full six steps below the chancel. Plastered semicircular tunnel-vault. Idiosyncratic classical-cum-Gothic capitals on the pillars of the nave arcades; segment-headed clearstorey windows above. Flat-ceilinged N aisle. In the broader S aisle, an opening high up into the SW Chapel of the Blessed Sacrament containing a wrought-iron screen and marble columns made by *Farmer & Brindley*. – Attached to the NE pier, stylized STATUE of Our Lady by *Hew Lorimer*, *c*.1945. – Hanging ROOD by *Nathaniel Hitch*, 1924, with a great sunburst behind the figure of Christ. – Wrenaissance PULPIT of 1924. – ORGAN by *Hill & Son, Norman & Beard*.

At the nave's W end, apsidal BAPTISTERY. Entrance through a semicircular arch enclosing another, the space between filled with a green tiled grille. Wrought-iron SCREEN with *fleurs de lis*, by *T. Elsey & Co.*, 1924. – Contemporary marble FONT, faintly Celtic, by *Farmer & Brindley*, its steepled canopy in gilded wood by *Hitch*.

At the SW, apse-ended CHAPEL OF THE BLESSED SAC-   44 RAMENT, its walls lined with green and black marble. Flanking the steps to the creamy marble altar, kneeling stone angels on tall marble pedestals. At the entrance, traceried wooden doors carved by Hitch, who was responsible also for the ALTARPIECE with its small figures of saints.

STAINED GLASS. E window (Annunciation and Nativity) by *Louis Davis*, 1913. – N chancel window (The Calling of SS Peter and Andrew; SS Peter and John at the Gate Beautiful) by *Pritchard*, 1958. – N transept ('For All the Saints'), colourful by *Karl Parsons*, 1936. – W window of N aisle (Christ the King) by *Louis Davis*. – Vigorous baptistery window (St John the Baptist) by *Douglas Strachan*, *c*.1923. – Chapel of the Blessed Sacrament (The Last Supper), horribly pictorial, by *Strachan*.

Fronting North Street is the RECTORY by *Reginald Fairlie*, 1937–8. Scots C17 style with pedimented dormerheads on the main block; single-storey range in front, all roofs inevitably pantiled.

BAPTIST CHURCH, South Street. Tudorish hall front added by *Gillespie & Scott*, 1901–2, to a chapel built in 1842.

BLACKFRIARS CONVENT, South Street. Of the Dominican   17 convent church begun *c*.1515 there survives only the N transept, for whose encroachment on the street permission was granted in 1525. Unusually, it has a semi-octagonal-apsed N end, perhaps influenced by Ladykirk Parish Church (Borders), built in 1500–4, which has similar but shorter apse-ended transepts.

Broad obtusely pointed S arch of two chamfered orders from the demolished nave. The corbels above must have supported the nave roof. Large W window, now missing its tracery. Each of the three apse windows seems to have been originally of the same size, but the centre one has been lowered, probably in the early C19, when its (already mutilated) loop tracery was replaced by a large-scale version of the tracery in the adjoining windows (intersecting round-headed arches under a circle). Over the windows, hoodmoulds studded with rosettes. Only fragments of the corner buttresses survive. In the remaining part of the parapet, a stone spout.

Inside, the roof is a pointed tunnel-vault with applied surface ribs meeting at a boss carved with symbols of the Passion. On one of the corbels from which the ribs spring, the arms of Hepburn (probably for John Hepburn, Prior of the Augustinian Convent of St Andrews Cathedral). Flattened ogee-arched aumbry in the s end of the E wall. The blocked door to its l., in the position of the altar, presumably dates from the c18, when the transept was incorporated in a house built against this wall.

CHURCH OF BLESSED MARY ON THE ROCK, The Scores. Not much more than foundations of the cruciform church demolished in 1559. Probably on or near the site of the Culdee house of St Andrews, it is said by the *Scotichronicon* to have been founded by Constantine II in the late c9. Before 1290 it had become a collegiate church and royal chapel.

Of the nave walls only the core remains. The stones were bedded in clay, which could suggest a date as early as the c10 or c11, but the foundations of a buttress at the NW corner and a single slightly projecting pilaster on the N wall make the c12 more likely. The choir and transepts, presumably added when the church was made collegiate, were built of ashlar, probably c13.

HOLY TRINITY, South Street. The *beau idéal* of a late medieval burgh church by *P. MacGregor Chalmers*, 1907–9, incorporating the tower and a few other remains of the Church of the Holy Trinity begun in 1411 and drastically reconstructed by *Robert Balfour* in 1798–1800.

The tall c15 W tower is L-plan, with a small stone spire over the NW jamb and a larger one over the main block. The walling rises unbroken to a sill course below the two-light trefoil-headed belfry openings. Above, a plain parapet on individual corbels.

Chalmers' church was ostensibly a restoration of the medieval church, but the walls (of Cullalo stone) were rebuilt, a SE chapel (the Hunter Aisle), vestry and session room added, whilst the design of the transepts and porch owed everything to conjecture. Details were culled from a variety of late medieval Scottish sources to make this a dictionary of architectural quotations.

Continuous nave and chancel with lean-to aisles. Boldly projecting rainwater spouts in the parapets. Clearstorey restored to the medieval size, but the cusped arched windows (Linlithgow Palace or Stirling Castle) are larger than the originals. S aisle window copied from Seton Chapel; rectangular window in N aisle from the St Leonard's Chapel. W gable intaken above the continuously corbelled parapet. Below the parapet, large beasts leaning out; like the rest of the sculpture they are by *James Young*. Window of five lancet lights (St

Machar's Cathedral, Aberdeen) above the two-arch richly carved doorway (St Mary's, Haddington, or St Mary's, Dundee). Carved angels lean over the E gable's parapet. Great E window a smaller version of Carlisle Cathedral's.

Tall crowstepped S porch (a memorial to John Knox) in the position of the C15 porch, detail taken from St Michael's, Linlithgow. Small gabled session house abutting the S transept. This stands on the site of a medieval transept or chapel but is considerably taller. Crowstepped gables to N and S. Big buttresses with image niches above coats of arms; finials of the Arbuthnot, Ladykirk and King's College, Aberdeen, type. Large S window a copy of the W window of St Mary's, Haddington. Below it, the door (Dryburgh Abbey's W door) with singing *putti* on the label stops. The English late Gothic chapel (Hunter Aisle) to the E had no predecessor here. Crenellated parapet studded with animal gargoyles. More beasts carved on the buttresses' sloping tops. On the N, a solid crowstepped vestry. It adjoins the N transept and organ chamber, very martial, with rainwater spouts firing from the angle-rounds.

Interior with continuous arcades, round-arched with cham- 41 fered mouldings. The responds and columns of the two W bays are original. Thereafter, every second pillar is C15, the rest of 1907–9, carefully reproducing the bell-shaped capitals and chamfered bases, but with carved decoration (Church of the Holy Rude, Stirling) applied to the chancel pillars. The chancel's dignity is further marked by slim clustered wall-shafts supporting only their foliaged capitals. Semi-elliptically arched wagon roof with applied ribs; at their intersections, bosses carved with Biblical scenes. Nook-shafted round-headed rere-arches in the clearstorey. Quadrant arches in the N aisle mark off the position of the organ. In this aisle's W bay, round-arched, hollow-chamfered C15 door into the tower.

The aisles open into the N and S transepts through two-bay arcades, the S original, the N conjectural. High on the N transept's E wall, a rather fussy arcade into the organ chamber. In the S transept, a wagon roof like that of the nave, the main ribs springing from wall-shafts. The pointed arch into the Hunter Aisle is decorated with little bosses carved with animals, fruit, angels, etc. More carved decoration on the piers of the Aisle's four-bay arcade to the S choir aisle and on the corbels of the wall-shafts which support the beams of the wooden ceiling.

Restrained oak FURNISHINGS of 1909, the chancel pews slightly more elaborate. – Contemporary open screen cutting off the chancel's E bay. – PULPIT by *Galbraith & Winton*, 1909, very expensive in alabaster and onyx on a base of the same green Iona marble as the chancel floor. On a bracket above, a carved dove which used to surmount the sounding board of the pulpit of 1800. – Late C19 stone FONT with lumpy carved saints. – ORGAN by *Henry Willis & Sons*, 1909; enlarged by *Harrison & Harrison*, 1974.

PANELLING on the Hunter Aisle's E wall of 1948 by *Whytock*

& Reid from *Leslie Grahame Thomson*'s design. – In the S
transept, two late medieval oak STALLS, their round arm-rests
carved with the arms of James IV and of Gavin Dunbar,
Archdeacon of St Andrews from 1503 to 1518.

Lots of STAINED GLASS. – E window (*Te Deum*) of 1910 by
Douglas Strachan, its fresh colours and neat drawing providing
the right foil for the architecture. – W window (Women in the
Bible), by *Strachan*, 1914, stronger-coloured and less disci-
plined. – In the clearstorey, regimental badges by *Alexander
Strachan*. – The N aisle's side windows are all by *Douglas
Strachan*: Christ as a Boy, realistic with deep blues, of 1912;
less successful his Joshua and Gideon of *c*. 1920; a strong David
of *c*. 1925, flanked by two clumsily drawn lights (Hezekiah and
Josiah) of 1950; Abraham and Melchisedek, after 1922; The
Minor Prophets, with a hint of Social Realism, *c*. 1920. – Unappealing E window (Our Lord and SS Luke and Andrew) by
A. Ballantine & Son, *c*. 1910. – In the S aisle, two narrative
windows ('Suffer the Little Children to come to Me'; Christ's
Mission) by *James Powell & Sons*, *c*. 1912. – This aisle's E
window (The Miracles of Christ), with small-scale drawing
and strong colours, is by *Douglas Strachan*, 1910. – By Strachan again (*c*. 1920) are the two small lights (The Perfect
Woman; The Perfect Knight) in the N transept's W wall. – The
transept's N window (*Benedicite*) is of *c*. 1912. – High up S
window (Christ Healing the Blind) by *Herbert Hendrie*,
c. 1930. – In the S transept's W wall, three small lights; two (SS
Thomas and Margaret) in primary colours, by *Sax Shaw*,
1968, the third (The Good Shepherd) by *Hendrie*, *c*. 1930. –
The transept's muddily drawn S window (The Resurrection
and Ascension) is by *Reginald Hallward*, 1910. – Small E light
(Justice) of *c*. 1920, by *Douglas Strachan*. – Windows in the
Hunter Aisle (Scenes from the Life of Christ) all by *Louis
Davis*, 1911. – In the War Memorial Shrine off the Hunter
Aisle, one light ('Fight the Good Fight'), very strongly
coloured, by *William Wilson*, 1950. – S window of session
house (Daniel and St Paul) by *Douglas Strachan*, *c*. 1925.

35   Black and white marble wall MONUMENT to Archbishop
James Sharp in the S transept. Erected in 1679, the year of
Sharp's assassination by Covenanters, it is said to have been
carved in the Netherlands, but the design could well be Scottish. Huge Corinthian aedicule; instead of a pediment, foliaged
scrolls frame a low-relief panel showing the Archbishop
holding up a church. Within the aedicule, a segment-headed
arch under Sharp's coat of arms. The arch frames a tomb-
chest resting on three skulls. On the chest, a figure of Sharp
at prayer, his mitre and pastoral staff laid aside; behind him,
marble relief of an angel emerging from a cloud to hold out a
martyr's golden crown, the point being made clear by the gilt
motto 'PRO MITRA'. The direct iconographical source for this
must be engravings of Charles I at prayer before his execution
in the *ΕΙΚΩΝ ΒΑΣΙΛΙΚΗ*. Dowsed torches flank the aedicule.
On its pedestal, low relief of Sharp's murder on Magus Muir.

HOPE PARK CHURCH, St Mary's Place. Originally United Presbyterian. By *Peddie & Kinnear*, 1864–5. Geometrical in hammerdressed rubble. Rose windows in the large transeptal gables. SW steeple; small spired tower at the NW. Hall added at the E by *Gillespie & Scott*.

MARTYRS' CHURCH, North Street. Originally United Free. By *Gillespie & Scott*, 1926–8. Chunky Scots Gothic gable front. (STAINED GLASS. One light (St Leonard) by *Marjorie Kemp*.)

ST ANDREW (Episcopal), Queen's Terrace. By *R. Rowand Anderson*, 1867–9. Large and prosperous First Pointed in snecked rubble. Cruciform, but the transepts do not project beyond the aisles, and the piend-roofed S transept is at the bottom of a tower completed to the original design in 1892 and taken down in 1938. In the E gable, three lancets beneath a rose window (Dunblane Cathedral's W front the obvious inspiration). Sturdy buttressed aisles, low clearstorey, large SW porch with an empty vesica for an image. Anderson's characteristically steep roof, unbroken from end to end, unifies the composition, red ridge tiles giving a welcome touch of colour.

Inside, the roof again comes to the rescue. Pointed wagon with kingpost trusses and collars, barely interrupted by the tall chancel arch. Nave arcades on alternate round and octagonal piers with stiffleaf capitals. The clearstorey's squatness is emphasized by the very broad pointed arches over its cinquefoil windows. Broad overarches again containing the paired lancets in the aisles. Blind arcade round the square-ended chancel.

The furnishings confirm the impression of solid wealth. – Mosaic REREDOS depicting a very stilted Ascension, made by *Powell & Sons* of London from *R. T. N. Speir*'s design, 1884. – Brasseagle LECTERN. – Oak PULPIT by *Sydney Mitchell & Wilson* (executed by *John S. Gibson*), a tight octagon with figures of the Evangelists in cusped niches.

STAINED GLASS. E window (SS Andrew, Peter and John) of *c.* 1870. – The S chancel window (Entombment and Resurrection) looks like *Hardman* of *c.* 1870. – N window of chancel (Jubal), stilted naturalism of 1964. – In the N aisle, The Raising of Tabitha, narrative style, *c.* 1880. – More decorative SS Gabriel and Michael, and Simeon and Anna, both of *c.* 1885. – Appalling depiction of Christ the Good Shepherd, *c.* 1900. – In the S aisle, two narrative windows (Solomon and Our Lord in the Temple; David playing before Saul) of *c.* 1885. – W window of this aisle (the Risen Christ), colourful by *Gordon Webster*, 1957. – W window of nave (Scenes from Christ's Life) by *Clayton & Bell*, 1893. – ORGAN by *Harrison & Harrison*.

Attached to the church's W end, very ecclesiastical HALL, Dec by *Hall & Henry*, 1893.

ST JAMES (R.C.), The Scores. Arts and Crafts Romanesque by *Reginald Fairlie*, 1909–10. Walls of crazy-paving pointed rubble; red tile fillets over the arched openings and under the eaves. Buttressed nave with transeptal chapels and a S porch. On the SE tower, a tall, corbelled parapet containing a small

43   octagonal spire. Inside, a braced wooden nave roof; plaster
saucer dome in the chancel. Extensive and expensive marble
cladding (by *Lomas* of Derby) in the chancel and chapels. –
STAINED GLASS. Three windows (St Peter, St Andrew, and
the Second Vatican Council), sketchily drawn and garishly
coloured, by the *Pluscarden Priory Benedictines*.

ST LEONARD, Donaldson Gardens and Hepburn Gardens. By
P. MacGregor Chalmers, 1902–4. Very perfect Romanesque
faultlessly executed in ashlar. The crowstepped saddleback sw
tower provides the cragginess needed to avoid blandness, its
huge belfry opening contrasting with the small scale of the
other detail.

Inside, a nave and w aisle, both with apsidal chancels. Over
the nave, a braced open roof. Round-headed arcade carried on
circular piers. The arrangement is of the High Presbyterian
sort advocated by the Scottish Ecclesiological Society, with
the COMMUNION TABLE placed in the chancel, the PULPIT
and READING DESK flanking the chancel arch. All these are of
1904, oak carved in low relief with Celtic-Romanesque
motifs. – PEWS also of 1904, several of their ends with low
reliefs. – In the aisle's 'chancel', marble FONT, Gothic, by *John
Hutchison*, 1891. – ORGAN at the aisle's s end, by *Willis*, 1904.
STAINED GLASS. Extensive scheme filling all the windows.
Beautifully rich colour in the N chancel windows (Christ the
True Vine, Christ the Bread of Life, the Madonna) by *Henry
Holiday*, 1904. – Also by *Holiday*, the w wall's N light (Our
Lord with the Doctors in the Temple), 1913. – Paler colours
and brittler drawing in the E wall's four N lights (St Leonard,
1943; The Crucifixion and Resurrection, 1926; Palm Sunday,
1928*; The Raising of Lazarus, 1934), all by *Margaret Chilton*.
Much less good is her later contribution, the nave's s window
(The Transfiguration, 1954), and the w wall's two s lights (Our
Lord Cleansing the Temple, 1946; St Margaret of Scotland,
1949). – The other three E windows (The Healing of the
Centurion's Servant; Our Lord with Disciples; War Scenes)
are by the *Stephen Adam Studio*, 1920–2, and rather
muddled. – Two intricately drawn w windows (The Baptism
of Our Lord; The Call of SS Andrew and Philip) by *Herbert
Hendrie*, 1933.

ST LEONARD'S CHAPEL. *See* Public Buildings: St Leonard's
School and Chapel, below.

ST MARY. *See* Streets: St Mary's Place, below.

PUBLIC BUILDINGS

BOYS' BRIGADE HALL, Kinnessburn Road. Brick with thrifty
half-timbering; by *James Gillespie & Scott*, 1899. Big semicircular windows in the broad gables.

CANONGATE PRIMARY SCHOOL, Maynard Road. By *Fife
County Council*, 1972. Single-storey, drydashed with low-
pitched roofs.

* Executed in partnership with *Marjorie Kemp*.

GIBSON HOSPITAL, Argyle Street. By *Hall & Henry*, 1880–2. Straightforward Jacobean, the ogee-roofed entrance tower an effective centre.

GREYFRIARS PRIMARY SCHOOL, Abbey Walk. By *David Henry*, 1888–9. Long and low with plenty of gables.

HARBOUR, The Shore. Haven at the mouth of the Kinness Burn, its outer harbour formed by two piers in the position of the wooden piers shown on a C16 map. The long N pier was rebuilt in stone (largely taken from the Castle) in 1656 and lengthened in 1761, 1783 and *c*.1830. In 1898–1900 *D. & C. Stevenson* extended it again, their concrete end contrasting with the horizontally and vertically laid rubble of the earlier extensions and repairs. Rubble quay on the W, probably C19. The SE pier, reached across an Edwardian suspension footbridge, is of coursed rubble, probably early C19. E groyne of 1900. To the S, quay walls form an inner harbour along the burn.

LANGLANDS PRIMARY SCHOOL, Kilrymont Road. By *Fife County Council*, 1957.

LAWHEAD SCHOOL, off Strathkinness Low Road. By *Fife County Council*, 1974.

MADRAS COLLEGE, South Street. Set well back from the street, 110 a suave Jacobean manor by *William Burn*, 1832–4. Dr Andrew Bell, son of a St Andrews hairdresser, had left £50 000 for the foundation of a school at his birthplace. Work began in the year of his death and the college opened two years later. The buildings were intended as a sympathetic foil for the surviving fragment of Blackfriars Convent (*see* above). This, isolated in the centre of the site's street frontage, dominates at first view. It was tied by tall railings (now gone) to the simple Tudor houses (the E tactfully enlarged by *David Henry* in 1889) which Burn provided for the English and Classical masters ('as remote from each other as the extent of the ground would admit') at the site's NE and NW corners.

The main school buildings stand behind a lawn (originally a gravelled playground). Two-storey front block, a procession of shaped gables over strapworked bay windows, the ends slightly broader and advanced with ball finials for emphasis. This block is joined by short screen walls to the broad low gables of the E and W ranges. Gateways in the links open into a quadrangle, the single-storey E, W and S ranges (intended respectively for the arithmetic, writing and English departments) hidden behind a round-arched groin-vaulted cloister walk. Towers with pierced parapets at the SE and SW corners. The cloister continues under the N range (housing the classical department). To the quadrangle it presents heavily corbelled oriels and broad gableted dormerheads.

Large additions, mercifully well hidden, at the back.

MADRAS COLLEGE (KILRYMONT), Kilrymont Road. By *Fife County Council*, 1966. V-plan main block, four curtain-walled storeys. On its N, a long one-storey green-tiled hall, its scalloped eaves annoyingly fussy. More tiling on the Sports Hall to the W.

OLD COURSE GOLF AND COUNTRY CLUB, off Guardbridge
Road. The name's implied elegance is belied by the blockwork
and render reality. By *Curtis & Davis* of New York, 1967–8;
enlarged 1982.

PUBLIC LIBRARY, Church Square. Built as the English School
in 1790 and refronted by *Robert Balfour*, 1811. Two storeys
of droved ashlar, with a very tall rusticated ground floor. The
porch looks an addition. It was converted to the City Hall by
George Rae in 1845 and the interior was recast in 1927.

THE ROYAL AND ANCIENT GOLF CLUB, Golf Place. This has
to count as a public building, but it is hardly worthy of the
club's reputation. It was begun by *George Rae*, 1853–4, a one-
storey lumpy Greek villa. *J. L. Fogo* added the w bay window,
1866. Upper floor by *John Milne*, 1880–2. Further additions
in 1900 by *James Gillespie & Scott*. Inside, the Big Room's
classical ceiling is of 1854.

Immediately to the s, PLAYFAIR MEMORIAL FOUNTAIN,
by *Robert S. Lorimer*, 1899. Tall corniced plinth with granite
basins, for humans (the water coming from dolphins' mouths)
on the long sides, for dogs at the ends. On top, a carved lion
holding the Playfair coat of arms.

ST ANDREWS MEMORIAL HOSPITAL, Abbey Walk. By *Charles
F. Anderson*, 1901–2. Recent additions in an updated version
of the undistinguished original.

ST LEONARD'S SCHOOL AND CHAPEL, South Street and The
Pends. Victorian girls' school occupying the site and some of
the buildings of a late medieval college whose chapel still
belongs to the University.

The college's ancestor was a Culdee hospital for the accommodation of six pilgrims to the shrine of St Andrew. This
hospital was enlarged by Bishop Robert, who placed it under
the care of the Cathedral's Augustinian canons in 1144. By
1413 its chapel had become also a parish church dedicated to
St Leonard. In the C15 the hospital became an almshouse for
aged women, but they gave 'little or no return in devotion or
virtue', so this use was ended. In 1512 Archbishop Alexander
Stewart and John Hepburn, Prior of St Andrews, converted
the hospital into the College of Poor Clerks of the Church of
St Andrew, a university college intended primarily but not
exclusively for the education of Augustinian novices in arts
and theology, the chapel continuing to double as a parish
church. Both church and college continued after the Reformation until 1747, when the college buildings were abandoned
after its union with St Salvator's College. In 1761 the parish
congregation followed the students to St Salvator's Chapel,
the St Leonard's Chapel being immediately unroofed and
having its w tower demolished. The college buildings were
sold to Professor Robert Watson in 1772 and the main s range
was converted to houses. In 1881 they were bought by the St
Andrews School for Girls, which moved in two years later,
changing its own name to St Leonard's School. The abandoned
chapel lost its w bay *c*.1837 to improve access from South

Street, but it was re-roofed in 1910 and the interior restored by *Ian G. Lindsay* in 1948–52.

The main entrance is by St Leonard's Lane off The Pends. On the l., MUSIC SCHOOL by *Morris & Steedman*, 1986, discreet but rubbly with a very large slated roof. Across the lane, a GATEWAY built *c.* 1600 E of the college's earlier entrance, with two moulded panel frames above the round-headed arch. Then a narrow court, its N side partly filled by the chapel, its S by the old college's domestic quarters, its W by Victorian school buildings.

The CHAPEL's N and S walls incorporate Romanesque masonry, but the stones in the S wall are clearly re-used and the N wall is built on late medieval foundations. A likely date for the present building's first stage is *c.* 1400 (i.e. shortly before the first recorded mention of St Leonard's Parish Church). This was of four bays, but after the foundation of the college in 1512 it was extended E by two further bays, the addition together with the previous E bay providing a collegiate choir. At the same time, new windows were made in the W part to match those of the addition. The tall W tower (demolished in 1761) was probably also part of this early C16 work.

The exterior is now unassuming. Against the S wall, a simple buttress near the W end; another (now bearing the Hepburn arms), stepped and gabled, marks off the two E bays. The windows of the choir are all of three lights with diagonally set cusps. The W window's upper part has been infilled, probably in the late C16, when a W gallery was erected inside, lighted by small windows placed under the wallhead. Roll-moulded door near the S wall's centre, presumably inserted *c.* 1512 to give access to the screen separating the choir from the parish church. A porch covering this door survived into the C18.

On the curtailment of the chapel, *c.* 1837, medieval fragments were placed in the W gable, among them two lancet-heads, a semi-octagonal doorhead, and the carved Hepburn arms with the initials PIH (for Prior John Hepburn). The gable's upper part (incorporating more medieval fragments) was built in 1910, when corbelling (the lowest corbel medieval) was introduced to the canted SW corner.

The restoration of 1948–52 gave the interior its general late medieval arrangement. Small windows high up in the N wall, presumably late C16 insertions to light the gallery. In the jambs of the S wall's two E windows have been three tiers of canopied image niches. In the r. window, only the l. jamb's top tier survives, but the l. window has all three tiers intact and also a credence ledge with a piscina at its E end. Aumbry to its E; a second aumbry beside the window of the choir's W bay (i.e. the E bay of the chapel before its extension of *c.* 1512). In the E gable, slit windows lighting wall passages which led from the N sacristy to the college's (demolished) E range. In the choir's N wall, a small window and basket-arched door into the sacristy. This now contains a tunnel-vaulted ground-floor room; an upper floor has been removed, perhaps in the late C16.

FURNISHINGS all of 1948–52, in best Jacobean Artisan Mannerist style. – SCREEN and ORGAN LOFT in the presumed position of the early C16 screen. – PULPIT in the nave. – In the choir, REREDOS with a painting of St Leonard by *Walter Pritchard*, 1956.

MONUMENTS. In the choir's N wall, Robert Stewart, Earl of March, †1586. Large monument of the basket-arched tomb-recess type, with very incompetent Corinthian pilasters; above, a panel space framed by small pilasters flanked by outsize scrolls; more scrolls flank the small inscription stone on top. – Peter Brown †1630, badly worn wall monument with paired Corinthianish columns (restored in cement). – Robert Wilkie †1611, the tomb recess a smaller and shallower version of the Stewart monument's; above, an heraldic panel in a steeply pedimented aedicule flanked by scrolls. – Several C16 FLOORSLABS. In the nave, Canon William Ruglyn †1502, with a cross on a six-step Calvary flanked by a Bible and chalice. – In the centre of the choir, John Wynram, heraldic, dated 1582. – Emmanuel Young †1544 and an anonymous 'chief master of the poor students', both with incised full-length effigies. – In the choir's NE corner, James Wilkie †1590, with smart heraldry.

ST LEONARD'S HOUSE, on the S side of the court, incorporates the college's S range, its E half built by Principal Peter Brown *c*.1617, its W by his successor Dr William Guild in 1655. In the C17 this range contained ten houses, each having one set of chambers (for two students) on each floor, the upper floor sets being reached by external wooden stairs. Evidence of a C17 origin survives only on the S (garden) side, where the range appears as a very unpretentious two-storey crowstepped building. Even here there is a bowed projection of *c*.1800 sticking out from the W half, and the second and third houses from the E were rebuilt in the early C19. On the N side, the late Georgian and early Victorian reconstruction was more thoroughgoing. *John Milne* gave the E half an asymmetrical oriel-windowed Tudor front in 1852–4. The W part was remodelled *c*.1800, mixing a pedimented centre with hood-moulds and a battlemented parapet. Inside, an entrance hall whose stair curves up one side to a landing carried across the end on Roman Doric columns.

On the court's W side, and with a N wing pushing towards the chapel, a large and boring block by *Gillespie & Scott*, 1900–1, its ogee-hatted SE tower the only hint at enjoyment. To its S, the crowstepped NEW BUILDING of 1926. Further S still, *Gillespie & Scott*'s SCIENCE BLOCK of 1908.

Boarding houses* spread E along The Pends. BISHOPSHALL (so named by Bishop Charles Wordsworth, who owned it from 1874 to 1887) was built as a University hall of residence (St Leonard's Hall) in 1867–8 and bought by the school in 1887.

* For St Nicholas, *see* Streets: Abbey Walk, below.

Unmemorably gabled and gableted, it is by *Brown & Wardrop*. Behind are the OLIPHANT MEMORIAL GATES of 1903 by *Robert S. Lorimer*. Heraldic supporters on the neo-Georgian gatepiers; elaborate wrought-iron overthrow. The next three buildings are all by *Gillespie & Scott*. ST RULE (1894–6) with a touch of Queen Anne but not of fun. – THE HOSPICE (1892–4), smaller and venturing a few Scots late medieval details. – The SANATORIUM (1899), timid Scots Renaissance.

TOWN HALL, South Street and Queen's Gardens. 1858–62, by *J. Anderson Hamilton* suppressing some of his usual exuberance. Baronial with a Flemish flavour. Big mullioned and transomed window in the crowstepped gable to South Street. On the gable's l., a fat low turret with a conical stone spire; on the r., a very tall spired rectangular turret, energetically corbelled out. Quieter elevation to Queen's Gardens extended s in 1885.

WEST INFANT SCHOOL, St Mary's Place. Small-scale Romanesque with a belfry, by *William Nixon*, 1846. Large additions of 1894.

WEST PORT, South Street. A symbol of civic pride on the main 101 approach to the town. The gate was built in 1589 by *Thomas Robertson*, mason in Blebo,* incorporating walling from the earlier gate on the site. The contract specified Edinburgh's Netherbow Port as the model.

Central round-arched pend gripped on the W by semi-octagonal towers. In the towers' front faces, tall gun slits. Above the towers and centre, a corbelled parapet punctured by cannon spouts and squarish gunholes set in moulded frames. Over the gate, relief panel of David I on horseback, carved by *Balfour Simmers*, 1844–5, a replacement for the original panel containing the royal arms. Much plainer E front. The ball-finialled buttresses standing like gatepiers each side of the pend were built in 1843, when guardhouses of 1589 were demolished. On the parapet, panel containing the City arms, by *Simmers*, 1844–5. The plain coped walls containing foot-gates which link the centrepiece to the houses each side are probably part of the earlier gate.

STREETS

ABBEY WALK

Street curving downhill towards The Shore, the Cathedral Precinct Wall (*see* above) on its N side. On the S, at the corner with Greenside Place, DAUPHIN HILL HOUSE, dated 1786 on a skew. Then, set well back, ST NICHOLAS, a boarding house of St Leonard's School, bleak neo-Georgian by *Reginald Fairlie*, 1930. A lane leads down to ABBEY PARK HOUSE, a classy late Georgian villa with a steep pediment and balustraded parapet, swamped in later additions. After Greyfriars

---

* Other masons known to have worked under Robertson on the West Port are *Patrick* and *John Arthur*, and *Walter Scott*.

Primary School (*see* above), St Leonards Fields of 1927,
tall, with thrifty crowsteps. Opposite the St Andrews Memorial Hospital (*see* above), Abbey Cottage, a rambling
Gothick *cottage orné*, presumably by *Robert Balfour*, who
owned it. It must be of *c*.1815, despite the date of 1787 over
the door. Behind it, a large late C19 Gasholder.

ABBOTSFORD CRESCENT, HOPE STREET AND HOWARD PLACE

A development laid out in 1847 on a field (Colonel Holcroft's
Park) which had been bought a year before by James Hope,
son-in-law of John Gibson Lockhart. Elevations for the houses
were produced by *John Chesser*. Most were not built until the
1860s, and the scheme was not completed until the 1890s.
Abbotsford Crescent begun in 1865 is austere Georgian
survival. Only the consoled cornices and round-headed doors
at its w end hint at the date. Much more obviously Victorian
is the detached Abbotsford House of 1869, with an Ionic
portico and steep pediment.
Howard Place is a convex crescent. Georgian survival again,
but with iron cresting on Nos. 1–7's parapet. Simpler Georgian
survival in Hope Street.

BALFOUR PLACE

Balfour House on the corner was built by the architect-
contractor *Robert Balfour* for himself, *c*.1800. Two-bay pedimented s front with cast-iron balconies under the first-floor
windows. The drydashed e addition is unwelcome.

BELL STREET

Laid out together with Greyfriars Garden (formerly North Bell
Street) in 1834, but elevations for the buildings were not
produced by *George Rae* until 1842, and they were only completed in 1858.
Nos. 1–35 on the e side are to Rae's design. Three-storey corner
block, the rest two-storey. Simple but elegant first-floor
window detail – cornices or pediments at the end, architraves
on the rest, all with aprons. Much of the ashlar stonework now
painted, and box dormers have begun to invade. Ground floors
altered with late Victorian and C20 shopfronts, at No. 17 with
bulbous Corinthian cast-iron columns of *c*.1885. Another cast-
iron shopfront at No. 39, part of *James Gillespie & Scott*'s
reconstruction of the building in 1886.
The w side's n part is shanty-town redevelopment. Nos. 14–38
are part of Rae's scheme. On No. 38's front to South Street,
an elaborate but small-scale Edwardian timber shopfront.

CASTLE STREET

Not much in South Castle Street. Harled and pantiled No. 11 of

*c.*1700, with a forestair; restored 1966. Beside it, the larger
rubble-built Nos. 13–15; forestair to the first-floor door, its
lintel dated 1735. Alterations were made in 1964.

In North Castle Street, All Saints' (Episcopal) Church and Castle
Wynd House (*see* Churches, above). Opposite, the rendered
Nos. 35–39, the S part C17 with a jettied upper floor, the
plain N extension probably C18, both marred by late Victorian
dormerheads. No. 41 is a late C18 remodelling of earlier work;
the l. windows were widened by *J. Donald Mills*, 1941. No.
43, late C18 with fluted pilasters at the door. At the street's N
end, CASTLEMOUNT on the W, with a plain late Georgian
front; large crowstep-gabled Edwardian addition facing The
Scores. On the E, CASTLEGATE, with a corner turret, was
designed by *Jesse Hall* for himself, 1879.

CHURCH STREET

Generally undistinguished Georgian and Victorian mixture.
Shopfront by *James Gillespie*, 1891, with cast-iron Corinthianish columns on the early C19 Nos. 7–9. No. 8, by *David
Henry*, 1891, its shopfront with tall Composite columns. Twin-
gabled No. 19, by *Hall & Henry*, 1885–6; granite shopfront
with foliaged capitals.

COLLEGE STREET

Mostly pleasant late Georgian. The harled No. 11 is of *c.*1530,
with a back jamb added *c.*1560. On the l. of the front, a
round-arched door; on the r., a chamfered pend arch. Interior
reconstructed 1967–70.

DOOCOT ROAD

In the new housing, the C16 BOGWARD DOOCOT: beehive type
with two stringcourses and a flat cornice.

DOUBLEDYKES ROAD

On the S, KINBURN HOTEL by *James Gillespie & Scott*, 1888–
90, a castellated double villa built in the style of fifty years
before. Then KINBURN PLACE, flat Jacobean of *c.*1860. On
the N, KINBURN HOUSE by *John Milne*, 1856, a castellated
bedstead in the early C19 Gillespie Graham manner.

EAST SCORES

SAINT GREGORY'S, by *Paul Waterhouse*, 1921, was built as
flatted fishermen's housing. Tamely pointed crazy-paved
rubble, Rosemary tiled roof, crowstepped gablets. The placid
NW corner tower quenches any risk of over-excitement. Determinedly fishing village picturesque sheltered housing at
KIRKHILL, by *Walker & Pride*, 1970.

ELLICE PLACE *see* NORTH STREET

GREYFRIARS GARDEN

Originally North Bell Street. Laid out in 1834, when plots were offered for sale with the condition that houses should be of two storeys and ashlar-fronted. Only two were sold in the first year, and in 1836 it was agreed that the w side should be kept as a garden ground.

No. 1 on the Market Street corner, built in 1841, observes the two-storey condition but on a huge scale. Corniced first-floor windows, their aprons decorated with rosettes set in lozenges; severe original shopfront. Nos. 2–10 were begun in 1836. Rusticated ground floor, much cut into by later shops, No. 5's with cast-iron Corinthian columns. No. 11 is of 1840–4, perhaps by *George Rae*, with cast-iron anthemion and palmette balconies; anta-pilastered doorpiece on the r. Then a return to the plain rusticated ground-floor treatment at Nos. 12–15. End block (Nos. 16–17) of 1844, with three-light windows.

HEPBURN GARDENS

A long stretch of villas with St Leonard's Church (*see* Churches, above) for punctuation.

Nos. 14–24 are by *James Gillespie & Scott*, 1906–10, three pairs of large semi-detacheds. Sub-Voyseyish variants on a theme, in harl and red brick. Further w, *Gillespie & Scott*'s HEPBURN HALL (formerly THE RIDGE) of 1913, Cotswoldy but in hard grey stone. In the porch, a panel with the Hepburn arms, moved here from the N garden wall of Deans Court (*see* North Street) in 1947. WAYSIDE is by *Robert S. Lorimer*, 1901–4, asymmetrical, with South African Dutch gables on the l., a pavilion roof and boat dormer on the r. NEW PARK SCHOOL, an 1860s Tudor villa swamped by additions. BALNACARRON of *c.*1900, multi-gableted and bargeboarded, with a V-plan oriel on the r.

HOPE STREET *see* ABBOTSFORD CRESCENT

HOWARD PLACE *see* ABBOTSFORD CRESCENT

KENNEDY GARDENS

A street of prosperous Victorian villas.

RATHELPIE at the e end is strongly gabled Tudor of *c.*1860, with a small sw tower. RATHMORE is by *John Milne*, 1861, a wavily bargeboarded lodge which has shot upwards, the height made almost ridiculous by the four-storey tower, its ogee-headed attic windows striking a Gothic note. LISCOMBE by *T. M. Cappon*, 1893–4, copies its dormer window's roof from a tower at Thirlestane. On the N side, WARDLAW HALL (former WESTERLEE), Baronial with a vengeance, by *Milne*, 1865–8.

KINBURN PLACE *see* DOUBLEDYKES ROAD

MARKET STREET

WHYTE-MELVILLE FOUNTAIN in the middle of the street. Red sandstone and polished granite, decorated with lots of carved foliage and gargoyles. It was designed by *R. W. Edis* and executed by *Earp*, 1880. Three tiers, the lowest basin circular, the upper two quatrefoils of diminishing size. On the middle basin's sides, panels carved with an inscription and two coats of arms. Fourth panel with a relief portrait of the bewhiskered George John Whyte-Melville, by *J. Edgar Boehm*.

Nos. 1–53 (N side). Nos. 1–5 on the South Castle Street corner are C17. Crowstepped gable to Market Street; in the back wing, a roll-moulded door. Then a drydashed block by *Walker & Pride*, 1982, slightly recessed from the building line, followed by plain C18 and C19 houses, No. 21 dated 1836, No. 33 a harled and pantiled intrusion. No. 45, hidden down a close, is a crowstepped house of *c*.1800; in its front a stone, perhaps C16, with the royal arms of Scotland.

Nos. 2–48 (S side). The harled gable of an Edwardian store is an unpromising start. Next, the crowstepped gable of the small No. 6, C18 but much altered. No. 8, early C19 with a rusticated ground floor, is followed by undistinguished Victorian and C20 buildings. On No. 16, an inserted panel with the arms and initials of Master Thomas Balfour and the date 1561. No. 34 (dated 1902) has a feeble corner turret to Baker Lane.

Nos. 55–79 (N side). The BUCHANAN BUILDING by *Cunningham & Jack*, 1964, stretches down Union Street as well as Market Street. In the Union Street front, a pair of panels carved by *Hew Lorimer* with characteristically stylized naturalism. On the College Street corner, crowstep-gableted CENTRAL BAR by *George Rae*, 1852.

Nos. 50–76 (S side). Plain start: Nos. 56–60 of 1949, No. 66 with a pend for access to CRAIL'S LANE's simple vernacular. Crowstepped gable front at No. 68, dated 1724, with a Quality Street shopwindow of 1950. The scale rises with the twin-gabled Nos. 70–72 (1860–1, probably by *George Rae*) and soars with the hammerdressed Baronial Nos. 74–76 (1873, probably by *John Milne*).

Nos. 81–149 (N side). First a pair of banks. Modernist classical BANK OF SCOTLAND by *Muirhead & Rutherford*, 1937. Late Georgian ROYAL BANK, its architraves early Victorian embellishments, its ground floor early C20. No. 85A (former CROSS KEYS HOTEL) was built in 1851, with a segmental pedimented doorpiece. The architect may have been *George Rae*, who extended it·E in 1864. Over the recessed entrance to Muttoes Lane is inserted a steep pedimented stone, probably C17, inscribed

THE LORD GAVE AND THE LORD HATH TAKEN BLESSED
BE THE NAME OF THE LORD

Nos. 89–93, Jacobean with large pedimented dormerheads, by *John Milne*, 1889. Then plain Victorian takes over, dotted with a few late Georgian bits and WOOLWORTH (No. 141) of 1935 with jazz-modern touches.

Nos. 80–140 (S side). A ragbag. No. 80 by *David Henry*, 1890, Jacobean with heraldic beasts flanking the corner gablets; its sturdy shopfront is of 1893–4, by *James Gillespie*. Late C18 No. 88, the two centre bays carried up under a pediment. The street is pinched by Nos. 88–90, late Victorian with a spired corner turret. Big Roman Doric columned doorpiece on the early C19 Nos. 92–94. Then plain late Georgian, interrupted by the large gableted dormers of No. 116 (1871–2, probably by *Jesse Hall*).

NORTH STREET

WAR MEMORIAL at the E end, by *Robert S. Lorimer*, 1922: stumpy cenotaph in front of a screen wall.

Nos. 1–33 (N side). First, two set-back pantiled houses, No. 1 late C18, No. 3 a drydashed rebuild of 1960. More drydash on the 1950s Nos. 5–11, over-large in scale, with eccentric traditional detail. Nos. 15–17, simple of *c.*1800. Nos. 19–21 with a forestair; the front has been Georgianized, but there is evidence of C17 windows. Late C18 No. 23, pantiled with minimal crowsteps. Plain late Georgian to the corner with North Castle Street.

Nos. 2–22 (S side). DEANS COURT on the corner was built in the early C16, L-plan, the main block fronting E, NW jamb. Stairtower, now reduced to a flat-roofed projection, in the inner angle towards the courtyard. The house was acquired and remodelled in the late C16 by Sir George Douglas. He was responsible for the courtyard's round-arched foot-gate, its thin hoodmould supporting etiolated attached columns rising to the wallhead. Within this frame, an aedicule borne on human head corbels and containing an eroded coat of arms. The archway's wrought-iron gate is of 1933 by *Reginald Fairlie*, who also made the larger gateway on the l. Douglas was probably also responsible for extending the jamb W and recasting the main block's windows with roll-moulded margins to match the new work's S windows. Heavy-handed conversion to a university hall of residence by *J. D. Mills*, 1931. Mills added a would-be Scots Renaissance door to the N wing's courtyard front, a shaped pediment to the E front, and a NW extension. The E and W gables were rebuilt in 1975. Inside, two C18 panelled rooms. In the courtyard, a large WELL. All this stands aloof from North Street, whose S side really begins with the early C18 pantiled No. 12 (MUSEUM), originally three houses but reconstructed as one in 1936: simply moulded doorpiece, crowsteps on the E gable. The pantiled No. 20 steps slightly forward. Its front now looks mucked-about Georgian, but the E gable's small second-floor window has a cornice of *c.*1600. OLD CASTLE TAVERN, late Georgian, on the corner of South Castle Street.

Nos. 35–75 (N side). No. 35 is plain Georgian dressed up with 1930s pantiles and large crowsteps to fit in with All Saints' Rectory (*see* Churches, above). GANNOCHY HOUSE, a desperately plain block by *Reiach & Hall*, 1971. For the Younger Hall and St Salvator's Hall, *see* University Buildings, above. Plain No. 65, of *c*.1800. COLLEGE GATE is by *J. C. Cunningham*, 1949–53, gutless Scots Renaissance. Squeezed into the SE corner of St Salvator's College (*see* University Buildings, above), the rubble-built No. 71. Before the Reformation the site was owned by the Knights of St John, but the present house is late C16, probably the work of Archbishop Patrick Adamson, who bought the property in 1572. L-plan with a NW jamb but also a conical-roofed SW tower. In the tower, a flourish of gunloops. The W gable's crowsteps are gableted; the plain E crowsteps are probably C18. Most windows altered but some still roll-moulded. Heavy crowstepped N addition by *David Henry*, 1912.

Nos. 24–82 (S side). Mostly austere late Georgian, but the small tenement at Nos. 30–32 has an early C17 core extended with slightly later outshots towards the street. No. 32's forestair is of *c*.1950. (Inside, a chimneypiece with an heraldic lintel dated 1618.) No. 52, with a Roman Doric columned doorpiece, is dated 1827 on its r. skewputt; large late C20 box dormer. Smaller dormer addition on No. 52A, its piended platform roof framed by masonry piers at the corners. No. 54 a shoddy intrusion by *J. C. Cunningham*, 1938–9. A few classy touches to the W: rusticated ground floors at Nos. 60 and 66, pilastered doorpieces on Nos. 62–64, pedimented doorpiece on the late C18 No. 70, crowsteps on the slightly earlier No. 72. Then, across Union Street, the Martyrs Church (*see* above) and humble SALVATION ARMY HALL of 1984. Just as humble the late C18 No. 82 against the gable of No. 19 College Street.

Nos. 77–129 (N side). No. 77's front was remodelled in the late C18, but the l. stairtower proclaims an earlier origin. The building history must be largely conjectural, but the present NW wing, which has a vaulted ground floor, seems to be C15, probably the house on this site owned by John Ray in 1459 and which had passed to Andrew Balfour by 1497. In the mid-C16 this house became an L-plan by the addition, perhaps in two stages, of a large front block, the work probably done for Hew Bontaveron, chaplain of the St Katharine's altar in St Salvator's College Chapel. The SW stairtower may be part of the mid-C16 work or may be a slightly later encroachment on the street. The house was remodelled in the late C17 and the NE wing containing a new stair added. The SW stairtower is rounded, except on the E, where its flat front is corbelled out at the eaves for a conical roof (by *Paul Waterhouse*, 1923–4, replacing a late C18 oversailing roof). In the tower's E front has been a first-floor door; above it, a round-headed niche for an armorial panel. In the main block's front, evidence of two C16 doors, the l. roll-moulded. Late C17 central door. In BUTTS WYND at the back, harled addition by *R. Rowand*

Anderson, 1891–2, when he converted the house to a students' union.

Nos. 79–81, urbane late Georgian with a rusticated ground floor, are by *Robert Balfour*. Then the set-back University Library (*see* University Buildings, above), followed by timid infill by *Cunningham, Jack, Fisher & Purdom*, 1974. The CRAWFORD CENTRE is a very smart villa built for the Lindsays of Wormiston, *c.*1812. Broad Roman Doric columned doorpiece; rosettes on its frieze and again under the eaves. Single-storey piend-roofed wings, their polished ashlar a contrast to the main block's broached stonework. On the l., mid-C19 stables with a fishscale-slated bellcote. The street now becomes cottagey with front gardens until the resolutely burgh-picturesque NEW PICTURE HOUSE (by *Gillespie & Scott*, 1930) muscles in, pushing an arcaded loggia over the pavement. Victorian ensues. Gableted No. 125 of 1863, probably by *Jesse Hall*. Steepled corner on No. 127 facing across Murray Park to ARGYLE HOUSE's fat ogee-roofed turret (by *Hall & Henry*, 1879–81). The TUDOR INN, interwar roadhouse Elizabethan.

Nos. 84–150 (S side). On the corner, the crowstepped gable of Nos. 22–24 College Street. In College Street, a forestair to the first-floor door, whose lintel is dated 1722. Nos. 84–86 North Street, rubble-built C18 houses with a pilastered doorpiece on No. 86. At the Muttoes Lane corner, planners' vernacular of 1985, covered in porridgey harl. Little better are *Walker & Pride*'s thin Scots Renaissance No. 94 and POLICE STATION of 1935. Rather bolder approach at the JOHNSTON CENTRE, by *Sinclair & Watt*, 1974; Spencean arcades under a blockwork first floor and slate-hung 'mansard'. Late Georgian resumes at Nos. 110–122. Then all is very plain until Nos. 140–146, by *George Rae*, 1844, with stylized acroteria on the ground-floor window pediments and heavy pilastered doorpieces. At the Greyfriars Garden corner, a gable with a big Roman Doric columned doorpiece.

ELLICE PLACE to PILMOUR LINKS (N side). In ELLICE PLACE, No. 1, very plain, by *James Gillespie*, 1876. No. 3 of *c.*1800, broached ashlar, with a pantiled roof. Nos. 4–6 (by *George Rae*, 1863) are taller: Elizabethan dormerheads over the top-floor windows; weird first-floor window surrounds suggestive of buckle work. Then PLAYFAIR TERRACE, by *George Rae*, 1846–52. Georgian survival ends (Nos. 1–3, and No. 8, with an unfortunate attic addition). In between, Nos. 4–5, Aegypto-Greek with giant anthemions on the gables; Nos. 6–7 less inventive, with smaller detail. PILMOUR PLACE was begun in 1820, a simple late Georgian terrace but without formal unity. PILMOUR LINKS, an undistinguished group, mostly late Victorian, dominated by the very large but unpompous RUSACKS MARINE HOTEL of 1887–92.

PILMOUR LINKS *see* NORTH STREET

PILMOUR PLACE *see* NORTH STREET

PLAYFAIR TERRACE *see* NORTH STREET

QUEEN'S GARDENS

Laid out in 1858 for houses on the E side, their gardens on the w, it was mostly built by 1864.

On the N corner, the Town Hall (*see* Public Buildings, above). No. 2 (BURGH OFFICES), by *David Rhind*, was built in 1869 as the COMMERCIAL BANK. Heavy segmental pedimented dormers and a Frenchy roof; bracketed stone balcony in the centre. Most of the houses are decent post-Georgian, their stonework of polished ashlar. On Nos. 16–17, columned door-pieces with foliaged caps and human head keystones (the carving by *Walker* of Edinburgh). For St Regulus Hall on the Queen's Terrace corner, *see* University Buildings, above.

QUEEN'S TERRACE

Begun in 1865.

For St Andrew's (Episcopal) Church, *see* Churches, above. Solid grey villas predominate. Secluded in a large garden, St Andrew's Rectory (by *James Gillespie & Scott*, 1896) has a touch of half-timbering. More colourful the half-timbering and glazed red brick of No. 16, dated 1897. In the street's E part, an aediculed gateway of *c.*1914 to the BOTANIC GARDENS; in its pediment, a re-used stone inscribed with a variant of the Keith motto:

> They.Have.Said. And.They.will
> Say.Let.Them.Be.Saying
> 1720

To its E, a second pedimented gateway, of 1984.

ST MARY'S PLACE

MANSEFIELD (No. 3) on the S is early C19, with giant angle pilasters and a Roman Doric doorpiece. Opposite, the old West Infant School (*see* Public Buildings, above). INCHCAPE HOUSE, coarse Jacobean of 1861, probably by *George Rae*. WEST PARK HOUSE demure late Georgian. No. 6 was built as a photographic studio in 1866: single-storey front block with heavy doorpieces, two-storey piend-roofed building behind. Then the harled front of the VICTORY MEMORIAL HALL, made out of *William Burn*'s ST MARY'S CHURCH of 1839–40. It faces LOCKHART PLACE, a pair of Georgian survival houses built in 1851 as part of James Hope's Abbotsford Crescent scheme.

ST MARY'S STREET

ASHLEIGH HOUSE (No. 37) was built as a fever hospital, *c.*1850. Three blocks joined by set-back lower links; broad eaves.

THE SCORES

Large Victorian villas (now mostly used by the University) built to enjoy the sea view.

At the E end, on the S, THE CASTLE HOUSE, late Victorian with a comfortable ogee-roofed centre; fat turret on the l. Beside it, KENNEDY HALL by *James Gillespie & Scott*, 1895–6, Baronial with a balustraded SE tower and conical-roofed NW turret. Then the bulk of St Salvator's Hall (*see* University Buildings, above). Opposite on the N, the pacific Baronial CASTLECLIFFE of 1869 by *David Bryce*. Typical of Bryce is the asymmetrical W front with its two canted bay windows, the l. corbelled out to a crowstepped gable, the r. under a ball-finialled parapet. Just as characteristic the S front's crowstepped gable gripped by turrets. Poor Edwardian additions on the S and NE, and worse extensions made more recently. Then KIRNAN, small (in this context), Baronial again. Much larger and fiercer is EDGECLIFFE, a double house of 1864–6 by *George Rae*; crowstepped and machicolated, with turrets corbelled diagonally across the corners of the gabled end bays. THE PRINCIPAL'S HOUSE by *John Starforth*, 1864–6, with a saddlebacked entrance tower. On the S, No. 10 (THE SWALLOWGATE), relaxed Scots Jacobean, by *R. Rowand Anderson*, 1895. No. 12 (CRAIGARD) of 1863 appears small and prickly by comparison. It is probably by *Jesse Hall*, who was responsible for No. 14 (ST KATHARINE'S LODGE) built as a short three-house terrace in 1856, the gables and bay windows managing to avoid symmetry. On the N, a very large but bleak crowstepped double villa (NORTH CLIFF and ROCKVIEW) by *Hall*, 1864, but only completed in 1881–2 by *John Milne*.

After the University Library (*see* University Buildings, above), No. 16, a tall crowstepped two-bay house of *c.*1895, and a contemporary double cottage (Nos. 18–20) by *Hall & Henry*. These face *James Gillespie*'s stolid Italianate PRESBYTERY of 1884. The one-storey No. 22 (THE WHAUM) is a pantiled survivor from the early C19. CANMORE on the N, by *James Gillespie & Scott*, 1985, with a three-storey bay window carried up as a broad-eaved tower, abuts the plain No. 31 Murray Park.

After Murray Park, only the S side is built up. It is a long bay-windowed terrace, beginning with Nos. 24–26 by *John Milne*, 1897–8. No. 30, also by *Milne*, with a Frenchy roof over its bay window. ST ANDREWS GOLF HOTEL, probably by *Hall & Henry*, *c.*1895; big and plain, but not deserving the new addition. GILLESPIE TERRACE was laid out by *George Rae*, 1849. Varied combinations of classical detail and bay windows, except at No. 2, where the windows are bows and the detail not classical. No. 6 is by *Jesse Hall*, 1865. At the end, two large houses, the l.'s two gables joined by a heavy Jacobean stone balcony; the r. (THE SCORES HOTEL) of 1880, more richly Jacobean but spoilt by a front addition. Finally, the red sandstone HAMILTON HALL (former GRAND HOTEL) by *James M. Monro*, 1895, huge but timid François I.

In front of Gillespie Terrace, the MARTYRS' MONUMENT, a squat flat-topped obelisk by *William Nixon*, 1842–3; segmental pedimented base with swags and guttae. To its W, an admirably frilly cast-iron BANDSTAND of *c.* 1890.

SOUTH STREET

Nos. 1–25 (N side). On the corner, THE ROUNDEL (No. 1), its skinny front block probably C16, but the regular five-bay fenestration and cavetto cornice look like a late C17 remodelling. Late C17 doorpiece, a lugged architrave enclosing a squashed ogee arch. C16 Gothic doorpiece in the projecting SE stairtower, whose flat roof and heavy parapet balusters are presumably part of the C17 reconstruction. In the house's E gable, stone carved with the Haldenstone arms. Piend-roofed late Georgian rear additions. (Inside, vaulted ground floor.)

No. 3 is C16, regularized in the C17. The original doors and windows had moulded surrounds; the later openings chamfered margins. No. 5's bland ashlar front of *c.* 1800 hides a C17 U-plan house with crowstepped N wings. In the garden wall, a BEE-BOLL incorporating the top of an ogee-arched aumbry of *c.* 1500. The building line steps forward at No. 7 (*c.* 1790); doorpiece with a fluted frieze. Then a couple of harled houses, both badly altered: No. 9 of *c.* 1600; Nos. 11–13, C18, but with a concrete tiled roof. Ashlar fronts on No. 15, late C19 Georgian survival, and the late C18 No. 17, with a dentil cornice and fanlit front door. No. 19's picturesque pantiled appearance dates from a reconstruction of 1935, but its built-up Gothic doorway is late medieval. The window on its r. has been made from a late C16 roll-moulded door. Above the present door, a sundial with a human head on top and dated 1734, brought here from Airth (Central) in 1935. The late C18 double house at Nos. 23–25 was raised, *c.* 1860, by an extra floor, its windows linked by sill and lintel courses in an early C18 manner and with a tall chimney-stack atop a vestigial shaped gablet.

Nos. 2–24 (S side). PRIORSGATE (No. 2) beside The Pends (*see* p. 367) is of *c.* 1785, built on the site of the E wing of Queen Mary's House. The two W bays seem to incorporate C16 walling, and C16 vaulted cellars survive inside. At the bottom of its back garden, a two-storey late Georgian garden building with pedimented gables.

QUEEN MARY'S HOUSE (No. 4) has a plain street-face dressed up only by the early C18 Gibbsian doorpiece on the l. The main front is to the garden, where its late C16 character shines through. L-plan* with a SW jamb; in the inner angle, a stairtower corbelled out to support a rectangular cap-house. To the stairtower's r., an early C18 porch with a rusticated round-arched door and urns on the steep pediment. At the jamb's SE corner, a second-floor oriel, possibly an early C17 addition, as may be the gable's crowstepped lean-to extension.

---

* Originally U-plan. The E wing was sold off in 1783 and Priorsgate built on its site.

The house was restored by *Reginald Fairlie* as a library for St Leonard's School in 1927. Inside, a vaulted ground floor (the main block's w vault removed), the kitchen having been in the jamb. Oak panelling of *c.*1600 in the jamb's second-floor room.

Nos. 6–8 are C18 with a late C19 top floor, No. 10 stolid late C18 enlivened by side lights flanking the door. The parapeted mid-C18 No. 14 is grander; Gibbsian doorpiece with beefy consoles under the pediment. Lower rear wing, its windows enlarged in the late C19; early C19 Roman Doric aediculed doorpiece. No. 22 is plain late Victorian. By contrast, the improbably picturesque No. 24 restored by *W. Murray Jack*, 1970–1, to a conjecture of what the C17 house on the site might have looked like. L-plan with a slated cat-slide roof on the jamb. The sash windows and main block's pantiles are C18 details. Above the garden wall's gate from Abbey Street, a marriage lintel dated 1721 which came from a demolished house in Baker Lane.

Nos. 27–103 (N side). Twin-gabled Tudor No. 27 (by *George Rae*, 1856) and late Georgian No. 29, united by a continuous shoddy shopfront. Another poor shopfront at No. 31 (*c.*1800). No. 33 is of *c.*1930, harled, with a red-tile roof. Then Nos. 35–39 of *c.*1800, with a later 'mansard', the polished ashlar contrasting with the late C18 No. 41's rougher stonework. Big cast-iron balconies on No. 43 (*c.*1830). After the plain C18 Nos. 45–47, the early C19 broached ashlar front of No. 49 concealing late C16 painted wooden ceilings. Unassuming late C18 and early C19 at Nos. 53–57. Nos. 59–61 were remodelled by *George Rae* in 1866 with a continuous first-floor hood-moulding. No. 63, *c.*1840, with delicately architraved first-floor windows. No. 65 of *c.*1820, tall and plain, its ground floor a reconstruction of 1974. In the gable of its back wing to Baker Lane, an inset stone carved with a crowned head.

ST JOHN'S HOUSE (Nos. 67–69) was begun *c.*1450 as an L-plan building with the hall in the back wing. The front block was rebuilt *c.*1600, its upper floor jettied out on corbels at the rear, and then raised from two to four storeys in the C18. Its windows seem to have been enlarged *c.*1850. The rear wing was extended and internally reconstructed in the C17 and C18. *W. Murray Jack*'s reconstruction of 1967–75 added a glass-walled staircase against the main block's N wall.

95   No. 71 is a tenement of *c.*1600, remodelled *c.*1800 with a wide Roman Doric columned doorpiece; late Victorian gabled dormers. Then the early C19 No. 73, bowing out to a new building line continued in the same urbane late Georgian manner by Nos. 75–81 and, more simply, by the contemporary Nos. 83–89. Tall No. 91, late C18 with a two-storey rear wing down Crail's Lane. No. 95, tactful infill of 1971; Nos. 97–99 dated 1874. More forceful, although only one storey, is the former POST OFFICE (later, Christian Institute, and now a shop) at Nos. 101–103, by *James Gillespie & Scott*, 1891–2: cast-iron columns in a stone frame, a pedimented attic pro-

jecting into the centre of the balustrade. At Nos. 105–107, a late Georgian tenement dressed up in the 1920s with Tudor detail *à la* Libertys. For Holy Trinity Parish Church, *see* Churches, above.

Nos. 34–78 (S side). No. 34 on the Abbey Street corner is late C18 but with a mid-C19 chimney gablet of the same type as Nos. 23–25. Then a large early C16 tenement (Nos. 36–38), its first-floor windows Georgianized. Above the r. second-floor window, a panel with the arms and initials of Prior John Hepburn, who owned the property in 1521. It was restored in 1968–72 by *W. Murray Jack*, together with the adjoining SOUTH COURT (Nos. 36–42). South Court is a back-to-front F on plan, the N, E and S ranges apparently built by the Lamond family in the late C16 and the E range extended S probably *c.*1660 by George Martine, whose arms are above the pend from the street. Regular four-bay N front, its windows' chamfered margins probably late C17. This range's courtyard elevation dates from the early C19, when a staircase was added. Inserted scroll-pedimented dormerhead dated 1642. The E range's two-storey bay window was added by *John Milne*, 1860–2. In the courtyard's SE corner, a crowstep-gabled stairtower, probably C17, behind a flat-roofed porch. The S range is Georgian but incorporates remains of a late C16 arcade of three segmental roll-moulded arches. The W arch was re-opened in 1968–72 as the entrance to a new pend to the garden. Here the E range's late C17 extension projects with a crowstepped gable. In the inner angle, part of a late C16 ashlar building. It has been very smart, with a would-be classical aediculed window in the jettied upper floor. Classy early C19 Roman Doric columned doorpiece.

No. 44 is plain late Georgian but with C16 cellars. Much grander No. 46, built *c.*1600 for the Balfours of Mountquhanie, whose arms are below the l. second-floor window, and remodelled in 1723 for Principal Hadow of St Mary's College with a corbelled parapet and crowstepped gables. W extension (No. 48) of 1880, in the same style but different stone. In the garden behind, a lectern DOOCOT, probably early C18.

No. 52's rendered front probably hides a C16 origin, but its present appearance is late Georgian, with a tall Roman Doric doorpiece. Outsize crowsteps on the E gable, its skewputt carved with the arms of Monypenny of Pitmilly. More render at No. 54 of 1859–60, perhaps by *George Rae*, mixing Thomsonesque Greek detail into a Jacobean outline; stone owls on the balcony above the slitlike door. No. 56 is a narrow late C18 cliff; its pilastered double door looks an insertion of *c.*1830. No. 58 a mess, C16 badly Georgianized. No. 60 is of the earlier C17 but with a late Georgian doorpiece and late C19 dormers; lower crowstepped rear wing. No. 62 (*c.*1800) has a boring street frontage but is much better to the garden, with a boldly projecting pedimented centre. After St Mary's College (*see* University Buildings, above), the early C19 Nos. 68–78 advance urbanely. No. 72's shopfront is by *James Gillespie*,

1903; Nos. 76–78's pilastered ground floor of 1970. Vernacular rear wing in the close behind No. 70.

Nos. 109–163 (N side). The classical ALBERT BUILDINGS (Nos. 109–121) on the W of Holy Trinity Church are by *William Scott*, 1844, their unity broken by selective stone cleaning. No. 121's shopfront by *James Scott*, 1906. Cottagey Nos. 123–125 of *c*.1930, with a broad Tudorish gablet. POST OFFICE (No. 127), plain classical of *c*.1840, its top floor added in 1866. At Nos. 129–131, C18 vernacular behind built-out shops. Ashlar tenement of 1850–5 (probably by *George Rae*) at Nos. 133–139; the r. half has been raised by one storey. No. 143's plain tenement of *c*.1800 was reconstructed by *W. Murray Jack* in 1960–3, the Victorian shopfront now incongruous in a polite ashlar surround. In the courtyard behind, the harled and pantiled No. 141, early C18 with a forestair. A touch of Norman Shaw Queen Anne at the narrow-fronted No. 145 of *c*.1900. Nos. 147–149 are by *Jesse Hall*, 1867, with a foliaged frieze; anthemion finials on top of the bargeboarded dormers. Nos. 153–155, early C19 with lugged architraved first-floor windows. Nos. 157–159 are Georgian replicas in painted blockwork of 1972. Severe tenement (Nos. 161–163) of *c*.1820 on the corner of Bell Street.

Nos. 80–118 (S side). On the corner with Queen's Gardens, splay-fronted classical-modern BANK OF SCOTLAND of 1960. Next door, JOHN MENZIES, interwar Art Deco without much art. Nos. 96–100, of *c*.1880. The late Victorian Nos. 102–104's drydash is redeemed by the thistle-finialled Jacobean dormers and cast-iron columned shopfront; C18 wing in the close behind. Across a small gap, partly filled by a garage, Nos. 108–110 of *c*.1780, small but smart provincial, with masonic symbols in the centre pediment. In the close behind the early C19 Nos. 112–114, a house dated 1734. The SOUTHGAIT HALL (No. 118) is of 1857, probably by *George Rae*, with thrifty but effective Jacobean detail at the first-floor windows and a heavy Roman Doric doorpiece. W extension in the same style by *John Milne*, 1894. The mansard roof is more recent. Madras College, Blackfriars Chapel and the Baptist Church follow (for all these, *see* Public Buildings and Churches, above).

Nos. 165–213 (N side). After the classy block on Bell Street's W corner (*see* Bell Street), plain early C19 tenements (Nos. 169 and 175) flanking the twin-gabled Jacobean Nos. 171–173 of *c*.1860, probably by *George Rae*. Nos. 177–179, C18, small and rendered. Polished ashlar at Nos. 181–187 of *c*.1850, with lugged architraves at the first-floor windows. Nos. 189–191 were built in 1800; Victorian shopfront adding punch. Built across the close behind the rendered Nos. 193–195 of *c*.1800, a much altered crowstepped building, probably C18. Big crowstepped dormerheads on the late C19 Nos. 197–199; the cast-iron columned shopfront of 1905 is by *Gillespie & Scott*. Late C19 No. 201; No. 203, drydashed infill. In the close behind, a three-storey brewery building of *c*.1800, with a piended pantiled roof. Symmetrical pair of Victorian shopfronts on Nos.

205–207 of 1737. Large bargeboarded dormers have been added to the C18 No. 209. Nos. 211–213, dated 1903, with a corner turret, abutting West Port.

Nos. 132–172 (S side). On the corner of Rose Lane, No. 132, Baronial with a corner turret, by *Hall & Henry*, 1904. In ROSE LANE, a pleasant vernacular group. At the foot, a small BREWERY of *c.*1800. In IMRIE'S CLOSE behind Nos. 134–136 South Street, an early C18 cottage used as a Burgher meeting house from 1749 to 1774; it was reconstructed by *James Gillespie & Scott*, 1950–4. Simple C18 rubble and pantiled house at Nos. 142–144 South Street. In ALISON'S CLOSE on the l., a plain C19 vernacular row. Behind the C18 Nos. 146–148 South Street, a pretty white-painted rubble group, partly reconstructed in 1939–49 by *J. C. Cunningham*. Large-scale late Georgian Nos. 150–154 South Street, the windows disconcertingly grouped 2/1. An appropriately ecclesiastical look was given to No. 156 of *c.*1800 when *Jesse Hall* remodelled it as a manse in 1871. Picturesque interwar rubble infill at No. 158, next to the rendered C18 Nos. 160–162. More infill but without much attempt to fit in at No. 164. The early C18 Nos. 166–168 was reconstructed by *Gillespie & Scott*, 1955–7; defiantly pink-harled, with a forestair. BRITANNIA HOTEL (No. 170) by *James Gillespie*, *c.*1870. The street ends with No. 172, very tall Georgian-Elizabethan of 1844, probably by *George Rae*.

UNION STREET

Known as the Foul Waste until *c.*1830, when it acquired the present name.

The Buchanan Building (*see* Market Street) fills the W side. On the E, early C19 houses. No. 5 has an absurd Ionic doorpiece with huge rosettes on the frieze; less endearing is its C20 'mansard'. No. 7 squeezes aprons between the first-floor sill course and a band course.

ST MARGARET'S HOPE   *1080*
0.8km. NW of North Queensferry

Accomplished neo-Georgian by *Ernest Newton*, 1916, its official look understandable since it was built to house the admiral commanding in Scotland. On the drive, an ARCHWAY, perhaps early C19; set into each side a C16 heraldic panel bearing the arms of the Napiers of Wrightshouse.

ST MONANS   *5000*

For most of its existence a fishing village, the natural harbour improved by a pier in 1865. Major C20 development gave the village burghal status in 1933 but did not enhance its approaches.

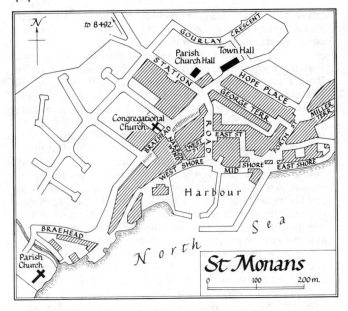

CHURCHES

CONGREGATIONAL CHURCH, Braehead. Built as a Free
Church, then successively United Free Church and Braehead
Parish Church. Gothic, by *David Horne* of Greenock, 1870.
Gable front with three lancets, a rose window and pyramidal
spire.

13 PARISH CHURCH, Braehead. Admirably sturdy-looking in its
cliff-top graveyard overlooking the sea. Building of the church
in 1362–70 was paid for by David II, who endowed it as a
chapel served by an unspecified number of chaplains. James
III transferred the chapel and endowments to the Dominicans
in 1471. The choir was blocked off from the rest and fitted up
for public worship in 1647 and two years later became a parish
church. The abandoned transepts, roofless by the late C18,
were restored by *William Burn* in 1826–8 and the whole building was brought back into use.

The church consists of a choir and transepts, with a steeple
at the crossing. The stub of a basecourse projecting from the
w wall suggests that a nave was begun but quickly given up.
Well-dressed ashlar masonry (partly reworked and renewed in
1826–8); by contrast the roofs' Cumberland slates (provided
in *P. MacGregor Chalmers*' repair of 1899) look very thin.
Splayed basecourse. Windows delineated by a stringcourse
below and hoodmoulds above, interrupted by the buttresses
along the choir's s side and at the E and s gables. Burn finished
the buttresses with obelisk pinnacles, except for those at the
corners, which he gave tall gabled finials. Against the choir's

N wall, an orangey-coloured lean-to vestry of 1826–8 on the site of the medieval sacristy.

Strong low crossing tower. At its NE corner, a slim round stairtower with crosslet windows. The main tower's tall W window was made by Burn and blocked in 1955 by *Ian G. Lindsay*, who provided a discreet rectangular light instead. Inside the corbelled parapet (rebuilt in 1899), an octagonal spire with small stone lucarnes. The lack of a weathercock makes it unnecessarily dumpy.

The window tracery was much renewed by Burn. The plate tracery in the S transept appears to be entirely by him. His also seem to be the intersecting tracery of the N transept's gable window and its W window's Y-tracery. The choir windows' designs are medieval: in the N openings, rectilinear tracery; in the S, curvilinear; in the E, curvilinear again but simpler. In the small semicircular light at the top of the E gable, radiating quatrefoils in mouchettes. Are these windows of the 1360s, or do they represent a late C15 remodelling, perhaps after the church was taken over by the Dominicans?

The limewashed interior's chaste appearance dates from 1955, when *Ian G. Lindsay* stripped plaster from the walls and removed Burn's plaster reproductions of medieval work. The chancel arch looks naked without Burn's mouldings. Simply shafted and chamfered C14 crossing arches to N and S. Panelled wooden ceilings of 1955 (replacing Burn's vaults) over the crossing and transepts. In the S transept's E wall, a rectangular aumbry which has had doors. Ogee-headed aumbry (again checked for doors) with a drain in its sill in the S wall. Ogee-headed piscina in the N transept's SE corner.

Over the four-bay chancel, elaborate late Gothic vault, its diagonal and transverse ridge-ribs springing from wall-shafts, the tiercerons from the tas-de-charge, and the intermediate longitudinal ribs from corbels set high up. Carved and painted heraldic bosses at the intersections. The outline of Burn's E doors (built up in 1955) is visible on the gable. In the S wall, a triple SEDILIA, the seat divisions corbelled out in a massive curve. Over each seat, blind tracery with round-headed arches containing cusped ogee arches. Similar blind tracery at the CREDENCE to the E. CONSECRATION CROSSES on the N and S walls. In the N wall, a chamfered door into the vestry. (Inside the vestry, remains of a credence niche and piscina.)

The FURNISHINGS are of 1955–61 and very simple. – On the chancel's E wall, a wooden PANEL painted with the burgh arms and the date 1792. It is thought to have been part of a gallery front removed in 1826–8. – MODEL BOAT hung in the S crossing arch, probably C18.

PARISH CHURCH HALL, Station Road. Demurely Classical, by *Robert S. Lorimer*, 1913. Gable frontage, with a Venetian window.

PUBLIC BUILDINGS

HARBOUR. A natural tidal harbour, with boatbuilders' slipways. A narrow approach from the sea, between the rocks. First came the central pier (now cased in cement), for which the Privy Council allowed donations from all over Scotland in the interest of impoverished residents and the nation at large. (Earlier records probably refer to a harbour at West St Monans, existing by 1649 but now largely disappeared.) Then the EAST PIER by *D. & T. Stevenson*, 1865, and finally the short WEST PIER and the deepening of both basins by *Charles Stevenson*, 1902.

TOWN HALL (formerly the School), Hope Place. 1866, by *Thomas Currie*, with additions of 1876. Gabled, with deep eaves.

DESCRIPTION

St Monans seems at first sight to have been swamped by C20 housing. To the NW a mass of red-tile roofs looking every whichway. To the NE the grey roofs of GOURLAY CRESCENT, with hoists on some of the rear dormers, by *C. F. Anderson* of St Andrews, 1933. STATION ROAD enters St Monans between them, past the Church Hall and then steeply down to the Harbour (for both, *see* above). Good views uphill, e.g. to the tall No. 26, white-harled early C19, and the sea-facing late Georgian villa at No. 35 George Terrace over a high retaining wall. Finally, harled and colour-washed C18 or early C19 fronts looking smugly across at each other, No. 3 restored for the East Neuk of Fife Preservation Society in 1971. Digressions on the way down start with INVERIE STREET, a high terrace with rooftops and sea view. Nos. 2–4 a double house, No. 6 a black whinstone bungalow with a chimney-gable, both *c.* 1840. SEAVIEW itself late Victorian, with fancy iron brackets for the rhones and daisies on the conductors. Congregational Church (*see* above) breaking a line of late Victorian fisher tenements. To the E, HOPE PLACE (for the former school, now Town Hall, *see* above) and GEORGE TERRACE, both lined with long, rather urban fisher tenements of *c.* 1890. Two storeys of grey stone with an attic (here called a garret) whose dormers have slide-out hoists for gear. Long rows of brick sheds to the rear, for the storage and tarring of nets. MILLER TERRACE to the E repeats the formula on a smaller scale, with a chimney-gabled shop at the near end (Guthrie's bakery). FORTH STREET is another way down, with No. 19 and the chimney-gabled No. 17 on the steepest slope, and the later chimney-gable of No. 11 (John Gowans, plumber). In ROSE STREET, first the sharp corner of No. 14, *c.* 1840, with plain slab cornice and bullseyed crowstep gable, all in orange ironstone. Then, after an awkward gap, the C18 No. 11, two harled storeys crowned with a projecting timber loft, windowed from end to end. No. 13 could be of 1719 (the owner has a charter of that date), but the upper floor has been added.

Two final digressions from Station Road. EAST STREET with imitation vernacular housing of 1970 and the more exotic BRAID COURT of 1974, both by *Baxter, Clark & Paul*. On the corner of WEST STREET, No. 2 with scrolled skewputt, possibly C17. Warehouses to the S and straight ahead, where a rubble block with hipped and pantiled roof, probably C18, closes the vista (Montador, fish merchant). To the N, a tall warehouse with ventilator has been excellently restored by *Baxter, Clark & Paul*, 1974.

EAST SHORE starts from the bottom of Forth Street. Opposite the big boatbuilding shed, No. 1, crowstepped and stuccoed. No. 5, formerly a Relief Meeting House of 1796 with a broad W gable, made into houses after 1847, has the first half of its date on an elegant keystone reset high in the wall; its neighbour has the other. The rest modernized or industrial vernacular (timber shed at No. 8, the boatbuilder James N. Miller). At the far end an early C19 house by itself, with chimney-gable and its own sea wall. MID SHORE starts with a gable of big orange crowsteps (actually in Forth Street). CLYDESDALE BANK with a prettily carved fascia of 1935. A slit vista up THE CRIBBS, where No. 2 has a surprise front garden and No. 5 a forestair and a chamfered wall which admits to an even narrower slit. No. 4 Mid Shore, C18 with mid-step skews, net-loft and hoist. No. 6 Victorian, with a hoist on its dormer. WEST SHORE has a concave curve and an up-and-down skyline. No. 1 C18 with crowsteps, No. 2 likewise, but the roof lifted another storey later. No. 3 with a red brick lum, No. 4 with a mid-C18 rusticated doorpiece and pillared forestair. At Nos. 5–7, early C18, a hipped projecting jamb with stone pedestal and baluster finials. Vaulted beer cellars in the back court. The last of this sequence of restorations (by *W. Murray Jack* for the National Trust for Scotland, 1968–70) is the POST OFFICE dated 1867. Then NARROW WYND climbs up towards the Congregational Church (*see* above), and West Shore henceforth has greater freedom of detail till couthiness returns at No. 20 (nicely arguing its wall-line with its neighbour) and harling at No. 21 and the forestaired No. 22, all with swept dormers. The W gable of the last house, No. 27, has a neat pantiled extension swept uphill and round the corner. In the two-sided WEST END the image slips a little. At No. 7 an Olde English front door and a Riviera sun-roof.

COAL FARM, 0.8km. E. Between this and the sea, the lower part of a C18 cylindrical rubble WINDMILL.

BALCASKIE. *See* p. 84.

NEWARK CASTLE. *See* p. 329.

SALINE

Village mostly developed in the C18 and C19, with some recent housing at the W end.

FREE CHURCH, Bridge Street. Disused. 1844, by *Lewis Mercer*. Broad-eaved rectangle. Segment-headed bellcote on the barge-boarded gable.

PARISH CHURCH, Main Street. By *William Stark*, 1808–10. Its ungainly appearance is not helped by the harling, first applied in 1838, but since renewed with too much cement in the mix. Standard Georgian preaching box dressed up with rather small Tudor windows (latticed glazing of 1905) and thin buttresses. At the w gable, the buttresses are paired and rise like flanking towers, the l. supporting a bellcote. Perhaps the effect was less awkward before *P. MacGregor Chalmers* steepened the roof-pitch in 1905. Sizeable hall of 1972 at the w.

Inside, the gallery round three sides carried on columns of clustered shafts may be a replacement of 1905, but if so it must have followed the original design. – FURNISHINGS by *Chalmers*, 1905. – STAINED-GLASS E window (Christ and symbols of Baptism and the Eucharist) by *John Blyth*, 1984, in strong colours.

SESSION HOUSE at entry to the churchyard, with Tudor detail, built by *Andrew Cairns*, 1819. – Remains of a probably contemporary HEARSE HOUSE at the SW corner.

PRIMARY SCHOOL, Oakley Road. Low front block by *Thomas Frame*, 1875. Roguish Gothic with a battered chimney and gabled bellcote. Tall plain w addition by *John Houston*, 1907. s extensions by *George Sandilands*, 1922–4.

DESCRIPTION

On the approach from Dunfermline, to the l., among the new houses of UPPER KINNEDDAR, is UPPER KINNEDDAR HOUSE, low early C19 Tudor made rambling by a late C19 addition in a plainer variant of the original style. In MAIN STREET, two set-back Tudor houses: on the r., the large-scale MANSE (by *Robert Hay*, 1849–50), with horizontal glazing; on the l., OCHILVIEW (dated 1851, extended w in the same style, 1901), its hoodmoulds' labels carved with human faces. Further down, a pretty early C19 Jacobean double cottage (YEW COTTAGE and IVY COTTAGE), with crenellated gate-piers to the front gardens. No. 21's door lintel is dated 1830. In OAKLEY ROAD beyond the School (*see* above), the crow-stepped CRAIG HOUSE, dated 1749 on a marriage stone above the door. The lumpy Parish Church (*see* above) stands at a crossroads. WEST ROAD leads out towards Dollar. On its r., CLAVERLEY, built in 1814–15 as the Parish School and Schoolhouse, the house being given a second storey in 1834, when its elegantly carved skewputts were re-used. Ionic portico on the late Georgian PRESTON FIELD.

To the r. of the crossroads, the pantiled DRUMCAPIE PLACE (dated 1786) with a splayed corner. NORTH ROAD exits ahead with a long straggle of weavers' cottages, several still pantiled. BRIDGE STREET off to the r. begins with a crowstepped double cottage (Nos. 1–3) of c. 1800 with massive scrolled skewputts, followed by an early C19 ashlar-fronted house (No. 5) with horizontal glazing. Just before the BRIDGE (its N side dated 1785), the old Free Church (*see* above) on the l.; on the r., a late Georgian tower with a big crosslet 'arrowslit'. At the road's bend to the N, the old CHURCHYARD; opposite, GATESIDE HOUSE, early C19, with scrolled skewputts. Further on, NORTHWOOD, built as the Manse in 1795–6 by *Robert Smith*, mason in Torryburn, to his own plain design. Just outside the village, TULLOHILL HOUSE, harled and crowstepped, with the date 1722 on a stone over the door. The two E bays, with an oval attic window in the gable, may be a slightly later addition. Irregular office courtyard on the S.

FARMS

DEVONSIDE, 1.3km. NE. Early C19 ashlar-fronted farmhouse with a central gablet above the main cornice; extravagant scrolled skewputts carved with foliage. – A screen wall hides the pantiled STEADING, its gable ends disguised by castellation.

HALLCROFT, 1.8km. N. Harled farmhouse, dated 1765. Fat cornice, rusticated doorpiece, and crowstepped gables. The ground-floor windows have been widened. At the back, a rubble and pantiled steading; in its N wall, a re-used stone with the date 1674.

KILLERNIE CASTLE. *See* p. 261.

SANDFORD HILL
2.8km. S of Wormit

4020

English Arts and Crafts villa poised on the edge of a former quarry; by *M. H. Baillie Scott*, 1913.* White-harled walls, the steep roofs covered with red Rosemary tiles. W (entrance) front a cottagey composition round two sides of a patio (complete with wishing well). Huge rectangular bay window projecting on the S. Off-centre bow disturbing the near symmetry of the twin-gabled E (garden) front. Inside, a two-storey drawing room with minstrels' gallery. Tactful but chimneyless hotel extension at the NW by *Robert Hurd & Partners*.

SCOTSTARVIT TOWER
3.3km. S of Cupar

3010

Beautifully executed tower house built for the Inglises of Tarvit 58 *c*.1500. It is L-plan, with the turnpike stair in the small SE jamb. Ashlar walls rising sheer to the parapet, carried on

---

* Replacing a smaller thatched house, designed by Scott and illustrated in his *Houses and Gardens* (1906), which was destroyed by fire.

Section

|⊢————————————|————————————|₁₀m

Second (hall) floor

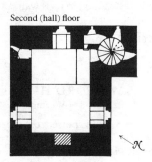

N

Scotstarvit Tower,
section and plan of second floor

double-member corbels, widely spaced except where they are
paired to carry wallhead chimneys on the N and W. Above this
level the work seems to be of the 1620s, executed for Sir John
Scott of Scotstarvit, who bought the estate in 1611. Parapet
with large gunloops. Within the parapet, crowstep-gabled attic
over the main block and a lucarned conical roof over the stair.
Above the door from the stair, heraldic panel carved with the
date 1627 and the arms and initials of Scott and his wife Dame
Anne Drummond.

Internally, the main block contains two high tunnel-vaulted
spaces one above the other, each divided by an entresol. Above,
an unvaulted top storey and attic. The lowest floor, lit only by
slit windows in the gables, was presumably a store (the kitchen

must have been outside the tower). On the entresol above (the floor now gone but its corbels surviving), comfortable windows with stone seats in the embrasures. Unusually for a living room there is no fireplace. The second-floor hall has similar windows but also a large fireplace in the w gable. At the NE corner, a garderobe; at the SE corner, another wall-chamber, entered from the stair and with only a small window into the hall. Below this window, a sink. The entresol above, again provided with window seats, has a small off-centre fireplace in the N wall, so perhaps this was originally two rooms. In the top room under the parapet walk, a larger w fireplace with a simple corbelled hood; blocked rectangular windows set high up. The attic's chimneypiece of 1627 is now at Hill of Tarvit (*q.v.*).

1km. WSW, an Iron Age HOMESTEAD, excavated by Bersu in 1946–7, comprising an oval bank 33m. by 27m. enclosing a round timber house of elaborate design *c.*17m. in diameter. The house showed at least three structural phases, in each of which the roof was supported on three circular post settings – the innermost free-standing, the others in continuous trenches.

SEAFIELD TOWER

1.9km. N of Kinghorn

2080

Ruined tower of *c.*1500 built on a small promontory jutting into the Forth. It has been L-plan with a small NE jamb containing a turnpike stair. Putholes show that the tunnel-vaulted ground floor has been subdivided horizontally. The first-floor hall has had a N fireplace. Jamb of a large E window. Wall-chamber, perhaps a garderobe, in the SW corner. The second floor's arrangement seems to have been the same but with a w fireplace. Corbels for the third floor. – Immediately on the N, a rubble wall, probably a later defence.

STAR

3000

Large hamlet with a good number of vernacular whinstone and pantiled cottages, but more than its fair share of late C20 bungalows.

PRIMARY SCHOOL. Very plain single-storey front block dated 1815. Late C19 addition on the w. On the E, a harled addition of 1925 by *George Sandilands*, who also covered all the roofs with flat red tiles. – In the playground, a late C19 PUMP by *Glenfield & Kennedy* of Greenock: fluted iron column, the water coming out of a lion's mask.

STARLEY HALL

1.9km. W of Burntisland

2080

Formidably Baronial villa of *c.*1865 built on a steep slope to enjoy dramatic views over the Forth. On the s front, a l. tower with corbelled parapet and rounds; on the r., a circular turret with canted cap-house.

STRATHAIRLY HOUSE
0.9km. E of Upper Largo

4000

C18 house given an ashlar front *c.* 1830, its centre pediment too small for the Ionic portico below. In the walled garden to the w, an C18 crowstepped lectern DOOCOT. – FARMHOUSE to the N, mid-C18 with a Gibbs surround to the door.

STRATHEDEN HOSPITAL
2.8km. SW of Cupar

3010

A large complex, the architectural merit hard to discern. It began with a two-storey block by *Peddie & Kinnear,* 1863–5. Additions by the same firm (latterly *Kinnear & Peddie*), 1869, 1879, 1888, and an Infirmary, 1891. Large extensions by *Gillespie & Scott,* 1892 and 1913. Nurses' Home by *A. D. Haxton,* 1929. Another extension by *Walter Alison,* 1937. Further accretions have followed.

STRATHENDRY CASTLE
2km. W of Leslie

2000

Rubbly T-plan tower house, probably built *c.* 1600 for Thomas Forrester and his wife Isobel Learmonth, whose arms and initials are above the S door. The only martial feature is the corbelled parapet walk across the E gable. The rear stairtower may have been rebuilt in 1699 by Sir Edward Douglas, who placed his initials and that date over its w door; its ogee roof is an alteration by *Henry F. Kerr,* 1906. The house occupies the NW corner of a small courtyard, apparently on the site of the original barmkin, but the present office ranges are by *William Burn,* 1824, remodelled by *David Bryce* in 1845 and again in 1943. Inside the house, a vaulted ground floor, originally a single room.

STRATHENDRY HOUSE
1.9km. W of Leslie

2000

By *William Burn,* 1824. A 'very handsome building, in the style of the old English manor-house of Queen Elizabeth's time', reported *The New Statistical Account* (1836); but quite unexciting.

STANDING STONE, *c.* 100m. W of the lodge, on the S side of the

A911. An irregular sandstone boulder 1.5m. high, apparently
the only survivor of a setting of four, beside which a cist and
an 'urn' were found in 1760.

STRATHKINNESS   4010

Hillside village of C19 vernacular cottages, many pantiled, now
bullied by recent development on the edges.

FREE CHURCH, Main Street. Now Village Hall. Lumpily
   detailed Gothic, dated 1867.
STRATHKINNESS CHURCH, Church Road. Built in 1863–4 but
   still unpretentious Georgian except for a Gothic bellcote.

STRATHMIGLO   2010

The right to create a burgh of barony was given to Sir William
Scott of Balwearie in 1509, but the first feus were not granted
until 1600. By the early C19 this was a weaving centre, with a
suburb of Cash Feus on the s bank of the Eden.

PARISH CHURCH, Kirk Wynd. Built by *George Kilgour* to his
   own design, 1783–4. Unassuming broad box with scrolled
   skewputts and round-headed windows. At the E gable, a
   narrow tower topped with a birdcage bellcote. sw vestry and
   porch of *c.*1925; above its door, a re-used stone inscribed

> JESVS CHRIST IS THE DOORE AND HE THAT ENTERES
> IN BE HIM SHALBE SAVED JOHN 10 9 1647

The interior was recast in 1848–9, the pulpit (since replaced)
being moved to the s wall and a semi-octagonal gallery put up
round the other three sides; simple box pews. – STAINED
GLASS in the s wall. In the large windows flanking the pulpit,
memorial windows ('Greater love hath no man than this ...';
'I have fought the good fight') of *c.*1920. – Contemporary
but better the gallery windows (Abram and Melchisedek). –
Ground-floor windows (Faith and Grace) of *c.*1890.

CHURCHYARD MONUMENTS. On the E wall, a large monument to the Cheapes of Wellfield, *c.*1881; heavy classical, with
a coat of arms on top. – To its s, wall monument to Francis
Moray, dated 1646, excruciatingly provincial Ionic aedicule,
now badly weathered. – At the SE corner, another aedicule,
probably early C18, framing a marble tablet topped by skulls
and a *putto* head. – Nearby, enjoyable collection of late C17
and early C18 headstones, rustically classical, decorated with
emblems of death. – More of the same type in the sw corner. –
In the centre, monument of *c.*1810 to James Cheape, a large
domed plinth rather like a small but solid version of the
Robertson Mausoleum in Greyfriars Churchyard (Edin-

burgh). – On the W wall, inept Ionic aedicule of 1760 to the Ireland family, inscribed:

DEATH FROMT 'IS STROKE NONE ARE EXEEM'D
THIS MOURNFUL TOMB DOTH GRACE
THE NAMES OF SUCH WHO WERE ESTEEM'D
AMONG THE FAITHFUL RACE
TH [*sic*] PARENTS DAUGHTER *A*ND a SON
WHOM NUMBERS MUCH DID PRIZE
FOR TaLENTS USEFULL ROUND THE PLACE
WHERE NOW HIS BODIE LYS

Pictish SYMBOL STONE at the entrance to the churchyard. It bears the head of a deer, and a disc with a notched rectangle symbol.

PRIMARY SCHOOL, High Street. By *George Sandilands*, 1934.

TOWN HALL, High Street. The hall itself is mid-C19, with a crowstepped gable; built into this, a skewputt carved with a head, perhaps C17. In front, steeple of 1734, the tower divided by band courses into five stages. Armorial panel above the first-floor window; on its sill, a large sundial. The fourth stage's clock faces are of 1921, replacing stone dials, but set in the original moulded frames. At the belfry, paired lancets, a surprisingly old-fashioned detail. Old-fashioned too the balustraded parapet. Broached spire of slightly egg-shaped profile.

DESCRIPTION

HIGH STREET, the main thoroughfare, is pleasant but without much personality. A few things worth picking out. Cubical sundial on the mid-C19 Nos. 19–23, and a mid-C18 rusticated doorpiece on No. 27. The crowstepped ROYAL HOTEL announces the burgh's centre. In the group round the Town Hall (*see* above), the mid-C18 No. 24 is of three storeys instead of the usual two; unfortunate ground-floor shop of *c.*1963. Pilastered doorpieces on Nos. 26–28, No. 26 of *c.*1830, No. 28 of *c.*1800 and more delicate. Scrolled skewputts on the white-painted STRATHMIGLO INN of *c.*1800. Further w, No. 89 (CLUNIE HOUSE) is heavy neo-classical of *c.*1840, with a balustraded porch in the recessed centre. Next door, No. 91 (LOMOND VIEW), its windows enlarged but a corniced doorpiece, rusticated quoins and scrolled skewputts still giving a touch of class. No. 95, dated 1875, Georgian survival but with weird detail. Opposite, the harled REFORMED PRESBYTERIAN CHURCH (by *George Page*, 1851–2), much altered on its conversion to a hall, *c.*1935. Beside it, the late Georgian Nos. 88–90, with a consoled pediment over the r. door. Then the Primary School (*see* above) on the N and, on the s, the late C19 Georgian survival MILLFIELD, with the ruins of the C18 WEST MILL beyond.

To the s, the plain Tudor WESTFIELD was built in 1847 as the Free Church Manse. In SKENE STREET and CASH FEUS, C18 and C19 cottages, No. 19 Skene Street with a pedimented doorpiece.

CORSTON TOWER, 1km. E. Only the E wall and fragments of the gables of the mid-C16 tower house of the Ramsays of Corston. Rubble-built with ashlar dressings. Ground-floor oval gun-loop. Second-floor garderobe at the NE corner. The house was of three storeys with an attic. A turnpike stair crowned with a cap-house projected from the SW corner.

PITLOUR. *See* p. 344.

STRATHTYRUM HOUSE
1.2km. W of St Andrews

4010

Two-phase Georgian mansion. The main block facing s was built *c*.1805 by *Robert Balfour*. Large and plain, except for the semicircular Roman Doric portico on the pedimented centre. This is an addition to the shorter mid-C18 house behind. N front with a three-bay centre, a rusticated bullseye in its pediment. (Early C19 Adamish interiors.)

STABLES, dated 1817; U-plan with pedimented ends. – MAUSOLEUM, dated 1781. Gothick, each front divided into three bays by big pinnacled piers. In the outer bays, diamond panels on the walls, a diamond-patterned parapet above. In the centre bays, elliptical arches (containing windows on three sides, a door on the fourth) supporting fluted parapets.

LODGE dated 1821, with a Roman Doric columned and pedimented porch. – Contemporary swagged GATEPIERS topped by urns.

STRUTHERS
4.9km. S of Cupar

3000

Farmhouse built by *William Martin*, wright, 1827; on the centre bay, a quatrefoil-in-circle finial.

STRUTHERS CASTLE to the W, now very ruined, was built for the Lindsays of the Byres, probably in the early C16. There seem to have been buildings round a roughly rectangular courtyard, its N and E ranges filled by the L-plan main house. E jamb projecting outwards from the E range. This jamb's gable still stands. At its ends, stepped buttresses topped by corbelled rounds. Were these an afterthought? At the s gable's E corner, base of another buttress. N of the N range, and now detached, another stepped buttress but with a conventionally tabled top. In the E range's W wall, tall round-arched windows, probably late C17 insertions.

TARVIT
1.2km. SE of Cupar

3010

The mansion house built for Patrick Rigg of Morton *c*.1790 was demolished in 1963. Its contemporary HOME FARM'S courtyard steading survives. Main front with a ball-finialled octagonal steeple over the pedimented centre. Round-headed overarches in the links to the piend-roofed end pavilions, whose first-floor rooms have large fanlights for windows.

TAYFIELD see NEWPORT-ON-TAY

4020

TAYPORT

Small town beside the Tay. The late C18 village's population increased substantially as a result of the settlement here of cottars cleared from their rural plots by agricultural improvement. Development as a jute manufacturing centre followed the rebuilding of the harbour as the s terminus of the Edinburgh & Northern Railway's ferry to Broughty Ferry in 1847. Tayport was made a burgh in 1888.

CHURCHES

OUR LADY STAR OF THE SEA (R.C.), Queen Street. By *Reginald Fairlie*, 1938–9. Studiedly simple rendered rectangle with an E apse. s porch broached to carry the slate-roofed octagonal tower; in its face, stone SCULPTURE of Our Lady by *Hew Lorimer*. SW hall.

ST MARGARET OF SCOTLAND (Episcopal), Queen Street. Humble but picturesque in red brick and half-timbering, only the window tracery disclosing its ecclesiastical function. It is by *T. M. Cappon*, 1899.

TAYPORT (former FERRYPORT-ON-CRAIG) PARISH CHURCH, Castle Street. Modestly ambitious late Georgian rebuild of the church erected in 1607. The long s wall, of cherrycock-pointed squared rubble, is of 1794, the rest of 1825. Two-storey galleried box with a semi-octagonal s apse. On the N, the C17 Scotscraig burial vault forms the base of a narrow tower of 1825, rising sheer to a corbelled eaves course under the slated spire. In the tower's N front, C17 armorial panels in a double frame.

Interior mostly of 1825, with a gallery round three sides. The s apse is filled by a huge ORGAN built by *John R. Miller* in 1899. – Late Victorian STAINED GLASS in the s wall, the smaller windows with medallions of sacred emblems (the *Agnus Dei*, Pelican, etc.) set in abstract designs. Figure subjects in the large windows flanking the pulpit.

CHURCHYARD MONUMENTS. Immediately NW of the church, a slab (now set upright) to Walter Key † 1695, with a scalloped border and emblems of mortality. – To its E, a weathered curly-pedimented aedicule put up by John Patie to his wife Margaret Duncan † 1798; in its centre an angel above a tablet bearing initials and a plough. – Wright's tools carved

on the headstone of William Dutch †1815, to its N. – To the
SW, Alexander Duncan †1813 with the inscription:

> See, here's a man laid low.
> That lived a pious lffe [*sic*].
> Respected, and Esteemed,
> For counsel, and Advice.
> His soul, we trust has fled,
> To yonder Rig¦ons high.
> To Prais Redeeming Love,
> To all Eternity.

– Further w, John Gregory †1854, carved with emblems of a
shipmaster. – To its NE, elegant Adamish stone of *c.*1780 to
the Robertson family, with roses and thistles in the middle of
its oval panels. – On its NE, a ship in sail on the headstone of
William Keay †1804. – To the E, William Dow †1804, a stone of
the same sort as Margaret Duncan's, the inscription beginning:

> See Mortals all Ive bid a dieu
> to Earthly things so soon most you
> to all belou most bid Fareuell
> And in the silent grave most Duell

– Aedicular stone with a curly pediment and roses on the fluted
pilasters commemorating Isabel Black †1823 and her husband
George Craig †1829, the inscription stating that 'They were
both related in the 6.ᵗʰ degree to JOHN BARON JOHNSTONE in
Annandale'.

TAYPORT PARISH (former FERRYPORT-ON-CRAIG FREE)
CHURCH, Queen Street. Bare Gothic of 1843. The gable front
is divided by pinnacled buttresses into a 'nave' and 'aisles';
parapet crowstepped over 'aisles', plain on the 'nave', whose
round window is filled with circles of masonry. Transepts were
added to the E end in 1866.

UNITED SECESSION CHURCH, Castle Street. Secularized. Built
in 1844; a Tudor door in the ball-finialled gable. Glasgow-
style STAINED GLASS of *c.*1900.

PUBLIC BUILDINGS

HARBOUR. By *Thomas Grainger*, 1847, for the Edinburgh &
Northern Railway, it was the s end of their ferry across the
Tay. Pier and two quays of rough ashlar.

LIGHTHOUSES, off Dalgleish Street. Both by *Robert Stevenson*,
1823, and originally identical round towers with domed lead
lanterns. Beside the EAST LIGHTHOUSE a simple cottage. The
WEST LIGHTHOUSE was heightened later in the C19 and given
a corbelled balcony under the lantern. Below, a terrace of plain
cottages.

PRIMARY SCHOOL, Queen Street. 1875–6, by *John Milne*. Plain
school board Gothic with a *flèche*. Frenchy spire at the back
engulfed in additions of 1938.

SCOTSCRAIG GOLF CLUB, Golf Road. Lightweight English
picturesque of 1896; extended in the same style 1907.

DESCRIPTION

The town is built along a bank sloping down to the Tay. At the bottom, the streets s and e of the Parish Church (WHITEN-HILL, BUTTER WYND, SCHOOL WYND, GREENSIDE PLACE, ROSE STREET and NELSON STREET) contain agreeable vernacular housing, mostly early C19. s of Greenside Place, a late C19 SAWMILL with timber-slatted drying sheds. Next to the Harbour (*see* above), the harled No. 11 INN STREET is of *c.*1800. Beside it, a large vaulted ICEHOUSE.

CASTLE STREET higher up is the main street, a small-scale small-town mixture, mostly Victorian. In WILLIAM STREET to the w, No. 36 began as a smart cottage-villa of *c.*1830: rusticated stonework; recessed Doric columns at the door. Gabled wings were added in the mid-C19. The heavy perron is of *c.*1930. Next door, No. 38, early C19 with an Edwardian porch filled with Glasgow-style stained glass. In ALBERT STREET, a late C19 terrace (Nos. 7–21) with round-arched doors and windows.

THORNTON

2090

Mining village developed from the late C19. A timber clock-tower on No. 47 Main Street provides a jolly central point.

FREE CHURCH, Station Road. Disused. Free Gothic by *William Williamson*, 1904–6. Red sandstone front; red brick sides. *Flèche* on the steep roof.

PARISH CHURCH, Main Street. A T-plan chapel-of-ease built in 1834–5; *James Robertson*, wright in Dysart, was the contractor. Birdcage bellcote, its sides pierced with holes, on the s gable. (STAINED GLASS. Two leaded windows by *Douglas G. Hogg*, 1972.)

PRIMARY SCHOOL, Station Road. 1904, by *James Gillespie & Scott*. Thrifty in red brick with sparing Queen Anne touches. Rear additions by *George Sandilands*, 1938.

TORRIE HOUSE *see* TORRYBURN

TORRYBURN

0080

A long village following the coast road along the Forth, it contains the three settlements of Torryburn, Low Torry and Newmills. Prosperous in the late C18, it declined in the C19 and has been largely redeveloped in the second half of the C20.

PARISH CHURCH, Main Street. Built 1799–1800. Rubble preaching box with a birdcage bellcote on the w gable. The n jamb is earlier, perhaps of 1696, when the building of an 'aisle' was suggested; in its N gable, a hoodmoulded Gothic light. The corner buttresses must be of 1800. The church was reconstructed in 1928, when plate tracery was inserted in the windows, a chancel added at the E, and the W porch raised to two storeys. Inside, STAINED-GLASS E window (The Risen Christ) of *c*. 1930.

At the churchyard gate, piend-roofed SESSION HOUSE with Gothic windows, of *c*. 1800. – Good collection of C17 and C18 HEADSTONES. W of the church, Agnes Hamilton †1690, with a curvy pediment and scrolled sides, the front carved with figures of tailors. – A little to the S, John Hinton, dated 1786, with incompetent pilasters; on top, a lion with cloth paws. – To its SE, a half-buried stone of *c*. 1700 with an Angel of the Resurrection. – SE of the church, a stone dated 1756, with an upturned ploughshare.

PRIMARY SCHOOL, off Main Street. By *John Houston*, 1912. Harled, with red sandstone dressings and bracketed eaves.

DESCRIPTION

On the entry from the E, the Parish Church (*see* above) is followed by the OLD MANSE built by *James Houston* and *James Sands*, 1768–70, with a Gibbsian doorpiece. Taller E addition of 1860. Then cottagey redevelopment of 1961. In LOW CAUSEWAY to the S, the estate wall of Craigflower (*see* below), followed by C18 and C19 vernacular houses. Among them, SHIP COTTAGE, with scrolled skewputts, its rusticated doorpiece recording its erection in 1745 and restoration in 1887; above, panel carved with a ship and the date 1747. At the W end of MAIN STREET, an C18 cottage terrace (THE NESS), now drydashed, but No. 2's door lintel is dated 1773 (its upper floor and scrolled skewputts are probably C19) and that of No. 4 1772.

LOW TORRY begins after the railway bridge. On the r., behind the Primary School (*see* above), TINIAN HOUSE of *c*. 1750, white-harled with vestigial crowsteps and a moulded doorpiece. On the street, a jolly brick and harl HALL of *c*. 1910, with Art Nouveau wooden brackets under the eaves. Vestigial crowsteps again on the late C18 HILLDROP, and upside-down scrolled skewputts on the pantiled ALBERT COTTAGE. The same crowstep detail, together with flattened skewputts, on No. 91 Main Street, dated 1771, its orangey rubble contrasting with its Edwardian red-tiled roof. The crowstepped No. 81 is C18 but with a pilastered doorpiece of *c*. 1840. Late C19 and early C20 sprawl before the gates of Torrie House (*see* below). On the S, a red sandstone sub-Renaissance range by *John Houston*, 1909–11, including the WEST FIFE TAVERN, with voluptuous engraved glass in the windows. Then C18 vernacular, rather altered. Crowstepped double house (Nos. 28–30 Main Street), dated 1712. No. 16, now covered with bullnosed render, is dated 1747. At right angles to the end of Main Street, a white-harled house (dated 1772) with crowsteps on the W skews and club skewputts on the E.

CRAIGFLOWER

Baronial country house of 1862, by *David Bryce* using some of his favourite motifs. On the asymmetrical entrance front, a shouldered-arch porch; on its parapet, a strapwork cartouche and obelisks standing on balls. On the r., a canted bay window corbelled out to a square-plan crowstepped gable. On the garden front's r., twin turrets grasping a gable. The more domestic range to its l. incorporates a remodelled late Georgian house. Converted to flats 1985.

TORRIE HOUSE

Only the stables and a couple of fragments of the Batty-Langleyish villa-mansion built *c.*1785 for Sir William Erskine and altered in the early C19 by the introduction of some large Tudor windows. House and stables formed a continuous long frontage looking s over Torryburn to the Forth.

The crenellated stables form a large courtyard open to the w. At each corner, a tower with blind Gothic first-floor windows and second-floor quatrefoil openings. The sw tower, originally part of the house and with a large Tudor window, has been remodelled to match the others. On the s front, an arcaded loggia; in its centre an open-pedimented ogee-arched opening. – Just s of the house, the drive is crossed by a BRIDGE of *c.*1810. Below its parapet, a stringcourse breaking into a bartizan at the centre. – The drive's s end at Torryburn village is marked by castellated GATES (round-arched for carriages, a pointed arch for pedestrians) and a LODGE with Gothic windows and a crenellated parapet. Quadrant screen walls topped by small obelisks.

FARMS

DRUMFIN, 1.1km. NE. Farmhouse built by *John Duncanson*, mason, 1836–7, probably from a design by *Robert Bonnar*: cottagey with horizontal glazing. Behind, large pantiled steading mostly by Bonnar, 1828–9. To the s, a round conical-roofed DOOCOT of *c.*1800.

OVER INZIEVAR, 2.3km. N. Harled house of 1835 with single-storey piend-roofed wings. Pantiled steading.

TULYIES, 0.5km. N. Standing stone with boulder setting, on the s side of the A985. The stone is 2.4m. high, with deeply weathered natural grooves and more than fifty cupmarkings on the lower part of the E face.

TOWNHILL see DUNFERMLINE

TULLIALLAN CASTLE
see KINCARDINE-ON-FORTH, p. 268

TULLIALLAN CASTLE (SCOTTISH POLICE COLLEGE) *see* KINCARDINE-ON-FORTH, p. 269

UPPER LARGO

Village clustered round the Parish Church.

LARGO PARISH CHURCH, Church Place. Large and well-sited 25 in a graveyard high above the surrounding street. Cruciform and at first sight deceptively of a piece, but the 'chancel' is of 1623, the central steeple is dated 1628, and the rest is of 1816–17 by *Alexander Leslie*.

Tall basecourse round the rendered 'chancel'. Two-thirds of the way up the E gable there is a crowstepped intake, its top framing a panel carved with the arms of Peter Black of Largo and the inscription:

FEAR GOD

P   B

1623

Hoodmoulded E window. Unconvincingly crenellated parapet, just low merlons sitting on a blocking course. Primitive obelisk pinnacles at the gable. The square tower straddles the 'chancel's' W end. Its parapet (merlons on a blocking course again) was added in 1816–17. Dumpy octagonal spire with stone lucarnes and a gilded weathercock. Clock-faces make it appear bulbous from a distance. Leslie's ashlar-built 'transepts' and 'nave' courteously quote the C17 work. So does the SE vestry added in 1894–5, when Perp tracery was inserted in the windows.

The interior is made uneasy by the tunnel-vaulted 'chancel' 26 (blocked off from the rest until 1826) not being centred on the 'nave'. It now has a chancel arch of 1894–5 whose clustered wall-shafts and foliaged corbels look too earnestly ecclesiastical. The contemporary hammerbeam roofs and traceried gallery fronts in the 'nave' and transepts are happier. Rearrangement of 1965 by *L. A. L. Rolland*, who designed the COMMUNION TABLE under the crossing and introduced the canopied PULPIT of 1815 from Newburn Church. – ORGAN by *David Loosley*, 1981.

STAINED GLASS. E window ('Praise the Lord'), E window of N 'transept' ('The Church's One Foundation') and rose window in that 'transept', all by *J. & W. Guthrie*, 1895. – S window ('Behold I make all things new'), crisply drawn in clean colours, after 1934. – Group of large and expensive early C19 WALL MONUMENTS, mostly with urns, in the E aisle; the one to General James Durham †1840 is signed by *David Ness*, and that to James Kettle †1820 by *J. Dalziel*. – The pulpit is balanced by the monument to Colonel John Falconer Briggs †1850, with a large trophy. – Less rumbustious the aedicule to Sir Philip Durham †1845, of whom the inscription says that he

PASSED HIS LATTER YEARS ... COURTED IN SOCIETY
AND GENEROUSLY SPENDING AN AMPLE FORTUNE

The rubble CHURCHYARD WALL was built in 1657. Early
C19 piend-roofed OFFERTORY HOUSES at the gate. Beside it,
a Pictish CROSS SLAB, bearing a cross with intertwined sea-
horses on the front. On the reverse, a Pictish beast or elephant,
disc and Z-rod, and a hunting scene. – A few GRAVESTONES
worth notice. Each side of the S 'transept', an C18 table stone
carved with emblems of mortality at one end and a winged
angel's head at the other. – Just to the E of this 'transept',
curly-topped stone with a recut inscription to John Fortune's
children †1755–69 on the back; on the front, full-length portraits (?) of Fortune and his wife standing on skulls, and an
angel of the Resurrection in the tympanum.

KIRKTON OF LARGO PRIMARY SCHOOL, North Feus. 1878,
by *John Melvin & Son*.

SIMPSON INSTITUTE, Main Street. By *Charles E. Tweedie*,
1890–1. Small-scale Scots Jacobean with an ogee-roofed belfry
of the type of St Ninian's, Leith (Edinburgh).

109 WOOD'S HOSPITAL, Woodlaw Park. By *James Leslie*, 1830, it
was built as an almshouse for sixteen inhabitants, each allotted
a sitting room and bedroom. Long, two-storey Jacobethan
front with steep pedimented dormerheads over the hoodmoulded windows. It is divided into four 'houses', each with
an advanced centre containing the Tudor arched door giving
access to four of the apartments. Gabled centrepiece (containing the communal hall) with a Gothick traceried window
under an ogee hoodmould; the gable's parapet has a cusped
underside and scrolls on top. The building was restored in
1975 by *Wheeler & Sproson*, who designed the white-harled
sheltered housing which now hides it from the road.

DESCRIPTION

At the village's SW entry, a concrete owl sits on the bowed gable
of No. 26 SOUTH FEUS, the first of a line of agreeable early–
mid-C19 houses enjoying open S views over the Forth; smart
pilastered doorpieces on the early Victorian No. 12 and
CARLTON. MAIN STREET proper begins with the crisply
harled late Georgian LARGO HOTEL opposite the lump of a
garage made out of the old FREE CHURCH of 1844. The
remainder is pleasant but nondescript C18 and C19.

CHURCH PLACE to the l. forms an oval round the Parish Church
(*see* above). At its SW, a couple of C18 harled houses, one with
a forestair. Just to their N, the late C18 GATEPIERS to Largo
House (*see* below), their fluted urn finials wrapped in swagged
bands. They now prelude suburban villas along the beginning
of the E drive. Half-hidden by trees to the church's NW is the
MANSE built in 1770 and heightened in 1837 (the back wing
probably showing the original height); little brackets under
the window sills. Vernacular cottages to the E lead to the corner
with NORTH FEUS, where more of the same progress up
the hill to the Primary School (*see* above). WOODLAW PARK

begins with Wood's Hospital (*see* above). At its end, on the l.,
EDEN COTTAGE, C18 with a Gibbsian doorpiece.

LARGO HOUSE

Roofless remains of the smart mansion house built for the
Durhams of Largo in 1750. *John Adam* supplied a chimneypiece and possibly the design.* Pedimented three-bay
centrepiece with a coat of arms in the tympanum. Segmental
pediment over the Ionic pilastered doorpiece, the flanking
windows' architraves enriched with egg-and-dart moulding.
The first-floor windows have bracketed sills. Bow at the back.
Wings and a rear extension were added in a darker-coloured
stone, 1831.

Ruinous STABLES to the NW with a centre pediment, built
by *Alexander & James Leslie* in 1815. – Probably of *c.* 1831
the bow-fronted whinstone SOUTH LODGE. Its GATEPIERS
have vermiculated rustication, a Greek key frieze and eagle
finials.

On the HOME FARM's W approach, a roofless late C17
DOOCOT. – Early C19 whinstone and pantiled STEADING. –
The harled FARMHOUSE is of about a century earlier. To its
S, the conical-roofed early C17 WOOD'S or LARGO TOWER,
the surviving SW tower of an early C17 house. Quatrefoil
gunloops in first-floor window surrounds. Corbelling for a
stair turret in the W inner angle with the lost rectangular main
block.

COATES HOUSE. *See* p. 128.
LAHILL. *See* p. 303.

VALLEYFIELD

0080

C18 and C19 settlement along the shore of the Forth, with a C20
mining village on the hill above.

LOW VALLEYFIELD is a straggle of smashed vernacular. HIGH
VALLEYFIELD was begun *c.* 1908. At the W end, early C19
brute-classical LODGES to the demolished Valleyfield House
introduce broad-eaved and red-tiled terraces of typical Fife
Coal Co. early C20 type.

WOODHEAD, 0.5km. W. Early C19 villa-farmhouse in the pretti-
est Gothick manner. Crenellated portico across the recessed
centre; a quatrefoil window above.

VICARSFORD CEMETERY

4020

2.9km. SE of Newport-on-Tay

Laid out *c.* 1890. Windy hilltop site with magnificent views,
the natural advantages and disadvantages of little concern to

---

* The masonry has the same diagonal droving as John Adam's Ballochmyle House
(Strathclyde).

residents. – GATEPIERS in the style of *c*.1700. – Broad-eaved
LODGE.

CHAPEL on the summit, designed by *T. Martin Cappon* and
built in 1895–7 as a memorial to Lady Leng. The site gives it
an importance quite disproportionate to its size. C13 French
Gothic, with the Sainte-Chapelle, Paris, the main inspiration.
Green copper roof a foil to the hard grey snecked rubble
masonry. Accomplished but routine carved gargoyles by *James
Bremner*. On the W, a small cloister arcade, its buttress pinnacles lavishly crocketed. Vaulted interior faced in creamy
Caen stone.

WEMYSS CASTLE
0.9km. SE of Coaltown of Wemyss

Perched above the Forth, the rubbly barrack-like house of the
Wemysses of Wemyss. Its present bleak appearance is due to
the reconstruction begun in the 1930s by *Stewart Tod*, who
removed Victorian additions without reinstating the C17 parapets.

The earliest part is a rectangular C15* tower which projects
as the N wing of the U-plan entrance (W) front. Its original
two lower floors are of cubed ashlar masonry. Inside, a vaulted
ground floor with a tight turnpike stair in the NE corner's wall
thickness. This tower probably occupied the SW corner of a
walled enclosure. The drum tower to the N may be contemporary. Rebuilding of the enclosure's E and (canted) N wall
seems to have taken place in the early C16, perhaps begun by
Sir David Wemyss († 1511) and continued by his son David (†
by 1544‡), providing a round tower at the SE corner and a
pimply projection at the NE. Chequer corbelling under the
parapet. At the same time extra accommodation was provided
in ranges built against the enclosure's inner faces, the E range
containing a hall. *c*.1600 the early C15 SW tower and the
early C16 additions were all reconstructed and heightened, the
parapets on the N and E becoming decorative stringcourses.

By the late C17 the house must have seemed cramped and
inconvenient, and in December 1669 David, second Earl of
Wemyss, signed a contract with *Robert Mylne* for the construction of an L-plan addition extending 35.7m. S of the
existing E range. This combined with the C15 tower to make
an irregular U-plan main front, the lower courtyard ranges
to the N appearing only as insignificant appendages. On the
seaward (E) front, the new block continued the height and
parapet of the existing, and a new SE tower (not mentioned in
the contract but clearly contemporary) balanced the rec-

---

* Possibly of 1421, the date which has been added to the margin of the C16 heraldic
panel above the entrance. A charter was signed at Wemyss in 1428.
‡ The heraldic panel over the entrance has the initials DV (for David Wemyss)
twice.

tangular turret added c.1600 on top of the early C16 round tower. A garden was laid out E and S of Mylne's extension.

Extensive further additions were made in 1874–6 by *Peddie & Kinnear*, who virtually infilled the U-plan's courtyard on the W and added bay windows above an arcaded terrace on the E. These additions were removed by *Stewart Tod*, who replaced Peddie & Kinnear's W block with a much narrower single-storey balustraded range and placed in its inner angle with the C15 tower a small belltower evocative of the Tolbooth tower at West Wemyss.

(The principal interiors are in Mylne's late C17 addition. At its N end, a grand oak scale-and-platt stair. S of this, the range seems to have been planned to contain a ground-floor family apartment, a first-floor state apartment, and second-floor bedrooms. By the late C19 the main living accommodation was concentrated on the ground floor, with the hall of c.1600 used as the dining room,* the family dining room S of the stairhall as the drawing room, the family drawing room and Earl's bedchamber beyond thrown into one as the library. In the recent reconstruction this library has again been made into two rooms (Second Drawing Room and White Sitting Room) but retaining the late C19 ceilings copied from that of the King's Bedroom above. In the first-floor state apartment the main rooms have late C17 plaster ceilings and early C18 pine panelling. In the State Drawing Room (later study) an overmantel painting showing Wemyss Castle on the l. and Macduff's Castle on the r., by *John van Sypen*, 1718. The King's Bedroom's ceiling is divided into compartments by foliaged strapwork, with small pendants at some intersections. In the panels, relief casts of Kings David and Alexander. Closet in the small SE tower, its simply compartmented ceiling's border enriched with leafy pendants; thistles, roses and *fleurs de lis* on the frieze. The SW jamb's bedroom has a more loosely composed and lightly modelled ceiling made by *John Nicol*. Star in the centre compartment; in the others, flying cherubs holding roses; *fleurs de lis* in the corners. It is very similar to the contemporary ceilings provided by James Baine for Holyroodhouse (Edinburgh).

The vaulted basement under the E range's N end was converted from a kitchen into a chapel by *Robert S. Lorimer* in 1897, its walls covered with blind arcading. It was intended as a memorial to Millicent Erskine Wemyss, whose richly carved monument is surmounted by a recumbent effigy carved by *Princess Louise*.)

WEST PITCORTHIE *see* KILRENNY

---

* In the late C17 arrangement it was perhaps a gallery.

3090

WEST WEMYSS

West Wemyss was made a burgh of barony in 1511, and a harbour was built in 1621. Salt-making was the main industry until replaced in the C19 by the coal trade and mining.

ST ADRIAN'S PARISH CHURCH, Main Street. Simple crow-stepped cruciform church of 1890–5, built of pink sandstone rubble. At the S gable, two crowstepped porches linked by a Gothic loggia. Spiral tracery in the gable's big rose window.

PRIMARY SCHOOL, off Broad Wynd. Built on a rough E-plan in 1896. Presumably it is by *Alexander Tod*. Harled, with octagonal Tudor chimneys.

TOLBOOTH, Main Street. Simple harled rubble block, probably early C18, but the sturdy pend arch on the r. looks earlier. In the centre, a tower with a small concave-sided spired roof. In its front wall, two panels. The lower has the arms and initials of David, Earl of Wemyss (1678–1720); the upper a coronet and an inscription said to have read:

> THIS FABRIC WAS BUILT BY EARL DAVID
> WEMYSS AND TOWN
> FOR THE CRIBBING OF VICE AND SERVICE TO
> CROWN

DESCRIPTION

At the W end, the HARBOUR's inner basin has been largely infilled. Ashlar and rubble wet dock by *J. & A. Leslie*, 1872–3. On its N, the white-harled late C18 Nos. 1–4 SHORE HEAD, with a central gablet; the window surrounds have been Victorianized. N of the inner basin, a three-storey store, late Georgian with a piended pantiled roof. To its E, Nos. 5–6 COXSTOOL, a jolly castellated house of *c*.1900. On the hill above, THE BELVEDERE, dated 1927, a large harled villa (now hotel) with shaped gables and an octagonal-lanterned belvedere. It looks across the road to the crowstepped and gableted red sandstone MANSE by *Robert S. Lorimer*, 1894–5.

MAIN STREET's dominant feature is the Tolbooth tower (*see* above) rising above the simple early C19 vernacular houses (restoration is in progress, 1988). There is also straightforward new housing, which also extends up BROAD WYND, at whose N end is a pantiled group built by the Wemyss Coal Co. to commemorate nationalization of its mines in 1947, the blocks linked by screen walls carrying concrete balusters of C17 type. Embedded in these houses, a mid-C19 hall, crowstepped with a small birdcage bellcote on one gable. At the end of Main Street, the Parish Church (*see* above), its graveyard wall's ball-topped GATEPIERS dated 1703, the entrance between them filled, *c*.1920, by *A. Stewart Tod*'s WAR MEMORIAL.

WINDYGATES

A village of late C19 and C20 workers' housing dominated by the Cameron Bridge Distillery.

PARISH CHURCH, Balcurvie Road. Originally United Free. Sturdy buttressed rectangle of *c.*1910. In the gable window, simplified Scots late Gothic tracery. On the N, a late C19 HALL which became the Free Church in 1899.

BALCURVIE PRIMARY SCHOOL, Balcurvie Road. Small Board school of 1874–6, enlarged in 1888–9, and almost doubled in size by a N addition in 1906–7.

CAMERON BRIDGE DISTILLERY. Founded by John Haig, 1824. Large group of C19 and C20 brick-built granaries, malt kilns and bonded stores. Three tall brick chimneys. In the middle, a railway line crossed by a mid-C19 lattice-sided cast-iron footbridge.

CAMERON HOSPITAL. The nucleus is the red sandstone CAMERON BRIDGE HOUSE built in 1849 for the distiller John Haig; *David Bryce* was his architect. Crowstepped villa with prominent chimneys. In 1911 the house became an Infectious Diseases Hospital, its ground developed with single-storey harled and tiled pavilions by *W. D. Telfer.* Two-storey ADMINISTRATION BUILDING and NURSES' HOME by *William Williamson & Hubbard,* 1938. – OUT-PATIENTS (formerly T.B. TREATMENT CENTRE) by *R. Forbes Hutchison, c.*1955. – S block by *John Holt, c.*1964.

DESCRIPTION. Entering from the S, Cameron Hospital (*see* above) is glimpsed among trees on the l. Beyond it, a path down to the Distillery (*see* above) across CAMERON BRIDGE, whose E cutwaters look C17; the rest belongs to a reconstruction of 1870. The main road loops across the River Leven at a high level. Below it on the r., BRIDGEND HOUSE by *Andrew Heiton Jun.,* 1869, a timid mixture of styles. At the N end of STATION ROAD, the WINDYGATES HOTEL, painted white and black, early C19 with an overdose of Venetian windows sadly deprived of their astragals. Opposite, a cast-iron CLOCK, its plaque stating that it was ERECTED FROM THE PROCEEDS OF SOCIAL BETTERMENT DAIRY SCHEME 1916. In LEVEN ROAD, mid-C19 Jacobean gatepiers to DURIE VALE, an early C19 farmhouse with scrolled skewputts and a consoled cornice over the door; Victorian bay window and E wing.

WORMIT *see* NEWPORT-ON-TAY

GLOSSARY

Particular types of an architectural element are often defined under the name of the element itself, e.g. for 'dogleg stair' see STAIR. Literal meanings, where specially relevant, are indicated by the abbreviation *lit*.

ABACUS (*lit*. tablet): flat slab forming the top of a capital, *see* Orders (fig. 16).

ABUTMENT: the meeting of an arch or vault with its solid lateral support, or the support itself.

ACANTHUS: formalized leaf ornament with thick veins and frilled edge, e.g. on a Corinthian capital.

ACHIEVEMENT OF ARMS: in heraldry, a complete display of armorial bearings.

ACROTERION (*lit*. peak): pointed ornament projecting above the apex or ends of a pediment.

ADDORSED: description of two figures placed symmetrically back to back.

AEDICULE (*lit*. little building): term used in classical architecture to describe the unit formed by a pair of orders, an entablature, and usually a pediment, placed against a wall to frame an opening.

AFFRONTED: description of two figures placed symmetrically face to face.

AGGER (*lit*. rampart): Latin term for the built-up foundations of Roman roads.

AGGREGATE: small stones added to a binding material, e.g. in harling or concrete.

AISLE (*lit*. wing): (1) passage alongside the nave, choir or transept of a church, or the main body of some other building, separated from it by columns or piers; (2) (Scots) projecting wing of a church for special use, e.g. by a guild or by a landed family whose burial place it may contain.

AMBULATORY (*lit*. walkway): aisle at the E end of a chancel, usually surrounding an apse and therefore semicircular or polygonal in plan.

ANNULET (*lit*. ring): shaft-ring (q.v.).

ANSE DE PANIER (*lit*. basket handle): basket arch (*see* Arch).

ANTA: classical order of oblong section employed at the ends of a colonnade which is then called *In Antis*. See Orders (fig. 16).

ANTEFIXAE: ornaments projecting at regular intervals above a classical cornice. See Orders (fig. 16).

ANTHEMION (*lit*. honeysuckle): classical ornament like a honeysuckle flower (*see* fig. 1).

A   P   A   P   A

Fig. 1. Anthemion and Palmette Frieze

APSE: semicircular (i.e. apsidal) extension of an apartment. A term first used of the magistrate's end of a Roman basilica, and thence especially of the vaulted semicircular or polygonal end of a chancel or a chapel.

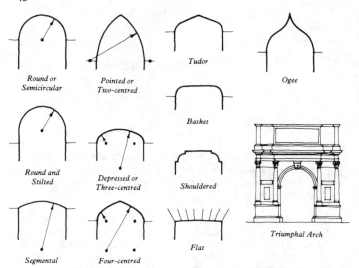

Fig. 2. Arch

ARABESQUE: light and fanciful surface decoration. *See* Grotesque.

ARCADE: series of arches supported by piers or columns. *Blind Arcade:* the same applied to the surface of a wall. *Wall Arcade:* in medieval churches, a blind arcade forming a dado below windows.

ARCH: for the various forms *see* fig. 2. The term *Basket Arch* refers to a basket handle and is sometimes applied to a three-centred or depressed arch as well as the type with a flat middle. *Transverse Arch:* across the main axis of an interior space. A term used especially for the arches between the compartments of tunnel- or groin-vaulting. *Diaphragm Arch:* transverse arch with solid spandrels spanning an otherwise wooden-roofed interior. *Chancel Arch:* across the w end of a chancel. *Relieving Arch:* incorporated in a wall, to carry some of its weight, some way above an opening. *Strainer Arch:* inserted across an opening to resist any inward pressure of the side members. *Triumphal Arch:* Imperial Roman monument whose elevation supplied a motif for many later classical compositions. *Blind Arch:* framing a wall which has no opening. *Overarch:* framing a wall which has an opening, e.g. a window or door.

ARCHITRAVE: (1) formalized lintel, the lowest member of the classical entablature (*see* Orders, fig. 16); (2) moulded frame of a door or window. Also *Lugged* or *Shouldered Architrave*, whose top is prolonged into lugs (*lit.* ears).

ARCHIVOLT: continuous mouldings of an arch.

ARRIS (*lit.* stop): sharp edge at the meeting of two surfaces.

ASHLAR: masonry of large blocks wrought to even faces and square edges. *Droved Ashlar* (Scots) is finished with sharp horizontal tool-marks.

ASTRAGAL (*lit.* knuckle): moulding of round section, and hence (Scots) wooden glazing-bar between window-panes.

ASTYLAR: term used to describe an elevation that has no columns or similar vertical features.

ATLANTES: male counterparts of caryatids, often in a more demonstrative attitude of support. In sculpture, a single figure of the god Atlas may be seen supporting a globe.

ATTACHED: description of a shaft or column that is partly merged into a wall or pier.

ATTIC: (1) small top storey, especially behind a sloping roof; (2) in classical architecture, a storey above the main cornice, as in a triumphal arch.

AUMBRY: recess or cupboard to hold sacred vessels for Mass.

BAILEY: open space or court of a stone-built castle; *see also* Motte-and-Bailey.

BALDACCHINO: tent-like roof supported by columns, e.g. over some monuments of the C17-18.

BALLFLOWER: globular flower of three petals enclosing a small ball. A decoration used in the first quarter of the C14.

BALUSTER (*lit.* pomegranate): hence a pillar or pedestal of bellied form. *Balusters:* vertical supports of this or any other form, for a handrail or coping, the whole being called a *Balustrade*. *Blind Balustrade:* the same with a wall behind.

BARBICAN: outwork defending the entrance to a castle.

BARGEBOARDS: boards, often carved or fretted, hanging clear of the wall under sloping eaves.

BARMKIN (Scots): enclosing wall.

BARONY: *see* Burgh.

BARROW: burial mound.

BARTIZAN (*lit.* battlement): corbelled turret, square or round, at the top angle of a building.

BASE: moulded foot of a column or other order. For its use in classical architecture *see* Orders (fig. 16). *Elided Bases:* bases of a compound pier whose lower parts are run together, ignoring the arrangement of the shafts above. Capitals may be treated in the same way.

BASEMENT: lowest, subordinate storey of a building, and hence the lowest part of an elevation, below the piano nobile.

BASILICA (*lit.* royal building): a Roman public hall; hence an aisled church with a clear storey.

BASTION: projection at the angle of a fortification.

BATTER: inward inclination of a wall.

BATTLEMENT: fortified parapet with upstanding pieces called merlons along the top. Also called Crenellation.

BAYS: divisions of an elevation or interior space as defined by any regular vertical features.

BAY WINDOW: window in a recess, with a consequent projection on the outside, named according to the form of the latter. A *Canted Bay Window* has a straight front and bevelled sides. A *Bow Window* is curved. An *Oriel Window* does not start from the ground.

BEAKER: type of pottery vessel used in the late third and early second millennia B.C.

BEAKHEAD: Norman ornamental motif consisting of a row of bird or beast heads with beaks biting usually into a roll moulding.

BEE-BOLL: wall recess designed to contain a beehive.

BELFRY (*lit.* tower): (1) bell-turret set on a roof or gable (*see also* Bellcote); (2) room or stage in a tower where bells are hung; (3) belltower in a general sense.

BELLCAST: *see* Roof.

BELLCOTE: belfry as (1) above, with the character of a small house for the bell(s), e.g. *Birdcage Bellcote:* framed structure, usually of stone.

BERM: level area separating ditch from bank on a hillfort or barrow.

BILLET (*lit.* log or block) FRIEZE: Norman ornament consisting of small blocks placed at regular intervals (*see* fig. 3).

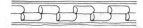

Fig. 3. Billet Frieze

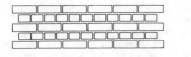

English

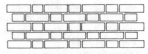

Flemish

Fig. 4. Bond

BIVALLATE: of a hillfort: defended by two concentric banks and ditches.

BLIND: *see* Arcade, Arch, Balustrade, Portico.

BLOCKED: term applied to columns etc. that are interrupted by regular projecting blocks, e.g. to the sides of a Gibbs surround (*see* fig. 10).

BLOCKING COURSE: plain course of stones, or equivalent, on top of a cornice and crowning the wall.

BOLECTION MOULDING: moulding covering the joint between two different planes and overlapping the higher as well as the lower one, especially on panelling and fireplace surrounds of the late C17 and early C18.

BOND: in brickwork, the pattern of long sides (stretchers) and short ends (headers) produced on the face of a wall by laying bricks in a particular way (*see* fig. 4).

BOSS: knob or projection usually placed to cover the intersection of ribs in a vault.

BOW WINDOW: *see* Bay Window.

BOX PEW: pew enclosed by a high wooden back and ends, the latter having doors.

BRACE: *see* Roof (fig. 22).

BRACKET: small supporting piece of stone, etc., to carry a projecting horizontal member.

BRESSUMER: (*lit.* breast-beam): big horizontal beam, usually set forward from the lower part of a building, supporting the timber superstructure.

BRETASCHE (*lit.* battlement): defensive wooden gallery on a wall.

BROCH (Scots): circular tower-like structure, open in the middle, the double wall of dry-stone masonry linked by slabs forming internal galleries at varying levels; found in W and N Scotland and probably dating from the earliest centuries of the Christian era.

BRONZE AGE: in Britain, the period from *c.* 2000 to 600 B.C.

BUCRANIUM: ox skull.

BULLSEYE WINDOW: small circular window, e.g. in the tympanum of a pediment.

BURGH: formally constituted town with trading privileges. *Royal Burghs*, which still hold this courtesy title, monopolized imports and exports till the C17 and paid duty to the Crown. *Burghs of Barony* were founded by secular or ecclesiastical barons to whom they paid duty on their local trade.

BUT-AND-BEN (Scots, *lit.* outer and inner rooms): two-room cottage.

BUTTRESS: vertical member projecting from a wall to stabilize it or to resist the lateral thrust of an arch, roof or vault. For different types used at the corners of a building, especially a tower, *see* fig. 5. A *Flying Buttress* transmits the thrust to a heavy abutment by means of an arch or half-arch.

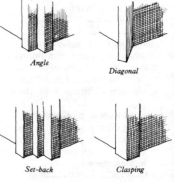

Angle

Diagonal

Set-back

Clasping

Fig. 5. Buttresses at a corner

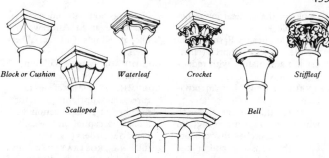

Block or Cushion   *Waterleaf*   *Crocket*   *Stiffleaf*

Scalloped   *Bell*

Fig. 6. Capitals   *Elided*

CABLE MOULDING or ROPE MOULDING: originally a Norman moulding, imitating the twisted strands of a rope.

CALEFACTORY: room in a monastery where a fire burned for the comfort of the monks.

CAMBER: slight rise or upward curve in place of a horizontal line or plane.

CAMES: *see* Quarries.

CAMPANILE: free-standing bell-tower.

CANDLE-SNUFFER ROOF: conical roof of a turret.

CANOPY: projection or hood over an altar, pulpit, niche, statue, etc.

CANTED: tilted, generally on a vertical axis to produce an obtuse angle on plan, e.g. of a canted bay window.

CAP-HOUSE (Scots): (1) small chamber at the head of a turnpike stair, opening onto the parapet walk; (2) chamber rising from within the parapet walk.

CAPITAL: head or top part of a column or other order; for classical types *see* Orders (fig. 16); for medieval types *see* fig. 6. *Elided Capitals:* capitals of a compound pier whose upper parts are run together, ignoring the arrangement of the shafts below.

CARTOUCHE: tablet with ornate frame, usually of elliptical shape and bearing a coat of arms or inscription.

CARYATIDS (*lit.* daughters of the village of Caryae): female figures supporting an entablature, counterparts of Atlantes.

CASEMENT: (1) window hinged at the side; (2) in Gothic architecture, a concave moulding framing a window.

CASTELLATED: battlemented.

CAVETTO: concave moulding of quarter-round section.

CELURE or CEILURE: panelled and adorned part of a wagon roof above the rood or the altar.

CENOTAPH (*lit.* empty tomb): funerary monument which is not a burying place.

CENSER: vessel for the burning of incense, frequently of architectural form.

CENTERING: wooden support for the building of an arch or vault, removed after completion.

CHAMBERED TOMB: burial mound of the Neolithic Age having a stone-built chamber and entrance passage covered by an earthen barrow or stone cairn.

CHAMFER (*lit.* corner-break): surface formed by cutting off a square edge, usually at an angle of forty-five degrees.

CHANCEL (*lit.* enclosure): that part of the E end of a church in which the altar is placed, usually applied to the whole continuation of the nave E of the crossing.

CHANTRY CHAPEL: chapel attached to, or inside, a church, endowed for the celebration of masses for the soul of the founder or some other individual.

CHECK (Scots): rebate.

CHERRY-CAULKING or CHERRY-COCKING (Scots): masonry techniques using a line of pinstones in the vertical joints between blocks.

CHEVET (*lit.* head): French term for the E end of a church (chancel and ambulatory with radiating chapels).

CHEVRON: zigzag Norman ornament.

CHOIR: (1) the part of a church where services are sung; in monastic churches this can occupy the crossing and/or the easternmost bays of the nave, but in cathedral churches it is usually in the E arm: (2) the E arm of a cruciform church (a usage of long standing though liturgically anomalous).

CIBORIUM: canopied shrine for the reserved sacrament.

CINQUEFOIL: *see* Foil.

CIST: stone-lined or slab-built grave. First appears in Late Neolithic times. It continued to be used in the Early Christian period.

CLAPPER BRIDGE: bridge made of large slabs of stone, some built up to make rough piers and other longer ones laid on top to make the roadway.

CLASSIC: term for the moment of highest achievement of a style.

CLASSICAL: term for Greek and Roman architecture and any subsequent styles inspired by it.

CLEARSTOREY: upper storey of the walls of a church, pierced by windows.

CLOSE (Scots): courtyard or passage giving access to a number of buildings.

COADE STONE: artificial (cast) stone made in the late C18 and the early C19 by Coade and Sealy in London.

COB: walling material made of mixed clay and straw.

COFFERING: sunken panels, square or polygonal, decorating a ceiling, vault or arch.

COLLAR: *see* Roof (fig. 22).

COLLEGIATE CHURCH: a church endowed for the support of a college of priests, especially for the singing of masses for the soul of the founder. Some collegiate churches were founded in connection with universities, e.g. three at St Andrews and one at King's College, Aberdeen.

COLONNADE: range of columns.

COLONNETTE: small column.

COLUMN: in classical architecture, an upright structural member of round section with a shaft, a capital and usually a base. *See* Orders (fig. 16).

COLUMNA ROSTRATA: column decorated with carved prows of ships to celebrate a naval victory.

COMMENDATOR: one who holds the revenues of an abbey *in commendam* (medieval Latin for 'in trust' or 'in custody') for a period in which no regular abbot is appointed. During the Middle Ages most Commendators were bishops, but in Scotland during and after the Reformation they were laymen who performed no religious duties.

COMPOSITE: *see* Orders.

CONDUCTOR (Scots): down-pipe for rainwater; *see also* Rhone.

CONSERVATION: a modern term employed in two, sometimes conflicting, senses: (1) work to prolong the life of the historic fabric of a building or other work of art, without alteration; (2) work to make a building or a place more viable. Good conservation is a combination of the two.

CONSOLE: ornamental bracket of compound curved outline (*see* fig. 7). Its height is usually greater than its projection, as in (*a*).

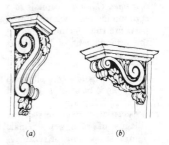

(*a*)   (*b*)

Fig. 7.   Console

COOMB CEILING or COMB CEIL-
ING (Scots): ceiling whose slope
corresponds to that of the roof.

COPING (*lit.* capping): course of
stones, or equivalent, on top of
a wall.

CORBEL: block of stone projecting
from a wall, supporting some
feature on its horizontal top
surface. *Corbel-course*: continuous projecting course of stones
fulfilling the same function.
Corbel Table: series of corbels
to carry a parapet or a wall-
plate; for the latter *see* Roof (fig.
22).

CORBIE-STEPS (Scots, *lit.* crowsteps): *see* Gable (fig. 9).

CORINTHIAN: *see* Orders (fig.
16).

CORNICE: (1) moulded ledge, decorative and/or practical, projecting along the top of a building or feature, especially as the
highest member of the classical
entablature (*see* Orders, fig. 16);
(2) decorative moulding in the
angle between wall and ceiling.

CORPS-DE-LOGIS: French term
for the main building(s) as distinct from the wings or pavilions.

COUNTERSCARP BANK: small
bank on the down-hill or outer
side of a hillfort ditch.

COURSE: continuous layer of
stones etc. in a wall.

COVE: concave soffit like a hollow
moulding but on a larger scale.
A *Cove Ceiling* has a pro-
nounced cove joining the walls
to a flat surface in the middle.

CREDENCE: in a church or chapel,
a side table, often a niche, for
the sacramental elements before
consecration.

CRENELLATION: *see* Battlement.

CREST, CRESTING: ornamental
finish along the top of a screen,
etc.

CROCKETS (*lit.* hooks), CROCK-
ETING: in Gothic architecture,
leafy knobs on the edges of any
sloping feature. *Crocket Capital: see* Capital (fig. 6).

CROSSING: in a church, central
space opening into the nave,
chancel and transepts. *Crossing
Tower:* central tower supported
by the piers at its corners.

CROWSTEPS (Scots): squared
stones set like steps to form a
skew, *see* Gable (fig. 9).

CRUCK (*lit.* crooked): piece of
naturally curved timber combining the structural roles of an
upright post and a sloping rafter, e.g. in the building of a cottage, where each pair of crucks
is joined at the ridge.

CRYPT: underground room
usually below the E end of a
church.

CUPOLA (*lit.* dome): (1) small
polygonal or circular domed
turret crowning a roof; (2)
(Scots) small dome or skylight
as an internal feature, especially
over a stairwell.

CURTAIN WALL: (1) connecting
wall between the towers of a
castle; (2) in modern building,
thin wall attached to the main
structure, usually outside it.

CURVILINEAR: *see* Tracery.

CUSP: projecting point formed by
the foils within the divisions of
Gothic tracery, also used to
decorate the soffits of the
Gothic arches of tomb recesses,
sedilias, etc.

CYCLOPEAN MASONRY: built
with large irregular polygonal
stones, but smooth and finely
jointed.

DADO: lower part of a wall or its
decorative treatment; *see also*
Pedestal (fig. 17).

DAGGER: *see* Tracery.

DAIS, or DEIS (Scots): raised platform at one end of a room.

DEC (DECORATED): historical
division of English Gothic architecture covering the period
from *c.* 1290 to *c.* 1350.

DEMI-COLUMNS: engaged columns, only half of whose cir-
cumference projects from the
wall.

DIAPER (*lit.* figured cloth): repe-
titive surface decoration.

DIOCLETIAN WINDOW: semi-
circular window with two mul-

lions, so called because of its use in the Baths of Diocletian in Rome.

DISTYLE: having two columns; cf. Portico.

DOGTOOTH: typical E.E. decoration applied to a moulding. It consists of a series of squares, their centres raised like pyramids and their edges indented (*see* fig. 8).

Fig. 8.   Dogtooth

DONJON: *see* Keep.

DOOCOT (Scots): dovecot. Free-standing doocots are usually of *Lectern* type, rectangular in plan with single-pitch roof, or *Beehive* type, circular in plan and growing small towards the top.

DORIC: *see* Orders (fig. 16).

DORMER WINDOW: window standing up vertically from the slope of a roof and lighting a room within it. *Dormer Head:* gable above this window, often formed as a pediment.

DORTER: dormitory, sleeping quarters of a monastery.

DOUBLE-PILE: *see* Pile.

DRESSINGS: features made of smoothly worked stones, e.g. quoins or stringcourses, projecting from the wall which may be of different material, colour or texture.

DRIPSTONE: moulded stone projecting from a wall to protect the lower parts from water; *see also* Hoodmould.

DROVED ASHLAR: *see* Ashlar.

DRUM: (1) circular or polygonal vertical wall of a dome or cupola; (2) one of the stones forming the shaft of a column.

DRY-STONE: stone construction without mortar.

DUN (Scots): a small stone-walled fort.

E. E. (EARLY ENGLISH): historical division of English Gothic architecture covering the period 1200-1250.

EASTER SEPULCHRE: recess with tomb-chest, usually in the wall of a chancel, the tomb-chest to receive the Sacrament after the Mass of Maundy Thursday.

EAVES: overhanging edge of a roof; hence *Eaves Cornice* in this position.

ECHINUS (*lit.* sea-urchin): lower part of a Greek Doric capital; *see* Orders (fig. 16).

EDGE-ROLL: moulding of semicircular or more than semicircular section at the edge of an opening.

ELEVATION: (1) any side of a building; (2) in a drawing, the same or any part of it, accurately represented in two dimensions.

ELIDED: term used to describe (1) a compound architectural feature, e.g. an entablature, in which some parts have been omitted; (2) a number of similar parts which have been combined to form a single larger one (*see* Capital, fig. 6).

EMBATTLED: furnished with battlements.

EMBRASURE (*lit.* splay): small splayed opening in the wall or battlement of a fortified building.

ENCAUSTIC TILES: glazed and decorated earthenware tiles used for paving.

EN DÉLIT: term used in Gothic architecture to describe attached stone shafts whose grain runs vertically instead of horizontally, against normal building practice.

ENGAGED: description of a column that is partly merged into a wall or pier.

ENTABLATURE: in classical architecture, collective name for the three horizontal members (architrave, frieze and cornice) above a column; *see* Orders (fig. 16).

ENTASIS: very slight convex deviation from a straight line;

used on classical columns and sometimes on spires to prevent an optical illusion of concavity.

ENTRESOL: mezzanine storey within or above the ground storey.

EPITAPH (*lit.* on a tomb): inscription in that position.

ESCUTCHEON: shield for armorial bearings.

EXEDRA: apsidal end of an apartment; *see* Apse.

FERETORY: (1) place behind the high altar where the chief shrine of a church is kept; (2) wooden or metal container for relics.

FESTOON: ornament, usually in high or low relief, in the form of a garland of flowers and/or fruit, hung up at both ends; *see also* Swag.

FEU (Scots): land granted, e.g. by sale, by the *Feudal Superior* to the *Vassal* or *Feuar*, on conditions that include the annual payment of a fixed sum of *Feuduty*. The paramount superior of all land is the Crown. Any subsequent proprietor of the land becomes the feuar and is subject to the same obligations. Although many superiors have disposed of their feudal rights, others, both private and corporate, still make good use of the power of feudal control which has produced many well-disciplined developments in Scotland.

FIBREGLASS: *see* GRP.

FILLET: narrow flat band running down a shaft or along a roll moulding.

FINIAL: topmost feature, e.g. above a gable, spire or cupola.

FLAMBOYANT: properly the latest phase of French Gothic architecture, where the window tracery takes on undulating lines, based on the use of flowing curves.

FLATTED: divided into apartments. But flat (Scots) is also used with a special colloquial

meaning. 'He stays on the first flat' means that he lives on the first floor.

FLÈCHE (*lit.* arrow): slender spire on the centre of a roof.

FLEUR-DE-LIS: in heraldry, a formalized lily as in the royal arms of France.

FLEURON: decorative carved flower or leaf.

FLOWING: *see* Tracery (Curvilinear).

FLUTING: series of concave grooves, their common edges sharp (arris) or blunt (fillet).

FOIL (*lit.* leaf): lobe formed by the cusping of a circular or other shape in tracery. *Trefoil* (three), *Quatrefoil* (four), *Cinquefoil* (five) and *Multifoil* express the number of lobes in a shape; *see* Tracery (fig. 25).

FOLIATED: decorated, especially carved, with leaves.

FORE- (*lit.* in front): *Fore-building:* structure protecting an entrance. *Forestair:* external stair, usually unenclosed.

FOSSE: ditch.

FRATER: refectory or dining hall of a monastery.

FREESTONE: stone that is cut, or can be cut, in all directions, usually fine-grained sandstone or limestone.

FRESCO: painting executed on wet plaster.

FRIEZE: horizontal band of ornament, especially the middle member of the classical entablature; *see* Orders (fig. 16). *Pulvinated Frieze* (*lit.* cushioned): frieze of bold convex profile.

FRONTAL: covering for the front of an altar.

GABLE: (1) peaked wall or other vertical surface, often triangular, at the end of a double-pitch roof; (2) (Scots) the same, very often with a chimney at the apex, but also in a wider sense: end wall, of whatever shape. *See* fig. 9. *Gablet:* small gable. *See also* Roof, Skew.

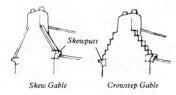

Skewputt

Skew Gable   Crowstep Gable

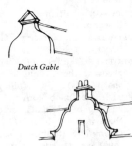

Dutch Gable

Curvilinear or Shaped
Gable at wallhead

Fig. 9.   Gables

GADROONING: ribbed ornament, e.g. on the lid or base of an urn, flowing into a lobed edge.

GAIT (Scots) or GATE: street, usually with a prefix indicating its use, direction or destination.

GALILEE: chapel or vestibule usually at the W end of a church enclosing the porch; *see also* Narthex.

GALLERY: balcony or passage, but with certain special meanings, e.g. (1) upper storey above the aisle of a church, looking through arches to the nave; also called tribune and often erroneously triforium. (2) balcony or mezzanine, often with seats, overlooking the main interior space of a building. (3) external walkway projecting from a wall.

GARDEROBE (*lit.* wardrobe): medieval privy.

GARGOYLE: water spout projecting from the parapet of a wall or tower, often carved into human or animal shape.

GAZEBO (jocular Latin, 'I shall gaze'): lookout tower or raised summer house overlooking a garden.

GEOMETRIC: historical division of English Gothic architecture covering the period *c.* 1250–90.

See also Tracery. For another meaning, *see* Staircase.

GIBBS SURROUND: C18 treatment of door or window surround, seen particularly in the work of James Gibbs (1682–1754) (*see* fig. 10).

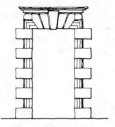

Fig. 10.   Gibbs Surround

GNOMON: vane or indicator casting a shadow on to a sundial.

GRC (glass-reinforced concrete): concrete reinforced with glass fibre, formed in moulds, often used for the multiple repetition of architectural elements.

GROIN: sharp edge at the meeting of two cells of a cross-vault; *see* Vault (fig. 26a).

GROTESQUE (*lit.* grotto-esque): classical wall decoration of spindly, whimsical character adopted from Roman examples, particularly by Raphael, and further developed in the C18.

GRP (glass-reinforced polyester): synthetic resin reinforced with glass fibre, formed in moulds, sometimes simulating the outward appearance of traditional materials.

GUILLOCHE: running classical ornament formed by a series of circles with linked and interlaced borders (see fig. 11).

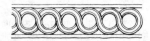

Fig. 11.   Guilloche

GUNLOOP: opening for a firearm.
GUTTAE: *see* Orders (fig. 16).

HAGIOSCOPE: *see* Squint.
HALF-TIMBERING: timber fram-

ing with the spaces filled in by plaster, stones or brickwork.

HALL CHURCH: (1) church whose nave and aisles are of equal height or approximately so. (2) (Scots C20): church convertible into a hall.

HAMMERBEAM: *see* Roof.

HARLING (Scots, *lit.* hurling): wet dash, i.e. a form of roughcasting in which the mixture of aggregate and binding material (e.g. lime) is dashed onto a rubble wall as protection against weather.

HEADER: *see* Bond.

HENGE: ritual earthwork with a surrounding bank and ditch, the bank being on the outer side.

HERITORS (Scots): proprietors of a heritable subject, especially church heritors who till 1925 were responsible for each parish church and its manse.

HERM (*lit.* the god Hermes): male head or bust on a pedestal.

HERRINGBONE WORK: masonry or brickwork in zigzag courses.

HEXASTYLE: term used to describe a portico with six columns.

HILLFORT: Iron Age earthwork enclosed by a ditch and bank system; in the later part of the period the defences multiplied in size and complexity. Hillforts vary in area and are usually built with careful regard to natural elevations or promontories.

HOODMOULD or label: projecting moulding above an arch or lintel to throw off water.

HORSEMILL: circular or polygonal farm building in which a central shaft is turned by a horse to drive agricultural machinery.

HUNGRY JOINTS: *see* Pointing.

HUSK GARLAND: festoon of nutshells diminishing towards the ends (*see* fig. 12).

HYPOCAUST (*lit.* under-burning): Roman underfloor heating system. The floor is supported on pillars and the space thus formed is connected to a flue.

ICONOGRAPHY: description of the subject matter of works of the visual arts.

IMPOST (*lit.* imposition): horizontal moulding at the spring of an arch.

IN ANTIS: *see* Anta.

INDENT: (1) shape chiselled out of a stone to match and receive a brass; (2) in restoration, a secretion of new stone inserted as a patch into older work.

INGLENOOK (*lit.* fire-corner): recess for a hearth with provision for seating.

INTERCOLUMNIATION: interval between columns.

IONIC: *see* Orders (fig. 16).

JAMB (*lit.* leg): (1) one of the straight sides of an opening; (2) (Scots) wing or extension adjoining one side of a rectangular plan, making it into an L or T plan.

KEEL MOULDING: *see* fig. 13.

Fig. 13. Keel Moulding

KEEP: principal tower of a castle. Also called Donjon.

KEY PATTERN: *see* fig. 14.

Fig. 12. Husk Garland

Fig. 14. Key Pattern

KEYSTONE: middle and topmost stone in an arch or vault.

KINGPOST: *see* Roof (fig. 22).

LABEL: *see* Hoodmould. *Label Stop:* ornamental boss at the end of a hoodmould.

LADY CHAPEL: chapel dedicated to the Virgin Mary (Our Lady).

LAIGH, or LAICH (Scots): low.

LAIRD (Scots): landowner.

LANCET WINDOW: slender pointed-arched window.

LANTERN: a small circular or polygonal turret with windows all round crowning a roof (*see* Cupola) or a dome.

LAVATORIUM: in a monastery, a washing place adjacent to the refectory.

LEAN-TO: term commonly applied not only to a single-pitch roof but to the building it covers.

LESENE (*lit.* a mean thing): pilaster without base or capital. Also called pilaster strip.

LIERNE: *see* Vault (fig. 26b).

LIGHT: compartment of a window.

LINENFOLD: Tudor panelling ornamented with a conventional representation of a piece of linen laid in vertical folds. The piece is repeated in each panel.

LINTEL: horizontal beam or stone bridging an opening.

LOFT: three special senses: (1) *Organ Loft* in which the organ, or sometimes only the console (keyboard), is placed; (2) *Rood Loft*: narrow gallery over rood screen, q.v.; (3) (Scots) reserved gallery in a church, e.g. a *Laird's Loft*, or a *Trades Loft* for members of one of the incorporated trades of a burgh.

LOGGIA: sheltered space behind a colonnade.

LONG-AND-SHORT WORK: quoins consisting of stones placed with the long sides alternately upright and horizontal, especially in Saxon building.

LOUIS: convenient term used in the antique trade to describe a curvaceous chimneypiece of Louis XV character.

LOUVRE: (1) opening, often with lantern over, in the roof of a room to let the smoke from a central hearth escape; (2) one of a series of overlapping boards to allow ventilation but keep the rain out.

LOZENGE: diamond shape.

LUCARNE (*lit.* dormer): small window in a roof or spire.

LUCKENBOOTH (Scots): lock-up booth or shop.

LUGGED: *see* Architrave.

LUNETTE (*lit.* half or crescent moon): (1) semicircular window; (2) semicircular or crescent-shaped surface.

LYCHGATE (*lit.* corpse-gate): wooden gate structure with a roof and open sides placed at the entrance to a churchyard to provide space for the reception of a coffin.

LYNCHET: long terraced strip of soil accumulating on the downward side of prehistoric and medieval fields owing to soil creep from continuous ploughing along the contours.

MACHICOLATIONS (*lit.* mashing devices): on a castle, downward openings through which missiles can be dropped, under a parapet or battlement supported by deep corbels.

MAINS (Scots): home farm on an estate.

MAJOLICA: ornamented glazed earthenware.

MANSARD: *see* Roof (fig. 21).

MANSE: house of a minister of religion, especially in Scotland.

MARGINS (Scots): dressed stones at the edges of an opening. 'Back-set margins' (RCAHMS) is a misleading term because they are actually set forward from a rubble-built wall to act as a stop for the harling. Also called Rybats.

MARRIAGE LINTEL (Scots): on a house, a door or window lintel carved with the initials of the owner and his wife and the date of the work – only coincidentally of their marriage.

MAUSOLEUM: monumental tomb, so named after that of Mausolus, king of Caria, at Halicarnassus.

MEGALITHIC (*lit*. of large stones): archaeological term referring to the use of such stones, singly or together.

MERCAT (Scots): market. The *Mercat Cross* was erected in a Scottish burgh, generally in a wide street, as the focus of market activity and local ceremonial. Most examples are of post-Reformation date and have heraldic or other finials (not crosses), but the name persisted.

MERLON: *see* Battlement.

MESOLITHIC: term applied to the Middle Stone Age, dating in Britain from *c*. 5000 to *c*. 3500 B.C., and to the hunting and gathering activities of the earliest communities. *See also* Neolithic.

METOPES: spaces between the triglyphs in a Doric frieze; *see* Orders (fig. 16).

MEZZANINE: (1) low storey between two higher ones; (2) low upper storey within the height of a high one, not extending over its whole area.

MISERERE: *see* Misericord.

MISERICORD (*lit*. mercy): ledge placed on the underside of a hinged choir stall seat which, when turned up, provided the occupant with support during long periods of standing. Also called Miserere.

MODILLIONS: small consoles at regular intervals along the underside of some types of classical cornice.

MORT-SAFE (Scots): device to assure the security of a corpse or corpses: (1) iron frame over a grave; (2) building or room where bodies were kept during decomposition.

MOTTE: steep mound forming the main feature of C11 and C12 castles.

MOTTE-AND-BAILEY: post-Roman and Norman defence system consisting of an earthen mound (motte) topped with a wooden tower within a bailey, with enclosure ditch and palisade, and with the rare addition of an internal bank.

MOUCHETTE: motif in curvilinear tracery, a curved version of the dagger form, specially popular in the early C14 in England but in the early C15 in Scotland; *see* Tracery (fig. 25).

MOULDING: ornament of continuous section; *see* the various types.

MULLION: vertical member between the lights in a window opening.

MULTI-STOREY: modern term denoting five or more storeys.

MULTIVALLATE: of a hillfort: defended by three or more concentric banks and ditches.

MUNTIN: post forming part of a screen.

MUTULE: square block under the corona of a Doric cornice.

NAILHEAD MOULDING: E.E. ornamental motif, consisting of small pyramids regularly repeated (*see* fig. 15).

Fig. 15.   Nailhead Moulding

NARTHEX: enclosed vestibule or covered porch at the main entrance to a church; *see also* Galilee.

NECESSARIUM: medieval euphemism for latrines in a monastery.

NEOLITHIC: term applied to the New Stone Age, dating in Britain from the appearance of the first settled farming communities from the continent *c*. 3500 B.C. until the beginning of the Bronze Age. *See also* Mesolithic.

NEWEL: central post in a circular or winding staircase, also the

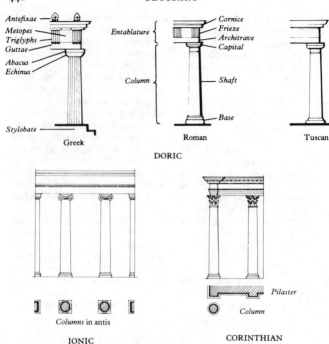

Fig. 16. Orders

principal post when a flight of stairs meets a landing.

NICHE (*lit.* shell): vertical recess in a wall, sometimes for a statue.

NIGHT STAIR: stair by which monks entered the transepts of their church from their dormitory to celebrate night services.

NOOK-SHAFT: shaft set in an angle formed by other members.

NORMAN: *see* Romanesque.

NOSING: projection of the tread of a step. A *Bottle Nosing* is half round in section.

OBELISK: lofty pillar of square section tapering at the top and ending pyramidally.

OGEE: double curve, bending first one way and then the other. *Ogee* or *Ogival Arch: see* Arch.

ORATORY: small private chapel in a house.

ORDER: (1) upright structural member formally related to others, e.g. in classical architecture a column, pilaster, or anta; (2) one of a series of recessed arches and jambs forming a splayed opening. *Giant* or *Colossal Order:* classical order whose height is that of two or more storeys of a building.

ORDERS: in classical architecture, the differently formalized versions of the basic post-and-lintel structure, each having its own rules of design and proportion. For examples of the main types *see* fig. 16. Others include the primitive Tuscan, which has a plain frieze and simple torus-moulded base, and the Composite, whose capital combines Ionic volutes with Corinthian foliage. *Superimposed Orders:* term for the use of Orders on successive levels, usually in the upward sequence of Doric, Ionic, Corinthian.

ORIEL: *see* Bay Window.

OVERARCH: *see* Arch.

OVERHANG: projection of the upper storey(s) of a building.

OVERSAILING COURSES: series of stone or brick courses, each one projecting beyond the one below it; *see also* Corbel-course.

PALIMPSEST (*lit.* erased work): re-use of a surface, e.g. a wall for another painting; also used to describe a brass plate which has been re-used by engraving on the back.

PALLADIAN: architecture following the ideas and principles of Andrea Palladio, 1508–80.

PALMETTE: classical ornament like a symmetrical palm shoot; for illustration *see* Anthemion, fig. 1.

PANTILE: roof tile of curved S-shaped section.

PARAPET: wall for protection at any sudden drop, e.g. on a bridge or at the wallhead of a castle; in the latter case it protects the *Parapet Walk* or wall walk.

PARCLOSE: *see* Screen.

PARGETING (*lit.* plastering): usually of moulded plaster panels in half-timbering.

PATERA (*lit.* plate): round or oval ornament in shallow relief, especially in classical architecture.

PEDESTAL: in classical architecture, a stand sometimes used to support the base of an order (*see* fig. 17).

Fig. 17. Pedestal

PEDIMENT: in classical architecture, a formalized gable derived from that of a temple, also used over doors, windows, etc. For the generally accepted meanings of *Broken Pediment* and *Open Pediment see* fig. 18.

PEEL (*lit.* palisade): stone tower, e.g. near the Scottish–English border.

PEND (Scots): open-ended passage through a building on ground level.

PENDANT: hanging-down feature of a vault or ceiling, usually ending in a boss.

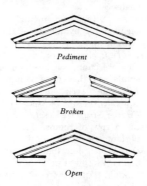

Pediment

Broken

Open

Fig. 18. Pediments

PENDENTIVE: spandrel between adjacent arches supporting a drum or dome, formed as part of a hemisphere (*see* fig. 19).

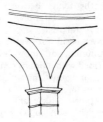

Fig. 19. Pendentive

PEPPERPOT TURRET: bartizan with conical or pyramidal roof.

PERISTYLE: in classical architecture, a range of columns all round a building, e.g. a temple, or an interior space, e.g. a courtyard.

PERP (PERPENDICULAR): historical division of English Gothic architecture covering the period from *c.* 1335–50 to *c.* 1530.

PERRON: *see* Stair.

PIANO NOBILE: principal floor, usually with a ground floor or basement underneath and a lesser storey overhead.

PIAZZA: open space surrounded by buildings; in the C17 and C18 sometimes employed to mean a long colonnade or loggia.

PIEND: *see* Roof.

PIER: strong, solid support, frequently square in section. *Compound Pier:* of composite section, e.g. formed of a bundle of shafts.

PIETRA DURA: ornamental or scenic inlay by means of thin slabs of stone.

PILASTER: classical order of oblong section, its elevation similar to that of a column. *Pilastrade:* series of pilasters, equivalent to a colonnade. *Pilaster Strip: see* Lesene.

PILE: a row of rooms. The important use of the term is in *Double-pile,* describing a house that is two rows thick.

PILLAR PISCINA: free-standing piscina on a pillar.

PINNACLE: tapering finial, e.g. on a buttress or the corner of a tower, sometimes decorated with crockets.

PINS (Scots): small stones pushed into the joints between large ones, a technique called cherry-caulking.

PISCINA: basin for washing the communion or mass vessels, provided with a drain; generally set in or against the wall to the s of an altar.

PIT-PRISON: sunk chamber with access above through a hatch.

PLAISANCE: summerhouse, pleasure house near a mansion.

PLATT (Scots): platform, doorstep or landing. *Scale-and-platt Stair: see* Stair.

PLEASANCE (Scots): close or walled garden.

PLINTH: projecting base beneath a wall or column, generally chamfered or moulded at the top.

POINTING: exposed mortar joints of masonry or brickwork. The finished form is of various types, e.g. *Flush Pointing, Recessed Pointing. Bag-rubbed Pointing* is flush at the edges and gently recessed in the middle of the joint. *Hungry Joints* are either without any pointing at all, or deeply recessed to show the outline of each stone. *Ribbon Pointing* is a nasty practice in the modern vernacular, the joints being formed with a trowel so that they stand out.

POPPYHEAD: carved ornament of leaves and flowers as a finial for the end of a bench or stall.

PORCH: covered projecting entrance to a building.

PORTCULLIS: gate constructed to rise and fall in vertical grooves at the entry to a castle.

PORTE COCHÈRE: porch large enough to admit wheeled vehicles.

PORTICO: in classical architecture, a porch with detached columns or other orders. *Blind Portico:* the front features of a portico attached to a wall so that it is no longer a proper porch.

POSTERN: small gateway at the back of a building.

POTENCE (Scots): rotating ladder for access to the nesting boxes of a round doocot.

PREDELLA: in an altarpiece the horizontal strip below the main representation, often used for a number of subsidiary representations in a row.

PRESBYTERY: the part of the church lying E of the choir stalls.

PRESS (Scots): cupboard.

PRINCIPAL: *see* Roof (fig. 22).

PRIORY: monastic house whose head is a prior or prioress, not an abbot or abbess.

PROSTYLE: with a row of columns in front.

PULPITUM: stone screen in a major church provided to shut off the choir from the nave and also as a backing for the return choir stalls.

PULVINATED: *see* Frieze.

PURLIN: *see* Roof (fig. 22).

PUTHOLE or PUTLOCK HOLE: putlocks are the short horizontal timbers on which during construction the boards of scaffolding rest. Putholes or put-lock holes are the holes in the wall for putlocks, and often are not filled in after construction is complete.

PUTTO: small naked boy (plural: *putti*).

QUADRANGLE: inner courtyard in a large building.

QUARRIES (*lit.* squares): (1) square (or sometimes diamond-shaped) panes of glass supported by lead strips which are called *Cames*; (2) square floor-slabs or tiles.

QUATREFOIL: *see* Foil.

QUEENPOSTS: *see* Roof (fig. 22).

QUIRK: sharp groove to one side of a convex moulding, e.g. beside a roll moulding, which is then said to be quirked.

QUOINS: dressed stones at the angles of a building. When rusticated they may be alternately long and short.

RADIATING CHAPELS: chapels projecting radially from an ambulatory or an apse; *see* Chevet.

RAFTER: *see* Roof (fig. 22).

RAGGLE: groove cut in masonry, especially to receive the edge of glass or roof-covering.

RAKE: slope or pitch.

RAMPART: stone wall or wall of earth surrounding a castle, fortress, or fortified city. *Rampart Walk:* path along the inner face of a rampart.

RANDOM: *see* Rubble.

REBATE: rectangular section cut out of a masonry edge.

REBUS: a heraldic pun, e.g. a fiery cock as a badge for Cockburn.

REEDING: series of convex mouldings; the reverse of fluting.

REFECTORY: dining hall (or frater) of a monastery or similar establishment.

REREDORTER (*lit.* behind the dormitory): medieval euphemism for latrines in a monastery.

REREDOS: painted and/or sculptured screen behind and above an altar.

RESPOND: half-pier bonded into a wall and carrying one end of an arch.

RETABLE: altarpiece; a picture or piece of carving standing behind and attached to an altar.

RETROCHOIR: in a major church, an aisle between the high altar and an E chapel, like a square ambulatory.

REVEAL: the inward plane of a jamb, between the edge of an external wall and the frame of a door or window that is set in it.

RHONE (Scots): gutter along the eaves for rainwater; *see also* Conductor.

RIB-VAULT: *see* Vault.

RINCEAU (*lit.* little branch) or antique foliage: classical ornament, usually on a frieze, of leafy scrolls branching alternately to left and right (*see* fig. 20).

Fig. 20.   Rinceau

RISER: vertical face of a step.

ROCK-FACED: term used to describe masonry which is cleft to produce a natural, rugged appearance.

ROCOCO (*lit.* rocky): latest phase of the Baroque style, current in most Continental countries between *c.* 1720 and *c.* 1760, and showing itself in Britain mainly in playful, scrolled decoration, especially plasterwork.

ROLL MOULDING: moulding of semicircular or more than semicircular section.

ROMANESQUE: style in architecture current in the C11 and C12 and preceded the Gothic style (in England often called Norman). (Some scholars extend the use of the term Romanesque back to the C10 or C9.)

ROOD: cross or crucifix, usually over the entry into the chancel.

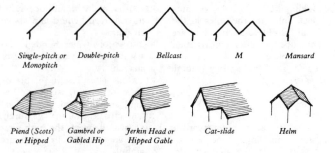

Single-pitch or   Double-pitch   Bellcast   M   Mansard
Monopitch

Piend (Scots)   Gambrel or   Jerkin Head or   Cat-slide   Helm
or Hipped   Gabled Hip   Hipped Gable

Fig. 21.   Roof Forms

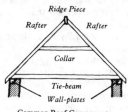

Ridge Piece

Rafter   Rafter

Collar

Tie-beam

Wall-plates

Common Roof Components

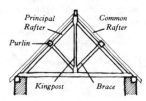

Principal   Common
Rafter   Rafter

Purlin

Kingpost   Brace

Roof with Kingpost Truss

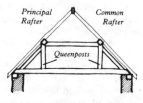

Principal   Common
Rafter   Rafter

Queenposts

Roof with Queenpost Truss

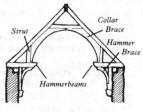

Collar
Brace

Strut

Hammer
Brace

Hammerbeams

Hammerbeam Roof

Fig. 22.   Roof Construction

The *Rood Screen* beneath it may have a *Rood Loft* along the top, reached by a *Rood Stair*.

ROOF: for external forms *see* fig. 21; for construction and components *see* fig. 22. *Wagon Roof*: lined with timber on the inside, giving the appearance of a curved or polygonal vault.

ROPE MOULDING: *see* Cable Moulding.

ROSE WINDOW: circular window with patterned tracery about the centre.

ROTUNDA: building circular in plan.

ROUND (Scots): useful term employed by the RCAHMS for a bartizan, usually roofless.

RUBBLE: masonry whose stones are wholly or partly in a rough state. *Coursed Rubble*: of coursed stones with rough faces. *Random Rubble*: of uncoursed stones in a random pattern. *Snecked Rubble* has courses frequently broken by smaller stones (snecks).

RUSTICATION: treatment of joints and/or faces of masonry to give an effect of strength. In the most usual kind the joints are recessed by V-section chamfering or square-section channelling. *Banded Rustication* has only the horizontal joints emphasized in this way. The faces may be flat but there are many other forms, e.g. *Diamond-faced*, like a shallow pyramid, *Vermiculated*, with a stylized texture like worms or worm-holes, or *Glacial*, like icicles or stalactites. *Rusticated Columns* may have their joints and drums treated in any of these ways.

RYBATS (Scots): *see* Margins.

SACRAMENT HOUSE: safe cupboard for the reserved sacrament.

SACRISTY: room in a church for sacred vessels and vestments.

SALTIRE or ST ANDREW'S CROSS: with diagonal limbs. As the flag of Scotland it is coloured white on a blue ground.

SANCTUARY: (1) area around the main altar of a church (*see* Presbytery); (2) sacred site consisting of wood or stone uprights enclosed by a circular bank and ditch. Beginning in the Neolithic, they were elaborated in the succeeding Bronze Age. The best-known examples are Stonehenge and Avebury.

SARCOPHAGUS (*lit.* flesh-consuming): coffin of stone or other durable material.

SARKING (Scots): boards laid on the rafters (*see* Roof, fig. 22) to support the covering, e.g. metal or slates.

SCAGLIOLA: composition imitating marble.

SCALE-AND-PLATT (*lit.* stair and landing): *see* Stair (fig. 24).

SCARCEMENT: extra thickness of the lower part of a wall, e.g. to carry a floor.

SCARP: artificial cutting away of the ground to form a steep slope.

SCREEN: in a church, usually at the entry to the chancel; *see* Rood Screen and Pulpitum. *Parclose Screen:* separating a chapel from the rest of the church.

SCREENS or SCREENS PASSAGE: screened-off entrance passage between the hall and the kitchen in a medieval house, adjoining the kitchen, buttery, etc.; *see also* Transe.

SCUNTION (Scots): equivalent of a reveal on the indoor side of a door or window opening.

SECTION: view of a building, moulding, etc. revealed by cutting across it.

SEDILIA: seats for the priests (usually three) on the s side of the chancel of a church; a plural word that has become a singular, collective one.

SESSION HOUSE (Scots): (1) room or separate building for meetings of the elders who form a kirk session; (2) shelter by entrance to church or churchyard for an elder receiving the collection for relief of the poor, built at expense of kirk session.

SET-OFF: *see* Weathering.

SGRAFFITO: scratched pattern, often in plaster.

SHAFT: upright member of round section, especially the main part of a classical column. *Shaft-ring:* motif of the C12 and C13 consisting of a ring like a belt round a circular pier or a circular shaft attached to a pier.

SHEILA-NA-GIG: female fertility figure, usually with legs wide open.

SHOULDERED: *see* Arch (fig. 2), Architrave.

SILL: horizontal projection at the bottom of a window.

SKEW (Scots): sloping or shaped stones finishing a gable which is upstanding above the roof. *Skewputt:* bracket at the bottom end of a skew.

SLATE-HANGING: covering of overlapping slates on a wall, which is then said to be *slate-hung.*

SNECKED: *see* Rubble.

SOFFIT (*lit.* ceiling): underside of an arch, lintel, etc.

SOLAR (*lit.* sun-room): upper living room or withdrawing room of a medieval house, accessible from the high table end of the hall.

SOUNDING-BOARD: horizontal board or canopy over a pulpit; also called Tester.

SOUTERRAIN: underground stone-lined passage and chamber.

SPANDRELS: surfaces left over between an arch and its containing rectangle, or between adjacent arches.

SPIRE: tall pyramidal or conical feature built on a tower or turret. *Broach Spire:* starting from a square base, then carried into an octagonal section by means of triangular faces. *Needle Spire:* thin spire rising from the centre of a tower roof, well inside the parapet. *Helm Spire: see* Roof (fig. 21).

SPIRELET: *see* Flèche.

SPLAY: chamfer, usually of a reveal or scuntion.

SPRING: level at which an arch or vault rises from its supports. *Springers:* the first stones of an arch or vaulting-rib above the spring.

SQUINCH: arch thrown across an angle between two walls to support a superstructure, e.g. a dome (*see* fig. 23).

Fig. 23.　Squinch

SQUINT: hole cut in a wall or through a pier to allow a view of the main altar of a church from places whence it could not otherwise be seen. Also called Hagioscope.

STAIR: *see* fig. 24. The term *Perron* (*lit.* of stone) applies to the external stair leading to a doorway, usually of double-curved plan as shown. *Spiral, Turnpike* (Scots) or *Newel Stair:* ascending round a central supporting newel, usually in a circular shaft. *Flying Stair:* cantilevered from the wall of a stairwell, without newels. *Geometric Stair:* flying stair whose inner edge describes a curve. *Well Stair:* term applied to any stair contained in an open well, but generally to one that climbs up three sides of a well, with corner landings.

STALL: seat for clergy, choir, etc., distinctively treated in its own right or as one of a row.

STANCHION: upright structural member, of iron or steel or reinforced concrete.

STEADING (Scots): farm building or buildings. A term most often used to describe the principal group of agricultural buildings on a farm.

STEEPLE: a tower together with a spire or other tall feature on top of it.

STIFFLEAF: *see* fig. 6.

STOUP: vessel for the reception of holy water, usually placed near a door.

STRAINER: *see* Arch.

STRAPWORK: C16 and C17 decoration used also in the C19 Jacobean revival, resembling interlaced bands of cut leather.

STRINGCOURSE: intermediate stone course or moulding projecting from the surface of a wall.

STUCCO (*lit.* plaster): (1) smooth external rendering of a wall etc.; (2) decorative plaster-work.

STUDS: intermediate vertical members of a timber-framed wall or partition.

STUGGED (Scots): of masonry that

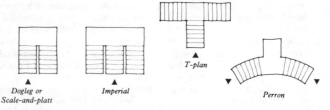

Dogleg or Scale-and-platt

Imperial

T-plan

Perron

Fig. 24.　Stair

is hacked or picked as a key for rendering; used as a type of surface finish in the C19.

STYLOBATE: solid structure on which a colonnade stands.

SWAG (*lit.* bundle): like a festoon, but also a cloth bundle in relief, hung up at both ends.

TABERNACLE (*lit.* tent): (1) canopied structure, especially on a small scale, to contain the reserved sacrament or a relic; (2) architectural frame, e.g. of a monument on a wall or free-standing, with flanking orders. Also called an Aedicule.

TAS-DE-CHARGE: coursed stone(s) forming the springers of more than one vaulting-rib.

TERMINAL FIGURE or TERM: upper part of a human figure growing out of a pier, pilaster, etc. which tapers towards the bottom.

TERRACOTTA: moulded and fired clay ornament or cladding, usually unglazed.

TESSELLATED PAVEMENT: mosaic flooring, particularly Roman, consisting of small *Tesserae* or cubes of glass, stone, or brick.

TESTER (*lit.* head): bracketed canopy, especially over a pulpit, where it is also called a sounding-board.

TETRASTYLE: term used to describe a portico with four columns.

THERMAL WINDOW (*lit.* of a Roman bath): *see* Diocletian window.

THREE-DECKER PULPIT: pulpit with clerk's stall below and reading desk below the clerk's stall.

TIE-BEAM: *see* Roof (fig. 22).

TIERCERON: *see* Vault (fig. 26b).

TILE-HANGING: *see* Slate-hanging.

TIMBER FRAMING: method of construction where walls are built of timber framework with the spaces filled in by plaster or brickwork. Sometimes the timber is covered over with plaster or boarding laid horizontally.

TOLBOOTH (Scots): tax office containing a burgh council chamber and a prison.

TOMB-CHEST: chest-shaped stone coffin, the most usual medieval form of funerary monument.

TOUCH: soft black marble quarried near Tournai.

TOURELLE: turret corbelled out from the wall.

TOWER HOUSE (Scots): compact fortified house with the main hall raised above the ground and at least one more storey above it. A medieval Scots type continuing well into the C17 in its modified forms, the L plan and so-called Z plan, the former having a jamb at one corner, the latter at each diagonally opposite corner.

TRACERY: pattern of arches and geometrical figures supporting the glass in the upper part of a window, or applied decoratively to wall surfaces or vaults. *Plate Tracery* is the most primitive form of tracery, being formed of openings cut through stone slabs or plates. In *Bar Tracery*

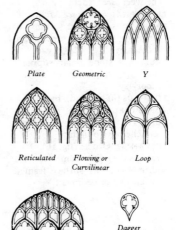

Plate   Geometric   Y

Reticulated   Flowing or Curvilinear   Loop

Perpendicular   Dagger   Quatrefoil   Mouchette

Fig. 25.   Tracery

the openings are separated not by flat areas of stonework but by relatively slender divisions or bars which are constructed of voussoirs like arches. Later developments of bar tracery are classified according to the character of the decorative pattern used. For generalized illustrations of the main types *see* fig. 25.

TRANSE (Scots): passage, especially screens passage.

TRANSEPTS (*lit.* cross-enclosures): transverse portions of a cross-shaped church.

TRANSOM: horizontal member between the lights in a window opening.

TREFOIL: *see* Foil.

TRIBUNE: *see* Gallery (1).

TRICIPUT, SIGNUM TRICIPUT: sign of the Trinity expressed by three faces belonging to one head.

TRIFORIUM: middle storey of a church treated as an arcaded wall passage or blind arcade, its height corresponding to that of the aisle roof.

TRIGLYPHS (*lit.* three-grooved tablets): stylized beam-ends in the Doric frieze, with metopes between; *see* Orders (fig. 16).

TRIUMPHAL ARCH: *see* Arch.

TROPHY: sculptured group of arms or armour as a memorial of victory.

TRUMEAU: stone pillar supporting the tympanum of a wide doorway.

TUMULUS (*lit.* mound): barrow.

TURNPIKE: *see* Stair.

TURRET: small tower, often attached to a building.

TUSCAN: *see* Orders (fig. 16).

TYMPANUM (*lit.* drum): as of a drum-skin, the surface framed by an arch or pediment.

UNDERCROFT: vaulted room, sometimes underground, below the main upper room.

UNIVALLATE: of a hillfort: defended by a single bank and ditch.

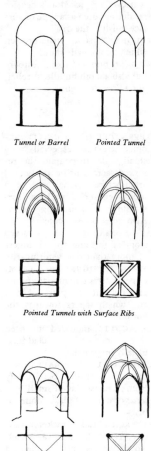

Tunnel or Barrel   *Pointed Tunnel*

Pointed Tunnels with Surface Ribs

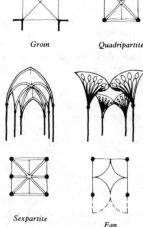

Groin   *Quadripartite*

Sexpartite   *Fan*

Fig. 26. (a)   Vaults

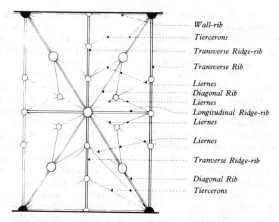

Wall-rib
Tiercerons
Transverse Ridge-rib
Transverse Rib
Liernes
Diagonal Rib
Liernes
Longitudinal Ridge-rib
Liernes
Liernes
Tranverse Ridge-rib
Diagonal Rib
Tiercerons

Fig. 26. (b) Ribs of a Late Gothic Vault

VASSAL: *see* Feu.

VAULT: ceiling of stone formed like arches (sometimes imitated in timber or plaster); *see* fig. 26a. *Tunnel-* or *Barrel-vault*: the simplest kind of vault, in effect a continuous semicircular arch. *Pointed Tunnel-vaults* are frequent in Scottish late medieval architecture but otherwise rare. A Scottish peculiarity is the *Pointed Tunnel-vault with Surface Ribs* which are purely decorative in intention. *Groin-vaults* (usually called *Cross-vaults* in classical architecture) have four curving triangular surfaces produced by the intersection of two tunnel-vaults at right angles. The curved lines at the intersections are called groins. In *Quadripartite Rib-vaults* the four sections are divided by their arches or ribs springing from the corners of the bay. *Sexpartite Rib-vaults* are most often used over paired bays. The main types of rib are shown in fig. 26b; *transverse ribs, wall-ribs, diagonal ribs*, and *ridge-ribs*. *Tiercerons* are extra, decorative ribs springing from the corners of a bay. *Liernes* are decorative ribs in the crown of a vault which are not linked to any of the springing points. In a *stellar vault* the liernes are arranged in a star formation as in fig. 26b. *Fan-vaults* are peculiar to English Perpendicular architecture and differ from rib-vaults in consisting not of ribs and infilling but of halved concave cones with decorative blind tracery carved on their surfaces.

VAULTING-SHAFT: shaft leading up to the springer of a vault.

VENETIAN WINDOW: *see* fig. 27.

Fig. 27.   Venetian Window

VERANDA(H): shelter or gallery against a building, its roof supported by thin vertical members.

VERMICULATION: *see* Rustication.

VESICA (*lit.* bladder): usually of a window, with curved sides and pointed at top and bottom like a rugger-ball.

VESTIBULE: ante-room or entrance hall.

VILLA: originally (1) Roman

country-house-cum-farmhouse, developed into (2) the similar C16 Venetian type with office wings, made grander by Palladio's varied application of a central portico. This became an important type in C18 Britain, often with the special meaning of (3) a country house which is not a principal residence. Gwilt (1842) defined the villa as 'a country house for the residence of opulent persons'. But devaluation had already begun, and the term implied, as now, (4) a more or less pretentious suburban house.

VITRIFIED: hardened or fused into a glass-like state.

VITRUVIAN SCROLL: running ornament of curly waves on a classical frieze. (*See* fig. 28.)

VOLUTES: spiral scrolls on the front and back of a Greek Ionic capital, also on the sides of a Roman one. *Angle Volute:* pair of volutes turned outwards to meet at the corner of a capital.

VOUSSOIRS: wedge-shaped stones forming an arch.

WAINSCOT: timber lining on an internal wall.

WALLED GARDEN: C17 type whose formal layout is still seen in the combined vegetable and flower gardens of C18 and C19 Scotland. They are usually sited at a considerable distance from a house.

WALL-PLATE: *see* Roof (fig. 22).

WATERHOLDING BASE: type of Early Gothic base in which the upper and lower mouldings are separated by a hollow so deep as to be capable of retaining water.

WEATHERBOARDING: overlapping horizontal boards, covering a timber-framed wall.

WEATHERING: inclined, projecting surface to keep water away from wall and joints below.

WEEPERS: small figures placed in niches along the sides of some medieval tombs; also called mourners.

WHEEL WINDOW: circular window with tracery of radiating shafts like the spokes of a wheel; *see also* Rose Window.

WYND (Scots): subsidiary street or lane, often running into a main street or gait.

YETT (Scots, *lit.* gate): hinged openwork gate at a main doorway, made of wrought-iron bars alternately penetrating and penetrated.

Fig. 28.   Vitruvian Scroll

INDEX OF ARTISTS

Abbey Studio (glass-stainers), 110, 186

Adam, John (mason), 353n

Adam, John (1721–92), 102, 103, 291, 423 and n; Pl. 68

Adam, Robert (1728–92), 291

Adam & Small (glass-stainers), 281

Adam, Stephen (glass-stainer, 1847–1910), 150

Adam (Stephen) Studio (glass-stainers), 161, 384

Adam, William (1689–1748), 19, 66n, 211, 306, 349

Adamson, Robert (builder), 86

Adesoun, Thomas (mason), 213n

Aitken, James, 290

Aitken, William (mason), 349

Alborn, Thomas (plasterer), 321

Alison, Andrew (mason), 110

Alison & Hutchison & Partners, 190

Alison, Walter (c. 1887–1950), 412

Alison (Walter) & Hutchison, 76

Allan, John, 121

Anderson, Charles F., 238, 386, 406

Anderson, George (mason), 273

Anderson, J. F., 299

Anderson, John (mason), 213n

Anderson & Ramage (plasterers), 236

Anderson, Robert, 337 and n

Anderson, Sir Robert Rowand (1834–1921), 38, 50, 53, 102, 104, 124, 146, 148, 149, 162, 178, 181, 185, 186, 197, 284, 289, 292, 306, 317, 319, 383, 395–6, 398; Pls. 40, 111

Anderson (Rowand) & Balfour Paul (Sir Robert Rowand Anderson, q.v.; Arthur Forman Balfour Paul, 1875–1938), 149

Anderson, T. S., 332

Andrew, Brother (wright), 295

Angus, George (c. 1792–1845), 36, 266, 270, 275

Annan (James) & Son (modellers), 223

Anstruther, Agnes Dorothea (d. 1941), 125, 126

Appleton Partnership, 98

Archibald, Henry (c. 1807–77), 305

Armour, C. H., 218

Arthur, Alexander (plasterer), 141n

Arthur, John (mason), 389n

Arthur, Patrick (mason), 389n

Atkinson, William (c. 1773–1839), 47, 269; Pl. 75

Bacon (Percy) & Bros. (glass-stainers), 312

Baird, John (1798–1859), 185

Baird & Thomson (John Baird, q.v.; James Thomson, 1835–1905), 194

Bald, Robert, 266

Baldie, Robert (d. c. 1890), 37, 229, 299, 311

Balfour, Andrew (builder), 185

Balfour, Robert (c. 1770–1867), 135, 137, 198, 257, 274, 309, 311, 380, 386, 390, 396, 415

Ballantine (A.) & Gardiner (glass-stainers, 1892–1905: Alexander Ballantine, d. 1906), 182, 218, 229, 249

Ballantine (A.) & Son (glass-stainers: Alexander Ballantine, d. 1906; James Ballantine II, q.v.), 76, 104, 150, 161, 335 and n, 382

Ballantine, James, II (glass-stainer, 1878–1940), 59, 174, 182

Ballantine (James) & Son (glass-stainers, 1860–92: James Ballantine, 1808–77; Alexander Ballantine, d. 1906), 39, 161, 180, 181, 280, 348

Ballingal, James (builder), 174

Ballingal, Niel, 320

Ballingall, James (mason), 354

Balsillie, John (wright), 137

Bannatyne, Robert (glazier), 321

Barclay, H. & D. (Hugh Barclay, 1828–92; David Barclay, 1846–1917), 50, 187, 188, 189, 190, 191

Barclay, James, 303, 318

Barclay, Thomas, 218, 303, 318, 320

Batchelor, Andrew, 71

Bawte, Henry (mason), 213n

Baxter, Alexander (carver), 353

Baxter, Clark & Paul, 407

Baxter, John, Jun. (d. 1798), 98, 235

Baxter, Robert (mason), 273

Bean, Andrew (plasterer), 141

Beaton, Walter (mason), 283n

Beattie, Thomas (sculptor, c. 1861–1933), 192, 240

Begg, Ian McKerron, 342

Bell, Hay, 160; Pl. 20

Bell, John (wright), 324 and n

Bell, Robert (d. 1859), 56, 226, 333

Berthault, Louis-Martin (?1771–1823), 103

Beveridge, David, 187

Beveridge, William (sculptor), 83

Binns, J. J. (organ builder), 280

Birrell, Ebeneezer, 93n

Birrell, George Smith (1838–76), 276

Birrell, Hugh (1794–1873), 86, 87, 123, 303, 309

Birrell, William, 77, 132, 167, 314, 315

Black, James (mason), 213

Black, Nicol (mason), 213n

Black, Roger (mason), 271n, 273, 291 and n

Black, William (schoolmaster), 174

Black, William S. (sculptor), 181, 335 and n

Blair, W. (glass-stainer), 348

Blanc, Hippolyte Jean (1844–1917), 188, 272, 313, 319

Blane, Roger (mason), 294n

Blyth, Alexander, 129, 130n, 174, 225 and n, 262

Blyth, John (glass-stainer), 207, 319, 348, 408

Blyth & Westland (1893–1913: Benjamin Hall Blyth, 1849–1917; David Westland), 107

Bodley, George Frederick (1827–1907), 39, 182

Boehm, Sir Joseph Edgar (sculptor, 1834–90), 393

Bonnar, Robert (c. 1793–1853), 195, 420

Bonnar, Stanley (sculptor), 232; Pl. 118

Bonnar, Thomas (d. 1847), 223n, 249

Bonnar, Thomas, Jun. (decorator, d. 1899), 141, 217

Bonthron, Henry (mason, c. 1757–1840), 283n

Bonthron, William (wright, c. 1795–1868), 274

Boucher, Thomas, 292

Bowman, John (mason), 135

Boyter, F., 348

Brandon Bridge-building Co., 282

Bremner, James (sculptor), 424

Briggs, William, 99

Brindley & Foster (organ builders), 281

Brooke (Joseph) & Co. (organ builders), 249

Broun, John (mason), 212

Brounhill, John (mason), 213

Brown, James (wright), 135

Brown, James (d. 1878), 288

Brown, James (fl. 1882), 67, 348

Brown, Thomas (1806–72), 56, 58, 105

Brown, Thomas, Jun., 191

Brown & Wardrop (1849–73: Thomas Brown, Jun.; James Maitland Wardrop, 1824–82), 48, 64, 389; Pl. 80

Browne, Sir George Washington (1853–1939), 285

Browne (Joseph) & Co. (sculptors), 223

Bruce, Sir William (c. 1630–1710), 45 and n, 46, 84, 85, 86, 306, 321n

Brunton, John (c. 1799–1862), 325

Bruyn, Nicolas de (engraver, 1565–1652), 82

Bryce, David (1803–76), 37, 47, 81, 82, 85, 100, 218, 228, 236, 252, 317, 338, 343, 398, 412, 420, 427; Pls. 79, 82; see also Burn & Bryce

Brydie, Andrew (wright), 70

Brydon & Robertson, 250

Bryson, Nathaniel (glass-stainer), 57, 104

Bunton, Sam, 53, 196

Burlison & Grylls (glass-stainers: John Burlison, 1843–91; Thomas John Grylls, 1845–1913; Thomas Henry Grylls, 1873–1953), 198

Burn & Bryce (1841–50: William Burn, q.v.; David Bryce, q.v.), 87

Burn, J. P., 208

Burn, James, 61

Burn, Robert (1752–1815), 65, 203

Burn, William (1789–1870), 36, 37, 47, 50, 51, 57, 80, 81, 82, 84, 86, 87, 103, 105, 115, 125, 126, 165, 177, 179, 221, 223, 224, 261, 285, 385, 397, 404, 405, 412; Pls. 27, 28, 81, 110

Burne-Jones, Sir Edward Coley (painter, 1833–98), 39, 207, 228, 281

Burnet (Frank) & Boston, 194

Burnet, Son & Campbell (1886–97: John Burnet, 1814–1901; Sir John James Burnet, 1859–1939; John Archibald Campbell, 1859–1909), 210

Burnett, Thomas Stuart (sculptor, 1853–88), 316

Burnie, David B., 190

Cairns, Andrew (builder), 408
Cairns, James Davidson (c. 1866–1947), 136
Cairns, John (mason, c. 1768–1853), 274
Cameron, Robert Macfarlane (d. 1921), 191, 293
Campbell, Allister (mason), 213n
Campbell, G. Charles, 105, 106, 107, 132, 204, 273
Campbell, James (builder), 291
Campbell, Judith, 135, 136
Cappon, Thomas Martin (c. 1864–1939), 42, 226, 335, 337, 392, 416, 424
Carnaby, John (plumber), 321
Carpenter, Richard Cromwell (1812–55), 53, 117; Pl. 98
Carr, David (d. 1986), 283; Pl. 117
Carrick, Alexander (sculptor, 1882–1966), 78, 271, 333, 378
Carstairs, David (wright), 69
Caslake, J., 83
Cassells, J., 232
Chalmers, John, 122
Chalmers, Peter MacGregor (1859–1922), 38, 112, 149, 186, 198n, 207, 249, 311, 312, 314, 376, 380, 384, 404, 408; Pls. 41, 42
Chalmers, Roderick (painter, d. 1747), 172
Chambers, Sir William (1723–96), 104
Chantrey, Sir Francis (sculptor, 1789–1841), 40, 301; Pl. 39
Chesser, John (1820–93), 53, 390
Chilton, Margaret Isabel (glass-stainer, b. 1875), 40, 311, 314, 384
Christie, John (plasterer), 321
Clark & Blyth, 266
Clark, Thomas (builder), 120
Clayton & Bell (glass-stainers: John Richard Clayton, 1827–1913; Alfred Bell, 1832–95; John Clement Bell, 1860–1944; Reginald Otto Bell, 1864–1950; Michael Charles Farrar Bell, b. 1911), 198, 383
Cleland, James (1770–1840), 140n
Clow, W. & A. (sculptors: William Clow, 1851–1935; Alexander Clow, 1861–1946), 120, 255, 349
Cockerell, Charles Robert (1788–1863), 103
Collins, E. V., 292
Comper, Sir John Ninian (1864–1960), 38
Constable, William (b. 1863), 75, 76; see also Lyle & Constable
Cook, Archibald, 251
Corstorphine, John, 275
Cottier & Co. (glass-stainers), 312

Cousans, Son & Co. (organ builders), 112
Cousin, David (1808–78), 194
Cousin & Gale (David Cousin, q.v.), 270
Cousin, George, 114
Covell Matthews & Partners, 193
Coventry, Thomas (mason), 349
Cowie, George (mason), 349
Craig, James (1744–95), 376
Crawford & Fraser, 117
Crichton, Richard (?1771–1817), 36, 46, 235, 259; Pl. 71
Cumming, Andrew, 93
Cunningham & Jack (John C. Cunningham; William Murray Jack), 393
Cunningham, Jack, Fisher & Purdom, 89, 373, 396
Cunningham, John C., 258, 350, 395, 403
Cunningham, Robert (mason), 65, 66
Currie, J. & T. W., 70
Currie, John (builder, c. 1779–1847), 212
Currie, John (c. 1840–1922), 137, 207, 208, 209, 210, 255
Currie, Thomas (wright, c. 1812–91), 207, 406
Curtis & Davis, 386
Dalziel, James (sculptor), 104, 421
Damesme, Louis-Emmanuel-Aimé (1757–1822), 103
Dannatt, Trevor (b. 1920), 47, 342
Davidson, Charles, 128
Davidson, John (mason), 163
Davidson, William (sculptor), 319
Davis, Louis (glass-stainer, 1861–1941), 379, 382
Dearle, John Henry (glass-stainer, 1860–1932), 312
Deas, Francis William (c. 1871–1951), 47, 59, 104, 172, 239, 327
Deas, G. B., 293
Department of the Environment, 270
Design Furniture Group, 59
Deuchars, Louis (sculptor, 1871–1927), 240
Dewar, A. & A. C., 128
Dewar, Alexander Cumming (d. 1932), 312
Dickson, R. & R. (Richard Dickson, 1792–1857; Robert Dickson, c. 1794–1865), 36, 47, 130, 131, 196, 197, 235, 236, 259; Pls. 71, 78
Dishington, George (surveyor), 120
Douglas, Campbell (1828–1910), 291
Douglas (Campbell) & Morrison (Campbell Douglas, q.v.; Alexander Morrison, fl. 1888–1906), 293

Douglas (Campbell) & Sellars (Campbell Douglas, q.v.; James Sellars, 1843–88), 37, 38, 162, 288, 289, 295

Douglas (Campbell) & Stevenson (Campbell Douglas, q.v.; John James Stevenson, 1831–1908), 50, 163

Douglas, John (1829–1911), 378

Doulton & Co. (tile-makers), 299

Dow, William, 281, 285, 300

Downie, James (builder), 259

Drake, Elizabeth (painter, b. 1866), 223

Drummond, John (wright), 213

Ducheman, Peter (mason), 213n

Duffus, George, 282

Dufour (wallpaper manufacturer), 141

Duncan, David (wright), 137

Duncanson, John (mason), 420

Dunfermline Burgh Council Architect's Department, 189, 190

Dunfermline District Council Architect's Department, 194

Dunn & Findlay (James Bow Dunn, q.v.; James L. Findlay, q.v.), 282

Dunn, James Bow (1861–1930), 113, 294, 333

Dunsterfield, George (plasterer), 46, 85, 86; Pl. 64

Durie Foundry, 329

Earp, Thomas (sculptor), 393

Easton, Gibb & Son Ltd (contractors), 356

Edis, Sir Robert William (1839–1927), 51, 393

Edward, Alexander (1651–1708), 321n

Eginton, William Raphael (glass-stainer, 1778–1834), 141

Elliot, Archibald (1761–1823), 51, 189

Elliot, James (1770–1810), 280

Elsey (T.) & Co. (smiths), 379

Fairlie, Reginald Francis Joseph (1883–1952), 38, 47, 76, 78, 106, 125, 131, 141, 187, 225, 262, 308, 309, 376, 377, 379, 383, 389, 394, 400, 416; Pl. 43

Fairlie (Reginald) & Partners, 375

Falconer, Thomas (d. 1796), 324

Farmer & Brindley (decorators), 133, 379

Faulkner-Brown, Hendy, Watkinson, Stonor, 378

Ferriby, E. A., 231

Fife County Council Architect's Department, 70, 71, 76, 94, 107, 123, 132, 152, 163, 172, 188, 189, 190, 191, 192, 233, 234, 235, 238, 250, 268, 282, 291, 294, 300, 309, 319, 340, 356, 384, 385

Fife Regional Council Architectural Services, 132, 163, 188, 189, 233, 234, 238, 287, 314, 336

Findlay, James L. (1868–1952), 101; see also Dunn & Findlay

Finlay, Morris, 161

Finlay, Thomas (mason), 125

Fisher, J., 268; see also Fife County Council Architect's Department

Fisher, James (mason), 83, 259n

Flemisman, Peter (sculptor), 214

Fogo, John Laurie, 386

Foley, John Henry (sculptor, 1818–74), 181

Forgan, George (builder), 212, 348

Forshaw, John Henry (1895–1973), 55, 205

Forster & Andrews (organ builders), 182, 266, 276

Forsyth, Edward L., 107

Fowler, William, 273

Frame, Thomas, 408

Frame (Thomas) & Son, 191, 239

Frame, William, 221n, 223

Fraser, John, 54, 193, 194

Fraser (John) & Son, 187

Fraser & Son (builders), 295

French, Thomas (mason), 213n, 373

Fulton, Robert, 261

Gady, John (mason), 213n

Gairdner, John, 374

Galbraith & Winton (sculptors), 381

Galloway, W. (sculptor), 219, 293

Gamley, Henry Snell (sculptor, 1865–1928), 49, 164

Gandy, John Peter (1787–1850), 103

Gardner, James (mason), 305

Gardner, William (mason), 305

Gascoyne, Alexander (glass-stainer), 281

Gauldie, Hardie Wright & Needham, 378

Gauldie, William, 151n

Gavinlock, Alexander (mason), 352–3

Gelton, Toussaint (painter, c. 1630–80), 85n

George (Ernest) & Peto (Sir Ernest George, 1839–1922; Harold Peto, 1828–97), 39, 313

Gern, August (organ builder), 312

Gibb (Sir Alexander) & Partners, 266

Gibbs, James (1682–1754), 65

Gibson & Hopewell, 107

Gibson, John S. (sculptor), 383

Gibson, Thomas (d. 1896), 118

Gilbert, Alexander (mason), 69, 349

Gilbert, George (mason), 69

Gilbert, John (mason), 69

Gillespie, James (1777–1855): see Graham, James Gillespie

Gillespie, James (1854–1914), 50, 51, 102, 127, 161, 283, 287, 292, 318, 391, 394, 396, 398, 401, 403

Gillespie (James) & Scott (James Gillespie, 1854–1914; James Scott, q.v.), 51, 54, 73, 130, 191, 231, 260, 263, 276, 299, 305, 318, 319, 320, 373, 375, 377, 378, 379, 383, 384, 386, 388, 389, 390, 391, 392, 396, 397, 398, 400, 402, 403, 412, 418

Gillespie, Kidd & Coia, 39, 232–3; Pl. 47

Gilpin, William Sawrey (1762–1843), 86

Glenfield & Kennedy (founders), 340, 411; Pl. 122

Glenrothes Development Corporation Architect's Department, 232, 233, 235

Good, Thomas (sculptor), 181

Gordon, Alexander Esmé (b. 1910), 106

Gordon & Dey (Alexander Esmé Gordon, q.v.; William Gordon Dey), 247

Gosman, John (mason), 137

Goudie, Isobel (glass-stainer), 180

Goulden, Richard Reginald (sculptor, d. 1932), 51, 188, 193

Gowan, Alexander (sculptor), 271

Graham, James Gillespie (1777–1855), 36, 47, 48n, 51, 53, 66, 79, 133, 140, 164, 165, 170, 198, 247, 249, 273, 284, 324, 338; Pls. 15, 74, 106

Grainger & Miller (Thomas Grainger, q.v.; John Miller, 1805–83), 54, 115, 164, 302; Pl. 108

Grainger, Thomas (1795–1852), 292, 319, 320, 417

Grant, Mary (sculptor, d. 1908), 40, 181

Gray, Charles W., 340

Gullen, C. Scott, 59

Gullen, W. & C. Scott, 65

Guthrie, J. & W. (glass-stainers: John Guthrie; William Guthrie), 421

Hadden, Thomas (smith, 1871–1940), 188, 192, 193

Hall & Henry (Jesse Hall, q.v.; David Henry, q.v.), 71, 383, 385, 391, 396, 398, 403

Hall, Jesse (1820–1906), 82, 83, 391, 394, 396, 398, 402, 403

Hallward, Reginald (glass-stainer, 1858–1948), 382

Hamilton, C. & F. (organ builders), 185

Hamilton, David (1768–1843), 47, 140, 141; Pl. 74

Hamilton, David & Thomas (organ builders), 198

Hamilton, James Anderson (1816–75), 50, 389

Hamilton, John (mason, d. ?1677), 84

Hamilton, Thomas (1784–1858), 37, 50, 65, 187, 258, 271; Pls. 96, 107

Hamilton-Paterson, Robert (b. 1843), 344

Harding, David (sculptor), 231, 232

Hardman (John) & Co. (glass-stainers: John Hardman, 1811–67; John Hardman Powell, 1828–95; John Tarleton Hardman, d. 1959; Patrick Feeny), 377, 383

Hardy, Dorsfield (painter), 126

Harris, John, 71

Harrison & Harrison (organ builders), 136, 381, 383

Harrison, Thomas (1744–1829), 46, 103 and n; Pl. 70

Hart, A. Vincent (glass-stainer), 335

Haxton, A. D., 107, 208, 311, 314, 412

Haxton & Walker, 312

Hay (D. R.) & Co. (decorators), 223 and n, 224

Hay, David Ramsay (decorator, 1798–1866), 341

Hay, George, 37, 280; Pl. 24

Hay, John (d. 1861), 37, 311

Hay, Robert (c. 1786–1864), 185, 192, 227, 228, 408

Heaton, Butler & Bayne (glass-stainers: Clement Heaton, 1824–82; James Butler, 1830–1913; Robert Turnill Bayne, 1837–1915; Clement John Heaton, fl. 1882–5; Clement James Butler, 1858–1929; Richard Cato Bayne, 1870–1940; Basil Richard Bayne, 1897–1953), 186

Heiton, A. & A. (Andrew Heiton, c. 1793–1858; Andrew Heiton, Jun., q.v.), 116

Heiton, Andrew, Jun. (1823–94), 238, 306, 312, 336, 427

Heiton & McKay (John F. McKay), 50, 283

Henderson, Alexander (plasterer), 343

Henderson, John (1804–62), 36, 115, 117, 121

Henderson, Peter Lyle Barclay (1848–1912), 50, 54, 187, 191, 316

Henderson, Robert (mason), 172
Hendrie, Herbert (glass-stainer, 1887–1946), 349, 382, 384
Henry, David (1835–1914), 67, 71, 137, 385, 391, 394, 395; see also Hall & Henry
Hill (William) & Son and Norman & Beard (organ builders), 160, 218, 379
Hilsdon, Henry (organ builder), 108
Hislop, J. W., 273, 292, 312
Hitch, Nathaniel (carver), 379
Hodkinson, Ian (conservator), 153; Pl. 90
Hogg, Douglas G. (glass-stainer), 418
Holford (William) & Associates, 378
Holiday, Henry (glass-stainer, 1839–1927), 39, 181, 377, 384
Holland, Henry (1745–1806), 103
Holme, F. & G., 50, 187
Holmes, D. (sculptor), 81
Holt, John (1914–77), 107, 189, 293, 427; see also South-East Regional Hospital Board Architect's Department
Honeyman & Keppie (John Honeyman, 1831–1914; John Keppie, 1863–1945; Charles Rennie Mackintosh, q.v.), 120
Hope, Alexander (mason, c. 1743–1815), 110
Hope, Thomas (mason, c. 1775–1836), 115
Horne, David, 404
Horne, James (smith), 353 and n
Horsburgh, Andrew (wright), 120, 263
Houston, James (builder), 419
Houston, John, 170, 186, 190, 195, 256, 257, 408, 419
Houston & Stewart (smiths), 83
Howie, John (sculptor), 168
Hradetzky (organ builder), 376
Hubbard, Henry, 293
Hurd (Robert) & Partners, 113, 157, 409
Hutchison, James (slater), 321
Hutchison, John (sculptor, 1833–1910), 384
Hutchison, R. Forbes, 283, 427
Hutchison, Robert (c. 1769–1845), 123, 130, 133, 164, 165, 218, 259 and n, 276, 305, 307, 318, 320, 324
Hutton, Robert (mason), 186
Inglis, John (wright), 129, 326
Ingram & Co. (organ builders), 75, 77, 186
Innes, James (slater, d. 1708), 321
Jack, William Murray, 70, 71, 73, 400, 401, 402, 407; see also Cunningham & Jack;

Cunningham, Jack, Fisher & Purdom
Jackson, Charles d'Orville Pilkington (sculptor, 1887–1973), 280
Jackson, Thomas (mason, d. ?1576), 213n
Jamieson (Auldjo) & Arnott (Ernest Arthur Oliphant Auldjo Jamieson, c. 1880–1937; James Alexander Arnott, 1871–1950), 193; Pl. 113
Jellson, John (mason), 305
Jennings, J. (glass-stainer), 198
Johnston, Alexander (1839–1922), 335
Johnston & Baxter (Alexander Johnston, q.v.; David W. Baxter, d. 1957), 335
Johnston, Charles Stewart Still (1850–c. 1924), 190
Johnston, Harvey, 163
Johnston, J. R., 355; see also Ministry of Public Building and Works
Johnston, Marcus Macdonald, 170, 293
Jones, Edward, 103
Jones & Willis (church furnishers), 185
Joseph, Samuel (sculptor, 1791–1850), 40, 301; Pl. 37
Just & Carver, 105, 341
Just, George (mason), 260, 262, 325n
Just, Robert, 325n
Kay, James (mason), 235n
Kellock, Alexander (wright), 226
Kemp, Marjorie (glass-stainer), 106, 258, 383, 384n
Kempe, Charles Eamer (glass-stainer, 1834–1907), 185
Kennedy, George Penrose (c. 1838–98), 270
Kennedy, John (mason), 169
Kerr, Henry Francis (1855–1946), 249, 412
Kilgour, George, 413
Kilgour & Nicoll, 283
Kilgour, Robert (wright, c. 1737–98), 271 and n, 294n
Kinnear, Charles George Hood (1830–94), 276, 277, 345; see also Peddie & Kinnear
Kinnear & Peddie (Charles George Hood Kinnear, q.v.; John More Dick Peddie, 1853–1921), 273, 284, 412
Kinross, John M. (1855–1931), 164, 214, 215
Kirkaldy Foundry, 271, 336
Kyle, Thomas (wright, d. 1704), 323 and n, 353
Laing, Alexander (d. 1823), 36, 46, 195, 288, 291, 294, 341

Laird (Michael) & Partners, 54, 284
Lamb, William (sculptor, 1893–1951), 335
Lavers, Barraud & Westlake (glass-stainers: Nathaniel Wood Lavers, 1828–1911; Francis Philip Barraud, 1824–1900; Nathaniel Hubert John Westlake, 1833–1921), 313
Lawson, J. B., 77
Lawson, James (wright), 273
Lees, William (c. 1777–1862), 56, 70, 87, 120, 135, 137, 263, 274
Leslie, Alexander (1754–1835), 36, 122, 125 and n, 260, 263, 304, 318, 334, 421; Pl. 25
Leslie, Alexander & James (builders), 423
Leslie, J. & A. (James Leslie, q.v.; Alexander Leslie, 1844–93), 426
Leslie, James (1801–89), 115, 282, 287, 422; Pl. 109
Lessels, John (1808–83), 125n
Lind, Harry, 191
Lindsay, Sir Coutts (1824–1913), 82
Lindsay, Ian Gordon (1906–66), 123, 146, 153, 387, 405
Lindsay, James, 50, 190
Lister, John, 303
Little, Robert, 115, 273, 284, 291
Little, William, 140, 141, 285
Little (William) & Son, 325
Loire, Gabriel (glass-stainer, b. 1904), 40, 340
Lomas (marble workers), 384
Lonsdale, Horatio Walter (painter, 1844–1919), 223, 224
Loosley, David W. (organ builder), 161, 421
Lorimer, Hew (sculptor, b. 1907), 255, 348, 379, 393, 416
Lorimer, Sir Robert Stodart (1864–1929), 47, 48, 51, 53, 67, 83, 87, 120, 125, 126, 162, 184, 192, 198, 199, 200, 201, 230, 239, 240, 255, 256, 277, 306, 307, 310, 319, 334, 347, 349, 374, 375, 386, 389, 392, 394, 405, 425, 426; Pls. 67, 83, 84
Louise, Princess, Duchess of Argyll (sculptor, 1848–1939), 425
Lowe, Graham (glass-stainer), 293
Lumsden, J., 293
Lyall, Henry (wright), 213n
Lyle & Constable (George A. Lyle; William Constable, q.v.), 76
Lyon, Andrew W. (decorator, d. c. 1933), 217, 223
McArthy & Watson (Charles McArthy; John Watson, d. 1924), 69

MacCallum, C. (sculptor), 293
McClure, David (painter, b. 1926), 216
McConnell, G. H., 189; see also Fife Regional Council Architectural Services
MacCulloch, John (mason), 169
MacDonald (F. A.) & Partners, 117, 189, 193, 238
McFarlane, Alexander (builder), 186
Macfarlane, James, 131
McFarlane, John (sculptor), 328
Macfarlane (Walter) & Co. (Saracen Foundry), 191
McGill, Alexander (d. 1734), 36, 46, 172; Pl. 22
McGilvray (sculptor), 204
McGlashan (Stewart) & Son (sculptors), 180, 181
Mackay & Co. (decorators), 149
Mackenzie, David, II (1832–75), 335
McKenzie, Kenneth (wright), 321
Mackintosh, Charles Rennie (1868–1928), 41, 204; Pl. 45; see also Honeyman & Keppie
McKissack (John) & Son (John McKissack, c. 1844–1915; James McKissack, 1875–1940), 292
McLachlan, John (d. 1893), 291
Maclaren (James) & Son (James Maclaren, 1828–93; John T. Maclaren, d. 1948), 163, 326, 335
McLennan, Sadie (glass-stainer), 150
McLeran, James, 341
McLundie, R. Douglas (glass-stainer), 185; see also Abbey Studio
McNeil, Cara (glass-stainer), 301
McNeish, Alexander (painter), 153; Pl. 90
Macrae, A. S., 303
Maile (G.) Studios (glass-stainers), 311
Malcolm, Robert, 263
Marshall, Edward (sculptor, 1598–1675), 149n
Martin (Hugh) & Partners, 232
Martin, Moses (mason), 213, 215
Martin, William (wright), 415
Marwick, Thomas Waller (c. 1901–71), 192
Masoun, Gilbert (mason), 213n
Masoun, William (mason), 213n
Matheson, Robert (1808–77), 178, 376
Matthew (Robert), Johnson-Marshall & Partners, 266
Matthews, James (1820–98), 281
Matthews & Mackenzie (James Matthews, q.v.; Alexander Marshall Mackenzie, 1848–1933), 37, 311
Mears (Sir Frank) & Partners, 250

Meffane, William (wright), 213n
Meik & Bouch, 115
Meik (Thomas) & Sons, 115
Meikle (William) & Sons (glass-stainers), 160, 161
Melville, John (plasterer), 321
Melvin (John) & Son (John Melvin, Sen., c. 1805–84; John Melvin, Jun., d. 1905; William Kerr), 422
Mercer, Alan, 355
Mercer, James A., 50, 187
Mercer, John (sculptor), 40, 149; Pl. 32
Mercer, Lewis, 408
Merlioun, Henry (mason), 295
Merlioun, John (mason), 213n
Millar, H. & R. (clockmakers), 69
Millar, James (builder), 103
Miller, James (1860–1947), 299
Miller, John R. (organ builder), 162, 335, 416
Mills, John Donald (1872–1958), 264, 375, 391, 394
Mills & Shepherd (John Donald Mills, q.v.; Godfrey D. B. Shepherd, 1874–1937), 310, 378
Milne, James (fl. 1811–34), 57
Milne, John (1822–1904), 50, 120, 123, 138, 163, 199, 282, 308 and n, 315, 332, 386, 388, 391, 392, 393, 394, 398, 401, 402, 417; Pl. 11
Ministry of Public Building and Works, 195, 232, 270, 355
Mitchell, Alexander (c. 1793–1859), 225n
Mitchell, Archibald (mason), 129
Mitchell, Arthur George Sydney (1856–1930), 41, 210, 270, 319
Mitchell, Joseph (1803–83), 74
Mitchell & Kinghorn (cabinet-makers), 313
Mitchell (Sydney) & Wilson (Arthur George Sydney Mitchell, q.v.; George Wilson, b. 1845), 189, 194, 207n, 383
Moffat (W. L.) & Aitken, 115, 234
Moffat, William Lambie (1808–82), 64
Monro, James Milne (d. 1921), 54, 398
Monroe, George (mason), 250
Monroe, John, Yr. (mason), 250
Morgan, William (carver), 323
Morris & Co. (glass-stainers and decorators), 207, 228, 281, 312, 328
Morris, James (builder), 86
Morris & Steedman (James Shepherd Morris, b. 1931; Robert Russell Steedman, b. 1929), 326, 387
Morrison, Robert (schoolmaster), 326

Morrocco, Alberto (painter, b. 1917), 232
Morton, William (wright), 213n
Motion, R. H., 94, 143, 190, 193, 195, 356
Mottashaw, G. W. (glass-stainer), 335
Mottram, Alfred Hugh (c. 1886–1953), 354, 355
Moxon & Carfrae (decorators), 200
Muirhead & Rutherford, 76, 188, 189, 190, 191, 194, 393
Multi Professional Architectural Practice of Edinburgh, 232
Murdoch, Alexander (sculptor), 76
Murray, Jean Pamela (glass engraver), 228
Murray, John, 271, 280
Mylne, John, Jun. (1611–67), 45, 88, 90, 306
Mylne, Robert (1633–1710), 45, 306, 424
Mylne, Robert (1733–1811), 344; Pl. 69
Needham, John, 163
Neilson, Alexander (sculptor), 151, 187
Neilson, Samuel (mason, d. 1753), 110; Pl. 18
Nesfield, William Andrews (1793–1881), 86
Ness, David (mason), 120, 263
Ness, David (sculptor), 85, 257, 421
Ness (David) & Co. (sculptors), 236
Newbigging, Thomas, 189
Newman, H. A., 163
Newton, Ernest (1856–1922), 403
Nicol, John (plasterer), 425
Nicoll, Peter (wright), 294n
Nisbet, Alexander (mason), 72
Nixon (painter), 200; see also Moxon & Carfrae
Nixon, William (c. 1810–48), 51, 178, 376, 377, 389, 399
Noble, Matthew (sculptor, 1818–76), 181
Norman & Beard (organ builders), 149, 161
Ochterlony, Sir Matthew Montgomerie (1880–1946), 181
Office of Works, H.M. (1851–77, Robert Matheson, q.v.; 1877–1904, Walter Wood Robertson, q.v.; 1904–14, William Thomas Oldrieve, q.v.; 1914–22, C. J. W. Simpson; 1922–43, John Wilson Paterson, q.v.; 1943–53, William A. Ross, 1891–1977; 1953–62, J. E. R. G. Kemp; 1962–9, H. A. Snow), 74, 142, 183, 189, 190, 283

Oldrieve, William Thomas (1853–1922), 178; *see also* Office of Works, H.M.

Oliver, Kenneth, 194

Orrock, Robert (master of works), 115

Orrok, James (mason), 226

Ower, C. & L. (Charles Ower, Jun., *c.* 1849–1921; Leslie Ower, *c.* 1852–1916), 96, 97, 335, 336

Page, George, 414

Papworth, John Buonarotti (1775–1847), 103

Parr (James) & Partners, 188

Parsons, Karl (glass-stainer), 379

Paterson (signwriter), 351n

Paterson, Alexander (wright), 84

Paterson, George (d. 1789), 235n, 270, 354n

Paterson, John, 115

Paterson, John Wilson (1887–1970), 245; *see also* Office of Works, H.M.

Paton, Sir Joseph Noel (painter, 1821–1901), 181, 182, 250

Paulin, George Henry (sculptor, b. 1888), 181

Paxton, Sir Joseph (1803–65), 191

Pearson, Frank Loughborough (1864–1947), 113

Peddie, John Dick (1824–91), 70, 72, 160

Peddie & Kinnear (John Dick Peddie, q.v.; Charles George Hood Kinnear, q.v.), 37, 73, 160, 264, 302, 383, 412, 425

Peebles, Robert (mason), 137

Peris, Robert (mason, d. 1587), 226

Phin, Walter (painter), 112

Pierson, Alexander, 273

Pilkington, Frederick Thomas (1832–98), 53, 117; Pl. 97

Pinfold, Michael (painter), 342

Pink, N. K. (glass-stainer), 110; *see also* Abbey Studio

Pinnan (James) & Son (modellers), 223

Playfair, James (1755–94), 48, 287, 353

Pluscarden Priory Benedictines (glass-stainers), 384

Porden, William (*c.* 1755–1822), 103

Powell (James) & Sons (glass-stainers and church furnishers: James Powell, d. 1840; Arthur Powell; James Cotton Powell; Nathaniel Powell), 113, 185, 377, 382, 383

Powell (James) & Sons (Whitefriars) Ltd, 185

Pritchard, Walter (painter), 379, 388

Property Services Agency, 191, 283, 287

Puttensen (bell-founder), 350

Rae, George (1811–69), 53, 101, 274, 375, 386, 390, 392, 393, 396, 397, 398, 400, 401, 402, 403

Ramsay, William, 325

Reiach & Hall, 395

Reid, Robert (1775–1856), 51, 374, 377

Rendel & Robertson, 282

Rhind, Alexander (sculptor), 319

Rhind, David (1808–83), 397

Rhind, John (sculptor, 1828–92), 71, 272

Richmond, William B. (sculptor), 377

Riss, Egon (1902–64), 292; Pl. 119

Ritchie, Alexander Handyside (sculptor, 1804–70), 186

Robertson, James (wright, *fl.* 1745), 305

Robertson, James (wright, *fl.* 1835), 418

Robertson, Malcolm (sculptor), 231, 232

Robertson, Thomas (mason, *fl.* 1589), 389 and n; Pl. 101

Robertson, Thomas (mason, *fl.* 1850s), 226

Robertson, Walter Wood (1845–1907), 180, 190, 374; *see also* Office of Works, H.M.

Robertson, William (builder), 311

Robinson, Robert (b. 1734), 236

Roche, John (mason), 110

Rodger, Lawrence Allan F., 235

Rodgie, 304

Rolland (L. A.) & Partners, 124, 306, 333, 334

Rolland, Lawrence Anderson Lyon (b. 1937), 79, 350, 421

Roos, Alexander, 51, 219, 223n

Ross-Smith, Stanley Patrick, 107

Rowan, William (overseer), 353

Roy, Nicolas (mason), 213, 215n, 216, 373

Ruid, Alexander (wright), 213n

Rushworth & Dreaper (organ builders), 106, 302

Russell, Alexander (founder), 336

Russell, Alexander L. (glass-stainer), 335

Sandilands, George, 71, 101, 106, 142, 163, 189, 292, 300, 319, 332, 408, 411, 414, 418

Sands, James (builder), 419

Sang, William Drysdale (*c.* 1850–1917), 292

Schotz, Benno (sculptor, 1891–1984), 233

Schultz, Robert Weir (1861–1951), 221, 223, 224

Scobie, Andrew, 107, 187, 188, 190, 194, 195, 249, 250

Scobie (Andrew) & Son, 94, 315, 339

Scobie, James T., 132, 193, 315

Scott, Gilbert Telfer, 132

Scott, J. M., 320

Scott, James (mason), 230

Scott, James (1861–1944), 402; *see also* Gillespie (James) & Scott

Scott, John (wright), 110

Scott, Mackay Hugh Baillie (1865–1945), 47, 409 and n

Scott Morton & Co. (decorators), 59, 240

Scott & Oswald (builders: William Oswald, *c.* 1793–1847), 274

Scott, Walter (mason), 389n

Scott, Walter Schomberg (b. 1910), 216, 219, 290

Scott, William (d. 1872), 402

Scottish Health Service Common Services Agency, 233, 356

Scovell, Charles Percy (organ builder), 182, 304

Scovell & Co. (organ builders), 136

Scrymgeour-Wedderburn, Henry James, 11th Earl of Dundee (1902–83), 53, 97

Shaw, Sax Roland (glass-stainer, b. 1916), 382

Shearer, James (1881–1962), 181, 188, 189, 192, 193n, 195, 344

Shearer (James) & Annand, 93, 193, 194

Shearer, Robert F., 356

Shiells, R. Thornton (1833–1902), 304

Sibbald, William (d. 1809), 115

Sim, Stewart, 117

Simmers, Balfour (sculptor, *c.* 1805–65), 389

Simpson, Ebenezer, 190

Simpson, Stedman, 77

Simpson, William Roger, 113, 115

Simson, William (builder), 345

Sinclair, Peter, 106, 204, 235

Sinclair & Watt, 396

Slater, J. (carver), 185

Small, J. W., 151

Smart, Alistair (sculptor, b. 1937), 190

Smart, Stewart & Mitchell (David Smart, 1824–1914; Donald Alexander Stewart; b. 1876; Robert Matthew Mitchell, d. 1949), 314

Smirke, Sir Robert (1780–1867), 103

Smith, Alexander P. (woodcarver), 198

Smith, David Forbes, 293, 299, 300

Smith, George (1793–1877), 73, 337, 338

Smith, Gilbert (mason, d. 1726), 88, 91

Smith, James (*c.* 1645–1731), 45, 46, 321 and n, 353 and n, 376; Pl. 66

Smith, James (*c.* 1779–1862), 70

Smith, John (clockmaker), 350

Smith, Robert (mason), 409

South-East Regional Hospital Board Architect's Department, 293

Speed, John (mason), 332

Speir, Robert Thomas Napier (1841–1922), 383

Spence (Sir Basil), Glover & Ferguson, 293

Spence, R. C., 342; *see also* Cunningham, Jack, Fisher & Purdom

Spy (cartoonist), 126

Staig, James (mason), 213n

Starforth, John (1823–98), 398

Stark, William (1770–1813), 103, 178 and n, 408

Steell, David George (painter, b. 1856), 201

Steell, Sir John (sculptor, 1804–91), 51, 218

Stevenson, Charles, 406

Stevenson, D. & C. (David Alan Stevenson, b. 1854; Charles A. Stevenson), 385

Stevenson, D. & T. (David Stevenson, 1815–85; Thomas Stevenson, 1818–87), 406

Stevenson, David Watson (sculptor, 1842–1904), 260

Stevenson, John (mason), 285

Stevenson, Robert (1772–1850), 137, 321, 417

Stevenson, W., 234

Stevenson, William Grant (sculptor, 1849–1919), 260

Stewart, Charles (wright), 163

Stewart, Donald Alexander (b. 1876), 225

Stewart, J. T. (glass-stainer), 160

Stewart, John (mason), 130

Stewart & Menzies (James W. Stewart; Duncan Menzies), 252

Stewart, Richard (wright), 213n, 217

Stirling, James Frazer (b. 1926), 51, 373

Stirling, William, I (1772–1838), 36, 104, 148, 150, 247n; Pl. 16

Stodart (sculptor), 83

Stokes, G. H., 191

Storrar, David, 164, 276

Storrar, J. G., 142

Strachan, Alexander (glass-stainer), 40, 59, 182, 382

Strachan, Douglas (glass-stainer, 1875–1950), 40, 181, 182, 281, 376, 379, 382

Swanston, John D. (1869–1956), 285

Swanston & Legge, 117
Swinton, John, 214, 225, 328
Sypen, John van (painter), 425
Tait, John (mason), 213n
Tait, John (1787–1856), 174
Tarbolton, Harold Ogle (1869–1947), 219
Taylor (organ builder), 69
Taylor, James (mason), 70, 135
Taylor, John (mason), 70
Taylor, Maurice E., 259; see also Fife County Council Architect's Department
Taylor, Michael (mason), 70
Taylor, Robert (mason), 70
Taylor (Robert) & Co., 263
Taylor, William (mason), 70, 137
Taylor & Young (Isaac Taylor, b. 1871), 49, 195
Telfer, W. D., 427
Telford, Thomas (1757–1834), 336
Thom, William (mason), 213
Thomas, William R., 202
Thoms & Wilkie (Patrick Thoms, c. 1874–1946; William Fleming Wilkie, 1876–1961), 38, 138, 165, 332
Thomson, James (carver, d. ?1704), 353
Thomson, Leslie Grahame (Leslie Grahame MacDougall from 1953; 1896–1974), 382
Thomson & Wilson (David Thomson, d. 1911; Charles Heath Wilson, 1809–82), 103
Tinto, Peter, 231, 232, 233; see also Glenrothes Development Corporation Architect's Department
Tod, Alexander, 127, 426
Tod, Alexander Stewart, 106, 108, 127, 204, 205, 424, 425, 426
Tod (Stewart) & Sons, 197
Tower, Walter E. (glass-stainer), 335
Trotter, Charles (cabinet-maker), 223
Turnbull, William (mason), 212
Turpie, Andrew (wright), 263
Tweedie, Charles E., 422
Ure, T. Hyslop, 132, 187, 189, 194, 256
Ure (T. Hyslop) & Beveridge, 313
Virtue, David, 110
Waddell, Andrew (wright), 84
Waddell, John Jeffrey (1876–1941), 57
Waddell (John Jeffrey, q.v.) & Young (T.P.W.), 198
Wailes, William (glass-stainer, 1808–81), 39, 187
Walker (carver), 397
Walker (organ builder), 182
Walker, Henry W., 77, 328

Walker (J. W.) & Sons Ltd (organ builders), 60, 207, 232
Walker, James Campbell (c. 1822–88), 50, 188, 328; Pl. 112
Walker & Pride, 162, 198, 280, 375, 391, 393, 396
Walker, Ruth Margaret Livingstone (glass-stainer, b. 1942), 257
Walker, William, 350
Ward & Hughes (glass-stainers: Thomas Ward, 1808–70; Henry Hughes, 1822–83), 39, 260
Wardrop, James Maitland (1824–82), 304
Wardrop & Reid (James Maitland Wardrop, q.v.; Charles Reid, 1828–83), 119, 194
Waterhouse, Paul (1861–1924), 47, 54, 132, 133, 193, 378, 379, 391, 395; Pls. 44, 114
Waterson, Alexander (wright), 273
Watson, Alexander (builder, c. 1794–1864), 86, 87
Watson & Salmond (John Watson, 1873–1936; David Salmond, 1876–1938), 270
Webster, Gordon (glass-stainer, b. 1908), 182, 377, 383
Weekes, J., Jun., 336
Weir, Robert Schultz: see Schultz, Robert Weir
Welsh, Archibald, 192
Wheeler & Sproson (Harold Anthony Wheeler, b. 1919; Frank Sproson), 53, 107, 110, 116, 132, 138, 154, 193, 232, 234, 282, 286, 290, 293, 351, 422; Pls. 46, 100
Whiston, Peter (b. 1912), 162, 212
White, Robert (builder), 212
White, Thomas, Jun., 236
Whitelaw, John, 131, 132
Whyte, David, 186
Whytock & Reid (decorators), 185, 381–2
Wilkie, Sir David (painter, 1785–1841), 301
Wilkie (David) & Son (wrights), 273
Wilkie, James (mason), 271
Wilkie, Peter (wright), 305
Wilkie, Robert (wright), 77
Wilkie, William (mason), 83
Wilkieson, David (wright), 235n
Wilkins, William (1778–1839), 103
Williams, Merlyn Christopher, 231; see also Glenrothes Development Corporation Architect's Department
Williamson, David (wright), 213n
Williamson, Faulkner-Brown & Partners, 378

Williamson & Inglis, 70, 79, 283
Williamson, William (1871–1952),
    50, 59, 76, 115, 181, 202, 271,
    272, 284, 287, 289, 293, 299,
    332, 333, 418; Pls. 10, 115
Williamson (William) & George B.
    Deas, 76
Williamson (William) & Hubbard,
    282, 283, 287, 293, 300, 427
Willis (Henry) & Sons (organ
    builders), 186, 335, 381, 384
Wilson, Andrew (mason), 70
Wilson (Hugh) & Womersley
    (Lewis), 193
Wilson, John (mason), 86
Wilson, John Bennie (1849–1923),
    108, 282
Wilson, Patrick (c. 1798–1871),
    110

Wilson, Samuel (plasterer), 240
Wilson, Thomas W.
    (woodcarver), 198
Wilson, William (glass-stainer,
    1905–72), 40, 77, 106, 182, 185,
    302, 309, 324, 348, 377, 382
Wimpey (builders), 235, 298
Wishart, David (mason), 354
Witt, Jacob de (painter, 1640–97),
    46, 85, 86, 256
Wright, William (wright), 213n
Wylie, David (wright), 135
Young, Andrew (painter), 112
Young (J.) & Sons (contractors),
    266
Young, James (sculptor), 380
Young, John, 174, 305
Young (R.) & Son, 191
Younger, William, 123

INDEX OF PLACES

Principal references are in **bold** type;
demolished buildings are shown in *italic*.

Abdie, 32, 36, 41, **57–8**
Abercrombie Parish Church, **86–7**
Aberdour, 25, 32, 40, 48, 54, **58–66**, 242; Pls. 10, 62, 80, 96
  Castle, 42, 43, 47, 48, 58, **60–4**; Pls. 48, 49, 51
  Otterston, **66**, 202
  Whitehill, 48, **66**
Airdrie, **66–7**, 127
Anstruther and Cellardyke, **67–75**; Pls. 36, 93
Anstruther Place or Dreel Castle, 72, 255n
Ardross Castle, 25, **75**
Arncroach, **75**
Auchterderran, Bowhill and Cardenden, 35, 50, 55, **75–6**
Auchtermuchty, 20n, 24, 27, 36, 41, 49, 52, 55, **76–9**
Auchtertool, 41, 49, 55, **79–80**, 202
Balbirnie House: *see* Glenrothes
Balbirnie Stone Circle: *see* Glenrothes
Balcarres, 35, 44, 47, 48, **80–3**, 261; Pls. 63, 84
Balcaskie, 45, 46, 47, 48, **84–7**; Pls. 64, 65
Balcomie Castle, **87–8**
Baldridgeburn: *see* Dunfermline
Balfarg: *see* Glenrothes
Balgonie Castle, **88–91**, 354; Pl. 52
Ballinbreich Castle, 42, **91–3**
Ballingry, Lochore and Crosshill, 35, 50, 55, **93–4**; Pl. 120
  Lochore House, 46, **94**; Pl. 72
Balmerino, 30, 31, 34, 53, 70n, **94–7**, 146, 329
  Drumnod Wood, 24, **97**
  Green Hill, 22, **97**
Balmule House, **97–8**
Balmuto, **98**
Balwearie Castle, **98–9**
Balwearie Tower: *see* Kirkcaldy
Bandon Tower, **99**
Barns Farm (Dalgety Bay), 21
Barns Mill, 25n
Benarty Hill, **99**
Benarty House, **99–100**
Bendameer House, **100**

Birkhill, 47, 97, **100**
Black Cairn Hill: *see* Newburgh
Blair Castle, **100–1**; Pl. 73
Blairhall: *see* Culross
Blebocraigs, **101**
Blebo House, **101**
Boarhills, **101**
Bogleys: *see* Kirkcaldy
Bonnytown, 27
Bowhill: *see* Auchterderran, Bowhill and Cardenden
Bow of Fife, **102**
Brackmont Mill, 23
Brankstone Grange, **102**
Broomhall, 46, **102–4**; Pl. 70
Brunton, 34, 36, 39, **104–5**
Buckhaven and Methil, 37, 38, 39, 53, **105–8**
Burntisland, 19, 50, 51, 53, 54, **108–18**; Pls. 97, 98, 108, 115
  churches, 32, 35, 39, 41, **108–13**; Pls. 18, 19
  Rossend Castle, 44, 108, **113–14**, 202, 203; Pl. 53
Cairneyhill, **119**
Cambo, **119**
Cameron, 36, **120**
Cardenden: *see* Auchterderran, Bowhill and Cardenden
Carnbee, **120**
Carnock, 36, 39, **120–2**
Cellardyke: *see* Anstruther and Cellardyke
Ceres, 34, 36, 39, 49, **122–4**; Pl. 29
Charlestown, 49, 50, **124**; Pls. 77, 121
Charleton, **125–7**
Charlottetown, **127**
Clatchard Craig: *see* Newburgh
Coaltown of Balgonie, 50, **127**
Coaltown of Wemyss, 53, **127–8**; Pl. 99
Coates House, **128**
Colinsburgh, 53, **128–9**
Collairnie Castle, 44, **129–30**
Collessie, 22, 25, 34, 36, 41, **130–1**
Cowdenbeath, 23, 38, **131–2**
Craigflower: *see* Torryburn

Craighall, 45-6
Craigluscar Hill, 23, **132**
Craigtoun Park (formerly Mount Melville), 47, 48, **132-3**
Crail, 29, 33, 42, 49, **133-40**, 262; Pls. 34, 85, 103
Crawford Priory, 46-7, 81, **140-1**; Pl. 74
Creich, 32, 34, 36, 39, 55, **142**
Crombie, 24, **142**
Crombie Point, **142-3**
Crossgates, **143**
Crosshill: *see* Ballingry, Lochore and Crosshill
Cruivie Castle, **143**
Culross, 19, 49, 52, 54, **143-58**, 166; Pls. 60, 86, 89, 90
 Abbey, 30, 31, 32, 34, 35, 40, 43, 143, **146-51**, 205; Pls. 16, 32
 Blairhall, **158**; Pl. 60
 Palace, 52, 146, **154-7**; Pls. 87, 88
Cults: *see* Kirkton of Cults
Cupar, 19, 42, 53, **158-68**, 240; Pls. 105, 106
 churches, 33, 34, 36, 37, 41, **160-2**; Pls. 20, 38
 public buildings, 49, 50, 51, 53, 54, **162-4**
 Preston Lodge, 52, **166-7**; Pl. 94
Dairsie, 35, 44, **169-70**; Pl. 21
Dalgety Bay, 21, 35, 36, **170-2**; Pl. 33
 Donibristle House, 36, 46, 48, 58, 64, 170, **172**; Pl. 22
Denmylne, **172-3**
Denork, **173**
Donibristle House: *see* Dalgety Bay
Doo Cave: *see* East Wemyss
Down Law, **173**
Dreel Castle: *see* Anstruther Place
Drumcarrow Craig, 24, **174**
Drumnod Wood: *see* Balmerino
Dunbog, **174**
Dunearn Hill, 23, 24, 25, **174**
Dunfermline, 21, 23, 42, 48-9, 50, 51, 52-3, 54, 55, **175-96**; Pls. 112, 114
 Abbey, 30, 31, 33, 34, 36, 39, 40, 43, 113, 114, **175-85**, 277, 308; Pls. 6, 7, 9, 27, 28, 31
 churches, 37, 38, 39, **185-7**; Pls. 40, 42
 Pittencrieff Park, 51, 175, **192-3**; Pl. 113
 standing stone, 21, **196**
Dunimarle Castle, 47, **196-8**; Pl. 78
Dunino, 55, **198**
Dunnikier House: *see* Kirkcaldy
Dunshelt, **198**
Dura House, **199**

Dysart: *see* Kirkcaldy
Earlsferry: *see* Elie and Earlsferry
Earlshall, 44, 47, 48, **199-202**
Easterheughs, **202-3**
Easter Pitcorthie: *see* Pitcorthie
East Lomond, 22, 23, 24, **203**, 217; Pl. 3
East Newhall: *see* Cambo
East Wemyss, 28, 35, 55, **203-5**
 Doo Cave, 28, **205**
 Macduff Cemetery, 41, **204**; Pl. 45
 Macduff's Castle, **204**, 425
Edenwood, 27, **205**
Elie and Earlsferry, 19, 25, **205-12**
Falkland, 37, 48, 49, 51, 52, **212-25**
 Palace, 43, 44, 106, 200, **212-17**, 328, 373; Pls. 54, 55
 House of Falkland, 47, **221-5**; Pl. 81
Fernie Castle, **225-6**
Flisk, **226**
Fordell Castle, 25, 35, **226-8**
Forgan, 32, 35, 39, 41, **228**
Freuchie, 25n, 54, **229**
Gateside, **229**
Gauldry, **230**
Gibliston House, **230**
Giffordtown, **230**
Gladney House (*Linktown, Kirkcaldy*), 291, 292n
Glasslie, 22, 217
Glassmount (Kinghorn), **272**
Glenduckie Hill, 24, **230**
Glenrothes, 39, 49, 53, 54, **230-7**, 303, 318; Pls. 46, 47, 118
 Balbirnie House, 46, **235-6**, 237; Pl. 71
 Balbirnie Stone Circle, 21, **236**
 Balfarg, 21, 236, **237**
 Rothes, 231, **237**
Grangemuir House, **237**
Grange of Lindores, 21, **237**
Green Craig, 24, **237-8**
Green Hill: *see* Balmerino
Guardbridge, 25n, **238**
Halbeath, **238-9**
Hallowhill (St Andrews), 29
Hill House, **239**
Hill of Tarvit, 47, 165n, **239-41**, 411; Pls. 1, 83
Inchcolm, 21, 30-2, 33, 34, 59, **241-6**; Pl. 8
Inchrye Abbey, 46
Innergellie, **247**
Inverkeithing, 33, 34, 36, 39, 49, 52, 54, **247-52**; Pls. 15, 104
Inzievar, 47, **252**; Pl. 82
Isle of May: *see* May
Kellie Castle, 43, 44, 46, 240, **252-6**, 351; Pl. 59
Kelty, **256-7**
Kemback, 35, **257-8**
Kennoway, **258-9**

Kettlebridge: see Kingskettle
Kilconquhar, 32, 36, 39, **259–61**
    Castle, 47, 81, **261**
Killernie Castle, **261–2**
Kilmany, 36, 39, 47, **262–3**
Kilrenny, 67, 73, **263–4**
Kilrie House, **264**
Kinaldy, **264**
Kincaple House, **264**
Kincardine-on-Forth, 19, 24, 36,
    39, 49, 53, 55, **265–70**, 275
    Tulliallan Castle, 43, **268–9**
    Tulliallan Castle (Scottish
      Police College), 47, **269–70**;
      Pl. 75
Kinghorn, 33, 41, 50, **270–2**; Pl.
    107
Kinglassie, 35, 41, **272–4**
Kingsbarns, 29, **274–5**
Kingsdale House, **275**
Kingskettle, 23, 36, 266, **275–6**
Kinloch (Collessie), 25
Kinloch House, **276–7**
Kinloss House, **277**
Kirkcaldy, 19, 22, 25, 55, **277–301**
    Balwearie Tower, 56, **301**
    Bogleys, **300**
    centre, 36, 37, 39, 50, 51, 52, 53,
      54, **277–87**; Pls. 24, 91, 92,
      117
    Dunnikier House (North; 1791–
      3), 46, **294**
    Dunnikier House (Pathhead;
      1692, now Path House), **298**;
      Pl. 61
    Dysart, 33, 36, 38, 49, 50, 52,
      53, 286, **288–91**, 295; Pl. 100
    Linktown, 50, 55, **291–2**; Pls.
      111, 119
    Pathhead, 54, **294–9**; Pls. 61,
      116
    other areas, **293–4**, **299–301**
    Ravenscraig Castle, 42, **295–8**;
      Pl. 50
    Torbain, 56, **301**
Kirkforthar, **301**
Kirkton of Cults, 23, 36, 40, **301–
    2**; Pls. 37, 39
Kirkton of Largo: see Upper Largo
Knockdavie Castle, **302**
Ladybank, 22, 40, 49, 54, **302**
Lady Mary's Wood (Kirkton of
    Cults), 23, **301–2**
Lahill, **303**
Largo House: see Upper Largo
Largoward, **303**
Lathrisk, 21
Lathrisk House, **303**
Lawhead (St Andrews), 23
Leslie, **303–7**
    Leslie House, 45, 47, 48, 84,
      231, 232, 233, **306–7**; Pl. 67
Letham, **307**
Leuchars, 26, 27, 29, 32, 41, **307–
    10**, 359; Pl. 11

Castle, 42, 83, **310**
Leven, 19, 37, 55, **310–12**
Limekilns, 37, 39, 48, 54, 104,
    312–13; Pls. 23, 57
Lindores Abbey: see Newburgh
Links Wood, 23, **314**
Linktown: see Kirkcaldy
Lochgelly, 40, **314–15**
Lochmalony, 22
Lochore: see Ballingry, Lochore
    and Crosshill
Logie, 55, **315**
Logie House, **315**
Lordscairnie, **315–16**
Lower Largo and Lundin Links,
    21, 22, 28, 54, **316–17**; Pl. 4
Lumphinnans: see Cowdenbeath
Lundin Links: see Lower Largo
    and Lundin Links
Lundin Tower, **317**
Luscar House, **317**
Macduff Cemetery: see East
    Wemyss
Macduff's Castle: see East
    Wemyss
Macduff's Cross: see Newburgh
Maiden Castle, **317–18**
Markinch, 32, 36, 37, 39, 41, 49,
    54, **318–20**
Masterton, 22
May, Isle of, 30, **320–1**
Melville House, 22, 45, 46, 90,
    321–3, 354; Pl. 66
Methil: see Buckhaven and Methil
Methilhill (Buckhaven and
    Methil), 22, **106–8**
Milton of Balgonie, **324**
Monimail, **324–5**
Moonzie, **325–6**
Morton, 20
Mossmorran, **326**
Mount Melville: see Craigtoun
    Park
Mountquhanie, **326**
Mugdrum, 25, **327**
Murrel, The, 47, **327**
Myres Castle, 24, **327–8**
Naughton, **328**
Nethertown: see Dunfermline
Newark Castle, **329–30**
Newburgh, 21, 22, 23, 26, 28, 38,
    49, **330–4**
    Black Cairn Hill, 23, **333**
    Clatchard Craig, 21, 23, 24,
      28
    Lindores Abbey, 25n, 28, 30,
      34, **330–1**, 332
    Macduff's Cross, 22, **333**
Newburn, 39, **334**, 421
Newport-on-Tay, 25, 51, **334–8**
    Tayfield, **337–8**
Newtonhall House, **338**; Pl. 79
Newton of Falkland, 54, **338**
Norman's Law, 23, 24, **338–9**
Norrie's Law, 22, 28, **339**

North Queensferry, 182n, **339–40**; Pl. 122
Oakley, 40, 55, **340**
Otterston: *see* Aberdour
Over Rankeillour, **341**
Pathhead: *see* Kirkcaldy
Pitcairlie House, **341**
Pitcorthie, 22, **342**
Pitcorthie House, 47, **342**
Pitcullo, 26, **342**
Piteadie Castle, **342–3**
Pitfirrane, **343–4**
Pitlessie, 54, **344**
Pitliver, **344**
Pitlour, **344–5**; Pl. 69
Pitscottie, 25n
Pitreavie, 23, **345**
Pittarthie Castle, 43, **346**
Pittencrieff Park: *see* Dunfermline
Pittenweem, 49, 52, **346–52**
Purin Hill, 25n
Raith House, 46, 48, 287, 301, **352–3**
Randerston, 25n, **353**
Ravenscraig Castle: *see* Kirkcaldy
Ravenshall, 24
Rossend Castle: *see* Burntisland
Rossie House, **354**
Rosyth, 38, 53, **354–6**
Rothes, 231, **237**
St Andrews, 23, 28, 29, 48, 49, 51–2, 53, 54, **357–403**; Pl. 95
　Castle, 42, 43, 357, **369–72**; Pl. 56
　Cathedral and Priory, 30, 31, 32, 34, 41, 310, 325, 357, **361–9**, 377, 386; Pl. 12
　churches, 33, 34, 37, 38, 39, 40, 357, **378–84**, 385; Pls. 17, 35, 41, 43, 44
　public buildings, 50, 371, 375, 376, 380, **384–9**; Pls. 101, 110
　St Regulus', 29, 30, 357, **358–61**, 362; Pl. 5
　University, 33, 34, 39, 40, 50–1, 54, 359, **372–8**, 386, 388, 398; Pls. 14, 30, 102
St Margaret's Hope, **403**
St Monans, 33, 38, 288, **403–7**; Pl. 13
Saline, 41, 55, **407–9**
Sandford Hill, 47, **409**

Scoonie, 28
　Manse, 55
Scotstarvit Tower, 24, 43–4, 240, 289, **409–11**; Pl. 58
Seafield Tower, **411**
Star, **411**
Starley Hall, **411–12**
Strathairly House, **412**
Stratheden Hospital, **412**
Strathendry, 22, **412–13**
Strathendry Castle, **412**
Strathendry House, **412–13**
Strathkinness, **413**
Strathmiglo, 21, 28, 41, 49, **413–15**
Strathtyrum House, **415**
Struthers, **415**
Tarvit, **415–16**
Tarvit House, 329
Tayfield: *see* Newport-on-Tay
Tayport, 38, **416–18**
Thornton, **418**
Tofts Law (Newport-on-Tay), 25
Torbain: *see* Kirkcaldy
Torrie House (Torryburn), 46, 420
Torryburn, 20, 22, 41, 46, **418–20**
　Craigflower, 47, 143, 419, **420**
　Tulyies, 22, **420**
Townhill: *see* Dunfermline
Tulliallan Castle: *see* Kincardine-on-Forth
Tulliallan Castle (Scottish Police College): *see* Kincardine-on-Forth
Tulyies: *see* Torryburn
Upper Largo, 19, 28, 39, 41, **421–3**; Pls. 25, 26, 109
　Largo House, 46, 422, **423**; Pl. 68
Valleyfield, **423**; Pl. 76
Vicarsford Cemetery, 42, **423–4**
Waukmill, 24, 25n
Wemyss Castle, 45, 46, 127, 128, **424–5**
Wemyss Hall: *see* Hill of Tarvit
West Flisk, 24
West Lomond, 22
West Pitcorthie: *see* Kilrenny
West Wemyss, 49, 425, **426**
Whitehill: *see* Aberdour
Windygates, 54, **427**
Wormit: *see* Newport-on-Tay

The National Trust for Scotland is proud to be associated with Penguin Books Limited in the preparation of *The Buildings of Scotland*.

The Trust exists to care for fine buildings and beautiful scenery. It was brought into being in 1931 by a few prominent Scots concerned at the destruction of much of the country's heritage of landscape and architecture.

In its care are more than 100 properties covering over 400,000 hectares. These include castles and great houses, gardens, mountains, islands, historic sites and a wide variety of small properties.

The Trust has won widespread recognition for its pioneer work in the restoration of the 'little houses' of towns and villages. The revolving fund which it set up for buying, restoring and reselling them has been widely imitated.

Like the National Trust, it is incorporated by Act of Parliament and is dependent for finance on legacies, donations and the subscriptions of its members.

The Trust's offices, from which fuller details may be obtained, are at 5 Charlotte Square, Edinburgh EH2 4DU.